Uncle John's BATHROOM READER. PLUNGES INTO MUSIC

By the
Bathroom Readers' Institute

Bathroom Readers' Press
Ashland, Oregon

UNCLE JOHN'S BATHROOM READER®
PLUNGES INTO MUSIC

For this expanded edition, a few select articles have been included from the following books: *The Best of Uncle John's Bathroom Reader* © 1995 Bathroom Readers' Press; *Uncle John's Ultimate Bathroom Reader* © 1996 Bathroom Readers' Press; *Uncle John's Giant 10th Anniversary Bathroom Reader* © 1997 Bathroom Readers' Press; *Uncle John's Great Big Bathroom Reader* © 1998 Bathroom Readers' Press; *Uncle John's Bathroom Reader Plunges Into History* © 2001 Portable Press; *Uncle John's Supremely Satisfying Bathroom Reader* © 2001 Bathroom Readers' Press; *Uncle John's Ahh-Inspiring Bathroom Reader* © 2002 Bathroom Readers' Press; *Uncle John's Bathroom Reader Plunges Into Great Lives* © 2003 Portable Press; *Uncle John's Unstoppable Bathroom Reader* © 2003 Bathroom Readers' Press; *Uncle John's Bathroom Reader Plunges Into History Again* © 2004 Portable Press; *Uncle John's Bathroom Reader Plunges Into Texas* © 2004 Portable Press; *Uncle John's Slightly Irregular Bathroom Reader* © 2004 Bathroom Readers' Press; *Uncle John's Bathroom Reader Christmas Collection* © 2005 Portable Press; *Uncle John's Bathroom Reader Plunges Into Michigan* © 2005 Portable Press; *Uncle John's Fast-Acting Long-Lasting Bathroom Reader* © 2005 Bathroom Readers' Press; *Uncle John's Bathroom Reader Plunges Into Hollywood* © 2005 Portable Press; *Uncle John's Bathroom Reader Plunges Into New Jersey* © 2005 Portable Press; *Uncle John's Bathroom Reader Plunges Into Ohio* © 2007 Portable Press.

For information, write:
The Bathroom Readers' Institute, P.O. Box 1117, Ashland, OR 97520
www.bathroomreader.com • 888-488-4642

Cover design by Michael Brunsfeld, San Rafael, CA (*Brunsfeldo@comcast.net*)

Uncle John's Bathroom Reader® *Plunges into Music*
by the Bathroom Readers' Institute

ISBN-13: 978-1-59223-824-8   ISBN-10: 1-59223-824-6

Library of Congress Cataloging-in-Publication Data

Uncle John's bathroom reader plunges into music.
p. cm.
ISBN 978-1-59223-824-8 (pbk.)
1. Music—Humor.
ML65.U58 2008
780—dc22
2007039215

Printed in the United States of America
Second Printing
2 3 4 5 6 7 8 9 12 11 10 09 08

iii

THANK YOU!

The Bathroom Readers' Institute sincerely thanks the people whose advice and assistance made this book possible.

Gordon Javna
Thom Little
Brian Boone
Amy Miller
Jay Newman
John Dollison
Julia Papps
JoAnn Padgett
Melinda Allman
Michael Brunsfeld
Angela Kern
Maggie McLaughlin
Dan Mansfield
Jef Fretwell
Stephanie Spadaccini
Jeff Cheek
Kyle Coroneos
Brândon Williams
David Harp
Debbie Pawlak
Gabriella Toth
J. Carroll
Jenness Crawford
Janet Spencer
Jennifer Payne
John Scalzi
Kathryn Grogman

Heather Holliday
Lisa Meyers
John Javna
Kerry Kern
Malcolm Hillgartner
Jahnna Beecham
Lea Markson
Maggie McLean
Bethanne Patrick
Megan Kern
Toney Lee
Vickey Kalambakal
Sue Steiner
Alan Reder
Sydney Stanley
Scarab Media
Nancy Toeppler
Karen Malchow
Laurel Graziano
Monica Maestas
David Calder
(Mr.) Mustard Press
Steven Style Group
Publishers Group West
Raincoast Books
Porter the Wonder Dog
Thomas Crapper

CONTENTS

Because the BRI understands your reading needs, we've
divided the contents by length as well as subject.

Short—a quick read
Medium—2 to 3 pages
Long—for those extended visits, when something
a little more involved is required
* Extended—for those leg-numbing experiences

OVERTURE

Music truly is the universal language. We're surrounded by it—on television and the radio, at the office, at the store, in the car, on the phone, even walking down the street (thanks to MP3 players). And what's the first thing most people do when there is no music? They start humming a tune. Not only is music woven into the fabric of every single civilization on Earth, recent findings show that humans were singing songs to each other before there even *was* civilization (see page 150).

So with that in mind, Uncle John asked, "How do we cram such a huge subject into a 500-page book?" Obviously we couldn't include everything, but we've gone out of our way to include something for just about everyone—no matter what your personal taste may be. Here's a partial setlist...

• **The birth of a genre:** Read about the mother of the blues and the father of bluegrass. Plus the roots of rock, country, folk, jazz, disco, rap, motown, heavy metal, opera, polka, and many more.

• **Playin' in the band:** Things that go bump on the stage, hit makers who hated their biggest hits, reunions that never happened, and others that did...but maybe shouldn't have.

• **Going (instru)mental:** What did they use before pianos? What's a mandocleta, a tin sandwich, a bronze lur, and an Aeolian harp?

• **Outsider music:** The guy who made a metal symphony out of his '82 Honda Accord, the bird that helped Mozart compose a concerto, wineglasses that sing, and the cave that plays itself.

• **Musical odds and ends:** Cartoon music, why gold records are gold, what's on the president's iPod (and why), and what happened when Ozzy Osbourne made music with Miss Piggy.

To our regular readers, you may notice a few "greatest hits" from past *Bathroom Readers*. They were just too good to not include in our first book dedicated to music—one we're really jazzed about! So settle in and have fun. We're off to go jam.

As always, Go with the Flow!

—Uncle John, the BRI staff, and Porter the Wonderdog

THE FIRST...

A bunch of musical firsts.

...pop album with printed lyrics: The Beatles' *Sgt. Pepper's Lonely Hearts Club Band*, 1967.

...singer to refuse a Grammy: Sinéad O'Connor won Best Alternative Album prize in 1990 for *I Do Not Want What I Haven't Got*. She declined the award to protest the Grammys' "extreme commercialism."

...foreign-language #1 pop song: "Sukiyaki," by Japanese singer Kyu Sakamoto. It went to the top of the Billboard charts in 1963.

...double album: Benny Goodman's *Live at Carnegie Hall*, 1938. First rock double album: Bob Dylan's 1966 *Blonde on Blonde*.

...American pop band to tour the Soviet Union: the Nitty Gritty Dirt Band, in 1977.

...musical guest on *Saturday Night Live*: Billy Preston. He beat the debut show's other guest, Janis Ian, by about 20 minutes.

...recorded yelling of "Free Bird!" at a concert: 1976, at the Fox Theater in Atlanta. The show was being taped for Lynyrd Skynyrd's live album, *One More From the Road*.

...music book published in the United States: *Seven Songs for Harpsichord or Forte-Piano*, by Francis Hopkinson, in 1788.

...first African-American recording artists: Pianist Willie "The Lion" Smith of Newark, New Jersey, who played on the 1920 song "Crazy Blues" by Mamie Smith's Jazz Hounds.

...British musician with a #1 single in the United States: It's not the Beatles—it's Mr. Acker Bilk, whose clarinet instrumental "Stranger on the Shore" topped the American charts in 1962.

...band to rock Antarctica: Nunatuk, a band made up of resident British researchers, who performed in Antarctica as part of a series of environmental awareness concerts in 2007.

...album released on CD: ABBA's 1981 album *The Visitors*.

Dolly Parton's first single: "Puppy Love." She was 13.

MUSICAL EBAY

*Want to own a piece of your favorite musician? Check the online auction
sites for stuff that used to belong to them. Just don't be too picky.*

• A plastic Christmas tree with ornaments, garland, and lights once owned by Syd Barrett of Pink Floyd. Someone paid $1,600 for it.

• Wanna rock? Somebody sold a stone with an image they claimed looked like Jerry Garcia of the Grateful Dead on it. Price: $450,000 (The rock came with a free yacht.)

• A program from Prince's 1996 wedding to Mayte Garcia called "Coincidence or Fate?" outlining the many spooky reasons why the two should marry. (Example: her middle name is Jannell, his father's first name and initial is John L.) Asking price: $600.

• A clock made of ivory elephant tusks purchased in the 1950s by country music star Jim Reeves ("He'll Have to Go") sold for $1,500.

• A microphone autographed by Britney Spears's ex-husband and failed rapper Kevin Federline, along with the words "America's most hated." Asking price: $100.

• Baseball isn't popular in England, which makes a baseball autographed by Paul McCartney rare (and strange). It sold in 2005 for $2,500.

• A coat hanger used to hang the suit that Elvis Presley was buried in fetched $15,000. (Suit not included, obviously.)

• A chair owned by Nirvana bassist Krist Novoselic—with a sweat stain attributed to bandmate Kurt Cobain—sold for $15,000.

• Somebody asked $5,000 for a wooden sake drinking box used by Bon Jovi guitarist Richie Sambora. (It didn't sell.)

• Remember the one-hit wonder Rednex, who had a hit with the country/disco song "Cotton Eye Joe" in 1995? In 2007 the band and everything that came with it—trademark, record deals, back catalogue—went on sale on eBay for $1.5 million. (No takers.)

• Martin Bulloch, drummer of the Scottish band Mogwai, sold his used pacemaker on eBay for $540.

COVER ME!

Some songs are so closely associated with certain musicians that it's hard to believe they weren't the first to perform them.

"RESPECT"
BEST-KNOWN VERSION: Aretha Franklin
ORIGINAL ARTIST: It's an Otis Redding song. When it came out on his 1965 album *Otis Blue*, it wasn't a hit or even a single. Franklin covered it two years later. When he heard her version, Redding reportedly said, "That little girl stole my song." He was right—it became a #1 hit and Franklin's signature song.

"GOT MY MIND SET ON YOU"
BEST-KNOWN VERSION: George Harrison
ORIGINAL ARTIST: Harrison's 1987 comeback hit was a cover of an obscure 1960s soul song recorded by James Ray and written by Rudy Clark (who also wrote "Good Lovin'" and "If You Gotta Make a Fool of Somebody"). Harrison had wanted to do the song ever since he was with the Beatles—he thought it was well written, but badly performed on Ray's recording. (He especially disliked the "horrible screechy women's voices singing those backup parts.")

"KILLING ME SOFTLY WITH HIS SONG"
BEST-KNOWN VERSION: Roberta Flack
ORIGINAL ARTIST: In 1971 Los Angeles-based singer Lori Lieberman saw Don McLean perform "American Pie" and was so moved by his concert that she wrote a poem called "Killing Me Softly with His Blues." Charles Fox and Norman Gimbel later wrote music for it, changing "blues" to "song," and Lieberman recorded it—but it went nowhere. Flack read an article about Lieberman on an in-flight magazine, thought the title of the song was great, and later, upon hearing it, decided to record it herself.

"TAINTED LOVE"
BEST-KNOWN VERSION: Soft Cell
ORIGINAL ARTIST: It's arguably *the* definitive 1980s synth-

"Sometimes, you let the hair do the talking." —James Brown

pop song, but Ed Cobb of the Four Preps wrote it in 1964 as a ballad for a little-known soul singer named Gloria Jones.

"MAMA TOLD ME (NOT TO COME)"
BEST-KNOWN VERSION: Three Dog Night
ORIGINAL ARTIST: Randy Newman wrote it, and Eric Burden and the Animals first recorded it in 1967. Newman later included the song on his 1970 album, *12 Songs*, which didn't receive much attention at the time. But later that year, the song became a #1 hit for Three Dog Night, who transformed Newman's slow, funk-influenced tune into a revved-up rock song.

"GREATEST LOVE OF ALL"
BEST-KNOWN VERSION: Whitney Houston
ORIGINAL ARTIST: Though it's one of Houston's best-known songs (and widely regarded as one of the sappiest ever written), it was first sung by George Benson for the 1977 Muhammad Ali movie *The Greatest*. So is the song about Ali? No—lyricist Linda Creed actually wrote it about battling breast cancer, which would later claim her life at age 37.

"DON'T KNOW MUCH"
BEST-KNOWN VERSION: Linda Ronstadt and Aaron Neville
ORIGINAL ARTIST: The song was cowritten and performed in 1980 by Barry Mann, who wrote dozens of hit songs in the 1960s, '70s, and '80s, and is best known for his 1961 hit recording of "Who Put the Bomp?" Bill Medley of the Righteous Brothers and Bette Midler both recorded "Don't Know Much," but it wasn't a hit until the Ronstadt/Neville duet was released in 1989.

"THAT'S WHAT FRIENDS ARE FOR"
BEST-KNOWN VERSION: Dionne Warwick and Friends
ORIGINAL ARTIST: Rod Stewart. He sang the song (written by Burt Bacharach and Carole Bayer Sager) for the end credits of the 1982 comedy film *Night Shift*. That version went largely unnoticed, but it became a smash hit when Warwick performed it with Elton John, Gladys Knight, and Stevie Wonder in 1986 to raise money for AIDS research.

BEHIND THE (SILLY) HITS

Throughout the history of pop music, novelty songs have occasionally ascended the charts. Here are the true stories of a few of them.

Song: "Hello Muddah, Hello Faddah"
Artist: Allan Sherman
Story: In the early 1960s, 11-year-old Robert Sherman spent a few weeks at a New York summer camp called Camp Champlain. He hated it. Robert wrote desperate letters to his parents begging them to come and get him. They refused, so Robert threw a butter knife at another camper to get himself sent home. (It worked; the other kid wasn't hurt.) But later that summer, to the surprise of Robert's father, songwriter Allan Sherman, Robert asked to *return* to Camp Champlain. Sherman encapsulated his son's hatred for camp and rapid change of heart into a single letter home (from the fictional "Camp Granada") and set it to Ponchielli's classical melody "Dance of the Hours." Released on Sherman's 1963 album *My Son the Nut*, "Hello Muddah, Hello Faddah" reached #2 on the singles chart.

Song: "Do the Bartman"
Artist: Bart Simpson
Story: In 1991 Michael Jackson guest-starred on *The Simpsons* as a man who's institutionalized…because he thinks he's Michael Jackson. Jackson became a big *Simpsons* fan and wrote "Do the Bartman" to be performed by Bart Simpson (voiced by Nancy Cartwright). But for legal reasons, Jackson wrote and produced the song under the pseudonym Bryan Loren. "Do the Bartman" was released at the height of the *Simpsons* craze in 1991 and became a #1 hit in Ireland, England, and was a staple on MTV.

Song: "A Boy Named Sue"
Artist: Johnny Cash
Story: In 1968 Shel Silverstein, a writer and illustrator best known for his children's books (*The Giving Tree*), was reading about the famous John Scopes evolution trial of 1925. He came

across a reference to a male attorney on the case who had the name of Sue Hicks. That inspired Silverstein to write "A Boy Named Sue," a song about a man seeking revenge against his father for giving him a woman's name. Silverstein sold the song to Columbia Records, who gave it to Johnny Cash, who recorded it live on his *At San Quentin* album in 1969. Cash usually sang serious songs about prison, pain, and heartache. But the silly "A Boy Named Sue" became the biggest hit of Cash's career, going to #2 on the pop chart and #1 on the country chart.

Song: "Short People"
Artist: Randy Newman
Story: Newman was well known in the 1970s for writing darkly funny, first-person story songs. In 1977 he scored a hit with "Short People," an ironic song about how ridiculous prejudice can be. (Sample lyric: "They got little hands and little eyes / and they walk around tellin' great big lies.") The song received a lot of media attention (and airplay) because many people thought Newman *actually* hated short people. Nevertheless, the song was a #2 pop hit. Despite its success, Newman dislikes the song—he feels it made him look like a lightweight songwriter and a hateful man—and still refuses to include it (even though it's his biggest hit) on his "greatest hits" albums.

Song: "Disco Duck"
Artist: Rick Dees
Story: In 1976 Dees was a Memphis disc jockey during the height of the disco fad. Inspired by a friend who did a Donald Duck impression, Dees wrote "Disco Duck," a novelty song about a man who goes to a disco party and dances so hard that he turns into a duck. Regional label Fretone Records released the song, and it was a moderate hit across the South. RSO Records then bought the rights and released it to the rest of the United States, where it went to #1. But not in Memphis—rivals of Dees's station wouldn't play it because they didn't want to promote the competition. Later, "Disco Duck" was featured in the hit film *Saturday Night Fever*. Unfortunately, it didn't make it onto the soundtrack album (which sold 40 million copies). Dees went back to his career as a deejay, and his *Weekly Top 40* radio show is still in syndication.

The play-by-play in Meat Loaf's "Paradise by the Dashboard Light" was by sportscaster Phil Rizzuto.

MUSIC NOTES

Some nuggets of rock 'n' roll trivia.

- Shortest hit single: "Some Kind-a Earthquake" by Duane Eddy (1959) at 1 minute, 17 seconds.

- Longest hit single: "Autobahn" by Kraftwerk (1975) at 22 minutes, 30 seconds.

- Avant-garde guitarist Yngwie Malmsteen's 1984 show at London's Marquee Club sold out in minutes. Why? Fans thought "Yngwie Malmsteen" was a pseudonym for Bruce Springsteen.

- In the early 1970s, the Beach Boys were in an experimental phase and considered changing the name of the band to just "Beach."

- Before he was in KISS, drummer Peter Criss was in a band called Lips.

- Who made it into the *Guinness World Records* as the loudest rock band? The Who: 126 decibels at a 1976 concert. Guinness later axed the category. Why? Hearing damage begins at 80 decibels. What?

- The Animals' classic 1964 hit "House of the Rising Sun" was reportedly captured in one take. The band was in the studio for a total of eight minutes: four to rehearse the song and four to record it. Cost of the studio time: $5.

- Best-selling artist of all time in Africa: Tupac Shakur. Best-selling artist of all time in Iran: Liza Minnelli.

- In 1981 a medley of pop songs by a group called Stars on 45 reached #1, resulting in one of the longest titles to hit the top of the charts. The song's full title: "Medley: Intro Venus / Sugar Sugar / No Reply / I'll Be Back / Drive My Car / Do You Want to Know a Secret / We Can Work It Out / I Should Have Known Better / Nowhere Man / You're Going to Lose That Girl / Stars on 45."

- The flip side of Napoleon XIV's 1966 single "They're Coming to Take Me Away, Ha-Haaa!" was "!aaaH-aH, yawA eM ekaT ot gnimoC er'yehT."

OUTSIDER MUSIC

"Outsider music" is experimental, musical art created by nonmusicians (often self-taught) for their own enjoyment or as a means of self-expression. It's usually recorded at home, and frequently disregards common musical structures, sounds, rhythm, and even melody. If you like your music weird, adventurous, unique—and oddly compelling—listen up.

BACKGROUND
Since 1975, Irwin Chusid has been a disc jockey on WFMU, a New Jersey radio station that plays underground—and often strange—music. In the late 1970s, a friend gave Chusid an LP called *Philosophy of the World* by a group called the Shaggs. Chusid had never heard anything like it: the band banged on their instruments without melody or rhythm and didn't seem to be playing in unison. Chusid thought it was baffling, terrible...and charming. As bad as it was, he thought it was undeniably earnest. Ever since, Chusid has combed flea markets and yard sales for what he calls "outsider music."

So what's the difference between outsider music and just plain bad music? According to Chusid, "passion, soul, idiosyncratic ideas, sincere self-expression, and guilelessness." More specifically, it's music created by people who lack the talent, tunefulness, or knowledge of musical structures found in mainstream popular music. Much of it is self-recorded and the results are bizarre and startling.

In 2000 Chusid wrote a book about outsider music titled *Songs in the Key of Z*. Here are some of his top picks.

THE SHAGGS. In 1966 four New Hampshire sisters (Betty, Dorothy, Helen, and Rachel Wiggin) were given used instruments by their father, who pulled them out of school and told them to become a rock band. They had only a few basic lessons before they made their album *Philosophy of the World*. The result: dissonant noise played by musicians who sound like they're playing their instruments for the first time (and independently of each other). It became a cult hit with fans of weird music—Frank Zappa called it one of the best albums ever made.

Carly Simon's father is the Simon of publishing giant Simon & Schuster.

WESLEY WILLIS. He recorded over 1,000 songs, almost all accompanied by the same demo track played on a cheap keyboard. Most of Willis's songs are about concerts he attended, and the lyrics usually follow the same pattern: "This band played at the Rosemont Horizon. About a thousand people were at the show. The jam session was awesome. It really rocked the (name of animal)'s (part of animal's anatomy)." Then he screams the band's name a few times, then sings another verse, adds in some keyboard sound effects, and ends with a popular advertising catchphrase, such as "Wheaties, breakfast of champions!"

LANGLEY SCHOOLS MUSIC PROJECT. In 1976 Hans Fenger was hired to teach music at five elementary schools in rural Langley, British Columbia. To interest the kids in music, he had them sing songs by the Beach Boys, the Eagles, and David Bowie. The kids were so enthusiastic that Fenger recorded them (arranged into a giant choir) in a school gym and handed out LPs of the recordings to their parents. Critics say the familiar songs performed by children in an echo-drenched gym are haunting and moving. "It touches the heart in a way no other music ever has, or ever could," said critic and jazz musician John Zorn. A CD of the performance was released in 2001.

JANDEK. Since 1978, Jandek (real name: Sterling Smith) has released more than 50 albums of folk, blues, and "noise rock." He goes through phases: He'll record acoustic songs on several records, then several records' worth of noisy experimental music, leading fans to believe that he records hundreds of songs at a time in one feverish session. The recordings vary from spoken word and a cappella singing to scream-filled electric guitar noisefests to stark acoustic folk songs, and Jandek plays all the instruments.

THE LEGENDARY STARDUST COWBOY. In the 1960s, this performer (real name: Norman Odom) invented a new kind of music that combined rockabilly with extremely fast hard rock. (It later came to be called "psychobilly.") His best-known song is the 1968 single "Paralyzed," in which Ledge (as he likes to be called) furiously strums on an acoustic guitar, then growls, snarls, and makes other noises, occasionally yelling out "Paralyzed!" The song reached the Billboard chart in 1968.

A standard CD is 4.7 inches in diameter.

WHAT'S THE DEFINITION OF PERFECT PITCH?

A: *An accordion thrown into a dumpster without hitting the sides. Here are a few other jokes that some musicians love...and some musicians hate.*

What's the difference between a lead guitar player and a large pizza?
A: A large pizza can feed a family of four.

Q: How do you get two piccolo players to play in perfect unison?
A: Shoot one.

Q: Why did God give drummers a half-ounce more brains than horses?
A: So they don't poop in the road during parades.

Q: What's the difference between an accordion and an onion?
A: No one cries when you chop up an accordion.

Q: What's the difference between a dead trombonist in the road and a dead skunk in the road?
A: The skunk might have been on his way to a gig.

Q: Why do bagpipers march when they play?
A: To get away from the noise.

Q: How do you know when the stage is level?
A: The drummer is drooling out of both sides of his mouth.

Q: Why are violas larger than violins?
A: They're not. Violinists' heads are smaller.

Q: What's the difference between an accordion player and a terrorist?
A: Terrorists have sympathizers.

Q: How do you make a million dollars singing folk music?
A: Start with two million.

Q: What do you get when you play New Age music backward?
A: New Age music.

Original title of "The Star Spangled Banner" was "The Defense of Fort McHenry."

SHOW THEM THE MONEY

Who's getting rich? In the dog-eat-dog world of music royalties,
it's usually not the performer. Here's a quick rundown
of who makes what from the music you buy.

PERFORMANCE VS. MECHANICS

Every time someone buys a CD, everybody involved in the album's creation and distribution—from the songwriter to the record label to the retailer—gets a piece of the sale, known as a *royalty*. Royalties are divided into two types—performance and mechanical—and who gets them makes a big difference to everyone's bank account.

Performance royalties are paid every time a song is performed in public. This includes concerts, radio, TV, films, commercials, Muzak, and even background music in restaurants, bars, and malls. Anyone using music publicly has to pay royalties to the songwriter and music publisher (the person who deals with the administrative tasks of making music). Performance royalties are collected and disbursed by one of several performance-rights agencies, the largest of which are the American Society of Composers, Authors, and Publishers (ASCAP); Broadcast Music Inc. (BMI); SoundExchange; and the Society of European Stage Authors and Composers (SESAC).

Mechanical royalties are payments by the record company, or label, to songwriters, publishers, and performers for music sold on a per-unit basis. This includes not only CDs but also videos, computer games, ringtones, downloads, sheet music, and even musical greeting cards. The current payment rate (set by Congress) is 8.5 cents for songs of five minutes or less in length; that amount is split between the songwriter and publisher. The recording artists get mechanical royalties too, but those can vary, based on the terms of their contract with their label.

HOW MUCH DOES EVERYONE GET?

Royalties are just a small slice of the CD pie. Retailers and record labels also get some of the money. Here's an approximate breakdown of who gets what from each CD:

Suggested retail list price:	**$15.98**
The store:	4.73
The record label (including marketing & distribution):	7.90
The manufacturer who packaged the actual disc:	.83
The songwriters and publishers:	.82
The recording artist:	1.70

WHAT ABOUT DOWNLOADS?

With millions of songs being downloaded each year, there's a whole new procedure for calculating music royalties, but labels still make the most. Apple iTunes, for example, charges 99 cents per song. Apple grosses about 34 cents per download, and the record label gets 47 cents. The songwriter and publisher share 8 cents and the artists and producers split the remaining 10 cents.

SO, WHERE'S THE REAL MONEY?

Even though they might not make big bucks off CD sales, there are two ways that musicians *can* make a substantial amount of money:

• They can double up. Some artists write, sell, produce, or start their own record labels, thereby increasing their royalties.

• Most, though, make their money with concerts. Tours and merchandising (the stuff that's for sale at live shows) generally make a lot more money than albums do. The Rolling Stones grossed $138 million in 2006 from their "A Bigger Bang" tour, but made only $12 million that year in record royalties. Even lesser-known bands can make a good living on the road by setting their own ticket prices and commanding more than 50 percent of the show's profits. So if you want to really help your favorite band, go to their concerts and buy one of their T-shirts. That'll spread the bucks around.

• Some people do get rich off of recordings, though. Merv Griffin, for example, owned all of the rights to "Think Music," the *Jeopardy!* theme song. Griffin acted as songwriter, publisher, and producer for the song (he hired studio musicians, who don't get royalties). Griffin's estimated royalties on the 30-second instrumental: more than $70 million.

...A. They all appeared on *The Muppet Show.*

KILLER ALBUMS

A lot of things can make a musician's once-promising career take a sudden nosedive. Sometimes it's the pressure to repeat past successes, sometimes it's self-indulgence...and sometimes it's just one really bad album.

Artist: Peter Frampton
Album: *I'm in You*
Story: In 1976 Peter Frampton released his breakthrough album *Frampton Comes Alive!*, which sold 16 million copies worldwide. At the time, it was the best-selling live album in history and made the singer a teen idol. The pressure was on to release a successful follow-up...and quick. So in 1977, Frampton released his next album. But rather than something cheery and poppy like *Frampton Comes Alive!*, he made *I'm in You*, an experimental funk-rock album. Strangest of all, it included very little of Frampton's signature guitar work. Instead, it featured synthesizers, pianos, overdubs, and even an eight-minute funk song. The album earned the respect of music critics who had dismissed Frampton as a lightweight pop star, but it was too weird for his young fans. Expected to top *Frampton Comes Alive!*'s sales, *I'm in You* sold only a million copies—a lot for some acts, but a disappointment for megaplatinum Frampton at the peak of his career. Frampton took a year off and attempted a comeback in 1978 by starring with the Bee Gees in *Sgt. Pepper's Lonely Hearts Club Band*, a movie adaptation of the Beatles' classic album. Critics hated it, audiences avoided it, and the soundtrack album, with Frampton and others singing Beatles songs, sold even more poorly than *I'm in You*. Frampton's career never recovered.

Artist: Mariah Carey
Album: *Glitter*
Story: In 2001 Carey signed an $80 million deal with Virgin Records, the biggest recording contract ever. But even at that price, Virgin considered it a bargain—Carey was well established as a pop icon, still hot after a string of hit records in the 1990s. Her first album for Virgin: *Glitter*, an album of cover songs from the 1980s, or songs that sounded like they *could* have been from

---

Got milk? Hanson, Billy Ray Cyrus, and Tony Bennett have all worn milk "mustaches" in ads.

the 1980s. The record was also the soundtrack to a film called *Glitter*, a remake of *A Star Is Born* with Carey playing a 1980s pop singer. The film, Carey's first starring role, received terrible reviews and bombed at the box office. But Virgin Records wasn't worried because musically, Carey had never made a misstep. It turned out to be a bad gamble: Not only did Carey's fans avoid the movie *Glitter*, they avoided the album, too. To complicate matters, the album hit stores on September 11, 2001, a day when most Americans were glued to their televisions, watching reports of the terrorist attacks on the World Trade Center and other sites. Pop records were the last thing on anyone's mind, and *Glitter* sold only 600,000 copies—a tenth as many as Carey usually sold. It ended a bad year; earlier in 2001, she'd had a nervous breakdown and left a long, nonsensical message to her fans on her Web site, then retreated from public life to recuperate in a hospital. Virgin lost so much money on *Glitter* that they bought out Carey's huge contract and kicked her off the label. She wouldn't have another hit album or song for four years.

Artist: Garth Brooks
Album: *In the Life of Chris Gaines*
Story: By 1998, 36-year-old country singer Garth Brooks was the third-best-selling musician of all time, behind only the Beatles. But success took its toll: Brooks was bored with country music and was considering retiring from the business altogether. Instead, he came up with an unusual solution: He created an alter ego for himself—a moody, long-haired, soul-patch-wearing Australian rock singer named Chris Gaines. According to Brooks's fictitious backstory, Gaines was a rock superstar in the 1980s, won the 1990 Grammy for Album of the Year, and was now making a "comeback" after a near-fatal car accident. Brooks appeared on TV as Gaines (Brooks hosted *Saturday Night Live* in 1999; Gaines was the musical guest). A Chris Gaines song called "Lost in You" reached the *Billboard* Top 5, but Brooks's huge fan base and the music press were bewildered, calling the project everything from self-indulgent to crazy. *In the Life of Chris Gaines*, a "greatest hits" collection, turned out to be Brooks's worst-selling album ever. A planned Chris Gaines movie was canceled and Brooks retired the persona.

Every song title on the soundtrack to *An American Werewolf in London* has the word "moon."

9 RANDOM LISTS ABOUT MADONNA

Our trivial tribute to a pop singer who still makes headlines more than 25 years into her unparalleled career.

13 VITAL STATISTICS
1. Full name: Madonna Louise Ciccone
2. Birthplace: Bay City, Mich.
3. Birthdate: August 16, 1958
4. Astrological sign: Leo
5. Measurements: 34-23-33
6. Height: 5 feet, 4 inches tall
7. Eye color: hazel
8. Natural hair color: dark brown
9. Birth order: the third of eight children
10. Saint's name taken at her confirmation: Veronica
11. Name taken as a Hebrew/Kabbalistic name: Esther
12. Homes: New York City, Los Angeles, London, and Skibo Castle in Dornoch, Scotland
13. Nicknames: Nonni (childhood), Maddy, Mo, Madge, Mads, Veronica Electronica

6 BOOKS SHE WROTE
1. *The Adventures of Abdi*
2. *The English Roses*
3. *Lotsa de Casha*
4. *Mr. Peabody's Apples*
5. *SEX*
6. *Yakov and the Seven Thieves*

2 BANDS SHE SANG IN BEFORE GOING SOLO
1. The Breakfast Club
2. The Millionaires (later renamed Modern Dance, Emanon, and Emmy)

2 THINGS SHE MUST HAVE
1. A bottle of vodka in her dressing room (to spray on her stage clothes to keep them "fresh").
2. Complete silence when she's sleeping. (That includes running water.)

3 RUN-INS WITH THE CATHOLIC CHURCH
1. 1987: Pope John Paul II urges fans not to attend Madonna's "Who's That Girl?" World Tour in Italy.
2. 1989: Catholic leaders condemn her "Like a Prayer" video—featuring burning

crosses, statues crying blood, and Madonna kissing a statue of a black saint that comes to life—as "blasphemous."

3. 2006: Vatican officials call her "Confessions" tour performance (hanging from a cross and wearing a crown of thorns) an open attack on Catholicism and insist it not be performed in Rome.

8 GOLDEN RASPBERRY AWARDS

1. 1986: Worst Actress for *Shanghai Surprise*

2. 1987: Worst Actress for *Who's That Girl?*

3. 1993: Worst Actress for *Body of Evidence*

4. 1995: Worst Supporting Actress for *Four Rooms*

5. 2000: Worst Actress for *The Next Best Thing*

6. 2002: Worst Actress for *Swept Away* (tied with Britney Spears for *Crossroads*)

7. 2002: Worst Screen Couple (with Adriano Giannini) for *Swept Away*

8. 2002: Worst Supporting Actress for *Die Another Day*

3 WORLD RECORDS

1. Top-earning female singer of all time (*Guinness World Records*)

2. Top-grossing concert tour by a female artist, for the 2006 "Confessions" tour. (*Billboard*)

3. Most costume changes in a movie (*Evita*): 85 (39 hats, 45 pairs of shoes, and 56 pairs of earrings). (*Guinness World Records*)

4 REVEALING QUOTES

1. "I won't be happy until I'm as famous as God."

2. "I'm ambitious. But if I weren't as talented as I am ambitious, I would be a gross monstrosity."

3. "I have the same goal I've had ever since I was a girl. I want to rule the world."

4. "Everyone probably thinks that I'm a raving nymphomaniac, that I have an insatiable sexual appetite, when the truth is I'd rather read a book."

2 RANDOM FACTS

1. Outside of the U.S. and Canada, the documentary *Madonna: Truth or Dare* was called *In Bed with Madonna*.

2. Her book *SEX* was originally titled *X*, but it was published within months of the release of Spike Lee's *Malcolm X*, so it was changed to *SEX*.

MUSICAL PRESIDENTS, PART I

*Some U.S. presidents were amazing musicians; some just dabbled;
others couldn't hit a note to save their lives. Here are a few
musical anecdotes from the annals of the Oval Office.*

GEORGE WASHINGTON (1789–97)

Washington was not very musical. "I can neither sing," he admitted, "nor raise a single note on any instrument to convince the unbelieving." Yet many in his family *were* talented musicians, and he hired a "music master" to come to Mount Vernon once a week to provide instruction. The lessons would often escalate into full-blown music parties. Some participants noted that Washington preferred a large group of musicians at these impromptu sessions. Why? To drown out his own inferior flute playing.

JOHN ADAMS (1797–1801)

Adams began a musical tradition that still endures today. On New Year's Day in 1801, he invited a local band of marines to play music at the Executive Mansion (before it was called the White House). Adams was so impressed with their skill, he urged Congress to draft a bill declaring them the official band of the young nation. Now dubbed the United States Marine Band, it is the oldest professional musical organization in the United States, and has played for every president since.

THOMAS JEFFERSON (1801–09)

A man of many talents, Jefferson is known to have played the cello, clavichord, and violin. As with many other passions in Jefferson's life (art, farming, architecture), it wasn't enough that he alone enjoyed them—Jefferson believed that the young nation would benefit from them as well. "Music is the favorite passion of my soul," he said, "and fortune has cast my lot in a country where it is in a state of deplorable barbarism." To counter this, Jefferson wrote essays on the virtues of music, urging his fellow countrymen to take up a musical instrument.

JAMES MADISON (1809–17)

James and Dolley Madison may have been the most social First
Family in history, entertaining guests on nearly every evening of
Madison's two terms in office. On one such evening, the Marquis
de Lafayette presented Madison with a lead crystal flute, made in
France. It bears the inscription "A S E President Madison des
Etats Unis" ("To His Eminence President Madison of the United
States"). Said to have been one of the president's most prized pos-
sessions, he sometimes played it for guests while Dolley accompa-
nied him on piano. The flute is now in the Library of Congress.

ABRAHAM LINCOLN (1861–65)

Although not much of a musician (he dabbled with the harmonica and Jew's harp), Lincoln's dark moods could often be swayed by
a simple American "sad, little song." In place of the classical pieces
that the Marine Band usually played, Lincoln requested popular
folk ditties. His favorite song, ironically, was the tune that rallied
the South. "I have always thought 'Dixie' one of the best tunes I
have ever heard," he said. Some of Lincoln's other favorites:
"When Johnny Comes Marching Home," "John Brown's Body,"
"The Battle Hymn of the Republic," and "Camptown Races."

ULYSSES S. GRANT (1869–77)

Grant hated music. He liked to tell people, "I only know two
songs: one is 'Yankee Doodle' and the other isn't."

CHESTER A. ARTHUR (1881–85)

Arthur was not a very public man. "I may be President of the
United States," he would say, "but my private life is nobody's
damned business." However, one item about Arthur's private life
did find its way to the press. According to an 1882 article from the
Washington Weekly Star: "President Arthur can make the banjo do
some lively humming when so disposed."

For more musical presidents, turn to page 289.

*   *   *

"I'd rather be a musician than a rock star." —**George Harrison**

Heavy! Liberace's last piano was decorated with 350 pounds of rhinestones.

THE ELVIS MOVIE GENERATOR

From 1956 to 1969, Elvis Presley made 31 movies with titles like Roustabout, Girls! Girls! Girls!, *and* Harum Scarum. *At a rate of more than two movies per year, they were by necessity low budget and formulaic, usually just a showcase for a handful of Elvis songs, a pretty girl, a chase scene, and a fight. Now you too can come up with your own Elvis movie plot... with Uncle John's patented Elvis Movie Generator.*

1) PICK A NAME FOR ELVIS'S CHARACTER

It should be something masculine, preferably one syllable.
Real examples: *Clint, Vince, Chad, Rick, Jess, Deke, Josh*
Or it can be playful and boyish, usually ending with the letter "y."
Real examples: *Jimmy, Johnny, Toby, Danny, Rusty, Lucky*

2) PICK A PROFESSION FOR ELVIS'S CHARACTER

He always has a job that requires lifting, throwing, and/or sweating. Extra points if it's dangerous or mildly threatening.
Real examples: *boxer, helicopter pilot, gambler, rodeo cowboy, life-guard, crop duster, waterskiing instructor, tour guide, soldier, racecar driver, pro bono doctor, Navy frogman, handyman*
Or it can be something a little more believable for Elvis.
Real examples: *rock 'n' roll singer, traveling singer, nightclub singer, coffeehouse singer, jazz singer, riverboat singer*

3) PICK A FUN-LOVING AND WHIMSICAL TITLE

A good title should contain one or more of the following: "Girls," "Love," "Rock," a city or state, an article of women's clothing, a nonsense word, two words that rhyme, or an exclamation point. Some examples we made up:
So Many Girls So Little Time, What a Night!, That Darn Girl, Gals-a-Poppin'!, Wackity Schmackity, Howdy Denver!, Drive Faster!, What's a Feller to Do?, Too Many Bikinis, Say Hey, Once Upon a Time in the Islands, Aloha Mexico

---

Neil Young and Jimi Hendrix stole a truck to get to Woodstock in time to perform.

4) CREATE A PLOT BY FILLING IN THESE BLANKS

In (*title of the movie*), Elvis plays (*character's name*), a (*character's profession*) who needs to raise $5,000 by the end of the week to (*get into the big race, stay out of jail, buy his airplane back, fix his motorcycle, etc.*). Will he do it in time? And will he win the heart of (*Judy, Valerie, Cathy, Lily, etc.*) in the process?

Here are a few we came up with:

• In **Stockholm Stockings**, Elvis plays **Dash**, a **lobster fisherman** who needs to raise $5,000 by the end of the week in order to **buy back his father's scuba business.** Will he do it in time? And will he win the heart of **Betty, the waitress in the local pie shop,** in the process?

• In **Racin'**, Elvis plays **Johnny**, a **motorcycle racer** who needs to raise $5,000 by the end of the week in order to **get enough money for the race entry fee.** Will he do it in time? And will he win the heart of **Sheree, the sheriff's daughter,** in the process?

• In **Turnpike**, Elvis plays **Lance**, a **singing truck driver** who needs to raise $5,000 by the end of the week in order to **buy a pony for the kids at the orphanage.** Will he do it in time? And will he win the heart of **Margie, the lady doctor who works in the orphanage,** in the process?

*　　*　　*

KEEPING UP WITH THE TIMES

A weekly summary of R&B music has been a part of *Billboard* magazine since 1942. Today its chart of rhythm & blues and rap songs is called the "Hot R&B/Hip-Hop Songs Chart." Here are some of its former—and somewhat politically incorrect—names:

1942–1945: "The Harlem Hit Parade"

1945–1949: "Race Records"

1949–1958: "Rhythm & Blues Records"

1973–1982: "Hot Soul Singles"

1982–1990: "Hot Black Singles"

Elvis once volunteered to be an FBI drug informant. (His services were refused.)

THE STRANGEST MUSICALS EVER MADE

Uncle John has always wanted a musical version of the Thomas Crapper story. And no—not done by a tuba band.

BAT BOY: THE MUSICAL (1997)
This award-winning off-Broadway musical was inspired by a batlike creature that was invented by—and frequently featured in—the tabloid newspaper *Weekly World News*. Violent, funny, and *very* R-rated, the play tells the story of a half-bat, half-boy who is adopted by a very ordinary family, who name him Edgar. They attempt to civilize him, but his taste for blood can't be overcome, the townspeople are afraid of him, and several people end up dead. Theater critic John Lahr of the *New Yorker* noted that "this is the only play in the history of the theater whose hero ends Act I with a rabbit in his mouth, and who moves on in Act II to an entire cow's head."

CHEE-CHEE (1928)
This play by the legendary musical duo of Richard Rodgers and Lorenz Hart put an end to their long string of successful shows. Why? It may have been the plot, based on a comic novel called *The Son of the Grand Eunuch*. In the story, the Chinese emperor's grand eunuch, Li-Pi-Sao, tells his son, Li-Pi-Tchou, that he wants him to take over his job. But Li-Pi-Tchou is in love with the beautiful Chee-Chee and doesn't want to become a eunuch. So the lovers flee and go through a series of scenes where Chee-Chee has to award some thief or bully sexual favors to get herself and Li-Pi-Tchou out of one predicament or another. The review in the *London Observer* was entitled simply, "Nasty! Nasty!"

THALIDOMIDE: A MUSICAL (1995)
This is the (musical) story of a man who was born with very short arms and "flipperlike" hands...and his search for love. It was written by Mat Fraser, who was born with short arms and flipperlike hands because his mother was one of the tens of thousands of

women around the world who took the drug thalidomide during her pregnancy. The musical is Fraser's humorous and very un-PC look at the drug's history and his own experience with prejudice. "I don't believe any subject is too dark for comedy or musical theater," Fraser said.

HEDWIG AND THE ANGRY INCH (1998)

This is just your basic off-Broadway musical about a gay East German rock singer named Hedwig who falls in love with a U.S. soldier and has a sex-change operation so he can marry him and go to the States. But the operation is botched and Hedwig ends up with an inch-long "mound of flesh" where his penis used to be. But they get married anyway, and Hedwig goes to live with the soldier in Kansas until the soldier runs off with another man. So Hedwig assembles a band of female Korean rock-and-rollers he calls "the Angry Inch" and starts touring. Then he falls in love with an innocent teenager who steals his songs and becomes a huge star, and Hedwig and the Angry Inch are forced to play in chain restaurants to survive. And they sing a lot of songs. So, you know, same old stuff. It was made into a film in 2001.

1776 (1969)

You recognize the year—but how about the Broadway musical? It's about the Second Continental Congress and the writing of the Declaration of Independence...and it's a musical comedy. That improbable combination somehow worked: It ran for three years (1,217 performances) and won three Tony awards (Best Musical, Best Featured Actor in a Musical for Ronald Holgate, and Best Director). Highlight: Thomas Jefferson, Benjamin Franklin, and two cohorts perform a high-stepping song and dance called "But Mr. Adams" in which they each try to get out of writing the Declaration. Sample lyric: "I cannot write with any style or proper etiquette/I don't know a participle from a predicate/I am just a simple cobbler from Connecticut." It was also made into a movie (now available on DVD).

*   *   *

"We hate critics. Most of them are fat and ugly and they criticize."
—Rob Pilatus, of Milli Vanilli

In the horror film *Trick or Treat*, Ozzy Osbourne plays a televangelist who denounces heavy metal.

CRAZED CONDUCTORS

You know that stereotype of the angry orchestra conductor hollering insults at his terrified musicians? Here we reinforce that stereotype.

"Already too loud!"
   —Bruno Walter, at his first rehearsal with an American orchestra, on seeing them reach for their instruments

"God tells me how the music should sound, but you stand in the way!"
   —Arturo Toscanini, to a trumpet player

"Come on, people, pick a note—preferably one that Debussy wrote!"
   —Johannes Dietrich

"Why do you always insist on playing while I am trying to conduct?"
   —Eugene Ormandy

"I never use a score when conducting my orchestra. Does a lion tamer enter a cage with a book on how to tame a lion?"
   —Dimitri Mitropolous

"You don't need to count here. You won't get lost because at the end, I will turn and look at you stoppingly!"
   —Leif Segerstam

"Never look at the trombones. You'll only encourage them."
   —Richard Strauss

"I can wait."
   —Arnold Schoenberg, when told that a soloist would need six fingers to perform his concerto

"Show me an orchestra that likes its conductor and I'll show you a lousy conductor."
   —Goddard Lieberson

"Boys, look like you're having fun, but don't have any."
   —Lawrence Welk

"After I die, I shall return to Earth as a gatekeeper of a bordello and I won't let any of you enter!"
   —Arturo Toscanini

"The conductor's stand is not a continent of power, but rather an island of solitude."
   —Riccardo Muti

"At last, fortissimo!"
   —Gustav Mahler, when he first saw Niagara Falls

Liszt-o-mania: In 1842 women fought over Franz Liszt's handkerchiefs as souvenirs.

WHY DOES THE RUBBED WINEGLASS SING?

It it physics…or fairies?

HEAR'S THE RUB
You've probably seen this, or done it yourself: Hold the base of a stemmed wineglass firmly to a tabletop, wet your finger, and rub it around the rim of the glass. A high, eerie sound sings out, and you can change the pitch by lowering or raising the level of liquid in the glass. More than that, you can increase the volume by rubbing the glass harder or faster. People have been known to perform with sets of wineglasses, playing entire complicated songs. An instrument was even invented based on the process: the Glass Armonica, built by Benjamin Franklin (see page 294). But how does it work?

The answer is that the sound comes from tiny, invisible music fairies that live inside wineglasses. When you rub the rim of the glass, you send strong vibrations through the fairies' environment, much like our environment can be vibrated by a strong earthquake. The sound you hear is the terrified screams of the fairies who are either running from their homes in horror or being crushed to death in the cataclysm.

OR NOT
Okay, we were just kidding. The wonderful sound made by rubbing a wineglass can be explained by simple physics.

Sound—all sound—is produced by the vibration of some kind of material, which in turn causes a vibrating wave of air that travels to our ears. (Sound vibrations can also travel through liquids and solids.) In this instance, rubbing the glass's rim causes it to vibrate, the same way that striking a bell causes *it* to vibrate.

Your finger is the key: As it rubs around the rim, it's repeatedly and rapidly sticking to—and then coming unstuck from—the glass. That's known as "slip-stick" motion, and it's a common phenomenon. It happens during earthquakes when tectonic plates slide against each other, it explains the sound produced by creaky hinges as well as the sound produced by a violin bow rubbed across a string. (Wetting your finger helps the slip-stick motion occur by removing the natural oils from your fingertip, making for better contact with the glass.) Your finger is actually creating a wave of vibrations through the glass, which cause it to wobble back and forth very rapidly—hundreds of times per second—changing its shape from round to oval again and again. That vibration causes the air around the glass to vibrate, creating sound waves that travel to your ears.

JUST ADD WATER

But why do different glasses "sing" different notes? And why does the pitch change if you add wine or water to the glass? Also simple: The pitch of the glass, like the pitch of a guitar string, is determined by its size, mass, and composition. Thin-walled glasses vibrate more rapidly, or at a higher frequency, than thick-walled glasses, just as thinner guitar strings vibrate faster than thicker ones. And, to our ears, that faster vibration results in a higher note. (If you want to know the frequency of a given glass, tap it with a spoon. That "ping" you hear is the same pitch it will produce when you rub its rim.)

Now for the water trick: Put more liquid in the glass, and the pitch is lower. Take some away, and the pitch is higher. That's because when you add water to the glass, the water vibrates *with* the glass. And the increased mass (just as with a thicker glass) results in a lower-frequency vibration—a lower note. This means that you can "tune" a set of glasses and play music with them, as people have been doing for more than 500 years.

EXTRAS

• You can make a glass sing without even touching it. Take two similar stemmed glasses and place them on a table an inch apart from each other. Rub the rim of one to make it sing, and the other one will also vibrate and produce sound. Then pour water into both glasses and do it again: You can see the water in the untouched glass vibrating.

• First wineglass-playing star: Irish inventor Richard Pockrich, who toured the British Isles in the 1700s, playing concerts on what he called his "Angelic Organ"—a box with wineglasses inside.

"DID I SHAVE MY LEGS FOR THIS?"

...and other great country song titles.

"Mama Get a Hammer (There's a Fly on Papa's Head)"

"Rednecks, White Socks and Blue Ribbon Beer"

"He Went to Sleep and the Hogs Ate Him"

"Redneck Martians Stole My Baby"

"If Fingerprints Showed Up on Skin, Wonder Whose I'd Find on You"

"It Ain't Love, but It Ain't Bad"

"Flushed from the Bathroom of Your Heart"

"She Feels Like a Brand New Man Tonight"

"She Got the Gold Mine (I Got the Shaft)"

"You're the Reason Our Kids Are Ugly"

"She Dropped Me in Denver (So I Had a Whole Mile to Fall)"

"Thank God and Greyhound She's Gone"

"She Broke My Heart at Walgreens (and I Cried All the Way to Sears)"

"Get Your Tongue Outta My Mouth (Cause I'm Kissing You Goodbye)"

"All My Exes Live in Texas (That's Why I Hang My Hat in Tennessee)"

"I Got in at Two With a Ten and Woke Up at Ten With a Two"

"Touch Me with More than Your Hands"

"My Wife Left Me for My Girlfriend"

"Get Your Biscuits in the Oven and Your Buns in the Bed"

"Drop-Kick Me, Jesus, Through the Goalposts of Life"

"I'm the Only Hell (My Mama Ever Raised)"

"Too Dumb for New York, Too Ugly for L.A."

"If You See Me Gettin' Smaller, It's 'Cause I'm Leavin' You"

The *Leave It to Beaver* theme is called "The Toy Parade."

MUSIC'S MOST...

Some of the undisputed record holders in the music world.

PROLIFIC SONGWRITER

In 1907 the owner of Pelham's Café in New York's China-town asked one of his waiters—one of his "singing waiters," a popular fad at the time—to write a promotional song for the restaurant. He wrote "Marie from Sunny Italy"—and it earned him 37 cents. That young waiter was Irving Berlin, and "Marie from Sunny Italy" was his first published song. Although he could play no instrument at the time, Berlin decided to become a song-writer, and to say he was successful would be an understatement of epic proportions. Over the next 50 years, Berlin wrote more than 3,000 songs. They include dozens of standards like "Anything You Can Do (I Can Do Better)," "A Pretty Girl Is Like a Melody," "Oh, How I Hate to Get Up in the Morning," "Blue Skies," "Easter Parade," "How Deep Is the Ocean," "Alexander's Ragtime Band," "Puttin' on the Ritz," "There's No Business Like Show Business," and two of the most famous songs in American music history, "God Bless America" and "White Christmas." He also wrote 19 musicals, including *Annie Get Your Gun*, and 18 film scores.

...TALKATIVE PERFORMER

On October 17, 2003, Dan Lloyd of Cardiff, Wales, had a sore throat. That's because Lloyd, who goes by the name "Rapper Ruff-stylz," had just finished a world-record round of rapping—nonstop for 10 hours and 34 minutes. By *Guinness* rules he was allowed to take a 15-minute break, but only once every four hours. And if the physical demands of the feat weren't grueling enough, it was freestyle rapping, so he had to make up all the words as he went along. "People were bringing up words for me to talk about and to rhyme" he said. "I really just went through hyperspace from one crazy subject to another." The previous record was 8 hours 45 minutes, set by Canadian rapper TO that same year.

...SPEEDY SONGWRITER

Writer's block is evidently not a problem for Canadian singer-

---

Woody Guthrie wrote "This Land Is My Land" as a protest of Irving Berlin's "God Bless America."

songwriter Kevin Bath. Between October 2006, and September 2007, he released one new CD of original songs...every week. Each recording contained eight songs, for a total of 416 songs written, recorded, and published in one year, which *Guinness World Records* acknowledged as a world record. The songs cover many musical styles, including rock, punk, country, reggae, folk, children's, instrumental, and one completely improvisational collection. (Some album titles: *Sponge Bath Square Pants*, *Punk Bath*, and *Grapes of Bath*.)

...RECORDED ELECTRIC BASSIST

Carol Kaye was 22 years old in 1957 when she was asked to play for a Sam Cooke recording session. She was a jazz guitarist by trade, playing clubs all over Los Angeles (she started at the age of 14), and thought the studio work would be a one-time thing. She was wrong. For the next five years, she worked as a regular session guitar player in Hollywood studios. Then, in 1963, a bass player failed to show up for a session at Capitol Records. Kaye grabbed a Fender electric bass and played the part. She was such a natural on the instrument that she quickly became the most coveted bass player in L.A., no matter what the style of music. She has since played on *more than 10,000 recordings*, many of which you've heard and just didn't know it was her. (Session players were almost never listed in the credits.) A small sample of some of the people she played for: the Beach Boys, Randy Newman, Barbra Streisand, Glen Campbell, Sonny and Cher, Dr. John, Taj Mahal, Quincy Jones, and the Doors. She also worked in film and television, recording theme and background music for *The Brady Bunch*, *M*A*S*H*, *The Cosby Show*, *The Love Boat*, and *Hawaii Five-0*. (Our favorite: she came up with the "dum dum, dum-dum-dum dum" part in the *Mission Impossible* theme song.) Her advice to aspiring session players: "Learn how to grab a parking place, don't be late, carry a pencil, don't be egotistical... oh, yeah, and know how to read music, be creative, and play your a** off."

*　　　*　　　*

Those who wish to sing always find a song.

—Swedish Proverb

Bill Haley once used the stage name "the Ramblin' Yodeler."

MUSIC TO GO SHOPPING BY

*Is that bland music you hear in the supermarket sending you
a secret message to spend more money? (Yes, it is.)*

SOMETHING IN THE AIR

In behavioral psychology, there's a specialty called *atmospherics*, is the study of how a store's environment—everything from the paint on the walls to the display layouts to the music—affects retail purchases. It's also the study of how to change a store's atmosphere to generate greater sales. The goal is to create an environment that's pleasant, so shoppers will linger. Ever since a seminal 1982 study by Ronald Milliman, a marketing professor at Western Kentucky University, retailers have been trying to figure out just what music to play to make shoppers spend, spend, spend.

Milliman examined how the tempo of the background music playing in a store affected shoppers. If the music had a laid-back tempo of 60 beats per minute, shoppers lingered longer than if it were a more lively 108 beats per minute—and both groups spent more time shopping than those in a store with no music at all. More time means more impulse buys; for every additional minute shoppers spend in a supermarket, they spend another $1.89. And slowing down the beat of the music has been shown to increase sales by 38.2 percent. It was the same with diners: Patrons at restaurants with laid-back music spent an average of 56 minutes eating, as opposed to an average of 45 minutes with faster beats—and they bought 3.04 more drinks.

KNOW YOUR AUDIENCE

So is that the solution? Slow the music down and sales go through the roof? Not quite. Atmospherics researchers have broken music into two different categories: background music (like Muzak) and foreground music (like Top-40 songs). If tempo were the only factor affecting shopping, the world would be overrun by elevator music. However, studies have also shown that the under-25 crowd

---

Palindromic pseudonym: Stevie Wonder released a 1968 album under the name Eivets Rednow.

will flee Muzak-soaked environments and linger around pop music. For older crowds, the reverse is true.

The details get even more specialized than that. Shoppers who aren't pressed for time will linger in stores playing unfamiliar music, but if they're on a schedule, they'll stay longer if they know all the songs. And in restaurants, the popularity of the music has far less effect than volume: Softer music means happier customers. (Song length hasn't been shown to have any effect at all.)

THE SEARCH CONTINUES

So what's a store owner to do? Pop songs or smooth jazz? Slow or fast? Loud or soft? Esoteric or well-known? In the end, what all this research has shown is that if customers like the music, they're more likely to keep shopping. And as long as taste in music is as varied as the channels on satellite radio, stores will continue to try to find the perfect tune to coax your money out of your wallet.

* * *

MYTH-CONCEPTION: THE MUSICAL

The Reel Story: In *The Sound of Music*, the von Trapp children are portrayed as having no musical abilities. Their governess Maria (played by Julie Andrews) has to teach them to sing and play instruments from scratch.

The Real Story: Don't believe the Hollywood version. Yes, the von Trapps were a real family from Austria who really did emigrate to the United States just before World War II, and they really were a family of singers. But they didn't learn it from their governess—they had always been gifted musicians, and the children were raised in a musical home. Their father, Georg von Trapp played the violin, accordion, and mandolin. Their mother Agathe played the piano and violin. Long before Maria arrived, the von Trapp home often sounded like a musical conservatory as the children practiced piano, violin, guitar, cello, clarinet, accordion, and recorder. When Maria joined the household, she taught the children madrigals (a type of secular singing) and masses and organized them into four-part harmonies.

STRANGE LAWSUITS

*Not even an artform as sacred as music can
escape the clutches of pesky lawyers.*

PLAINTIFF: Slipknot, a heavy-metal band
DEFENDANT: Burger King
LAWSUIT: In a 2005 ad campaign for their new "chicken fries," Burger King showed mock-concert footage of a heavy-metal band called Coq Roq, whose members wore grotesque masks and costumes to resemble monstrous chickens. Slipknot sued, claiming Burger King had stolen their stage act (they dress up in grotesque masks and costumes) and that the Burger King ads would confuse their fans into thinking that it was actually *them* in the commercials. Burger King argued that lots of heavy-metal bands (such as KISS and Marilyn Manson) perform in costume, and that Coq Roq wasn't intended to resemble Slipknot.
VERDICT: A district court threw out the case.

PLAINTIFF: Peter Frampton
DEFENDANT: Surf clothing manufacturer Billabong
LAWSUIT: In 2004 Billabong came out with a bikini bottom that featured a 1970s-era picture of Frampton and the phrase "Baby I love your waves"—a take-off on a line from one of Frampton's best-known songs, 1975's "Baby, I Love Your Way." Billabong also used the image and phrase on a line of T-shirts. Only problem: They used Frampton's face and lyric without permission...and without paying him.
VERDICT: Settled out of court, but Billabong no longer sells the bikini or T-shirts.

PLAINTIFF: Bryan O'Lone, a 16-year-old concert pianist
DEFENDANT: Yelena Ivanov, president of the Young Pianist Competition of New Jersey
LAWSUIT: In preparation for the 2005 competition at Carnegie Hall, O'Lone had rehearsed Chopin's "Sherzo No. 2." But when he arrived at the recital hall, the event schedule indicated he'd be per-

forming Beethoven's "Pathetique," a piece he didn't know. O'Lone reported the mix-up to contest officials, who told him he had to perform the Beethoven piece. When the time came, O'Lone went on stage and played the Chopin piece he'd rehearsed. In the middle of the performance, Ivanov stormed onto the stage, shut the keyboard cover on O'Lone's hands, and told the audience he'd been kicked out of the competition. O'Lone and his parents sued Ivanov (for "public embarrassment"), asking for an apology and $350.
VERDICT: Pending.

PLAINTIFF: Evel Knievel, 1970s motorcycle daredevil
DEFENDANT: Kanye West, 2000s rap star
LAWSUIT: In the video for his 2006 single "Touch the Sky," West plays a character named "Evel Kanyevel" who attempts to jump over the Snake River Canyon on a rocket-powered motorcycle. Knievel sued West, claiming that West stole his look (West wears a Knievel-esque stars-and-stripes jumpsuit) and because of the video's similarity to his own 1974 real-life jump over the Snake River Canyon. It added that the "vulgar and offensive sexual images" in the video hurt Knievel's image and reputation with children.
VERDICT: The two met at Knievel's Tampa condo in late November 2007 and made a secret settlement. "I thought he was a wonderful guy and quite a gentleman," the 69-year-old daredevil said of the 29-year-old rapper. (Knievel died on November 30, just days after the meeting.)

PLAINTIFF: The State of Illinois
DEFENDANT: The Dave Matthews Band
LAWSUIT: In 2004 one of the band's tour buses was driving across Chicago's Kinzie Street Bridge. The driver decided that the bridge's open metal grating made it a great place to empty the bus's septic tank, so he illegally dumped about 100 gallons of human waste into the Chicago River below. Oops. It landed on a tour boat. The state sued the Dave Matthews Band for $70,000 in civil penalties and threatened criminal charges.
VERDICT: In addition to settling the lawsuit by paying $200,000 to the state, the band donated $50,000 to the Friends of the Chicago River and $50,000 to the Chicago Park District.

None of Frank Sinatra's 29 partners on *Duets* or *Duets II* (1993–94) recorded with him in the studio.

I WANT MY MTV!

*Filmed performances by big stars seems like a no-brainer—
who wouldn't want to watch? So why did it take so
long for the industry to figure it out?*

A LONG AND WINDING ROAD

The earliest ancestor of the music video was the *soundie*, a black-and-white 16mm film recording of a musician performing before a live audience. The first soundies appeared in 1940, and all the big singing stars and bandleaders recorded them: Bing Crosby, Cab Calloway, Duke Ellington, even Lawrence Welk. Eight to ten three-minute soundies from different artists fit on a single film reel, which would be sent to diners, bars, and nightclubs all over the country. Patrons could drop a dime in a Panoram—a video jukebox with a small viewing screen—and watch a soundie.

There were a few problems, though: Viewers couldn't choose which video they wanted to see (the way they could choose songs in a jukebox) because the reel just ran continuously. Other issues were technical: The reels didn't last very long and the Panoram's mechanics were unreliable—often, the reel wouldn't slip into the correct playing position and would instead be thrown off balance inside the machine. Then a repairman had to be called in to fix it.

But it was the advent of television after World War II that really led to the decline of soundies. With musical variety shows like *The Ed Sullivan Show* playing for free, why would anyone waste a dime on a Panoram? By the mid-1960s, bands like the Beatles and the Rolling Stones had begun producing film clips of their songs to promote their albums. Most of these early videos aired on music TV shows like *Shindig* and *Hullabaloo*. But it would be another 30 years before music videos got their own TV station.

THANK QUBE

In 1977 a cable system called Qube debuted in Ohio. Among its 30 channels, Qube had several unique ones: Star, which became the Movie Channel; Pinwheel, which became Nickelodeon, and

Sight on Sound, which featured concert footage and other types of musical programming.

A former disc jockey and radio program director for New York's WNBC, Bob Pittman, noticed how popular Qube was in its local market and used some of Qube's concepts on a local New York TV show called *Album Tracks*. In 1979 he got a job with the Warner Satellite Entertainment Company, and the following year he pitched the idea of a station that aired videos produced by record companies.

VIDEO REINVENTS THE RADIO STAR

Warner execs loved the idea and gave him the green light, and on August 21, 1981, at one minute past midnight, MTV debuted. It was a good deal for Warner: The record companies provided the videos at their own cost, so the station's content was basically free. The first video: the Buggles' "Video Killed the Radio Star." (Second video: Pat Benatar's "You Better Run.")

At that time, the station only had about 125 videos, but within months, MTV was the most-watched cable network Warner owned. For his part, Pittman pushed hard to make the station unique. His target audience was under 30, so he hired flashy design houses to create ads to appeal to those viewers. He also wanted the station's IDs to be unique; Pittman felt that viewers should never turn to MTV and be confused about what they were watching.

The result: in every market where MTV was shown, record sales went up. Stores reported that albums by groups like Duran Duran and the Stray Cats—artists with limited radio play—were flying off shelves simply because their videos were on MTV. In markets where MTV wasn't available, Pittman ran ads urging viewers to call their cable companies and say "I want my MTV!" Thousands of fans did just that, and by 1983, MTV was available in most areas from New York to Los Angeles.

THE STATION'S SEGREGATED CHILDHOOD

As MTV's popularity and viewership increased, critics began to attack it. In particular, they slammed MTV for excluding African American artists. The station shot back, saying that its rock music format wasn't compatible with funk, R&B, or rap—in other words, with the stereotypical black music styles. The argument continued

Manfred Mann's Earth Band's "Blinded by the Light" includes the melody of "Chopsticks."

until 1982, when Michael Jackson's *Thriller* album hit record stores. His record company, CBS, demanded that MTV show Jackson's "Billie Jean" video. ("Billie Jean" was the album's third single, but the others, "Wanna Be Startin' Something," and "The Girl Is Mine," didn't have videos.) If it didn't, CBS would pull *all* of its videos—which made up 25 percent of MTV's programming. MTV caved. "Billie Jean" became a #1 hit and was the first video by an African American artist to air on MTV.

MTV DOES NOT PLAY WELL WITH OTHERS

It wasn't long before MTV had competition. Country Music Television launched in 1983, and many other imitators, like Cable Music Channel (CMC), hit the airwaves. Most fizzled, but commercial TV began to pay attention to videos, too. Shows like *Friday Night Videos* (on NBC) and *Night Tracks* (on WTBS) ran for years. MTV responded by demanding exclusive rights to videos from the record companies, and in most cases, it got them. These exclusive contracts soon turned MTV into the major player in video distribution (and also gave the station a reputation as a bully).

WORLD DOMINATION?

Initially, MTV's primary demographic was young people. To attract an older audience, MTV launched VH1 in 1985. The station also began tweaking its own all-music format to hold on to younger viewers. By 1987, music videos were interspersed with programs like the game show *Remote Control* and Weird Al Yankovic's *AL-TV*, which aired song parodies. About the same time, MTV Europe, MTV Australia, and MTV Japan debuted. MTV India and MTV Asia followed in the 1990s, and MTV *Internacional*, a weekly show, expanded into MTV Latin America.

Today, your chances of stumbling onto a video when you turn to MTV (or even MTV2) are slim. Sitcoms, reality shows, dramas, and celebrity news rule. You want videos? Go to MTV's Web site—or YouTube.

Bonus: Which videos did MTV play *after* the first two, the Buggles and Pat Benatar? The next six were "She Won't Dance" (Rod Stewart), "You Better You Bet" (the Who), "Little Susie's on the Up" (Ph.D.), "We Don't Talk Anymore" (Cliff Richard), "Brass in Pocket" (the Pretenders), and "Time Heals" (Todd Rundgren).

Gladys Knight won first prize on *Ted Mack's Amateur Hour* TV show when she was 7 years old.

FIRST RECORDS

Buying your first album or single is a rite of passage. Here's what some celebrities picked for their first purchases.

- **Bruce Springsteen:** Elvis Presley's "Jailhouse Rock"
- **Dave Matthews:** *Magical Mystery Tour* by the Beatles
- **Lou Reed:** Fats Domino's *The Fat Man*
- **Rob Zombie:** *The Alice Cooper Show*
- **John Mayer:** Debbie Gibson's *Out of the Blue*
- **Mandy Moore:** "Wind Beneath My Wings" by Bette Midler
- **Elvis Costello:** "Twist and Shout" by the Beatles
- **Paul Rudd** (actor, *Anchorman, Knocked Up*): "Wichita Lineman" by Glen Campbell
- **Chris Martin** of Coldplay: *Thriller* by Michael Jackson
- **David Furnish** (Elton John's partner): *Caribou* by Elton John
- **Trisha Yearwood:** *Barry Manilow's Greatest Hits*
- **Kelly Clarkson:** Guns N' Roses' *Appetite for Destruction*
- **Courtney Love:** Marlo Thomas's *Free to Be You and Me*
- **David Gilmour** of Pink Floyd: "Rock Around the Clock" by Bill Haley and His Comets
- **Levon Helm** of the Band: "School Days" by Chuck Berry
- **Morrissey** of the Smiths: Marianne Faithfull's "Come and Stay with Me"
- **Kurt Cobain:** "Seasons in the Sun" by Terry Jacks
- **Iggy Pop:** "Red River Rock" by Johnny and the Hurricanes
- **Janis Joplin:** a Leadbelly collection
- **Eric Clapton:** *The Chirping Crickets* by Buddy Holly and the Crickets

B. B. King wrote jingles for Colgate, Pepsi, and AT&T.

MUSICAL
WORD ORIGINS

*Because we always wanted to know where
the word "music" came from.*

DRUM. This word comes from the Middle Dutch term
tromme, which is believed to be onomotopaeic in origin. It
became the English *drum*, as a noun, in the early 1500s.

DOO-WOP. This music style, begun in the 1950s and characterized by rich vocal harmonies, was named for the nonsense syllables
sung behind the lead. First song that actually had the phrase "doo-
wop" in it: "When You Dance," a 1955 hit by the Turbans. It didn't
become an official word, however, until 1969.

MUSIC. It became an English word around A.D. 1250. It comes
from the Middle French *musique*, which came from the Latin
musica, which came from the Greek *mousikos*, which referred to
any art ruled by Zeus's nine daughters who protected the arts,
known as the *Mousae*, or Muses.

TREBLE. From the Latin *triplus*, meaning "triple." It was first
used as a musical term in English the 1300s, describing the third,
and highest, part in three-part harmony. Today it refers generally
to the higher frequencies in music (as opposed to the lower *bass*
frequencies).

PSALM. The old Greek verb *psallein* meant "to pluck a stringed
instrument." That became *psalmos*, which meant something along
the lines of "the sound of a harp," and then came to mean a song,
especially a sacred song of the Jewish tradition, as in the psalms of
King David.

SEA SHANTY. Shanties are songs sung by sailors in a tradition
going back at least to the 1500s. They're often call-and-response
songs and were used like other work songs—to establish a rhythm

for repetitive tasks and to help keep the crew's spirits up. An example you probably know: "Blow the Man Down." ("Give me some time to blow the man down.") The term comes from the French *chantez*, meaning "Sing!" (the command from of *chanter*, "to sing"). It became an English word in the 1860s.

CHORD. From the Middle English *cord*, which was simply a shortened version of *accord*. The musical meaning, which is three or more notes played simultaneously—or "in accord" with one another—came into use in the 1500s. The first recorded use of the written word with an "h" was in 1608.

CELLO. It's short for the Italian *violoncello*. The Italian suffix *-one* denotes largeness, so a big viola would be a *violone*—and that was originally the name of the double bass (which looks like a big viola). The suffix *-cello* denotes smallness. In the 1600s, a new instrument, larger than a viola but smaller than a violone, came into use and was given the name *violoncello*—basically "big little viola." It came into English in the early 1700s, and in the 1850s, it started being shortened to *cello*.

MELODY. This goes all the way back to the ancient Greeks. Their word *melos* meant "song," and *aoidein* meant "to sing," and they were combined to form *melodia*, the word for "music." That went to Old French as *melodie*, and then to English in the 1200s as "melody."

CLEF. A clef is a symbol placed at the beginning of the staff in sheet music, signifying the designated pitch range of the music (as in treble clef or bass clef). It came into English use in the late 1500s from the Latin *clavis*, meaning "key."

*   *   *

RANDOM FACT ABOUT WORLD MUSIC

American bluegrass music is very popular in the Czech Republic. The Czechs developed a taste for it when bluegrass artists like Bill Monroe and Jimmie Rodgers were played over Armed Services radio during World War II.

James Brown's wife once tried to get her traffic tickets dismissed because of "diplomatic immunity."

ATTACK!

Both on and off the stage, a rock show can be a pretty hazardous place.

MEAT SABBATH. The giant hand (a stage prop) was supposed to fling a bunch of meat into the first few rows of the crowd at the 1981 Ozzy Osbourne concert, but it fell a little short. "The stage crew had been trying it out all day," recalled Osbourne, "so the elastic wasn't quite as springy during the show. So I'm standing there, I put my foot on this lever and several @*&%$ pounds of offal slowly come up and splat all over the back of my head!"

I'LL CHECK YOUR LEVELS! When Led Zeppelin was playing a concert in Vancouver, British Columbia, their manager, Peter Grant, saw what he thought was a bootlegger in the front row illegally recording the show with fancy equipment. Grant ran up to the man, ripped away his microphone, and beat him up. Oops. The "bootlegger" was actually a health official with the Canadian government testing the decibel levels in the arena. (Assault charges were filed against Grant, but were later dropped.)

BUZZWORTHY. It might have been funnier if Dave Grohl had gotten stung by the bee (tragic, but funnier). Yet for the up-close fans at that 1997 Foo Fighters concert, watching Grohl duck and spin around his mike stand in between song lyrics to avoid the bee that was attracted to the his saliva-soaked microphone (due to Grohl's incessant gum-chewing), that sight alone was pretty funny.

THE BIG BANG. The High Numbers were just another English club-band until one night in 1964 when Pete Townshend raised his brand-new Rickenbacker 12-string above his head. "The neck poked through the ceiling. When I pulled it out, the top of the head was left behind." Townshend's friends were all laughing at his predicament, so he pretended he'd done it on purpose and smashed the rest of the guitar. Not to be outdone, drummer Keith Moon then kicked over his bass drum. The crowd went wild. After they changed their name to The Who, the band went on to smash hundreds more instruments over the next few years.

"I am the best Keith Moon-type drummer in the world." —Keith Moon

"HAIL TO THE CHIEF"

It's the official anthem of the president of the United States. It must, by decree, be played every time the president arrives at a formal function. (Uncle John wants to know how he can get his own anthem, too.)

THE BOATING SONG

The melody to "Hail to the Chief" began as an old Scottish air by the same name—a highlander ditty that was sung by boatmen while rowing on the lochs. The tune was "borrowed" in 1810 by an English songwriter named James Sanderson, who was writing music for a London play called *The Lady of the Lake*, based on a popular poem by Sir Walter Scott. The play took its storyline from the legend of King Arthur, but centered around a Scottish folk hero—the "Chief" in the updated version of the song. The play caught on quickly in England and soon found its way to America, where it first ran in New York City in 1812. When the sheet music was published in Philadelphia a short time later, a few new lyrics were added to the song by a man named L. M. Sargent, who retitled it "Wreaths for the Chieftain." But most people simply referred to the song by its first line: "Hail to the chief who in triumph advances!"

BIRTHDAY MUSIC

On February 22, 1815, the song was first performed in the presence of a president, James Madison, at a celebration commemorating George Washington's 83rd birthday (Washington had died in 1799). The event received so much favorable press that sales of the song's sheet music doubled by the next day. Thirteen years later, the still-popular tune was played by the United States Marine Band on July 4, 1828, when President John Quincy Adams arrived at the groundbreaking of the C&O Canal in Maryland. By that time, hundreds of sets of lyrics had been published—most of them satirical. But it was the catchy melody, not the words, that people responded to. Over the next few years, the song was played not just for presidents but for assorted visiting dignitaries (even some Indian chiefs were greeted with "Hail to the Chief"). It would take the work of two First Ladies for it to be associated solely with the *Commander*-in-Chief.

The U.S. Air Force is the only military branch that doesn't own its service song...

PARTYING HARD AND WALKING TALL

• Julia Gardiner Tyler, wife of President John Tyler, was a fan of the song. In 1844 she requested that the Marine Band play it whenever the president arrived at their social gatherings, of which there were many, so that the president could make a grand entrance. The band agreed, and a tradition was born.

• The next president, James K. Polk, was so short in stature and unassuming in nature that he often went completely unnoticed when he entered a room. This irritated First Lady Sarah Polk so much that she went to the conductor of the Marine Band and ordered him to play the song every time her husband arrived at any formal function. After two consecutive terms of playing "Hail to the Chief" at every presidential function, the custom was firmly in place, but it still wasn't official.

UNDIGNIFIED

Chester A. Arthur hated the song, and when he became president in 1881 he ordered John Philip Sousa, the Marine Band leader at the time, to write a new presidential anthem. Sousa got to work and presented the president with two songs, one called "Presidential Polonaise" and another called "Semper Fidelis." Arthur loved "Presidential Polonaise," and the Marine Band played it throughout his term. But the public never really took to it, and when Arthur died shortly after leaving office, the song died with him. Meanwhile, the Marine Band adopted "Semper Fidelis" (Latin for "always faithful") for their theme song. When Grover Cleveland took office in 1885, "Hail to the Chief" quietly resumed its place as the unofficial presidential entrance song. And by this point it was becoming taboo for the tune to be used to honor any other public figure.

But the song remained unofficial until President Harry Truman, a piano player and amateur musicologist, decided to research its origins in 1953. Excited by the song's storied history, Truman ordered that it be named the official theme song of the president of the United States. In 1954 the U.S. Department of Defense (because of the song's military nature) made it official—that "old Scottish boat song" had earned its place as an American institution.

THE OFFICIAL (AND NOT SO OFFICIAL) LYRICS

The words to "Hail to the Chief" have changed often over the years, but the original lyrics are credited both to Sir Walter Scott as well as a lyricist named Albert Gamse:

> Hail to the chief we have chosen for the nation,
> Hail to the chief! We salute him, one and all.
> Hail to the chief, as we pledge cooperation
> In proud fulfillment of a great, noble call.

And over the years, many people have had fun with the words. The song has been satirized in dozens of movies and television shows, not to mention political campaigns. Here are two alternate versions from the 1996 movie *My Fellow Americans*:

> Hail to the chief, he's the chief and he needs hailing.
> He is the chief so you all had better hail like crazy.
>
> —President Russell P. Kramer (Jack Lemmon)

> Hail to the chief, if you don't I'll have to kill you.
> I am the chief, so you'd better watch your step, you bastards.
>
> —President Matt Douglas (James Garner)

* * *

BABY, YOU CAN PLAY MY CAR

You know those grooves cut into highway shoulders that make loud noises when you drive over them, hopefully to wake you up if you've fallen asleep? Well, a Japanese engineer had the ingenious idea of "tuning" them so a car's tires can play a melody while you're driving down a section of road. The grooves are "tuned" by simply having more or fewer of them on the road over a given distance: The more there are, the higher the pitch that's produced. That way you can have a stretch of road with differently tuned grooves…and as you drive a melody is sounded. So far three of the roads exist, in Hokkaido, Gunma, and Wakayam prefectures, and they each play different tunes. (Optimum driving/playing speed: about 28 mph).

NAME THAT FICTIONAL MUSICIAN

See if you can name these made-up—but well-known—musical characters who appeared in films, books, and TV shows. (Answers on page 507.)

THE SAX MAN

He's a jazz saxophone player who befriends a little girl and tells her his life story: He got his break on *The Tonight Show* with Steve Allen, recorded one album, *Sax on the Beach*, spent all his money on a $1,500-a-day habit—buying Fabergé eggs—and once appeared on *The Cosby Show*. He died in 1995, leaving his saxophone to the little girl. His sax part was played by Los Angeles-based sax great Dan Higgins, and his voice was read by the late actor Ron Taylor. Who was he?

THE OLD-TIMEY BAND

This foursome travels through the South after scoring a huge hit—and not knowing anything about it. They had only recorded it to get a few bucks from a blind DJ who paid people to "sing into the can" in his studio. The song would later get three of the band-members pardoned by the governor (they were also escapees from prison). Who are they?

THE UNIVERSAL BLASTER BAND

The "biggest, loudest, richest rock band in the history of history itself" was so loud that they had to put their amplifiers in another building while they played so the noise from the speakers wouldn't kill them. The recommended listening distance for audience members: 37 miles from the stage, inside a concrete bunker. The band's lead singer had to take a yearlong hiatus—which he spent being dead—for tax purposes. Who were they?

THE SWEETHEARTS OF FOLK

This husband-and-wife folk duo were known as "the sweethearts of folk music" and were one of the biggest folk acts of the 1960s. They recorded seven albums before a disastrously bitter split,

---

The Doobie Brothers were originally called Pud.

after which the husband recorded three solo efforts: *Cry for Help* (featuring the single "May She Rot in Hell"), *Songs from a Dark Place*, and *Calling It Quits*, the cover of which featured him digging his own grave. Many years later, they reunited to sing their signature hit, "A Kiss at the End of the Rainbow," for a film documentary. Who were they?

THE FOLK TOON SINGER
He became the archetypal rock star in 1970. By 1978 he was so famous that he made the cover of *Rolling Stone*...for the second time. In the 1990s, he moved to Vietnam and became the number-one act in the country, later moving back to the United States and shocking his audience by releasing a country album under a new name (he added "Ray" to his first name). After that, he became a big supporter of Internet file sharing, and now gives away all of his music for free. And although he's entirely fictional, you really can download his music on the Internet. Who is he?

THE VANISHING STAR
This New Jersey rocker disappeared almost as soon as he appeared in 1983. And though he appeared in 1983, he actually played in the 1960s, having been born in the 1930s. (Confusing, huh?) His band cruised to the big time with a Springsteen-like hit from their first album, *Tender Years*. Then they recorded a second album, *Season in Hell*—but the record label refused to release it. After that, he vanished and was never seen again. Or he returned from the dead. Maybe. Who was he?

THE "DISCOVERED" MASTER
He's the long-lost son of one of the most famous composers in history, having been born in 1807 "at the age of 65." He was "discovered" in 1965 by a composer in Iowa, who has since released several albums of the lost master's work, four of them winning Grammy Awards (for Best Comedy Recording). The albums include *Black Forest Bluegrass*, *A Little Nightmare Music*, and a 2007 live album featuring the hit "Beethoven 5th Symphony Sportscast." Who is he?

For the answers, turn to page 507.

Song that received *American Bandstand*'s lowest rating ever: "The Chipmunk Song" (1958).

THE REUNION-NOTS

Sooner or later every old musical group reunites for a concert tour or comeback album. But a few resist the temptation—and sometimes for interesting reasons.

• The Beatles broke up in 1970. Almost immediately, they were offered millions of dollars to reunite, but they refused. Then in April 1976, *Saturday Night Live* producer Lorne Michaels jokingly made an on-air offer to the band: If all four Beatles appeared on his show, he'd give them $3,000, to be split four ways. "You divide it up any way you want," Michaels said. "If you want to give less to Ringo, that's up to you." A month later, Michaels upped the offer…to $3,200. Amazingly, it nearly worked: Paul McCartney and John Lennon were actually watching *SNL* together in Lennon's New York apartment and considered heading down to the show's live taping…but ultimately decided not to go.

• With international hits like "Dancing Queen" and "S.O.S., " the Swedish disco band ABBA was the world's most popular band in the 1970s. They broke up in 1982 and never hinted at a reunion. Then in 1999, a musical based on their songs, *Mamma Mia!*, became a smash hit in England and rejuvenated interest in the group. In 2000 a concert promoter offered the four members of ABBA $1 *billion* to reunite for a 100-date concert tour. Amazingly, they turned it down. The group didn't think they could compete with the past. "All we could see was a disappointed audience," said ABBA's Bjorn Ulvaeus. "How could we live up to what we were?"

• The Smiths were one of the biggest British bands of the 1980s, and a major influence on alternative rock. They broke up in 1987 and lead singer Morrissey went on to a successful solo career. Then in 1996, drummer Mike Joyce successfully sued Morrissey and Smiths guitarist Johnny Marr for $1 million worth of unpaid royalties. Angry and offended, Morrissey vowed never to play with the Smiths again. In 2005 the group was offered $5 million for a single performance at a Coachella, California, music festival. Morrissey told a reporter, "I would rather eat my own testicles than re-form the Smiths, and that's saying something for a vegetarian."

What's a *mondegreen*? A misheard song lyric such as "'Scuse me, while I kiss this guy..."

UNSUNG HEROES

You may not recognize their names, but you've heard their music more times than you know. These teams of studio musicians have played on hundreds of hit records over the last 50 years.

THE WRECKING CREW

That's the nickname these musicians from the 1960s gave themselves after the old line studio players, who hated rock, complained that they were "wrecking the business." The band, which included Hal Blaine (drums), Joe Osborne (bass), Larry Knechtel (keyboards), Glen Campbell (guitar), and Leon Russell (piano), were producer Phil Spector's "go-to" guys.

♪ The Wrecking Crew played on six consecutive Record of the Year Grammy winners: "A Taste of Honey" by Herb Alpert and the Tijuana Brass (1966), "Strangers in the Night" by Frank Sinatra (1967), "Up, Up and Away" by the Fifth Dimension (1968), "Mrs. Robinson" by Simon and Garfunkel (1969), "Aquarius/Let the Sunshine In" by the Fifth Dimension (1970), and "Bridge Over Troubled Water" by Simon and Garfunkel (1971).

Selected Hits: "Be My Baby" by the Ronettes • "Surf City" by Jan and Dean • "You've Lost That Lovin' Feeling" by the Righteous Brothers • "I Got You, Babe" by Sonny and Cher • "Mr. Tambourine Man" by the Byrds • "California Dreamin'" by the Mamas and the Papas • "This Diamond Ring" by Gary Lewis and the Playboys • "Good Vibrations" by the Beach Boys • "I'm a Believer" by the Monkees • "River Deep, Mountain High" by Ike and Tina Turner

MUSCLE SHOALS RHYTHM SECTION

Jimmy Johnson (guitar), Roger Hawkins (drums), David Hood (bass), Barry Beckett (keyboards), and Donny Short (lead guitar) are known as the "Swampers" by the music legends who've come down to Muscle Shoals, Alabama, to record with them since 1967.

♪ The musicians were given the nickname "Swampers" during a recording session with Mick Jagger because of the swampy land in Muscle Shoals. They were referenced by name in Lynyrd Skynyrd's "Sweet Home Alabama."

♪ The Muscle Shoals Sound Studios was founded in 1969 in an old casket warehouse. Their first client was Cher.

Selected Hits: "Mustang Sally" by Wilson Pickett • "Old Time Rock 'n' Roll" by Bob Seger • "Respect" by Aretha Franklin • "High Time We Went" by Joe Cocker • "Tonight's the Night" by Rod Stewart • "Kodachrome" by Paul Simon • "When a Man Loves a Woman" by Percy Sledge • "Sweet Soul Music" by Arthur Conley • "The Harder They Come" by Jimmy Cliff • "Chain of Fools" by Aretha Franklin • "Wild Horses" by the Rolling Stones • "Land of a Thousand Dances" by Wilson Pickett • "Lay Down Sally" by Eric Clapton

THE A TEAM

Immortalized by John Sebastian in his song "Nashville Cats," these superpickers—including Bob Moore (bass), Buddy Harman (drums), Grady Martin, Hank Garland, Chet Atkins, Harold Bradley (guitar), Hargus "Pig" Robbins (keyboards), Floyd Kramer (piano), Pete Drake (steel guitar), and Charlie McCoy (harmonica)—have played on hundreds of country hits over the past half-century.

Selected Hits: "Oh, Pretty Woman" by Roy Orbison • "Stand by Your Man" by Tammy Wynette • "Just Like a Woman" by Bob Dylan • "Crazy" by Patsy Cline • "King of the Road" by Roger Miller • "El Paso" by Marty Robbins • "Big Bad John" by Jimmy Dean • "I'm Sorry" by Brenda Lee

THE MEMPHIS SOUND

In 1958 the Royal Spades were a band of white kids from Memphis who loved black music. When sax player Packy Axton's mother opened a studio called Satellite Records (later Stax-Volt) to record local talent, they changed their name to the Mar-Keys and became the house band. Local black musicians soon joined, led by keyboard player Booker T. Jones, drummer Al Jackson Jr., and sax man Andrew Love. In 1962 guitarist Steve Cropper and bassist Donald "Duck" Dunn split off from the Mar-Keys to join Jones and Jackson as Booker T. and the MGs ("Memphis Group"), and Love and trumpeter Wayne Jackson still play as the Memphis Horns. But together this assembly of black and white musicians wrote the book on what came to be called classic Southern soul.

First major film musical to have an all-black cast: King Vidor's *Hallelujah,* in 1929.

Selected Hits: "Try a Little Tenderness" by Otis Redding • "Soul Man" by Sam and Dave • "Midnight Hour" by Wilson Pickett • "Knock on Wood" by Eddie Floyd • "Dock of the Bay" by Otis Redding • "Son of a Preacher Man" by Dusty Springfield • "Suspicious Minds" by Elvis Presley • "Let's Stay Together" by Al Green • "Shaft" by Isaac Hayes • "I'll Take You There" by the Staples Singers • "Born Under a Bad Sign" by Albert King • "Cry Like a Baby" by the Box Tops • "Mercury Falling" by Sting • "Storm Front" by Billy Joel

THE FUNK BROTHERS

They worked in a basement called the "Snake Pit" and churned out legendary Motown hits hour after hour from 1958 to 1973. The band included Benny Benjamin (drums), James Jamerson (bass), Joe Messina, Larry Veeder (guitar), Earl Van Dyke, Joe Hunter (piano), Hank Crosby (saxophone), Paul Riser (trombone), and Herbie Williams (trumpet). They claim to have played on more hit records than the Beatles, Elvis, and Frank Sinatra combined.

♪ Recording sessions began at 10 a.m. and were over at 1 p.m. The musicians were on call seven days a week.

♪ Originally, each band member was paid $10 per song. It usually took about an hour to record each song, but sometimes less.

Selected Hits: "Dancing in the Street" by Martha and the Vandellas • "Stop! In the Name of Love" by the Supremes • "My Girl" by the Temptations • "I Can't Help Myself" by the Four Tops • "Ain't That Peculiar" by Marvin Gaye • "Reach Out, I'll Be There" by the Four Tops • "Do You Love Me" by the Contours • "Tears of a Clown" by Smokey Robinson and the Miracles • "My Guy" by Mary Wells • "Please Mr. Postman" by the Marvelettes • "Cloud Nine" by the Temptations • "I Want You Back" by the Jackson Five • "Going to a Go-Go" by the Miracles • "What's Going On" by Marvin Gaye

Random Session Notes:

• Drummer Hal Blaine of the Wrecking Crew played a set of tire chains in Simon and Garfunkel's "Bridge Over Troubled Water."
• Billy Joel played piano on the Shangri-Las' teenage angst classic "Leader of the Pack." He was 16.

NYPD blues? Eddie Money is a graduate of the New York City Police Academy.

BIRTH OF A GENRE

No one person creates a popular musical genre all by themselves—
usually it evolves from a combination of influences over time.
But a few people came very close to making that claim.

CLIFTON CHENIER—ZYDECO
Long before Clifton Chenier came along in the 1950s,
people in the Deep South were already playing amped-up
accordion- and fiddle-based Cajun music. But Louisiana native
Chenier, now called the "King of Zydeco," blended that Cajun
music with local Creole style, blues, jazz—and the R&B-flavored
rock 'n' roll of fellow Louisianians Professor Longhair and Fats
Domino. The fast-paced music that resulted set the standard for
the genre known as zydeco. Chenier would take the sound all over
the world with his Zydeco Ramblers, earning his greatest fame in
1983 when his album *I'm Here!*—which was recorded in one
eight-hour session—won a Grammy. He died four years later at
the age of 62. About the music that's nearly impossible to sit still
to, Chenier said, "If you can't dance to zydeco, you can't dance—
period."

DICK DALE—SURF ROCK
In the 1950s, Dick Dale, son of a Lebanese father and a Polish
mother (his name is actually Richard Mansour) started messing
around with the sound of his electric guitar. Working directly with
guitar maker Leo Fender, Dale invented a heavily reverbed, loud,
lightning-fast guitar style—with Arabic-influenced scales—that
would strongly influence the new music genre known as "surf
rock." In 1961 he released "Let's Go Trippin'," regarded by many
as the first surf-rock song. Dale, already known by that point as
the "King of the Surf Guitar" to his surfing buddies, said he wanted
to pattern his style on that of Gene Krupa, the famous jazz drummer, and create "sounds of native dancers in the jungles along
with Mother Nature's creatures and the roar of the ocean." Dale's
biggest hit: 1962's "Misirlou," which reached a whole new audience in 1994 when it was featured in the Quentin Tarantino film
Pulp Fiction.

Composers Antonio Vivaldi and Antonin Dvorak both died broke.

JAMES BROWN—FUNK

By the mid-1960s, James Brown had already made a name for himself with a string of R&B hits like "Please Please Please" and "Night Train." But in 1967 he broke new ground with the release of "Cold Sweat," now widely regarded as the first true funk song. Brown had created similar songs in the past, but "Cold Sweat" was different—it put the emphasis of the song emphatically on the beat, taking the focus away from the melody almost entirely (the song has, basically, only two chords). Its effect on the music world was immediate: "'Cold Sweat' deeply affected the musicians I knew," legendary soul producer Jerry Wexler said. "It just freaked them out. No one could get a handle on what to do next." Brown liked "Cold Sweat" so much that he used it as a blueprint for future songs, and other performers—notably Sly and the Family Stone and George Clinton—did, too. Soon, funk became its own genre.

ENNIO MORRICONE—SPAGHETTI WESTERN

Morricone, an Italian composer born in 1928, almost single-handedly invented this genre of film scoring. All you have to do is think of Clint Eastwood in his early Western phase. Hear that music? That plaintive whistling, banging, shouting, ringing…and that twangy electric guitar? That's "Italo Western" music, as it's sometimes called. Morricone first created it in 1964 when he began his famous collaboration with director Sergio Leone on the film *A Fistful of Dollars*. He went on to develop the sound in more than 30 Westerns, and hundreds of other directors were influenced by his work. In the years since, bands all over the world—like Tokyo's Los Rancheros, Norway's Los Plantronics, and Germany's Motorpsychos—have made the sound part of their act. (Uncle John recommends the album *For a Few Guitars More: A Tribute to Morricone's Spaghetti Western Themes.*)

WINSTON GRENNAN—ONE DROP

If you're a fan of reggae, you've probably heard Winston Grennan play the drums. And even if you haven't, you'd probably recognize the sound he created: the "one-drop" rhythm that is the foundation of reggae music. Grennan was born in Duckenfield, Jamaica, in 1944 into a family of musicians. By the time he was 20, he was one of the most sought-after session drummers in the Kingston ska and "rocksteady" studio scene, precursors to the coming reggae boom. Grennan would play on recordings by such early reggae stars as Toots Hibbert, Jimmy Cliff, Peter Tosh, and Judy Mowatt (not to mention folk and rock stars such as Peter, Paul and Mary; Paul Simon; and the Rolling Stones). It was with reggae superstar Bob Marley that he developed the one drop: The *1* in the 1-2-3-4 beat cycle is completely dropped, with the emphasis put on the *3*. Years later, he told the Baltimore *City Paper*, "I was searching for something of my own, that I could say, 'Well, I do this.' So I started to practice a thing called 'one drop'…and that groove was *the* groove."

FELA—AFROBEAT

In the 1950s, Nigerian musician Fela Anikulapo Kuti, who later became known simply as "Fela," formed a band called Koola Lobitos in London, where he was attending college. There he started blending West African highlife music—already a fusion of African and Western music that featured West African drums, guitars, and horns—with jazz and funk music. He returned home to Nigeria in 1963 and built the sound around huge bands—he would tour at one point with an ensemble of 80 singers, dancers, and instrumentalists—and dubbed the music "Afrobeat." By the 1970s, Fela was one of the most popular musicians in Africa, and in the 1980s he was nearly as famous in Europe and, to a lesser extent, in the United States. Today, thousands of Afrobeat bands play around the world; since his death in 1997, Fela birthday bashes featuring Afrobeat bands have sprung up in many major cities (look for one near you on October 15).

BILL MONROE—BLUEGRASS

In the 1930s, the Monroe Brothers—Bill Monroe and his brothers Birch and Charlie, all in their early twenties—started playing what's now known as "old-timey" music for radio shows in South Bend, Indiana. By 1945 Monroe had assembled a band whose lineup included Earl Scruggs on banjo, Lester Flatt on guitar, Chubby Wise on fiddle, Howard Watts (aka Cedric Rainwater) on stand-up bass, and Monroe on mandolin. The band's name: the Blue Grass Boys. And the distinctively acoustic sound they

---

Early bloomer: Elton John won a scholarship to the Royal Academy of Music at the age of 11.

forged would come to be known as "bluegrass." More than 150 musicians would play in the Blue Grass Boys over the years, with Bill Monroe at the helm until his death in 1996. He was inducted into the Country Music Hall of Fame in 1970, the International Bluegrass Music Hall of Honor (with Flatt and Scruggs as the first honorees) in 1991, and the Rock and Roll Hall of Fame in 1997 (as an "early influence")—he's the only person ever to be honored by all three. And his song "Blue Moon of Kentucky" was adopted by the State of Kentucky in 1989 as its "Official Bluegrass Song."

* * *

WARNING: KARAOKE MAY BE HAZARDOUS TO YOUR HEALTH

• In August 2007, a man at a bar in Seattle, Washington, had just started singing "Yellow" by the band Coldplay when a woman in the audience yelled, "I can't stand that song!" Then she jumped onto the stage and started punching the singer. The woman was restrained by other audience members and police were called. She was arrested on karaoke-related assault charges.

• In July 2007, a 30-year-old man at Shangri-La Chinese restaurant in Liverpool, England, was singing karaoke when the crowd started heckling him. He walked off the stage and directly into the audience, where he proceeded to punch one of the hecklers in the face, leaving a cut that required 40 stitches. The singer was arrested on karaoke-related assault charges.

• In August 2005, an English tourist in Burgas, Bulgaria, attacked two men who were performing a version of Queen's "We Are the Champions." The tourist told police he attacked the men for "bad singing." He was arrested on karaoke-related assault charges.

• As of 2007, the song "My Way," made famous by Frank Sinatra, had been pulled from nearly all the karaoke machines in Manila in the Philippines. Newspapers reported that drunken, out-of-tune versions of the song had been the cause of hundreds of fights and scores of arrests (on karaoke-related assault charges).

Irving Berlin could only play piano in the key of F sharp.

A CYMBAL OF SUCCESS

From the sultans to the Beatles, the Zildjian
family gets a bang out of business.

THE BIG BANG

The tinny clang of the cymbal can be heard in many different kinds of music: Buddhist monks use them to enhance meditation; rock and jazz drummers add high points to their beats with them; every orchestra percussionist has at least one cymbal to hit when a little accent is needed; and belly dancers accompany their graceful gyrations with small cymbals that fit into their hands. Many of these instruments are manufactured in Massachusetts by the oldest family business in America—and one of the oldest continuously operating businesses in history.

Their story starts in Constantinople (now Istanbul), Turkey, in 1623. An Armenian alchemist, Avendis I, developed a secret formula for a metal alloy that made cymbals sound better with a more resounding ring. The Ottoman sultan Murad IV was so impressed that he gave Avendis the Turkish name *Zildjian*, meaning "cymbal smith." The company has been handed down to family members ever since...through an astounding 14 generations.

ON THE MARCH

Cymbals were introduced to Europe in the 17th century (probably by Turkish military bands), and 100 years later they started showing up in European classical music. By the 19th century, such renowned composers as Hector Berlioz and Richard Wagner demanded that only Zildjian cymbals accompany their orchestral works when performed live. The family took advantage of their growing reputation and started sending representatives to Paris and London.

In the early 1900s, things were looking good as the business expanded once again, this time sending exports to the United States. In 1929 the Zildjians' first American factory opened in Quincy, Massachusetts. The timing was awful: People were more focused on the recent crash of the stock market than the crash of an expensive cymbal—the Great Depression made instruments a tough sell.

Antonio Vivaldi composed **488** concertos, more than any other composer.

But Avedis Zildjian III (the 12th generation after his name-sake) was an innovator. In the 1930s, he courted drummers involved in the increasingly popular genre of jazz, and when the famous drummer Gene Krupa needed a thinner cymbal, Avedis was his man. Zildjian's various styles of cymbals—thin splash, ride, crash, hi-hat, and sizzle—were soon used in all types of percussion ensembles. The company was on its way again.

STARR POWER
In the 1940s, the United States entered World War II. Since the War Production Board had restricted nonmilitary use of copper and tin, both crucial metals in the Zildjian alloy, the company seemed doomed...but, thanks to military bands, it did fine.

Then in 1964, the British Invasion rocked the United States with the Beatles' first appearance on Ed Sullivan's TV show. When aspiring drummers saw the Zildjian logo on Ringo Starr's drum set, demand for the brand exploded. By 1976 they were the most popular cymbals in the world, and Avedis was able to pass on a very lucrative company to his sons Armand and Robert.

A new problem arose in the early 1980s, however, when Robert quit the family business to found a rival company in Canada called Sabian. But the Zildjians remained a staple of American music. Armand (a drummer who kept a set of left-handed drums in his office) saw cymbal making as an art. He loved and perfected the Zildjian sound and worked closely with musicians (who said he treated them like family).

CYMBAL MINDED
As the company splashes its way into the future, one link with the past has never changed—the alloy formula of 1623. For nearly four centuries, it has remained a family secret, passed down from father to eldest Zildjian son. But these days, the eldest Zildjian son is a daughter—actually, two daughters. Craigie Zildjian runs the company, while her sister Debbie is vice president of human resources, the first woman to oversee the melting room...as well as the secret formula.

THE FATHER OF COUNTRY MUSIC

Jimmie Rodgers's recording career was short—only six years—but it was long enough to establish country music as a national phenomenon and pave the way for generations of country artists to come.

THE SINGING BRAKEMAN

Jimmie Rodgers' plaque at the Country Music Hall of Fame says that his "name stands foremost in the country music field as the man who started it." And indeed, there was no such thing as country music in 1927 when Jimmie Rodgers recorded his first songs for the Victor Talking Machine Company. There was "hillbilly" music, songs and tunes that were shunned by music aficionados and mostly unknown outside the hollows of Appalachia and the farmlands of the American South and West. But in that year, talent scout Ralph Peer, who also discovered the Carter Family (see page 190), arrived in Bristol, Tennessee, looking for new talent. Peer paid Rodgers $100 to record two of his songs: "Sleep, Baby, Sleep" and "The Soldier's Sweetheart." By the end of 1927, Rodgers was a success, traveling east to record and release more songs—including the first of his "Blue Yodels," a series of "white blues" songs featuring a distinctive yodeling style that was emotional, either plaintive or happy, instead of simply an ornamental part of the song. The record sold an astonishing half a million copies, and Jimmie Rodgers was established as a star.

HE'S BEEN WORKING ON THE RAILROAD

But before he hit it big on the radio, Jimmie Rodgers was just a Mississippi boy. Born in 1897, he lost his mother when he was seven, and from then until his early teens he was raised by an aunt who was a music teacher and who exposed him to all sorts of popular music. When he was 12, he entered and won an amateur singing contest, and, apparently hooked by his success, ran away from home twice in the following two years to perform in traveling medicine shows.

The black and white keys on Mozart's piano were the reverse of today's.

Jimmie returned to his father's house in 1911 but kept running away. Each time, his father hauled him back; finally, he gave Jimmie an ultimatum: school or work. Jimmie chose work and settled into a job on the railroad as a water boy. Promoted to brakeman, he held the job for 15 years, but he was still hooked on singing. He taught himself to play guitar, banjo, and mandolin and often performed for his peers, earning himself the nickname "the Singing Brakeman." He also learned the blues from the African Americans who worked with him; eventually, Rodgers incorporated that style into his own, combining hillbilly songs with the African American blues. In his spare time, he performed in tent shows and on the new medium of local radio.

"TB BLUES"

It wasn't the success of his records that ended the Singing Brakeman's railroading career, however, but the ravaging illness of tuberculosis. Three years before he was discovered by Ralph Peer, Rodgers was diagnosed with TB. At just 27 years old, he was already on his second marriage and the father of two children. He ignored his doctors' advice to take it easy because he needed to make a living. He continued on as a brakeman until he was finally fired for being too frail to do the work. When he was discovered by Ralph Peer in 1927, he was working at a series of odd jobs. But by 1928, he was so popular that his start power has been compared to that of Elvis Presley.

JIMMIE SUPERSTAR

Over the next five years, Rodgers headlined concerts across the country, delighting audiences with songs that reflected the hard times of the Depression and the rowdy, hard-drinking boisterousness of the laboring man. He focused on the common man because, as Rodgers once said, "The underest dog is just as good as I am, and I'm just as good as the toppest dog." He sang sentimental songs, too, about mother and home, and loss and longing. And he yodeled the blues like no one before or since. His performances of the classic "Frankie and Johnny" and the lament of "In the Jailhouse Now" became iconic country music tunes. He even starred in a short movie in 1929 titled appropriately, *The Singing Brakeman*. He performed with cowboy/humorist Will Rogers, newcomer

Louis Armstrong, and the Carter Family. But his worsening tuberculosis dogged him every step of the way.

LOSS OF A LEGEND

At a 1933 recording session in New York City, Rodgers was so weak that he had to lie on a cot in the back room between songs, trying to regain the strength to stand at the microphone. On the eighth day, he recorded his last song, the simple and gentle "Years Ago." Two days later, he died in a New York hotel of a pulmonary hemorrhage, a result of his tuberculosis. As he'd predicted in his 1931 song "TB Blues," he'd lost his battle with the deadly disease. He was only 35.

In 1961, Jimmie Rodgers was among the first artists inducted into the Country Music Hall of Fame. He made it into the Rock and Roll Hall of Fame as an Early Influence in 1986 and was honored at the museum's American Music Masters series in 1997. Rodgers inspired everyone from Hank Williams to Merle Haggard, and folk superstar Bob Dylan once called him "one of the guiding lights of the twentieth century, whose way with song has always been an inspiration to those of us who have followed the path…He was a performer of force without precedent with a sound as lonesome and mystical as it was dynamic. He gives hope to the vanquished and humility to the mighty."

A note from Uncle John: This Jimmie Rodgers should not be confused with pop singer Jimmie Rodgers, who charmed early rock 'n' roll fans with his hit songs "Honeycomb" (1957) and "Kisses Sweeter than Wine" (1958).

*　　*　　*

HELLO?

In 1972 someone from United artists made a call to Don Arden, manager of the new band the Electric Light Orchestra, to find out the title of their debut album. The UA rep couldn't get in touch with Arden and made a note: No answer—and ELO's debut album came out with the title *No Answer*.

BAGPIPER'S FUNGUS

Recent studies have found that professional musicians often suffer from some very real—but very odd—ailments. Here are a few.

FIDDLER'S NECK

The name might sound silly, but according to a study of regular violin and viola players by Dr. Thilo Gambichler of Oldchurch Hospital in London, the friction of the instrument's base against the left side of the neck (for right-handed players) can cause lesions, severe inflammation, and cysts. What's worse, said the study, published in the British medical journal *BMC Dermatology*, it causes *lichenification*—the development of a patch of thick, leathery skin on the neck, giving it a "bark-like" appearance.

GUITAR NIPPLE

A similar report issued in the United States cited three female classical guitarists who suffered from *traumatic mastitis*—swelling of the breast and nipple area—due to prolonged friction from the instrument's body. The condition can strike male players, too.

BAGPIPER'S FUNGUS

Recent medical reports have detailed the dangers of playing Scotland's national instrument. Bagpipes are traditionally made of sheepskin coated with a molasses-like substance called treacle. That, the report said, is a perfect breeding ground for various fungi, such as *aspergillus* and *cryptococcus*. Bagpipers can inadvertently inhale fungal spores, which, according to Dr. Robert Sataloff of Thomas Jefferson University Hospital in Philadelphia, can lead to deadly lung—and even brain—diseases.

TUBA LIPS

Many long-term tuba players develop an allergic reaction to nickel, an ingredient in brass. The allergy can result in dermatitis of the lips and can sometimes develop into chronic eczema. Strictly speaking, the condition can also affect the chin and hands, and can be contracted from any number of brass instruments (but "tuba lips" is more fun to say).

CODAS AND TUTTIS

And other musical terms that you may find helpful one day.

Canon: Literally "rule" in Latin; a composition that begins with a basic melody line, which is repeated by other instruments or voices following a pre-established rule (e.g., wait two measures to begin). An a cappella example is the song "Row, Row, Row Your Boat" (a cappella canons are called "rounds").

Libretto: The text—or spoken parts—of an opera or musical. Literally, "little book."

Break: Common in jazz, a short, improvised solo taken by one member of a band

Coda: Closing section of a piece of music

Minuet: Slow, graceful dance, and the music for it, played in 3/4 time

Suite: A collection of several short instrumental compositions

Chord: Three or more different notes played or sung simultaneously in harmony

Symphony: Usually used to indicate a three- or four-movement orchestral piece

Opus: Used to number a composer's works, as in "Liszt, Opus 1." (The plural is not used, as it would cause confusion—the plural of opus is "opera.")

Carol: English in origin, a lyrical song of joy, usually religious in nature and most commonly used for Christmas songs

String quartet: A group of four instruments, usually two violins, a viola, and cello

Timbre: The quality of sound, often given in terms like "harsh," "bright," "warm," and so on

Baroque: Style of European classical music dating from about 1600 to 1750. Characterized by emotional, flowery style.

Madrigal: A complex, multi-part, lyrical composition for voices only. Madrigals have their roots in the 14th century, but were further developed in the 16th and 17th centuries. The different parts are polyphonic, moving independently of each other.

First downloadable single to sell over 1 million copies: Gwen Stefani's 2005 "Hollaback Girl."

Chamber music: From the 1500s, compositions written for two to ten musicians and meant for small gatherings (chambers) rather than theaters. Usually instrumental; never featuring a conductor.

Atonal: Music written without any specific key

Romantic era: European music era running from the early 19th to the early 20th century, characterized by focus on emotion rather than formal rules and structure

Nonet: A composition written for nine instruments

Concertmaster/concert-mistress): The first violin in an orchestra. Leads orchestra in tuning; plays any given violin solos (in concertos, guests may play solos).

Tutti: Passage in which an entire ensemble or orchestra plays without a soloist

Pastoral/pastorale: A composition meant to evoke a simple, idyllic, often rural setting

Glissando: From the French *glissander*—to glide; to glide or slide from one pitch to another, rather than stopping and starting again

Étude: A piece of music written solely to improve technique (études are often also performed or recorded for artistic purposes)

Phrase: A recognizable unit of music; a musical "sentence"

Falsetto: The upper register of the human voice, called "head voice" rather than the lower "chest voice." Also a style of "artificial" singing by men used to reach the higher pitches normally sung by women.

Scordatura: Literally "mistuning" in Italian, a retuning of a string instrument for a desired effect. (Popularly used as "alternate tunings" on guitars, but also used for stringed instruments in orchestras.)

Oratorio: An extended composition for solo voices, choruses, and orchestra, with a religious subject. (Handel's *Messiah* is the most famous.)

Fugue: A technique in which a composer introduces a tune, after which other instruments, coming in at different times, repeat the theme with alterations. Usually written for two to six instruments or voices.

For more musical terms, turn to page 281.

SATCHMO

Louis "Satchmo" Armstrong is best remembered for his gravelly voice, for his intrepid trumpet, and for introducing the world to jazz. Get to know the man Wynton Marsalis calls "the embodiment of jazz music."

THE FOUNDING FATHER OF JAZZ

Louis Armstrong is called one of, if not *the*, most influential artist in the history of jazz music. He basically invented the now-ubiquitous feature of jazz—the improvised solo; was one of the first "scat" singers; is one of the most recognized cornet and trumpet players—and singers; and his recordings of songs like "April in Paris," "Pennies from Heaven," and "Mack the Knife" remain hugely popular today. As jazz trumpeter Max Kaminsky wrote, Louis Armstrong was "the heir of all that had gone before—and the father of all that was to come."

BORN IN THE BATTLEFIELD

Armstrong was born on August 4, 1901, in a rough section of New Orleans known as the Battlefield, where the toe-tapping sounds of dance halls, brothels, honky-tonks, and even funerals surrounded and inspired him. When he was just six years old, Louis joined three other boys who were singing on street corners for tips, and a few years later, he bought himself an old cornet from a pawnshop. He also started hanging around with local musicians like Joe "King" Oliver and Bunk Johnson.

In 1913 Louis' life changed dramatically when, on New Year's Eve, he fired a gun into the air in celebration. He was arrested and sent to reform school. There he met Peter Davis, the man in charge of the school's music program. Davis gave him a bugle and his first formal musical training. He also put Louis in the school's band and eventually made him the group's leader. When 13-year-old Louis emerged from the reform school, he was a polished musician.

A NEW KIND OF MUSIC

Armstrong went home to his mother and sister (his father had left the family when Louis was a baby) and got jobs delivering coal and newspapers in New Orleans to earn money for his family. But he always found time for music and often sat in with a popular local blues group called Kid Ory's Band, which featured Joe Oliver, one of the local musicians Armstrong admired (and one of the city's best cornet players). Oliver mentored the youngster for several years, but it was a relationship that the New Orleans establishment frowned upon. In those days, jazz was controversial, and the mainstream population considered many early jazz musicians to be unsavory characters. Most came from dangerous neighborhoods like the Battlefield, and most were African American.

Oliver left New Orleans for Chicago after white police officers arrested him when a fight broke out at a bar where he was playing. Believing the arrest was racially motivated, Oliver decided to leave the South for good. This left a gap in Kid Ory's band. Armstrong took over on the cornet.

DOWN HOME CHICAGO

Meanwhile, Joe Oliver found huge success in Chicago. His King Oliver's Creole Jazz Band played a regular gig at the Lincoln Gardens, the Windy City's most famous dance hall. Oliver's influence would prove tremendous…both on jazz (his recordings introduced many white musicians to a genre often considered exclusively "black") and on Louis Armstrong, who said that Oliver "did more for young musicians…than anyone I know of." In 1922 Oliver offered Armstrong a job with the Creole Jazz Band. The pay: $52 per week. Armstrong couldn't pass up an opportunity to reunite with his mentor and earn some decent money. He left for Chicago right away.

He became tremendously popular very quickly, as Chicago had never seen or heard anyone like Louis Armstrong. Joe Oliver let his protégé have what they called "cutting contests" with other horn blowers in which one cornet player tried to outblow the others. The contests were great publicity for the band, especially since Armstrong could defeat the best Chicago had to offer. The electrifying sounds of his cornet also made him a standout in Oliver's band, and the group's growing popularity led to their first record in 1923. The songs included "Just Gone," "Canal Street Blues," and "I'm Going Away to Wear You Off My Mind," classics that marked the beginning of modern jazz.

In 1924 Armstrong received an offer from Fletcher Henderson, one of Harlem's most famous bandleaders. He invited Armstrong to join his orchestra, which played regularly at the Roseland Ballroom, a famous all-white dance hall in New York City. Armstrong's cornet didn't blend well with Henderson's sound, though, so before moving to New York, he traded up to the cornet's louder, brighter-sounding cousin…the trumpet.

STEPPING OUT OF THE ORCHESTRA

Once in New York, Armstrong brought his unique "New Orleans style" to Henderson's group. But Armstrong wasn't satisfied just to play: he wanted to sing, too. Each Thursday night at the Roseland, vaudeville acts competed in an amateur night for prizes. Armstrong and his trumpet showed up one Thursday evening and belted out a show-stopping version of "Everybody Loves My Baby, but My Baby Don't Love Nobody but Me." The delighted audience awarded him first place. From then on, Armstrong sang and played in Henderson's orchestra at the Roseland every week. Word of his talent quickly spread throughout New York, and he even backed up greats like Bessie Smith and Ma Rainey on their early recordings. (Later in his career, Armstrong sang nearly as much as he played. Two reasons: his high-pressure trumpet playing style was damaging his cheeks, and he could make more money as a singer.)

GETTING THE HEEBIE JEEBIES

In 1925 Armstrong found his way back to Chicago, where he joined a studio band at Okeh Records. Very few jazz recordings were made at that time, but the music was popular and the company saw a potential market for jazz records. The studio band featured Armstrong on trumpet and vocals, his wife Lil Armstrong on piano, Kid Ory on trombone, Johnny Dodds on clarinet, and Johnny St. Cyr on banjo. They were called the Hot Five, and with Armstrong as their leader, their music delivered the definitive sounds of jazz and scat singing. Scat was a style Armstrong had picked up as a kid on the streets of New Orleans; as an adult, he popularized the style and was the first to record it. The Hot Five tune "Heebie Jeebies" was the first recording to include scat singing, and it became one of the band's biggest hits.

Nigerian-born singer Sade's real name is Helen Folasade Adu.

In 1927 the Hot Five turned into the Hot Seven with the addition of Pete Briggs on tuba and Baby Dodds (Johnny's brother) on drums. Their recordings continued to be top sellers.

AMBASSADOR SATCHMO

Armstrong went to London in 1932 and, on arrival at the Howard Hotel, was met by an English journalist who called him "Satchmo," a distorted version of "Satchelmouth," the nickname Armstrong had gotten years before for the way his cheeks grew oversized (like stuffed satchels) when he blew his horn. "Satchmo" became Armstrong's favorite nickname and eventually caught on with the public.

Throughout the 1940s and '50s, new kinds of music emerged—bebop and rock 'n' roll—and the big band and jazz music that was popular during World War II started to fade from public view. But Armstrong and his new band (called Louis Armstrong and the All Stars) continued to play it, traveling to Africa, Europe, South America, and Asia. The U.S. State Department even sponsored several of these tours, engaging Armstrong as an informal ambassador who introduced jazz, a distinctly American art form, to the rest of the world.

PUTTIN' ON THE HITS

For the next three decades, Louis Armstrong racked up some of the biggest hits in musical history. As late as 1964, he made it to Billboard's top spot—which the Beatles had held for 14 consecutive weeks—with his version of "Hello, Dolly." And in 1967 he released what would become one of the most recognizable numbers of his long career, "What a Wonderful World."

By the fall of 1968, Armstrong's health was failing, but despite his doctor's warning to take it easy, he continued to perform live. On July 6, 1971, it caught up to him when, the night after performing at the Waldorf Astoria's Empire Room in New York, he suffered a heart attack and died. He was buried in New York's Flushing Cemetery. In 1999 *Time* magazine included him on their list of the 100 most important people—period—of the 20th century. (And in 2001 the main airport in New Orleans was renamed the Louis Armstrong New Orleans International Airport.)

Sonny Bono's epitaph: "And the beat goes on."

MUSICAL STUDIES

*Scientists around the world conduct all sorts of studies on the
effects of music...including some very* strange *studies.*

SHARK TAIL

In 2006 scientists at the Blackpool Sea Life Centre in England couldn't get two of their sharks, Bloodnose (the male) and Lucy (the female) to mate. They tried piping in Barry White music through speakers perched above the sharks' tank. It didn't work, and neither did Mozart, Beethoven, or an opera by Puccini. The song that finally got Bloodnose and Lucy going: "My Heart Will Go On," the love ballad from the movie *Titanic*, as sung by Celine Dion.

THIS OPERA IS AWESOME, DUDE

Psychologists at the University of Leicester in England conducted a study to look for a link between the kind of music a person likes and his or her behavioral traits. After surveying 2,500 people, the scientists found that classical music fans were the most likely to have smoked marijuana, blues fans were the most likely to have gotten a speeding ticket, and opera fans were the most likely to have ingested hallucinogenic mushrooms. Most likely to have both taken drugs *and* have a criminal record: fans of techno music. Least likely to take drugs or engage in criminal behavior: fans of musical theater.

iMPLANT

BT Laboratories, a British electronics research and development firm, says it's about 15 years away from musical breast implants. Using the same technology that allows a handheld device like an iPod to hold thousands of songs on a computer chip, BT scientists say a similar chip could be embedded in a breast implant. A small music player would be embedded in the other implant. The wearer would listen to the music via wireless headphones. "It's hard for me to think of breast implants as just decorative," said BT's Ian Pearson. "If a woman has something implanted permanently, it might as well do something useful."

Glockenspiel means "play of bells" in German.

NEUTRON DANCE

In 1994 choreographer Nicola Hawkins and composer Deborah Henson Conant created "The Interpretive Dance of the Electrons," a short ballet. Consisting largely of seemingly random—but very precise—movements, the ballet mimics the behavior of subatomic particles. The ballet was performed live just once (dancers included Hawkins, along with three Nobel Prize winning scientists) at the 1994 Ig Nobel Prize ceremony, an award for strange or useless scientific research.

THE GREAT GIG IN THE SKY

Dr. David Demko, a gerontologist (someone who studies the science of aging), writes a monthly column for *Blender* magazine called "When Will Your Favorite Rock Star Die?" After analyzing the medical histories, genetic factors, and lifestyle traits of rock and pop stars, Demko determines when they're likely to die. He says Sting, a yoga and exercise enthusiast, will live to age 93. Other stars he's profiled include Ozzy Osbourne (he'll live to 65), Whitney Houston (she'll live to 59), and Michael Jackson (he'll live to 76). But according to his calculations, Demko says Rolling Stones guitarist Keith Richards should have died in 1996. "He should have passed away at age 52. I'm not sure how he does it, but he defies all conventional wisdom."

*   *   *

MUSIC POP QUIZ

Harold Lloyd Jenkins was born in Friars Point, Mississippi, in 1933. He started his first band, the Phillips County Ramblers, when he was 10. At the age of 18 he was recruited by the Philadelphia Phillies to play baseball, but got drafted into the Army and served in the Korean War. In 1957 he returned to music and changed his name. In 1958 had his first hit with "It's Only Make Believe." He became a country music superstar and remained one until his death in 1993. The name he chose for himself came from two towns he saw on a road map—one from Arkansas and one from Texas. Can you guess it?

Answer: Conway Twitty

TWANG! A BRIEF HISTORY OF THE ELECTRIC GUITAR

"More than any other instrument," says Charlie McGovern of the Smithsonian Institution, "the electric guitar has been the dominant shaping force in American music in the last half-century." It's a relatively new instrument whose history is still being written. Here's a quick summary of what we know so far.

GONNA NEED A BIGGER SOUND

The 1920s are known as "The Roaring Twenties" and a large part of that "roar" was the music. This was the "Jazz Age," and the number of bands, and audiences for them, multiplied enormously all across the country. The 1920s also happened to be a time when the popularity of the acoustic guitar soared. It wasn't until that decade that steel-string guitars came into prominence. The increased volume of these new instruments led to more and more bands accepting them into their ranks, but they still had a hard time being heard. As one critic observed:

> In the Chicago and New Orleans jazz bands...the guitar had a rough time. No matter how hard the frustrated picker picked, he was usually drowned out by all sorts of horns and some bully on an 88-key, 500-pound piano.

Guitarists tried all kinds of tricks to be heard:

• They tried connecting megaphones to guitars.

• They used bigger and bigger instruments.

• They put microphones up against the strings. Logical...except that the technique usually produced too much feedback.

It wasn't working. Then, in 1924, one imaginative musician and instrument maker had an idea.

ELECTRIFYING FIRST

Since 1919 Lloyd Allayre Loar had been the leading luthier and sound engineer for the Gibson Guitar Company. (Instruments made by Loar, especially his mandolins, are among the most coveted in the world today.) He was also a virtuoso musician on several stringed instruments, and had long been interested in getting

---

The word "guitar" comes from the Greek *kithara*, a seven-stringed lyre.

better—and louder—sound from instruments; in the course of that goal he was the first person to put f-holes (like the holes in violins) in guitars and mandolins (that was in 1922). He also looked into electrifying stringed instruments. That led to him developing what we now know as a *pickup*—a device that "picks up" vibrations and converts them into electrical charges which are then converted into sound in an amplifier. Loar's device was a simple magnet surrounded by a wire coil that was placed under the bridge of the guitar. It was primitive, but it worked, and he built prototypes of electric violas and basses. (The Gibson company was also a leader in speaker and amplifier technology at the time—which helped Loar's work a lot.)

CLUELESS
Unfortunately, the Gibson board of directors didn't think there'd be much of a market for electric instruments, and declined to add them to their product line, so in 1924 Loar left the company. In the 1930s, he formed his own company, Vivi-Tone, selling electric guitars, mandolins, violas, and even claviers, and for various reasons, the company failed. One of the problems: Loar's pickups were *electrostatic*, meaning they picked up the vibrations of the instrument's bridge or body, not the vibrations of the strings themselves. They worked—and improved versions of that kind of pickup are popular today—but they just didn't sound very good. The next big step in the electric guitar's development would cure all that.

THE 1930s
By the late 1920s instrument makers and musicians all over the country were experimenting with their own ways to electrify guitars. One of them was Los Angeles musician George Beauchamp, and in 1930 he hit the jackpot. As the company history says today:

> By 1930 many people familiar with electricity knew that a metal moving through a magnetic field caused a disturbance that in turn could be translated into an electric current by a nearby coil of wire.

Beauchamp figured out that the moving piece of metal could be a metal string on an instrument—and invented the *electromagnetic* pickup, the heart of the electric guitar. In 1931 he teamed up with designer and entrepreneur Adolph Rickenbacker and founded the

Electro String Instrument Corporation (it later became the Rick-enbacker International Corporation) in Los Angeles, and started selling electric guitars. One of the famous models: the "Frying Pan Electro Hawaiian Guitar," so named because it was a lap-steel, or Hawaiian-style, guitar, and with its long neck and round body—it looked like a frying pan.

Around the same time, the Dobro Company (also in Los Angeles) started selling electric Spanish guitars, and in Seattle a year later, Paul Tutmar founded Audiovox, the first company to manufacture electric guitars exclusively. By 1935 the idea was out there, musicians liked it, and the big companies—Gibson, Epiphone, and National—took notice and started selling electrified guitars. The era of the electric guitar was taking shape.

GUITAR HEROES

Once the product was available on a wide basis, guitar players began showing the world what could be done with it. In the mid-1930s, for example, Aaron "T-Bone" Walker pioneered the stunts and styles of future rock 'n' roll greats like Chuck Berry and Jimi Hendrix, strutting across the stage, doing splits, and playing the guitar behind his back. He also experimented with volume and feedback, demonstrating that it was the guitar and amplifier *together*—not the guitar alone—that made a new instrument.

But the guitarist who made the biggest difference and helped catapult the electric guitar to new prominence was Charlie Christian, who played with Benny Goodman's band from 1939 to 1941. He is credited with creating an identity for the electric guitar as a solo instrument, playing staccato, hornlike, lead parts—a radical departure from the normal approach at the time—playing chords and being part of the rhythm section. Christian's style and technique were revolutionary and helped innovate a new jazz genre: bebop. In fact, his impact was so great that Frederic Grunfeld, author of *The Art and Times of the Guitar*, wrote, "There is the guitar before Christian and the guitar after Christian, and they sound virtually like two different instruments."

THE SOLID-BODY GUITAR

The next great leap forward in the electric guitar story came from two electronic geniuses. The first was Les Paul, a jazz guitarist who began experimenting with electric sounds in the late '20s (by jamming his mother's phonograph needle into the top of his guitar and plugging it in). Paul recognized what many before him had: all electric guitars until that time were amplified hollow body guitars, and that hollow body was creating feedback and distortion. Paul logically figured that an un-hollow—or solid—body would help, so in the late 1930s he created an instrument he called "The Log." It was a section of 4"x4" wooden fence post with a bridge, a neck, and a pickup on it—and a guitar body attached just for looks. He brought it to Gibson, and again, the guitar maker missed an opportunity to revolutionize the guitar world. Paul kept going back...and Gibson kept turning him down. "They laughed at me for 10 years," he told the *Washington Post* in 2005. "They called me 'the guy with the broomstick with the pickups on it.'"

It wasn't until somebody else came out with a commercially successful solid-body electric guitar in 1950, that the folks at Gibson finally got the message. In 1952, after working with Paul on the design, they released the aptly named Gibson Les Paul electric guitar. But who was the guy who introduced that first solid-body electric? Leo Fender.

BEND IT LIKE FENDER

Unlike Les Paul, Leo Fender wasn't a musician—he just loved tinkering with electronics. In 1938 he opened the Fender Radio Service in Fullerton, California, and musicians started coming in to get their electric guitars fixed. In 1946 that led to the opening of the Fender Electric Instrument Company, and, in 1950 the introduction of a solid-body electric guitar he called the *Broadcaster*. However, another musical instrument company (drum maker Fred Gretsch) owned the name "Broadcaster," so in 1951 he renamed it the *Telecaster*.

The Telecaster was a huge hit, but it wasn't until 1954, when Fender created the most popular electric guitar of all time—the *Stratocaster*—that the electric guitar came into its own. The Strat had a whole new look, with a sleek shape and beveled edges. And it came with a tremolo arm, or "whammy bar"—a metal bar extending from the guitar's bridge, which a player used to rapidly vary the tension of the strings. These and a host of other innovations made the Stratocaster revolutionary in the 1950s...and

...was by local bandleader Gage Brewer in Wichita, Kansas, in 1932.

opened the door to the electric guitar's immense popularity. Incredibly, the first Strats sold for only $75. How much are they worth today? If you have one, it can bring in as much as $20,000 as a collectible. But Eric Clapton's black 1956 model recently broke the record for a Stratocaster, selling for $959,000.

THE BIG THREE

There are of course many other respected electric guitar makers out there: Epiphone (John Lennon played one), Vox (Brian Jones of the Rolling Stones played one), Ibanez (Jerry Garcia played one), Gretsch (George Harrison, Chet Atkins, Bo Diddley, and John Fogerty played them), and Kramer (Eddie Van Halen played one) are just a few. But the Telecaster, the Les Paul, and the Stratocaster are by far the most famous and recognizable.

• The Telecaster was an immediate hit after its release and has remained popular ever since. Some famous players: Muddy Waters, Syd Barrett, Buck Owens, Waylon Jennings, Jimmy Page (the lead part on "Stairway to Heaven" was done on a telecaster), Keith Richards, and Bruce Springsteen (it's the guitar on the cover of the *Born to Run* album)

• Famous Les Paul players: Neil Young, Duane Allman, Slash, Marc Bolan, The Edge, Carlos Santana, Noel Gallagher, Dave Grohl, Pat Metheny, Joe Walsh, Peter Frampton, Slash, and Frank Zappa.

• The first big star to use Fender Stratocaster: Buddy Holly. Television appearances in 1957 and 1958 with his Stratocaster, just a few years after its first release, helped establish it with rock 'n' rollers. In the early 1960s Dick Dale, the "King of the Surf Guitar," did it again. Some other notables: Ike Turner, Eric Clapton (he got his first Strat in 1970, and it's the guitar sound you hear on *Layla*), David Gilmour, Jimi Hendrix, Mark Knopfler, and Stevie Ray Vaughan.

*   *   *

"One guitar player has an orchestra in his hands."

—Jeff Buckley

Before its introduction in 1949, the RCA 45-rpm record was code-named "Madame X."

WAS JOHN FOGERTY REALLY STUCK IN LODI?

And other burning questions about famous songs.

SONG: "LODI"

QUESTION: Was John Fogerty ever "stuck in Lodi"?

BACKGROUND: Fogerty wrote "Lodi" for Creedence Clearwater Revival's 1969 album, *Green River*. The song is about a guy who dreams of becoming a rock star but ends up working as an unsuccessful bar singer in the dismal town of Lodi, California. "If I only had a dollar," Fogerty sings, "for every song I sang / Every time I had to sing while people sat there drunk / You know I'd catch the next train, back to where I'd been / Oh Lord, stuck in Lodi again."

ANSWER: Nope. Fogerty grew up in El Cerrito, California, about 50 miles from Lodi. But Stu Cook, who played music with Fogerty from their early teens until the breakup of CCR in 1972, said they'd never been to Lodi. "We played around close to Lodi, because it was a very small town," he told *Creem* magazine in 2006. "It was really going nowhere and it didn't seem to be going anywhere. More of a state of mind than a piece of real estate."

SONG: "I'VE BEEN EVERYWHERE"

QUESTION: Did Hank Snow really go to all those places?

BACKGROUND: The 1962 song by country superstar Hank Snow (and later covered by Johnny Cash) tells the tale of a hitchhiker roaming around the United States and beyond, and is famous for its breakneck-speed lyrics listing off town after town. The first verse alone: "I've been to Reno, Chicago, Fargo, Minnesota, Buffalo, Toronto, Winslow, Sarasota, Wichita, Tulsa, Ottawa, Oklahoma, Tampa, Panama, Mattawa, La Paloma, Bangor, Baltimore, Salvador, Amarillo, Tocopilla, Barranquilla, and Padilla."

ANSWER: He could have: Snow was one of the most popular country stars in the U.S. and Canada (he was born in Nova Scotia) for six decades, sold more than 80 million albums, and played *thousands* of concerts, so it's possible that he really had been to all those towns and cities (91 of them) in the song. But the trouble is, Snow didn't write the song. It was originally written by an Australian country songwriter named Geoff "Tangletongue" Mack in 1959, whose original lyrics listed a bunch of Australian town names ("I've been to Wollongong, Geelong, Kurrajong, Mullumbimby, Mittagong..."). It became a hit Down Under in 1962 for another Aussie singer, Lucky Starr. Mack wrote the song, so the story goes, when a bad case of heartburn kept him up one night and he needed something to distract him. He pulled out a map, and the rest is...geography. (Mack wrote the American version, too.)

SONG: "YOU'RE SO VAIN"

QUESTION: Will we ever find out who's "so vain"?

BACKGROUND: You've probably heard the story: Carly Simon's 1972 #1 hit had that tantalizing line, "You're so vain, you probably think this song is about you." Ever since the song came out, people have been guessing who the song was written about. Some of the suspected egos: Mick Jagger (he sang backing vocals on the song), Warren Beatty, Kris Kristofferson, British playboy William Donaldson (Simon's onetime fiancé, until he was caught with another woman), and James Taylor (Simon's ex-husband). And Simon has played it up over the years, dropping hints in scores of interviews.

ANSWER: Probably. In 2003 Simon "donated" a dinner date and the answer to "Who's so vain?" to a charity auction. NBC executive Dick Ebersol won with a $50,000 bid. He was sworn to keep the name secret—but he was allowed to give out one clue: "The letter 'E' is in the person's name." That eliminated only Donaldson. A year later, Simon added an "A." That eliminated Kristofferson. Uncle John's guess is that she'll tell the world sometime in the next few years.

SONG: "A DAY IN THE LIFE"

QUESTION: What is Blackburn Lancashire, and why does it have 4,000 holes in it?

BACKGROUND: Every Beatles fan knows the line from Lennon and McCartney's masterpiece on 1967's *Sgt. Pepper's Lonely Hearts*

Club Band: "I read the news today, oh boy, four thousand holes in Blackburn Lancashire..." It goes on to say: "Although the holes were rather small, they had to count them all / Now they know how many holes it takes to fill the Albert Hall..."

ANSWER: Blackburn is a town in northwestern England, in the county of Lancashire. While he was writing the song, Lennon came up with some of its impressionistic lyrics by reading snatches of newspaper columns, including a January 7, 1967, *Daily Mail* article about a plan to fill the potholes—4,000 of them—in Blackburn's roads. And the link to Albert Hall, London's famous concert venue? That was imagination. "There was still one word missing in that verse when we came to record," Lennon later said in an interview. "I knew the line had to go: 'Now they know how many holes it takes to—something—the Albert Hall.' It was nonsense verse, really, but for some reason I couldn't think of the verb. What did the holes do to the Albert Hall? It was Terry [Doran—a friend] who said 'fill.' And that was it."

SONG: "DOWN BY THE RIVER"
QUESTION: Did Neil Young really "shoot his baby"?

BACKGROUND: On Neil Young's second solo album, 1969's *Everyone Knows This Is Nowhere*, is one of his most famous songs, "Down by the River." The chorus bellows: "Down by the river, I shot my baby / Down by the river, I shot my baby...dead..." Ever since then, an urban legend has circulated claiming that the song is about Young's girlfriend, who died after he "shot" an overdose of heroin into her veins.

ANSWER: No. Young made the song up. In the liner notes to his 1977 compilation album *Decade*, he said that he wrote the song, along with "Cowgirl in the Sand," while lying in bed with a 103° fever.

SONG: "HOUSE OF THE RISING SUN"
QUESTION: Was there really a brothel called the "Rising Sun"?

BACKGROUND: Long before the Animals had a #1 hit with it in 1964, this song was a classic American folk tune. But nobody's quite sure where it came from. Folklorist Alan Lomax wrote in 1941 that the music came from an old English ballad, and the lyrics—at least as we know them today—were written by two

Kentuckians named Georgia Turner and Bert Martin in the 1930s (the oldest known recording is from 1934). Other experts disagree. In any case, the song has been recorded countless times, by artists ranging from the Weavers to Bob Dylan to Sinead O'Connor. The song is about a woman telling her sad story of working in a brothel in New Orleans. The first verse, as reported by Lomax: "There is a house in New Orleans / they call the Rising Sun / and it's been the ruin of many a poor girl / and me, O God, for one." (The Animals changed the lyrics so the narrator is a man, the son of a ruined gambler.)

ANSWER: Nobody's sure of that, either. Some tourism-minded New Orleanians say there was such a house of ill repute from 1862 to 1874, located at 826-830 St. Louis Street. It was run, according to the guidebook *Offbeat New Orleans*, by a madam named Marianne LeSoleil Levant, whose surname means "the Rising Sun." But acoustic blues legend Dave van Ronk, who taught the song to Bob Dylan, told a different story: Old photos of the New Orleans Prison for Women, he said, showed a "rising sun" emblem on its entrance. So, he insisted, the song was about that prison, not a brothel.

*   *   *

OUR HERO

American singer and songwriter Bill Withers, known for hits like "Just the Two of Us" and "Lean on Me," got his break in 1971 at the age of 32. He was working at a Los Angeles factory making airplane parts when Booker T. Jones of Booker T. and the MGs agreed to produce his song "Ain't No Sunshine." The part where Withers sings "I know, I know, I know..." 26 times in a row was just a placeholder—he meant to fill that in with more lyrics later. "Then Booker T. said, 'No, leave it like that,'" Withers later recalled. "So I left it like that." The song went to #3 on the pop chart and won the Grammy for Best R&B Record in 1972, and Withers never looked back. (Oh—we forgot to mention that he's our hero because the airplane parts he was making when he recorded "Ain't No Sunshine" were toilet seats for 747s.)

MUSIC LESSONS

Our first page of advice centers on composing and performing.

"It's been very important throughout my career that I've met all the guys I've copied, because at each stage they've said, 'Don't play like me, play like you.'"

—Eric Clapton

"Do it again on the next verse, and people think you meant it."

—Chet Atkins

"Just don't give up trying to do what you really want to do. Where there is love and inspiration, I don't think you can go wrong."

—Ella Fitzgerald

"The most perfect technique is that which is not noticed at all."

—Pablo Casals

"It's a funny thing about music. The worst thing you can do is think."

—Neil Young

"If you sing loud enough and hit the drums hard enough, everything's going to be all right."

—Don Dixon

"Music has to breathe and sweat. You have to play it live."

—James Brown

"A painter starts with a blank canvas and as a musician, your canvas is silence. You don't want to cover it all up. So if you know what you're doing as a musician, you play the silences. You can't fall into that trap of trying to get everything in and playing so fast. You have to take time and pace yourself. Otherwise, technically you may make people go 'wow,' but it doesn't make good music."

—Keith Richards

"Get around, be on the scene, play it clean, be seen, be keen, and be over eighteen."

—Willie "the Lion" Smith, advising a young pianist in 1923

"Music should always be an adventure."

—Coleman Hawkins

"Don't bullsh*t...just play."

—Wynton Marsalis

In the 1944 film *To Have or Have Not*, Lauren Bacall's singing was dubbed by Andy Williams.

FAILED COMEBACKS

They came, they saw, they conquered. They went away.
Then they tried to come back...which didn't go so well.

MICHAEL JACKSON
In the 1980s, Michael Jackson could do no wrong. He was one of the hottest pop stars in the world, with a string of top-selling albums and songs. But by 2001, his music had been overshadowed by his bizarre behavior and eccentric personal life. In an attempt to put himself back on top, he released a single, "You Rock My World," which actually made it to the top 10. To keep the momentum going, he hired a British film crew to make a documentary about him. But instead of lionizing the singer, the film made Jackson look alarmingly weird. *Living with Michael Jackson* depicted, among other things, Jackson dangling his infant son over a balcony and admitting to sleeping in beds with children. This led to Jackson's arrest on child-abuse charges, a controversy that haunted his career from then on.

PAT BOONE

In the 1950s, Boone was a pop star who performed sanitized versions of R&B songs. He had his last hit in 1962, then became a televangelist and gospel singer. In 1997 Boone tried to reach out to young audiences with sanitized, swing versions of heavy metal songs by Judas Priest and AC/DC on an album called *In a Metal Mood: No More Mr. Nice Guy.* Boone promoted the album with an appearance on the American Music Awards dressed in a black leather vest with no shirt underneath. Instead of winning new fans, Boone was mocked and his album bombed. He also alienated much of his conservative fan base and was fired from *Gospel America*, the religious TV show he hosted.

VANILLA ICE

In 1990 Vanilla Ice (real name: Robert Van Winkle), a white rapper from Miami, hit #1 with "Ice, Ice Baby," the best-selling rap single of all time. Ice's popularity declined rapidly after it was discovered that "Ice Ice Baby" used music sampled from Queen's song

"Under Pressure" without permission. Then, to make matters worse, he was sued for stealing dance moves, and his claim that he was from a tough Miami ghetto was proven false (he was actually from Dallas, Texas). Vanilla Ice was soon a laughingstock, mocked by other rappers and on TV comedy shows for being a phony. In 1994 he released what he hoped would be a comeback album, *Mind Blowin'*, presenting himself as a violent thug who smoked a lot of marijuana—themes popular in rap music at the time. Once again, he was derided as a phony and the album tanked.

NEW KIDS ON THE BLOCK

This boy band was a cultural phenomenon in the 1980s, selling more than 70 million albums. But by 1992, kids and teenagers had moved on to rap and grunge rock. So in 1994, the group abandoned its squeaky-clean image and released *Face the Music*, an attempt at R&B and rap music. The first single, "Dirty Dawg," featured a cameo from a rap duo, and the video was so violent that it was banned in some markets. "Dirty Dawg" was a dud, the album sold poorly, and the band split up soon afterward.

*   *   *

PIANO ISLAND

Off the coast of Xiamen City, China, is the small island of Gulangyu with a population of less than 20,000—also called "Piano Island" or "The Island of Music." The Chinese name for the island literally means "drum waves islet," after the sound the waves make on the island's reef. But Piano Island is best known for its piano museum, the largest in China, which has a collection of antique pianos, from miniature pianos and player pianos to circular pianos and accordion-style ones. Island residents also personally own more than 620 pianos—that's a piano in one out of every five homes, more per capita, say officials, than anywhere else on Earth. Many of China's most famous pianists grew up here, including Cheng-zong Yin, who in 1967 set up a piano in Tiananmen Square and started playing in defiance of the communist government's decree that piano playing was illegal.

King Frederick II of Prussia (1712–86) wrote 120 flute concertos, more than any other composer.

THE *OTHER* SOPRANOS

If you're a man, perhaps you need a little reminder that your life is pretty good. Well, just be glad you weren't born in Italy in the 1700s. (Now cross your legs and read this story.)

THE ULTIMATE SACRIFICE

Who were the *castrati*? They were boys who were castrated in an effort to fill the Catholic Church's need for singing talent. The practice appeared in Europe as early as the 1500s, but historians estimate that between 1720 and 1730 (the height of the craze), 4,000 boys between the ages of nine and twelve who showed even vague musical promise were castrated each year. By that time, the practice was limited almost entirely to Italy, but its seeds had been planted years earlier when the Church, having banned women from singing in choirs (religious officials thought women's voices were too seductive for the church) turned to young boys, whose sweet tones were preferable to the shrill soprano falsettists.

Castration prevented puberty, and without the male hormone *testosterone*, a castrato's vocal cords remained small and immature throughout his lifetime, which kept his voice high. And because his bone joints didn't harden, he also grew unusually tall and developed a large chest cavity, which gave him extra lung capacity. With rigorous training, the combined effect was tremendous vocal flexibility, a high range, pure tone, and extraordinary endurance. The very best could hold a note for up to a minute without taking a breath.

THE GOOD LIFE

Many poor parents willingly sacrificed their sons to this cause in the hope that they'd find fame and fortune. Cardinals, church fathers, choir directors, and composers signed up the castrati for shows and performances. The boys dedicated their youth to a rigorous musical and vocal training regime. But only a few went on to stardom. The rest made careers in cathedrals, church choirs, and the theater.

Many historians consider the castrati who did make it "the original pop stars." Women swooned for them onstage and off; one young castrato was welcomed to the city of Florence by the town's

The Vienna Philharmonic, founded in 1842, hasn't had a permanent conductor since 1901.

wealthiest and most influential citizens. And though their voices were as high as a soprano's, they rarely played women's roles in operas—they were cast instead as the brave young heroes. (Male sopranos played the female roles until women were allowed on the stage in the late 18th century.)

BEST OF THE BEST
At their peak the castrati were employed by all of Europe's opera houses and church choirs, and the century's biggest composers, such as George Frideric Handel and Christoph Willibald von Gluck, wrote operas and vocal music specifically with castrato voices in mind. And the singers demanded enormous annual salaries: Records show some being paid as much as £1,500 (the equivalent of about $245,000 today).

The most famous castrati of them all: Carlo Maria Broschi (1705–82)—known on the stage as Farinelli. He was hired by the king of Spain, Ferdinand VI, for an undisclosed (but assumed to be very large) sum of money to serenade the king every night beneath his bedroom window. The job lasted 25 years. Ferdinand credited the youthful-sounding singer with single-handedly lifting his depressed spirits and helping him find the mental strength to attend to his affairs of state.

DOWNFALL OF THE DRAMA QUEENS
The reign of the castrati waned in Italy by the mid-1800s. The Catholic Church had long condemned the practice (and threatened to excommunicate participants), and, bowing to public opinion, the Italian government made castration illegal in 1870.

But historians say that it was largely the conceit of the castrati themselves that brought about their demise. Most of the performers became spoiled and egotistical; they often changed the scores to highlight their voices. Leading composers Rossini, Wagner, and Verdi all grew frustrated with their tampering and simply stopped writing for them. At the same time, the devoted but temperamental opera-loving public lost interest in the castrati, turning instead to the female soprano, whose timbre had become fashionable. Alessandro Moreschi, the world's last professional castrato and director of papal music for the Vatican, died in 1922. (Recordings of him are still widely available.)

Farrokh Bulsara was called "Britain's 1st Asian pop star." Stage name: Freddie Mercury, of Queen.

MODERN MOZARTS

When you think of composers, you probably think of the old guys: Bach, Beethoven, and Mozart. But there are many modern (living) classical composers who have earned a listen, too. Here are just a few—some that you may know...and some that you probably don't.

JOHN ADAMS

Most Americans haven't heard of him, but Adams is one of the most celebrated composers in the world today. His best-known work: *Nixon in China*, an opera written about President Richard Nixon's 1972 trip to the communist nation. (Uncle John's favorite line: Henry Kissinger sings to Chou En-Lai, "Premier, please, where's the toilet?") *Nixon in China* won the 1989 Grammy for Best Contemporary Composition, and has since been performed at major opera houses all over the world. In 2002 Adams, 55 years old and having written dozens of major works already, was commissioned by the New York Philharmonic to compose a musical work to commemorate the anniversary of the attacks on the World Trade Center. The resulting choral piece, *On the Transmigration of Souls*, won the 2003 Pulitzer Prize for Music, and then a recording of its premiere performance won classical music's "triple crown" in 2005, taking the Grammys for Best Classical Recording, Best Orchestral Performance, and Best Classical Contemporary Composition.

PHILIP GLASS

Philip Glass may be the best-known living classical composer, but his revolutionary minimalist compositions met with a lot of resistance when he began in the late 1960s—so much so that Glass, who studied philosophy at the University of Chicago and music at Juilliard, couldn't find a steady job playing music and had to work as a cab driver and a plumber to pay his bills. Glass kept at it, though, and eventually people came around. His rise to fame began with 1976's *Einstein on the Beach*—a five-hour opera. He composed several more operas, all of which are still performed regularly at opera houses worldwide, as well as literally hundreds of chamber music pieces, concertos, symphonies, and more over the

---

The harp, first documented in Egypt in 4000 B.C., is believed to owe its design to a hunter's bow.

decades. In 1983 he branched out into film, scoring the experimental documentary *Koyaanisqatsi*, his first commercial success. That was followed by Errol Morris's *The Thin Blue Line* in 1988, Martin Scorcese's *Kundun* in 1997, and Peter Weir's *The Truman Show* in 1998. Glass has even composed some pop music...sort of. His 1986 album *Songs from Liquid Days* features lyrics by Paul Simon, Suzanne Vega, and David Byrne. Today Glass is considered one of the modern classical era's most influential composers, and he continues to compose, perform, and record prolifically.

GLENN BRANCA

You know what classical music needs? More electric guitars. At least we think so—and so does Branca. He writes works for traditional classical instruments, too, but Branca is known primarily for writing compositions for electric guitars—sometimes lots of them. Examples: 1981's *Indeterminate Activity of Resultant Masses* (for drums...and 10 guitars), and his *Hallucination City: Symphony for 100 Guitars*, which was performed at the World Trade Center in June 2001. (Guitarists mentored by Branca include Lee Ranaldo and Thurston Moore of the highly influential alternative rock band Sonic Youth.)

*   *   *

TOP 10 HITS OF 1956

1. "Heartbreak Hotel"
—*Elvis Presley*

2. "Don't Be Cruel"
—*Elvis Presley*

3. "My Prayer"
—*The Platters*

4. "Lisbon Antigua"
—*Nelson Riddle*

5. "Hound Dog"
—*Elvis Presley*

6. "The Wayward Wind"
—*Gogi Grant*

7. "Poor People of Paris"
—*Lee Baxter*

8. "Que Sera, Sera"
—*Doris Day*

9. "Memories Are Made of This"
—*Dean Martin*

10. "Rock And Roll Waltz"
—*Kay Starr*

Black Sabbath released its self-titled first album on Friday the 13th, February 1970.

NOW HEAR THIS!

The personal music player was a revolution in technology that
changed the way people listened to music. And it all started
with the Sony Walkman. Here's the story.

THE PRESSMAN

In the mid-1970s, a team of Sony engineers headed by Mitsuro Ida created the Pressman—a portable tape recorder that could fit into a shirt pocket. As Sony expected, it quickly became standard equipment for journalists. But there was one small problem: The Pressman recorded in mono, and radio journalists preferred working in stereo. They requested a stereo version.

Sony's engineers put their best into it, shrinking stereo components, trying to get them into a small, pocket-sized case. They almost made it—but could only fit in the playback parts and two tiny speakers. Since the whole point was to come up with a tape recorder, the attempt was an embarrassing and expensive failure. Still, the quality of the sound was surprisingly good. So Ida kept the prototype around the shop instead of dismantling it. Some of the engineers started playing cassettes on it while they worked.

THE MISSING LINK

One day Masaru Ibuka wandered by. Although he'd co-founded the company with Akio Morita, he was considered too quirky and creative to fit into day-to-day operations. So he was made "honorary chairman"—a title that gave him much respect, little authority, and lots of time to wander the halls of Sony.

Ibuka stopped to watch the Pressman engineers working on their design problem. He heard music coming from the unsuccessful prototype and asked, "Where did you get this great little tape player?" Ida explained that it was a failure because it couldn't record.

Ibuka spent a lot of his time roaming around, so he knew what was going on all over the company. He suddenly remembered another project he'd seen that was being developed on the other side of the building—a set of lightweight portable headphones.

Longest time between #1 albums: 37 years, for Johnny Cash. (1969 to 2006.)

"What if you got rid of the speakers and added the head-phones?" he asked Ida. "They'd use less power and increase the quality of the sound. Who knows, maybe we can sell this thing even if you can't record on it." The engineers listened politely and respectfully—while privately thinking the old man had finally lost it. Why make a tape recorder that can't record?

LISTENING WELL

Ibuka took the gadget, with headphones attached, to Morita. He too was skeptical...until he heard the quality of the stereo music. To the shock of the engineering team, Morita gave it a green light. It was dubbed the Walkman, to go along with the Pressman.

The marketing department thought it was a terrible idea. They projected that the company would lose money on every unit sold. Even the name seemed wrong. According to American distribu-tors, "Walkman" sounded "funny" to English ears. So Sony rolled the product out as the "Soundabout" in the U.S. and the "Stow-away" in England. Their 1979 publicity campaign—a low-budget, lukewarm affair aimed at teens—got virtually no results. It seemed as though the Walkman's critics were right.

As it turned out, though, Sony had just targeted the wrong market. Teens had boom boxes...it was *adults* who wanted the Walkman. The little unit was perfect for listening to Mozart while jogging or the Stones while commuting, and was small enough to fit into a briefcase or the pocket of a business suit. To Sony's surprise, white-collar workers discovered the Walkman on their own. It became a sudden, raging success. Sony had prepared an initial run of 60,000 units; when the first wave hit, they sold out instantly. Within a few years, millions of personal cassette players had been sold.

But the Walkman's greatest innovation was the idea behind it—a slim, portable, personal music player. In 1984 Sony struck gold again with the release of the Discman, a portable CD player. And of course that was just the beginning: In 2001, Apple changed the music industry when it rolled out the iPod (for that story, turn to page 304). And now we can play MP3s on our cell phones—and who knows where it will go next? And it's all from a failed prototype that didn't get thrown away...and that some-body thought was a cool idea.

THE SUICIDE SONG

"Gloomy Sunday" is a ballad that's been covered by dozens of performers, from Billie Holiday to Björk. But some say it's more than just a sad song… it actually causes people to kill themselves. Or is it all just a coincidence?

PIANO MAN

In 1933 Hungarian songwriter Rezso Seress was working as a piano player in a Budapest restaurant called Kispipa Véndegló. The 34-year-old was struggling to make it as a composer, but he hadn't published any songs yet.

Then his girlfriend dumped him—because, she said, he was always depressed about his dismal music career. Seress grew even more despondent about the break up, but he channeled his sadness into his songwriting. With the help of a lyricist named Laszlo Javor, Seress wrote a somber ballad called "Szomorú Vasárnap," or, in English, "Gloomy Sunday." The song was a lament about someone whose lover has died, leading the narrator to thoughts of suicide. Here's one translation:

Sunday is gloomy, my hours are slumberless.
Dearest, the shadows I live with are numberless.
Little white flowers will never awaken you,
Not where the black coach of sorrow has taken you.
Angels have no thought of ever returning you.
Would they be angry if I thought of joining you?
Gloomy Sunday.
Gloomy is Sunday; with shadows I spend it all.
My heart and I have decided to end it all.
Soon there'll be candles and prayers that are sad, I know.
Death is no dream, for in death I'm caressing you.
With the last breath of my soul I'll be blessing you.
Gloomy Sunday.

THE SONG REMAINS THE SAME

Seress added "Gloomy Sunday" to the repertoire of songs he played at the restaurant. Even though it had been gut-wrenching to write (and audience members were visibly saddened by it), Seress thought "Gloomy Sunday" was the best thing he'd ever written, and he made a serious effort to get it published by a sheet-music

Tinkle, tinkle: Up until the 1800s, the triangle often had jingling rings strung on it.

company. (In Europe in the 1930s, records were available, but songs were far more popular as sheet music to be played at home on the piano.)

Seress sent the song to music publishers in Hungary, France, and England. They all turned him down, and all for the same reason. As one of the rejection letters said, "It's the terrible compelling despair about it. I don't think it would do anyone any good to hear a song like that."

Finally, in 1935, a music publisher agreed to release "Gloomy Sunday." The song became a moderate hit, providing Seress a modest income from the royalties. Things were beginning to look up.

IT'S GOT A GOOD BEAT AND YOU CAN DIE TO IT

According to the legend that has since sprung up around the song, trouble began in February 1936 when Budapest police investigated the first in a series of strange deaths. Joseph Keller, a shoemaker, was found dead with a suicide note consisting of the words "gloomy Sunday" and a request that his grave be decorated with 100 of the "little white roses" mentioned in the now-popular song. After Hungarian newspapers reported the connection between the suicide and the song, morbid curiosity made sales of "Gloomy Sunday" sheet music and recordings skyrocket.

But, eerily, so did the number of suicides allegedly related to the song:

• Two people were found in Budapest's Danube river, each clutching the sheet music of "Gloomy Sunday."

• As a band of Roma (Gypsy) street musicians performed the song, two people shot themselves.

• A man went into a nightclub and asked the band to play "Gloomy Sunday." They did, and he walked out into the street and shot himself.

• At a dinner party in a wealthy home, the song drifted from the party to the servants' quarters. Two maids heard the song and slashed each others' throats.

And, in perhaps the most bizarre twist, a Budapest woman who killed herself by drinking poison was later identified as Rezso Seress's ex-girlfriend—the inspiration for the song. Her suicide note consisted of two words: "Gloomy Sunday."

B.B. King named his guitar "Lucille" after nearly losing it in a fire...

After 18 suicides were supposedly linked to the song, Budapest police took action. They asked musicians, orchestras, and radio stations to stop playing the song and ordered stores to stop selling its sheet music and recordings, effectively banning the song.

But even the ban didn't stop the deadly effects of "Gloomy Sunday." Fueled by the controversy over what the press had begun to call "the Hungarian Suicide Song," "Gloomy Sunday" became a bestseller all over Europe. And in the next few months, it was linked to even more suicides, including a shopkeeper in Berlin who hung herself with the sheet music at her feet and a man in Rome who heard a beggar sing the song and then jumped off a bridge to his death.

ANARCHY IN THE U.K. (AND U.S.)

Curiosity about the song soon reached the United States, where a Hollywood songwriter named Sam M. Lewis composed an English translation (those are his lyrics at the start of this article). In 1936 the song was recorded by Hal Kemp and His Orchestra, one of the most popular bands of the era. It reportedly took 21 takes for them to cut the song because it upset the musicians. Unfortunately, the song's reputation had followed it from Europe, and an Ohio college student named Phillip Cooks reportedly became its latest victim: Accounts said that he listened to the song repeatedly, then took his own life in May 1936.

In 1941 Billie Holiday recorded the song—arguably the most famous version—which became a best seller in the United States and England. But her record label, fearful of more suicides, had hired Sam M. Lewis to add a third, more uplifting verse to the song. In it, the narrator says that the loss and despair were all just a dream, and that everything's actually great. The happy ending didn't help—later that year, a New York typist killed herself, leaving a request that Holiday's version of "Gloomy Sunday" be played at her funeral.

Because of all the hysteria over the song, BBC Radio in England would only play an instrumental version of "Gloomy Sunday." One day in 1941, a London policeman heard that version being played repeatedly from an apartment window. When he investigated, he found an automatic phonograph playing the record on repeat next to a dead woman holding an empty bottle of pills. After that, the BBC banned all versions of "Gloomy Sunday," a ban that stayed in effect until 2002.

MAYBE EUROPE IS JUST DEPRESSING

Ultimately, "Gloomy Sunday" was linked to nearly 100 suicides, a fact that troubled its songwriter, Rezso Seress, for years. He once told a reporter, "I stand in the midst of this deadly success as an accused man. This fatal fame hurts me. I cried all of the disappointments of my heart into this song and it seems that others with feelings like mine have found their own hurt in it." He never had another successful song, and became another "Gloomy Sunday" casualty when he jumped out of a Budapest window to his death in 1968.

It's been debated for years: Did people really kill themselves because one incredibly sad song destroyed their will to live? Some say no, and point out that Europe in the 1930s was not a happy place. World War II was well underway for many countries, and just around the corner for others. Fascism was on the rise, and economic depressions had crippled the continent.

And Hungary, the birthplace of the "Suicide Song," had one of the highest suicide rates in the world in the 1930s. (It still does, for reasons that would probably take an army of psychiatrists to figure out.) The song hit a sensitive nation in a sensitive spot, at just the right time. And the suicides never reached epidemic proportions in other countries—though, unfortunately, the song's reputation undoubtedly helped its sales. After the 1940s, no other suicides were linked to the song until 1997, when Scottish singer Billy Mackenzie took his own life. His band, the Associates, had recorded "Gloomy Sunday" several years earlier. It was a distant coincidence, but the Gloomy Sunday conspiracy theorists took note.

CODA

Today the song remains a favorite of musicians, both for its haunting lyrics and melody and for its dark legend. It's been covered dozens of times in recent years by artists including Ray Charles, Lou Rawls, Branford Marsalis, Marianne Faithfull, Björk, Sarah McLachlan, Sinead O'Connor, and Elvis Costello.

ANCIENT INSTRUMENTS: THE BRONZE LUR

Unless you had spegesild med løgsovs for lunch recently, you've probably never heard of this instrument.

ONE BOGGY MORNING
In 1797 a farmer named Ole Pedersoen was digging for peat in an old bog in eastern Denmark when he found six strange objects. They were S-shaped tubes made of bronze, with one end flared, and they were enormous—more than seven feet long. They turned out to be musical instruments—horns, to be exact—and they were nearly 3,000 years old.

Five of those instruments ended up in the Danish National Museum in Copenhagen (the sixth, through somewhat mysterious circumstances, found its way to Russia). Nearly 60 more of the horns were later found around Scandinavia, Latvia, and northern Germany.

More than 30 years later, the five horns in the Danish National Museum caught the attention of curator C. J. Thomsen. In the process of organizing the museum's many ancient artifacts, Thomsen had decided to classify all of them according to what they were made of: stone, bronze, and iron. He conjectured (correctly, it was later proven) that this would put them in chronological order. That's how we got the terms Stone Age, Bronze Age, and Iron Age.

The instruments had simply been called "horns," but Thomsen gave them the old Nordic name *lur*, which meant "hollowed-out log." Another type of lur, the wooden Viking horn, was already well known to museums. But these tall bronze lurs were much older.

PAIRFECT

The well-preserved lurs were still playable, and their striking design was so simple that it was no mystery how they were played: They were shaped like flattened fish hooks, with a thin mouthpiece coming straight out from the player's mouth for more than a foot. The tube then curved around the side of the player's head and upward and forward again. From there, it grew slightly in diameter and rose until it was nearly four feet above the player's head. Way up at the top, a decorative flat plate, about 10 inches in diameter, was attached to the end of the tube. It's believed the player would hold the segment attached to the mouthpiece with one hand and the upward-curving tube with the other.

But here's the cool part: Lurs come in pairs. One lur is designed to curve to the right of a player's head, while its companion lur curves to the left. They were meant to be played by two people side by side, with the lurs rising up around them symmetrically.

LET'S PLAY

And what does a bronze lur sound like? In 1893 Danish musicologist and composer Angul Hammerich held a lecture on the lurs in Copenhagen and had professional musicians demonstrate on the instruments. The tone, it was reported, was similar to a trombone or trumpet. Today you can easily find modern recordings of these 3,000-year-old horns on the Internet, and on a 2003 CD called *From the Danish Past and Present* by the Royal Danish Brass. The album has several songs played on the ancient instruments, including four of the six horns that were found by farmer Ole Pedersoen on that day back in 1797.

*   *   *

THE DA VINCI CODA

In November 2007, a musician and computer technician in Rome claimed to have found a musical score hidden in Leonardo da Vinci's famous painting, *The Last Supper*. Giovanni Maria Pala told reporters that when five equally spaced lines are drawn across the painting, objects such as loaves of bread and the hands of Jesus and the apostles fall on the lines like the notes on a staff. The notes, he says, represent a piece of "sacred music." Only catch: they have to be played backward. The music is described as a "Bachlike passage" about 40 seconds long, which Pala calls a "hymn to God."

The bugle fanfare played at the start of a horse race is a tune called "First Call."

MUSIC AWARDS SHOWS BY THE NUMBERS

Since they started, these awards shows have done little to promote music…but they're sure given us a lot of statistics.

THE GRAMMYS

1: Number of times a single artist has won the coveted Big Four—Record of the Year, Album of the Year, Song of the Year, and Best New Artist—at the same ceremony. Christopher Cross won these honors in 1981 for his self-titled album and the song "Sailing."

8: From 1967 to 1974, Aretha Franklin won this many consecutive awards for Best Female R&B Vocal Performance: "Respect," "Chain of Fools," "Share Your Love with Me," "Don't Play That Song," "Bridge over Troubled Water," "To Be Young, Gifted and Black," "Master of Eyes," and "Ain't Nothing Like the Real Thing."

12: The age of the youngest person ever nominated for a Best Male Country Vocal Performance Grammy: Billy Gilman, in 2001 (he lost to Johnny Cash).

14: The age of the youngest person to *win* a Grammy. In 1997 LeAnn Rimes won not one, but two awards: Best New Artist and Best Female Country Vocal Performance for "Blue."

31: Most Grammys won by an individual: the late Sir Georg Solti, who conducted the Chicago Symphony Orchestra for 22 years. (He was nominated 74 times.)

1957: Year the first Grammys were awarded.

$2,500: Cost of a ticket to the 2007 Grammy Awards Ceremony.

COUNTRY MUSIC ASSOCIATION AWARDS

5: The most CMA Awards won in a single year. Johnny Cash did it in 1969, and Vince Gill repeated the feat in 1993.

A Baby Grand piano is 5'11" long. Professional Grand: 6'. Concert Grand: 8'11" or longer.

10: The most nominations for CMA Awards in a single year, by Alan Jackson in 2002. Merle Haggard had held the record since 1970 with nine nominations.

14: Number of years that Brooks and Dunn have won the Vocal Duo of the Year award. They claimed that category from 1992 through 1999 and from 2001 through 2006. (Montgomery Gentry won in 2000; Sugarland won in 2007.)

19: Total number of CMA awards won by Brooks and Dunn. They hold the record, but Vince Gill is just one trophy away from sharing the title.

$550: Cost of a ticket to the 2008 awards show. If you want to go to the after-show party, you'll have to pay another $3,900.

1968: Year the CMA Award show was first broadcast, making it the longest-running annual music awards program on network television. (The CMAs were first held in 1967, but that show wasn't on TV.)

AMERICAN MUSIC AWARDS

8: The most American Music Awards won in a single year. Michael Jackson won eight in 1983 for *Thriller*, and so did Whitney Houston in 1993 for *The Bodyguard* soundtrack.

22: The most American Music Awards won by a group, by Alabama.

23: The number of AMAs that record-holder Whitney Houston has won as a solo artist.

$1,782: Cost of a ticket to attend the 2007 AMA show (this one includes the post-show party).

1973: The year the American Music Awards began. Dick Clark created the show because ABC executives wanted a piece of the music industry awards pie after the Grammy Awards moved to CBS. From the AMAs' inception, controversy has surrounded the show, which some critics believe favor the most popular musicians and groups and not necessarily the most talented.

In 1991 *Star Trek*'s Data (Brent Spiner) released an album titled *Ol' Yellow Eyes Is Back.*

MUSICAL COMEDY

Are they musicians who do comedy? Or are they comedians who do music? We don't know—but we love what they do.

VICTOR BORGE

Victor Borge was a piano prodigy: He learned to play at three and won a scholarship to the Copenhagen Music Conservatory at the age of eight. But his real love was comedy, and before World War II, he appeared in Copenhagen music halls doing comic impersonations of Adolf Hitler. When the Nazis invaded Denmark in 1940, Borge—who was Jewish—fled to the United States. He spoke no English but learned the language quickly by watching American movies.

Borge's big break came in 1941 when he got a job appearing regularly on Bing Crosby's radio show. Soon after, he had a program of his own, and in 1953, he opened a one-man show on Broadway. In all of his performances, Borge merged music and comedy. He played the "Minute Waltz" as a duet—reducing it to 30 seconds, as he and a partner started at opposite ends of the piece. And among his most famous routines were his "phonetic punctuations," in which he spit and made rude noises to indicate punctuation (such as commas, periods, and exclamations points) as he recited songs and stories. And he kept up his habits of falling off his piano bench and sitting on his keyboard for laughs into his 90s.

Borge died in 2000, just days after giving a concert in Denmark. He said, "I have always worked for two audiences at the same time. One is sophisticated, the other not musically oriented. Nobody must be bored."

Borge quote: "Laughter is the shortest distance between two people."

TOM LEHRER

In the 1940s, while a mathematics student at Harvard University, Lehrer began writing musical parodies. In one, he sang the periodic table to the tune of the "Major General's Song" from the operetta *The Pirates of Penzance*. Lehrer's song ends with the lines "These

The word piccolo means "small" in Italian.

are the only ones of which the news has come to Harvard / And there may be many others but they haven't been discarvered." Then, in the 1950s and early '60s, he toured internationally, singing pieces like "The Masochism Tango," "The Weiner Schnitzel Waltz," "Smut," "Poisoning Pigeons in the Park," and his anthem about nuclear war, "We Will All Go Together When We Go." After a few years, though, he gave up show business to become a mathematics professor at MIT.

Lehrer reemerged a decade later, writing songs for the children's TV show *The Electric Company*, and in 1998 he performed onstage for the first time in 25 years at the Lyceum Theatre in London. But he hasn't played before an audience since.

Lehrer quote: "It is sobering to consider that when Mozart was my age, he'd already been dead for a year."

ALLAN SHERMAN

Allan Sherman grew up in Southern California, where he started writing music and plays in 1942, including a musical for his high school's senior class. But he started his show-biz career producing TV programs like the game show *I've Got a Secret*, which he also created. In 1958 he was fired after airing an episode that all the execs thought would flop. (It did.) Between jobs, Sherman started writing down the song parodies he'd been playing for his friends for years. With the support of several Hollywood comics such as Harpo Marx, Jack Benny, and George Burns, he was signed by Warner Bros. in 1962 to record some of those songs, including "Sarah Jackman" (sung to the tune of "Frere Jacques") and "The Streets of Miami" (to the tune of "The Streets of Laredo"). The album, *My Son, the Folk Singer*, became one of the fastest-selling albums to date. The following year, he released the album that would make him famous, *My Son, the Nut*, and included a song called "Hello Muddah, Hello Fadduh." The song was a hit; it climbed to the #2 spot on the Billboard chart and earned Sherman a Grammy and an appearance on *The Tonight Show*.

Sherman continued to write parodies—tunes with titles like "Here's to the Crabgrass" and "Hail to Thee Fat Person"—until he died in 1973 at the age of 48.

Sherman quote: "Somewhere, over the rainbow, way up tall. There's a land where they've never heard of cholesterol."

"WEIRD" AL YANKOVIC

Alfred Yankovic picked up his first musical instrument (the accordion) the day before his seventh birthday, and he learned rock 'n' roll, he says, by playing along to Elton John's "Goodbye Yellow Brick Road" with his accordion. While in college in the late 1970s, he started writing and recording song parodies. He sent two of the recordings to Los Angeles–based disc jockey Dr. Demento (Barry Hansen), who played odd and funny music on his national radio show. By 1982 the young satirist had a record deal, a degree in architecture, and a nickname: "Weird Al."

Yankovic plunged into his new career and found a niche singing parodies of well-known pop songs. Over the years, his hits have included "My Bologna," "I Lost on *Jeopardy!*" "Another One Rides the Bus," "Eat It," "Smells Like Nirvana," "Like a Surgeon," and "Amish Paradise."

"Weird Al" has won three Grammys, sold millions of albums, and been awarded 13 gold and six platinum records. His 2007 release, *Straight Outta Lynwood*, debuted in *Billboard*'s Top 10 and was nominated for two Grammys. And just in case his audience worries he'll run out of material, Yankovic says he's still got "plenty of warped ideas" and will keep recording.

Yankovic quote: "I'm still a geek on the inside. That's the important thing."

*   *   *

HARE CUERVO?

Having brass bands play at weddings and festivals has been a tradition in India for more than a century. Today, Indian folk melodies and tunes from popular "Bollywood" films are the songs most commonly played at such events. But sometimes international hits find their way into the mix, too. That explains why you could be wandering through an Indian city or village and hear a brass band pumping out a raucous version of "Tequila!"

Regis Philbin sings "Pennies From Heaven" on *Who Wants to Be a Millionaire—The Album.*

CELEBRITY ORCHESTRA

Some people play Fantasy Football—Uncle John plays Fantasy Orchestra.
These famous folks actually do play these instruments (or did).

STRING SECTION

Violin: Albert Einstein, Jack Benny, Ben Franklin, Meryl Streep

Viola: Jimi Hendrix (his first instrument)

Cello: Condoleeza Rice, Louis Braille, Paula Zahn, Thomas Jefferson

Bass violin: Dick Smothers

Harp: Harpo Marx

WOODWIND SECTION

Flute: John Quincy Adams, George Eastman (founder of Kodak), Frederick the Great (King of Prussia), Alyssa Milano (*Who's the Boss?*)

Clarinet: Woody Allen, George Segal

Oboe: Julia Roberts

Trombones: Jonathan Frakes (Riker on *Star Trek*), Fred "Mister" Rogers

Saxophone: Jennifer Garner, Vince Carter (NBA player), Alan Greenspan (former Federal Reserve chairman)

BRASS SECTION

Trumpet: Montel Williams, Peter Weller (*Robocop*), Richard Gere, Prince Charles

Cornet: Drew Carey

Baritone horn: Neil Armstrong (1st man on the moon)

Tuba: Andy Griffith

PERCUSSION

Rosie O'Donnell, Tipper Gore, Johnny Carson, chef Emeril Lagasse, Hugh Laurie (*House, M.D.*), John Stamos

GUEST SOLOISTS

Piano: Katie Couric, Alexander Graham Bell, Ansel Adams (photographer), Dustin Hoffman

Organ: Albert Schweitzer

Accordion: Jimmy Stewart, John Smoltz (MLB pitcher), Charlie Chaplin, Richard Nixon

Concertina: Mahatma Gandhi

Guitar: Dave Barry (humor columnist), Louis XIV (King of France), Steven Seagal

Banjo: Steve Martin

CONDUCTOR

Werner Klemperer (*Hogan's Heroes*), David Odgen Stiers (*M*A*S*H*)

The world's largest playable harp is in Santa Fe, New Mexico. It's 13 feet tall.

A (BAD) NIGHT
AT THE OPERA

One of Uncle John's favorite movies is the Marx Brothers' A Night at the Opera. The Marxes perform some unbelievable antics on opening night...but are they so far-fetched? Here are some real-life examples of what can happen at the opera. (Honk-honk!)

CARMEN GET IT

A performance of *Carmen* was being staged in Mexico City. The singer playing the part of Don José had a long wait between acts 3 and 4, so he decided to dash out for a beer in a local tavern. No sooner had he entered than he was arrested by a couple of cops who saw his scruffy costume, thought he was a bum, and dragged him off to jail. When he insisted he was a tenor singing in the opera, they accused him of being drunk. He could only convince them...by singing. (They let him go.)

DUMB GIOVANNI

In 1958 Cesare Siepi was playing the lead in *Don Giovanni* with the Vienna State Opera. The script called for him to descend into hell using a stage lift. So Cesare said goodbye to the world, and stepped into the netherworld. But the lift got stuck halfway down, leaving his head and shoulders visible to the audience. Stage technicians brought the lift back up and tried to lower it again, but it got stuck a second time and was raised back to stage level. Cesare sang in Italian, "Oh my God, how wonderful—hell is full!"

JUST LIKE LEMMINGS

In the opera *Tosca*, two soldiers are to execute the character Cavaradossi while the heroine, Tosca, watches in horror. Prior to the performance in San Francisco in 1961, the director had too little time to instruct the firing squad. He told them, "When I cue you, march on stage, wait until the officer lowers his sword, then shoot." When they asked how to exit the stage, he said, "Exit with the principal characters." The soldiers marched onstage and were amazed to see two people against the execution wall: Tosca and Cavaradossi. They hadn't been told which one to shoot—so when the officer dropped his sword, they had to choose—and they shot Tosca. Wrong. Cavaradossi dropped dead 20 yards away, while the person they had just shot ran over to him weeping and wailing in Italian. Tosca then climbed to the top of the castle battlement to commit suicide. The firing squad, having been instructed to exit with the principal characters, followed her, leaping to their deaths as the curtains closed.

NOISE POLLUTION

When *The Wreckers* opened in England in 1901, King Edward VII came to the opening. Conductor Sir Thomas Beecham later asked the king's private secretary if the king had liked the music. "I don't know," was the reply. "But you were sitting right next to him—surely he must have said something!" "Oh, yes—he did. He woke up three-quarters of the way through and said, 'That's the fourth time that infernal noise has roused me!'"

DEADPAN PERFORMANCE

In 1849 *Charles VI* premiered in Paris. At the beginning of the aria called "Oh God, Kill Him!" a member of the opera company fell dead. The next night, at the same point in the production, a member of the audience died. When the orchestra leader fell dead at the third performance, Napoléon III banned the opera for good.

SLAPSTICK OOPERA

In 1960 the diva playing the role of Donna Elvira in *Don Giovanni* in New York was to make her entrance in a sedan chair carried by two porters, then step out and begin singing. Unfortunately, she weighed a lot and the two porters struggled with the sedan chair. The porter in front set his burden down to get a better grip, which threw all the weight on the porter in the rear, who in turn threw the chair forward. The violent rocking of the chair caused the soprano inside to fall forward into a somersault, and she promptly got stuck. The porters couldn't see inside the sedan chair, had no idea what had happened, and carried her onstage like that. There was nothing for her to do except sing upside down from the chair. When they carried her offstage at the end of the song, an axe was needed to extricate her from the chair. Her first act upon regaining her freedom was to slap the two porters.

A CAPPELLA U.

*Want to see a good singing group? Go to the closest university—
you'll probably get to choose between a bunch of them.*

YALE LOUDER

One chilly January in 1909, a group of a cappella singers at
Connecticut's Yale University decided to start practicing
indoors at Mory's Temple Bar, a well-known private club near the
school's campus. The Varsity Quartet, as they were known, was
made up of members of Yale's Glee Club and had been around for
about a decade. The songs they sang covered many styles, often
from popular musical revues of the day, and featured the singers'
four-part harmonies and unique arrangements. The weekly practices soon became popular music events, and after a while the
group decided they needed a better name. One member, Denton
"Goat" Fowler, suggested "Whiffenpoofs," a nonsense word coined
by comedian Joseph Cawthorn for the 1908 Victor Herbert musical, *Little Nemo*. (A whiffenpoof, according to Cawthorn, was a
type of fish he'd caught.) The name was accepted.

Over the decades, the singing Whiffenpoofs became an
entrenched Yale tradition—and they still exist today. Some of the
songs in their repertoire over the decades include "Bye Bye Black-
bird," "Between the Devil and the Deep Blue Sea," and "Deep
River," and go all the way to Bob Marley's "Waiting in Vain."
They are now a 14-member group, and they've performed in
movies, on TV, at Carnegie Hall, at the Rose Bowl, and even at
the White House. They remain the country's oldest collegiate a
cappella group...but they aren't the only one.

I MAJORED IN "AIN'T SHE SWEET"

After the Whiffenpoofs, glee-club singing groups slowly started
popping up at campuses around the country. In 1927 the Double
Quartet, or DQ, an eight-member group, formed at Amherst College in Massachusetts; in 1936 a group of students from the all-
female Smith College in Massachusetts visited a Yale picnic—and
that year started the Smiffenpoofs, the country's first female collegiate singing group; the Nassoons were formed at Princeton in

1941; and in 1946 the Krokodiles started singing at Harvard. (These groups all still exist and still perform today.)

A CAPPELLA NATION

Starting in the 1980s, it practically became a prerequisite for a school of higher education to have an a cappella singing group. Today there are more than a *thousand* on college campuses all over the U.S. and Canada (and even some in Europe), with more than 20,000 students involved. They cover a wide range of musical genres, including rock, country, hip-hop, jazz, gospel, folk, and comedy, just to name a few. Some song examples: Pat Benatar's "Hit Me with Your Best Shot" (The Buffalo Chips, University of Buffalo); "Simcha G'dola," a fast and percussive Jewish devotional song (Pizmon, the Jewish Theological Seminary, New York, NY); "Save a Horse, Ride a Cowboy" from country duo Big and Rich (the Hullabahoos, University of Virginia); and "Let's Get It Started" by the Black Eyed Peas (the Beelzebubs, Tufts University).

There are groups for men only, groups for women only, coed groups, some class-specific groups from freshmen to senior, and some are open to any student of any grade willing to audition. Many schools therefore have more than one group...and some have more than a dozen (Cornell and Yale each have 18). They have state and national organizations, and there are even competitions: The Varsity Vocals International Championship of A Cappella is held every year to determine the year's best group. (2006 winners: Vocal Point, from Brigham Young University.)

THE RULES OF GLEE CLUB

Competition for spots on the more esteemed clubs can be fierce. You have to be able to sight read, have a certain amount of dancing and acting ability, maintain a grueling practice, performance, and promoting schedule (while going to school), and...oh yeah... you have to be able to sing really, really well.

The Whiffenpoofs, for example, are a registered non-profit organization with a substantial budget—they have an international touring schedule, and also find time to record and sell CDs. (You can hire them to play at your wedding for around $3,500.) Having a membership on your resume can be a huge help to someone going into the music business, whether it's performing, teaching, or some other musical application. Some famous alumni from the most prestigious groups: Senator Prescott Bush (President George W. Bush's grandfather—Yale's Whiffenpoofs); actress Mira Sorvino (Harvard's Veritones); Diane Sawyer (Wellesley's Blue Notes); Art Garfunkel (Columbia University Kingsmen); and Cole Porter (Yale's Whiffenpoofs).

NAME THAT TEAM

A lot of the groups have humorous or "punny" names. Some of our favorites:

• Treble in Paradise (American University)

• The Pitchforks (Arizona State)

• BC Sharps (Boston College)

• Shirley Tempos (Brandeis)

• ARRR!!! (Brown University. They sing sea shantys, which they refer to as singing *a capirate*)

• The Packabelles (University of North Carolina Asheville)

• Chord on Blues (University of Pennsylvania)

• The Ransom Notes (University of Texas)

*　　*　　*

RANDOM MOVIE QUOTE

Lucas: The first thing you need is a name. Then you'll know what kind of band you've got.

Mark: Right, right. I was thinking about, um, Marc. How does that sound?

Lucas: Is that with a C or with a K?

Mark: Well my name is with a K, so I was thinking my band's name could be with a C. That way it's kind of that psychedelic, you know, trip thing.

Lucas: Always play with their minds.

—*Empire Records* (1995)

THE SINCEREST FORM OF FLATTERY

If the real thing can't come to play your town, consider a tribute act.

I WANT TO HOLD YOUR SPAM

Possibly the very first official "tribute band," a relatively unknown musical act that mimicked a well-known musical act, was formed in 1975...as a joke. That year Monty Python alum Eric Idle formed the Rutles, a band that parodied (and paid homage to) the Beatles, as a skit for his new television show. The Rutles never found major mainstream success, but they did make a "mockumentary" film, *All You Need Is Cash*, in 1978. The movie featured such stars as John Belushi, Bill Murray, Gilda Radner—and even George Harrison—and the soundtrack was nominated for a 1979 Grammy for Best Comedy Recording. (The 2002 follow-up film, *The Rutles 2: Can't Buy Me Lunch*, focused on their "reunion tour.")

Nowadays, the largest group of tribute performers is *definitely* Elvis impersonators (some people call them the "Elvii"). In the documentary *Almost Elvis*, the filmmakers estimate that there are more than 35,000 impersonators worldwide. Plus, numerous contests crown the top Elvis every year. The largest—the Elvis Contest and Convention European Championships—takes place every January (Elvis's birth month) in Blackpool, England, where the winner takes home about $2,000 and gets the chance to perform in the contest's showcase exhibition.

Like the Elvii, most tribute artists try to emulate their originals' look, style, and sound. Some, though, try to stand out.

• Gabba is a British band that plays ABBA songs...but with a Ramones-inspired punk sound.

• AC/DShe is an all-female band that plays the songs of AC/DC.

• Dread Zeppelin covers Led Zeppelin with a reggae twist—and an Elvis-impersonator lead singer.

BIG BUSINESS

Tribute bands have a reputation for being small time and playing for niche audiences in tiny clubs. Not so. Many tribute bands have their own fan bases and sell thousands of concert tickets. Rain, for example, is a Beatles tribute band from California. The five-man group has been playing together since the late 1970s and does about 200 shows every year. And singer Tim Owens went from playing in the Judas Priest tribute band British Steel to actually becoming the lead singer for Judas Priest.

Although the originals rarely openly endorse their tribute bands, they're also unlikely to denounce them—probably because the tribute bands pay licensing fees for the music they record. Plus, the tribute bands offer free advertising. Says one imitator: "We're spreading their brand...so it's good for them."

THE NAME GAME

In honor of the great imitators and the fans who love them, we've compiled this list of some of our favorite tribute-band names:

BEATLES
The Fab Faux, A Hard Night's Day

TOM PETTY
Petty Theft

LED ZEPPELIN
Led Zepagain, Led Zepplica

MADONNA
Mandonna (all-male), Madonnabes

VAN HALEN
In Halen

JOHNNY CASH
Cash'd Out, A Band Named Sue

THE BYRDS
The Byrd Brains

AD/DC
BC/DC (from British Columbia)

GRATEFUL DEAD
The Deadbeats

ABBA
Björn Again

STING
Stung, Stingchronicity

PINK FLOYD
Floydian Slip, Pink Side of the Moon

2 LIVE CREW
2 White Crew

METALLICA
Harptallica (played on harp)

POISON
Posein'

KISS
MiniKiss (all little people)

ROLLING STONES
Rolling Clones

ALANIS MORISSETTE
Alanis Moreorless

SHANIA TWAIN
Shania's Twin

STEELY DAN
The Steely Damned

MÖTLEY CRÜE
Mostley Crue

...the audience booed. They wanted to hear "Whole Lotta Love."

TV HITS

Sometimes a TV show gets so popular that its audience can't get enough of it, even pushing a song from the show onto the pop chart.

SHOW: *Cheers*
SONG: "Where Everybody Knows Your Name"
STORY: In 1982 songwriter Gary Portnoy was working with collaborator Judy Hart Angelo on tunes for a Broadway musical called *Preppies* when the producer of a new TV sitcom, *Cheers*, asked if he could use one of the songs ("People Like Us") as the show's theme. *Preppies'* producers said no, so Portnoy and Angelo wrote another song for the *Cheers* producers. They didn't like it. So Portnoy and Angelo wrote another one. They didn't like that one, either. Finally, the duo wrote a song called "Where Everybody Knows Your Name." The producers loved it, and used it (sung by Portnoy) to play during *Cheers'* opening credits. The song quickly became a radio hit, but the show, initially, didn't catch on. Eventually, thanks in part to the song's popularity, *Cheers* went on to become one of the biggest shows on TV.

SHOW: *Family Ties*
SONG: "At This Moment"
STORY: L.A.-based pop band Billy Vera and the Beaters had a minor hit in 1981 with this ballad. But they hit the jackpot when the song was featured in three episodes of the show *Family Ties* in 1985 and '86—Alex (Michael J. Fox) and his girlfriend Ellen (Tracy Pollan) called it "their song." Radio stations across the country began getting requests for the once-forgotten song, dug out their copies, and in January 1987, "At This Moment" was the #1 song in the country.

SHOW: *Cops*
SONG: "Bad Boys"
STORY: When *Cops* premiered in 1989, it used the appropriately titled (but completely unknown) "Bad Boys" for its theme song, performed by an obscure reggae group called Inner Circle. Strangely,

---

Trumpeter Wynton Marsalis first played with the New Orleans Philharmonic when he was 14.

the song wasn't released as a single until 1993, four years after *Cops* went on the air. "Bad Boys" immediately hit the top 10 and went on to sell more than seven million copies.

SHOW: *The Greatest American Hero*
SONG: "Believe It or Not"
STORY: In the late 1970s and early '80s, Joey Scarbury was a session singer and songwriter for hire. Then TV composer Mike Post gave him his big break, selecting him to the sing the theme song for a new show called *The Greatest American Hero*. The song, whose official title is "Theme from *Greatest American Hero* (Believe It or Not)," went to #2 in 1981. The show ran for three seasons, and though Scarbury never had another hit, he continued to write songs for radio and TV.

SHOW: *Welcome Back, Kotter*
SONG: "Welcome Back"
STORY: In 1975 TV producer Alan Sachs was preparing a sitcom called *Kotter*, about a man who returns to his rough Brooklyn neighborhood to teach high school. Sachs told his agent, Dave Bendet, that he wanted a "Lovin' Spoonful or John Sebastian type of song" to use for the theme. The Lovin' Spoonful (with Sebastian as its leader singer) had had a string of pop hits in the 1960s, such as "Do You Believe in Magic?" and "Summer in the City." Coincidentally, Sebastian was also a client of Bendet's, so Sachs quickly hired him. Sebastian wrote a minute-long song called "Welcome Back," which he feared would get rejected because it didn't have the word "Kotter" in it. But Sachs liked the song so much that he changed the name of the show to fit the song— *Kotter* became *Welcome Back, Kotter*. The show was an instant hit in the fall of 1975, fueling demand for the song. Sebastian wrote and recorded a second verse, and the song was released as a single. It went to #1 on the pop chart.

* * *

"Rock 'n' roll has become respectable. What a bummer."

—**Ray Davies**

In 2007 the number of recorded CDs sold was about equal to the number of blank CDs sold.

ORIGIN STORIES

Straight from the horses' mouths.

"We did consider the name 'Beetles,' but Jerry [Allison] said, 'Aw, that's just a bug you'd want to step on,' so we immediately dropped that."

—Niki Sullivan, of Buddy Holly's group, the Crickets

"Back in the late days of the Acid Tests, we were looking for a new name. We'd abandoned the Warlocks; it didn't fit any more. One day we were all over at Phil Lesh's house smoking DMT. He had a big Oxford dictionary, opened it, and there were the words 'grateful dead,' those words juxtaposed. It was one of those moments, you know, like everything else on the page went blank, diffused, just sort of oozed away, and there was GRATEFUL DEAD, big black lettered edged all around in gold, man, blasting out at me, such a stunning combination. So I said, 'How about Grateful Dead?' And that was it."

—Jerry Garcia

"The band's name means the act of dying, but, like, really mega!"

—Dave Mustaine, of Megadeth

"We'd nailed up this ad: 'Band looking for a tough singer.' We'd gotten a few replies, one of them from a guy called Ozzy. As we were going to see him I told my pal, 'I hope it's not the Ozzy that goes to my school, 'cause he scares me.' It was."

—Geezer Butler, of Black Sabbath, on discovering Ozzy Osbourne

"There was this guy who sold tomatoes, this black gentleman, and his name was the Captain. He had beefsteak tomatoes, actually, but he used to say his tomatoes were as big as beef hearts."

—Captain Beefheart

"I was playing in an all-night jam session, and I had cut my finger and I didn't know it. When they turned the lights on at the end, the organ keyboard was covered in blood. So I called everybody over and said, 'Wouldn't this make a great album cover for a band called Blood, Sweat and Tears?' And so we called it that, except we didn't take the picture because no one had a camera."

—Al Kooper, of Blood, Sweat and Tears

Alanis Morissette appeared on *Star Search* in 1989, but lost to a singing cowboy named Chad.

CRAZY ABOUT MUSIC

But maybe not as crazy as these people.

I FEEL SHOT!

In January 2007, two men in Atmore, Alabama, got into an argument over the late "Godfather of Soul," James Brown, who had died just weeks earlier. What was the argument about? How tall Brown was. Dan Gulley Jr., 70, apparently became upset when David James Brooks Jr., 62, implied that Brown was short. So he shot him. Brooks went to a police station and was taken to a hospital; Gulley went to the station and turned himself in. (Brown was reportedly 5' 6" and, according to some sources, wore lifts in his shoes. Editors' note: Please don't shoot us.)

KNOCK OVER BEETHOVEN

In 2003 a violinist in the Beethoven Orchestra in Bonn, Germany, informed a fellow violinist that he had hit a wrong note during a rehearsal. When the second violinist hit the note—wrongly—again, the first one punched him. Then other musicians took sides and an orchestra-sized brawl broke out. The violent violinist who started the melee was fined the equivalent of $600. (Bonus: It was a public rehearsal.)

YOU'RE OUT!

On May 20, 1997, Chad Curtis, a baseball player for the Cleveland Indians, told teammate Kevin Mitchell that he didn't like the lyrics—or the volume—of a rap song playing on the clubhouse stereo. Mitchell disagreed, and their "artistic differences" erupted into a scuffle. When the dust settled, Curtis ended up on the 15-day disabled list with a thumb injury (he fell onto the clubhouse Ping Pong table during the fight). Mitchell was released from the team.

JINGLE HELLS

Workers' unions, noise-pollution activists, and even a member of the British parliament took the side of shopworkers in Britain in December 2006 against the "torture" of having to listen to

Christmas music. "If they're exposed to the same songs over and over," said Val Weedon, national coordinator of the U.K. Noise Association, "it's no different than being tortured." Lord Beaumont of Whitley, a member of the House of Lords, agreed: "It would certainly have an adverse effect on me," he said. "It would drive me to murder."

IT TAKES A VILLAGE PERSON

Some priests, a security guard, and three teenagers walk into an art museum...no, really. In January 2007, a group of Catholic priests were walking through the London Art Museum when they saw three teenage boys standing in front of a painting of Jesus... and singing the Village People's song "YMCA" (Jesus was apparently the "Y"). The outraged priests chased the boys through the museum, aided by a security guard. The boys were caught and charged with public mischief.

*   *   *

TOP OF THE J-POPS

Japan has a company that compiles statistics about record sales, similar to *Billboard* magazine in the United States. It's called Oricon (the name comes from a combination of the English words "original" and "confidence"). The bestselling albums on the Oricon chart for 2007:

1. *Home*, by Mr. Children

2. *Black Cherry*, by Koda Kumi

3. *The Best Damn Thing*, Avril Lavigne

4. *All Singles best*, Kobukuro

5. *A Best 2 -White*, Ayumi Hamasaki

6. *A Best 2 -Black*, Ayumi Hamasaki

7. *Ai Am Best*, Ai Otsuka

8. *Can't Buy My Love*, Yui

9. *Exile Evolution*, Exile

10. *Greatest Hits*, Sukima Switch

THE UKE

In the 1960s, many Americans were introduced to the ukulele when they saw it on TV, strummed by the strange, long hands of Tiny Tim. But the little instrument has a bigger history than that, and—like so many Hawaiians—it traces its ancestry far beyond the Islands.

ISLAND HOPPER

On August 23, 1879, a British sailing ship named the *Ravenscrag* pulled into Honolulu Harbor carrying a group of newcomers to the Hawaiian Islands: 419 men, women, and children from the Portuguese island of Madeira—and a small, guitarlike instrument called the *machete* (pronounced *mah shet*). Over the following decades, the little instrument would evolve into the signature instrument of the Hawaiian Islands.

Madeira, an eastern Atlantic island about 500 miles southwest of Portugal, was settled by the Portuguese in the 1400s. Somewhere around 1850, musicologists say, the *braguinha*, a small, four-stringed, guitar-shaped instrument, was introduced from Europe. It was known locally as the machete, and became a popular instrument in the island's rich musical culture.

In 1879, when British sugar growers promised good wages to laborers willing to work the cane fields in Hawaii, thousands of Portuguese took up the offer—and they brought their music with them. According to an article in the *Hawaiian Gazette* from September 1879, the imported music was an instant hit: "Madeira Islanders recently arrived here have been delighting the people with nightly street concerts." The article describes the "very sweet music" played "on strange instruments which are a kind of cross between a guitar and banjo." That was the machete, and the soon-to-be ukulele.

HAWAIIANIZE IT

As the story goes, four men from the *Ravenscrag* started it all: woodworkers Manuel Nunes and José do Espírito Santo, and musicians Augusto Dias and João Fernandes. Within months, Nunes had opened a woodworking shop in Honolulu, employing Dias and Santo, and soon ads were listed in local newspapers offering

Starting small: Neil Young's first instrument was the ukulele.

their products—including machetes. And the design of their instruments soon began to change.

Machetes traditionally had metal strings and were tuned to "open G"—meaning that when the strings were strummed "open" (without being fretted), they played a G chord. At some point in the 1880s, that design was changed to four gut strings (from sheep or cats) and the tuning was changed to the now-famous "My dog has fleas" (G-C-E-A), an "open-C" tuning. In another important change, machetes were now made with wood from the Hawaiian koa tree, famous to for its durability, beauty, and rich tonal qualities.

Nunes is recognized as the first mass producer of the instrument, but it was Dias and Fernandes who helped give it the boost that would spread its popularity throughout Hawaii. Dias and Fernandes became musicians of note in Honolulu, and through their playing became acquainted with Hawaii's royal family, including the "Merry King," King David Kalakaua. The king was a music lover, and he fell in love with the machete, eventually learning to play it himself. The royal thumbs-up for the instrument was a big boost, and sales started to soar. Nunes, Santo, and Dias would have a monopoly on the market for the next 30 years.

MY FLEA HAS LEAPS

But how did the machete come to be called the ukulele? The Hawaiian word *ukulele* literally means a louse or flea (*uku*) that jumps or dances (*lele*). There are a handful of theories about why Hawaiians began to call the instrument by that name:

• A player's quickly moving fingers resemble jumping fleas.

• One machete player, an aide to King Kalakaua, was very small and quick, and had the nickname "Ukulele." The instrument was named after him.

• Hawaiians already had a two- or three-stringed instrument called the *ukeke*, and the more versatile new instrument was called a *ukeke lele*—a "dancing ukeke."

• The spelling derives from *ukelele*, which means "strike-jump," describing how the instrument was played.

The u-k-e spelling, though not the accepted one by strict

ukuleleists today, is actually the original spelling. The u-k-*u* spelling was introduced in a *Hawaiian Gazette* article in 1895. In any case, most of the makers spelled it with a *u* in their advertisements and on the instruments—so that's the spelling that's used today.

LITTLE BIG TIME

Business improved for Nunes, Santo, and Dias over the years (and a few of their ukuleles still survive, and they're worth a fortune). Then, in the 1890s, orders started coming in from the mainland, thanks to a group of Hawaiian musicians who played at the 1893 World's Columbian Exposition in Chicago. Over the next decade, more would play at World's Fairs all over the country. But it was in 1915 that the popularity of the ukulele started to explode.

That year, 17 million people went to the Panama-Pacific International Exposition in San Francisco, a seven-month fair celebrating the completion of the Panama Canal, where the "Hawaiian Pavilion" was one of the attractions—and the ukulele was the star of the show. By 1917 Hawaiian music was the bestselling music in the United States. It was a boon for Nunes— the only one of the original three makers still living—and for up-and-coming ukulele makers such as James Anahu and Jonah Kumalae. They all had more business than they could handle, but they were about to get some serious competition: By 1920 the biggest guitar makers on the U.S. mainland, companies like Martin, Gibson, and Harmony, were selling thousands of ukuleles per year.

ALOHA

The ukulele boom lasted through the 1920s, bolstered by popular performers like Cliff "Ukulele Ike" Edwards and Roy "Wizard of the Strings" Smeck (Smeck played at Franklin D. Roosevelt's inauguration in 1933), but sales declined later in the 1930s. By the 1960s, the ukulele was virtually gone from popular music— until a strange character named Tiny Tim started singing "Tiptoe Through the Tulips" on *Rowan and Martin's Laugh-In*, and subsequently the *The Ed Sullivan Show* and Johnny Carson's *Tonight Show*, among others.

Tiny Tim, with his oiled locks, enormous nose, and high falsetto voice, caused ukulele sales to…well, do nothing. He sold millions of albums, but the ukulele remained an obscure instrument and today is treated mostly as a novelty by the general public. But there have always been devoted players and fans, especially in Hawaii, and popular ukulele clubs and festivals have sprung up all over the world. And as of 2007, sales have seen their first significant rise in decades, signaling that a new "ukulele boom" could be on the horizon.

*　　　*　　　*

POLITICALLY INCORRECT HITS

• **"Indian Giver."** This was the title track to a 1969 album by the 1910 Fruitgum Company (also known for the hit song "Simple Simon Says"). Sample lyrics: "Indian giver, Indian giver / You took your love away from me." The album went gold and the song was later recorded by the Ramones and Joan Jett and the Blackhearts.

• **"If You Wanna Be Happy."** This 1963 song by Jimmy Soul featured these lyrics: "Say man / Hey baby / Saw your wife the other day / Yeah? / Yeah, she's ugly. / Yeah, she's ugly but she sure can cook." It went to #1 on the Billboard chart and was Jimmy Soul's only hit.

• **"He Hit Me (and It Felt Like a Kiss)."** This Phil Spector-produced song by The Crystals was released in 1962. But it was actually written by legendary songwriting team Gerry Goffin and Carole King. They reportedly wrote it after singer Little Eva rationalized being beaten up by her boyfriend by saying "he loved her." If the song was supposed to be satirical, it didn't come across that way, and was widely criticized. One of the song's verses: "He hit me (ba-dat-shoo-wah) and it felt like a kiss / He hit me (ba-dat-shoo-wah) and I knew he loved me / If he didn't care for me, I could have never made him mad / But he hit me and I was glad."

Extra: In 2005 the British band Spiritualized released a spoof of the song called "She Kissed Me (and It Felt Like a Hit).

I HATE MY SONG

Sometimes pop stars record a song…and regret it.

SONG: "Shiny Happy People"
ARTIST: R.E.M.
BACKGROUND: The communist Chinese government issued a propaganda leaflet during the 1989 pro-democracy Tiananmen Square protests, claiming that protesters were alone in their dissent and that the rest of China was "shiny happy people holding hands." Michael Stipe of R.E.M. wrote a song based on that leaflet—the sappiest, most brainless pop song he could imagine. It was supposed to be a satirical joke mocking people who ignore tragedy and world events. It didn't work. Most people thought "Shiny Happy People" was a catchy pop song, not a *parody* of a catchy pop song. It reached the Billboard Top 10, one of only four R.E.M. songs to do so. It was such a contrast to R.E.M.'s usual straightforward, socially conscious music that Stipe issued a public apology for the song. The band never played "Shiny Happy People" live after 1991 and, despite it being one of their few actual hits, they refused to include it on their 2003 greatest hits album.

SONG: "The Flame"
ARTIST: Cheap Trick
BACKGROUND: In 1988 Cheap Trick was recording their album *Lap of Luxury*. The band hadn't had a hit in nearly a decade and Epic Records told them they'd be dropped from the label…unless they recorded a song called "The Flame." The band preferred to play harder power-pop music and songs they'd written themselves, like their hits "I Want You to Want Me" and "Surrender." "The Flame" was a radio-friendly love ballad written by songwriters Bob Mitchell and Nick Graham, who'd been hired by Epic. The members of Cheap Trick loathed the song, but recorded it and put it on *Lap of Luxury* because they didn't want to lose their recording contract. Epic Records was right: the song went on to become Cheap Trick's first and only #1 hit song. The band still hated it, though, and only began to play it live in 2001.

SONG: "We Are the World"
ARTIST: USA for Africa
BACKGROUND: Dozens of 1980s pop stars (including Michael Jackson, Lionel Richie, Bruce Springsteen, and Kim Carnes) agreed to be part of "We Are the World" because it was for a good cause—the proceeds went to help relieve the Ethiopian famine. But at least two singers thought the song itself (written by Richie and Jackson) was pretty mediocre—they were just afraid to admit it at the time. In 2005, twenty years after the song was recorded, Billy Joel told a reporter that "most of us there didn't like the song, but nobody would say so. Cyndi Lauper leaned over to me and said, 'It sounds like a Pepsi commercial.' I didn't disagree."

SONG: "Old Time Rock & Roll"
ARTIST: Bob Seger and the Silver Bullet Band
BACKGROUND: It's a classic rock-radio staple and Tom Cruise became a star when he danced to it in his underwear in the 1983 movie *Risky Business*. Seger co-wrote the song, but his backing group, the Silver Bullet Band, hated it. According to Seger, they thought it had cheesy lyrics and it didn't mesh with their usual sound the way previous hits "Night Moves" and "Hollywood Nights" did. Seger asked the band to try it out during a few concerts in Germany. The crowds loved it, so even though the band hated it, they recorded it. After it became their biggest hit, Seger told the *Detroit Free Press* in 1994, "they started becoming quieter about it."

SONG: "Smells Like Teen Spirit"
ARTIST: Nirvana
BACKGROUND: It's arguably the most important rock song of the 1990s. It brought grunge and alternative rock into the mainstream. Critics hailed it as an anthem for a generation of disaffected teenagers ("With the lights out / We're less dangerous / Here we are now / Entertain us"), which made lead singer Kurt Cobain very uncomfortable. He didn't want to be the voice of a generation or make hit records; he wanted Nirvana to remain an underground punk band. Result: he hated "Teen Spirit." After the song became a smash hit (it reached #6 on the pop chart) and made Nirvana rich and famous, Cobain would play the opening riff at concerts, say "I don't think so," then launch into a different song.

WAYLON JENNINGS:
A FIVE-SONG BIOGRAPHY

*Can five songs really tell the story of this country-music outlaw
who fought the Nashville system? Let's find out.*

BACKGROUND

Texas native Waylon Jennings may have done things the hard way. But in the process, he helped launch the "outlaw" music genre with fellow Texan Willie Nelson, jolting country music out of the comfortable mainstream rut it had settled into by the late 1960s. Jennings's stripped-down sound and uncompromising standards served as an inspiration for countless artists who followed him, ranging from Travis Tritt to Metallica. Here's a quick trip through his career, with stops at milestone songs.

1. BUDDY HOLLY AND "JOLE BLON"

Jennings, born in 1937 in Littlefield, Texas, met up with Buddy Holly in 1955 in Lubbock, where the young Jennings was working at radio station KLLL. Holly took a shine to Jennings and helped him with his career, working on songs with his him and producing his first single, the Cajun-tinged "Jole Blon," in 1958. Jennings also served as a backup member of Holly's band, the Crickets, playing bass for him during Holly's final tour. Jennings was supposed to be on the plane trip that claimed Holly's life on February 3, 1959, but gave up his seat to fellow Texan, "The Big Bopper" J. P. Richardson, who had a bad head cold and wanted to get some extra rest.

Jennings was devastated by Holly's death and spent the better part of two years mourning his friend. "Buddy was the first guy who had confidence in me," he later told a reporter. "Hell, I had as much star quality as an old shoe. But he really liked me and believed in me."

2. "ONLY DADDY'LL WALK THE LINE"

In 1960 Jennings hit the road. After stops in Phoenix and Los Angeles, he landed in Nashville in 1965 with an RCA contract.

Neil Diamond was his high school's fencing champion.

Luck gave him Johnny Cash as a roommate; the two developed a life-long friendship. Jennings's first hit was "That's the Chance I'll Have to Take" in 1965; from there, his popularity grew, culminating in 1968 with a string of Top 10 country hits, including "Only Daddy'll Walk the Line," in which he griped about being wrapped around a woman's little finger. But despite his popularity, Jennings wasn't satisfied with the work and began to chafe under what he saw as the musical restrictions of Nashville, where producers tried to tame his honky-tonk sound to make it safe for middle-of-the-road audiences.

3. "THIS TIME"

Jennings started on the outlaw path in 1970, when he took a chance on a young songwriter named Kris Kristofferson and used his songs for the albums *Singer of Sad Songs* and *Ladies Love Outlaws*, which laid the foundation for the tougher, rawer "outlaw" country sound. Then in 1972, Jennings got RCA to let him produce his own work and choose his musicians; with that new freedom he released his first masterpiece, 1973's *Honky Tonk Heroes*, which featured 10 songs written by Billy Joe Shaver and wrenched a number of emotional performances out of Jennings, from the wistful "We Had It All," and the wry opening guitar lines of the title track to the wanderlust classic "Willy the Wandering Gypsy and Me."

Jennings was doing it his way, and it finally paid off: In 1974 he charted his first #1 hit with "This Time." The Country Music Association voted him Male Vocalist of the Year in 1975. Pop stardom hit when *Wanted! The Outlaws*, a compilation album featuring Jennings, his wife Jessi Colter, and Willie Nelson, hit #1 on the pop chart.

4. THE SUPERSTAR YEARS: "GOOD OL' BOYS"

The late 1970s and early 1980s were very good for Jennings. He scored a string of ten #1 hits, including three with his old friend Willie Nelson, with whom he recorded the classic *Waylon & Willie* in 1978, an album that featured the ironic hit "Mammas Don't Let Your Babies Grow Up to Be Cowboys." He also achieved international fame by singing "Good Ol' Boys," the theme song he wrote for the hit TV show *The Dukes of Hazzard*, and becoming "The

Balladeer," the show's off-screen narrator who described the zany goings-on of Hazzard County. The *Dukes* theme song was one of his 10 #1 country hits. Jennings topped off this period of his career in 1985 by joining forces with old friends Nelson, Cash, and Kristofferson to form The Highwaymen, outlaw country's first and only "supergroup," whose album *Highwayman* featured a #1 song (called "The Highwayman") about reincarnation.

5. "MOST SENSIBLE THING"

Things slowed for Jennings after the mid-1980s, as he switched labels from RCA to MCA, then to Epic, and later to smaller labels like Justice, for whom he recorded 1996's *Right For the Time*, featuring the retrospective ballad "Most Sensible Thing," in which he looked back at some of the excesses of his earlier days. He also became a spokesman for education: The high-school dropout earned his GED in 1989 and then became a proponent of the program. He also released a children's album called *Cowboys, Sisters, Rascals & Dirt* in 1998, which provided pre-schoolers a little taste of outlaw country with songs like "All My Sisters Are Girls," and "Dirt," a salute to, well, getting dirty.

In his final years, Jennings struggled with failing health, primarily diabetes. In 2001 his foot was amputated due to complications brought on by the disease, which would later contribute to his death in February 2002.

A LASTING LEGACY

As a gauge of Jennings's influence on music, one need look only as far as the contributors to *I've Always Been Crazy* and *Lonesome, On'ry & Mean*, the two tribute discs released in 2003. There you'll find not only country stars Kris Kristofferson, Travis Tritt, and Kenny Chesney, but also a few surprises like Henry Rollins, Metallica's James Hetfield, and jazz chanteuse Norah Jones, whose smoky take of "Wurlitzer Prize (I Don't Want to Get Over You)" makes a good argument for music lovers not getting over Jennings anytime soon.

* * *

Random music fact: Ancient Greek physicians prescribed music to cure hangovers.

SACHS-HORNBOSTEL

*No, it's not a German curse word, it's a system used
all over the world to classify musical instruments.*

SACHS ON SAX

Musical instruments have a long history—and a remarkably complex family tree. Over the centuries, music historians have devised many systems for classifying the dizzying array of instruments. The oldest known system goes back to at least the fourth century B.C., when the Chinese developed a simple system based on what the instrument was made of, such as stone, wood, clay, or bamboo. In the first century B.C., musicians in India devised a system that separated instruments into four categories: those with vibrating strings; vibrating columns of air; percussion instruments that produce sound by the entire instrument vibrating, like bells; and percussion instruments that produce sound via skin membranes, like most drums.

Many centuries later, in the 1880s, Belgian music scholar Victor-Charles Mahillon, curator of the Brussels Conservatoire museum, used a system similar to the Indian one when he compiled a catalog of the museum's 1,500 instruments. In turn, his system was adapted in the early 1900s by musicologists Erich Moritz von Hornbostel and Curt Sachs, who expanded and improved on Mahillon's work in their 1914 paper titled *Systematik der Musikinstrumente*. Their system is still the most widely used instrument classification system in the world today. The Sachs-Hornbostel (or Hornbostel-Sachs) system divides all instruments into five major classifications, each of which is further divided, with those divisions divided again, and so on, into hundreds of different groups.

CLASS ACTS

The five major classifications of instruments are:

1. Idiophones, which produce sound by vibrating themselves (for example, bells, cymbals, gamelans, gongs, rattles, washboards).

2. Membranophones, which produce sound via vibrating membranes (congas, snare and bass drums, steel drums, talking drums).

3. Chordophones, which produce sound through vibrating strings (banjos, dulcimers, guitars, harps, lutes, pianos, ukuleles, violins).

4. Aerophones, which produce sound via vibrating columns of air (clarinets, flutes, harmonicas, trumpets, whistles).

5. Electrophones, which include instruments that produce sound solely through electronic means (such as theremins, moog synthesizers, drum machines, or electric organs).

BREAK IT DOWN

The Sachs-Hornbostel system is based on the Dewey decimal book-classification system, with every instrument having a number assigned to it—some of them very long. Each number in the entry corresponds to some characteristic of the instrument. The first number is always 1, 2, 3, 4, or 5—corresponding with the five main categories listed above. After that, each number has its own meaning.

If an instrument's Sachs-Hornbostel number begins with "11," for example, the instrument is an *idiophone*—the first "1" tells us that. The second "1" tells us that it is a "struck idiophone," like a cymbal or a xylophone. If the number begins with "12," it's a "plucked idiophone," like a Jew's harp or an *mbira* (sometimes called an African thumb piano). If the number begins with "24," the "2" tells us it's a *membranophone*, and the "4" means it's a "singing membranophone," where the membrane doesn't produce sound itself, but modifies other sounds—as in the kazoo, which makes a sound when you hum into it.

FOR EXAMPLE...

The Uncle John's Sachs-Hornbostel number quiz (say *that* three times fast): What musical instrument is designated by number "423.121.22"? To find out, you have to know what each number means:

4: It's an aerophone (the fourth of the five major categories).

42: It's an instrument in which the vibrating column of air is enclosed within the instrument.

423: The player's lips cause the air to vibrate directly in the instrument (as opposed to a reed instrument, for example).

423.1: The player's lips are the only means of changing the pitch (unlike the valves on a trumpet, for example).

423.12: The instrument is shaped like a tube (unlike a conch-shaped instrument, which is rolled into layers).

423.121: The instrument is end-blown (as opposed to side-blown, like a flute).

423.121.2: The tube is bent or folded.

423.121.22: The instrument has a mouthpiece.

What instrument has the Sachs-Hornbostel number 423.121.22? The bugle. (It's not the only instrument. The bronze lur is another that has that designation. For more on that ancient instrument, go to page 99.)

DISHARMONY

In spite of being the most popular system for musical instrument classification in the world, the Sachs-Hornbostel system has received its share of criticism over the years. "This classification is convenient, but not necessarily logical, as some instruments may belong to more than one class," says musicologist and musician Henry Doktorski of Duquesnes University in Pennsylvania. "The Jew's harp may be classified as an aerophone or a plucked idiophone. The aeolian harp may be classified as an aerophone or a chordophone."

Doktorski goes on to point to American composer Guy Klucevsek, who wrote a composition for solo accordion titled "Eleven Large Lobsters Loose in the Lobby" in 1991. The accordion, according to the Sachs-Hornbostel system, is an aerophone. But in "Eleven Large Lobsters Loose in the Lobby," the player doesn't use the bellows and reeds—he only produces sounds by tapping the keys and pressing the register switches. So, in that particular piece, the accordion is an idiophone—a percussion instrument.

Curt Sachs and Erich Moritz von Hornbostel wouldn't have a problem with the controversies, though, because they knew their system would grow and change through the ages. It was intended to be, as they described it, an "open-ended discussion." Kind of like music.

interview on National Public Radio, where he played, among other things, the "William Tell Overture." After that, Wilson was hired by the cable channel TVLand to make a series of promotional videos. The ads show Wilson's hands playing the theme songs to old shows like *The Odd Couple*, *The Addams Family*, and *The Dick Van Dyke Show*.

HOW TO MAKE HAND FARTS

The sound produced by hand music is created the same way your lips create sound in the mouthpiece of a brass instrument—except your palms act as your lips. You "shake hands with yourself," as R. A. Miller puts it, palms together, fingers folded between the thumb and fingers of the other hand, with one thumb over the other. (Many manualists use different versions of that technique, so see what works best for you.) You've got to create a small pocket of air between your palms, then squeeze it out. For the high notes, Wilson says, squeeze the air up through the top of your folded hands where the thumbs meet. For the low, truly flatulent-sounding notes, emit the air, naturally, out of the bottom. (Start with the high notes—they're supposed to be easier to control.)

It takes a lot of practice, but if you've got, er, a lot of time on your hands, you can learn to do it. The first trick is to make a sound at all; then you can begin to control the pitch. After that, you should be able to produce whatever fart notes you want and, finally, play a fart tune. Then you can get on TV and become a star.

GIVE 'EM A HAND—AND ANOTHER ONE

A few more handy tips about hand-flabulous music around the world:

• Bruce "Handman" Gaston has been playing his hands with bandmate and guitarist Ken Purcell all over the world since 1992. You can find their album, *Mr. Handman: Amazing Feats on Musical Hands* on the Internet. Highlight: A hand-fart version of "When I'm 64."

• Type "hand-farts" and "Bohemian Rhapsody" into an Internet search engine. You won't be disappointed.

LET'S DANCE!

*Even non-dancers (like Uncle John) will like
the stories behind these dance crazes.*

THE TWIST

You can thank Dick Clark for this dance craze—as host of TV's *American Bandstand*, he was always on the lookout for the next big fad. In 1959 he heard a little-known Hank Ballard b-side called "The Twist." Clark loved the song and urged Ballard to perform it on *Bandstand*, but Ballard wasn't interested. So Clark searched around Philadelphia (where the show was based) and found a part-time chicken plucker named Ernest Evans who was known for his ability to mimic popular singers. Before Evans could perform, however, Clark insisted he find a good stage name. Clark's wife, Barbara, suggested modeling it after Fats Domino: "Fats" became "Chubby," and "Domino" became "Checker." So the newly-christened Chubby Checker sang "The Twist" on *Bandstand* and it was an immediate hit. The single shot to #1, and *the* dance craze of the 1960s was born. So why was the Twist so popular? First, as a non-contact dance, it was novel and rebellious enough to appeal to teenagers, but safe enough for the conservative media. Second, the Twist is easy—even non-dancers (like Uncle John) could do it. "It's like putting out a cigarette with both feet and wiping your bottom with a towel," explained Checker.

Typecast: "The Twist" turned Checker into a star. He followed it up with a string of successful dance songs (to this day, he's the only recording artist to have had five albums in the Top 12 at the same time). Yet the song also took a toll on Checker's artistic dreams. "In a way, 'The Twist' really ruined my life," he lamented years later. "I was on my way to becoming a big nightclub performer, and 'The Twist' just wiped it out. It got so out of proportion. No one ever believes I have talent."

THE WALTZ

Even people who can't dance (like Uncle John) can recognize the familiar 1-2-3, 1-2-3 rhythm of the waltz. Although these days it's associated with high society, when the waltz was introduced in

European ballrooms in the early 1800s, it was shunned by "respectable" people. For one, the music came from peasant yodeling melodies of Austria and Bavaria. Worse yet: the close proximity of the two dance partners. Even poet Lord Byron, a notorious rake, claimed that the "lewd grasp and lawless contact" of the waltz "does not leave much to mystery to the nuptial night."

Nevertheless, the waltz caught on and became the standard dance of the upper classes in Europe and the United States. Most of the credit for that goes to Austrian composer Johann Strauss. In the mid-1800s, he re-worked the peasant melodies and turned them into layered compositions which were embraced by Viennese royalty. This made Strauss the "waltz king." He toured Europe with his orchestra, taking the music (as well as the dance) to Germany, Poland, and Russia. It soon found its way to England, then the United States...and eventually into Earth's orbit.

Revolver: Perhaps the most wisely recognized waltz is Strauss's 1867 work, "The Blue Danube"—it was so popular in Austria that it became the country's unofficial anthem. The piece also became a staple of American pop culture when Stanley Kubrick used it in his 1969 film *2001: A Space Odyssey* to accompany the delicate dance of a passenger shuttle orbiting a space station as it prepares to dock—which makes sense, as the word "waltz" comes from the German *walzen*, meaning "to revolve."

THE POLKA

This fast-paced dance is simple to learn, even for Uncle John. And it has a fun origin story, too...depending on who's telling it. The Bohemian version—the one most often cited—claims that in 1834 a young peasant girl named Anna Slezak was bored one Sunday and decided to make up a new dance. She choreographed a hop-step-close-step pattern while singing a Czech folk song ("Uncle Nimra Brought a White Horse"). A local schoolmaster walked by and asked Anna to show it to him; he wrote down the steps and then introduced the polka (from the Czech word *pulka*, meaning "half-step") in ballrooms in nearby Prague. The Polish version is similar: In the 1830s, a Bohemian man was visiting Poland when he saw a little girl dancing the polka (which may actually date as far back as the 1600s) and took the dance back home to Prague, where it was christened *polka*, meaning "Polish woman."

The polka is thought to have been the inspiration for polka-dots,...

Either way, thanks to the Bohemian army, the dance spread from dance hall to dance hall all over Europe, making it a huge fad in the mid-19th century. Much like rock 'n' roll would be 100 years later, the polka was embraced by the youth culture and vilified by grown-ups, who had only recently accepted the much slower waltz as their dance of choice.

Squeeze Box: For most of the 19th century, most polkas were written for violins. But as Polish immigrants emigrated to America in the 20th century, they brought along their accordions (invented around the same time the polka became popular), a much more versatile instrument that allowed a single musician to play melody, harmony, rhythm, and bass—perfect for polka parties! The polka's second golden age really took full swing in the Midwest after World War II, where millions of European refugees settled and brought their culture with them. Polka legends such as Frank Yankovic and Lawrence Welk helped legitimize the lively music for adults—many of whom were appalled by rock 'n' roll.

MORE WAYS TO SHAKE YOUR BOOTY

The Macarena: The song by Los del Río about a sensuous Spanish woman took the U.S. by storm in the mid-1990s. VH1 called it the "#1 Greatest One-Hit Wonder of All Time."

Hully Gully: A popular line dance from the 1960s, popularized by the 1960 song "Hully Gully," by the Olympics. John Belushi dances the hully gully in the 1980 film, *The Blues Brothers*.

Electric Slide: A disco line dance created by the famous disco dancer Ric Silver in 1976. It came from a song called "Electric Boogie," written by Bunny Wailer (from Bob Marley's band).

Charleston: Though it's associated with white "flappers" in speakeasies of the 1920s, the dance actually came from the song of the same name by African-American pianist James P. Johnson, who wrote it in the predominately black Charleston, South Carolina.

Achy-Breaky: The 1992 song made Billy Ray Cyrus a country superstar, and ushered in a new era of line dancing—not just in America, but all over Europe as well. And it's still going strong today.

Limbo: Created in Trinidad in the 1950s, the name comes from the word "limber," which you must be in order to do this dance. It became a fad in 1962 thanks to Chubby Checker's "Limbo Rock."

...which, in turn, were the inspiration for the game Twister.

ONE-HIT WONDERS

For some reason, certain songs have incredible mass appeal at a particular moment...which the performers are never able to re-create. Here are a few memorable examples.

Song: "99 Luftballoons"
Artist: Nena
Story: Carlo Karges, the guitarist for German pop singer Nena, was at a Rolling Stones concert in the early 1980s. At a dramatic point in the show, a batch of red balloons was released into the air. As they drifted upward and away in a large blob, Karges thought they resembled a weird aircraft. This inspired him to write "99 Luftballoons," a Cold War protest song in which a bunch of floating balloons are mistaken for nuclear missiles, triggering a global war. Despite being sung in German, the song hit #2 on the U.S. charts in 1984.

Song: "Lovin' You"
Artist: Minnie Riperton
Story: Riperton, a trained opera singer, moved to Florida with her husband Richard Rudolph in the early 1970s to raise their baby daughter, Maya, and try their hand at writing pop songs. In 1973 Stevie Wonder hired her to sing on his album *Fulfillingness' First Finale*, which led to a record contract for Riperton. "Lovin' You" is a ballad Riperton and Rudolph wrote about Maya that showcases Minnie's ability to hit *extremely* high notes. The song spent a week at #1 in 1974, but Riperton never had much chance to score another hit. In 1979 she died of cancer at age 31. (The song's inspiration, Maya Rudolph, became a comedian and a star on *Saturday Night Live*.)

Song: "Spirit in the Sky"
Artist: Norman Greenbaum
Story: In 1969 singer-songwriter Greenbaum was working on a farm in Petaluma, California, semiretired from the music business. One night he saw country singer Porter Wagoner on TV singing a

---

Producer Babyface got his nickname from Parliament bassist Bootsy Collins.

song about a preacher (Greenbaum can't remember the name of the song) and he decided to try to write a religious rock song. The result: "Spirit in the Sky," a hard rock/gospel song about trusting God and "what a friend we have in Jesus." (Greenbaum isn't a Christian; he's Jewish. He wrote about Jesus because he figured Christianity had more commercial appeal than Judaism.) "Spirit in the Sky" went on to sell two million copies in 1970, but it's probably better known for being included in more than 20 movies, including *Contact*, *Apollo 13*, and *Michael*.

Song: "The Ballad of the Green Berets"
Artist: Staff Sgt. Barry Sadler
Story: In the 1960s, Sadler was a medic in the U.S. Army's Special Forces, also known as the Green Berets (for the hats the unit wore). Sadler suffered a leg injury in the Vietnam War and was sent home to recover. A friend suggested to Sadler, an amateur musician, that he write a song about the Special Forces. Sadler did, and sent it to publisher Chet Gierlach, who in turn sent it to journalist Robin Moore, who'd written a book about the Green Berets. Moore and Sadler recorded the song, and it became a huge hit on Armed Forces Radio before its release on RCA Records in January 1966. It shot to #1 and became the best-selling song of the year. Sadler left the military to pursue a singing career, but he never had another hit. He died in 1989 after being shot under mysterious circumstances in Guatemala.

Song: "I'm Too Sexy"
Artist: Right Said Fred
Story: During a 1990 rehearsal, a computer being used by the English dance band Right Said Fred malfunctioned and began to play a snippet of a recording over and over. Singer Richard Fairbass started riffing lyrics to the strange musical loop and ad-libbed the line, "I'm too sexy for my shirt." Richard and his brother Fred then wrote a whole song around the lyric, a tongue-in-cheek listing of all the things the singer is "too sexy for." (The brothers were inspired by the vain, arrogant models who worked out at the gym they managed.) Self-released by the band in 1991 (and then picked up by Gut Records), "I'm Too Sexy" became a #1 hit in the United States and England.

First-ever song to debut at #1: "You Are Not Alone" by Michael Jackson (1995).

VIDEO TREASURES

The next time you're in a video store and don't know what to rent, check out one of Uncle John's favorite music-themed movies.

THE LAST WALTZ (1978) *Documentary*
Review: "The last concert of the rock group The Band in San Francisco after 16 years on the road. Perhaps the best movie of a rock concert, one that also features many of the most influential performers of the era (including Clapton and Dylan), together with some brief but revealing interviews with the band members." (*Halliwell's Film and Video Guide*) *Director*: Martin Scorsese

FEAR OF A BLACK HAT (1994) *Comedy*
Review: "This rap mockumentary about 'N***** With Hatz' is the best hip-hop film of all, taking on obvious targets (misogynist lyrics) and sacred cows (political rap) alike. For N.W.H. leader Ice Cold (Rusty Cundieff), everything is a metaphor. Defending the song 'Booty Juice,': 'on the political tip, all we saying is, we gonna get that a**.'" (*Rolling Stone*) *Director:* Rusty Cundieff

KOYAANISQATSI (1983) *Documentary*
Review: "Using aerial, slow-motion, and fast-motion photography, the camera glides across the American landscape, revealing an astonishing panorama of natural and manmade wonders. Set to a hypnotic score by Philip Glass, with no dialogue, this mesmerizing and gloriously beautiful film is a stunning sight and sound experience." (*Great Movies You've Probably Missed*, by Ardis Sillick and Michael McCormick) *Director:* Godfrey Reggio

LISZTOMANIA (1975) *Musical/Fantasy*
Review: "This film on the life and enormous popularity of Franz Liszt is one of the most outrageous film bios. Other famous composers are parodied, including Richard Wagner, depicted as a vampire. Casting Roger Daltrey as Liszt would normally be an enormous error, but because of the way Russell chose to depict the famous pianist as a bit of a rock star, Daltrey is ideal." (*The Scarecrow Video Movie Guide*) *Director:* Ken Russell

THE ROSE (1979) *Drama*

Review: "Bette Midler plays a young, talented, and self-destructive blues-rock singer. The best exhibition of the rock 'n' roll world outside of documentaries. Electrifying film features an incredible collection of songs." (*Videohound's Golden Movie Retriever*) *Director:* Mark Rydell

THE UMBRELLAS OF CHERBOURG (1964) *Musical/Foreign*

Review: "A curious experiment in which all of the words were sung. This would suggest a work of featherweight romanticism, but *Umbrellas* is unexpectedly sad and wise, a bittersweet reflection on the way true love sometimes does not conquer all. Catherine Deneuve plays a young woman who is head over heels in love with a local garage mechanic (Nino Castelnuovo). But a rich man falls in love with her, which begins a slow, indirect process that might lead to a proposal of marriage. A surprisingly effective film, touching and knowing and ageless." (*Roger Ebert*) *Director:* Jacques Demy

THE GLENN MILLER STORY (1954) *Biography*

Review: "The life story of famous bandleader Miller, who disappeared in a plane during World War II. Jimmy Stewart delivers a convincing portrayal with music that had all of America tapping its feet. Miller's music is the highlight of the film, with guest appearances by Louis Armstrong and Gene Krupa." (*Video Movie Guide*) *Director:* Anthony Mann

SPARKLE (1976) *Drama*

Review: "Three Harlem siblings form a vocal trio called Sister and the Sisters. Pretty soon, they're knocking 'em dead in local talent shows—and who wouldn't with music written and arranged by the great Curtis Mayfield? The filmmakers left plenty of room for vibrant recording-studio and in-concert scenes of the women singing knockout songs that should have become pop standards." (*Entertainment Weekly*) *Director:* Sam O'Steen

*   *   *

"God had to create disco music so that I could be born and be successful."

—Donna Summer

Rick James joined the Navy at 15, went AWOL, fled to Canada, and joined a band with Neil Young.

JUZT NUTZ

Each year, The Onion's A.V. Club receives thousands of records from up-and-coming bands, some with really, really strange names. Here are a few that we can print (but we can't vouch for their music).

- Dear and the Headlights
- The Dead Kenny Gs
- Human Being Lawnmower
- Happy Butterfly Foot
- Orb of Confusion
- Best Fwends
- The Color Fred
- Tigers Can Bite You
- To Live and Shave in L.A.
- Butt Stomach
- Shapes Have Fangs
- Harmonica Lewinsky
- Earth Dies Screaming
- Shoot for the Stars…and Kill Them
- Secret Lives of Freemasons
- Unicorn Dream Attack
- Chevy Metal
- The Pleasures of Merely Circulating
- Garrison Killer
- Penguins with Shotguns
- DD/MM/YYYY

- Mel Gibson & the Pants
- Doofgoblin
- Ringo DeathStarr
- General Patton & His Privates
- Let's French
- The Shark That Ate My Friend
- I Would Set Myself on Fire for You
- Dyslexic Speedreaders
- Clown Vomit
- Les Breastfeeders
- Happy Mothers Day, I Can't Read
- Neil Diamond Phillips
- Broke Up This Year, Alas
- Juzt Nutz
- If Your Hands Were Metal That Would Mean Something
- We All Have Hooks For Hands
- The House That Gloria Vanderbilt

Who's Al Dvorin? The guy who said "Elvis has left the building."

MUSICAL MAYHEM

*Elvis was known for his jumpsuits. These artists
made headlines with their lawsuits.*

MICHAEL JACKSON VS. PAUL MCCARTNEY
The Feud: The 1980s started out friendly between
Michael Jackson and Paul McCartney: They recorded
three songs in 1982 and '83—"The Girl Is Mine," "Say, Say, Say,"
and "The Man." But that changed in 1984 when Jackson asked
his friend McCartney for investment advice. McCartney's
response: publishing. Typically, songwriters share the rights to
their songs with a music publishing company that promotes and
markets the songs to the public; each gets 50 percent of the songwriting royalties. Publishing rights to most of the Beatles' songs
changed hands several times: In 1963 the Beatles signed with a
company called Northern Songs, and Northern sold them to
another music publisher, the Associated Television Corporation
(ATV). In 1984 ATV put them up for auction. McCartney and
Yoko Ono, John Lennon's widow, tried to buy the songs back
from ATV, but Jackson, taking McCartney's earlier advice about
investing in publishing, outbid them: He paid $47.5 million for
ATV's collection. This meant that even though McCartney and
Ono retained their 50 percent royalty rights, Jackson also got 50
percent of the profits for doing nothing...except coughing up the
$47.5 million.

Resolution: McCartney never did manage to get the rights back
from Jackson, and the pair's professional relationship seemed to
cool. (They never recorded together again.) Then in 1995, Sony
Music paid Jackson $95 million to form the Sony/ATV Music
Publishing Company. That split the royalty rights yet again. Now,
Jackson owns 25 percent, Sony owns 25 percent, and McCartney
and Ono own 50 percent.

ROGER WATERS VS. DAVID GILMOUR

The Feud: By the early 1980s, Pink Floyd had become one of the
most successful rock bands in the world. They'd released their
most famous albums—*The Wall, Dark Side of the Moon, Animals,*

and *Wish You Were Here*—and they'd sold tens of millions of records. But in 1985, bass player Roger Waters abruptly declared the band defunct, calling it "a spent force creatively." Guitarist David Gilmour had other ideas, and the following year, he (and the band's drummer, Nick Mason) announced that Pink Floyd would go on…without Waters.

That infuriated Roger Waters, who had been the band's primary lyricist and creative force (or so he said). He sued Gilmour, saying that because Gilmour wasn't an original band member, he had no right to continue using the name. (The two also argued about songwriting credits on *The Wall* and other albums.) For the next 20 years, the men didn't speak.

Resolution: A court eventually declared that Waters could retain the rights to most of the band's early albums, but Gilmour and the others were allowed to continue playing as Pink Floyd. (They had to pay Walters royalties for any of the old songs they performed.) But then in 2005 came a surprising turn of events: Gilmour, Waters, and the other members of Pink Floyd buried the hatchet long enough to play a charity concert called Live 8, though they declined to mount a reunion tour.

DAVID LEE ROTH VS. EDDIE VAN HALEN AND SAMMY HAGAR VS. EDDIE VAN HALEN

Feud: Van Halen formed in 1974 with Eddie Van Halen on guitar, Alex Van Halen on drums, Michael Anthony on bass, and David Lee Roth as the lead vocalist. Two years later, the group was discovered by KISS bassist Gene Simmons, who saw them playing at an L.A. nightclub and arranged for them to record an album. That album, called *Van Halen*, went platinum in just six months and subsequent records—especially *1984*—turned the group into superstars. But by the mid-1980s, the band members weren't getting along with each other as well as their records were with the public. In particular, David Lee Roth and Eddie Van Halen had a falling-out over two issues: First, Roth didn't like the band's new direction—Eddie was infusing keyboards into the band. Second, Eddie had played guitar on Michael Jackson's 1983 song "Beat It" without first clearing it with the band, which infuriated Roth. Finally, in 1985, the tensions erupted and Roth quit the band.

Enter Sammy Hagar, an established solo artist with "There's

Only One Way to Rock," "Red," and "I Can't Drive 55," who took over lead vocals. (Rumor has it that Eddie Van Halen's first choice to replace Roth was Scandal's Patty Smyth, but she turned him down.) With Hagar on board, Van Halen went on to release some of its most successful albums, including 1986's 5150, the band's first album without Roth, and their first album to hit #1 on the Billboard chart. The group lasted 11 years with Hagar on vocals, but in 1996, another falling-out caused a second rift. That year, Hagar and Eddie Van Halen argued over the lyrics to the song "Humans Being." Eddie thought Hagar's lyrics were cheesy and rewrote the song; Hagar was angry at the criticism and quit...or so says Eddie Van Halen. Hagar claimed he was fired. Either way, Van Halen was, once again, without a lead singer.

Resolution: At the MTV Music Awards in 1996, Roth announced that he was once again the lead singer for Van Halen. But word soon got out that he was mistaken —the rest of the band only had a short-term reunion in mind, and that fell through. Over the next few years, the band worked with several singers, including Gary Cherone of Extreme, Mitch Malloy...and Roth and Hagar, whose complicated returns and departures boggled the minds of fans and music journalists. Sammy Hagar reappeared in 2004, recording three new songs for the band's second greatest-hits album and joining the group on its 2004 world tour. Finally, in 2007 Van Halen embarked on a reunion tour featuring Roth and Wolfgang Van Halen, Eddie's son—who reportedly replaced bassist Michael Anthony after Anthony was fired because of his friendship with Sammy Hagar.

*   *   *

THE MUSIC MADE ME DO IT

In February 2000, police in New Iberia, Louisiana, were called to break up a fight at a teen dance at a skating rink. No kids were arrested—but the rink's owner and manager were. They had put rap music on the sound system, which the officers claimed caused the fight. "The music itself cranked the crowd up in a sense," a police spokesman said. (Charges were later dropped.)

American rock band with the most Top-40 hits: The Beach Boys, with 36.

MY DINGO HAS FLEAS

*Proving that drummers aren't the only animals in the
music world, here are news stories about real
animals and real music (more or less).*

DINKY

If you're ever in Australia, be sure to take a trip to Jim's Place, a hotel, restaurant, and bar just south of Alice Springs in the heart of the Outback. There you may get a chance to see Dinky the Dingo. Dingoes (wild dogs) aren't unusual in Australia, but this one is—he sings. Dinky was found as a puppy in the late 1990s (his mother had died after eating poisonous bait) and given to the restaurant's owner, Jim Cotterill. When Cotterill's daughters started taking piano lessons, the family was surprised to find that Dinky wanted to sing along. Now if anyone starts playing the piano at Jim's, Dinky hops up on the keyboard and starts howling along with whatever's being played. "It's not the dingo howl you hear in the hills at night," said a reporter for the Australian Broadcasting Corporation. "It really is an attempt to vocalize using an impressive variety of sounds." In 2004 Dinky achieved international fame when he was chosen as the subject of a Trivial Pursuit question (he won the honor in a contest for "the most trivial person or thing in Australia"), and now tourists from around the world come to hear him sing.

ELLIE AND THE PACK O' DERMS?

In 2000 two American scholars—elephant expert Richard Lair and Columbia University neurologist (and composer) David Sulzer—released a CD of elephants making music. The two men were living in Thailand, where they designed and built heavy-duty versions of traditional Thai instruments—gongs, wooden slit drums, a xylophone-like *renat*, and even a harmonica. Then they showed six elephants at the Thai Elephant Conservation Center how to make sounds with them...and let them do what they wanted. "I thought we would just train elephants to hit something," Sulzer told the *New York Times*, "and I would tape that and have to paste it together with other things." He ended up recording the "Thai Elephant Orchestra" exactly as they played—because, he says, they actually played music. "I have no doubt they're improvising," he said. "And composing, which is the same thing." Sulzer even put a "sour" key in the middle of a xylophone played by Praditha, a seven-year-old female. "She avoided playing that note—until one day she started playing it and wouldn't stop."

DREAM WEAVERS

Scientists at the University of Chicago made a surprising discovery in 2000: Birds sing in their dreams. And they may do it to learn songs. The team recorded the brain activity of four young Australian zebra finches, and mapped the birds' neural firing patterns while they sang. Then the birds' patterns were recorded while they slept. "The zebra finch appears to store the neural firing pattern of song production during the day," Professor Daniel Margoliash told *Science* magazine, "and reads it out at night, rehearsing the song, and, perhaps, improvising variations." The finding not only shed light on how animals learn, he said, but humans, too. "The beautiful songs of birds could have much to teach us about how we learn."

DEEP RIVER BLUES

In January 2001, the Rowland Institute for Science in Cambridge, Massachusetts, studied the effects of music on three carp fish— Beauty, Peppy, and Oro—and got some surprising results. Researcher Ava Chase placed loudspeakers next to the fish's aquarium and played either classical music (Bach) or blues (John Lee Hooker) to them. A button was placed in the tank that the fish could press. When classical music was playing, pressing the button did nothing. But when blues was playing, pressing the button resulted in a food reward. In time, the fish learned to press the button only when they heard the blues...even when an artist they hadn't heard before, like Muddy Waters, was played. "Prior to these experiments, there was skepticism about whether carp could discriminate one piece of music from another," Chase said. "Now it appears they can appreciate tunes, melodic patterns, and even genre."

Chinese mythology says the founder of music was Ling Lun, whose bamboo flutes mimicked birds.

THE REPLACEMENTS

*What happens when a famous band replaces
the person who was the group's voice?*

G ENESIS
Original Lead Singer: Peter Gabriel
What Happened? Creative differences within the band
and personal issues in Gabriel's life (notably family troubles)
came to the fore during the creation of the band's 1974 prog-rock
magnum opus, *The Lamb Lies Down on Broadway*, prompting
Gabriel to quit.

Replacement: Phil Collins, who was already in the band as the
drummer. His ascension came after the band auditioned a number
of famous singers, including Jeff Lynne (ELO), Phil Lynott (Thin
Lizzy), and teen heartthrob David Cassidy (yes, really).

Did It Work Out? Did it ever. The band's 1976 album, *A Trick of
the Tail*, outsold all the other Genesis albums combined and got
the band started on its move away from its progressive-rock roots
and toward radio-friendly arena rock, where they'd find great success in the 1980s.

Bonus Round: Phil Collins left Genesis in 1996 to focus on solo
work, and Genesis's two remaining members, Tony Banks and
Mike Rutherford, recruited Ray Wilson (formerly of the little-
known band Stiltskin) and released 1997's *Calling All Stations*. It
flopped, and Wilson was fired from the band. Collins reunited
with Genesis for a world tour in 2007.

JOURNEY

Original Lead Singer: Steve Perry. (He wasn't actually the group's
original lead singer; others before him included keyboardist Gregg
Rolie, guitarist Neal Schon, and singer Robert Fleischman. But
Perry was the singer during the band's most popular era, from 1977
through 1987.)

What Happened? After a decade-long hiatus following the band's
1986 *Raised on Radio* album, Journey reunited for 1996's *Trial by
Fire*. But their tour plans were delayed when a hiking accident

required Perry to undergo hip replacement surgery, which he was reluctant to do. Annoyed by their lead singer's indecision—he couldn't continue touring without the surgery—the band decided to go on without him.

Replacement Lead Singer: Steve Augeri, former lead singer of the band Tall Stories, which had not had notable success. Augeri was working as a manager of a Gap store in New York City when he was tapped as Perry's replacement.

Did It Work Out? Sort of. Augeri's vocal delivery was reminiscent of Perry's, and the band had a minor hit, "All the Way," in 2000. But the album, *Arrival*, didn't chart well (it topped out at #56, far below the #3 debut of *Trial by Fire*), and fans were ambivalent about the substitution of Augeri for the popular Perry. Nevertheless, Journey remained a big concert draw, especially when touring with other 1980s bands such as Def Leppard.

Bonus Round: In July 2006, Steve Augeri developed voice problems and was temporarily replaced on tour by Jeff Scott Soto. Soto was officially named the band's lead singer in December 2006…and then was tossed out in June 2007. A few months later, the band hired 40-year-old Arnel Pineda, a singer from the Philippines, after guitarist Neal Schon saw videos of him singing Journey songs…on YouTube.

THE CARS

Original Lead Singers: Ric Ocasek and Benjamin Orr

What Happened? The band rode high in the early 1980s with a series of hit singles and albums, but after 1987's critically and commercially disappointing *Door to Door*, the Cars ran out of gas and disbanded. In 2000 Orr—the bassist and singer on "Drive," the band's most successful single—died of pancreatic cancer. Ocasek, the better-known former front man, continued with a solo career and as producer for other bands and musicians, including Weezer, No Doubt, and the Killers.

Replacement Lead Singer: Todd Rundgren, who had a notable career in the 1970s as a solo artist ("Hello It's Me") and as a record producer (Hall and Oates, XTC, Meat Loaf, Cheap Trick, and others).

First jazz band led by a woman: Sophie Tucker's Five Kings of Syncopation (1914).

Did It Work Out? Not especially well. The group Rundgren joined in 2005 called itself the New Cars and had only two original members: guitarist Elliot Easton and keyboardist Greg Hawkes. (It also included former members of Utopia and the Tubes.) The group released a single ("Not Tonight") that went nowhere.

There was no bad blood between Ocasek and the New Cars—Ocasek gave his blessing to the endeavor, although he perpetrated a fake feud between himself and Rundgren on the comedy show *The Colbert Report* in 2006. (The "feud" was conveniently timed with the New Cars' "Roadrage" tour.)

ALICE IN CHAINS

Original Lead Singer: Layne Staley

What Happened? He died. As the band rose to fame with hits like "Man in a Box" and the *No Excuses* album, Staley was struggling with a heroin addiction that took an increasing toll on him—as well as on the band. During performances, guitarist Jerry Cantrell, whose voice sounded a lot like Staley's, was often called on to pick up the verses when Staley wandered offstage. Staley sang with the band for the last time when they opened for KISS on July 3, 1996, and he worked in music only fitfully after that. On April 19, 2002, family members found his remains in his Seattle condo; he had died an estimated two weeks earlier. The cause of death was an overdose from a "speedball"—a mixture of heroin and cocaine. Staley was 34.

Replacement Lead Singer: William DuVall, also the lead singer and guitarist for the Atlanta-based group Comes the Fall.

Did It Work Out? So far, so good. Alice in Chains went on a promotional tour for a greatest hits album in 2006, playing club dates with DuVall as the front man. The fan reaction was positive, and DuVall joined the band again on tour in 2007, this time as Alice in Chains opened up for Velvet Revolver (a supergroup of musicians from Guns N' Roses and Stone Temple Pilots). DuVall has since been given the title of the band's lead singer, and Alice in Chains' Web site reports that the group is working on a new album.

THE STORY OF MUSIC, PART I

What did the first music sound like? How long have human beings been playing music? And did they play fart songs? Readers keep asking us these questions, so we decided to dig around for the answers.

AH ONE...AH TWO...
The first musical era—as counted by historical musicologists—is called Prehistoric Music, and refers to all the music played by peoples before the invention of writing and the beginning of civilization. Note that this means different eras for different populations, since people around the world progressed at different rates and in different ways over the ages. As for the earliest prehistoric music of all, that could go back a very long way.

Consider that there is not a single race on Earth without music as an important and integral part of their culture. That, many experts say, suggests that some form of music, however primitive it may have been, was already an integrated part of human activity before the time when modern humans first left Africa, beginning the migrations that would eventually populate the globe. That was, they estimate, in the neighborhood of 100,000 years ago.

FROM THE BIRDS?

What did the earliest music sound like? No one really knows. But it's not hard to imagine the first human music being influenced by the more "musical" sounds in the world around us: birdsong, the howling of wolves or coyotes, or the wind sounding notes through a hollow log or in a cave. The earliest human music was probably an imitation of that. Rhythm was probably another early music ingredient: people clapping their hands or beating a stick on a hollow log. As humans developed better toolmaking abilities, actual instruments like primitive drums and horns, and even flutes, began to be played.

THE NEANDERTHAL FLUTE

The oldest instrument in the world is believed by some to be the "Neanderthal Flute": a five-inch, hollow section of a bear's thigh bone with four holes bored into it, in a line and of basically equal diameter. (The two middle holes are intact; the other two partial ones are at either end of the broken bone but still plainly visible.) The holes, some archaeologists say, align perfectly with what would have been notes on the diatonic scale—our "Do Re Mi" scale.

The broken bone flute was found in 1998 in a cave in modern-day Slovenia—and it's about 45,000 years old. That would make it the oldest known instrument by more than 30,000 years. But many archaeologists think the whole story is hogwash. The holes, they say, are in the bone for the same reason that animals' bones often have holes in them: because the teeth of carnivores put them there. If the holes happen to be in the right place to play proper musical notes, it was due to lucky bites by a hungry (and perhaps unknowingly musical) wolf. The "Neanderthal flute" debate continues among musicologists to this day.

The oldest *known* instruments are still very old: In 1999 six intact flutes were found in a Neolithic site in the east-central Chinese province of Henan. Carbon dating puts them at between 7,000 and 9,000 years old. They're made from the wing bones of red-crowned cranes, and they have five, six, seven, or eight holes…and some are still playable.

THE ANCIENTS

The Prehistoric Era ends with the coming of the first civilizations in the Middle East around 4000 B.C. The next spot on the timeline is the Ancient Era, which runs until the fall of the Roman empire in A.D. 476. Some big moments in the Ancient Era:

• In the 26th century B.C.—more than 4,600 years ago—a clay tablet is inscribed with numerous symbols in ancient Mesopotamia (modern-day Iraq), the area known as the Cradle of Western Civilization. The symbols describe 26 different instruments, including several stringed instruments like the harp and lyre, and some unknown ones. It also has symbols shown to be musical notation, describing the tuning of different strings and the intervals between them—making it the oldest known notation system in the world.

Some Chinese classical music is more than 3,000 years old.

There are also extensive remains of elaborate lyres and harps found in tombs from the same era.

• By 4000 B.C., basic zithers—wooden boxes with a hole or holes cut into one face, over which strings are strung—and harplike stringed instruments are being made and played in China. Flutes are (as we said) already being played there.

• Similar instruments are played at the same time in the Indus Valley civilizations, the ancestors of modern India.

• No known records show that the ancient Egyptians had notated music, but their writings and paintings clearly show that music was an important part of their lives, with many instruments developed there over the millennia. These included several types of stringed instruments, drums, castanets, bells, rattles, rams' horns, and silver and bronze trumpets.

THE FIRST SONG

In about 1500 B.C., the port city of Ugarit, now known as Ras Shamra in modern-day Syria, was a highly developed and cosmopolitan urban center. And back then, someone in Ugarit "wrote" something on a clay tablet. About 3,400 years later, in the 1950s, Professor Anne Draffkorn Kilmer of the University of California at Berkeley began studying the tablet, which had been found at an archaeological site. The writing was Hurrian cuneiform script (the Hurrians settled Ugarit), and Professor Kilmer spent the next 15 years working to translate the symbols, finally finishing in 1972. It turned out to be a song—and it's the oldest known notated song in the world. And it had not only words (to a hymn to "Nikkal," the wife of the Moon God), it had musical notes—and they weren't that dissimilar to the notes used in the diatonic scale— again, the "Do Re Mi" scale—that is the bedrock of Western music. Before the discovery, musicologists believed that no such scale existed until ancient Greeks devised one some 1,100 years later. And not only that—the Ugarit song had harmony parts notated. Until then, musicologists had also believed that harmony didn't exist at all in ancient music.

But that's not the end of the story—not by a long shot. Turn to page 346 for Part II of The Story of Music.

"THE NEXT BOB DYLAN"

Ever since Bob Dylan took the music world by storm in the early '60s, many talented singer-songwriters have been heralded as "the new Dylan." But was the title, as onetime "new Dylan" John Prine called it, "the kiss of death"?

PHIL OCHS

Ochs was a contemporary of Dylan who quit his job as a journalist to play the New York folk scene in the early 1960s. At the time he played mostly political folk songs like "Too Many Martyrs," about the civil right movement, and "I Ain't Marchin' Anymore," about the Vietnam War. When Dylan switched from folk to rock in 1965, Ochs thought he "sold out." But Ochs eventually abandoned folk, too. His 1967 album *Pleasures of the Harbor* combined his protest-song cynicism with rock, pop, and orchestral arrangements and included his only hit song, "Small Circle of Friends." In 1970 he reinvented himself again, singing 1950s-style rock 'n' roll and performing in a gold lamé jumpsuit. In 1976 he committed suicide, a year after performing with Joan Baez at a concert to celebrate the end of the Vietnam War.

STEVE FORBERT

In 1976, 21-year-old Steve Forbert moved from his rural home in Mississippi to New York to make it as a folk singer, just as the 20-year-old Bob Dylan had in 1961 (though Dylan was from Minnesota). Forbert built up a local following by playing his gravelly voiced story songs in clubs, and in 1978 was signed by CBS Records. In 1980 his song "Romeo's Tune" made it to #11 on the pop chart. With that song, Forbert switched from playing rural-inspired folk to electric folk rock, earning him more comparisons to Dylan. But the parallels ended there; Forbert never had another hit.

WILLIE NILE

This Buffalo-based singer-songwriter moved to New York City in the early 1970s to become, in his words, "a modern-day troubadour." He played folk clubs there for nearly a decade before getting signed to Arista Records, which led to a tour, opening for the Who in 1980. *New York Times* rock critic Robert Palmer called Nile "the next Bob Dylan: one of the most gifted singer-songwriters to emerge from the New York scene in years." He never caught on with American audiences, although his songs "Everybody Needs a Hammer" and "Hard Times in America" were smash hits in Europe. He released another album in 1981, but his third album was inexplicably delayed by Geffen Records for several years. By the time it was finally released in 1991, the momentum was gone, and the album sold poorly.

FRED NEIL

Another contemporary of Dylan, singer-songwriter Neil played shows in the folk-music scene in New York's Greenwich Village in the early 1960s before recording two critically acclaimed solo albums. But his biggest successes came as a songwriter: He wrote "Candy Man" for Roy Orbison and the Dylan-esque "Everybody's Talkin'" for Harry Nillson. Neil's been cited as an influence by many singer-songwriters, including Tim Buckley, David Crosby, and, strangely enough, Bob Dylan, whom Neil took under his wing when Dylan first came to New York. Neil seemed destined for stardom, but he didn't want to be famous. He stopped making music completely in 1971 and moved to Coconut Grove, Florida. The royalties from "Candy Man" and "Everybody's Talkin'" kept him comfortable for the rest of his life. He died of natural causes in 2001.

BRUCE SPRINGSTEEN

His debut album, 1973's *Greetings from Asbury Park, NJ*, showcased Springsteen's ability to perform in styles from folk to country to rock, all with high-volume poetic lyrics delivered at machine-gun speed. One critic wrote, "It's like Dylan's 'Subterranean Homesick Blues' played at 78 RPM, a typical five-minute track busting with more words than this review." In spite of rave reviews, the album sold only 25,000 copies in its first year. That all changed when rock critic Jon Landau wrote an article called "The Best Dylan Since 1968." It sang the praises of the rising star from New Jersey: "I've seen the future of rock and roll, and it's called Bruce Springsteen." Other critics and listeners began to take notice, and Springsteen was often compared to Dylan for his political songs and world-weary lyrics. 1975's *Born to Run* (produced by Landau) made Springsteen a superstar—and the only "new Dylan" to live up to the label.

MUSICAL TV EPISODES

When a TV shows airs an all-musical episode, we sometimes wonder if the writers just ran out of ideas. But some of those episodes turn out to be wildly popular…and sometimes they even take the show in a new direction.

I LOVE LUCY

One of the first TV shows to do a musical episode was *I Love Lucy*. In "Lucy Goes to Scotland," which aired in 1956, Lucy fell asleep and dreamed that she'd traveled to Scotland. Loosely inspired by *Brigadoon* (a 1947 Broadway musical in which American tourists stumble onto an enchanted Scottish village), the episode had Lucy discovering that she was scheduled to be sacrificed to a two-headed dragon (played by Fred and Ethel). But her bodyguard (Ricky) fell in love with her and vowed to protect her from the dragon. The episode featured numbers like "I'm in Love with a Dragon's Dinner" (sung by Ricky) and "Two Heads Are Nay Better Than One" (sung by Fred and Ethel).

COP ROCK

This was an entire police-procedural *series* (à la *Law and Order*) told in song. In the middle of briefings, cops would burst into synthesized pop-rock numbers—many composed by Randy Newman (of "Short People" and *Toy Story* fame). The cops sang about their jobs, and bad guys told their tales (one black-market adoption agent sang, "I'm the baby merchant / Tots 'r' us"). Aside from the bizarre format, writing and producing an entire musical every week was labor intensive and time consuming. Some producers estimated that it took three times longer to produce a *Cop Rock* episode than it did on a regular TV series. Despite its lofty concept, the show bombed, running for just three months in 1990.

XENA: WARRIOR PRINCESS

By the middle of the show's 1998 season, the main characters of this show—Xena and Gabrielle—had each caused the death of the other's child and declared their eternal hatred. With such a rift between them, they needed a special episode to resolve their differences. So the writers came up with a musical—"The Bitter

Suite"—in which Xena and Gabrielle traveled to the fictional land of Illusia. In the cartoonish sequences that followed, the two were guided by tarot card symbols to forgive each other. Lucy Lawless, who played Xena and had long aspired to a career in musical theater, sang all her own parts. (Renee O'Connor, who played Gabrielle, probably had no such aspirations; she was dubbed.)

They did a second musical episode in 2000. "Lyre, Lyre, Hearts on Fire" told the story of a fight for a magical lyre. The means: a battle of the bands. Unlike the first musical, this was a variety show of familiar songs and featured an eight-months-pregnant Lucy Lawless dancing and belting out the song "War" (as in "What is it good for? Absolutely nothin'").

SCRUBS

It wasn't surprising that this wacky medical comedy/drama aired a musical episode, but the show—titled "My Musical"—was surprising for the level of talent it employed. Most of the songs were written by Jeff Marx and Bobby Lopez, the creative team behind the hit Broadway show *Avenue Q*, and starred Stephanie D'Abruzzo, who was part of the play's original cast. The plot: A patient named Patti Miller was afflicted with a condition that made her see everything around her as a musical. The show's cast performed numbers like "For the Last Time, I'm Dominican" and "Everything Comes Down to Poo" as they tried to diagnose her ailment. In the end, the patient had brain surgery...and the music went away.

BUFFY THE VAMPIRE SLAYER

Toward the end of *Buffy*'s 1997–2003 run, Buffy died, went to heaven, and returned to life after her friends resurrected her. Soon after, in this episode, titled "Once More, With Feeling," a demon forces everyone in town to sing out their inner thoughts and feelings, Broadway-style. While the other musical episodes on this list were humorous one-offs, "Once More, With Feeling" actually changed the direction of the series: Buffy was forced to reveal to her friends that she resented them for bringing her back from the dead, while a relationship between two other characters began to crumble after they both sang about their doubts. A cast recording album of the episode was released, and it's even been produced onstage in small theaters around the country.

The pianist at the premiere of Wagner's only symphony: a 13-year-old girl named Clara Weick.

PASS ME THE EARPLUGS

Check out these masters of the musically awful.

SO BAD IT'S...STILL BAD

Florence Foster Jenkins, known in her day as the "Diva of Din," had the unfortunate combination of supreme confidence, lots of money...and little talent. Born in 1868, she came from a wealthy family and married a wealthy husband, which made it possible for her to spend her time taking voice lessons. She started giving concerts in 1912, and even though all the voice lessons did nothing to improve her singing, her concerts were hits. Why? The extravagant costumes (one of her most famous had wings and a crown), the dissonant sound, and Jenkins's self-assurance created a "so bad it's good" feel. Audiences loved her. The shows continued into the 1930s, and she played to increasingly packed rooms. Despite fierce criticism (which Jenkins attributed to professional jealousy) and the fact that many audience members are said to have laughed until they cried, Jenkins was undaunted, comparing herself to Frieda Hempel, Luisa Tetrazzini, and other opera divas of the day.

Jenkins's life and career were also the source of many stories:

• In one oft-repeated tale, she was in a taxi accident, and afterward she sent the cabbie a box of cigars in gratitude because, ever since the accident, she could hit "a higher F than ever before."

• When she sang the classical piece "Clavelitos" onstage, she often punctuated her phrases by throwing flower petals from a basket into the audience. During one performance, she got so carried away that she tossed the basket as well. (When the audiences roared for an encore, she had assistants gather up the petals so she could repeat it.)

• Her rendition of Mozart's "Queen of the Night Aria," recorded in the early 1940s, became famous even though it sounds something like a cat meowing through a flute: She misses cues, flubs passages, stops for a breath whenever she feels like it, and misses important high notes entirely.

Jenkins's fame peaked in October 1944 with her Carnegie Hall debut. The show sold out, and the box office turned away 2,000

Paul Hewson's stage name, Bono, is short for Bono Vox, which means "good voice" in Latin.

people. Jenkins had become a cult favorite, loved for the enthusiastic disaster that was her soprano voice. She died just a month
later at the age of 76. Three albums of Jenkins's work were compiled after her death and are still available today: *Murder on the
High C's*, *The Glory (????) of the Human Voice*, and *Muse Sur-
mounted: Florence Foster Jenkins and Eleven of Her Rivals*. And her
story was turned into a 2005 Broadway play, called *Souvenir*. In
what can only be called poetic justice, *Souvenir* star Judy Kaye
earned a Tony nomination for screeching the part of Jenkins.

THE SINGING GRANDMA

Elva Miller, a California housewife, probably would have remained
just another woman belting out gospel songs in her local church if
not for a few albums that she recorded and released herself in the
1960s. Arranger Fred Bock heard those albums and shopped them
around to different companies until Capitol Records signed her up
as a joke artist. Her first album, titled *Mrs. Miller's Greatest Hits*,
was released in 1966 when Miller was 59.

That record consists of Miller singing hits of the day, such as
"The Girl from Ipanema," "Yellow Submarine," and "Downtown." On the album, Miller drifts out of tempo with the orchestral background, forgets words, giggles, and even performs
specialty bird calls (achieved by whistling around a piece of ice
on her tongue). Despite these eccentricities, the record sold
250,000 copies in its first three weeks. Miller even traveled to
Vietnam to perform for the American troops stationed there.

Was her tin ear entirely genuine? In an interview with *Life*
magazine, Miller revealed that while recording in the studio she
was often encouraged to deliberately pull half a beat ahead of or
behind the music's tempo. But there's plenty of bad music out
there—it takes a certain extra-high level of atrociousness to hit
the charts.

CAPTAIN KIRK'S GREATEST HITS?

In 1968, at the height of his popularity as *Star Trek's* Captain Kirk,
William Shatner recorded an album called *The Transformed Man*.
In the liner notes, Shatner says that hearing the full album for the
first time "was deeper and more satisfying than anything I had
ever experienced."

The concept: to combine speeches from Shakespeare with dramatic readings of lyrics from pop hits, thus showing the connection between the two forms of "poetry." The liner notes explain that the pairings were intended to illustrate how one could walk the line between genius and madness. Unfortunately for Shatner, the album strayed a little too far toward madness. His version of "Mr. Tambourine Man," for example, included increasingly frantic and tortured calls for the tambourine man, and "Lucy in the Sky with Diamonds" offered overly earnest descriptions of cellophane flowers. *The Transformed Man* might have faded into obscurity if it weren't for the release of another album: 1988's *Golden Throats*, a compilation of (really bad) covers by famous people that included several of Shatner's tracks.

Although he has always defended the project, Shatner has also been known to spoof it, performing at the 1992 MTV Music Awards and releasing a similar album with *Star Trek* co-star Leonard Nimoy (Mr. Spock), on which Nimoy performed his own song, "The Ballad of Bilbo Baggins."

* * *

THAT SONG SMELLS GREAT!

First there were wax cylinders, then 78s, then LPs, then 8-tracks, then cassettes, then CDs, now MP3s. What's next? A German company called Optimal Media Production makes a variety of novelty CDs. Could one of these be the next big musical format?

• **The Freestyle Disc.** Utilizing the CD player's laser-reading function, this disc makes full-color, 3-D images "float through the room" as the music plays.

• **The Perfume Disc.** A scent is embedded in the disc, and when the CD player shines a laser light on the disc to play the music, a pleasing aroma is released.

• **The Vinyl-Look Disc.** It's a CD that plays on standard CD players, but it's made out of black polycarbonate. Result: It looks and feels like a tiny, old-fashioned record.

• **The Vinyl Disc.** One side is a CD. Flip it over, and you can play it on a record player (if you still have one).

Brian Wilson and his psychiatrist, Dr. Eugene Landy, recorded a rap song called "Smart Girls" (1988).

LAUGH TRACKS

From pithy to perplexing, it's another batch of amusing musical quotes.

"Say you write a song about a chandelier, and the chandelier gives off light. And the light is the color red and red reminds you of the color you're not supposed to wear around a bull. So you name the song 'Cow.'"

—Billy Corgan

"I play the harmonica. The only way I can play is if I get my car going really fast, and stick it out the window."

—Steven Wright

"I like to think of us as Clearasil on the face of the nation. Jim Morrison would have said that if he was smart, but he's dead."

—Lou Reed

"The other day I was in a gym in Kansas, and the worst songs were playing on the radio. And then *my* song came on. I was like, 'Oh no! I'm one of them!'"

—Jewel

"I'm not a snob. Ask anybody. Well, anybody who matters."

—Simon LeBon, of Duran Duran

"We just write down a bunch of words and pray to God they make sense. And if we don't, it doesn't matter—we're artists."

—Tom DeLonge, of Blink-182

"It's a lot cooler to write a song about a painful experience than it is to punch somebody in the face—which I've done, too. Thank God for music."

—Morgan Grace, songwriter

"We don't want to censor your songs. What we want to do is change your song. You're the younger generation; you believe in change."

—Rocco Laginestra, president of RCA, to Paul Kantner of Jefferson Airplane

"It's ill-becoming for an old broad to sing about how bad she wants it. But occasionally we do."

—Lena Horne

"There's a basic rule which runs through all kinds of music, kind of an unwritten rule. I don't know what it is. But I've got it."

—Ron Wood

Ha ha! The predecessor to the trombone was called the *sackbut*.

THE STORY OF "SILENT NIGHT"

At one time or another, Haydn, Mozart, and Beethoven were each assumed to be the creators of this Christmas carol—the melody is considered so beautiful in its simplicity that one of the great composers must have written it. The true identity of its composer was a mystery for nearly 200 years, until it turned out the story of the song was just as humble as the song itself.

SILENT ORGAN

Just before an 1818 Christmas Eve midnight mass at the Church of St. Nicholas in Oberndorf, Austria, Father Josef Mohr decided to do something special for the service. He wanted to create a new song based on the poem "Stille Nacht! Heilige Nacht!" ("Silent Night! Holy Night!"), which he'd written for Christmas mass two years earlier. Mohr gave the poem to the church's organist, Franz Gruber, and asked him to come up with a melody. Unfortunately, the church's organ was out of commission —mice had gnawed through the bellows—so Gruber improvised and came up with a melody in just a few hours…on guitar.

That night at mass, Mohr and Gruber sang the song as a duet. The choir, in four-part harmony, joined in for the last two lines of each of the song's six verses. It was a modest, unassuming world premiere.

ALL AROUND THE WORLD

Mohr published various versions of "Stille Nacht! Heilige Nacht!" in the 1820s and 1830s, each arranged for different instrumental accompaniments. It grew in popularity in Austria, Germany, and other German-speaking regions when it became a standard in the repertoire of traveling folk singers, and it was performed in venues ranging from great cathedrals to small music halls. For the next few years, the melody and lyrics remained almost completely intact. In 1839 the song was performed in the United States— and in English—for the first time at a Christmas mass at New York City's Trinity Church. The translation, titled "Silent Night,"

A 2003 survey of Austrian mall workers found that the nonstop playing of Christmas carols…

was written by Reverend John Freeman Young, the Episcopal bishop of Florida.

WHERE CREDIT IS DUE

Despite the rapid spread and popularity of the song, the identity of its composers got lost along the way. Mohr's credit as lyricist was never in doubt—after all, he was the one who got the song published in the first place. But many publishers declined to credit Gruber, and the melody was considered so sophisticated that musicologists and historians assumed that one of the great composers of the 19th century wrote it, with Franz Josef Haydn most often cited.

Finally, in 1995, Mohr and Gruber were vindicated when an original manuscript of "Stille Nacht! Heilige Nacht!" was discovered in Austria. In the corner of the document were the words "melodie von Fr. Xav. Gruber." This was authentication historians were looking for, and Mohr and Gruber were both officially credited as co-creators of the popular Christmas carol—one that's been translated into more than 300 languages since the night it premiered nearly 200 years ago.

*   *   *

DAY-O

The "Banana Boat Song" was made famous by Harry Belafonte in the 1950s. He made it so popular, in fact, that many people think he wrote it. Not only did he not pen the tune, but Belafonte's version isn't the only one out there. The song is an old Jamaican folk song typically sung by dock workers who've finished the night shift and want to be paid so they can go home. Eric Connor, a man from Trinidad, was the first to record a version of the tune in 1951; he called it "Day Dah Light." A year later, a folk group called the Tarriers also recorded it. Belafonte's 1955 version was actually the third recording. He met composer Irving Burghie, a Juilliard graduate whose mother was Jamaican, in New York. Burghie wrote down the song, added some of his own lyrics, and gave it to Belafonte, who made it a #1 hit.

HITS OF THE 1970s: A QUIZ

*Now it's time to find out how much you know about a
few of the hits of the '70s. (Answers on page 509.)*

1. "You Don't Bring Me Flowers," a duet by Barbra Streisand and
Neil Diamond, was a #1 song in 1976. How did this unlikely pair
get together?
a) They each recorded the song separately, and a disc jockey
spliced the two recordings together.
b) They ran into each other at a recording session and—as a
joke—decided to record the sappiest song they knew.
c) It was the dying request of Diamond's mother that he record a
song with Streisand—her favorite singer.

2. Led Zeppelin's "Stairway to Heaven" was the most-requested
FM song of the decade…but some Christian fundamentalists cite
it as an example of devil worship in rock. Robert Plant, the
group's singer, composed the lyrics. He says…
a) Even he doesn't know what they mean.
b) It's strange that fundamentalists would criticize it, because he's
a born-again Christian.
c) He purposely put "satanic" messages on the record to shock his
critics. "If they're idiotic enough to play it backwards, they deserve
it," he said.

3. Cheap Trick's "I Want You to Want Me" sold a million copies
in 1979. It was an incredible turnaround for the group. Their third
album had just flopped, and Epic Records had pretty much given
up on them. So how did they become stars?
a) An L.A. deejay became their champion, urging listeners to
write to Epic and release "I Want You to Want Me" as a single.
b) The group was asked to tour as an opening act for the Rolling
Stones, which sparked new interest in their album.

c) Somehow, a quickie album that they made exclusively for the Japanese market wound up receiving airtime on U.S. radio.

4. The #1 song of 1975 was "Love Will Keep Us Together," by the Captain & Tennille, who were, according to news reports, blissfully married. But few of the fans who heard the song knew it was really about...

a) Two men.

b) Two pets—a dog and a chipmunk.

c) A mother and child.

5. Melanie had a huge hit in 1971 with "Brand New Key." She had an innocent voice, but the lyric "I've got a brand new pair of roller skates, you've got a brand new key" sounded like it was about sex to most people. The truth would have disappointed them—the song was really inspired by...

a) A new pair of roller skates she got for her birthday.

b) A McDonald's hamburger.

c) A sporting goods store near her house.

6. The Bee Gees were the hottest group of the late '70s, and the record that started their meteoric comeback—before *Saturday Night Fever* was released—was "Jive Talkin'," a #1 hit in 1975. The song actually started out as...

a) "Jive Walkin'"—inspired by the British comedy troupe Monty Python and their "Department of Silly Walks."

b) "Drive Talkin'"—inspired by a rickety wooden bridge.

c) "Hive Stalkin'"—inspired by their hobby of keeping bees.

7. One of the biggest-selling records of the '70s was Terry Jacks's "Seasons in the Sun." He didn't plan to release it as a single, but...

a) His paperboy heard his demo tape and really liked it...then brought his friends to Jacks's house to hear it.

b) The Beach Boys heard his demo tape and talked about recording it themselves. Jacks figured if they liked it, it must be good.

c) He'd recently broken up with his wife, Susan Jacks (of the Poppy Family), and needed a quick $10,000 to pay his divorce lawyer.

First Canadian female artist to receive a U.S. gold record: Anne Murray, for "Snowbird" (1970).

FROM TROUBADOURS TO VAUDEVILLE

Traveling musicians have been singing for their supper for centuries.

INSPIRATION FROM AN UNLIKELY PLACE

The first traveling musicians known to write down their lyrics were the *Goliards*, clergymen and scholars who crisscrossed Europe during the 12th century, visiting famous teachers or great libraries. They sang in Latin, the language of the Church, but their songs were often satirical or even profane. Their only surviving work, a collection of verses called the *Carmina Burana*, includes both reverent prayers and bawdy drinking songs.

Around the same time, and likely inspired by the Goliards, poets and musicians who called themselves "troubadours" took to the roads of southern France. Most were aristocratic men who composed playful songs mainly about love, chivalry, and heroism. The best-known was William IX, Duke of Aquitaine. Like most noblemen, he traveled with an entourage that included singers and instrumentalists who played the music he wrote. After a while, though, the aristocratic troubadours stopped traveling—they wrote songs and sent their musicians out to play these songs at different castles.

The troubadour tradition expanded to other parts of Europe, where the performers took on different names. In northern France, they were called *trouveres*; in Germany, *minnesingers*. But wherever they were, they continued to travel the countryside entertaining locals. Eventually, an entire industry built up around them. Regular routes were established and scribes followed the singers, writing down their songs. About 300 of those songs (out of an estimated 2,500) survive today.

ROAD SONGS

The troubadours lasted only until the 13th century, but their music and poetry deeply influenced Western culture. Not only were they among the first groups to flower artistically after the dreary Middle Ages, but they changed the way people looked at music. Music was no longer the austere domain of the church—it was becoming fun and popular among the common people.

IT'S TIME TO GET ORGANIZED

Another group that appeared around this time were the minstrels. Like troubadours, they sang, played instruments, and traveled from town to town. But minstrels were usually illiterate and less refined than the troubadours; they sometimes wrote their own songs, but often played songs or told stories composed by others. They could be male or female, and they traveled to castles, inns, festivals, and weddings—anywhere they might earn a hot meal, some money, or a good night's sleep by a warm fire.

Despite their reputation as wanderers, the minstrels were the first musicians to organize. In the 14th century, a few "minstrel schools" were set up where they could learn new songs and techniques, swap gossip, and repair instruments. By the turn of the 16th century, they had set up musicians' guilds, or unions, all over Europe. The guilds formalized training, provided steady employment, and required that all minstrels join a guild...or quit. Some independent minstrels continued to roam, never joining the guilds. Guild musicians complained that the independent minstrels stole their songs and undercut their prices. (Some Christian scholars and theologians went so far as to call them "ministers of Satan.")

THE AGE OF EXPLORATION

Times were hard for the musicians who traveled from place to place, so to relieve the financial stress, some signed up for long sea voyages. Onboard, they played hymns during church services, marked the changing hours and shifts with trumpet calls and drums, and even went ashore to help make friends with the natives. The pay was decent, and shipboard musicians got the opportunity to travel to many exotic places: India, Africa, the Philippines, the Americas—Sir Francis Drake even took several musicians around the globe in 1580.

Once in the New World (they were among the first to get there), musicians were a part of almost every colony. Some settled down, but others continued to travel...and they lived on the fringes of society. For that reason, historians didn't pay much attention to them. But we know from diaries and letters that medicine shows and itinerant singers followed the wagon trains west, and musicians played at mining camps, pioneer villages, or anywhere audiences might gather.

HOORAY FOR VAUDEVILLE!

By the 1830s, more people were working in cities and earning enough to have extra money for cheap entertainment. Theaters were built to host circus acts, minstrel shows, dancers, singers, and musicians for a few performances; then the acts moved on to the next town.

By the 1890s, these touring troupes and the theaters where they performed had evolved into an organized entertainment circuit: vaudeville. No one is sure where the word comes from, but one possible explanation goes back to a 15th-century troubadour named Olivier Basselin. He traveled and sang his songs in Normandy, France, along the valley of the Vire River a place called the *vau de Vire*—which could be the origin of the word "vaudeville."

Most of the performers who worked the vaudeville circuit never made it big. Like the troubadours of old, they lived hand-to-mouth and toured the country, playing in small clubs and theaters. Some did become stars, however, including Jack Benny, Judy Garland, George Burns, Bob Hope, Fanny Bryce, and Charlie Chaplin.

Vaudeville died out in the 1930s when movies took over as the most popular form of entertainment. Many of the theater chains that once hosted the traveling shows—places like the Fox in Detroit and the Orpheum in Los Angeles—converted to movie palaces. Some vaudeville theaters, though—like the Wiltern in Los Angeles or the Hammerstein Ballroom in New York—continued to host music groups and still do today. Everyone from Gwen Stefani to the Rolling Stones has played those clubs, proving that the tradition of the traveling musician is alive and well.

*   *   *

"Never did I think I'd become family entertainment."

—**Jimmy Buffett**

Jerry Lee Lewis and televangelist Jimmy Swaggart are cousins.

WHY GOLD?
WHY PLATINUM?

*We've all seen pictures of Elvis or some other singing star in front
of a wall of gold records. Now the industry has platinum—and
even mega-platinum—records. But what does it all mean?*

PAINT IT GOLD

In 1941 the Glenn Miller Orchestra recorded a song for
the film *Sun Valley Serenade*. The song, "Chattanooga Choo
Choo," turned out to be enormously popular—much more so
than the movie—and in just three months it sold more than a
million copies.

RCA Victor, Miller's label, decided to come up with a special
way to reward Miller for the song's success. So during a radio
broadcast on February 10, 1942, they presented him with a surprise
gift: one of the master records of "Chattanooga Choo Choo"…that
they'd spray-painted with gold lacquer. Miller had received the
first—unofficial—"Gold Record."

In 1958 the Recording Industry Association of America
(RIAA) borrowed the gimmick and issued the first *official* "Gold
Record"—also for passing the million-sales mark—to Perry Como
for his song "Catch a Falling Star." Later that year, the first Gold
Album was awarded to the film soundtrack of *Oklahoma!* for
reaching $1 million in sales (not copies sold).

PRECIOUS METALS

Since the 1950s, the criteria for winning a Gold Record have
changed several times (selling one million, whether it's copies or
dollars, isn't nearly the accomplishment it was 50 years ago). New
categories of recordings have also been added. Today, awards are
given for Single, Shortform Album/EP, Full-Length Album, and
Multi-Disc Set. And new "metals" have been added, too:

Gold: 500,000 copies sold in the United States

Platinum: One million copies sold

Multi-Platinum: Two million copies sold

Paul McCartney and film critic Roger Ebert were born on the same day (June 18, 1942).

Diamond: Ten million copies sold (only awarded to singles and albums)

But that's not all: There are three categories for music videos, and they have different sales criteria. For Music Video Single, Gold designates 25,000 copies sold; Platinum 50,000 copies; and Multi-Platinum 100,000 copies. For Music Video Longforms and Multi-Box Music Video Sets, Gold means 50,000 copies sold, Platinum 100,000, and Multi-Platinum 200,000.

THE TOPS

Ten million copies is a lot, but more than 100 albums have reached that milestone. Here are the top 10 best-selling albums of all time (U.S. sales):

1. The Eagles, *Their Greatest Hits 1971–1975* (1976)
   Copies sold: 29 million

2. Michael Jackson, *Thriller* (1982)
   Copies sold: 27 million

3. Pink Floyd, *The Wall* (1979)
   Copies sold: 23 million

4. Led Zeppelin, *Led Zeppelin IV* (1971)
   Copies sold: 23 million

5. Billy Joel, *Greatest Hits Volume I & Volume II* (1985)
   Copies sold: 21 million

6. AC/DC, *Back in Black* (1980)
   Copies sold: 21 million

7. Garth Brooks, *Double Live* (1998)
   Copies sold: 21 million

8. Shania Twain, *Come on Over* (1997)
   Copies sold: 20 million

9. The Beatles, *The Beatles (The White Album)* (1968)
   Copies sold: 19 million

10. Fleetwood Mac, *Rumours* (1977)
    Copies sold: 19 million

GOLD EXTRAS

- First Platinum single: Johnny Taylor's "Disco Lady."

Pete Townshend & John Entwistle of the Who played in a Dixieland band called the Confederates.

• In 2000 the RIAA launched Los Premios de Oro y Platino, a new award for Spanish-language artists. Criteria: sales of 100,000 copies gets a Disco de Oro (Gold Record); 200,000 a Disco de Platino (you can figure that one out); and 400,000 a Multi-Platino award. Note: The lyrics must be at least 51% Spanish.

• Different countries around the world have their own "gold" standards. Examples: In Sweden, a Gold Album is awarded after 20,000 sales, and Platinum goes for 40,000. In Hungary, 7,500 copies gets Gold; 15,000 gets Platinum. In Switzerland, sales of 15,000 singles or albums earns a Gold award, and 30,000 gets Platinum.

• Best-selling single: Elton John's "Candle in the Wind 1997," an update of his 1973 song, "Candle in the Wind." He rewrote it in August 1997 to honor his close friend, Princess Diana, who had died earlier that month. He sang it in public only once, at her funeral in Westminster Abbey on September 6, 1997. Since then, it's earned a Multi-Platinum designation, with more than 11 million copies sold...and that's just in the United States. Around the world, it's sold about 35 million copies.

• The RIAA will only give awards to recordings made after the year they began giving away the awards—1958. Several songs recorded before that would easily receive Diamond status...but never will. Most notable: Bing Crosby's version of Irving Berlin's "White Christmas," which was recorded in 1942. The 2007 *Guinness Book of Records* puts its sales at an estimated 50 million copies, the best-selling single of all time.

* * *

WHAT ELSE WOULD YOU EXPECT FROM A GUY NAMED ZOMBIE?

Heavy metal singer Rob Zombie is a vegetarian. That's probably why he volunteered to record a message for the People for the Ethical Treatment of Animals in 2007. When listeners called PETA's hotline during the week before Thanksgiving, they heard Zombie describing in graphic detail the tortuous factory-farming methods that many turkeys endure.

Former Doobie Brother Jeff "Skunk" Baxter now advises Congress on missile defense.

THE SLAVE PRINCE OF ROCK 'N' ROLL

The story of that person known by a name he stopped
using, then known by a symbol that nobody quite
got, who then went back to his real name.

DO WHAT WE TELL U

In 1992 Warner Bros. was trying to renew a contract with one of their biggest stars, Prince. With 13 albums and mega-hits like "1999," "Purple Rain," "Little Red Corvette," and "When Doves Cry" behind him and his contract coming to a close, the label didn't want to lose the hitmaker to a competitor. And they succeeded. In September 1992, Prince agreed to a six-album, $100 million deal—the largest recording contract in history at the time.

But despite all that money (along with full creative freedom), Prince was unhappy. The contract stipulated that Warner owned the master tapes (in other words, the rights) to all of Prince's recordings, both new ones and old, dating back to the beginning of his time at Warner—all the way back to 1978. (The label owning the masters is standard industry practice.) Warner also wanted Prince to space out his next six albums over a 10-year period. Prince, who's so prolific he reportedly has thousands of unreleased songs, felt that them telling him how much to record and when to release it amounted to restricting his artistic freedom. And he was about to make his displeasure known.

SYMBOLIC RESPONSE

The name of Prince's first album under his new contract: ♀. What's that? It's not a word, it's a symbol—a combination of the "male" and "female" symbols with an arrow and a swirly flourish. But because it's a symbol, it's *completely unpronounceable*. Then in early 1993, after ♀ had reached #5 on the album chart, Prince got angry. He thought that the album and the singles hadn't performed as well as they should have, and blamed Warner for not working hard enough to promote it. He felt like disrespected,

---

Can you hear them all? On his debut album, *For You*, Prince played 27 different instruments.

hired help. So, when he appeared in concert, on TV, and in music videos, he did so with the word "slave" written on his face.

NAME GAME

That's not all. Prince further lashed out at Warner in a press release, saying that they'd used him as a "pawn" to "produce money." And because they'd trademarked the name Prince and used it as a "main marketing tool to promote all the music" that he wrote, he said, they had ruined his name. So Prince changed his name to... ⚤.

One reporter coined the phrase "The Artist Formerly Known as Prince" (TAFKAP) as a pronounceable substitute for the unpronounceable symbol. It stuck. Most people thought the name change was just TAFKAP being vain, or at least eccentric, but it was actually a savvy strike at Warner to let them know he wasn't happy with their treatment or his new contract. It was also a promotional tool—any time the media referenced ⚤, they were also promoting the album of the same name.

SIGN O' THE TIMES

Things remained ugly between the artist and the label, with ⚤ refusing to record any new material for Warner, contract notwithstanding. ⚤ and Warner agreed to release a three-CD greatest-hits collection in fall 1993. Though it was a triple album (and all old material, except for three songs extracted from Prince's vault of unreleased music), it counted as one album on the six-album deal.

Then in early 1994, to prove to Warner and to the world what he was capable of doing on his own, ⚤ released a single called "The Most Beautiful Girl in the World" on his own record label, NPG Records. It was Prince's...er, ⚤'s biggest hit since his mid-1980s heyday, peaking at #3 on the pop chart.

Warner was just as fed up with ⚤ at that point as ⚤ was fed up with Warner, but they still wanted to at least try and get their money's worth.

• In August 1994, Warner released *Come*, an album of "new" vault songs, then a few months later came *The Black Album*, an unreleased Prince double album recorded in 1986. Both releases were against ⚤'s wishes—he'd wanted to release another album called *The Gold Experience* in the summer of 1994. ♀ claimed that *Come* was "old material," while *The Gold Experience* was "new material," despite the fact that both albums had been recorded at the same sessions in 1993. Warner ultimately released *The Gold Experience* in September 1995.

• ♀ had now satisfied four albums of his six-album contract, mostly with material he thought was sub-par, but he wanted to burn through the six-album deal as quickly as possible.

• In 1996 Warner released two more albums of old Prince vault songs: the soundtrack to the Spike Lee movie *Girl 6* in March, and *Chaos and Disorder* in July. *Chaos and Disorder* turned out to be the worst-selling album of Prince's career, but he didn't care. The six albums were done. He was a free man.

AND THEN HE PARTIED LIKE IT WAS...

In November 1996, ♀ released a triple album called, appropriately enough, *Emancipation* on his own NPG Records. It went double-platinum, outselling all six Warner releases. Then in 1999 (a year he'd anticipated since his 1982 hit "1999"), ♀ started going by a new (old) name: Prince. It seems he had had another contract with Warner, for music publishing, that expired on December 31, 1999. Prince said the end of the contract "emancipated the name I was given before birth—Prince—from all long-term restrictive documents. I will now go back to using my name instead of the symbol I adopted to free myself from all undesirable relationships."

No more ♀. No more TAFKAP. Prince was just Prince again.

RANDOM PRINCE TRIVIA

• In 1996 Prince announced that his next album, *Crystal Ball*, would be released only through his Web site. He also said he wouldn't send out any albums until 50,000 copies were pre-ordered. (It took him a full year to actually release the album.)

• Songs Prince wrote for other artists include: "I Feel For You" by Chaka Khan, "Jungle Love" by the Time, "Round and Round" by Tevin Campbell, "Manic Monday" by the Bangles, "Nothing Compares 2 U" by Sinéad O'Connor, and "Stand Back" by Stevie Nicks.

...the Byrds' ninth album. It mistakenly went to press as *Untitled.*

- Prince usually wrote for others under assumed names. Among his pseudonyms: Mr. Goodnight, Jamie Starr, the Kid, Joey Coco, Christopher Tracy, Alexander Nevermind, Austra Chanel, Tora Tora, Azifwekaré, and Christopher.

- Prince had a long string of female musical protegees in the 1980s and '90s, some of whom he was linked with romantically. They included: Vanity, Candy Dulfer, Apollonia, Rosie Gaines, Sheena Easton, Martika, Wendy and Lisa, Diamond and Pearl, Jill Jones, Carmen Electra, Ingrid Chavez, Tamar, Nona Gaye, and Sheila E.

- In 2004, despite not having had a hit album in years, Prince stayed in the Top 5 of the *Billboard* album chart for most of the summer with his *Musicology* album. Reason: Most of the copies "sold" were actually copies that Prince gave away for free—one to each person who attended one of his concerts.

- Who's Prince's biggest influence? James Brown. "Without James Brown," he once said, "I'd be driving a snowplow in Minneapolis."

*　　*　　*

CRITICAL SUCCESS

Addie, Jessie, and Effie Cherry first took to the stage in the 1890s to earn some extra money when times were hard on their Iowa farm. The sisters sang their own songs, recited essays while dressed in funny costumes, and even performed an operetta called *The Gipsy's Warning*. Unfortunately, they did all these things badly.

Billy Hamilton, a local critic, wrote a scathing review of the sisters' act that was reprinted in a Des Moines newspaper. How scathing? He said: "The mouths of their rancid features opened like caverns and sounds like the wailings of damned souls issued therefrom. They pranced around the stage…like strange creatures with painted faces and hideous mien."

The Cherry Sisters sued and took their case to the Iowa Supreme Court. The judge, however, had seen their act and decided in favor of Hamilton and his paper. The case set a precedent, protecting critics from libel when they wrote unflattering reviews.

First live performance of a music synthesizer: by pianist Paul Bley at Lincoln Center, in 1969.

A MUSICAL IS BORN

Some musicals are so famous that they are familiar even to people who never go to plays. Here are the origins of some favorites.

SHOWBOAT (1927)

Oscar Hammerstein, Jerome Kern, and producer Florenz Ziegfeld were sick of the light, upbeat musicals that had made them famous. They wanted to do something with adult themes like alcoholism, interracial relationships, and marital troubles—even if no one came to see it. But they needn't have worried. Their adaptation of Edna Ferber's novel about life on a riverboat opened in 1927 to rave reviews and sold out so often that Ziegfeld considered staging a second production in a nearby theater to handle the overflow. So far, the show has had five Broadway revivals, more than any other musical in history.

GREASE (1972)

Originally a five-hour rock 'n' roll musical written by two amateur writers for a Chicago community theater. A producer bought the rights and had it trimmed by more than half before taking it to New York. Interesting sidelight: George Lucas's film *American Graffiti* is usually credited with starting the 1950s nostalgia boom, but this play opened off-Broadway on February 14, 1972—a year before *American Graffiti* premiered. It ran for 3,388 performances, and the 1978 film version was the #1 box-office film of the year.

WEST SIDE STORY (1957)

In 1949 Arthur Laurents and Jerome Robbins came up with an idea to do a modern New York slums-set musical version of *Romeo and Juliet* about a forbidden love amongst racial gangs called *East Side Story*. The plot was about a teenage Catholic American boy who falls in love with a Jewish Israeli girl. By 1950, they shelved the idea after a Broadway play called *Abie's Irish Rose* had a similar plot. Laurents and Robbins decided to revisit it in 1954 after reading an article about street riots in Los Angeles. They changed the musical to *West Side Story* and the racial groups from Catholics and Jews to Polish and Puerto Rican immigrants. They hired 25-

year-old composer Stephen Sondheim to write the lyrics and convinced Leonard Bernstein to compose the songs. The result: a dark, violent musical that was deliberately aggressive to reflect the passions of the angry, adolescent teenage characters. It opened on Broadway in 1957. Audiences and critics were stunned by its originality: *West Side Story* was the first musical with a tragic ending (not changed from *Romeo and Juliet*), and the music was technically intricate with atonal melodies and music in minor keys. Nevertheless, it was a hit, running for 985 performances.

OKLAHOMA! (1943)

Based on a play called *Green Grow the Lilacs*, which had a limited run in the 1930–31 Broadway season. A woman who'd helped produce it thought it would make a good musical and approached composer Richard Rodgers with the idea. He was interested, but his partner Lorenzo Hart—who'd become an unreliable alcoholic —wasn't. Rodgers's solution: he teamed up with lyricist Oscar Hammerstein...who hadn't had a hit in years and was considered a has-been. Together they wrote a musical called *Away We Go!* When it got to Broadway, it was renamed *Oklahoma!* and played to sellout crowds. It established Rodgers and Hammerstein as a team.

RENT (1996)

Playwright Billy Aronson came up with an idea in 1988 to create a musical based on Puccini's 1896 opera *La Boheme*, but about young artists dealing with AIDS in modern-day Greenwich Village (and not tuberculosis in 19th century Paris). He hired 29-year-old composer Jonathan Larson, who completely took over the project and conceived it as a rock musical. He named it *Rent*. The title refers to the characters' dingy lofts, but it also means "torn apart," fitting for a play in which nearly all the main characters are dying of AIDS. Larson spent three years writing *Rent* and another five developing it with a theater workshop. It debuted on Broadway in April 1996 and caused a sensation. Critics called it the most important musical of the last 20 years and it went on to win the Pulitzer Prize and the Tony for Best Musical. Tragically, Larson never got to see the fruit of his efforts: he died of a brain hemorrhage the night before *Rent* debuted.

WHY DISCO HAPPENED

Love it or hate it, disco music will always be associated with the 1970s.
But did it all begin and end in that decade? Not by a long shot—
it actually had its roots in World War II Paris.

LE RÉSISTANCE

When you think of disco, what comes to mind? Probably polyester, mirror balls, and lines of dancers doing the Hustle. But surprisingly, the seeds that would one day grow into disco were first planted by the Nazis.

During their brutal occupation of France in World War II, the Germans outlawed any form of art and music that they deemed "impure." The American jazz movement, which had experienced a renaissance in Paris in the 1930s, was high on the Nazis' cultural hit list. In 1940 Hitler's army began to shut down any cabaret that featured the "rhythms of belly-dancing negroes" and sending offenders to internment camps. (At the same time, however, the Nazis formed their own jazz band called Charlie and His Orchestra to broadcast taunting, satirical propaganda songs to the Allies over the radio.)

THE BEAT GOES ON

Unwilling to give up their beloved jazz, partying Parisians formed secret nightclubs that required passwords to get in, changed locations frequently, and tried to stay as quiet as possible. And without any jazz bands left, their only choice was to play records. The most famous club, Le Discotheque (French for "The Record Library"), opened on rue de la Huchette in 1941. With a *discaire*, or disc jockey, spinning jazz records all night long, the main attraction was dancing. Thumbing their noses at the occupying Reich, Le Discotheque and other underground clubs opened their doors to blacks and homosexuals, the same groups who would first embrace disco music 30 years later. The main ingredients that would result in disco in the 1970s were now in place.

LET'S DO THE TWIST!

When the Twist dance craze swept the United States in the early 1960s, it drew thousands of patrons to nightclubs like the Peppermint Lounge in New York City and the Whiskey a Go-Go in Los Angeles. Nightclub owners realized what the French had already figured out: As long as they played music that had the right beat, people would turn out in droves to dance. They also realized that it was cheaper to hire a deejay to play records than to pay a band (and deejays were far less temperamental). By 1965 more than 5,000 discotheques had popped up in the United States.

As the 1970s began, the innocence and idealism of 1960s counterculture had mostly been quashed by the escalating war in Vietnam and a conservative president in the White House. But the newfound sexual freedom that had begun in 1967's "Summer of Love" had blossomed with the first widespread use of the birth control pill in the early 1970s. The sexual revolution was now in full swing, and it was about to find its perfect partner: disco.

DO THE HUSTLE!

Just like in 1940s Paris, minorities and homosexuals were welcome in American underground dance clubs of the early '70s, and quickly became their primary patrons. While the Twist and similar dances featured two partners who danced without touching each other, the dancing in these new clubs was much more intimate—especially after salsa dancing spiced things up. Salsa, a style popular among Cuban immigrants on the Miami club scene, eventually blended with swing in a new dance called "disco swing," which spread around the country, one discotheque at a time.

In the Northeast, the dance was dubbed the "New York Hustle," later shortened to the Hustle (and then treated with many variations in the late 1970s). But each style shared the same elements: the couple moved side to side, then back and forth, while swiveling their hips and rotating around each other.

By 1973 the word "disco" was being used to describe both the discotheque scene and the music most often played there. The term entered the mainstream when *Rolling Stone* repeatedly used it in an article titled "Discotheque Rock '72: Paaaaarty!" But which record, exactly, was the first true disco song isn't quite as clear. Some music historians cite 1973's "Soul Makossa" by Manu

An average pop song is 3 min. long. The *longest* song on the Ramones' 1st album: 2:24 min.

Dibango. "Law of the Land" by the Temptations is another strong candidate, as is Gloria Gaynor's 1974 megahit "Never Can Say Goodbye." And still others cite the song "The Hustle" by Van McCoy, released in 1975, as the first song to truly have that "disco sound." But what exactly *is* the disco sound?

The simple answer is a combination of beat, tempo, instrumentation, and song length. The disco beat typically has four beats per measure, with equal emphasis on every beat: BUMP BUMP BUMP BUMP. Rock and funk beats typically have four beats per measure as well, but with emphasis on the second and fourth beats: ba BUMP ba BUMP. Disco is also much faster paced than most rock or funk, sometimes up to 120 beats per minute. The faster, the better.

ADDING MOULTON TO THE MIX

But what about that other staple of discotheques, the "long dance mixes" that kept people on their feet for hours? That idea was mostly the work of pioneering record producer (and occasional fashion model) Tom Moulton. During a photo shoot at a Long Island nightclub in 1971, he was amazed by the energy on the dance floor. "I got a charge of it, all these white people dancing to black music." The only problem was that the songs were usually three minutes long and had slightly different beats, making it difficult for dancers to stay in a groove. Inspired, Moulton went home to his studio and spent 80 hours remixing and editing soul songs together, over and over, altering their speeds to keep a continuous beat going. Result: a 45-minute tape of nonstop, thumping dance music. His tape was a hit at the Sandpiper Club in Fire Island, New York, and as word of the extended mix spread, budding disco artists wanted "Tom Moulton mixes" of *their* songs.

That led to another problem: The 7-inch single (45 rpm), which was common at the time, could only hold four to five minutes of music, not nearly enough to make an extended dance record. So Moulton experimented with larger formats, and created what would become the disco deejay's favorite: the 12-inch single. In 1974 Moulton was given the chance to extend a single called "Do It 'Til You're Satisfied" by B.T. Express from three minutes to nearly six. The extended dance song was a huge success, peaking at #2 on the Billboard pop chart.

Ringo Starr appears in an apple juice commercial in Japan. (*Ringo* means "apple" in Japanese.)

He was then brought in to mix Gloria Gaynor's debut album, *Never Can Say Goodbye*. With the focus on making the best dance record possible, Moulton filled side one of the album with a non-stop 18-minute dancing experience. Each of the three songs smoothly segued into the next, and the vocal sections were limited to one minute at the beginning of each track, allowing melody and beat to carry the rest of the song. Record executives were skeptical about the experiment, but Moulton proved his case when *Never Can Say Goodbye* became a huge hit on dance floors across the country. It solidified the golden rule for disco deejays and recording artists alike: Keep the beat going.

BIG BOYS WON'T TRY

Although disco scored a few early hits, for the most part, radio steered clear of it. The songs were often too long for airplay, and they needed thumping bass speakers to sound their best. As the large record companies ignored disco, dozens of independent labels cropped up, some only to produce one single before folding. But these small record companies fueled the growing dance scene: Labels like WestEnd, Prelude, and SalSoul were in high demand, producing a library of disco music with thousands of dance tracks. "Disco is the best floor show in town," reported writer Truman Capote. "It's very democratic, boys with boys, girls with girls, girls with boys, blacks and whites, capitalists and Marxists, Chinese and everything else, all in one big mix."

By 1976 the beat, the sound, and the underground dance-club scene—all of disco's components—were firmly in place. But a Hollywood movie was about to infiltrate that big mix and take disco to worlds where no disco dancer had gone before.

Shake that thang all the way over to page 451 for the story of disco's rise...and demise.

* * *

Roundball rock. NBA players who've released rap albums: Kobe Bryant, Allen Iverson, Jason Kidd, Shaquille O'Neal, Gary Payton, David Robinson, and Tony Parker (in French).

Tin Pan Alley was a specific place: W. 28th St. between Broadway and 6th Ave. in New York.

SWAN SONGS

When someone dies, whether it's sudden or not, the last thing he or she did often seems poignantly appropriate. For a musician, that's often a song.

JOHN COLTRANE
Date of Death: July 17, 1967 (age 40)
Last Song: "A Few of My Favorite Things."
Story: The man considered one of the most influential saxophone players in jazz history played his last concert on April 23, 1967, at the Olatunji Center of African Studies in Harlem. That night, Coltrane and his band performed a version of the Rodgers and Hammerstein classic "My Favorite Things," which had long been his signature song. They stretched it out to 34 minutes in a cacophonous, swirling deluge of sound, described as "frightening" and "Picassoesque" by both those who loved it and hated it. Coltrane knew at the time that he was dying of liver cancer; he'd be gone three months later. The performance was released 43 years later, in 2001, on the album called *The Olatunji Concert.*

OTIS REDDING
Date of Death: December 10, 1967 (age 26)
Last Song: "(Sittin' on the) Dock of the Bay"
Story: In his seven years of recording, Redding had never cracked the top 20 on the charts before. But when his song "Dock of the Bay" came out in January 1968, it held the top spot for four weeks. He recorded it on December 6 and 7, 1967—just a few days before he was killed in a plane crash.

MICHAEL HUTCHENCE
Date of Death: November 22, 1997 (Age: 37)
Last Song: "Possibilities"
Story: This song was written by the former lead singer of INXS for his first solo album, simply titled *Michael Hutchence.* He had been working on the album, while recording and touring with INXS, since 1995. He recorded "Possibilities" just three days before

---

Who are William, Saul, Jeffrey, and Mike? Axl, Slash, Izzy, and Duff of Guns N' Roses.

his death, which some believe was a suicide; others said it was an accident resulting from autoerotic asphyxiation. *Michael Hutchence* was released in 1999.

BING CROSBY
Date of Death: October 14, 1977 (age 74)
Last Song: "Once in a While"
Story: Crosby ended his final recording session on October 11 at BBC studios in London with the 1937 standard. Three days later, after playing golf with friends in Spain, he uttered a now-famous line as he walked off the course: "That was a great round of golf, fellas." A few seconds later, he died from a massive heart attack. What wasn't widely known until 2001 was that the *very* last song he sang was on that golf course. The summer 2001 issue of *BING* magazine, put out by the still-active "Club Crosby" fan club, carried an interview with Valentin Barrios, who played that round of golf with Crosby that day. "There were some construction workers building a new house just off the ninth hole," Barrios recounted. "The workers recognized Bing and motioned for him to come over to them. Bing was very happy to be recognized and walked over to the men, who asked for a song. The last song Bing Crosby sang, which I remember vividly, was 'Strangers in the Night.'"

GEORGE HARRISON
Date of Death: November 29, 2001 (age 58)
Last Song: "Horse to Water"
Story: Harrison wrote the song with his son Dhani for old friend and pianist Jools Holland (you can hear it on Holland's album *Small World Big Band*). Harrison recorded it in his home on October 1, in the midst of his battle with throat and brain cancer. With his characteristic dark sense of humor, he asked that his songwriting credit be listed as "RIP Limited."

*　　　*　　　*

"We want to be the band to dance to when the bomb drops."
—Simon Le Bon, of Duran Duran

Nashville nicknames: Music City, USA; Cashville; Nashvegas; and Titan Town.

THE POWER OF MUSIC

Does it live inside you?

"Music is nothing separate from me. It is me. You'd have to remove the music surgically."
—**Ray Charles**

"Music expresses that which cannot be said and on which it is impossible to be silent."
—**Victor Hugo**

"The only thing better than singing is more singing."
—**Ella Fitzgerald**

"I think people who can truly live a life in music are telling the world, 'You can have my love, you can have my smiles. Forget the bad parts, you don't need them. Just take the music, the goodness, because it's the very best and the part I give most willingly.'"
—**George Harrison**

"Music can name the unnameable and communicate the unknowable."
—**Leonard Bernstein**

"Good music is good no matter what kind of music it is."
—**Miles Davis**

"Music gives a soul to the universe, wings to the mind, flight to the imagination, and life to everything."
—**Plato**

"When you are listening to a rock 'n' roll song the way you listen to the Stones' 'Jumping Jack Flash,' that's the way you should really spend your whole life."
—**Pete Townshend**

"If the king loves music, it is well with the land."
—**Mencius, Chinese philosopher**

"Music should be something that makes you gotta move, inside or outside."
—**Elvis Presley**

"Music at its essence is what gives us memories."
—**Stevie Wonder**

"If you're looking for youth or longevity, just take a dose of rock 'n' roll. It keeps you going. Just like the caffeine in your coffee."
—**Hank Ballard**

"I don't listen to music. I hate all music." —Johnny Rotten

ELVIS BY THE NUMBERS

*We're not superstitious at the BRI, but we always try to include
at least one Elvis page in every book. One year we forgot...
and we were all shook up. We hope this makes up for it.*

TWELVE VITAL STATISTICS
1. Driver's license number (Tennessee): 2571459
2. Waistline, 1950s: 32 inches
3. Waistline, 1970s: 44 inches
4. Blood type: O
5. Shoe size: 11D (he wore size-12 combat boots)
6. Social Security Number: 409-52-2002
7. Draft number: 53310761
8. Checking account number: 011-143875
9. Length of his wedding to Priscilla Beaulieu: 8 minutes
10. Phone number (Memphis): 397-4427
11. Phone number (Beverly Hills): 278-3496
12. Phone number (Palm Springs): 325-3241

NICKNAMES OF SIX GIRLFRIENDS AND MISTRESSES
1. Ann-Margret: "Bunny," "Thumper," "Scoobie"
2. Malessa Blackwood: "Brown Eyes"
3. Margrit Buergin: "Little Puppy"
4. Dolores Hart: "Whistle Britches"
5. Ursula Andress: "Alan"
6. Ginger Alden: "Gingerbread," "Chicken Neck"

FIVE CODE NAMES FOR THE "MEMPHIS MAFIA" (ELVIS'S HANGERS-ON)
1. James Caughley: "Hamburger"
2. Joe Esposito: "Diamond Joe"
3. Lamar Fike: "Bull"
4. Marvin Gamble: "Gee Gee"
5. Charlie Hodge: "Slewfoot," "Waterhead"

FIVE ADVANTAGES TO BEING IN THE "MEMPHIS MAFIA"

1. Salary of $250 a week (1950s) to $425 a week (1960s)
2. Cadillacs, jewelry, women, and down payments on homes given as gifts
3. Free lodging (mobile homes on the grounds of Graceland)
4. Gold TCB ("Taking Care of Business") necklaces and .38-caliber pistols provided free of charge
5. Elvis never leaves Graceland without you.

SIX DRAWBACKS TO BEING IN THE "MEMPHIS MAFIA"

1. On call 24 hours a day
2. No paid vacations
3. No pensions
4. No matter how stupid or dangerous the request that Elvis makes of you, if you don't fulfill it, you're out of a job.
5. Outsiders disparage you as Elvis's "fart catchers."
6. Elvis never leaves Graceland without you.

ELVIS'S FAVORITE BIBLE PASSAGE

Matthew 19:24, "It is easier for a camel to go through the eye of a needle than for a rich man to enter the kingdom of God." (The passage haunted Elvis toward the end of his life.)

THREE TIPS FROM ELVIS FOR STAYING HEALTHY

1. "I eat a lot of Jell-O. Fruit Jell-O."
2. "The only exercise I get is on the stage. If I didn't get that, I'd get a little round around the tummy, as much as I eat."
3. "I have never tasted alcohol."

SIX WOMEN WHO CLAIM TO BE ELVIS'S WIFE, DAUGHTER, OR THE MOTHER OF HIS CHILDREN

1. Lucy deBarbin: Claims Elvis fathered her daughter Desiree on August 23, 1958.

2. Ann Farrell: Claims she married the King in Alabama in 1957, after refusing to sleep with him "unless they were man and wife."

3. Candy Jo Fuller: Claims to be Elvis's daughter after he had an affair with her mother in the 1950s. Claims Elvis paid child support for many years.

4. Zelda Harris: Claims the King married her in Alabama in 1960, "after just one date."

5. Barbara Jean Lewis: Claims she and Elvis dated for a year in the mid-1950s and that she gave birth to Elvis's daughter, Deborah Delaine Presley, in 1955. (In 1988 Deborah sued the Presley estate demanding her "fair share." She lost.)

6. Billie Joe Newton: Claims Elvis married her and fathered three children by her, the first when she was only nine years old. Claims Elvis divorced her in 1956 "because Colonel Tom Parker demanded it."

Note: None of these women have any proof to back up their claims. Most claim that the documentation—marriage certificates, birth certificates, divorce papers, etc.—has been lost or destroyed.

SIX FORGOTTEN MOMENTS IN ELVIS HISTORY

1. December 30, 1970: Tours FBI headquarters in Washington, D.C.; sought and obtained permits to carry firearms in every state.

2. July, 1971: Spends $55,000 on a stretch limousine that matched the one he saw in the movie *Shaft*.

3. January 2, 1972: Buys a $10,000 robe inscribed "The People's Champion" and gives it to Muhammad Ali.

4. March 31, 1973: Ali wears the robe that Elvis gave him for his fight against Ken Norton. Ali loses the fight.

5. September 1, 1975: Elvis is sworn in as deputy sheriff (honorary) of Shelby County, Tennessee.

6. December 18, 1975: Elvis spends the day obsessing over (1) the supernatural, (2) the occult, (3) his weight, and (4) his fear of becoming impotent. Loved ones describe him as "a physical and mental wreck."

*   *   *

"Ambition is a dream with a V-8 engine."
—Elvis Presley

OZZY OSBOURNE MEETS MISS PIGGY

*Ladies and gentlemen, we now bring you a few of
the strangest collaborations in music history.*

ROB ZOMBIE AND...LIONEL RICHIE

In 2003 horror-metal-rock singer Rob Zombie became a horror-movie director with the release of his film *House of 1000 Corpses*. He contributed five songs to the soundtrack, one of them a remake of the Commodores' classic song, "Brick House." When he decided to cover the song, he called former Commodores frontman Richie and asked him to listen to it. "He played this track for me," Richie later told *Rolling Stone*, "and it blew me away. Because he Zombarized it." Richie ended up contributing vocals for the song...because, he said, Zombie "wasn't saying *howwwse* right."

THE SAN FRANCISCO SYMPHONY AND...METALLICA

The thrash metal band teamed up with the acclaimed orchestra, led by composer Michael Kamen, for two sold-out shows in 1999. The resulting album, *Metallica—S&M with the San Francisco Symphony Orchestra*, features 21 songs, played by the band and accompanied by Kamen's orchestral arrangements. If that wasn't surprising enough to Metallica fans, the album got rave reviews...and the band and Kamen won a Grammy for the song "The Call of Ktulu."

OZZY OSBOURNE AND...MISS PIGGY

On his 2005 album *Prince of Darkness*, Ozzy Osbourne does a version of the Steppenwolf song "Born to be Wild"...as a duet with Miss Piggy. Excerpt: "I like smoke and lightning," Osbourne sings, and Miss Piggy squeals, "Oh, I do too!"

ELTON JOHN AND...EMINEM

Elton John ruffled some of his fans' feathers when he accepted an invitation to sing with the rapper at the 2001 Grammy Awards ceremony. The reason: Eminem was infamous for the anti-gay lyrics in his songs, including 18 mentions of an anti-gay slur on his album *The Marshall Mathers LP*, which won a Grammy for Best Rap Album that night. The openly gay Sir Elton said he knew he'd get flak for his decision to perform a duet of Eminem's song "Stan," but that he "hoped to influence" Eminem.

YO-YO MA AND...CONDOLEEZZA RICE
In 2002 Ma, a celebrated cellist, received the news that President Bush was about to award him the National Medal of Arts. When Ma found out that Rice, who was then Bush's National Security Advisor, was also a classically trained pianist, he asked to perform a piece with her at the ceremony. She accepted, and they played Brahms's "Violin Sonata #3 in D Minor." It was reported to be one of the highlights of the evening.

DUKE ELLINGTON AND...JIMMY STEWART
Otto Preminger's 1959 film *Anatomy of a Murder* has a jazz sound-track scored by Ellington, and he had a small on-screen cameo as a roadhouse owner named "Pie Eye." Stewart, who was taught to play piano as a boy by his mother, a skilled pianist, joins Ellington in the film for a jazz duet.

AIMEE MANN AND...MERV GRIFFIN
Alternative folk-rocker Mann appeared as a guest in April 2004 on *The Late Late Show with Craig Kilborn*. Also appearing that night was Merv Griffin. Griffin is best known as a '70s talk-show host and TV producer, but he started his career as a singer in the 1940s, and released several albums over the years. The duo performed a version of the jazz standard "Tenderly."

DUSTY SPRINGFIELD AND...JIMI HENDRIX
The British pop princess known for such hits as "I Only Want to Be with You" and "Son of a Preacher Man" wasn't exactly an acid-rocker. But in 1968 she had her own TV show, *It Must Be Dusty*, on BBC and attracted some of the biggest stars of the day. One was Hendrix, who played a rocking version of "Mockingbird" with Springfield. (Most of the film was lost, but a portion of it survives and can be seen on the Internet.)

DAVID BOWIE AND...BING CROSBY

Bowie shocked his—and Crosby's—audience when he put in a now-famous appearance on *The Bing Crosby Christmas Special* in 1977. They sang a bizarre (and slightly creepy) version of "The Little Drummer Boy."

STREISAND AND...STREISAND AND...STREISAND

In her 2001 TV special *Barbra Streisand, Timeless: Live in Concert*, Barbra Streisand performed a duet with 15-year-old Barbra Streisand look-alike Lauren Frost, who was portraying...a young Barbra Streisand. That's almost a Barbra Streisand/Barbra Streisand duet, but it got even more surreal when a giant video screen lowered down from the roof while they were singing. On the screen was Barbra Streisand, in a scene from her 1983 film *Yentl*, singing the song "A Piece of the Sky." Streisand and Frost (playing Streisand) sang the song with the 1983 Streisand, and the Streisand/Streisand/Streisand *trio* became an instant favorite of Streisand fans everywhere.

*　　*　　*

POP MUSIC ANAGRAM QUIZ

Unscramble each of these anagrams to find the name of a pop star or band.

1. Yea armchair!

2. Very bolo!

3. Multi-bearskin jet

4. Lard-fed pep

5. Ai! S.O.S!

6. Eat new sky

7. Hairy camera!

8. Be girly jam

9. Spoon god

10. Miking eel, you

11. Is so merry

12. These bleat

13. Fish, toe, frog

14. Silver spy eel

15. O, pant lordly!

ANSWERS

1. Mariah Carey, 2. Loverboy, 3. Justin Timberlake, 4. Def Leppard, 5. Oasis, 6. Kanye West, 7. Mariah Carey, 8. Mary J. Blige, 9. Snoop Dog, 10. Kylie Minogue, 11. Morrissey, 12. The Beatles, 13. Foo Fighters, 14. Elvis Presley, 15. Dolly Parton

The world's oldest known song, written in Hurrian on a clay tablet, is about 3,400 years old.

COUNTRY'S FIRST FAMILY

The Carter Family's impact is far reaching—they saved Appalachian music for posterity, began the country music recording industry, and inspired the careers of legends like Johnny Cash and Waylon Jennings.

EVERYTHING'S RELATIVE

A. P. (Alvin Pleasant) Carter, founding father of the Carter Family, was born in Poor Valley, Virginia, in 1891. He played the fiddle as a little boy and wrote his first song in 1911. Local girl Sara Dougherty was a singer, and when the two met in 1914, A.P. was smitten. They married a year later and settled in Poor Valley. The couple often sang and played music together at church meetings or gatherings with friends. In the 1920s, they asked Sara's cousin Maybelle to join them, and the trio that would become the Carter Family was born.

Sara and Maybelle loved music as much as A.P. did and were blessed with clear, pure voices. Maybelle was already a whiz on the autoharp, banjo, and fiddle. Now she taught herself how to play guitar and perfected a flowing, rhythmical style of flatpicking later known as the "Carter scratch." Sara played autoharp and sang the lead with her powerful alto voice. The trio performed old folk tunes, gospel hymns, mountain ballads, and A.P.'s original songs: hillbilly music was about to go national.

THANKS TO RALPH

The man who made it all possible was Ralph Peer. In 1927, Peer was looking for recording artists for his record label, the Victor Talking Machine Company. The new medium of radio was introducing new types of music to American audiences, and the symphonies and operas that were Victor staples weren't selling as well as they had just a few years before. Ralph Peer suspected that rural music—the "voice of the people"—might just be the genre that would drag Victor into the present.

He placed ads in the local newspapers in and around Bristol, Tennessee, announcing auditions and recording sessions. A.P. read one of the ads and hauled Sara and Maybelle (who was eight months pregnant at the time) to Bristol in a car borrowed from his brother (and Maybelle's husband) Eck. There, the trio recorded six songs and were paid $300.

AMERICAN IDOLS

Victor released a trial record of two of the Carters' songs. It sold so well that in 1928 the company invited the family to come to its recording studio in Camden, New Jersey, to make more records. The Carters recorded a dozen songs—including their famous "Wildwood Flower"—and were paid $600. Within two years, their records had sold more than 700,000 copies.

Inspired, A.P. started collecting old, near-forgotten songs. He traveled the remote hills and valleys of Appalachia in a quest for obscure tunes that would have been lost had he not tracked them down. He wrote down the words of the songs but couldn't read music, so he hummed the tunes from memory for Maybelle and Sara to learn. The girls couldn't read music either, which drove the New York sheet music producers crazy when they tried to translate the Carter songs into musical notes.

D-I-V-O-R-C-E

As rewarding as A.P.'s scouting trips were, his absences from home made Sara unhappy. She didn't like the life of a singing star. Lonely and overworked, with kids to raise and a farm to run, she was becoming more and more distant from her husband. She often refused to make personal appearances, so A.P.'s sister Sylvia filled in for her. Finally, she fell out of love with A.P.—and in love with his cousin, Coy Bays. Sara and A.P. divorced in 1936, but it would be six years before Sara and Coy got together: his family moved him to California to keep him away from Sara.

Surprisingly, A.P. and Sara's breakup wasn't the end of the Carter Family. For one thing, Ralph Peer persuaded the ex-couple that they didn't have to be a couple to continue performing together, so the group stayed together professionally for a time. But more importantly, the next generation was coming along behind them. A.P. and Sara's daughter Janette joined the Carter Family radio shows in 1939. And Maybelle's three young daughters—Helen, June, and Anita—also became part of the act.

Carnegie Hall—now a National Historic Landmark—was slated for demolition in 1960.

UNDER THE INFLUENCE

In 1938 the family started singing on the most powerful radio station in North America—XERA, which broadcast from a 500-kilowatt transmitter just over the Texas border in Mexico so it could evade U.S. laws restricting broadcast range. Now that they could be heard across America—and even into Canada—the Carter Family's influence spread to future generations of country performers. A teenaged Chet Atkins listened in Georgia; young Johnny Cash tuned in in Arkansas (and loved hearing little June yodel); Waylon Jennings listened in Texas.

Sara took the opportunity one night to dedicate a song to Coy Bays, her "friend in California." She sang the plaintive "I'm Thinking Tonight of My Blue Eyes," and when Bays heard it, he hopped in his car and drove all night to find her. They were married three weeks later.

Eventually, A.P. returned to his farm and country store in Poor Valley, and Maybelle formed a new group—Mother Maybelle and the Carter Sisters—with her three girls. Performing on the radio and in personal appearances, the group struggled at first, but by 1950 were performing at the Grand Ole Opry. When June Carter went solo (she also eventually married Johnny Cash), Maybelle, Anita, and Helen kept the family's songs alive—often as Cash's backup singers on his records and his television show.

MUSIC FOR THE AGES

Among the Carter Family's most enduring songs are "Will the Circle Be Unbroken?" with its universal theme of loss, grief, and hope; the uplifting "Keep on the Sunny Side"; and "Will You Miss Me When I'm Gone?" Legions of stars—from Johnny Cash to Emmylou Harris to Joan Baez—have rerecorded old Carter Family songs, and folk singers Woody Guthrie and Bob Dylan both rearranged Carter Family songs to create the hits "This Land Is Your Land" and "The Times They Are a-Changing."

A.P. died in 1960 after a long illness, Maybelle passed away in 1978, and Sara in 1979. And though the original Carter Family is gone, their music remains popular and beloved. The old recordings have been remastered and still sell well throughout America and Europe. In 2005 the group was posthumously awarded a Lifetime Achievement Award at the Grammys.

GO FAR IN LIFE: BE A MUSICIAN

On page 27, we told you about some of the presidents and their musical abilities. Well, that's no fluke. An education in music could lead to great things.

MUCH ADO ABOUT NOTING
The scientific research leaves little doubt: There is a direct correlation between music education and success later in life. Studies suggest that no matter how old you are, learning to play a musical instrument can make you an all-around smarter person. And even if you're not the musician type, it seems that simply *listening* to certain kinds of music can aid in learning.

THEORY: *Students with extensive musical training excel in other academic subjects, too.*
STUDY: "Nations' Emphasis on Music Education and Their Academic Standing in the World," conducted by the International Association for the Evaluation of Educational Achievement (IAEEA), 1988. This report looked at the school systems of three countries—Hungary, the Netherlands, and Japan—whose students consistently score among the highest in the world at math, reading, and science.
RESULTS: It's true. All three of these high-achieving nations *require* music and vocal training in elementary and middle schools. A related U.S. study, "Music Majors and Medical School," found that American students who majored in music were far more likely to be accepted into competitive medical schools than nonmusicians. It also studied the reading scores of 7,500 university students, and found that music majors repeatedly earned the highest scores— they beat out those who majored in biology, chemistry, math...and even English.

THEORY: *Students who are musicians cope with stress better than nonmusicians.*
STUDY: "Musicians and Emotional Health," conducted by the

Divine wind: The bagpipe is mentioned in the Bible (Daniel 3:5).

University of Texas. This 1998 study gave 362 first-year university students three tests that measured their emotional health, performance anxiety, and alcohol consumption.

RESULTS: The musicians in the group performed better on all of the tests than nonmusicians. They generally had a brighter outlook and drank less.

THEORY: *Listening to baroque music helps you think.*

STUDY: "Baroque Music and Learning a Foreign Language," by Georgi Lozanov, a Bulgarian psychologist. In the 1950s, Lozanov created a learning regimen in which some of his students were taught a foreign language while listening to music in the background. But it was a specific type of music: baroque (a style of 17th- and 18th-century classical music), and he played only slow selections that ran at 60 beats per minute. In a second control group, students were taught in silence.

RESULTS: Lozanov found that the baroque group 1) could learn a foreign language much faster than nonlisteners could, and 2) retained nearly 100 percent of the language when tested again four years later. Lozanov claimed that the human mind has an "optimum learning state" that occurs when "heartbeat, breath rate, and brain waves are smoothly synchronized and the body is relaxed, but the mind is concentrated and ready to receive new information." He claimed that his students could learn up to 1,200 new words a day using his baroque-music method.

A later study performed by an Australian doctor named John Diamond confirmed Lozanov's results by proving that the opposite is also true: Diamond found that certain musical rhythms could actually prevent learning and retention while studying. Any song with an interrupted beat—such as most rock and hip-hop songs—makes concentration more difficult. Unlike baroque, rock and rap songs are "out of sync with the body's pulse," according to Diamond.

*   *   *

"A hundred years from now, it's Yoko Ono the world's going to remember, not John Lennon or the Beatles."
—**Charlotte Moorman, performance artist**

BANNED MUSIC

Sssshh! Uncle John said we couldn't put this article in the book, but that just made us want to read it more.

Song: "The Pill" (1975)
Artist: Loretta Lynn
Story: After country superstar Lynn penned this song about a woman who feels liberated by birth control, the song was banned by country stations all over the United States. "I thought, 'Gee, what's wrong with these people?'" Lynn later said. Controversy was nothing new to the singer. Two of her earlier songs had also been blacklisted: 1966's "Dear Uncle Sam," which was something of an antiwar song, and her 1972 song "Rated X," which railed against the stigma faced by divorced women. Lynn proudly remains one of the most banned country artists in history. "I haven't done anything in my life that I'm ashamed of," she said in 2007.

Song: "Four or Five Times" (1951)
Artist: Dottie O'Brien
Story: O'Brien was a popular big-band singer in the 1950s and '60s, primarily with a group called Red Nichols and His Five Pennies. In 1951 she recorded this song, which radio stations refused to play because they felt its lyrics were too racy ("What I like best / is to have someone who is true / who will love me, too / four or five times"). Interestingly, the song had been around for many years and was recorded dozens of times by male singers, but had never been banned before. (That same year, Dean Martin's "Wham Bam, Thank You Ma'am" was banned for similar reasons.)

Song: "White Christmas" (1957)
Artist: Elvis Presley
Story: In 1957 Portland, Oregon, radio station KEX banned the playing of Presley's version of the famous Christmas song. Why? Because he was Elvis—who, because of his hip-gyrating performances and radically new music, was considered by some to be a menace. KEX disc jockey Al Priddy played the song anyway... and was fired.

The first Gold Record single was awarded to Perry Como in 1958 for "Catch a Falling Star."

Song: "Rumble" (1959)

Artist: Link Wray

Story: Radio stations all over the country refused to play this song because, they said, it promoted fighting. What was their rationale? Probably just the title—the song was an instrumental, featuring Wray's "rumbling" guitar…and no lyrics. Despite the ban (or maybe because of it), it sold a million copies.

Album: *Unfinished Music No.1: Two Virgins* (1968)

Artist: John Lennon and Yoko Ono

Story: When a shipment of 30,000 copies of *Two Virgins*—which pictured John and Yoko naked on the cover—arrived at the Newark, New Jersey, airport in early 1969, police seized them, claiming the albums were "pornography." The albums were never returned to the record company, and local stores that carried the record were raided. Many other towns around the country also banned the album.

Extra: In 1969 actress Sissy Spacek, then 19 years old and trying to make it in the music business, recorded a bubble-gum pop song denouncing the *Two Virgins* cover. The song was written by producer Artie Wayne, and Spacek released it under the name "Rainbo." It was called "John, You Went Too Far This Time." It flopped.

Song: "Cortez the Killer" (1975)

Artist: Neil Young

Story: Young's guitar ballad about conquistador Hernán Cortés's brutal conquest of Aztec Mexico was banned…in Spain. Fascist leader Generalissimo Francisco Franco felt it was insulting to the Spanish people.

Song: "We Were All Wounded at Wounded Knee" (1973)

Artist: Redbone

Story: In 1973 members of the American Indian Movement (AIM) seized the town of Wounded Knee on the Oglala Sioux Pine Ridge Reservation in South Dakota and held it for 71 days, demanding changes in the tribal government. Less than a month after the standoff ended, the all-Native American band Redbone released the song "We Were All Wounded at Wounded Knee," recalling the infamous massacre of an estimated 300 Sioux by U.S. Cavalry in 1890. (You may remember Redbone for their hit song "Come and Get Your Love.") The Wounded Knee song went to #1…in the Netherlands, and got extensive airplay in other European countries, where American Indian causes have long been popular. But it was barely heard in the United States, where radio stations banned it for being too provocative and antigovernment.

BONUS "BANS"

Album: *Jazz from Hell* (1986)
Artist: Frank Zappa
Story: Fred Meyer, a retail chain in the Pacific Northwest, put an "Explicit Lyrics" warning sticker on this album. But, just like Link Wray's "Rumble," it had no lyrics. It's an instrumental album.

Artist: Bob Dylan
Story: For a while in 1968, a radio station in El Paso, Texas, stripped all the Dylan songs from their playlists. Why? Because they couldn't understand what he was saying. (They allowed his songs to be played…if someone else was singing them.)

*   *   *

RANDOM MOVIE QUOTE

Bill: Ted, while I agree that, in time, our band will be most triumphant. The truth is, Wyld Stallyns will never be a super band until we have Eddie Van Halen on guitar.
Ted: Yes, Bill. But I do not believe we will get Eddie Van Halen until we have a triumphant video.
Bill: Ted, it's pointless to have a triumphant video before we even have decent instruments.
Ted: Well, how can we have decent instruments when we don't really even know how to play?
Bill: That is why we need Eddie Van Halen!
Ted: And that is why we need a triumphant video.
Bill and Ted: Excellent!
—*Bill & Ted's Excellent Adventure* (1989)

Blues-playing brothers Edgar and Johnny Winter are both albinos.

MUSICAL WORD ORIGINS

Because we always wanted to know where the word "boogie" came from.

RAGTIME. This term for the turn of 20th century music genre, known as the first truly American music style and a precursor of jazz, was coined around 1896. One of its characteristics is its heavily syncopated rhythm, meaning that it emphasized the off beat, or "weak beat," in the music's structure. That gave the music what the "King of Ragtime," piano player Scott Joplin, called a "weird and intoxicating" effect. According to some, it also gave it a "ragged" beat, or "ragged time," which was later shortened to "ragtime."

SKA. This music style, combining Caribbean rhythms (*calypso* from Trinidad and *mento* from Jamaica) with American jazz (especially the horn arrangements), originated in Jamaica in the 1950s. Some sources say it got the name "ska" in 1964, possibly a shortening of the word scat (as in scat singing). Another theory: Ska guitar legend Ernest Ranglin reportedly said the word describes the scratchy guitar style used in the music. He was instructed, he said, to "Play it like 'ska ska ska,'" and the name stuck.

BOOGIE-WOOGIE. In the 11th century, the French used the word *boulgre* to refer to a sect of Bulgarian heretics who were accused of being sexual deviants. The word came to English in the 14th century as "bougre," for heretics in general. By the 19th century, it had become "bogy," meaning a "hobgoblin," and then "bogeyman." When that word came to the United States in the late 1800s, it was used as a racist term for blacks and a slang term for sex. In the 1910s, a new style of piano-based dance music, characterized by steady, driving rhythms and walking bass lines, started being played by black musicians in bordellos and saloons. Whether it's because of its association with sex, suggestive dancing, or African Americans (or a combination of all three) is unknown, but that style of piano playing soon came to be called "boogie woogie." First recording to use the term: Clarence "Pinetop" Smith's *Pinetop's Boogie Woogie*, from 1929.

Nick Cave, David Lee Roth, Henry Rollins, and Sting are all published authors.

THE SOUND OF MUZAK

You hear it in the elevator, in your dentist's office, at the supermarket—even in the reptile house of the Bronx Zoo. Here's the inside story on the music you love to hate.

WAR BABY

During World War I, General George Squier, a pioneer in radio communications, figured out how to send several messages simultaneously over electric power lines—which proved quite useful on the battlefields. Squier believed that if his system could broadcast messages in times of war, it could broadcast music, news, and entertainment in times of peace. So after the war, he pitched his idea to a New York utility company as a way to make extra money off existing power lines. They liked the idea and founded Wired Radio, Inc. in 1922.

Wired Radio began broadcasting from the balcony of a power plant to residential customers in the Lakeland area of Cleveland. For 11 cents per month, listeners could tune to three music channels and one all-news channel via a special receiver plugged into their electrical outlets. This was moderately successful at first, but the company knew it couldn't last. Why would anyone keep paying Wired Radio's monthly fee when they could listen to a regular radio for free? So they began looking for a new way to make money from Squier's invention.

WHISTLE WHILE YOU WORK

In the 1930s, using the name Muzak (a takeoff on Kodak), Wired Radio decided to peddle background music for hotels, restaurants, and offices. They came up with a new sales pitch, too: listening to the music would actually make employees work harder. The claim seemed outlandish at the time, but Muzak backed it up with a 1937 British study called "Fatigue and Boredom in Repetitive Work," which concluded that people work harder when listening to the "proper" music.

Once again, sales were slow...and might have stayed that way, if Britain hadn't been gearing up for World War II. The English government had also read "Fatigue and Boredom in Repetitive

---

Ted Nugent makes and sells his own line of beef jerky called "Gonzo Meat Biltong."

Work" and arranged for a special BBC music program to be piped
into airplane, tank, and munitions factories to prevent fatigue.

When production in some factories increased as much as six
percent, word quickly got back to Washington. The U.S. military
hired Muzak to provide the same service to American defense
plants… and *their* productivity went up 11 percent. Muzak had
finally found a product that people wanted to buy.

TAKEOFF

After the war, Muzak expanded into bank lobbies, insurance
companies, medical and dental offices, department stores…and,
of course, elevators. Why play music in an elevator? In the 1940s
and '50s—when most office buildings phased out elevator operators—passengers were left alone for the first time. "People were
nervous and tense," explains a Muzak franchiser, "because they
no longer had anyone to talk to in the elevator." Muzak filled
the void.

"STIMULUS PROGRESSION"

Over the years, Muzak programming became more scientific (or
pseudoscientific, depending on whom you believe). The company
calls it "stimulus progression." Here's how it works:

• Each song the company records is rated according to tempo,
rhythm, instrumentation, and size of orchestra; then it's given an
overall "stimulus value."

• Using a computer, Muzak programmers create a broadcast schedule divided into 15-minute segments. The songs in each segment
are always organized in *ascending* order of their stimulus value, "to
provide people with a lift." Each 15-minute segment ends with 60
seconds of silence.

• Faster segments are played at 10:00–11:00 a.m. and 3:00–4:00
p.m., when employees are more likely to need a lift. Slow segments are played at 1:00–3:00 p.m. and after 6:00 p.m., when
employees are thought to be the most energetic.

IN THE RED

In the '70s, Muzak faced a new problem. To save money, the company, which had been acquired by Westinghouse, stopped hiring

The Vinaccia family, inventors of the mandolin, may have built the first six-string guitar in 1779.

unionized American musicians. Instead, they contracted with a nonunion Communist orchestra—the Brno Radio Orchestra of Czechoslovakia—to record most of the songs in the company's music library. Few, if any, of the Eastern European musicians had ever heard songs like "Born Free" and "Raindrops Keep Falling on My Head." The result was a strange Muzak that even regular customers, people who *liked* Muzak, thought was terrible. By the early '80s, cancellation rates were so high that Westinghouse sold Muzak to department store heir and media mogul Marshall Field V.

The New Muzak

In 1987 Muzak did a major overhaul of its image. It banned Communist orchestras—as well as harmonicas, tubas, fluegelhorns, and "any instrument that would sound dated or hokey." Organs in particular had been a big problem—Jane Jarvis, a previous Muzak programming vice president, moonlighted as the organist at Shea Stadium, and some felt the Muzak produced under her direction was more suited for a ballgame than an elevator or department store. They also added vocals, ending a 50-year tradition. Prior to the format change, human voices had only been heard on Muzak in 1981, when an announcer broke the news that American hostages had been released from Iran, and on Good Friday in 1985, when Muzak joined radio stations worldwide in a simultaneous broadcast of "We Are the World."

Today, Muzak broadcasts via satellite to 200,000 customers and more than 100 million "listeners" around the world. It is heard in just about every kind of workplace imaginable, including churches, prisons, mental institutions, the Pentagon, and at least one German brothel that the company knows of.

MUZAK FACTS

• According to one survey, more than 75 percent of Americans recognize the Muzak name, making the trademark as big a household word as Coca-Cola, Kleenex, and Xerox. The bad news: more than 50 percent of the respondents in the same survey said they don't like listening to it.

• Many songwriters, including Bruce Springsteen, refuse to sell Muzak the rights to their songs. Not so with Paul Simon—"When I hear my song on an elevator," he says, "I know I've got a hit."

Mick Fleetwood of Fleetwood Mac estimates that he spent $8 million...on cocaine.

- President Dwight D. Eisenhower played Muzak in the White House—and Lyndon Johnson liked it so much he bought a local Texas franchise. He even had Muzak speakers installed in the trees of the LBJ Ranch.

- Andy Warhol claimed Muzak was his favorite music.

- Neil Armstrong listened to Muzak during the *Apollo XI* voyage to the moon.

- During the fall of Saigon in 1975, State Department staffers evacuated the American embassy compound with Muzak playing in the background.

- Studies show that even cows and chickens increase productivity when "functional" music is played in the background.

- 7-Elevens in British Columbia, Canada, and Seattle, Washington, use Muzak to keep juveniles from loitering in front of the stores. The tactic has proven quite effective, but it drives Muzak nuts. "I'm opposed to a negative use of a positive thing in our lives," company official Tom Evans complains. "If they want to torture people, why don't they just blast air-raid sirens?"

*　　*　　*

TWO FASCINATING BOOKS ON MUSIC

- *This Is Your Brain on Music* (2006), by musician, engineer, and lifelong audiophile Daniel J. Levitin. Said the *Boston Globe:* "It segues deftly from a crash course in pitch, timbre, melody, and other music characteristics to the electrochemical processes of the brain and the elucidation of such topics as 'ear worms,' those insipid jingles and pop songs that get infuriatingly stuck in our heads."

- *Musicophilia: Tales of Music and the Brain* (2007), by celebrated neurologist (and author of *Awakenings*) Oliver Sacks. Some of the chapters: "Papa Blows His Nose in G," about people who can determine the exact pitch of sounds; "A Hypermusical Species: Williams Syndrome," about people with a musical type of autism; and "A Bolt from the Blue," about a man who was struck by lightning… and thereafter was crazy for classical piano music.

CHECK THE LABEL, PART I

*For a musician, getting signed by a big-name label can make
a career. Here are the star-making stories behind some
of America's most influential record companies.*

SUN RECORDS

The Story: In 1952 DJ-turned-record-producer Sam Phillips opened Sun Records at 706 Union Avenue in Memphis. Phillips had been producing local artists since 1949, but producing alone didn't make much money and he could hardly pay his bills. So he decided to cut out the middle man and both produce and distribute the albums himself in an effort to keep more of the profits. Phillips had a reputation for being open to new things and being willing to listen to just about anyone who came into his studio. In particular, he loved black rhythm and blues and wanted to bring that kind of music to white audiences. And so, not surprisingly, Sun's first release (in March 1952) was a song called "Drivin' Slow" by a 16-year-old saxophone player named Johnny London. But it was Elvis Presley—who came into Sun Studios in 1954 to record two songs for his mother's birthday—who proved to be the star Phillips was looking for. The first songs they recorded: "That's When Your Heartaches Begin" and "My Happiness."

A year later, Elvis Presley was on the verge of stardom and Sam Phillips found himself in a quandary: Elvis needed a big record label to back him, and Phillips needed money to expand his own enterprise and attract more talent. So in 1955, Phillips sold Presley's contract to RCA Victor for $35,000, the most anyone had ever paid for a new artist. Presley, of course, became the "King of Rock 'n' Roll," and Sun Records got a reputation as the place where rock (and rockabilly) music was born. Over the next 14 years, Sam Phillips worked with everyone from Johnny Cash to B. B. King. Finally, in 1969, he sold Sun to Mercury, and today, the old studio on Union Avenue is the Sun Studios Museum.

Major Recording Stars: Elvis Presley, Johnny Cash, Carl Perkins, Roy Orbison, Jerry Lee Lewis, B. B. King

CAPITOL RECORDS

The Story: In 1942 singer and songwriter Johnny Mercer teamed up with movie producer Buddy DeSylva and Glen Wallichs, the owner of Music City (the largest record store in Los Angeles at the time), to start Capitol Records in a small office of the Music City building at the corner of Sunset and Vine. Theirs was the first record label based on the West Coast, and their hope was to become a viable competitor for the three largest New York labels: RCA Victor, Columbia, and Decca. By 1946 Capitol had sold more than 40 million albums and had achieved its goal.

The label's first releases were instrumentals by Paul Whiteman, often called the "King of Jazz," and his orchestra, one of the most popular music acts of the 1920s. From there, Capitol went on to sign Bing Crosby, Peggy Lee, Nat King Cole, and others. The label's first million-selling release: Ella Mae Morse's "Cow Cow Boogie" in 1942.

By 1956 Capitol Records had established itself as one of the top four record labels in the United States, and the execs thought a new home was in order. Architect Welton Becket designed the 13-story Capitol Tower to be built on Vine Street near Hollywood Boulevard. The building was the first round office tower, and it resembled a stack of records. Today, it's a Hollywood landmark, and its spire blinks "Hollywood" in Morse code. (And for all you Beatles fans, John Lennon's star on the Walk of Fame is just steps from Capitol's front door.)

Major Recording Stars: Frank Sinatra, The Beatles, the Beach Boys, Pink Floyd, Heart, Shirley Bassey, Judy Garland, Grand Funk Railroad, Radiohead, Duran Duran, Dean Martin, Garth Brooks, Blondie, Jimi Hendrix

RCA RECORDS

The Story: The company known today as RCA Records opened in 1901 as the Victor Talking Machine Company. It made phonographs and phonograph records; among Victor's recording artists were opera singer Enrico Caruso, classical cellist Victor Herbert, and country music stars Jimmie Rodgers and the Carter Family. By 1929, when the Recording Company of America (RCA) bought the company, Victor was the premier phonograph producer in the United States and one of the biggest in the world.

The new company was called RCA Victor, and almost immediately the execs set about changing the way artists were promoted and records were made. Early on, Victor had introduced the "red seal," an ornamental seal added to its classical records in an effort to make them seem special. (Victor's president had actually "borrowed" the idea from an English phonograph company, but RCA Victor made it famous.) RCA continued and expanded the practice, assigning red seals to only the most exclusive clients (like orchestras conducted by the great Arturo Toscanini).

RCA also changed the way records were formatted. Early records were 78 rpm, meaning they revolved 78 times every minute. But 78s broke easily and could play only five minutes of music. In 1948 RCA Victor's rival Columbia introduced a 12-inch, 33-rpm long-playing record that was sturdier and could play for up to 25 minutes without a break. In response, RCA Victor started using 7-inch 45s. These records were smaller than Columbia's but held the same amount of music; they also had less surface noise. And to make the 45s even more attractive, RCA Victor produced them in red, blue, and other vibrant colors. Within a few years, 45s were the most popular record format...thanks primarily to the advent of rock 'n' roll music. Younger audiences liked the small, sleek records, and RCA's sales boomed.

By the late 1960s, 45s were on the way out—12-inch LP (long-playing) records complete with elaborate album covers became popular, and the little 45s and their paper packaging were less attractive. But RCA Victor was still going strong, recording popular artists like John Denver and ZZ Top. Over the years, RCA dropped Victor from its name (though the name still exists as the company's classical music department) and split into several different labels. But all of them continue to produce and record new artists today.

Major Recording Artists: Paul Anka, Harry Belafonte, Dinah Shore, Nina Simone, the Foo Fighters, Kelly Clarkson, Benny Goodman, Lena Horne, Don McLean, Lou Reed, the Strokes

For the histories of more record companies,
turn to page 380.

On waking from a diabetic coma, Jerry Garcia's first words were, "I'm not Beethoven."

WHO WROTE "THE ITSY-BITSY SPIDER"?

...And those other ditties we sang when we were kids?

"**ROCK-A-BYE BABY**"
Originally "Hush-a-Bye Baby," this song came from what was purported to be the oldest poem written by Europeans in (or near) the New World: The Pilgrims wrote it aboard the *Mayflower* in 1620. Or it was written by Wampanoag Indians and translated by Pilgrims. Or it was written by a Pilgrim boy watching Wampanoag Indians put their babies in cradles in trees. Or it was written by a relative of Davy Crockett. Or it was written in England in the 1700s. With all these stories floating around, no one knows for sure where it came from. But it is old, with records of it dating back to at least the 1700s.

"I'VE BEEN WORKING ON THE RAILROAD"
Also of unclear origins, this song may have descended from an African American work song called "Louisiana Levee." Others say it was an adaptation of a hymn sung by Irish Americans, many of whom made up the crews that built the railroads in the American West. It was first published in 1894 under the name "Levee Song" in *Carmina Princetonia*, an annual songbook put out by Princeton University. That version doesn't have the "Someone's in the kitchen..." part, which was added later. "Dinah," who appears in the original and in the later "kitchen" verse, was a slang term referring to any African American woman. "Dinah blow your horn" is believed to be a plea by the workers for "Dinah" to send out the signal that it was lunchtime.

"WABASH CANNONBALL"
In 1853 the Lake Erie, Wabash, and St. Louis Railroad Company was formed to connect railways in Ohio, Indiana, and Illinois. Not long after that, somebody—train-hopping hobos, said George Milburn in *The Hobo's Hornbook*—wrote this song about a fictional train on that route. "Listen to the jingle, the rumble and the roar /

As she glides along the woodland, over hills and by the shore /
Hear the mighty rush of the engine, hear the merry hobos squall /
To rumble through the jungle on the Wabash Cannonball." It was
first published in 1882 as "The Great Rock Island Route" by J. A.
Roff, and the Carter Family had a hit with it in 1929. The version
recorded in 1936 by Roy Acuff and the Smoky Mountain Boys is
on the Rock and Roll Hall of Fame's list of "500 Songs that
Shaped Rock and Roll."

"BUFFALO GALS"

This song was popular long before Jimmy Stewart and Donna
Reed sang it in *It's a Wonderful Life*. It was first published in 1844
under the title "Lubly Fan" (or "Lovely Fan," "Fan" being short
for Fannie). Its author is believed to have been one of the first
blackfaced minstrels, John Hodges, also known as "Cool White,"
though most musicologists believe other versions of the song
existed previously. The names of many towns and states have
been substituted for "Buffalo" over the years—"Roundtown Gals,"
"Johnstown Gals," "Louisiana Gals"—but some believe "Buffalo"
stuck with the song because the western New York town was a
major stopping point for the mid-1800s minstrel circuit. Others
say the song came from Buffalo itself: It was about men working
on the Erie Canal who were calling to the prostitutes—the Buffalo gals—on the city's notorious Canal Street. The melody itself, it
is believed, is of German origin.

"THE ITSY-BITSY SPIDER"

It was probably originally written as "The Incy-Wincy Spider,"
and it's still sung that way by many people—and nobody knows
where it came from. The earliest reference to the song about the
spider who goes "up the waterspout" only to come back down
again, dates back to a 1947 issue of *California Folklore Quarterly*.
It's been a favorite children's song since at least then.

"GO TELL AUNT RHODY"

This song about Aunt Rhody and her old grey goose is believed to
have come from an opera—*Le Devin du Village* ("The Village
Soothsayer"), written in 1752 by Jean-Jacques Rousseau. The song
was published separately as "Rousseau's Dream, an Air with Varia-

tions for the Piano Forte" in 1814 by J. B. Cramer in London. The origin of the English lyrics is unclear, but one account says they were first published in 1944 in the book *Play Songs of the Deep South* by Altona Trent-Johns—featuring "the play songs of Negro children"—under the title "Run, Tell Aunt Nancy." But some experts believe the lyrics are much older.

"HOME ON THE RANGE"

In 1872 an Indiana doctor named Higley Brewster decided to retire and move west to Smith County, Kansas. There he penned a poem titled "Western Home." People liked it so much that they told him he should set it to music, so he gave the lyrics to Dan Kelley, a member of a Kansas band called the Harlan Brothers Orchestra. The song became a local hit and was published in Kansas newspapers in 1873. But it wasn't the song we know today—it didn't have the words "home on the range" in it. The original words were "A home, a home, where the deer and the antelope play..." But as the song made its way west, reportedly sung by cowboys, the words gradually changed. In 1910 musicologist John Lomax printed a version he heard in Texas—"Home, home on the range..."—and that's the way it's been ever since. In 1947 it was made the state song of Kansas, and today it's one of the best-known American songs of all time.

*　　*　　*

TOP 10 HITS OF 1958

1. "Volare (Nel Blu Dipinto Di Blu)"
   —Domenico Modugno
2. "All I Have to Do Is Dream"
   —The Everly Brothers
3. "Don't"　　*—Elvis Presley*
4. "Witch Doctor"
   —David Seville
5. "Patricia"　　*—Perez Prado*
6. "Tequila"　　*—The Champs*
7. "Catch s Falling Star"
   —Perry Como
8. "Sail Along Silvery Moon"
   —Billy Vaughn
9. "It's All in the Game"
   —Tommy Edwards
10. "Return to Me"
    —Dean Martin

SECRETS OF THE STRADIVARIUS

The violins made by Antonio Stradivari are considered by many to be the most perfect instruments ever made. Here's the story of these mysterious instruments and the man behind them.

MUSIC MAN

Antonio Stradivari was born in Cremona, Italy, in 1644. As a young man he came under the tutelage of a famous violin maker named Nicolo Amati. He proved a gifted student and, before his training was even completed, began putting his own labels on the violins he made, using the Latin form of his name, *Stradivarius*. He was about 22 years old.

Amati himself was a member of one of the most famous violin-making families in Italy. Of all the members of the Amati family, Nicolo was considered the most gifted craftsman—and yet even *his* violins couldn't compare to those of his pupil Stradivari.

As early as 1684, Stradivari began to experiment with the details of violin making in search of better sound. He found it, of course, and in the process gave the violin its modern form—shallower in construction, less arched in the belly and back, with an improved bridge and a new varnish, deeper and darker than the yellower varnish Amati had used.

In the 19th century, a few more changes were made to the design of violins so that they could be heard more easily in large auditoriums. But for the most part, all modern violins follow the style established by Stradivari more than 300 years ago...only they don't sound nearly as good as the original. When Stradivari died in 1737, he took many of his secrets to the grave with him.

Or did he?

SOLVING THE MYSTERY

It's estimated that Stradivari made more than 1,100 instruments in his lifetime; more than 450 of his violins survive to this day, as do numerous violas, cellos, guitars, and even a few harps. Many of his tools survive too, as do many of the patterns and molds that he

---

Martina McBride once worked as a T-shirt vendor at Garth Brooks concerts.

used to fashion his instruments. But without his expert skills and knowledge, they're useless—even when experienced craftspeople use his original equipment. No one, Stradivari's admirers claim, has been able to make a violin as good as an original Stradivarius.

Stradivari has been dead for more than 250 years now, and people are still arguing over what it is that makes his musical instruments sound so beautiful. People have studied Stradivarius violin slivers under electron microscopes and taken violins to the hospital to have them CAT scanned. Some people have even taken these priceless instruments apart to precisely measure every piece and tiny detail of their construction, hoping to learn their secrets.

"You have to put in a thin blunt knife and ease it around to separate the pieces, breaking the glue," explains Sandra Wagstaff, who cracked open her $2.2 million Stradivarius violin in 2001. "You hear, 'Click, click, click,' and if it goes quiet, you stop. *Immediately*, because that means you're cutting into the wood."

What do we have to show for more than two and a half centuries of such efforts? Not much. Music experts still can't agree on anything—what the secret is, whether there really *is* a secret, and if there is, whether Stradivarius even *knew* what it was.

Theory #1: It's in the man. Like Picasso paintings, Stradivarius violins get their beautiful sound from his unique—and irreproducible—techniques. "The real secret," says violin dealer Robert Bein, "is that Stradivari was an artist, and those instruments are imbued with that X-factor that we recognize as art. So the secret died with him."

Theory #2: It's in the varnish. Stradivari apparently used three layers of varnish: the first coat consisted of silica and potash, which was allowed to soak into the bare wood to give it strength; the second coat probably consisted of egg whites and honey or sugar; and the third coat was a mixture of gum arabic, turpentine, and a resin known as Venetian red. But—at least according to this school of thought—the details of Stradivari's varnish recipes may remain a mystery forever.

Theory #3: It's in our heads. "If the audience sees you've got a Strad, you must be good because only good players have Strads," explains Dr. Bernard Richardson, a musical acoustics specialist at the University of Cardiff in Wales. "There was no secret. We know the tools he used, the techniques he used, and the wood he used, so there's no reason people should not make exactly the same instruments."

Gregg Alf, a Michigan violin maker, agrees. "There's a lot of mumbo-jumbo about the Stradivarius mystique," he says. Alf and his partner, Joseph Curtin, took apart a famous Stradivarius known as the Booth Stradivarius, measured it carefully, and built a precise replica—even down to the scratches—that, like the original, has a beautiful sound. Just *how* beautiful is open to interpretation, but it later sold at Sotheby's for $33,000, the highest price ever paid for a violin made by someone who isn't dead yet. Alf argues that, with practice, he'll be able to make replicas as good as or even better than the originals, especially considering that the originals have been aging and deteriorating for more than 250 years.

Theory #4: It's in the bugs. According to this theory, Stradivari didn't have any secrets at all—tiny microbes in the wood he used are what give his violins their wonderful sound. In Stradivari's day, when trees were cut down, the logs were thrown into the river and floated downstream to Venice, where they might soak in a lagoon for two or three years before they were finally sold. In this time the wood became waterlogged, allowing for rich growth of bacteria and fungus. These lifeforms ate away much of the pectin in the sap and also the *hemicellulose*, the organic material that holds moisture in wood.

With the hemicellulose gone, the wood became lighter, drier, and 50 times more permeable to varnish than ordinary wood. Stradivari's varnish contained 20 or more different minerals that caused it to dry with a hard, gemlike finish that gave the wood excellent sound characteristics, unlike the gummy, oil-based varnishes that are popular today.

"This combination of highly permeable wood and a very hard composite varnish, which happened to be used by all craftsmen of the period, even on furniture, is what accounts for these remarkable acoustic properties," theorizes Dr. Joseph Nagyvary, a biochemist at Texas A&M University. "Stradivari was a marvelous craftsman, but the magnificent sound of his instruments was a lucky accident."

"Do you know why they haven't made any good violins in Italy for a hundred years?" Nagyvary asked in 1986. "In the 1840s, they dammed up the rivers."

Theory #5: The worms helped, too. In 2001 Dr. Nagyvary

revised his theories to give some credit for Stradivari's success to woodworms. Actually, the lack of them: Stradivari happened to be in business at a time when the region of Cremona was suffering through a woodworm epidemic. So Stradivari treated his wood with borax, a preservative, to keep the worms out. The borax also bound the molecules of the wood more tightly together, so in using this treatment, Stradivari unknowingly improved the wood's acoustic properties.

The epidemic passed at about the same time that Stradivari died, Nagyvary says, so subsequent violin makers from Cremona stopped treating their wood. When the sound quality of their instruments declined, they mistakenly assumed that Stradivari's "secrets" must have died with him...or so the theory goes.

LUCKY FIND?

If you ever happen to see an old violin at a flea market or a garage sale and notice that the label reads "Stradivarius," go ahead and buy it if you want. But don't pay a lot of money for it and don't get your hopes up—it's probably a fake.

As we said earlier, Stradivari was largely responsible for establishing the standard design for modern violins. Later violin makers followed his standard...and communicated as much by labeling their violins "Stradivarius" too. This was not intended to defraud, it was just a maker's way of stating that the violin's design was inspired by Stradivari and not by Amati or some other master craftsman. Over time, the true intent of these labels was forgotten...and as a result, hundreds if not thousands of unintentionally "fake" Stradivarius violins are still in circulation.

Even the experts have been fooled: In 1999 the Ashmolean Museum in Oxford, England, had to admit that it "might" have a fake in its collection after a violin nicknamed "the Messiah," previously described as "a flawless Stradivarius jewel," was found to be made from a spruce chopped down after Stradivari's death.

*   *   *

"I inherited a painting and a violin which turned out to be a Rembrandt and a Stradivarius. Unfortunately, Rembrandt made lousy violins and Stradivari was a terrible painter."

—Tommy Cooper, comedian

KEITH URBAN LEGENDS

And other fake stories about famous people.

THE LEGEND: Keith Richards once had his blood replaced with "clean" blood at a Swiss clinic to beat an addiction to heroin.

THE TRUTH: Richards has admitted to heroin addiction and has made several attempts to break it over the years. In 1973, some accounts say, he did receive some sort of dialysis-type treatment to "filter" his blood, but the idea of getting a "blood change" to treat an addiction isn't medically possible.

HOW IT SPREAD: Richards says he started the rumor himself: "Someone asked me how I cleaned up, so I told them I went to Switzerland and had my blood completely changed. I was just fooling around. I opened my jacket and said, 'How do you like my blood change?' That's all it was, a joke. I was *@%$ing sick of answering that question. So I gave them a story." Also, in his 2003 book *I Was Keith Richards' Drug Dealer*, onetime Richards friend (and drug dealer, by his account) Tony Sanchez also claims that Richards had his blood "changed."

LEGEND: When singer Mariah Carey was asked about the death of King Hussein of Jordan in February 1999, she confused him with basketball player Michael Jordan. "I'm inconsolable at the present time," she told CNN. "I was a very good friend of Jordan. He was probably the greatest basketball player this country has ever seen. We will never see his like again."

THE TRUTH: It never happened.

HOW IT SPREAD: The story appeared on an Internet chat site, falsely attributed to *USA Today* and CNN, and it spread from there.

LEGEND: John Denver was an Army sniper in Vietnam.

THE TRUTH: Denver never served in the Army or any other branch of the military. He was inducted in 1964, but he was classified 1-Y—not qualified for service—because he was missing two toes due to a lawnmower accident when he was a boy.

New York City's Metropolitan Opera seats 4,065 people. (Ohio State's stadium holds 101,000.)

HOW IT SPREAD: Nobody knows exactly who started this one, but it began in the early 1970s. Similar stories have been spread about another "nice guy," Fred Rogers of *Mr. Rogers' Neighborhood.* He wasn't a sniper, either.

LEGEND: Frank Zappa, in a "gross-out" competition, once ate a spoonful of feces onstage. Sometimes the claim is that he merely defecated onstage.

THE TRUTH: From *The Real Frank Zappa:* "For the record, folks: I never took a @#*% on stage, and the closest I ever came to eating @#*% anywhere was at a Holiday Inn buffet in Fayetteville, North Carolina, in 1973."

HOW IT SPREAD: "This legend originated in the mid-1960s," according to urban-legend investigators Snopes.com, "no doubt inspired by the eccentricities of Frank Zappa's music and appearance." In a 1993 interview in *Playboy,* Zappa called it "somebody's imagination run wild. Chemically bonded imagination."

LEGEND: Country-music singer Keith Urban, at a concert in North Dakota in July 2006, made all the Canadians in the audience leave—because their government hadn't supported the United States in the war in Iraq.

THE TRUTH: Urban played at the North Dakota State Fair in Minot on July 21, 2006, but no credible reports have ever been found of him having asked any Canadians to leave. And several Canadians who were at the concert wrote to various Internet sites, saying that they hadn't been thrown out of the show.

HOW IT SPREAD: Via fake e-mails that made the rounds of the Internet sometime in late 2006. Here's a sample: "What an ass!!! No more Keith Urban for me!!! (or Garth Brooks) This big-shot western singer asked all Canadians to stand up at the Minot Fair. After everyone stood up, he asked them all to leave the stands because they were not helping out fighting with USA troops… Pass this around and see how his record sales do in Canada!"

LEGEND: U2 frontman Bono, while performing a show in Glasgow, Scotland, asked the crowd for a moment of silence. Then he slowly clapped his hands for a few moments and said, "Every time I clap my hands, a child in Africa dies." An audience member then yelled out in a thick Scottish brogue, "Well, stop *@#!ing doing it, then!"

THE TRUTH: It was actually British comedian Jimmy Carr who said the famous line…in his comedy act. Carr was making fun of Bono and other celebrities who appeared in a 2005 charity commercial in which they said a child died from extreme poverty every three seconds—every time they snapped their fingers. Carr quipped, "I watched that, and couldn't help thinking, 'Well, stop clicking your fingers!'"

HOW IT SPREAD: Via hoax e-mails in 2006 regarding the concert in Glasgow—or New York, or London, or various other places. Even some newspapers fell for it and reprinted the stories, including Australia's *Sunday Mail.*

* * *

ORIGIN OF A SONG

In the mid-1970s, Amanda McBroom was an unknown songwriter living in Los Angeles. While driving down the freeway one afternoon, she heard a song called "Magdalena," by Leo Sayer. One line caught her attention: "Your love is like a razor / My heart is just a scar." Initially, McBroom loved the lyric, but moments later, she realized she didn't agree with the sentiment…and that got her thinking: What is love, anyway? As she continued toward home, some lyrics came to mind, and she had to repeat them to herself over and over so she wouldn't forget them before she could write them down. When she arrived at home, she raced to her piano and within minutes, she'd written a song. She titled it "The Rose." A year later, she offered it to a producer making a movie of the same name. The film's execs didn't like the song, though; they thought the gentle melody just wasn't rock 'n' roll enough for the project, so they rejected it. But the movie's star, Bette Midler, loved McBroom's ballad and insisted that the producers use it in the film. When the movie was released in 1979, it and its title song were huge hits, and in 1980, both were nominated for Golden Globe Awards. The film lost, but McBroom's song took home a statue. (So did Bette Midler, for Best Actress.)

MUSIC LESSONS 2: THE BIZ

You've practiced a lot and have finally made it big. Way to go!
Now you have a whole new set of skills to learn.

"Map out your future, but do it in pencil."

—John Bon Jovi

"Learn to play two chords, and then get yourself a lawyer before learning the third."

—Tony Iommi, of Black Sabbath

"The days of the half-stoned pop star with long black hair, staggering down the corridor clutching a bottle of Jack Daniels and thinking he's Keith Richards, are over. It's not that I sit in an office with a fax machine, but I do keep an eye on what's going on."

—Noel Gallagher, of Oasis

"Don't object so much. You'll live longer."

—Mike Nesmith, of the Monkees

"The music business is a cruel and shallow money trench, a long plastic hallway where thieves and pimps run free, and good men die like dogs. There's also a negative side."

—Hunter S. Thompson

"Never hate a song that's sold a half million copies."

—Irving Berlin

"The amount of money one needs is terrifying."

—Ludwig Van Beethoven

"You're a local band until you get a record contract, and then all of a sudden Bruce Springsteen is your competition."

—Sammy Llana, of the BoDeans

"Only become a musician if there is absolutely no other way you can make a living."

—Kirke Mechem, American composer

"The more you get, the more you get."

—Tom Petty

"If you don't go for as much money as you can possibly get, then I think you're stupid."

—Mick Jagger

"If you're gonna sell out, make sure they're buying."

—Martha Davis, of the Motels

Most popular first dance song at U.S. wedding receptions: "Unforgettable" by Nat King Cole.

THE UNLUCKY 27 CLUB

Coincidence or not, many of rock's most innovative performers died...at the age of 27.

JIM MORRISON

The Doors signed their first record label contract in August, 1966. In less than five years, they were international rock 'n' roll superstars—and they were finished. Morrison, their enigmatic lead writer and singer, was dead. After the recording of their last album, *L.A. Women*, in March 1971, Morrison got an apartment in Paris. There he reportedly carried on with his history of alcohol and substance abuse, and died in July. The official death report filed by the French police lists heart failure as the cause of death, but others offer a different story. Some of Morrison's friends (in particular, Sam Bennett, who wrote a 2007 book on the subject) have claimed that the singer actually died of a heroin overdose in the bathroom of a Left Bank nightclub. To avoid bringing negative publicity to the popular club, Morrison's girlfriend, Pamela Courson, and others carried him home and placed him in the bathtub in an effort to clean him up. Courson's involvement, though, remains unclear, and she took her secrets to the grave: she herself died of a heroin overdose three years later. **Morrison's age at time of death: 27.**

KURT COBAIN

Cobain's story is even shorter. His band, Nirvana, was one of the early breakouts of the grunge rock scene. Their second and hugely influential album, *Nevermind*, was released in 1991, and as it soared in popularity (eventually knocking Michael Jackson's *Dangerous* out of the top *Billboard* spot), grunge went mainstream. The sudden stardom was difficult for Cobain, and like so many before him, he found refuge in alcohol and drugs. On April 5, 1994, he was found dead of a self-inflicted shotgun wound to his head at his home near Seattle. (Conspiracy theories persist that Cobain's wife, Courtney Love, played a role in his death. But that's another story.) **Cobain's age at time of death: 27.**

JANIS JOPLIN

Joplin, too, struggled with drug and alcohol addictions for years, but by 1970 seemed to be turning her life around. In late September she was in Hollywood putting the finishing touches on what became her final album, titled after her nickname, *Pearl*. She'd kicked her heroin habit by this time (or so she thought) but continued to drink heavily. When she got into a fight with her boyfriend on the night of October 3—he stood her up to play strip poker with another woman—she sought comfort in heroin. When Joplin didn't show up at the recording studio the next day, her bandmates called the police, who found her body in her hotel room. The official cause of death was heroin overdose. Tragically, she missed the success of the album *Pearl*, the biggest-selling of her career, with songs like "Mercedes Benz," and her chart-topping "Me and Bobby McGee," both of which became rock 'n' roll classics. **Joplin's age at time of death: 27.**

JIMI HENDRIX

The songs "Purple Haze," "Manic Depression," "Hey Joe," "The Wind Cries Mary," "(Let Me Stand Next to Your) Fire", "Are You Experienced?," "Foxey Lady," and "Red House" are among the most famous in the history of rock 'n' roll. Hendrix released them all on one album, *Are You Experienced*, in 1967. It was also his *first* album. Three years and just two albums later he was gone. On September 18, 1970, his girlfriend, Monika Dannemann, found him unconscious in bed and noticed traces of vomit around his nose and empty packets of sleeping pills on the floor. Instead of calling for an ambulance, though, she phoned Eric Burdon, a friend and the lead singer of the Animals. Together, they cleared the apartment of drugs and then finally summoned help. At first, it seemed like Hendrix might survive the overdose. The ambulance technicians assured Dannemann that he was breathing and would be fine. But on the way to the hospital, he started choking and was pronounced dead on arrival. An autopsy revealed sleeping pills, barbiturates, and amphetamines in his system. Rumors of foul play persisted in the months after Hendrix died, and Scotland Yard investigated. But they found no new evidence and eventually dropped the case. **Hendrix's age at time of death: 27.**

Jimi Hendrix's only #1 hit: "All Along the Watchtower" (1968).

THAT'S NOT ALL

• Brian Jones, guitar player and founding member of the Rolling Stones. Cause of death: drowning, related to drug and alcohol abuse, 1969. **Jones's age at time of death:** 27.

• Alan Wilson, lead singer and founding member of Canned Heat ("On the Road Again" and "Going Up the Country") Cause of death: barbiturate overdose, 1970. **Wilson's age at time of death:** 27.

• Gary Thain, bassist for Uriah Heep ("Easy Livin'," "Sweet Lorraine"). Cause of death: heroin overdose, 1975. **Thain's age at time of death:** 27.

• Ron "Pigpen" McKernan, keyboardist and founding member of the Grateful Dead. Cause of death: gastrointestinal hemorrhage, related to alcoholism, 1973. **McKernan's age at time of death:** 27.

• Pete Ham, singer and guitarist for Badfinger ("Come and Get It," "No Matter What"). Cause of death: suicide by hanging, 1975. **Ham's age at time of death:** 27.

*   *   *

26 MUSICIANS WHO HAVE APPEARED ON U.S. POSTAGE STAMPS

Roy Acuff	Howlin' Wolf
Leonard Bernstein	Scott Joplin
Eubie Blake	Lead Belly
Hoagie Carmichael	Glenn Miller
Patsy Cline	Charles Mingus
Nat "King" Cole	Thelonius Monk
John Coltrane	Jelly Roll Morton
Tommy Dorsey	Charlie Parker
Duke Ellington	Jimmie Rodgers
Benny Goodman	Ritchie Valens
Woody Guthrie	Muddy Waters
Bill Haley	Hank Williams
Buddy Holly	Bob Wills

On their 1976 *Worldwide Texas* tour, ZZ Top's stage props included live longhorn cattle.

QUIZ: WOMEN WHO ROCK

Careful—the questions get harder as you go. (Answers are on page 512.)

1. Her video for "Love Is a Battlefield" was the first to include dialogue as well as the musical performance.

2. She worked at the Playboy Club before her band had its first U.S. hit with "Heart of Glass."

3. Before this new-wave frontwoman formed her wildly successful band in 1978, she attended Ohio's Kent State University—and was on campus during the 1970 Kent State shootings.

4. *Rolling Stone* magazine featured only two women on its 2003 list of the 100 greatest guitarists of all time. This 1980s rocker was one of them. (Joni Mitchell was the other.)

5. Publications from *Rolling Stone* to the *Village Voice* heralded her band's sophomore album—1994's *Live Through This*—as a musical masterpiece. *Time* even called it one of the top 100 albums of all time.

6. Born in Scotland and the daughter of a big band singer, this rock star studied piano at the City of Edinburgh Music School before joining her first band at the age of 16...and that's no "garbage."

7. This gravelly voiced rocker was a member of her high-school glee club before hitting it big in the 1960s. She was inducted into the Rock and Roll Hall of Fame in 1995.

8. She's been called "punk's poet laureate" and is one of America's most influential singer-songwriters, yet she's had only three Top 20 singles in her career—"Because the Night," written with Bruce Springsteen, is the best known.

9. This influential punk and new wave groundbreaker changed her name in the 1970s because, she says, people would "stare at my surname and could not pronounce it." She picked her new name as an homage to a Native American tribe because she "hated cowboys."

10. This San Francisco rocker went to the same college as first daughter Tricia Nixon, and has been called the "Queen of the Summer of Love." But she retired from music in the late 1980s and today works as a painter.

Black Oak Arkansas' first album (1971) came with a deed to one square inch of land in Arkansas.

HOT FUN IN THE SUMMERTIME

Woodstock may have laid the foundation, but in the 1990s, three new music festivals retooled sweaty summer rock 'n' roll for a new generation.

LOLLAPALOOZA

Back in 1991, Perry Farrell—lead singer for Jane's Addiction —was frustrated that mainstream radio and media largely ignored America's independent rock scene. So he decided to organize a rock festival that would showcase both successful and unknown independent talent. Farrell chose the name *Lollapalooza* after hearing the word in a Three Stooges film, and gave the festival another unique twist: it would tour. Woodstock and other festivals were held in fixed locations; people had to travel to them. But Lollapalooza traveled to 21 different cities around the United States and played to more than 600,000 fans.

Lollapalooza also included nonmusical acts, including a troupe of martial artists and a circus sideshow that sometimes played the main stage. There were tents displaying art pieces, virtual-reality games, information tables for political and environmental activists, television-smashing pits, jungle gyms, and tattoo and piercing parlors. Farrell continued the annual festival until 1996, when he sold the rights to the William Morris Agency.

Original lineup: Jane's Addiction, Ice-T, Nine Inch Nails, Living Colour, Siouxsie and the Banshees, Rollins Band, Body Count, Butthole Surfers, Violent Femmes

LILITH FAIR

Before 1996, the thinking in the music industry was that female artists didn't have enough fans to sell out big rock shows; the bill needed to be "balanced" with better-known male performers. To prove the concert promoters wrong, singer Sarah McLachlan booked a tour with Paula Cole. After the success of that tour, McLachlan decided to front her own all-female summer music festival. She called it Lilith Fair, after the first wife of Adam who left the Garden of Eden to explore the world. Despite industry skepti-

Frank Sinatra, Bill Haley, and the Monkees all had songs covered by the Sex Pistols.

cism, the festival sold out in 1997, earning more than $16 million and becoming the year's best-selling tour.

The festival lasted only three years, but it had a huge impact. Lilith Fair was instrumental in launching careers—Jewel, the Dixie Chicks, and Nelly Furtado all played there—and in introducing audiences to new musical genres. Said Queen Latifah: "I wanted to do this because I was excited about playing to a different audience than I might normally play to at a hip-hop show." McLachlan always insisted that the Lilith Fair was more about music than politics. She said, "We're just here to put on a great musical show and I think any social or political issues are secondary, although very important, because it is a music festival first and foremost."

Original lineup: Sarah McLachlan, Emmylou Harris, Sheryl Crow, Indigo Girls, Patty Griffin, Lisa Loeb, Jewel, Meredith Brooks, Shawn Colvin, Paula Cole, Fiona Apple, Suzanne Vega, Dar Williams, Juliana Hatfield, Susanna Hoffs, Leah Andreone

OZZFEST

This festival—organized by Sharon, Ozzy, and Jack Osbourne—came about because Lollapalooza organizer Perry Farrell wouldn't let Ozzy play on that bill in 1995. (Farrell said Ozzy wouldn't be a big enough draw.) So in 1996 the Osbournes decided to start their own festival and devote it to heavy metal. Ozzfest debuted with 13 bands playing two sold-out shows in Los Angeles and Phoenix. Over the years, more bands signed on, and the show began to tour, even heading to Europe in 1998, 2001, and 2002. Ozzfest also became a place that nurtured new talent: Linkin Park, System of a Down, Incubus, and many others gained national exposure on the festival's stages.

Ozzfest continued to be popular into the new millennium, and in 2007 Sharon Osbourne announced that the festival would be free that summer. She was concerned that high ticket prices (in some cases, more than $200 each) made rock shows inaccessible to young fans. Despite many in the music industry saying it couldn't be done, Sharon and Ozzy managed to put the show on for free: they got media sponsors and gave away tickets (more than 420,000) on the Internet.

Original lineup: Ozzy Osbourne, Slayer, Fear Factory, Danzig, Biohazard, Sepultura, Prong, Neurosis

CARTOON COMPOSERS

Ever wonder who you're listening to when you watch your favorite cartoon characters pummel each other into elastic oblivion?

CARL STALLING

A discussion of cartoon music without Carl Stalling would be like a discussion of classical music without Mozart. Stalling was there right at the beginning, scoring the first Mickey Mouse cartoon ever made, *Plane Crazy*, and helped create the "click track"—a metronomic timer that allowed musicians to sync up the music they were composing to the action going on in the cartoon.

Born in 1891 and raised in Missouri, by the time Stalling was 12, he was playing the piano for his local silent movie house. In 1928 he was working a similar gig in Kansas City when his talents came to the attention of Walt Disney, who was making his cartoons there. Stalling worked directly with Disney for two years, scoring the first "Silly Symphonies," Disney cartoons that relied on music and animation, rather than dialogue, to tell the story.

But Stalling's best-known work started in 1936 when he joined the Warner Bros. Studio as in-house composer for its animated films. There, Stalling had something he didn't have before: access to an immense library of songs and scores from the Warner Bros. library. He went nuts with it, incorporating fragments of popular tunes into his own compositions to highlight entrances or events on-screen. The most famous example of this was Stalling's regular use of Raymond Scott's "Powerhouse" theme, a jazzy assembly-line tune that he used to punctuate scenes of construction or mechanical mayhem; it showed up in 40 separate Warner Bros. cartoons.

From *Porky's Poultry Plant* in 1936 through *To Itch His Own* in 1958, Stalling composed scores for over 600 Warner Bros. cartoon shorts, creating many of them in less than a week. Stalling retired in 1958, and died in 1972. His music continued to be used well after his death: his most recent composer credit was in 2004.

SCOTT BRADLEY

Stalling's counterpart at Metro-Goldwyn-Mayer was Scott Bradley, who created the music for the scenes in which Tom and Jerry tried

A "Motown" is a poker term for two jacks and two fives—jacks on fives. (Get it? Jackson Fives!)

to bash each other's brains out. Despite the mayhem on screen, Bradley's work is generally considered to be some of the more complex and difficult in animation, which befits his background. The Arkansas-born musician was trained at a conservatory and studied under avant-garde composer Arnold Schoenberg.

Bradley got his start in animation in 1931 when he worked with famed Disney animator Ub Iwerks. A few years later, Bradley worked with producers Hugh Harman and Rudolf Ising, who were producing cartoons for the MGM studio. When MGM decided to produce its cartoons in-house in 1937, Bradley came along, and like Stalling, he took advantage of his corporate parent's music catalog to nick useful bits from pop songs and other scores. Over time, though, he did more original work on scores, including incorporating Schoenberg's atonal avant-garde techniques. MGM closed down its animation shop in 1957; when it did, Bradley retired. He passed away in 1977.

THE SHERMAN BROTHERS

They are Robert B. and Richard M., and they're responsible for some of the most memorable Disney songs, including the unforgettable "It's a Small World."

The Sherman brothers came from a musical family. Their father Al Sherman was a songwriter in his own right, and one of the favorite Sherman family stories tells how the cost of Robert Sherman's birth in 1925 was paid for by the timely arrival of a royalty check for one of Al's songs. In the early 1950s, Al challenged his sons to start writing music together, and by 1958, the Sherman brothers had produced their first Top 10 song, "Tall Paul," for America's favorite Mouseketeer, Annette Funicello. This brought them to the attention of Walt Disney, who hired the brothers as his company's in-house composers.

The Shermans composed songs for a number of classic Disney animated movies, including *The Sword and the Stone*, *The Jungle Book* and *The Aristocats*, as well as for the company's live-action films. One of these films, *Mary Poppins*, brought the brothers a pair of Academy Awards, for original song ("Chim Chim Cher-ee") and for Best Score. The brothers would be nominated for Academy Awards seven more times. After Walt Disney died in 1966, the Sherman brothers worked on other animated films outside the

Disney camp, most notably the 1973 animated version of *Char-lotte's Web*, but they still occasionally work for Disney (in 2000 they provided new songs for *The Tigger Movie*).

BOB DOROUGH

An entire generation of Americans learned math, history, and sci-ence from Bob Dorough without ever knowing who he was. So who was he? He wrote and sang many of the songs featured in *Schoolhouse Rock!*, the series of educational shorts that ran on ABC from 1973 through 1986, with occasional revivals afterward.

Prior to the *Schoolhouse Rock!* phenomenon, Dorough had a career as a jazz pianist, composer, and lyricist. Among the people he worked with: Lenny Bruce, Mel Tormé, and Miles Davis (who featured Dorough as a vocalist on his 1967 *Sorcerer* album).

But it was *Schoolhouse Rock!* that brought Dorough the most success. The gig came about when advertising exec David McCall noticed that his son could remember rock lyrics but not his multi-plication tables. So he hired Dorough to whip up a song about math, which became "Three Is a Magic Number." Later, anima-tion was added and McCall pitched the idea of the shorts to ABC children's programming exec Michael Eisner (who later became CEO of Disney). Eisner bought the concept, and kids across America started learning math to Dorough's ditties.

Although Dorough was the primary songwriter for *Schoolhouse Rock!*, Lynn Ahrens, a Tony-winning composer (for *Ragtime*), also deserves mention; she penned some of the most famous history and science songs in the series, including "Interplanet Janet" and "The Preamble." If you can sing the preamble to the U.S. Consti-tution, thank Ahrens.

*   *   *

POLITICALLY CORRECT

In 1964 Dusty Springfield played two concerts in Johannesburg, South Africa. They were both before mixed-race audiences—as her contract demanded. The government of South Africa approached Springfield and told her she had to play for white-only audiences. She refused. And she was deported.

THE HISTORY OF OPERA IN THREE PAGES

Here are some of the notable firsts in opera. Because opera spans more than 400 years, hundreds of composers and librettists, and thousands of operas, we limited it to the historic highlights.

- **1597:** *Dafne*, by Jacopo Peri, becomes the first opera. It's based on a Greek tragedy but is written in Italian. Today, the prologue and a single aria (a solo vocal piece) are all that remain of it.

- **1600:** *Euridice*, also by Peri, is performed. It is the earliest opera whose complete score survives today.

- **1607:** *L'Orfeo*, a "play in music," becomes the world's first opera that continues to be performed regularly today. Composer Claudio Monteverdi wrote it for the court of Mantua, Italy. Its music and story are balanced, which forms the foundation of modern opera.

- **1637:** Opera goes commerical. The Teatro San Cassiano, the first public theater (tickets are sold), opens in Venice.

- **1630s:** The rest of Europe is astonished at the success of Venetian opera. The genre quickly becomes a fad, as almost all of the cultures try to absorb it and make it their own, but find it more difficult than it seems. The Germans are the first to try, but they change the language (to German, of course) and ultimately fail because even German audiences are used to hearing opera in Italian. The French run into a similar problem when they bring in Italian composers to teach opera writing (in French) to their own composers. The Spanish effort to mimic Italian opera (called the *zarzuela*) is somewhat successful—but only when it doesn't stray too far from the Italian style. The Russians take the easiest approach: They simply import operas straight from Italy, in Italian. As for the English, opera is altogether too ridiculous for their tastes, until...

- **1670:** Another type of opera takes shape in England. Shakespeare's plays (and some other theatrical works) are set to music.

Then in 1689, British composer Henry Purcell's *Dido and Aeneas* is performed for a girls' school in London. The opera is widely regarded as the first official English opera.

- **1778:** The Teatro alla Scala, or La Scala, is founded in Milan, Italy. It is still one of the most famous opera houses in the world.

- **1781:** Twenty-five-year-old Wolfgang Amadeus Mozart enters the operatic scene with *Idomeneo,* which many critics consider the greatest *opera seria,* or serious opera, ever written.

- **1786:** Mozart lifts opera to new heights with *The Marriage of Figaro.* Up to this point, *arias* (solo pieces, often with haunting melodies) and *recitatives* (the singing-to-move-the-story-along part between the arias) are neatly divided. But Mozart blended the two together, and his recitatives become an integral part of the opera. Of course, he can't please everyone; the Austrian emperor complains that Mozart's operas have "too many notes."

- **1805:** Beethoven enters the arena with *Fidelio.* The unsuccessful opera proves to be the only one he ever composes.

- **1859:** The French Opera House in New Orleans opens and establishes the city as the "Opera Capital of North America."

- **1873:** Organized by African Americans, the Colored American Opera Company (the first opera company in Washington, D.C.) opens with a production of *The Doctor of Alcantara,* by German composer Julius Eichberg.

- **1874:** The precursor to modern musicals, the operetta *Die Fledermaus* by Johann Strauss, premieres in Vienna.

- **1876:** The world's longest opera, a 16-hour sequence (divided into four parts), Richard Wagner's *The Ring of the Nibelungen,* premieres at the Bayreuth Festival in Germany.

- **1883:** The Metropolitan Opera in New York opens with Gounod's *Faust.*

- **1905:** Louis Adolphe Coerne's opera *Zenobia* is the first American opera to be performed in Europe.

Jimi Hendrix plays a comb and wax paper "kazoo" on the 1968 recording of "Crosstown Traffic."

• **1929:** Opera is broadcast over the radio for the first time. Which opera? Puccini's *Madame Butterfly*.

• **1925:** The world's first *atonal* (music that abandons traditional harmonies, ignores major and minor scales, and has no sense of key) operatic masterpiece, Alban Berg's *Wozzeck*, shocks audiences and critics with its eclectic score and graphic storyline about the exploitation of the poor.

• **1934:** Virgil Thomson's *Four Saints in Three Acts* (with a libretto by poet Gertrude Stein) finally legitimizes American composers as true operatic contributors on the world's stage.

• **1940:** Opera is televised for the first time when the New York Metropolitan Opera performs select scenes from *Pagliacci*, *Carmen*, and other works on NBC. The show is broadcast to about 2,000 households in the United States—the extent of the NBC network at the time. Three years later, the first complete opera, *Hansel and Gretel* by German composer Engelbert Humperdinck, is telecast.

• **1955:** Marian Anderson becomes the first African American member of the Metropolitan Opera Company.

• **1976:** Philip Glass's first opera, *Einstein on the Beach*, premieres and is praised as "one of the seminal artworks of the century." Glass has become one of the most influential and prolific modern opera composers, with 22 to his credit (so far).

• **2004:** Luciano Pavarotti, called the "King of the High Cs," gives his final operatic performance in *Tosca* at the Met in New York on March 13. (Pavarotti died of pancreatic cancer in September 2007.)

*   *   *

ENUFF ALREADY

You might remember Enuff Z'Nuff—an American "hair metal" band who enjoyed some success in the 1980s alongside groups like Skid Row, Poison, and Whitesnake. Today, they're one of the most popular bands in Hungary.

Music to our rears! The iCarta, a combination iPod and toilet paper holder (it costs about $99).

CHAMPAGNE MUSIC

In the 1950s, when rock 'n' roll began to monopolize the charts, Lawrence Welk waltzed into America's living rooms…and remained the premier proponent of politeness and polka for the next 30 years.

ACCORDION BOY

Around 1918, while he was still a teenager, Lawrence Welk made a deal with his father: If the elder Welk would buy him an accordion, Lawrence would stay on the family farm until he was 21. His father took the offer, and young Welk remained in the rural, German-speaking community of Strasburg, North Dakota until March 11, 1924—the day he turned 21—and off he went to become a musician.

Within three years Welk had his own band, the Novelty Orchestra (later renamed the Hotsy Totsy Boys and, still later, the Honolulu Fruit Gum Orchestra). They played in ballrooms, hotels, and on radio stations across the Midwest. In 1938, according to a legend perpetuated by Welk, a radio listener gushed that the band's music was "effervescent, like champagne." From then on, his group was known as The Champagne Music of Lawrence Welk.

Continued success took the band across the country and eventually to Southern California, where a 1951 late-night appearance on a Los Angeles TV show caused a flood of calls to the station. Welk got his own local show out of it, *The Dodge Dancing Party*, which ran for four years until 1955, when ABC started airing it nationally on Saturday nights as *The Lawrence Welk Show*.

BUBBLING OVER WITH ENTHUSIASM

The show was comfortably predictable: A musical number from the band (with featured solos) began the show, followed by vocal performances by the "Champagne Lady" (a featured vocalist, such as Alice Lon or, later, Norma Zimmer), dance numbers (in later years, by former Mouseketeer Bobby Burgess), and for the first 13 years, a performance by the "lovely" Lennon Sisters. At the end of the show, Welk would invite women from the audience to dance with him to the closing theme, "Bubbles in the Wine" (later "Champagne Fanfare"). Every show had a theme, such as Easter,

Fourth of July, "Battling Accordions," "Songs With 'Baby' in the Title," The Gay '90s, or a certain Broadway musical, like *The Music Man*. The songs were light and familiar—a mixture of waltzes, polkas, ballads, standards, novelty songs, and show tunes, many of which were 40 or 50 years old at the time. No rock, no jazz.

Audiences loved Welk's wholesome variety of barbershop quartets, ballroom dancers, old-fashioned music, and endless cascades of bubbles. At a time when Elvis Presley was shocking audiences with his sex appeal, Welk was banning cigarette and beer advertising on the show. He refused to hire comedians for fear of raunchy antics, and he once fired a favorite female performer for showing "too much knee." The show, with Welk's trademark phrases "ah-one an' ah-two" and "wunnerful, wunnerful," may not exactly have been pulse-pounding entertainment, but his fans were devoted and the show maintained high ratings for decades.

DON'T WORRY, STAY SAPPY

Not even the network cancellation of the show in 1971 could burst the Welk bubble. Though the show's ratings hadn't dropped, sponsors weren't interested in his sedate, older audience. So Welk campaigned on his own for the show and got distribution deals with more than 250 independent television stations in the U.S. and Canada. New shows were produced for syndication until 1982.

By the time of his death in 1992, Welk had amassed a business empire—a music library, resorts in California and Missouri, a home-video line, and several record labels. At one point, Welk was the second-richest performer in show business, outearned only by Bob Hope. Not bad for a squeaky-clean bandleader whose heavy accent often led to memorable mispronunciations, such as the time he wanted band members to be sharp and attentive, and told them to "Pee on your toes!"

RANDOM WELK FACTS

• Lawrence Welk didn't learn to speak English until he was 21.

• Show sponsors included Geritol, Sominex, and Aqua Velva.

• Welk had a #1 hit in 1961: the instrumental song "Calcutta."

• "The farmers come in from their hard day milking the cow and tending the crops and they want to put their feet up and drink beer and listen to the polkas." —Lawrence Welk, on his audience

---

The full title of Fiona Apple's *When the Pawn* album is 90 words long—the longest title ever.

ROLLING STONE

The origin of the best-known American music magazine.

ROCK TALK

In the mid-1960s, a young rock-music fan started the first magazine in the United States dedicated to rock music, offering cultural commentary and critical reviews. It was called *Crawdaddy!* and its publisher, 17-year-old Paul Williams, was a freshman at Swarthmore College, a small school in Pennsylvania. Since age 14, Williams had self-published a handwritten, mimeographed science-fiction magazine (or "zine") called *Within*. By the time he'd graduated from high school in 1966, he was much more interested in rock music. So he changed *Within* to *Crawdaddy!*, named after the London club where the Rolling Stones played their first concert.

At the time, jazz and folk music were already treated seriously by journalists at magazines like *Down Beat*, and Williams wanted *Crawdaddy!* to legitimize rock music in the same way. "*Crawdaddy!* will feature neither pin-ups nor news briefs; the specialty of this magazine is intelligent writing about pop music," Williams wrote in the first issue of the magazine in February 1966.

Williams persuaded record stores, bookstores, and newsstands in Philadelphia, New York, and Boston to carry *Crawdaddy!* at a cover price of 25¢ per copy. It was so successful that after a year (seven issues), Williams dropped out of school, hired some writers, and moved the magazine to a tiny office in Greenwich Village.

BETTER THAN ANYTHING HIPPER

Crawdaddy! caught the eye of Ralph Gleason, a music writer for the *San Francisco Chronicle*. The new magazine, he said in a 1967 article, was "devoted with religious fervor to the rock scene. The quality of the magazine matches the dedication of its contributors in writing, analysis, and thoughtful speculation."

At the time, Gleason was mentoring a 21-year-old Berkeley dropout named Jann Wenner. Wenner had written a music column for the college paper, and spent most of his time at Bay Area rock 'n' roll clubs, passing out flyers and trying to hang out with

---

Q: What band went through incarnations as Sigma 6, T. Set, Meggadeth, and the Abdabs?...

rock musicians. He wanted to be involved with music, but wasn't sure how. When he read Gleason's article on *Crawdaddy!*, Wenner got an idea.

Rock 'n' roll was more than just music in San Francisco in the summer of 1967. The city was the center of the countercultural movement, and the rock music generated there (by bands like Jefferson Airplane and the Grateful Dead) was at the center of a cultural shift. Based on the *Crawdaddy!* model but with a San Francisco mindset, Wenner wanted to start a magazine that dealt with rock in the context of the broader culture—one that talked about politics, pop culture, trends, and society, or what Wenner later called "the things and attitudes that the music embraces."

A MAN WITH A PLAN

Wenner wasn't the first person to write about the counterculture and its music, and he wasn't even the first in San Francisco. There had been other music magazines, including the *Mojo-Navigator*, but they had small circulations and were often handwritten and had a radical bent. Although those magazines were hip and vital, Wenner felt that they were poorly written and off-putting to mainstream readers. Wenner wanted his magazine to earn him a living, so it would need to be professional and marketable. His plan: "better than anything hipper and hipper than anything better." The politics would be left-leaning, but not radical. And music, not politics, would be the focus.

Wenner had no money to start a magazine, so he borrowed $7,500 from his wife's parents. With Gleason's guidance, a list of record-label contacts he stole from a radio station, and a run-down printer's studio on San Francisco's Market Street, Wenner started *Rolling Stone* magazine. He got the name from the Muddy Waters blues song "Rollin' Stone," which is also where the Rolling Stones got their name. Wenner was publisher and editor in chief, and Ralph Gleason was named contributing editor.

HE'S GOT ISSUES

Rolling Stone #1 was released on November 9, 1967. It was a 16-page, newspaper-size format, which was the cheapest way to print it. The cover image was a still photo of John Lennon from the

1967 antiwar film *How I Won the War.* Wenner printed 40,000 copies. Only 6,000 of them sold.

But Wenner kept putting out issues, and the magazine slowly grew more popular among rock fans and musicians. To boost *Rolling Stone's* visibility and viability, Wenner instituted a number of novel ideas. Some were gimmicky, like when he ran an ad offering a free roach clip with a paid subscription. But one idea paid off unexpectedly well when Wenner appealed to his readers—obsessive rock-music fans—asking them to send him articles. On the Letters page, he printed a note that said "Help!! Send us something we might like to print. Maybe we'll print it; maybe we'll pay you." Some of the magazine's first writers (who eventually became the biggest names in music journalism) were hired this way, including Lester Bangs, Greil Marcus, Cameron Crowe (just 15 at the time), and Robert Christgau. Sportswriter Hunter S. Thompson showed up in person in Wenner's office with a six-pack of beer. His book, *Fear and Loathing in Las Vegas,* was first serialized in *Rolling Stone.*

SOUNDS BAD

Trying to keep his magazine afloat by any means necessary, Wenner also engaged in some questionable editorial practices. According to *Rolling Stone: The Uncensored History* by Robert Draper, Wenner sometimes slanted articles to please advertisers. In one instance, he ordered a writer to pan a Jimi Hendrix release on Capitol Records at the request of Warner Bros. Records, who had signed Hendrix after he left Capitol. Draper also claims that interview subjects were allowed to review articles written about them before publication, a practice that seemed to run contrary to *Rolling Stone's* image of journalistic integrity. Wenner also briefly fired Greil Marcus after the writer gave a nasty review (opening line: "What is this s***?") to Bob Dylan's 1970 album *Self Portrait,* produced by *Rolling Stone* advertiser Columbia Records.

But the magazine did occasionally criticize the industry's sacred cows. In a 1968 issue, writer Jon Landau called Eric Clapton of the band Cream "the master of blues clichés." Four issues later, Wenner wrote that "Cream is good at a number of things; unfortunately, songwriting and recording are not among them." Clapton allegedly read both articles and disbanded Cream soon after.

COVER OF ROLLING STONE

In the early '70s, the magazine's circulation and popularity continued to grow. Then, in 1973, the band Dr. Hook and the Medicine Show released a song called "The Cover of *Rolling Stone*," all about what a milestone it was for a musician to appear on the cover of the magazine. The song was a hit, landing Dr. Hook, appropriately, on the cover of *Rolling Stone* in March 1973. *Rolling Stone* had officially made it. By 1975 it had over a million readers.

Today, after 40 years and more than 1,000 issues, *Rolling Stone* still has a readership of 1.3 million readers and, despite competition from newer magazines like *Spin, Blender,* and *Vibe,* it's still the world's best-selling music magazine. Even more remarkably, it's still privately owned; Wenner and his ex-wife Jane are the only two shareholders. Jann Wenner is still the editor and publisher at age 61. And while the Wenners have turned down various offers to sell the magazine, it's estimated that *Rolling Stone* is now worth at least $2 billion—all from a $7,500 investment in 1967.

*   *   *

SACRED HARP

Sacred Harp singing takes its name from a book of songs called *The Sacred Harp*, which was published in 1844 and includes tunes like "Amazing Grace," "Wondrous Love," and "Rock of Ages." The style has its roots in the American South, where hymn singing was considered an important part of spiritual life. Sacred Harp singers perform a cappella, and they insist that the emphasis is on participation, not performance. In fact, Sacred Harp singers don't put on concerts or shows at all; anyone who's there is expected to join in.

The style may be best known, though, for its unique musical notation. Sacred Harp sheet music includes oddly shaped notes—squares, ovals, diamonds, and triangles—that are supposed to make it easier for singers to read the music. Each shaped note corresponds with a syllable—*fa, so, la,* or *mi*—and singers need only to memorize what shape goes with what syllable to learn to read the music.

GUESS WHO'S PLAYING AT THE COUNTY FAIR?

*On a recent (and luckless) trip to Reno, Nevada, Uncle John was
astonished to see the names of bands on the marquees that he thought
were long defunct. It made him wonder if any other old acts were
still out there touring. Turns out there are...and they could be
coming soon to a racetrack or county fair near you.*

FOGHAT. "I Just Want to Make Love to You" put this band
on the charts in 1972. And 1975's "Fool for the City" and
"Slow Ride" took them to stardom. Slowly, they went down-
hill from there and broke up in 1984...then reformed in 1986...
then broke up again...then reformed...it's a long story. But as of
today, the band known as Foghat is still alive and touring.
Remaining original members: One—drummer Roger Earl.

.38 SPECIAL. This band, formed in 1975 in Jacksonville, Florida,
was fronted by vocalist Donnie Van Zandt, brother of legendary
Lynyrd Skynyrd vocalist Ronnie Van Zandt. They shot up the
charts in 1981 with "Hold on Loosely," hit a #1 bull's eye in 1982
with "Caught Up in You," and blasted their way to the top again
in 1983 with "If I'd Been the One." They've been shooting mostly
blanks since then...but they're still touring.
Remaining original members: Two out of six—Van Zandt and
Larry Junstrom, who was the original bassist for Lynyrd Skynyrd.

LOVERBOY. The 1980s band from Calgary, Alberta, that turned
out hits like "Turn Me Loose," "Lovin' Every Minute of It," and
"Working for the Weekend," is still going strong. In November
2007, they released their 12th album, *Just Getting Started* (their
first studio album in 10 years), and they're still touring regularly.
Remaining original members: Four out of five. The fifth, bassist
Scott Smith, died in 2000.

Sea shantys such as "Drunken Sailor" were the only songs allowed by the Royal Navy in the 1800s.

10CC. They formed in 1972 as a quartet with Graham Gouldman (who wrote the Yardbirds' "For Your Love" and the Hollies' "Bus Stop" in 1965), Eric Stewart, Kevin Godley, and Lol Creme. The band scored huge hits with "I'm Not in Love" (1975) and "The Things We Do for Love" (1977).

Remaining original members: Since 2004 Graham Gouldman, the primary singer and songwriter for the band, has been out there touring with a group called "10cc featuring Graham Gouldman and Friends." (And in 2006 he started recording with original bandmate Kevin Godley as "GG/06." So maybe they'll be touring, too.)

REO SPEEDWAGON. In the early 1980s, they topped the charts and were seemingly always on the radio with songs like "Time for Me to Fly" and "Keep on Loving You." They broke up in the late '80s, but got back together numerous times over the years with different lineups. Today they continue to release albums and do concerts, mostly at small venues like county fairs and casinos.

Remaining original members: One out of five—Neil Doughty, the keyboard player.

STARSHIP. Founded in 1965 as "Jefferson Airplane," they became "Jefferson Starship" in 1974, then, briefly, "Starship Jefferson" (an angry post-internal-lawsuit move), "Starship" in 1985, and finally "Jefferson Starship—The Next Generation" in 1991. They're still on the road today...as two different bands. Jefferson Starship—The Next Generation has two members from the original 1965 Jefferson Airplane lineup: guitarist/vocalists Paul Kantner and Marty Balin; and "Starship Featuring Mickey Thomas," Thomas being the vocalist on such Jefferson Starship hits as "Jane" (1979) and "We Built This City" (1985).

Remaining original members: It's hard to say, given that they reinvented themselves and altered lineups so many times since 1965. It's easier to list three original members who *aren't* with the band anymore: Guitarist Jorma Kaukonen and bassist Jack Casady, who still perform as the cult-favorite duo Hot Tuna; and Grace Slick, who retired from the music business in 1988.

WHAT A CONCEPT

Concept albums tell a story through a series of songs. Some famous examples: The Who's Tommy *and Pink Floyd's* The Wall. *It's not as easy as it sounds. Here are a few who have tried...and flopped.*

Artist: Emerson, Lake, and Palmer
Album: *Tarkus* (1971)
Concept: Set to classically-inspired rock music played on synthesizers, *Tarkus* is about a half-armadillo/half-tank robot who battles with a lion/scorpion/human hybrid named Manticore. Bonus: Manticore rides around on an electric pterodactyl.

Artist: KISS
Album: *Music from "The Elder"* (1981)
Concept: KISS's comic-book image was getting stale by 1981, so the group decided to try something different: this album about a mystical child warrior who grows up to fight evil spirits. It was supposed to be the soundtrack for a movie called *The Elder*, but the album sold so poorly that the movie was never made.

Artist: Saga
Album: *The Chapters* (2005)
Concept: Humanity is about to be destroyed! In *The Chapters*, here's how we're saved: Benevolent aliens reanimate the brain of Albert Einstein and place it in a half-human/half-robot body. The super-genius Einstein-bot comes up with a plan to save the day.

Artist: Masters of the Hemisphere
Album: *I Am Not a Freemdoom* (2000)
Concept: A colony of lake creatures lives peacefully near an island called Krone Ishta until it's taken over by Freemdoom, an evil dog/businessman. Freemdoom drains the lake around the island in an attempt to force the sea creatures to buy air-lungs. In a weird musical statement about capitalism, it turns out that air-lungs are made in a factory owned by...Freemdoom.

Artist: Wendy O. Williams
Album: *Maggots: The Record* (2000)
Concept: Giant maggots eat everybody in New York City. (It probably flopped because it wasn't far-fetched enough.).

Artist: Rock Plaza Central
Album: *Are We Not Horses?* (2006)
Concept: It's a cruel world. Robot horses who think they're real horses slowly come to the heartbreaking realization that they are, in fact, robot horses.

Artist: Clawjob
Album: *Space Crackers* (2006)
Concept: Two scientists travel into space to seek a remedy for a worldwide famine that threatens mankind. Unfortunately, upon their return, they find that 50 million flesh-eating aliens have invaded Earth and eaten almost everybody.

Artist: Frank Zappa
Album: *Joe's Garage* (1979)
Concept: After his girlfriend leaves him to become a rock groupie, Joe seeks revenge. As the story unfolds, he contracts a venereal disease, gives all of his money to a cult religion, and ends up in an intimate relationship with a piece of "kitchen machinery" named Sy Borg. (Unlike the others on this list, Zappa *meant* for this album to be humorous. And it didn't flop—it's still a favorite of Zappa fans.)

*　　*　　*

DICK CLARK'S (FIRST AND) LAST 'STAND

• First song played on the first episode of *American Bandstand* on August 5, 1957: "Whole Lotta Shakin' Goin' On" by Jerry Lee Lewis.
• Last song played on the last episode of *American Bandstand* on October 7, 1989: "We Can't Go Wrong" by the Cover Girls.

MUSIC CLASS

So you want to get a musical education? Check out some of the most celebrated conservatories in the world.

THE JUILLIARD SCHOOL (New York)
Humble beginnings: Frank Damrosch—the godson of Franz Liszt—wanted to create an American music academy that could compete with the great conservatories of Europe. So in 1905 he founded the Institute of Musical Art. Damrosch and his business partner took in 100 students, but by 1910, demand was so great that they had to move to a bigger building.

In 1919 a wealthy New York textile merchant named Augustus D. Juilliard died, leaving a will with directions that the bulk of his fortune go toward helping further music education in the United States. The trustees appointed to fulfill that goal created the Juilliard Graduate School in 1924, and two years later, it merged with Damrosch's school, forming the Juilliard School. Today, Juilliard is made up of six divisions that offer degrees in music, dance, drama, and other performing arts-related curriculum, and the school offers a joint degree with Columbia University.
Notable alumni: Yo-Yo Ma, Nina Simone, Itzhak Perlman, Wynton Marsalis, actress Bebe Neuwirth, actor Robin Williams, composer John Williams, and Broadway star Patti LuPone.

BERKLEE COLLEGE OF MUSIC (Boston)
Humble beginnings: Lawrence Berk, a musical composer and arranger for radio, founded the school in 1945, initially calling it the Schillinger House of Music in honor of his music teacher, famed composer and music theorist Joseph Schillinger. In 1954 he changed the named to Berklee, after his son, Lee Berk, though the young man never actually studied music. (The school had expanded its curriculum by then and no longer just taught Schillinger's principles, so Berk thought the original name was outdated.)

With 3,800 students, today Berklee is the world's largest music college. It also has the distinction of being first in many areas: Berklee was the first music school to offer guitar as a field of study, the first to blend popular music and a strict conservatory education, and the first college to offer a songwriting curriculum.

Notable alumni: Melissa Etheridge, Branford Marsalis, Quincy Jones, and singers Paula Cole, John Mayer, and Aimee Mann.

THE JACOBS SCHOOL OF MUSIC (Bloomington, Indiana)

Humble beginnings: Charles Campbell was teaching German at Indiana University in the early 1900s, but he loved music. In 1907 he organized a recital at the university and put the entire proceeds of the show into a fund to establish a music school. In 1909 he taught the first classes (though they were noncredit classes) and the next year, the Indiana University School of Music was up and running.

The school recently changed its name thanks to a huge endowment in 2005 from philanthropists Barbara and David Jacobs, but its curriculum has remained consistent over the years—focusing primarily on classical music education and offering degrees in everything from music theory to voice to cello.

Notable alumni: Songwriter Hoagy Carmichael, opera singers Sylvia McNair and Angela Brown, songwriter and record producer Booker T. Jones, jazz trumpeter Chris Botti, and violinist Joshua Bell.

ST. PETERSBURG CONSERVATORY (Russia)

Humble beginnings: By the early 1800s, St. Petersburg had become a premier stop on the calendars of some of the world's greatest musicians: Franz Liszt, Richard Wagner, and Robert Schumann all performed there. But despite the city's emerging reputation as a center of art and culture, it lacked a school to train its own talent. So Russian composer and pianist Anton Rubinstein founded the St. Petersburg Conservatory in 1862. The school was Russia's first public music academy, and it turned out pianists, composers, cellists, and others who went on to play in the country's state and private symphonies, choirs, and operas.

The conservatory endured despite Russia's political upheaval during the 20th century. After the Communists came to power and renamed the city Leningrad, the school's name also changed— at different times, it was called both the Petrograd Conservatory and the Leningrad Conservatory. Today, with its original name

---

Barry Manilow's "I Write the Songs," by Bruce Johnston, was about Beach Boy Brian Wilson.

restored, the St. Petersburg Conservatory is still open and offers undergraduate and graduate degrees.

Notable alumni: Composer Pyotr Ilyich Tchaikovsky, choreographer George Balanchine, and composer Sergei Prokofiev.

THE EASTMAN SCHOOL (Rochester, New York)

Humble beginnings: George Eastman, the founder of Kodak, established the school because, he explained, "The life of our communities in the future needs what our schools of music and of other fine arts can give them." In 1921, its first year, the Eastman School had 104 students. Over the years, the school has grown steadily, and today about 900 students are enrolled in undergraduate and graduate programs that include music education, theory, and jazz composition.

Notable alumni: Violinist Michael Klotz, composer Jeff Beal, opera singer Renee Fleming, jazz musician Chuck Mangione, composer Charles Strouse, and Doriot Anthony Dwyer, a principal flutist with the Boston Symphony and one of the first women to hold such a prestigious position.

ROYAL ACADEMY OF MUSIC (London)

Humble beginnings: Earl John Fane (also known as Lord Burghersh) founded the academy in 1822. Fane was a composer and violinist who wanted to offer England's musicians a place to study that rivaled the great academies in Italy, which was the center of classical music at the time. He teamed up with French harpist Nicolas-Charles Bochsa, and the two managed to convince England's King George IV to grant their school a royal charter in 1830. (A royal charter gave the institution legal and legitimate standing within the British government.) Today, the school remains a public institution, hosts about 650 students, and is part of the University of London. The academy also maintains one of the largest music museums in the world. It includes more than 200 stringed instruments (many crafted by the Stradivari family) and the papers and artwork of Yehudi Menuhin, one of the most famous American-born violinists and composers.

Notable alumni: Annie Lenox, Elton John, and Sir Arthur Sullivan (composer of *The Pirates of Penzance*)

TIPPER VS. MUSIC

People around the world have been trying to regulate music for centuries, but in the 1980s, Tipper Gore launched the first campaign to rate albums. Here's the story of how a vice president's wife took on graphic lyrics in music and won...sort of.

DARLING TIPPER

In 1984 Tipper Gore, wife of then-senator Al Gore, bought Prince's *Purple Rain* album for her 11-year-old daughter, Karenna. They put on the CD and Gore liked it...until she got to "Darling Nikki," a very sexually explicit song, and one Gore thought was inappropriate for an 11-year-old. Had she known, she never would have bought the album.

Gore did some more "research" on the level of vulgarity in popular music—she watched MTV for a few hours and found more songs that troubled her, including Van Halen's "Hot For Teacher," and Mötley Crüe's "Looks That Kill." "The images frightened my children, they frightened me," she said. "The graphic sex and the violence were too much for us to handle."

She started talking to some friends—wives of prominent Washington businessmen and politicians—and decided to use her influence to do something about it. With Susan Baker (wife of treasury secretary James Baker), Pam Howar (wife of powerful realtor Raymond Howar) and Sally Nevius (wife of Washington city council chairman John Nevius), Gore formed the Parents Music Resource Center, or PMRC, in 1985.

PMRC's stated goal: to raise parental awareness of "the growing trend in music towards lyrics that are sexually explicit, excessively violent, or glorify the use of drugs and alcohol." The group even suggested that the increase of some crimes in the previous 30 years directly correlated with the popularity of rock music—rape was up 7% since 1955 and teenage suicide was up 300%.

PMRC TO RIAA: X, V, D/A, O!

In early 1985, the PMRC sent a letter to the Recording Industry Association of America (RIAA, the music industry trade organi-

---

Bobby Pickett titled his song "Monster Mash" to cash in on the "mashed potato" dance craze.

zation) and asked it to stop releasing sexually explicit or violent recordings, or at the very least, give albums a rating so parents could judge for themselves if the music is appropriate for their child. "Exercise voluntary self-restraint," the letter read, "perhaps by developing guidelines and/or a rating system, such as that of the movie industry." Gore actually had a very specific labeling program in mind. Sexual content would be marked with an "X," violent content would be marked with a "V," drugs and alcohol mentions got a "D/A," and promotion of occult themes got an "O." The letter, signed by the wives of over 20 Washington politicians and businessmen, was sent to 62 record companies as well. Only seven responded and all refused to implement any changes.

THE LINK BETWEEN MUSIC AND HEARING LOSS

In 1985, using their clout (i.e., their husbands), the PMRC convinced the United States Senate to hold hearings on the alarming content of popular music. The PMRC testified, detailing their concerns about the harmful effects of sex and violence in music. Several major musicians testified against the PMRC. John Denver said he was "strongly opposed to censorship of any kind," partially because censors often misinterpret music. (In 1973, when the government was in the midst of an anti-drug-song crackdown, the FCC asked many radio stations to refrain from playing Denver's song "Rocky Mountain High," even though the song is really about enjoying nature.) Dee Snider of the band Twisted Sister argued a similar point: Gore said his song "Under the Blade," which Snider said he wrote about an upcoming surgery, was about bondage and rape. "Mrs. Gore was looking for sadomasochism and bondage, and she found it. Someone looking for surgical references would have found those as well."

But Frank Zappa gave the most pointed commentary. "The proposal is an ill-conceived piece of nonsense which fails to deliver any real benefits to children, infringes the civil liberties of people who are not children, and promises to keep the courts busy for years dealing with the interpretational problems inherent in the proposal's design."

Zappa even went so far as to suggest that the RIAA and Congress had made a deal: The RIAA would agree to some meaningless, superficial labeling (to look good in the public eye). In return, Congress would pass a bill that the RIAA was strongly lobbying for: the Home Recording Act, which would outlaw copying music onto blank tapes (the RIAA said unauthorized copying had cost them billions in lost sales).

CENSORSHIP? OH, BE QUIET

Gore repeatedly assured the Senate and the public that what she was trying to do was create accountability, and let parents know what kind of music their kids were listening to—that it was definitely *not* censorship. But was it? While the PMRC's most-talked-about goal was a labeling system, it actually had some other demands, too. They wanted to:

- establish a rating system for albums *and* concerts
- require song lyrics to be printed on album covers
- have albums with explicit cover art kept under store counters
- make record companies break contracts with performers who engaged in violent or sexually explicit onstage behavior
- pressure radio and television to not air objectionable artists

Some of those points were unrealistic (it would be impossible to print an entire album worth of lyrics on the cover of a CD or cassette), but politicians ultimately found themselves having to agree that forcing record companies or radio stations to ban any musicians the PMRC found offensive would violate the artists' First Amendment rights.

DID IT STICK?

On November 1, 1985, before the hearings were even over, the RIAA bowed to the pressure of the PMRC (and growing public sentiment—a national poll said 75 percent of Americans favored a labeling system). Ultimately the RIAA agreed to place stickers reading "Parental Advisory: Explicit Lyrics" on albums deemed offensive. Record companies would do so (and determine what albums would get stickers) at their own discretion. Every objectionable album would get the same sticker, not a specific label as Gore had initially proposed. The "Parental Advisory" sticker would have no legally binding effect on stores. It didn't prevent stores from selling stickered albums to minors, nor did it require them to keep offensive albums behind the counter, unless they wanted to. Wal-Mart opted not to carry stickered albums at all (a policy that still stands).

THE OPPOSITE EFFECT

So did labeling curb "offensive" music, or at least get kids to stop listening to it? Probably not. In fact, in *Heavy: The Story of Metal*, a documentary about 1980s hard rock, members of the bands Mötley Crüe, Quiet Riot, and Poison all claim their album sales went up after getting stickered. "The sticker almost guaranteed your record would be bought by rebellious kids," said Mötley Crüe's Nikki Sixx.

*   *   *

MASSACHUSETTS: THE MUSICAL STATE

Bet you didn't know that the great state of Massachusetts is one of the most "officially" musical in the country. Here's a list of their musical state symbols:

- **Official Song:** "All Hail to Massachusetts," by Arthur Marsh

- **Official Folk Song:** "Massachusetts," by Arlo Guthrie

- **Official State Ceremonial March:** "The Road to Boston," composer unknown

- **Official Patriotic Song:** "Massachusetts (Because of You Our Land Is Free)," by Bernard Davidson

- **Official Glee Club Song:** "The Great State of Massachusetts," words by George A. Wells, music by J. Earl Bley

- **Official Polka Song:** "Say Hello to Someone from Massachusetts," by Lenny Gomulka

- **Official Ode:** "Ode to Massachusetts"

- **Official Blues Artist:** Henry St. Clair Fredericks, better known as Taj Mahal

WHO'S THAT SONG ABOUT?

*Many pop songs are written about specific people. Here are the stories
about the inspirations behind some famous songs. (But we
still don't know who "You're So Vain" is about.)*

"SOMETHING," "LAYLA," "WONDERFUL TONIGHT"

In 1966 George Harrison married model Pattie Boyd, who inspired him to write the ballad "Something" (Frank Sinatra called it "the greatest love song ever written"). Harrison later became close friends with another famous guitarist, Eric Clapton. When Boyd and Harrison had marriage troubles, she confided in Clapton, who fell in love with her but, because of his friendship with Harrison, was unable to act on it. So *he* wrote a song about Boyd—"Layla," named for a Persian love poem about unrequited love. Harrison and Boyd divorced in 1977, and she married Clapton two years later. Clapton then wrote "Wonderful Tonight," *also* about Boyd. While "Wonderful" is widely believed to be a sweet love song about a man telling his wife how beautiful she looks, it was actually based on Clapton's complaints about how long it took Boyd to get ready for a party.

"OUR HOUSE"

In 1969 Graham Nash was having an affair with fellow musician Joni Mitchell, and they shared a house in Los Angeles' Laurel Canyon, a hippie enclave at the time. Nash wrote "Our House" about that experience. But despite the song's lighthearted bohemian references, Nash says it's actually about wanting to ditch the hippie lifestyle; he preferred the stability of his fairly conventional life with Mitchell. But by the time "Our House" became a hit in the late 1970, Nash and Mitchell had already split up.

"RING OF FIRE"

Johnny Cash performed it, but his future wife, June Carter, wrote it—about him. In 1962 singing partners Carter and Cash were married to other people, but their own relationship was deepen-

---

Circus music commonly used to introduce clowns: the 1897 tune "Entrance of the Gladiators."

ing. One night, Carter came up with the song while she was driving around aimlessly, worried that Cash's drinking and drug abuse would lead him to death and destruction—and, because she was so attracted to him, would bring her down along with him. Carter's sister Anita first sang the song, but Cash added a horn arrangement (an idea he said came to him in a dream), rerecorded it, and made it one of his signature songs. Cash and Carter married in 1968 (and he credits her with helping him beat drugs).

"THE GIRL FROM IPANEMA"

In 1962 two Brazilian songwriters named Antonio Carlos Jobim and Vinicius de Moraes were sitting in a bar near Ipanema beach. When a particularly striking woman named Heloisa Pinheiro sashayed past on her way to the beach, both men let out an "Ahhhhhh." They did that every day when she walked by. And they wrote a song about her—"The Girl from Ipanema." Jobim gave the song to Brazilian guitarist João Gilberto, who put it on the album *Gilberto/Getz*, a collaboration with American saxophonist Stan Getz. The song, sung by Astrud Gilberto, became a huge international hit and won the Grammy Award for Record of the Year. It also put the bossa nova style of Brazilian music on the map.

"SWEET CAROLINE"

In 1963 Neil Diamond was reading a magazine and saw a picture of President John F. Kennedy and his daughter, six-year-old Caroline. Caroline was dressed up in horse riding gear and standing next to her pony. "It was such an innocent, wonderful picture," Diamond said. "I felt there was a song in there." But he didn't actually write the song until four years later, when he was sitting in a Memphis motel room suffering from writer's block. He remembered the picture of the carefree little girl, and he wrote the song in an hour. "Sweet Caroline" was released in 1969 and reached #4 on the chart, one of the biggest hits Diamond ever had. But the inspiration behind "Sweet Caroline" was a mystery until 2007. Always having a fondness for the song, Kennedy asked Diamond to perform it live at her 50th birthday party. He did, and afterward he told Kennedy—and the world—that she was the real "Sweet Caroline."

The piano piece "Chopsticks" was written by 16-year-old Euphemia Allen.

LOST LEGEND: MA RAINEY

Say hello to the singing powerhouse who came to be known as the "Mother of the Blues."

BORN TO SING

The blues is now so ingrained in our popular culture that it's easy to forget it wasn't always that way. And one of the reasons blues music is so popular today is the work of a woman who's also largely forgotten: Gertrude Pridgett, otherwise known as "Ma Rainey."

Pridgett was born in 1886 in Columbus, Georgia, to a family of minstrel show performers traveling around the South. In 1902 the 16-year-old, according to her account, heard a young girl perform a "blues" song at a theater in St. Louis. Pridgett liked the sound of it, and started incorporating the style into her own shows—but only as the last song. It was a novelty; most Americans had never heard of the blues.

In 1904 Pridgett married a fellow singer, William "Pa" Rainey, and changed her name to "Ma Rainey." Together they traveled throughout the South in a loop known as the "chitlin' circuit," playing in juke joints, saloons, and tents—the only places where black musicians could play at the time—from Georgia to Missouri to Texas and back. Along the way, they often heard "country blues" sung by their fellow performers, and they began to incorporate it more and more into their act. "Her ability to capture the mood and essence of black rural Southern life," wrote Daphne Harrison in *Black Pearls: Blues Queens of the 1920s*, "quickly endeared her to throngs of followers throughout the South."

INTO HISTORY

In 1916 Rainey separated from her husband and started her own band, Madam Gertrude Ma Rainey and Her Georgia Smart Sets. Rainey—a short, dark, plump, and extremely free-spirited

---

Melba toast is named after Australian opera singer Dame Nellie Melba.

woman—wowed audiences with her glittery, rhinestone-beaded costumes and an ostrich feather fan, her huge voice belting out songs that combined the bawdiness of minstrel show songs with the hard-luck sound of the blues. Historians credit Rainey's work with the Smart Sets as being one of the primary reasons the popularity of the blues spread around the country during the 1910s, setting it up for the national explosion that was soon to come.

RECORD GROWTH

Ma Rainey's reputation grew over the next several years, and in 1923 she reached a new—and much larger—audience when she started recording for Paramount Records, billed as "the Mother of the Blues." She was 37 years old at the time, with nearly 25 years of performing behind her. She would go on to record more than 100 songs with Paramount—more than 20 of them her own compositions—and sang with the biggest stars of the day, including Louis Armstrong and saxophonist Coleman Hawkins. Soon she was performing all over the North, and could be heard on radio shows across the country. Her songs, like "C.C. Rider" and "Bo Weavil Blues," chronicled the hard lives of blacks in the South, but that's not all: Some of them were exceedingly racy for their time, openly talking not only about sex, but homosexual sex (most historians believe Rainey was bisexual).

Rainey became one of the biggest stars of an era now known as "Classic Female Blues," which peaked in the mid-'20s. Other stars of the day were Mamie Smith, Ethel Waters, and Bessie Smith—a younger singer Rainey mentored when they both performed with a traveling circus several years earlier. Bessie Smith would go on to become the highest-paid black singer of the 1920s.

END OF THE LINE

By the late '20s, Classic Female Blues had run its course, and Rainey made her last recording in 1928. She continued performing until 1935, and finally returned home to Columbus, Georgia, where she bought a house and two theaters. She ran the theaters and sang in the town's Friendship Baptist Church until she died of a heart attack in 1939. By then, she had faded into such obscurity that her death went largely unnoticed; her obituary listed her as a

A guitar pick is a *plectrum*—a tool used to pluck or strum a stringed instrument.

housekeeper. But the blues continued to develop and spread over the following decades, and in time, musicians, historians, and fans began to recognize her role. Now dozens of her recordings are available on CD.

BACK IN THE SPOTLIGHT

New audiences discovered Rainey in 1984 when playwright August Wilson's *Ma Rainey's Black Bottom* opened on Broadway. Named for one of Rainey's most popular songs, the play takes place at a 1927 Rainey recording session.

1983 Ma Rainey was inducted into the Blues Foundation Hall of Fame in Memphis, Tennessee, and in 1990 to the Rock and Roll Hall of Fame. In 1992 her home in Columbus, located at 805 Fifth Avenue, was listed in the National Register of Historic Places. In 2006 its restoration was completed, and it's now open to the public as a blues museum, known simply as the Ma Rainey House.

* * *

RANDOM MUSIC FACTS

• Since 1955 piano keys have been made of plastic, not ivory.

• Purdue University had the first collegiate marching band (1886). They were also the first to play on a sports field and make a formation—they formed a giant "P" (1907).

• Clarinets are made from the wood of the granadilla tree.

• Most frequently sung songs in English: "Happy Birthday," "For He's a Jolly Good Fellow," and "Auld Lang Syne."

• Mozart wrote the opera *Don Giovanni* in one sitting. It was first performed the very next day with no rehearsals.

• There are more than 10 million pianos in the U.S.

• British scientists say chickens produce more eggs if they listen to easy listening or Top 40 radio. (They hate heavy metal, opera, and jazz.)

The song "Midnight Train to Georgia" was written on an airplane.

FILM MUZIK

Just how big of a role does music play in the movies?
Here are some thoughts from those who write the
music…and those who hear it on the screen.

"A movie starts with a writer alone in a room, conjuring something out of vapor…and it ends with a score composer talking to himself in a little room, conjuring something out of vapor."

—**Danny Elfman (***Batman,***
Spider-man, The Simpsons)**

"In California, they like to pigeonhole you. From the time I began working for Hitchcock, they decided I was a big 'suspense' man. I think I'd enjoy writing a good comedy score, but I've never had the luck to be offered such films. Mancini gets the cheerful ones."

—**Bernard Herrmann
(***North by Northwest,***
Psycho, Taxi Driver)**

"I suffer by not being able to be coherent, but I don't care. I could be musically coherent all the time, but then I probably wouldn't be able to stir up feelings in people."

—**Ennio Morricone
(***The Good, the Bad and the***
Ugly; The Untouchables)**

"When producers say, 'This scene really doesn't work and we need some help here,' you realize what they're saying is that the music can make or break the movie."

—**Hans Zimmer (***Pearl***
Harbor, Batman Begins)**

"There's nothing worse than when music is used to tell the audience what they should be feeling. Unfortunately, it happens all the time."

—**Martin Scorsese, director
(***Taxi Driver, Raging***
Bull, The Departed)**

"Music is a big factor in help-ing the illusion of the film come to life, the same way that music brings back differ-ent periods of our lives."

—**Francis Ford Coppola,
director (***The Godfather***)**

"You can take almost any visual film sequence and change its emotion and feel-ings by the use of music."

—**Norman Jewison, director
(***Jesus Christ Superstar,***
Rollerball, Moonstruck)**

George Gershwin's last tune: "Love Is Here to Stay," for the 1938 film *The Goldwyn Follies*.

"Writing film music is a very lonely profession. When you finally perform it, you're performing for an audience who really knows nothing about music—the producer and director."

—Jerry Goldsmith (*Chinatown, Patton, Star Trek: The Motion Picture*)

"As musicians, we like to think we don't need visual aids to project music. The music should be able to engage us aurally and intellectually without a visual distraction…but people are visual addicts, stimulated by computer or movie screens. For that generation, it's hard to listen to Beethoven and be completely engaged in a way that we would prefer them to be."

—John Williams (*Star Wars, E.T., Harry Potter*)

"We do not go to the cinema to hear music, but we require it to deepen and prolong in us the screen's visual impact."

—Maurice Jaubert, French film composer

"Film music should have the same relationship to the film drama that somebody's piano playing in my living room has on the book I am reading."

—Igor Stravinsky, 20th-century classical composer

*   *   *

CAN MUSIC MAKE YOU…

…**love me?** No. In January 2007, a 55-year-old man in Darlstad, Sweden, upset that his girlfriend had broken off their relationship—four months earlier—went to her home and sang love songs outside her door for several hours. She called the police. He was arrested and charged with harassment.

…**quit smoking?** Yes, if you're a chimpanzee. A chimp in a Shaanxi province (China) safari park quit smoking in 2005 after 16 years. She had first started, zoo officials said, after her mate died in 1989 by scavenging butts left by park visitors. When her health started to deteriorate, zoo staff started trying to wean her off cigarettes. The chimp had a hard time of it at first, they said, but they were able to calm her down by giving her a Walkman, through which she listened to pop music…and eventually did stop smoking.

Paul McCartney, Nancy Sinatra, and Louis Armstrong all recorded songs for James Bond films.

THE MUSICAL CONDOM

*Music is so powerful and all-pervasive in our world that everything
seems to sing these days. Even prophylactics. Honest.*

MUSICAL SNORKEL. For the swimmer who needs a
musical soundtrack, there's a snorkel with an FM radio
receiver built right into it. The sound is transmitted
through your teeth so, according to the manufacturer, no earpiece
is required. (*Jaws* music not recommended.) Price: $129.

MUSICAL SUIT. In the 1990s, drummer Mick Fleetwood of the
band Fleetwood Mac often performed while wearing his "drum
suit": a costume into which he'd sewn several pads from an electronic drum set, each one of which created a different sound. He'd
play his signature extended drum solos while walking through the
audience...hitting himself.

MUSICAL TOOTHBRUSH. Sir George Reresby Sitwell was a
British aristocrat—and an eccentric writer—who lived from 1860
to 1943. Some of his unpublished works: *Wool-Gathering in
Medieval Times and Since, Acorns as an Article of Medieval Diet,* and
Lepers' Squints. He was also an eccentric inventor. Some of his
creations: a tiny pistol for shooting wasps, and an "egg" filled with
rice and smoked meat inside a synthetic shell, designed as a
portable meal for travelers. But the best one: a toothbrush that
played the Scottish ballad "Annie Laurie" as you brushed your
teeth. Although it's unclear whether Sitwell intended to market
his inventions to the world, none of them ever caught on.

MUSICAL WINE CASE. English keyboardist Nick Holland
came up with this idea in 1998 while taking some time off from
touring. "I love red wine, and once the band had finished a gig,
everywhere was closed so we couldn't have a drink," he told the
Oxford Mail. So he decided to make a sort of instant pub: a velvet-
lined case that holds a bottle of wine, two glasses, a corkscrew—
and plays your choice of music, accompanied by flashing lights,
when you open the lid. Holland says the case has other positive

---

Can you name the oldest form of Irish dance music? It's the jig, of course.

qualities, too: "A friend of mine is now in a relationship thanks to this wine case," he said. "He went to a field with a young lady and took the case with him. He ended up in the field for four hours and they've been together ever since." At last report, he'd sold 15 of the cases for about $325 each.

MUSICAL CONDOM. This invention gives a whole new twist to the phrase "Shall I put on some romantic music?" In 1996 Hungarian novelty shop owner Ferenc Kovacs invented a condom that's fitted with a tiny microchip like the ones in musical greeting cards. The chip is activated when a condom is…er, um—unfurled, and it comes with your choice of songs: "Arise, Ye Worker" (Kovacs is an ardent Communist), or a tune called "You Sweet Little Dumbbell."

MUSICAL PICTURE FRAME. From the U.S. Patent Office, patent #5271173: "A musical picture frame for generating music for a picture frame and creates an elegant and romantic atmosphere for the memory. With fingers pressing on the pressure seat, the rubber conductor will be forced to contact with the PC board circuit and proper music will then be generated." As far as we can tell, that means: music plays when you press the picture frame.

MUSICAL POTTY CHAIR. Proving that everything a kid touches these days emits some kind of annoying sound, one inventor has a patent (#4509215) on a musical potty chair. But this potty chair plays music *only* when the child makes a "deposit," serving as a reward for a job well done (a key to the potty-training process). No word on whether this one has ever hit the market, but Uncle John sure hopes so.

*　　*　　*

SECRET IDENTITY

In 1993 an anonymous electronica "group" called the Fireman released an album titled *Strawberries Oceans Ships Forest*. It did well in dance clubs and with music critics. The unlikely identity of the Fireman was revealed later that year: Paul McCartney.

The music to Nat King Cole's 1954 hit ballad "Smile" was composed by Charlie Chaplin.

CLASSICAL HIT MAKERS

*Here's a look at the lives of three of history's
most renowned classical composers.*

JOHANN SEBASTIAN BACH (1685–1750)

Bach spent most of his life not far from his birthplace of Eisenach, Germany, and was virtually unknown as a composer during his lifetime. Yet his compositions influenced generations of future composers, from Beethoven to the Beach Boys.

Bach came from a musical family: his father was a music director in Eisenach, and taught young Johann to play the violin and harpsichord. Orphaned at 10, the boy went to live with his brother, Johann Christoph, a church organist, who taught him organ and music composition. By the time he was 18, Bach was a church organist himself and was writing music; one of his most famous pieces, "Toccata and Fugue in D Minor," was composed during this time.

In 1703 Bach got a job as a member of the court chamber orchestra in nearby Weimar. Five years later, he became the concertmaster, leading the violin section and playing all the solos. He also continued to play the harpsichord and composed some of the orchestra's music. Bach took inspiration from great Italian composers like Vivaldi and Corelli and adapted their works for the organ and harpsichord. He composed the Brandenburg Concerti while working in Weimar, though these famous compositions were not appreciated in their time—the sheet music was put away and forgotten until it was rediscovered in the 19th century.

In 1723 Bach moved to Leipzig, where he spent the rest of his life and composed most of his famous pieces, including "Mass in B Minor" and "The Art of Fugue." In all, he wrote more than 1,000 works (both religious and secular) and is considered to be one of the greatest composers in the history of Western music.

WOLFGANG AMADEUS MOZART (1756–1791)

Born in Salzburg, Austria, his full name was Johannes Chrysostomus Wolfgangus Theophilus Mozart. He was a prodigy who learned to play the keyboard at three and was composing at five.

Of J. S. Bach's 20 children, 10 died in infancy. 4 became well-known composers and musicians.

By the age of six, he was touring Europe, acclaimed as a virtuoso. Mozart played for European royalty, everyone from Empress Maria Theresa to Marie Antoinette. They showered him with money and gifts, and he was his family's primary moneymaker, a fact that would cause problems for most of his life.

Mozart's father Leopold was a bit of a stage parent; he devoted his life to making his son famous, and when Mozart got older, Leopold wanted him to get a steady composing job so he could continue to support the family. Mozart did take such a job, as a court musician for the archbishop in Salzburg, but he was unhappy there. The salary was barely adequate, and Mozart wanted to compose operas. He became less and less content in Salzburg. This, coupled with the archbishop's attitude (he treated the young man like a servant), ultimately led Mozart to quit his job and move to Vienna to try to establish himself as a freelance musician.

Work in Vienna was lucrative, but Mozart was a terrible money manager and had a penchant for gambling. As a result, he always had financial problems (according to legend, he was so poor at times that he burned his furniture to keep warm). Even so, people loved his music and paid to hear him play. He composed and played his most famous works in Vienna: *The Magic Flute* and his Mass in C Minor, among others.

Masked Man

The end of Mozart's life was tragic…and mysterious. In July 1791, a masked stranger asked Mozart to write a Requiem Mass. Even though he was only 35, Mozart had a premonition that the work would be his last. He told friends that he'd been poisoned and had to complete this work as his own requiem before he died. Working frantically, he dictated portions of the requiem from his bed. True to his premonition, Mozart died while completing the composition.

It turned out that the man who commissioned the piece was Austrian Count von Walsegg, who wanted people to believe that he'd written a great requiem for his wife. The count hid his identity so that no one would know he'd actually hired a composer. Furthermore, there's no evidence that Mozart was poisoned. A letter later revealed that Mozart had eaten pork cutlets several weeks before he died. Some of his symptoms resembled those of trichinosis, which can be contracted by eating undercooked pork.

LUDWIG VAN BEETHOVEN (1770–1827)

Beethoven was born in Bonn, Germany, and like Mozart before him, displayed impressive musical talent at a very young age. By the time he was eight, he could play the organ, viola, and piano and had performed for the royal court in Bonn. But he wasn't the prodigy Mozart was, much to his father's dismay. Johann van Beethoven was ruthless when it came to molding his son into a pianist and composer: he made the boy practice through the night and even beat him when he made mistakes. At the age of 11, Beethoven became an apprentice to Christian Gottlob Neefe, organist to the royal court in Bonn. Neefe wrote, "Beethoven [is]...a boy of 11 years, and of most promising talent." Beethoven often took over for Neefe when he was unable to play for the court, and the boy quickly earned a reputation as a "wunderkind."

Life in Vienna

In 1792, 22-year-old Beethoven moved to Vienna. He'd wanted to study with Mozart, but the composer died the year before, so Beethoven decided to train with Joseph Haydn instead. (Mozart and Haydn were close friends, and Haydn was an accomplished composer and musician, sometimes called the "Father of the Symphony.") The compositions he wrote during this period showed Haydn's influence as Beethoven focused on traditional symphonies and piano sonatas, including No. 8 (the "Pathetique Sonata") and No. 14, better known as the "Moonlight Sonata." But over the course of his life, Beethoven's style evolved to include works that expressed his personal struggles and the politics of his time. He wrote the "Waldstein Sonata," numerous concertos, and his final symphony, the Ninth.

Beethoven was both talented and prolific, but most historians agree that one of the things that makes his career so extraordinary was that he was also deaf. He was born able to hear but suffered from tinnitus (ringing in the ears) throughout his childhood. No one knows exactly what caused the illness—everything from lead poisoning to childhood abuse to syphilis has been suggested. But by the time Beethoven was 45, he was completely deaf and was unable to hear the music he played. Over the years, he used various hearing aids to help during concerts. One included a piece of wood attached to the piano; Beethoven held the wood in his teeth so he could feel the piano's vibrations and follow the music.

Conductor Leopold Stokowski founded the American Symphony Orchestra when he was 80...

STARVING FOR THEIR ART?

Beethoven, Mozart, and their contemporaries were celebrities in 18th-century Vienna, but they often had trouble paying their bills. Music was extraordinarily important to the Viennese. Organ grinders on street corners played bits of symphonies. In almost every coffeehouse, accomplished musicians played instruments and sang operas. And people who didn't play an instrument were considered uncultured. But even though music mattered so much, musicians were usually undercompensated. Churches employed musicians in their choirs and even commissioned composers to write original pieces for special masses. Mostly, though, only the aristocracy could afford to employ full-time musicians, and they were not generous.

Pay Scale

Mozart was probably the best paid of his contemporaries, but that didn't keep him solvent. During his young adulthood, Mozart made about 450 florins a year as music director for the archbishop of Salzburg. For writing the opera *Cosí fan tutte* in 1790 he was paid 900 florins, about twice what his contemporaries would have made, and, by his death, he brought in about 1,000 florins a year. In contrast, Mozart's brother-in-law Franz Hofer drew only about 20 florins a year as a violinist at St. Stephen's Church in 1787.

Wealthy patrons and the nobility sponsored Beethoven throughout much of his life. But they almost never paid him enough and were unreliable sources of income. Many times during his life, Beethoven was broke and supplemented his income by giving piano lessons. In 1800 he made 600 florins.

How much was a florin worth in the 18th century? It's nearly impossible to adjust the cost of living over the span of 200 years and make the conversion from florins to dollars. But consider this: civil servants' wages at the time ranged from 700 florins a year for menial positions to 20,000 florins a year for high-level positions.

*   *   *

"Sometimes I hate music. I spend some of my most miserable hours on stage performing. But I've also spent my best ones."

—Linda Ronstadt, 1970

...and signed a six-year recording contract at age 94. (He died a year later.)

OH, FRANKIE!

You might be surprised at the role that trickery played in helping an up-and-coming singer get the "lucky break" he needed.

BACKGROUND

In 1942 a young singer named Frank Sinatra gave a performance at New York's Paramount Theater. Until then, his career had gotten little attention. But that night was different— Sinatra played to a packed house and gave such a powerful performance that about 30 bobby-soxers passed out and several had to be taken away in ambulances. The publicity generated by that incident helped catapult Sinatra to superstardom in less than a year.

BEHIND THE SCENES

The decisive moment in Sinatra's career actually came a few weeks *before* the Paramount show, when his press agent, George Evans, saw a teenage girl throw a rose on stage while Sinatra was singing. "I figured if I could pack the theater with a bunch of girls screaming, 'Oh, Frankie,' I'd really have something," he recounted later.

So Evans paid a dozen teenage girls $5 each to sit in the front rows during the performance and swoon. Rehearsing with them in the basement of the Paramount, he taught some of them to faint in the aisles during the slow songs, and taught others to scream "Oh, Daddy," when Sinatra sang "Embraceable You." He made sure the theater was full by giving away free passes to schoolkids on vacation. He even rented the ambulance that waited in front of the theater to take the girls away.

MASS HYSTERIA

Evans paid only 12 girls, but in a classic example of the power of suggestion, hundreds of others got caught up in the "excitement." About 20 girls who *hadn't* been paid to pass out fainted…and the whole crowd went crazy. The next time Sinatra played the Paramount, recalls a promoter, "they threw more than roses. They threw their panties and their brassieres. They went nuts, absolutely nuts." Sinatra-mania was born. Ol' Blue Eyes went on to become the most popular singer of his generation. But Evans wasn't around to enjoy it. Sinatra fired him a few years later in a dispute over money.

Garth Brooks's college major: Marketing. (Good pick? He's the best-selling solo artist of all time.)

A MUSICAL IS BORN

Proving it's harder than just saying, "Hey, kids, let's put on a show," here are the origins of more great musicals.

CATS (1982)

When T. S. Eliot first wrote *Old Possum's Book of Practical Cats*, a children's book of verse, he circulated it just to his friends; it wasn't published until years later. The same thing happened when Andrew Lloyd Webber, a fan of the book, put some of the poems to music. At first, he only entertained friends with them. Eventually Webber decided to turn them into a short, one-act musical…then changed his mind and began working on a full-length performance. Until January 2006, *Cats* was the longest-running musical in Broadway history, earning more than $100 million since it opened.

MAN OF LA MANCHA (1965)

In the late 1950s, a TV/film writer named Dale Wasserman went to Madrid to do research for a movie. The local press mistakenly reported that he was there to write a play about Don Quixote—which sparked his curiosity. Wasserman became so interested in Quixote and author Miguel Cervantes that he traveled all over Spain, retracing their steps. This, in turn, inspired him to write a TV drama called *I, Don Quixote*, which aired on CBS in 1959. He expanded it into the musical *Man of La Mancha* in the early 1960s.

GYPSY (1959)

In 1957 actress and burlesque dancer Gypsy Rose Lee published her autobiography, *Gypsy*, which focused on her early years as a vaudeville performer with her sister as well as her strained relationship with Mama Rose, her domineering "stage mother." Theater producer David Merrick read an excerpt of the book in *Harper's* and approached Lee for permission to turn *Gypsy* into a stage musical. Jerome Robbins, another major theater producer, had read the book and also wanted to do a musical, so he and Merrick teamed up with a *third* producer who wanted to make a *Gypsy* musical, Leland Heyward. Broadway star Ethel Merman had asked Heyward to produce her next show, and she felt she'd be perfect to play Mama Rose. Irving Berlin and Cole Porter both turned down offers to write the music, so the job went to Jule Styne (on Merman's demand) while Robbins's *West Side Story* lyricist Stephen Sondheim wrote the words. It opened in 1959, played on Broadway for two years, and produced the standard "Everything's Coming Up Roses."

ANNIE (1977)

Lyricist Martin Charnin was browsing in a bookstore, doing some last-minute Christmas shopping, when he saw a book called *Arf: The Life and Hard Times of Little Orphan Annie*. He bought it for a friend and intended to wrap it and give it away. Instead, he stayed up that night reading it...and decided to turn it into a musical. Ironically, although the musical was a smash, the movie it inspired in 1982 was such a huge financial disaster that it even caused the *play's* ticket sales to plummet...and ultimately forced it to close in 1983.

LES MISÉRABLES (1987)

French playwright Alain Boubil got the idea after seeing *Jesus Christ Superstar* on Broadway: he figured that if pop-rock music could be used to tell the story of Jesus, why not tell the story of the French Revolution? Boubil wasn't sure how to do it...until he saw *Oliver!*, adapted from the Charles Dickens novel *Oliver Twist*. He decided to adapt a classic novel from the period...and settled on Victor Hugo's novel *Les Misérables*.

*   *   *

THERE'S SOMETHING DRUMMING IN DENMARK

One of the most popular bands in Denmark is Safri Duo. But they're not a typical band—there are only two members, and they both play percussion. One of their biggest Danish hits was "The Bongo Song," which prominently features bongos. They also do marimba-only remakes of classical music and in 2002 recorded a version of Michael McDonald's "Sweet Freedom," on which McDonald actually sang lead vocal.

---

30 artists turned down "Bye Bye Love" before the Everly Brothers made it a #1 hit.

DEM BONES

And other body parts found in song titles.

"Hot Legs"
(Rod Stewart)

"Pink Toenails"
(Dixie Chicks)

"Popsicle Toes"
(Michael Franks)

"The Scalp Song"
(Simpson College
fight song)

"Go for the
Throat"
(Iggy Pop)

"Protect Ya Neck"
(Wu-Tang Clan)

"Do Your Ears
Hang Low?"
(traditional)

"Hips Don't Lie"
(Shakira)

"Baby Got Back"
(Sir Mix-a-Lot)

"Thigh High
Nylons"
(Mustard Plug)

"Muscle of Love"
(Alice Cooper)

"I Want My Rib
Back"
(Kenny Chesney)

"Waist Deep in
the Big Muddy"
(Pete Seeger)

"Spleen" (Staind)

"Dem Bones"
(spiritual)

"Clavicle"
(Alkaline Trio)

"Skull and
Crossbones"
(Stormwitch)

"Red Right Ankle"
(The Decemberists)

"Ankle Deep"
(Tom Petty)

"Sea Legs"
(The Shins)

"Willie and the
Hand Jive"
(Johnny Otis)

"Black Finger-
nails, Red Wine"
(Eskimo Joe)

"Fingernail Moon"
(Annie Lennox)

"Lips of an
Angel" (Hinder)

"Skin"
(Rascal Flatts)

"Cheek to Cheek"
(Irving Berlin)

"These Eyes"
(The Guess Who)

"Lyin' Eyes"
(The Eagles)

"Eye in the Sky"
(The Alan Parsons
Project)

"Bette Davis Eyes"
(Kim Carnes)

"Put Your Head
on My Shoulder"
(Paul Anka)

"Heel"
(The Toadies)

"Head, Shoulders,
Knees, and Toes"
(children's
traditional)

Frédéric Chopin and Jim Morrison are both buried in Pere Lachaise cemetery in Paris.

EATIN' THE
TIN SANDWICH

*The history of the harmonica will take you to China,
Africa, Europe, the Mississippi Delta, and beyond...*

BLOWING IN THE WIND

When musicians like Bob Dylan and John Lennon became famous in the 1960s, they did it with a little help from the harmonica. And they gave the harmonica a boost, too. Sales of the tiny instrument skyrocketed when folksingers and rock musicians brought it back into the limelight. But it wasn't the first time the "mouth harp" became a sensation.

From the 1920s until the 1940s, the harmonica was one of the most popular instruments in the country. The biggest blues, jazz, country, and hillbilly bands—and even theater companies—had harmonica players as part of their acts. Harmonica classes became a regular part of curriculums in many public schools. By the 1930s, the German company M. Hohner, the biggest maker of harmonicas worldwide, was selling more than 25 million a year.

Where did the easy-to-carry instrument originate? That's a very old story.

THE SOUND OF OLD SHENG-HAI

Most musicologists agree that the earliest predecessor to the harmonica was developed in China between 3,000 and 5,000 years ago. It was a three-foot-long instrument made of bamboo pipes called the *sheng*, which means "sublime voice." Although neither the sheng nor its ancient sisters, the *naw*, the *yu*, and the *ho*, looked anything like a harmonica, they all had one important feature in common: free reeds.

A reed is a thin strip of cane, wood, plastic, or metal that vibrates when air passes over it. A "free-reed" instrument, like the accordion or harmonica, produces sound from a reed vibrating inside a chamber—the vibrating reed produces a single note and doesn't touch anything else.

"Fixed-reed" instruments, like the clarinet and the saxophone, use a reed that vibrates against some other part of the instrument. On the clarinet or sax, it's the mouthpiece, which is attached to a tube with holes in it. Cover the holes and you change the pitch.

The *sheng* had multiple free reeds set inside bamboo tubes, which allowed chords (multiple notes that sound good together) to be played. For thousands of years, the sheng and similar instruments were played all over China and Southeast Asia.

FREEING THE PITCH

Fixed-reed instruments had been played in Europe for centuries (and some say that even those were introduced from Asia), but free-reeds had not. In 1776 French Jesuit missionary Pierre Amiot sent several shengs from China to Paris—and people who heard them loved them. Within a few years, European instrument makers were building their own free-reed devices, making instruments such as the harmonium and the reed organ.

In 1821 a 16-year-old named Christian Friedrich Ludwig Buschmann was experimenting with different ways to combine pitch pipes in order to create a new instrument. He soldered together 15 pipes of different pitches, similar to the sheng and, without knowing it, made the next big step toward the modern harmonica.

THE INS AND OUTS

Buschmann's harmonica, known as the *aura,* was an immediate hit, and soon other instrument makers began experimenting with the design. In 1825 a man named Richter (his first name is unknown) came up with the idea of a 10-hole, 20-note configuration, one row of reeds activated by inhaling, the other by exhaling.

Richter arranged the notes with the common person in mind: no matter where the mouth is placed, it would always play notes that were in harmony—that sounded good—together, whether inhaling or exhaling. That's why the instrument is called a "harmony-ca"—it's always in harmony. Richter's three-octave model has barely changed at all. (Pretty impressive when you consider that a grand piano has an eight-octave range but weighs about 1,000 pounds—4,000 times as much as a harmonica.)

HARMONIC CONVERGENCE

In 1857 Matthias Hohner, a clock maker from Trössingen, Germany, visited a harmonica maker in Vienna, Austria, and decided to make his own instruments. He started making them in his kitchen with the help of his family, and sold 650 harmonicas the first year. In 1862 relatives in the United States urged him to export some of the instruments. He did, and by 1887 was producing more than a million harmonicas a year, with sales across Europe and the United States.

BLEND IT LIKE HOHNER

One of the things that helped make the harmonica so successful was its musical flexibility. It could play romping *Biergarten* music, plaintive European folk songs, and even complex classical music. And it was small and inexpensive, so even poor people could afford one. By the late 1800s, African Americans in the South, who had their own musical traditions that could be traced back thousands of years, were inventing a new kind of music: the blues. And the "mouth harp" would be part of it. The "bending" of the notes—using air direction and pressure to slide between notes—would become the trademark sound of the blues. The popularity of the music would soon influence other new styles of American music—jug band, Dixieland, jazz, and swing—and would help carry the harmonica to even greater popularity.

THE GOLDEN YEARS

The 1920s began the first golden age for the harmonica. Two new technologies were sweeping the country: radio and recording. That meant that people could become national stars relatively quickly—and so could the instruments they played: Vernon Dalhart's 1925 recording "Wreck of the Old 97," with Dalhart singing and playing harmonica, became country music's first million-seller.

By the end of the 1920s, hundreds of artists were making recordings, and many of them featured the harmonica. And it wasn't just for accompaniment: all-harmonica bands became hot tickets. Then, in the late 1930s, a musical virtuoso named Larry Adler gave it another boost: Adler played classical and jazz as a harmonica soloist. How popular was he? From the 1940s until he died in 2001, he regularly played with the biggest stars of the day:

Jack Benny, George Gershwin, Billie Holiday, and later, Sting and Elton John.

ELECTRIFIED

The harmonica went into decline in the 1950s, but bluesmen like Little Walter, Howlin' Wolf, and Sonny Boy Williamson kept it alive, creating a modern blues-harp sound that would be carried on by James Cotton and Charlie Musselwhite. By the 1960s, the harmonica was back, thanks first to the folk music craze and then to Beatlemania.

Since then, harmonica players like Stevie Wonder, John Mayall, Huey Lewis, Delbert McClinton, Magic Dick (J. Geils Band), Neil Young, Bruce Springsteen, Charlie McCoy, Mickey Rafael (Willie Nelson's band), and John Popper (Blues Traveler) continue to show the world what one little instrument can do.

HARMONICA TRIVIA

• Nicknames for the harmonica: the Harp, the Tin Sandwich (Cowboy dialect), the Mississippi Saxophone (Blues lingo), and the Mouth Organ (from the German *mundharmonika* or *mundorgan*).

• Presidents Lincoln, Wilson, Coolidge, and Reagan were all harp players of varying ability. Lincoln reportedly wrote a letter to Hohner, telling how he enjoyed playing the harmonica to relax.

• The best-selling record of 1947 was "Peg O' My Heart" by a harmonica trio called the Harmonicats. After the Harmonicats' success, the musicians union decided to classify the harmonica as an instrument. Before that, they called it a toy.

• On December 16, 1965, astronaut Wally Schirra played "Jingle Bells" on the harmonica—from *Gemini VI*, at an altitude of 160 miles above Earth.

• In 1986 the M. Hohner Company sold their billionth harmonica.

• Currently, the most expensive harmonica in the Hohner catalog is a "Chord 48" (the size of a baseball bat, with hundreds of reeds). Cost: $1,500.

• More expensive, but not in the catalog: the solid gold, gem-encrusted model that Hohner presented to Pope Pius XI in the 1930s.

In 1972 the Raspberries released a raspberry-scented scratch-and-sniff album cover.

AMERICAN IDOL
BY THE NUMBERS

The incredible success story of this show is still unfolding. But one thing's for sure—American Idol is a ratings phenomenon…and a starmaker. Here are some of the show's impressive statistics. (So far.)

4: Final ranking of Season 5 contestant Chris Daughtry. A fan favorite, he was asked to front the rock band Fuel after his elimination, but declined. Good move—his debut album, *Daughtry*, has sold over 3.8 million copies—more than winners Ruben Studdard (2.4 million over three albums), Fantasia Barrino (2.1 million over two albums), and Taylor Hicks (700,000 from one album).

17: Age of the youngest *American Idol* winner, Season 6's Jordin Sparks. The previous year's winner, 2006's Taylor Hicks, holds the title for oldest idol. (He was 29.)

19: Number of sellout shows during the 2006 American Idols *Live!* Tour. The tour grossed $35.2 million on 59 dates and had a total attendance of 645,782 people. Top attendance was on July 30 in Greensboro, North Carolina, when 15,337 fans showed up. It was the most successful tour since they began in 2002.

27: Number of albums released by eliminated *American Idol* contestants. The most successful "loser" was Season 2 runner-up Clay Aiken, who has sold more than 6.5 million records. The least successful? Season 3's eighth-place contestant, Jon Peter Lewis. His 2006 album, *Stories from Hollywood*, sold only 1,000 copies (but it did get him a mention in the *Bathroom Reader*).

62: Number of songs released by *American Idol* alumni that have made Billboard's Hot 100 list. Kelly Clarkson has the most charted hits (10).

229: Total number of episodes through the end of Season 6.

300%: Increase in viewership between Season 1 and the finale of Season 6. The first season averaged only 12.7 million viewers, compared to 30.6 million in year six.

In the '30s, jazz musicians called gigs "apples." They called New York City "the *Big Apple*."

$750: Weekly stipend—including wardrobe budget—given to Season 4 contestants. (The show is tight-lipped about these numbers, and the amount from Season 4 seems to be the only one that's been leaked.) Season 4 runner-up Bo Bice explained the secret to living on such a small amount: "Make a fried baloney sandwich, mustard on one side of the bread and mayonnaise on the other, add some cheese, then a little cup of ramen. It's a good meal, man."

130,000: Difference in votes between Season 2 winner Ruben Studdard and runner-up Clay Aiken. Out of more than 24 million votes, Studdard received 50.28 percent and Aiken got 49.72 percent, making it the closest finale in the show's history.

9.5 million: Number of copies sold of Season 4 winner Carrie Underwood's debut album, *Some Hearts*. Underwood is also the only Idol to earn an American Music Award, Billboard Music Award, and Grammy in the same season (2006–2007) and the only Idol to win (or even be nominated for) Best New Artist at the Grammys.

16.1 million: Total albums sold by Season 1 winner Kelly Clarkson. She is also the first *American Idol* artist (and only the fifth recording artist in history) to have her first three albums debut in the top three on the Billboard 200.

64.5 million: Record-setting number of text messages sent during the fifth season. (Only Cingular customers could vote via text message, which makes the figure even more impressive.)

37.7 million: Number of viewers for the debut of the show's sixth season, a record for *American Idol*. The season's premiere was also the highest-rated prime-time telecast of the 2006–2007 season on any network.

$923 million: Net worth of Simon Fuller—TV producer, talent agent, and *American Idol* creator. He devised the British phenomenon *Pop Idol* in 2001 and brought the show to America soon after. Fuller also created the TV show *So You Think You Can Dance?* and negotiated David Beckham's move to the Los Angeles Galaxy, which netted the soccer star a reputed $250 million.

How high did Prince's song "7" get on the pop chart? It made it to #7.

ROCKET 88

The story of the first rock 'n' roll song.

BACKGROUND
Ike Turner and His Kings of Rhythm were a popular rhythm-and-blues group in the South in the late 1940s and early '50s. Turner, the band's manager, had earned a reputation as a stellar boogie-woogie pianist and songwriter. In traveling with bands of all genres around the country since the age of nine (and working as a sideman at recording sessions), Turner developed a distinctive, hard-driving style that combined jazz, blues, and country techniques.

One night after a 1951 gig at the Riverside Hotel in Clarksdale, Mississippi, Turner got a call from his friend B. B. King. The bluesman had set up a recording session for Turner and his band in Memphis with a producer named Sam Phillips. For the session, Turner decided to write a brand-new song called "Rocket 88."

The song was about the Oldsmobile 88, a model that had debuted two years earlier. It was the fastest American-made car at the time, with a powerful engine known as a "Rocket V8." Like a lot of blues and R&B songs, the lyrics could be interpreted as metaphors for sex, but Turner insists the song really is an ode to the car. Lyrics include: "V-8 motor and this modern design / my convertible top and the girls don't mind / sporting with me, riding all around town for joy / blow your horn, Rocket, blow your horn."

RECORDING
Turner didn't have much time to write the song—the band had to drive the 75 miles from Clarksdale to Memphis the next day. So he borrowed heavily from a couple of other songs. He stole the car theme (and some lyrics) from a 1947 song by Jimmy Liggins called "Cadillac Boogie." He took the melody, piano line, and even the title from a 1949 instrumental by boogie-woogie pianist Pete Johnson called "Rocket 88 Boogie."

But when the band arrived in Memphis on March 3, they discovered that guitarist Willie Kizart's amplifier, stored in the car's trunk, had been damaged by water during the trip. Kizart tried to plug some holes in the amp by stuffing them with paper. It didn't quite work, but he and Turner didn't mind; it gave his guitar a fuzzy, raw, feedback-laden sound that they actually liked. To Kizart's guitar and Turner's piano they added a stand-up bass, a driving drum beat, and a saxophone solo.

For unknown reasons the song wasn't credited to Ike Turner and His Kings of Rhythm, possibly because Turner was under contract elsewhere and couldn't record under his own name. Instead, the song was credited to Jackie Brenston and His Delta Cats, a band that didn't actually exist, although Brenston, Turner's regular sax player, sang the song. (The songwriting credits also say Brenston cowrote the song, but Turner wrote it alone.)

Released in April 1951, the song was a national hit on black radio stations, and the 45 sold well. It went to #1 on the R&B chart for six weeks (the pop chart, at the time, was for white artists only). "Rocket 88" became Turner's first commercial success. In the mid-1960s, he'd become a household name when he teamed up with a young singer named Anna Mae Bullock...whom he renamed Tina Turner.

WHY IT'S THE FIRST

With the money he made from producing "Rocket 88," Sam Phillips started Sun Records, which allowed him to record some of rock 'n' roll's earliest superstars, including Jerry Lee Lewis, Carl Perkins, and Elvis Presley. As someone who helped shape and define the rock 'n' roll sound, Phillips is an authority. And he says "Rocket 88" is, without a doubt, the first rock 'n' roll song.

Turner didn't just pull "Rocket 88" out of thin air (especially since he lifted so much of it from other songs). Dozens of blues, jazz, and swing songs have a similar dance beat, or fuzzy electric guitars, or a mixture of country and R&B elements. What makes "Rocket 88" the first rock 'n' roll song is that it had *all* of those elements.

• It combined a hard-charging country melody with a "jump blues" boogie-woogie piano riff.

• Turner's lineup consisted of guitar, drums, bass, saxophone, and piano—instrumentation that most early rock 'n' roll bands would later duplicate.

The Beatles' "All You Need Is Love" opens with a few bars of the French national anthem.

- Its lyrical themes, cars and sex, appealed to teenagers.
- It was a #1 hit on the R&B chart, which featured songs popular with both black and white audiences.
- Turner's guitar style blended country, jazz, blues, and R&B. Music historians now define rock 'n' roll as the same combination.

INFLUENCE

Just after Ike Turner had a hit with "Rocket 88," the country group Bill Haley and the Saddlemen recorded a cover of it that became a hit in the northeastern United States. After that success, Haley broke up the Saddlemen and formed the Comets, a rock group, that went on to record "Rock Around the Clock" in 1954. That recording would become the first rock 'n' roll song to go to #1 on the pop chart—and, along with "Rocket 88," set the style for rock 'n' roll for years to come.

*   *   *

IMPORTANT DATES IN MUSIC HISTORY

1898: Thomas Edison perfects the invention of the phonograph, making recorded sound possible. His first recording: a recitation of "Mary Had a Little Lamb."

1923: The first movie with recorded sound is shown in Los Angeles. It shows a couple dancing to music played by four musicians.

1957: Ricky Nelson sings Fats Domino's "I'm Walkin'" on his sitcom *The Adventures of Ozzie and Harriet*. Nelson's singing becomes a weekly fixture on the show and turns him into one of rock 'n' roll's first teen idols.

1970: On April 10, Paul McCartney announces that the Beatles have broken up.

1988: On April 12, 1960s icon Sonny Bono is elected the Republican mayor of Palm Springs, California. The day before, his ex-wife, Cher, wins an Oscar for *Moonstruck*.

2006: The last original episode of *Soul Train* airs.

Boxer "Sugar" Ray Leonard's full name: Ray Charles Leonard. (He was named after Ray Charles.)

INFLUENTIAL UNKNOWNS

They inspired everyone from Janis Joplin to the Rolling Stones, but we bet you don't know most of their names. Here are some of the most influential musicians never to make it big on the world's stage.

ERIK SATIE
Genre: Classical
Story: Satie was a pianist and composer in the late 19th and early 20th centuries who disregarded the era's popular romantic music styles to create minimalist and avant-garde compositions. His pieces often had mysterious and esoteric names like "Chilled Pieces," "Drivelling Preludes (for a Dog)," and "Dried up Embryos." Some included very specific instructions: "Vexations," for example, directed the performer to rest in silence before playing the piece 840 times in a row. Satie often used typewriters, foghorns, rattles, and other noisemaking devices in his compositions. In 1917 he collaborated with Pablo Picasso and Jean Cocteau to create a surrealist ballet, *Parade*, which featured awkward dancing and noisemakers instead of instruments in some parts. It landed Satie in jail for several days and earned him the label "cultural anarchist" from one critic.
Influence: "Classical" music in the 20th century was dominated by minimalist, experimental, avant garde composers who rejected traditional musical conventions. This was all done by Satie first, which heavily influenced composers such as John Adams, Philip Glass, and John Cage.

BIG STAR
Genre: Rock
Story: Big Star's tightly crafted pop combined the jangly, guitar-based pop of the 1960s (like the Byrds) with hard-charging 1970s Southern rock (like the Allman Brothers Band). The result was a new kind of music, later called "power pop." Chris Bell, Andy Hummel, and Joey Stephens formed the band in Memphis in 1971 and a few months later Alex Chilton joined them as co-frontman alongside Bell. (At age 20, Chilton was already an established artist, having had a #1 single with "The Letter" as

lead singer of the Box Tops.) Big Star was only together until 1975, but recorded two critically acclaimed albums in that time: *#1 Record* and *Radio City.*

Influence: Dozens of bands have cited Big Star as an influence. Their mixture of gently ringing guitars, hard-rock riffs, and tight melodies are evident in the music of groups like R.E.M., the Gin Blossoms, and the Replacements, who had a hit with the song "Alex Chilton." Cheap Trick most closely followed Big Star's power pop. That band even covered Big Star's "In the Street," used as the theme song for *That '70s Show.*

NEU!

Genre: Electronica

Story: NEU! (pronounced "noy") formed in Germany in 1971 and consisted of studio engineer Konrad Plank, drummer/guitarist Klaus Dinger, and keyboardist/guitarist Michael Rother. The band's self-titled 1972 debut laid the template for what would become electronic music by introducing a hypnotic, repetitive beat. NEU! called it the *motorik beat,* usually four quarter-note hits (three bass drum beats followed by one snare) repeated throughout a song. NEU! also pioneered the use of synthesizers and drum machines in pop music and was the first band to release "remixes" of their songs, now standard in dance music. The band broke up in 1975.

Influence: Members of NEU! worked with another German electronic band called Kraftwerk, who, with their 22-minute long hit "Autobahn," are frequently cited as the inventors of electronic music. NEU!'s beats and techniques were also used by bands like Devo, U2, and Radiohead.

GRAHAM BOND ORGANISATION

Genre: Blues-rock

Story: Before the mid-1960s, British rock was clean-cut pop, like the early Beatles. Graham Bond was one of the first to introduce the blues to British rock, making it grittier and more experimental. Bond was a jazz musician, but as the club scene shifted to rock 'n' roll music in the early 1960s, so did he, forming a band called the Graham Bond Organisation in 1963. (He played organ and sang—other members of the group included Ginger Baker and Jack

Bruce, who later formed the group Cream with Eric Clapton.) Bond brought technical proficiency and complexity to British rock, leading to long, bluesy guitar and organ solos. He also introduced the Hammond organ and the mellotron to rock. Yet, in spite of the band's impressive chops, The Organisation's music was largely unpalatable to popular music audiences: The group focused on creating whole albums (as opposed to radio-friendly singles) and was unwilling to alter its work for mainstream success. In 1965 Bruce and Baker left the band. Bond continued to play and record until 1973. He committed suicide in 1974.

Influence: British rock in the late 1960s was a direct result of Bond's influence and that blues-rock sound came to define the sound of the 1960s. Bond's sound inspired the Who, Eric Clapton, Blind Faith, the Yardbirds, early Fleetwood Mac, and Led Zeppelin, and American acts such as Janis Joplin, the Doors, and the Grateful Dead.

THE MONKS

Genre: Rock

Story: In 1964, five American GIs stationed in Germany decided to start a band: Gary Burger (lead guitar/vocals), Larry Clark (organ), Dave Day (banjo), Eddie Shaw (bass guitar), and Roger Johnston (drums). Calling themselves the Torquays, they played Chuck Berry and Beatles covers. After the men were discharged from the army, they decided to stay in Germany, changed the band's name to the Monks, and kept playing, but veering away from typical rock conventions, mostly basing their songs around rhythm instead of melody or chord progressions. Their lyrics were often inane and sometimes macabre—in one song, the Monks juxtaposed references to the escalating Vietnam War with nursery rhymes. Their onstage presence was equally peculiar: they often wore monk robes or all black, sometimes played with nooses around their necks, and shaved their hair in the style of Franciscan monks, with a bald circle at the top of their heads. The band abruptly broke up in 1967 when some members wanted to move back to the United States.

Influence: Jimi Hendrix saw a Monks show in 1965 and was intrigued by the band's use of feedback and the "wah-wah" pedal. The Monks' experiments with atonal, aggressive, unpolished music about dark themes hugely influenced the Velvet Underground. The music—and the "let's try it out" ethic—is a direct ancestor of punk rock.

WANDA JACKSON

Genre: Rockabilly, Country

Story: Called "the nice lady with a nasty little voice," Wanda Jackson began her career singing gospel and country music in the 1950s. But while recording her first album in 1958, she was one song short and included a crowd-pleaser from her live shows: "Let's Have a Party." More than any of the other songs, that one showcased her raw, growling vocal style. The song became a hit, and further encouraged by her boyfriend, Elvis Presley, Jackson recorded more rockabilly music during the 1950s, before returning to country in the 1960s, and then to gospel.

Influence: Jackson's "nasty little voice" paved the way for future female rock singers (Pat Benatar, the B-52s) and harder-edged country singers, such as Tanya Tucker and Loretta Lynn. Jackson still records and tours.

*　　*　　*

TOP 10 HITS OF 1960

1. "Theme From *A Summer Place*" —Percy Faith

2. "He'll Have To Go" —Jim Reeves

3. "Cathy's Clown" —The Everly Brothers

4. "Running Bear" —Johnny Preston

5. "Teen Angel" —Mark Dinning

6. "It's Now Or Never" —Elvis Presley

7. "Handy Man" —Jimmy Jones

8. "I'm Sorry" —Brenda Lee

9. "El Paso" —Marty Robbins

10. "The Twist" —Chubby Checker

WHAT'S OPERA, DOC?

Confession: Uncle John's main connection to opera comes solely from the classic Bugs Bunny cartoon in which Elmer Fudd sings "Kill de wabbit" while thunder and lightning rock the background. It still brings a tear to his eye.

"No opera plot can be sensible, for in sensible situations people do not sing."
—W. H. Auden

"Opera is when a guy gets stabbed in the back and instead of bleeding, sings."
—Robert Benchley

"One can't judge Wagner's opera *Lohengrin* after a first hearing, and I certainly don't intend hearing it a second time."
—Gioachino Rossini

"*Parsifal* is the kind of opera that starts at six o'clock and after it has been running for three hours, you check your watch and it says 6:20."
—David Randolph

"If you can sell green toothpaste in this country, you can sell opera."
—Sarah Caldwell

"In opera, there is always too much singing."
—Claude Debussy

"When an opera star sings her head off, she usually improves her appearance."
—Victor Borge

"An unalterable and unquestioned law of the musical world required that the German text of French operas sung by Swedish artists should be translated into Italian for the clearer understanding of English-speaking audiences."
—Edith Wharton

"An exotic and irrational entertainment."
—Samuel Johnson

"The prelude to Wagner's *Tristan und Isolde* reminds one of the old Italian painting of a martyr whose intestines are slowly unwound from his body on a reel."
—Eduard Hanslick

"Oh how wonderful, really wonderful opera would be if there were no singers!"
—Gioachino Rossini

The 1957 Bugs Bunny cartoon *What's Opera, Doc?* adapted music from various Wagner operas.

A BRIEF HISTORY
OF THE JUKEBOX

Jukeboxes played a critical role in developing popular music. Without them, there would have been no market for blues, jazz, or country music, and the record industry might not have survived. Hard to believe? Read on.

THAT'S AN EARFUL

When Thomas Edison invented the "Edison Speaking Phonograph" in 1877, it was an accident—he was actually trying to create a telephone answering machine. When that didn't work, he suggested a new use for it: a dictation machine for business executives. The one thing Edison did *not* want his proud machine used for was entertainment. But that's precisely what happened.

On November 23, 1889, a man named Louis Glass bought an Edison machine, installed a coin slot, and set it up inside the Palais Royale Saloon in San Francisco. Edison's phonograph didn't have much in common with 20th century jukeboxes: it played a wax cylinder, it had no electric amplifiers (just four listening tubes, so only four people could use it at a time), and it could play only a single song over and over.

But most people had never even seen a phonograph…so it was quite a novelty. The machine—which cost a nickel to play a two-minute song—reportedly brought in more than $15 a week, big money in 1889. Glass set up a dozen more around San Francisco and raked in the profits.

THE AMERICAN ENTERTAINER

Word of the money-making machine quickly spread. Dozens of saloons around the country copied the idea, and within a year a whole new industry had sprung up to capitalize on the fad.

Seventeen years later, the first true "juke box" was introduced. It was called the "Automatic Entertainer"—a slightly misleading name, since it had to be cranked by hand. But it did play the new 10-inch discs instead of Edison's wax-and-cardboard cylinder recordings. It also offered more than one selection; it had a huge 40-inch horn instead of listening tubes (though you still couldn't hear it unless you were standing nearby); and it could even tell the difference between real coins and "slugs."

Its most impressive feature, however, was its record-changing mechanism. This was mounted inside a glass cabinet at the top of the machine, and customers could actually watch the machine pick their record and play it. For most people, that was worth a nickel by itself. They would stand and gawk as the machine performed for them. Thereafter, the jukebox was as much of an attraction as the music it played.

AN ELECTRIFYING DEVELOPMENT

The Automatic Entertainer and its descendants dominated the industry for the next 20 years. But they were still missing something: volume.

In 1927—at about the same time that the electric guitar was being developed—the Automatic Music Instrument Company (AMI) changed that. They introduced the world's first electrically amplified music-playing machine. "Electrical amplification was the single most important technical improvement in the history of the machine," Vincent Lynch writes in *Jukebox: The Golden Age*. "Suddenly the jukebox was capable of competing with loud orchestras. It could entertain large groups of people in large halls, all at once, for a nickel."

The timing couldn't have been better. In the late 1920s and early 1930s, radio was the hot new medium. It threatened to make both jukeboxes *and* phonographs obsolete.

But as soon as jukeboxes could be heard in crowds, they found a profitable new home: speakeasies. Alcohol had become illegal in 1920, and rather than stop drinking, millions of Americans started frequenting these illegal bars. They needed entertainment. "Automatic phonographs" were the perfect solution: they were cheaper and less risky than big bands, and more entertaining than a piano player. In small, low-rent speakeasies, they were also the only way to get around the prejudice and elitism of radio, which shunned most "race" music such as jazz and rhythm and blues in favor of classical and mainstream pop hits.

1940s Wurlitzer Jukebox slogan: "The magic that changes moods."

Because of this, black speakeasies—known as *juke joints*
(originally slang for prostitution houses, *juke* came to mean
"dance")—preferred to get their music from automatic phonographs. "For all practical purposes," says one music critic, "there
was no place a black musician could have his records heard on a
large scale but the jukebox." In time, the machines became so
closely associated with juke joints that they became known as
jukeboxes.

Well…to be fair, it wasn't just booze that saved the jukebox.
Because of the Great Depression in the 1930s, most families
couldn't afford their own Victrola phonographs and records. But
they *could* afford to pop an occasional nickel into a jukebox.

THE GOLDEN AGE

Jukeboxes were a thriving industry in the late 1930s; their impact
on the recording industry is hard to imagine today. In 1939 jukeboxes used 30 million records. In 1942 that number was up to
about 60 million—half of all records produced that year.

But competition from network radio, home phonographs, and
other sources grew increasingly fierce. One way jukebox manufacturers distinguished themselves was by making their machines as
pleasing to the eye as they were to the ear. As late as 1937, jukeboxes had been virtually indistinguishable from the large wooden
radios of the day. "But from then on," says Charles McGovern of
the Smithsonian Institution, "the jukebox was more than a source
of music. It was a showpiece, a spectacle with lights, color, and
observable mechanical motion."

Manufacturers experimented with new designs involving glass,
chrome, ornate metals, bubble lights, mirrors, special lighting, and
plastics—which had just been invented—to give their machines
beautiful new art deco designs that would stand out in any environment. Even the names of the machines were flashy: some popular models included Singing Towers, the Throne of Music, the
Mother of Plastic, and the Luxury Light-Up.

But the most famous design of all was the Wurlitzer 1015, better known as "The Bubbler," thanks to its famous bubble tubes,
which was introduced in 1946. In the next two years the company
manufactured and sold more than 60,000 of them, making it the
most popular jukebox in history and establishing Wurlitzer as the

industry giant. "In most peoples' minds," says McGovern, "the 1015 is *the* Jukebox."

THE HEYDAY

Post-war sales of all jukeboxes were enormous: by the late 1940s there were more than 700,000 of them in the United States, filling nearly every bar, bowling alley, malt shop—even gas stations and schools—with music. But mechanically they weren't all that different from the ones that had been around in the 1930s. Most jukeboxes contained about 20 records and played between 20 and 40 songs (depending on whether they could play the "B" sides).

That changed in December 1948, when the Seeburg company introduced the Model M100-A, a jukebox that wasn't nearly as sleek or fancy as the competition, but had a whopping 100 selections. Because it offered so many musical choices, it had the potential to make a lot more money than any other jukebox on the market. The golden age of jukeboxes was over—beauty would never again count as much as performance and profitability.

THE JUKEBOX BUST

The market for jukeboxes grew through the 1960s, but by the 1970s, it started to decline. There were lots of reasons: splintering musical genres, FM radio, cassette tapes, the rising cost of records (which forced operators to charge more for each play), and even drunk-driving laws. "That was a 'problem' I heard about from Virginia to Mississippi," says a veteran jukebox distributor. "The fact that the drunk driving laws were being enforced meant that a lot of bars started closing down. It took away a big market."

By 1992 there were fewer than 180,000 jukeboxes in America. Recently, compact-disc technology has created a new market for them—and there's talk of developing "digital" jukeboxes. But none of them is likely to be as exciting or important as the originals. To most of us, the machines that shaped pop music in America are just collector's items or curiosities.

*   *   *

"Rock 'n' roll is not so much a question of electric guitars as it is striped pants."

—David Lee Roth

KEYS AND SLURS

More helpful musical terms. (For others, see page 69.)

Concerto: A composition written for a solo instrument accompanied by an orchestra

Overture: Musical introduction to an opera or other large musical work

Requiem mass: A musical mass for the dead, usually with soloists, chorus, and orchestra

Nocturne: Music meant to evoke a dreamy, "nighttime" mood

Trill: Rapid alternation between notes that are a half tone or whole tone apart

Recitative: Solo vocal style (used in genres like opera) characterized by loose rhythm; similar to normal speech

Impromptu: First used in the title of six compositions by Bohemian composer Jan Vaclav Vorisek, it refers to short, written piano pieces with an improvised "feel" to them

Interlude: Short instrumental music played between scenes in a play or opera

Reprise: A repetition of music or a theme in a composition, often with some changes

Leitmotif: Literally "leading motive," this refers generally to the dominant theme in a piece of music. More specifically, it refers to the basic recurring melodic theme, representing an idea, person, etc., in an opera (common to operas by Wagner).

Harmony: The playing of two or more notes simultaneously; also the interval relationship between the notes (thirds, fifths, and so on)

Key: The "home note" of the scale the piece uses. If you sing the "Do Re Mi" song with the first "Do" being an A—the song will be in the key of A. If you sing Do as F—it's in F. (Most songs and compositions don't stay exclusively in one key throughout their length.)

Modulation: Shifting to another key in the middle of a song or composition

Drone: A sustained musical sound, usually low, played under a melody. Also a part of an instrument that produces a sound, such as the drones on a bagpipe.

Vibrato: Quick, pulsating variation in pitch in a sung or played note

Tremolo: Quick repetition of the same note, often on the violin, or the rapid alternation between two notes (on a piano)

Dissonance: Notes that "sound bad" together

MUSICAL NOTATION TERMS

Legato: Indicates notes to be played continuously, rather than with separation between them

Staccato: Indicates notes to be played in short, separated bursts, as opposed to legato

Adagio: A relatively slow tempo

Presto: Very fast

Largo: Very slow

Grazioso: Played gracefully

Crescendo: A gradual increase in volume

Diminuendo: A gradual decrease in volume

Allegro: Literally "cheerful" or "merry"; a relatively fast tempo

Accelerando: A gradually increasing tempo

Grave: Played slowly and seriously

Pizzicato: Instruction to pluck, rather than bow, a string instrument like a cello or violin

Slur: A musical instruction to play a succession of notes without interruption; e.g., in one bow movement on a violin

Rubato: A direction to allow a player or singer some rhythmic freedom for emotional effect. Common during the Romantic period.

*   *   *

2-2-2 LOOKIN' OUT MY BACK DOOR

Creedence Clearwater Revival is the number-one #2 band of all time. They had five songs reach #2 on the pop chart—more than any other act—without ever reaching #1. Those five hits were: "Proud Mary," "Bad Moon Rising," "Green River," "Travelin' Band," and "Lookin' Out My Back Door."

Just a coincidence: Duran Duran members Andy, John, and Roger Taylor are not related.

ROCK 'N' ROLL HEAVEN

It's human nature to have a grim fascination with death. And when a famous person dies suddenly, we get even more curious. Here we respectfully present the grisly details about musicians who died of decidedly unnatural causes.

Star: Duane Allman
Story: The legendary lead guitar player for the Allman Brothers Band (and a session player on some of rock's most revered albums, including Eric Clapton's *Layla and Other Assorted Love Songs*) was enjoying a break in Macon, Georgia, after the release of the Allman Brothers' *At Fillmore East* album in 1971. On October 29 he was riding his Harley Sportster down a Macon street when an oncoming truck turned in front of him and stopped in his lane. Allman lost control of the bike, which flipped over and fell on top of him. He died from internal injuries in a hospital a few hours later. Age: 24. (A popular urban legend says that Allman hit a peach truck—hence the title of the band's next album, *Eat a Peach*. The legend is false.)

Star: Stiv Bators
Story: One of punk rock's early American pioneers, Bators was made famous by his work as guitarist and vocalist for the Dead Boys in the mid-1970s. He went on to play in various punk bands in Europe from 1980 until June 1990, when he was struck by a car while reportedly wandering drunk on a street in Paris. He was taken to a hospital, but went home without receiving treatment. He later died in his sleep, apparently due to a concussion. (You can see Bators in John Waters's 1981 cult-classic film *Polyester* and in the 1988 movie *Tapeheads*.) Age: 40.

Star: Tommy Bolin
Story: Bolin made a name for himself as a guitarist for the hard-rock bands Zephyr, the James Gang, and Deep Purple (he was Ritchie Blackmore's replacement during the band's final year). On December 3, 1976, Bolin was opening for Jeff Beck at the Jai-Alai Fronton sports arena in Miami. It was the first night of a tour to

promote Bolin's new solo album. He began his set with a 15-minute version of his song "Post Toastee," a moody contemplation of the mid-'70s rock scene's druggy excesses. The show went smoothly, but later that night, Bolin's girlfriend found him unconscious in his hotel room. In the morning, she called paramedics, but it was too late: Bolin was dead of "acute multiple drug intoxication," the drugs being alcohol, cocaine, barbiturates, and heroin. Age: 25.

Star: Chet Baker
Story: The legendary American jazz trumpeter and smooth-voiced singer (notable performance: "My Funny Valentine") had battled a heroin addiction since the 1950s. In 1988 he was spending most of his time living and playing in Europe. On May 13 of that year, Baker fell—or jumped—from a second-story window of an Amsterdam hotel and died from head injuries. Stories that he was pushed out the window, possibly by an angry drug dealer, have circulated since his death. But friends of Baker have argued that the door to the hotel was locked from the inside and there was no sign of a struggle. Cocaine and heroin were found in his room, but his death was officially ruled an accident. Baker was 59.

Star: "Dimebag" Darrell Abbott
Story: Abbott played lead guitar for the influential 1980s and '90s heavy-metal band Pantera and later for Damageplan. On December 8, 2004, Damageplan was performing at the Alrosa Villa in Columbus, Ohio, when 25-year-old Nathan Gale walked onto the stage and shot Abbott in the back of the head five times. Gale killed three other people who tried to stop him before a police officer shot and killed him. No official motive was ever determined, but Gale's friends told the press that he had both a history of mental illness and an obsession with Pantera—he believed they were "stealing his music." Abbott was 38. (The song the band was playing when he was killed: "Breathing New Life.")

Star: Aaliyah
Story: This R&B and hip-hop sensation saw her first album, 1994's *Age Ain't Nothing but a Number*, go platinum when she was only 15

years old. Her next album, *One in a Million*, went double-platinum. In July 2001, the young superstar was still on the rise with the release of her third album, *Aaliyah*. But just a month later, tragedy struck. On August 25, 2001, Aaliyah and eight others boarded a twin-engine Cessna 402B at an airport in the Bahamas, where she had finished shooting a music video. Just after takeoff, the plane crashed 200 feet past the runway, killing everyone on board. It was later revealed that the pilot, Luis Morales III, had lied to get his pilot's license and wasn't authorized to fly a twin-engine Cessna 402B—and he had alcohol and cocaine in his system at the time of the crash. Not only that, the plane was overloaded by several hundred pounds. Aaliyah was just 22 years old.

Star: Robert Johnson

Story: Robert Johnson recorded only 29 songs in his life, and they are the scratchy recordings typical of his era—the 1930s. But that didn't keep him from becoming one of the greatest influences on blues music—and even rock 'n' roll—in history. (His songs were later recorded by Eric Clapton, Led Zeppelin, the Rolling Stones, and B. B. King, just to name a few.) Little is known about his life, and much of what is "known" about it is actually legend. That's also true of his death. All agree that he died on August 16, 1938, near Greenwood, Mississippi. Most agree he was poisoned by a jealous husband and developed pneumonia a few days later. Johnson died at the age of 27.

Star: Keith Moon

Story: Moon is probably more famous for his overindulgent rock 'n' roll lifestyle than for his work as a drummer for the Who. Known for trashing hotel rooms, bathrooms, bars, houses, drum sets, and himself, that kind of mayhem would end up killing him young—even though, at the time, he was trying to get sober. On September 7, 1978, he had dinner with his girlfriend, Annette Walter-Lax, and Paul and Linda McCartney, then went home. That night he died of an overdose of medication he was taking—ironically—to help him quit drinking alcohol. The autopsy estimated he had taken 28 of the pills. Moon was 32.

BARD OF
THE BACKWOODS

*Regarded as one of the most influential musicians of the 20th century,
Hank Williams crammed a whole lot of life into just 29 years.*

HANKS A LOT

Hank Williams is often called the "Hillbilly Shakespeare" because he wrote or recorded more than 100 country classics. In just four years, he had eleven #1 hits and his songs reached the Top 10 of the country chart 36 times. Known for his simple melodies and melancholy lyrics, he is generally considered one of the most important country singer-songwriters of all time—a superstar by 25 who was dead at 29.

ON THE RISE

Williams was born in 1923 in Alabama, and he was a frail child, afflicted with chronic back pain due to spina bifida. Because he was often sick, his mother gave him his first guitar when he was eight so he could entertain himself. He taught himself to play and credited a local black musician named Rufe Payne, known in music circles as Tee-Tot, as the mentor who taught him the blues.

At just 16 years old, Williams quit school for a career in music. He played first at town square dances and then moved on to gigs at honky-tonks—small beer joints where he played with his band, the Drifting Cowboys.

THE HIT MAKER

In 1943 he met and married Audrey Mae Sheppard, a fellow singer who also played the stand-up bass. She took over managing her husband's career and orchestrated his move to Nashville in 1946, where he eventually landed a recording contract with MGM. Williams's first MGM release was the country blues song "Move It on Over," which was an immediate hit and rocketed up the country chart. (The song resurfaced as a hit in 1978 when George Thorogood and the Destroyers recorded it.)

Williams's first #1 song, "Lovesick Blues," topped the country chart for 16 weeks in 1949 and crossed over into the pop chart as well. That success earned him his first appearance at the Grand Ole Opry. (He performed there more than 20 times during his career.) At that debut on June 11, 1949, he received an unprecedented six encores.

From there, Williams blazed a trail of hits through Nashville. The songs included "Honky Tonkin" (1947), "I Saw the Light" (1948), "I'm So Lonesome I Could Cry" (1949), "You're Gonna Change (or I'm Gonna Leave)" (1949), "My Son Calls Another Man Daddy" (1950), "Hey Good Lookin'" (1951), "I Can't Help It (If I'm Still in Love with You)" (1951), "Cold, Cold Heart" (1951)—which was also recorded by and became a big hit for crooner Tony Bennett in the early 1950s—"You Win Again" (1952), and "Jambalaya (On the Bayou)" (1952).

THE FALL

As his fame grew, Williams became known as much for his drinking and unpredictability as for his talent. He suffered from insomnia and chronic back pain, and spent most of his waking hours under the influence of alcohol and drugs. He often showed up for concerts drunk, if he showed at all. He was fired by the Opry in August 1952 and also had several run-ins with the police for destroying property and playing with guns, though he was never arrested.

On January 1, 1953, after a New Year's Eve performance in Knoxville, Tennessee, Williams hired a driver to take him to Canton, Ohio. (He had to take the car because the weather was too bad to fly.) Before he left, he was given two shots of morphine and vitamin B12 to help ease his back pain during the trip. Two hours into the journey, the young driver—Charles Carr, a 19-year-old student on Christmas break from Auburn University—was stopped by the police for reckless driving. The trooper questioned him about Williams, who appeared to be asleep in the back seat. Carr explained that Williams had been drinking (on top of taking the sedatives) and had asked that he not be disturbed. Carr drove on until 6:30 a.m., when he stopped at a gas station in Oak Hill, Virginia. He looked into the back seat and Williams was unresponsive. Carr checked again, but to no avail—Hank Williams was dead. The cause of death was listed as "acute ventricular dilation" —a heart attack. He was just 29.

The last single Williams released before his death was the ironic "I'll Never Get Out of This World Alive," which reached #1 in January 1953, just a few days after his death. He had three more #1 hits later that year: "Your Cheatin' Heart," "Kaw-Liga," and "Take These Chains from My Heart."

AN AWARDING CAREER

In 1961 Hank Williams was the first person inducted into the Country Music Hall of Fame. (In tribute to his lasting impact on rock and folk music, he was inducted into the Rock and Roll Hall of Fame in 1987 in the "Early Influences" category.) Also in 1987, he was awarded the Lifetime Achievement Award from the National Academy of Recording Arts and Sciences. Country Music Television named Williams the second-most influential man in country music. (His son Hank Williams Jr. ranked 20th, and Johnny Cash was first). Williams received a posthumous Grammy in 1989 for a dubbed recording of "There's a Tear in My Beer" with his son, Hank Williams Jr.

*　　*　　*

Whether it was his lifestyle or his music, Hank Williams has been the inspiration for dozens of country songs. Here's a sampling.

"The Ghost Of Hank Williams" (The Kentucky Headhunters)

"I Think Hank Woulda Done It This Way" (The Blue Chieftains)

"Are You Sure Hank Done It This Way" (Waylon Jennings)

"Hank Williams Said It Best" (Guy Clark)

"I Feel Like Hank Williams Tonight" (Jerry Jeff Walker)

"Has Anybody Here Seen Hank" (The Waterboys)

"Hank Williams, You Wrote My Life" (Moe Bandy)

"The Car Hank Died In" (The Austin Lounge Lizards)

"Hank Williams Wouldn't Make It Now in Nashville, Tennessee" (Eleven Hundred Springs)

"If You Don't Like Hank Williams" (Kris Kristofferson)

After *Dark Side of the Moon*, Pink Floyd planned an album of sounds made by household objects.

MUSICAL PRESIDENTS, PART II

More musical moments from the White House. (Part I begins on page 27.)

T HEODORE ROOSEVELT (1901–09)
Roosevelt was not musically inclined, but his daughter Alice made musical history when she requested that the Marine Band learn to play some ragtime—a growing fad of early jazz that was looked down upon by the elite. According to a band member:

> Miss Roosevelt came up [at a White House reception] and said, "Oh, Mr. Santelmann, do play the 'Maple Leaf Rag' for me." "The 'Maple Leaf Rag'?" he gasped in astonishment. "Indeed, Miss Roosevelt, I've never heard of such a composition, and I'm sure it is not in our library." "Now, now, Mr. Santelmann," laughed Alice, "Don't tell me that. The band boys have played it for me time and again when Mr. Smith or Mr. Vanpoucke was conducting, and I'll wager they all know it without the music."

She was right, and they did play it for the First Daughter. It was one of the first instances of jazz being taken seriously as a musical form, and helped begin its long road to gaining wide acceptance.

WARREN HARDING (1921–23)

Harding's brief term was riddled with corruption and controversy. One of his few escapes was music—he played almost every kind of horn. As a young man in Marion, Ohio, Harding organized the Citizen's Cornet Band, and was so enthusiastic about leading the band, he plunged it into debt by purchasing fancy uniforms so they could participate in music contests. His gamble paid off when they placed third in a statewide competition (the $200 prize more than paid for the uniforms). As president, he brought the Citizen's Cornet Band to Washington and made them available to play at political rallies, for both Republicans and Democrats.

CALVIN COOLIDGE (1923–29)

When it came to music, the man known as "Silent Cal" (for his legendary quietness at dinner parties) had this to say: "To heal the

---

Led Zeppelin's "Houses of the Holy" is on their *Physical Graffiti* album, not *Houses of the Holy*.

unrest and lack of understanding now in evidence in our land, we must bring into our national consciousness a peaceful presence that will dispel confusion as light dispels darkness—and that peaceful presence can largely be music."

FRANKLIN D. ROOSEVELT (1933–45)

The wheelchair-bound Roosevelt was quite proficient on the piano, and was so fond of music in general, he often said that "singing should come before speaking." In 1938 Roosevelt took time out of his busy schedule to help design a grand piano to be built by Steinway & Sons. It was decorated with a gilded scene illustrating folk dances from around the world, and had legs in the shape of gilded eagles. The piano, which Roosevelt often played, still stands in the East Room of the White House today.

HARRY S. TRUMAN (1945–53)

Truman loved to play the piano. He once played so hard that one piano leg went through the White House floor. Growing up, Truman had one of the best music instructors in Kansas City, and showed early promise, but ultimately gave it up. Why? "I decided that playing the piano wasn't the thing for a man to do. It was a sissy thing to do. So I just stopped. And it was probably all for the best, I wouldn't ever have been really first-rate. A good music-hall piano player is about the best I'd have ever been. So I went into politics instead and became President of the United States."

JOHN F. KENNEDY (1961–63)

JFK took piano lessons during his school years—but as a 1962 New York Times article detailing Kennedy's childhood reported, "Anybody studying this boy's character when he was practicing scales would have said he'd never grow up to become President of the United States."

LYNDON B. JOHNSON (1963–69)

In his retirement years on his ranch in Texas, LBJ reportedly liked to drive his white convertible around the property blaring the song "Raindrops Keep Fallin' on My Head" by B. J. Thomas.

For Part III of Musical Presidents, turn to page 417.

CAB CALLOWAY'S JIVE DICTIONARY

In the 1930s and '40s, Cab Calloway and his band were famous for tunes like "Minnie the Moocher" and "St. James Infirmary." But he was also known as a "hep-cat," identified with outrageous zoot suits and jive talk. His guide on how to talk like a hipster was published in the 1940s.

APPLE: The big town, the main stem

BARBEQUE: The girlfriend, a beauty

BARRELHOUSE: Free and easy

BATTLE: Crone, hag

BEAT IT OUT: Play it hot

BEAT UP THE CHOPS: To talk

BEEF: To say, to state

BLIP: Something very good

BLOW THE TOP: To be overcome with emotion or delight

BUST YOUR CONK: Apply yourself diligently, break your neck

CLAMBAKE: Every man for himself

COOLING: Laying off, not working

CORNY: Old-fashioned, stale

CUBBY: Room, flat, home

CUPS: Sleep

CUT RATE: Low, cheap person

DICTY: High-class, nifty, smart

DIME NOTE: $10 bill

DRAPE: Suit of clothes, dress

DRY GOODS: Dress, costume

DUKE: Hand, mitt

FALL OUT: To be overcome with emotion

FEWS AND TWO: Money or cash in small quantity

FRAME: The body

FROMPY: A frompy queen is a battle

FRUITING: Fickle, fooling around with no particular object

GATE: A male person

GLIMS: The eyes

People who make and repair guitars are called **luthiers**.

GOT YOUR BOOTS ON: You know what it's all about, you are wise

GOT YOUR GLASSES ON: You are ritzy or snooty, you fail to recognize your friends

GUTBUCKET: Low-down music

HARD: Fine, good

HEP CAT: A guy who knows all the answers, understands jive

HOME-COOKING: Something very nice

ICKY: A stupid person, not hip

IN THE GROOVE: Perfect

JACK: Name for all male friends

JEFF: A pest, a bore

JELLY: Anything free, on the house

KILL ME: Show me a good time, send me

LEAD SHEET: A coat

LILY WHITES: Bed sheets

MAN IN GRAY: The postman

MESS: Something good

METER: Quarter, twenty-five cents

MEZZ: Anything supreme, genuine

MITT POUNDING: Applause

MOUSE: Pocket

MURDER: Something excellent or terrific

NEIGHO POPS: Nothing doing, pal

OFF THE COB: Corny, out of date

OFF TIME JIVE: A sorry excuse, saying the wrong thing

PIGEON: A young girl

POPS: Salutation for all males

POUNDERS: Policemen

QUEEN: A beautiful girl

RUG CUTTER: A very good dancer

SALTY: Angry or ill-tempered

SEND: To arouse the emotions (joyful)

SET OF SEVEN BRIGHTS: One week

SLIDE YOUR JIB: Talk freely

SOLID: Great, swell, okay

TOGGED TO THE BRICKS: Dressed to kill

TRUCK: To go somewhere

WRONG RIFF: Saying or doing the wrong thing

The Swedish group ABBA sang their English songs phonetically.

THEY'RE INSTRUMENTAL

*We've told you about electric guitars, violins, and cymbals—
here, we'll introduce you to the creators of three more
of the greatest musical instruments ever made.*

BARTOLOMEO CRISTOFORI
Cristofori was born in 1655 and lived in Padua, Italy, where he became a talented harpsichord maker. At the age of 32, he became the official musical instrument maker for the court of Prince Ferdinand de Medici in Florence. In this position, Cristofori had the responsibility of caring for Medici's vast music and instrument collection, and repairing and designing harpsichords.

He became interested in redesigning the harpsichord to overcome its primary limitation: no matter how much or how little pressure was used to play it, the volume could not be controlled because it was a plucking instrument. So Cristofori substituted hitting for plucking. He engineered a hammer device that rebounded immediately, creating a prolonged vibration (the basic design incorporated in standard acoustic pianos today), used strings that were thicker than the harpsichord's, and even developed the first soft pedal, which kept the hammers from hitting too many strings.

Cristofori called his new instrument a *gravicembalo col piano e forte*, or "large harpsichord with soft and loud," but eventually the name was shortened to *pianoforte*, or "soft loud," and finally just to piano. It took time for the piano to become popular because it was expensive to make; only royal families could afford one at first. But by the 1760s, pianos were everywhere.

In Today's Market: Only three of Cristofori's pianos exist today (it's estimated he made around 20 of them), and all three are in museums—in New York, Rome, and Leipzig. In the late 1990s, a Japanese piano maker spent three years building a replica of a Cristofori piano—to the tune of 10 million yen ($90,000). The highest price ever paid for any piano was $1.2 million for a Steinway purchased at a 1998 Christie's auction in London; in the 1880s, it would have sold for $1,200.

The inspiration for the Beatles' song "Good Morning" was a 1967 Kellogg's Corn Flakes ad.

BENJAMIN FRANKLIN

In addition to inventing bifocals, beginning the library system, and signing the Declaration of Independence, Franklin invented the glass armonica in 1761. He said, "Of all my inventions, the glass armonica has given me the greatest personal satisfaction." Franklin's inspiration for the instrument came while he watched a concert being played with musical glasses. Knowing he could improve the sound quality and make the glasses easier to use, he decided to create a new instrument. With the help of a glass-blower, Franklin placed 37 glass bowls (in 23 different sizes) horizontally along a spindle that was rotated using a foot treadle. He painted the discs different colors to identify notes, and by wetting his fingers and touching the rims, Franklin could create bell-like sounds.

When Franklin introduced his new instrument to Europe (he served as a diplomat in France during the American Revolution), it was enthusiastically received. Marie Antoinette took lessons; Beethoven and Mozart wrote music for it; even Tchaikovsky's "Dance of the Sugar Plum Fairy" in The Nutcracker was originally written for the armonica.

But unfounded rumors and superstitions in the 1830s brought a swift and sudden end to the armonica's popularity. People reported mental illness, nervous disorders, and losing the feeling in their hands after playing it. (Some historians attribute these ailments to lead poisoning from the glass.)

In Today's Market: The instrument disappeared from public view until the 1980s when the owner of a small glassblowing company, who had seen an armonica in a German museum, brought it out of obscurity. Today, Finkenbeiner Inc. in Waltham, Massachusetts, manufactures armonicas from glass quartz (no lead)—a custom design can be yours for just $7,165. Franklin's original armonica remained in a third-floor bedroom at his Philadelphia home until his daughter auctioned his personal effects soon after his death in 1790. In 1814 (24 years after his death), it was valued at $18. Today, it's in the possession of Pennsylvania's Franklin Institute.

RUDOLPH WURLITZER

Wurlitzer was born to a family of German instrument makers (they focused on traditional stringed, brass, and woodwind instruments). At 22, he immigrated to the United States to set up a business selling his family's products, and in 1856, he opened his own production plant in Cincinnati. (Later, the company expanded and moved its headquarters to New York State.)

A savvy businessman and salesman, Wurlitzer soon had a thriving business manufacturing and selling music boxes, coin-operated pianos, jukeboxes, and theater organs—most famously, the "Mighty Wurlitzer," a pipe organ originally designed to accompany silent movies as a one-man band. Ultimately, it became the music source for many old theaters, town halls, and churches during the first half of the 20th century. The biggest Wurlitzer ever built belonged to Radio City Music Hall in New York City—its 4,410 pipes had to be housed in 11 separate rooms. That organ took four weeks to install in 1932 and remains a popular attraction today.

In Today's Market: Restorations of many Mighty Wurlitzer organs are taking place across the United States, and costs can climb into the $600,000 range. In the 1930s, the organs cost about $20,000 each.

* * *

WHO WAS THAT MASKED BAND?

Background: In 1969 *Rolling Stone* reviewed a self-titled LP by a group called the Masked Marauders. Although no names were listed on the album, said *Rolling Stone* writer Greil Marcus, the mysterious musicians were almost certainly Mick Jagger, Bob Dylan, John Lennon, Paul McCartney, and George Harrison. Could the Masked Marauders be the most incredible (not to mention the most secretive) rock band of all time?

What Happened: *Rolling Stone* readers started asking for the album at record stores but couldn't find it. Stores had never heard of it, because it didn't actually exist—Greil Marcus had made the whole thing up. To capitalize on the hoax, he hired a band (the Cleanliness and Godliness Skiffle Band) to record a Masked Marauders album. It was released to stores, at which point Marcus admitted that it had all been a put-on to parody the many "supergroups" of the late '60s.

TWO-ETS

That's like "duets"—but with a #2 in it.

STEVE AND EYDIE

Come Together: The former Sidney Liebowitz (he changed it to "Steve Lawrence") and the former Edith Gormezano (she changed it to "Eydie Gormé"), both Brooklyn natives, had solo careers in the early 1950s before teaming up personally (they were married in 1957) and musically (with the release of the album *Steve & Eydie* in 1958).

Hits: They won a Grammy in 1960 with their duet "We Got Us" and an Emmy in 1978 for the television special *Steve & Eydie Celebrate Irving Berlin*. Lawrence and Gormé also maintained successful solo careers. They each had their biggest hits in 1963: Lawrence with "Go Away, Little Girl" (written by Carole King) and Gormé with "Blame It on the Bossa Nova." Gormé garnered a second Grammy in 1967 for "If He Walked into My Life."

Aftermath: Thought they were history? Wrong. Now in their 70s, they still tour and still have a large fan base despite the fact that neither of them has been on a Billboard Top-40 chart since 1963.

PORTER WAGONER AND DOLLY PARTON

Come Together: In 1967 Porter Wagoner was on top of the country music world, with a 15-year string of hits and his own syndicated TV show. But he had a problem: the featured female singer on his show, Norma Jean, was leaving. To replace her, Porter tapped an up-and-coming singer and songwriter named Dolly Parton, whose debut album, *Hello I'm Dolly*, was moving up the charts.

Hits: It was probably the smartest thing Wagoner ever did. The duo of Porter and Dolly was a smash from the release of their first single together ("Just Between You and Me," which reached #7 on the country chart), and between 1967 and 1974, when Parton left to focus on her solo work, the duo released a dozen albums, all of which made the Top 20. The song Parton wrote to Wagoner to ease the departure, "I Will Always Love You," became a huge solo hit for her, reaching #1 on the country singles chart in April 1974 and again in 1982. (Whitney Houston's 1992 version ruled the charts for a record-setting 14 weeks).

Aftermath: When the duo broke up it wasn't pretty. They refused to appear together or even speak to each other. (The cover of the 1980 album *Porter & Dolly*, featuring previously unreleased recordings, had separate pictures of them, pasted together to look like they were standing next to each other.) They eventually reconciled, however. Parton inducted her old duet partner into the Country Music Hall of Fame in 2002, and stayed in contact with him until his death in 2007.

CAPTAIN & TENNILLE

Come Together: Daryl Dragon and Toni Tennille met in 1971, while Dragon was a keyboardist for the Beach Boys and Tennille was staging a musical in San Francisco. They helped each other professionally—she hired him as a musician for her play, and he helped her get a gig singing backup with the Beach Boys—and they started doing shows together in Los Angeles.

Hits: In 1975 they signed with A&M Records, and hit #1 on the *Billboard* pop chart with their first single, "Love Will Keep Us Together." It turned out to be the biggest-selling single of the year, and won a Grammy. To celebrate, they got married. In 1976 they reached #4 with "Muskrat Love"—and played at the White House during bicentennial celebrations (Queen Elizabeth was in the audience) and in 1977 starred in their own short-lived television show. In 1979 they capped off their career with "Do That to Me One More Time," their second and final #1 song.

Aftermath: Toni Tennille sang backup on several albums by other artists in the 1970s, including Elton John's *Caribou* and Pink Floyd's *The Wall*, and made several solo albums. The duo is still together—they released a Christmas album in 2007, which included four brand new songs.

MICKEY AND SYLVIA

Come Together: In the early 1950s, Mickey "Guitar" Baker was in his late 20s and an East Coast session player; Sylvia Vanderpool was a teenage singer with trumpeter Oran "Hot Lips" Page for Columbia Records. They met when Sylvia hired Mickey to give her guitar lessons, and they soon started performing as a duo.

Hits: RCA heard about them and signed them up. In 1957 the sensuous "Love is Strange" went to #1 on the R&B chart. ("Sylvia / Yes, Mickey? / How do you call your loverboy? / COME HERE, loverboy.") Baker is considered one of the important early electric guitar masters, and the song's trebly, melodic guitar riff is said to have influenced scores of major artists afterwards, including Buddy Holly, the Beatles, and the Rolling Stones. Mickey and Sylvia had a few more lesser hits with "There Ought to Be a Law" and "Baby You're So Fine."

Aftermath: The two were done in 1962. A few years later Sylvia married Joe Robinson, and they started the All Platinum record label. In 1973 she had another hit with the very risque "Pillow Talk." (She had wanted Al Green to sing it, but he refused, calling it "too dirty.") In 1974 Joe and Sylvia started another label: Sugar Hill Records, which produced several hip-hop classics, including the Sugarhill Gang's 1979 "Rapper's Delight" and Grandmaster Flash and the Furious Five's "The Message."

*　　*　　*

A LUCKY HIT

The hit musical *Hair* had been on Broadway for about a year when the vocal group the Fifth Dimension arrived in New York City to perform at the Americana Hotel in 1969. "Billy [Davis, of the group] lost his wallet in a cab," recalls Florence LaRue (also a group member). "He didn't know where he'd lost it, but a gentleman called and said he'd found it and wanted to return it. Billy was grateful, but the man didn't want a reward. He just said, 'I would like you to come and see a play that I've produced.'

"Well, as it happens, he was the producer of the play *Hair*. And as we were sitting there listening to 'Aquarius,' we all looked at each other and said, 'This is a song we've got to record. It's just great.'" They took the song to their producer, who suggested that they combine it with "Let the Sunshine In." They recorded it in Las Vegas, where they were performing. "'Let the Sunshsine In / Age of Aquarius' was the quickest thing we ever recorded," says LaRue. "And it was our biggest hit."

THE FIFTH BEATLE

Almost from the moment Beatlemania hit, various people—all crucial to the band's success—laid claim to the title of "the fifth member of the Fab Four."

PETE BEST

Best has the best claim to being the fifth Beatle because he's the only one who actually *was* a Beatle. He was the band's drummer from 1960 to 1962, and played with the Beatles during the band's gigs in Hamburg, Germany. Best was a mediocre drummer by most accounts (judge for yourself—Best's drumming can be heard on the Beatles' *Anthology I*), but he stayed in the band because his teen-idol good looks attracted female fans, and because his mother, Mona Best, was the band's promoter. When the Beatles got a record deal, producer George Martin told manager Brian Epstein that Best wasn't a good enough drummer. This coincided with the feelings of the other members of the band, who were already planning to ditch him anyway. Epstein fired Best in August 1962 and he was replaced by Ringo Starr. Best's fans rioted that night at a concert at the Cavern Club; George Harrison ended up with a black eye.

Epstein immediately placed Best with another band he managed, Lee Curtis and the All Stars, but that didn't last long either, and Best spent most of the early and mid-1960s bouncing around minor bands who capitalized on Best's former Beatle status. Eventually, Best himself got tired of it and got a job at a bakery, and then later worked as a civil servant in Liverpool. After he retired in 1988, Best hit the road again with a new band and now spends his time making appearances in which he again capitalizes on his former relationship with the most popular band in the world.

BRIAN EPSTEIN

He was the Beatles' manager from 1961 to 1967, but before he met the Beatles, he'd never managed a musical group before—he was the record department manager of the North End Music Store, which his family owned. Epstein was also something of a frustrated creative type; he had attended theater school for a couple of years before dropping out and going to work in the store.

When he saw the Beatles perform in Liverpool's Cavern Club in 1961, he realized they were something special and became their manager and their champion. His first order of business: a new look. Epstein came up with the idea to dress the band in suits with matching mop-top haircuts. Next, he got them a record contract, which he accomplished in less than six months.

Once the band stopped touring in 1966, there was little for Epstein to do. It also didn't help that the Beatles had come to believe Epstein had botched a number of business deals for them. Epstein, who had dabbled in drugs for some time, died in 1967 from an overdose (although it's unclear if it was an accident or a suicide). Lennon later said that after Epstein's sudden death, the Beatles started to fall apart.

GEORGE MARTIN

When Brian Epstein played the Beatles' demo for him, Martin wasn't a rock record producer. He was an executive, the head of Parlophone Records, a small and underfunded division of EMI. He agreed to sign the band and produce them, but rather than hammer the Beatles into a preexisting idea of what they should sound like, Martin gave the band room to experiment and the opportunity to develop their own material. After the Beatles' first single, "Love Me Do," sold poorly in England, the record company wanted the band to hire an outside writer. Martin vetoed the idea and let the band release another single, the Lennon-McCartney song "Please Please Me." It went to #1.

He also had the technical experience the Beatles needed; although the band is credited with innovating the use of tape loops and overdubs on *Revolver* and *Sgt. Pepper's Lonely Hearts Club Band*, Martin first used loops and overdubs on the 1955 comedy album *Mock Mozart*. Ultimately, Martin produced everything the Beatles ever did (except for their final album, *Let It Be*), wrote the string and horn arrangements for the band's later songs, and is credited with moving the Beatles' sound away from simple rock 'n' roll into more experimental territory. After the Beatles broke up, Martin continued to work with Paul McCartney and Ringo Starr, and has since worked with an eclectic group of musicians ranging from Celine Dion and Elton John to Kate Bush and Ultravox. Martin was knighted in 1996 and retired

from production work in 1998 as the most commercially successful producer of all time.

NEIL ASPINALL

Aspinall was a childhood friend of George Harrison, but got to
know the Beatles when he rented a room in Pete Best's house during the band's early 1960s Liverpool days. When he got a car, the
Beatles asked him to be their road manager, hauling their equipment and setting it up at gigs around town. After Best was fired
from the band in 1962, Aspinall planned to quit in protest, but
Best talked him out of it. Good idea. Not long after, they hired
Mal Evans to be their road manager and Aspinall got promoted to
personal assistant, a job he held when the band became successful.
Aspinall helped find all the photographs of famous people needed
for the cover of *Sgt. Pepper's Lonely Hearts Club Band* and stood in
for band members during sound checks and dress rehearsals of TV
performances. He even contributed to the music when asked. He
played harmonica on "Being for the Benefit of Mr. Kite," lute on
"Within You Without You," and was one of the drunken-sounding
chorus members on "Yellow Submarine." (Previous musical experience: none.)

But his biggest contribution to the Beatles was as a businessman. When he became the band's driver, Aspinall had been studying to be an accountant. That was all the training the Beatles
required when they made Aspinall the managing director of Apple
Corps, their record company and corporate umbrella. This was no
easy task, since under the band's management Apple hemorrhaged
money and contributed to the stress that ultimately broke up the
Beatles. Aspinall hung in there and continued in the role even
after the band broke up, since the need to administer the Beatles'
affairs didn't end once the Fab Four stopped working together.
Still managing director of Apple to this day, Aspinall manages the
Beatles' legacy.

MAL EVANS

In the early 1960s, Evans worked for the telephone company in
Liverpool and hung out at the Cavern Club, where he eventually
became a bouncer. It was in this capacity that he got to know Brian
Epstein and the Beatles. In 1963 Epstein asked Evans to become the

Beatles' road manager, replacing Neil Aspinall, who had been promoted to personal assistant. From then on, Evans was a constant presence hanging around the Beatles. (He can even be seen lurking around the "rooftop concert" in the *Let It Be* documentary.) When they were on tour, Evans was their errand boy and bodyguard, and he filmed them constantly. After the band stopped touring in 1966, Evans, like Aspinall, became a catchall assistant and even played on some songs: homemade kazoo on "Lady Madonna," saxophone on "Helter Skelter," and the anvil in "Maxwell's Silver Hammer." Evans eventually discovered the band Badfinger and brought them to McCartney, who signed them to Apple. (Evans coproduced their first album.) At Apple Corps, Evans was an executive personal assistant until 1968, when the Beatles' new manager, Allen Klein, fired him. Evans went on to try producing records. It didn't work out: He produced Who drummer Keith Moon's *Two Sides of the Moon* in 1975, but his version was thrown out and the album was rerecorded. Evans died in 1976 of a gunshot after drunkenly pointing an unloaded rifle at a Los Angeles police officer.

Three more fifth Beatles:

• **Tony Sheridan** was a singer based in Hamburg, Germany, who used the Beatles as his backup band in the early 1960s. When he got a record deal in 1962, he asked the Beatles to play as session musicians on his German hit, "My Bonnie." The song was credited to "Tony Sheridan and the Beat Brothers."

• **Stuart Sutcliffe** had been close friends with John Lennon since childhood, so Lennon let Sutcliffe, a bass guitarist, join his band the Quarrymen, which later developed into the Beatles. Sutcliffe was a better painter than musician, so he quit the band in 1961 to become an artist. A year later, at age 21, he died of a brain hemorrhage.

• **Billy Preston** played piano with the Beatles in their Hamburg days and reunited with the group when George Harrison invited him to play on "Get Back" and "Let It Be" in 1969. Preston almost *did* become the fifth Beatle: After recording "Get Back," Lennon asked Preston to join the band outright, but the others said no. Preston went on to a successful solo career in the 1970s, with two #1 hits ("Will It Go Round in Circles" and "Nothing From Nothing"), and played on countless tracks by other artists.

RANDOM QUOTES

…about music and musicians.

"Some people say we have thirteen albums that all sound the same. That isn't true. We have fourteen albums that all sound the same."
—**Angus Young, of AC/DC**

"If Beethoven had been killed in a plane crash at the age of 22, it would have changed the history of music…and of aviation."
—**Tom Stoppard**

"It's like a Bob Dylan song that you've loved for years and years, and then you read an interview and he says, 'Oh, it's about a dog that was run over in the street.' You're like, 'What? That song colored and altered my opinion of life for three years! What do you mean it's about a dead dog in the street?!'"
—**Michael Stipe, of R.E.M.**

"Sometimes a woman can really persuade you to make an ass of yourself."
—**Rod Stewart**

"Everybody argues, then we do what I say."
—**Bono**

"I'm very driven, even though I don't drive."
—**Debbie Gibson**

"It's actually come as quite a shock to learn just how many people don't like me."
—**Phil Collins**

"I've been imitated so well I've heard people copy my mistakes."
—**Jimi Hendrix**

"I would introduce myself, 'Hi, I'm Glenn Frey from the Eagles.' And they would just look at me like, 'Well, you must be the placekicker because you're not big enough to play football.'"
—**Glenn Frey**

"The worst thing that ever happened to me was when platform shoes went out of style."
—**John Oates, of Hall & Oates (he's 5'5")**

"A typical day in the life of a heavy metal musician consists of a round of golf and an AA meeting."
—**Billy Joel**

Cher currently holds the record for longest amount of time between #1 hit singles: 25 years.

HOW iPOD CHANGED THE MUSIC BUSINESS

The "personal music player" revolution started with the Sony Walkman, which evolved into the Discman. Then the advent of the MP3 shook up the music industry…and it hasn't stopped shaking yet.

THE BLAME GAME

Despite what execs say about pirated MP3s costing them money, the record industry was in a tailspin *before* the iPod came along. Industry analysts blamed flagging CD sales on a variety of things: First, many of the early sales of CDs came from people replacing their LP and tape collections. Once they'd done that, they didn't need to buy additional copies, and CD sales slowed. Another factor was "social sharing"—making a CD for a friend or family member—an activity that started long before the advent of the Internet and is impossible to regulate. In fact, one market research study showed that more than a third of all music is acquired this way. Other critics blame poor sales on the high price of CDs. The final reason analysts put forward: music put out by major record labels just wasn't very good, and that's why no one was buying.

UNITED FRONT

The iPod arrived into that climate in October 2001. But it wasn't even the first MP3 player on the market. In the fall of 1998, Eiger Labs had introduced the MP Man, and Diamond Multimedia followed quickly with the Rio PMP300. Both sold well that Christmas season—they were small enough to fit in the palm of your hand (each was about the size of a deck of cards)—but there was a drawback: They had only 32MB of memory, which meant they could hold only 30 minutes of music. Apple solved that problem by including a miniature hard drive. Result: the first iPods could hold about 4,000 minutes, or roughly 1,000 songs.

Another problem with the early MP3 players was that the record industry claimed they encouraged piracy—people were copying music from CDs and from the Internet without paying for them. From the start, Steve Jobs, CEO of Apple Computers, wanted to work with the record industry and open a digital music store. The logic was clear: the more people who bought music digitally, the more iPods he could sell. Jobs succeeded in uniting the five major record labels—Universal, Warner, EMI, BMG, and Sony—in one online store. Rumor has it that he got Universal, the largest record company, to agree by hinting that Apple was planning to buy it. Whether or not this was true, once Universal signed, the others followed, and the iTunes store opened in 2003.

A NEW HOPE?

The iTunes store was an immediate success. Sales of songs hit the 10 million mark just four months after the store opened. Seventy million songs sold in the first year, 129 million the second, and 323 million the third. Today, iTunes sells 76 percent of all digital music, making it the third-biggest seller of music—period—after retailers Wal-Mart and Best Buy. A key to its success was the uniform pricing—all songs cost 99 cents. Soon after iTunes opened, the five record labels jockeyed for independent pricing schemes, while Jobs wanted to lower the price per song overall. An iTunes competitor, Rhapsody, lowered its price to 49 cents per song in 2004 (it ate the loss) and discovered that at half the price, people bought six times as many songs. But record labels still refused to go below 99 cents, fearing that cheaper prices might devalue their product.

IS THE CD DEAD?

Another fear: Ever since the iTunes store opened its digital doors, industry watchers have been predicting the death of the album. When consumers can buy any song for a buck and play those songs in any order they want on their iPods, why would they pay for an entire CD? What analysts discovered, however, is that albums in general are in no danger, and some genres—particularly jazz, classical, and concept albums—are actually strong sellers.

One type of CD, however, is feeling the effects of iTunes: the compilation. For years, the record industry relied on income generated by repackaging old hits in an endless array of "Best of" albums. It's far cheaper to rerelease old songs or "greatest hits" collections than record new ones. But with the rise of iTunes, people can buy whatever golden oldies they want and make their own compilations, so the income from repackaging is drying up.

Still, record labels are trying to make their way through the changing music market. Some have started signing contracts with new artists for just two or three songs. The hope is that those songs will get enough airtime on the radio to sell over iTunes and to sell cell phone ringtones, another growing source of revenue. Then, if the group takes off, they might get an album, but in the meantime, the label takes less of a risk.

EXTRAS

• The idea of accessing music via the Internet wasn't born with the iPod. In the late 1980s, a team of European engineers developed a way to encode and compress digital audio information into a file that could be relatively quickly transmitted over the Internet. It was called ISO-MPEG Audio Player-3—or MP3 for short. It's still the most popular digital music format on the Internet.

• First song compressed into an MP3 file: the song "Tom's Diner," by Suzanne Vega. One of the MP3's chief developers, Karlheinz Brandenburg, used the song as a model, refining the technology until that song sounded "right." This has lead some people to say that all MP3s are "tuned" to "Tom's Diner."

• By 1995 MP3s were common on the Internet—but they still weren't easy for consumers to work with. Then, in 1999, Northeastern University student Shawn Fanning invented Napster, the first successful MP3 swapping application.

• Several musicians, including Dr. Dre, Madonna, and the band Metallica, as well as the Recording Industry Association of America, sued Napster. Napster lost the case, and was forced to shut down in 2001. At its peak it had more than 25 million users.

• How successful is the iPod? According to Apple, more than 119 million have been sold worldwide.

• In July 2007, Apple announced that more than 3 billion songs had been purchased and downloaded via the iTunes Store. (If each song were three minutes long, it would take about 17,000 years to listen to them all.)

• "I get the Shuffle and then I shuffle the Shuffle." —President George W. Bush, showing reporters the iPod Shuffle that he received as a gift from U2 singer Bono in 2005.

TV MU$IC

Now for a boob-tube break.

T HAT'S WHAT I WANT
Since the rise of television in the late 1940s, there has
been one major obstacle to overcome when adding music
to TV shows: money. The budgets of most programs were (and
still are) very low, especially when compared to feature films.
After the costs of the writers, actors, sets, and crew are tallied up,
very little is left over to spend on scoring the show. Using existing
songs can be very expensive because of copyright considerations,
and hiring composers to score unique music for every single
episode can cost even more. These limitations have led television
music supervisors over the years to come up with some pretty
inventive solutions. Here are a few that have shaped the way we
watch TV.

Solution 1: ALTER AN EXISTING WORK

Hardly anyone can listen to the "William Tell Overture" and not
think of *The Lone Ranger.* But pioneering television music supervisor David Chudnow had to make sure that the opposite was also
true: When listening to the theme for the 1949 TV show *The
Lone Ranger,* the viewer wasn't *supposed* to think of Gioachino
Rossini's 1829 "William Tell Overture." Why? Because the Rossini
piece was actually owned outright by the *radio* version of *The Lone
Ranger,* and securing the rights for the transition to television was
beyond the show's budget. That was the case for nearly all of the
shows that switched from radio to television: the music would
have to be paid for again. On *The Lone Ranger,* Chudnow worked
around this by hiring NBC staff arranger Ben Bonnell to come in
and change a few notes and cues (the term for each individual
piece of music within a film or TV score)—just enough that even
if the viewer recognized the source work, the lawyers wouldn't be
able to prove that it was the exact same song. (Just for fun, listen
to the original and then the TV theme and see if you can spot the
subtle differences.)

Other early programs used the same tactic. The theme for the

Superman TV show starring George Reeves was slightly altered from the original radio score. This became the standard practice.

Solution 2: USE THEMES OVER AND OVER AND OVER

Even for shows that could afford to compose an original opening theme song, having to score cues for every episode presented a whole new challenge. Chudnow found one solution for this: He created MUTEL (short for "Music for Television"), a vast library of music cues that TV producers could mine and use, paying only a one-time fee. And the common practice was to alter existing cues from radio and B-movies to create the tracks for MUTEL. The result was a similar musical feel for most early TV shows: *Racket Squad*, *Captain Midnight*, *Annie Oakley*, and *Ramar of the Jungle* all culled their music from MUTEL. Soon more music libraries started popping up, but it quickly became obvious that more unique music was needed to give new shows their own identities.

Solution 3: HIRE A COMPOSER...ONCE

As television grew in the 1950s and '60s, the networks started making more money from advertisers. Higher-profile shows, such as CBS's *I Love Lucy*, could now afford a composer to score the opening theme and various cues—one that could be played when Lucy entered the apartment, one when she messed something up, another when she started crying, and so on. Once the composer's initial work was done, he was paid his fee, and then the show had its own unique musical library to cull from.

This would be the norm in episodic television for the next three decades—opening theme by an established composer and then incidental music by younger composers. The practice became even cheaper in the 1980s with the increased use of synthesizers and electric guitars to score television shows. As more and more shows went this route, it became harder for them to stand out...which led to the next big thing: songs.

Solution 4: BALLAD BREAKS

Ever notice how many of today's prime-time one-hour dramas include at least one pop song, often appearing over a montage right before the end of the episode? One of the first shows to do

---

First rap LP with an "Explicit Lyrics" warning label: 2 Live Crew's *As Nasty as They Wanna Be* (1989).

this was *Miami Vice*, which ran on NBC from 1984 to '89. And, as one of NBC's most successful shows, its budget allowed producers to use famous pop songs, such as "In the Air Tonight" by Phil Collins.

But most shows don't have the budget for big-name music. Enter Alexandra Patsavas. She's the music supervisor for *The O.C.*, *Grey's Anatomy*, *Private Practice*, *Chuck*, *Supernatural*, and many other shows. She spends most of her time listening to music samples from record companies, going to concerts, and debating with TV executives over the legal rights to the songs she wants to use. Her preference is indie rock and up-and-coming bands. It's a win-win situation: The songs cost far less than established hits, and the bands get an incredible amount of publicity. Two popular bands that first made their marks thanks to Patsavas: Snow Patrol and the Fray, both of which received Grammy nominations after getting mainstream exposure on *Grey's Anatomy*.

Solution 5: FAIR USE

A music supervisor's favorite song is a free song. Fortunately, there are thousands of tunes that fall in the category of public domain. The most prolific user of public domain songs: *The Simpsons*.

Solution 6: JUST GO FOR BROKE

Today, broadcast television faces more competition than ever before—DVDs, video games, and the Internet are all vying for our attention. So how do shows like *Criminal Minds*, *Lost*, and *Heroes* stand out? They go for that "major motion picture feel." Gone are the cheesy synths. Now full orchestras are making their way back into television on a large scale for the first time since the 1960s. Sure it costs more, but an orchestral score can make a show feel more like an "event." On the CBS drama *Criminal Minds*, producers have brought in veteran film composer Mark Mancina (*Training Day*, *Twister*, *Speed*) to give that show the movie feel. It's helped to make *Criminal Minds* one of the most successful dramas on television.

What will be the next innovation be? Will classical music make an unexpected return? Will silence be the next big trend? Stay tuned.

THEY'RE UNREAL, MAN!

*Lots of movies and TV shows feature made-up singers or bands.
Can you match the imaginary performer to the movie or
TV show it's from? (Answers on page 513.)*

1. Jet Screamer

2. The Electric Mayhem

3. Stillwater

4. The Pinheads

5. Conrad Birdie

6. Zack Attack!

7. The Wonders

8. Jesse and the Rippers

9. Sausalito

10. Future Villain Band

11. driveSHAFT

12. Hanover, Hardy & Dixon

13. Johnny Bravo

14. The Weird Sisters

15. Otis Day and the Knights

16. Wyld Stallyns

a) *Harry Potter and the Goblet of Fire*

b) *Saved by the Bell*

c) *The Jetsons*

d) *That Thing You Do!*

e) *Bill and Ted's Excellent Adventure*

f) *Full House*

g) *Lost in Translation*

h) *Sgt. Pepper's Lonely Hearts Club Band*

i) *Almost Famous*

j) *Back to the Future*

k) *Bye Bye Birdie*

l) *The Brady Bunch*

m) *The Muppet Show*

n) *Lost*

o) *Holiday Inn*

p) *Animal House*

A person who makes bows for violins and other instruments is called an *archetier*.

SEVEN INSTRUMENTS BIGGER THAN A TUBA

Okay, lots of instruments are bigger than a tuba—the piano, the harp, the bass violin, even some percussion instruments. But a tuba's still pretty big (a B-flat tuba has 18 feet of brass tubing). Here are some that are bigger —and stranger—than anything you'll ever seen in an orchestra.

1. THE GIANT TUBA

Well, of course a giant tuba is larger than a tuba. And this one is really giant. Built in the early 1900s by the prestigious brass instrument makers Besson & Company in London, it weighs 112 pounds and stands more than 8 feet tall. After it was built, the tuba served as a wall ornament at the factory for a few decades. Then, when the company moved to Edgeware, England, in 1948, it was displayed over the factory's entrance. There it remained, unplayed, for more than 50 years—until the company finally sold it in 2001. The tuba is now in the Horniman Museum in Forest Hill, South London. (People do play it occasionally, and they say it sounds like...a giant tuba.)

2. THE WANAMAKER ORGAN

This enormous pipe organ—so large that it's now housed in a building seven stories tall—was manufactured by the Los Angeles Art Organ company for the 1904 St. Louis World's Fair. It bankrupted the company with its then-astronomical cost of $105,000. Philadelphia merchant John Wanamaker bought it in 1909, had it shipped home in 13 freight cars, and installed it in his department store, where it still sits today (though the store is now a Macy's). The largest operational pipe organ in the world, it's an official National Historic Landmark and is valued at more than $50 million. It has six full keyboards, one on top of the other; 42 foot controls; dozens of rows of stops and controls; and, measuring from one inch to 32 feet in length—a grand total of 28,541 pipes. The entire thing weighs more than half a million pounds, and it's housed in Macy's seven-story-tall Grand Court. The sound? "Amazing" is the word heard most often, but don't trust us: You can hear it yourself. The official Wanamaker Organist (there have been only four since 1911) gives two performances per day.

3. THE SINGING STONES

In this unusual instrument, installed in a home in Vashon Island, Washington, a 20-foot-long, wing-shaped wooden soundbox is suspended from the ceiling. Hanging from the box are 35 wires, from 8' to 17' in length. And suspended on the wires are more than 100 rocks, ranging from potato- to football-size. The weight of the rocks pulls the wires tight, and the tonal qualities of the rocks, each meticulously chosen, influences the sound produced. So how *is* the sound produced? The creators, interactive instrument makers Ela Lamblin and Leah Mann, stand on a 20-foot-long platform behind the strings and walk, run, and dance back and forth as they stroke the wires with rosin-coated gloves. It sounds like an orchestra of rubbed wine glasses and violins.

4. THE SWAN BELL TOWER

It's a 270-foot-tall, copper-and-glass, needle-topped tower over-looking the Swan River in Perth, Australia. The tower houses 18 huge, tuned bells, the largest weighing more than 3,200 pounds. The bells are rung by groups of people pulling ropes attached to large wheels that swing the bells' clappers. One of the amazing things about the Swan Bell Tower is the story of the bells: Twelve of them spent their first several hundred years in the St. Martin-in-the-Fields Church on Trafalgar Square in London. They were rung for New Year's celebrations as well as for national events, like England's defeat of the Spanish Armada in 1588. (They date back to the 1300s.) In 1988, to commemorate Australia's bicentennial, those 12 bells, along with new ones, were given by the Church of England to the University of Western Australia, where they're now housed in that tall bell tower. Want to play them? Contact the staff—you can train to become a ringer.

5. THE ÜBERORGAN

This is one of the largest—and strangest—instruments ever made. Created for an installation at the Massachusetts Museum of Contemporary Art in 2000, artist Tim Hawkinson had to meet the challenge of filling up the space he was offered: six rooms encompassing 15,000 square feet. He did it by using more than 14,000 square feet of polyethylene (usually used to cover greenhouses) to make 12 "bus-sized," see-through "balloons" connected by thousands of feet of transparent tubing, all hanging from the ceiling. "They look like whales suspended in the air and hovering about you," Hawkinson said. The balloons act like bladders on bagpipes, each having an aperture containing a reed, which are connected to large tubular horns, each producing a different note in the chromatic scale.

The coolest part is how the Überorgan is played: In the largest room of the installation is a rack holding a 24-inch-wide mylar scroll, as well as a bunch of electronic equipment, from which wires go off in every direction. As you watch, the scroll is unrolled as it's pulled up to the high ceiling, and painted on the clear mylar are black dots and dashes, like the paper used in a player piano roll. The scroll passes through a roller on the ceiling, goes down to the floor, where it passes through another roller, up and down again several times, and finally back to the rack in a continuous loop. On its way it passes through a sensor that, based on the dots and dashes, electronically sends signals to valves on the balloons, telling them to release air and sound their notes. The dots and dashes are instructions to play hymns and popular songs (one being "Swan Lake"). Tired of the programmed music? Stop the scroll and sit at the instrument's keyboard and you can play the massive bladders yourself. The Überorgan was such a hit that it's been disassembled and moved to several other museums around the country, including the Getty Center in Los Angeles, where it was on exhibit for six months in 2007.

6. THE RIVERSIDE CHURCH CARILLON

A carillon is a musical instrument comprised of specially made, stationary (nonswinging) bronze bells, usually housed in a church's bell tower. The bells are sounded by clappers controlled by a keyboard with hand and foot pedals. This carillon was donated by John D. Rockefeller Jr. to the Riverside Church in New York City in 1925 in memory of his mother. It has 74 bells, spanning six octaves, housed in a tower 392 feet tall. The bells range in weight from 10 pounds to 20 tons, for a collective total of 200,000 pounds. It is the largest carillon by size and total weight in the world. The sound is rich, mournful, and powerful—and can be heard from several miles away.

7. THE GREAT STALACPIPE ORGAN

Called the largest musical instrument in the world, this "organ" was designed in 1954 by Pentagon mathematician and scientist Leland W. Sprinkle of Springfield, Virginia. It's actually a vast series of underground caves inside Luray Caverns near Shenandoah National Park in Virginia. The "instruments" that produce the music are *stalactites*—mineral formations, often shaped like icicles or draperies, that hang down from the ceilings of the caves. That technically makes the Great Stalacpipe Organ a *lithophone*, an instrument that makes music by striking rocks. The stalactites there have long been known for producing musical tones when struck, ever since the sprawling cave system was discovered in 1878. Sprinkle took it much further when, between 1954 and 1957, he shaved hundreds of stalactites in several caverns that span about 3 ½ acres—in effect, tuning them. He then connected electronically controlled, soft-headed mallets to them. The mallets in turn are connected to a large, specially made organ console with four stacked keyboards on which the stalactites can be "played." And you can actually play recognizable tunes. The warm, ethereal sound can be heard all over the 64 acres of the underground site, and Sprinkle himself played the instrument for years. The owners of the privately owned caverns still keep up the organ today, and have even released recordings of it. (No, it's not *rock* music.)

*   *   *

QUEENS OF THE STONED AGE

In 2007 the hard-rock band Queens of the Stone Age played a concert for the residents of a Los Angeles drug rehabilitation center. The band only played one song before clinic authorities pulled the plug and had security remove the band. Reason: The Queens of the Stone Age played their hit song "Feel Good Hit of the Summer," which consists entirely of the repeated lyrics "nicotine, valium, vicodin, marijuana, ecstasy and alcohol. C-c-c-c-c-cocaine."

First live musical performance to use an electric light show: Scriabin's *Poem of Ecstasy* (1908).

MYTHIC MUSIC

*Every world culture has its own mythology, and many are steeped
in the universal language of music. Here are some tales from
around the world that employ the power of song.*

THE MAGICAL HARP
Country: Ireland

Background: In Irish mythology, the Dagda was the king
of a group of gods known as the Tuatha Dé Danann. His most
prized possession was a beautiful harp of great size, made of the
finest wood and adorned with gold and jewels. When the Dagda
swept his hand across the strings, the seasons fell into their correct
order, critical to early Ireland's agrarian culture. On the battlefield,
one chord from the Dagda's great harp gave courage to his soldiers
and struck fear in the enemy.

Story: One night, a rival race of gods called the Fomorians stole
the harp. The Dagda and three of his finest warriors set out on a
mission to retrieve it from the abandoned castle where the Fomorians were hiding. Just as the Fomorians were enjoying a feast, the
Dagda burst through the door and saw his harp hanging on the far
wall. In his booming voice, he commanded, "Come to me, O my
harp!" The instrument began to shake and suddenly flew off of the
wall, straight into the hands of its owner. Before the Fomorians
could do anything, the Dagda began to play the Music of Tears
and the Fomorians began to cry. Then he played the Music of
Mirth and the Fomorians began to laugh uncontrollably. Then he
played the Music of Sleep…and they drifted off into unconscious-
ness. The Dagda and his men stole away into the night with the
harp.

THE MAGICAL VEENA
Country: India

Background: The *veena* is an Indian instrument that resembles a
lute. It's often depicted being held by Saraswati, the four-armed
goddess of music, as she sits on a lotus flower.

Story: A group of mischievous gods called the Gandharvas once
stole all the *soma* plants from the world (soma sap was used to

make an elixir for the gods). At the behest of the other gods, Saraswati traveled to the garden of the Gandharvas to retrieve the stolen plants. Once inside the garden, she sat down and began to create beautiful melodies on her veena. The Gandharvas were transfixed by the music and begged Saraswati to teach them the songs. "Only if you give back the soma plants," replied the goddess. Overjoyed, the Gandharvas agreed. And once they learned the music, they became celestial musicians whose melodies were said to be more intoxicating than anything of earthly origin. And the songs Saraswati played are believed to be the basis for *ragas* and *raginis*, the two main melodic forms of Indian classical music.

THE MAGICAL PIPE

Country: Germany

Background: One of the best-known musical myths is also one of the darkest. It tells of the Pied Piper of Hamelin, who was hired to rid the town of its rat infestation in the year 1284.

Story: The piper lured the rats out of town by playing a special tune on his magical flute. Once the rats were gone, the townspeople refused to pay the piper. So he returned while the adults were all in church...and played a new song. This one enchanted the town's children, who followed the Pied Piper away from their homes.

Most early versions of this tale told that the children were led to the same place as the rats, the Weser River, where they all drowned. In another version they were taken to a cave, never to be heard from again. But there's a third version with a happier ending in which the Pied Piper, feeling remorseful, returns the kids to the grieving townspeople...but only after he is paid several times his original fee.

THE MAGICAL LYRE

Country: Greece

Background: Orpheus was the son of the Greek god Apollo, who gave his son a beautiful lyre. Orpheus learned to play it with such skill that whoever heard it became enchanted—men, women, beasts, and even the rocks and trees.

Story: One day, Orpheus happened upon the beautiful young maiden, Eurydice, and seduced her with a song on his lyre. The two fell in love and were married. But soon after the wedding, a poisonous viper bit Eurydice and she died. Devastated, Orpheus played such sad songs that the other gods wept. At their urging, Orpheus traveled down to the underworld to convince the god Hades to free Eurydice and return her to the world of the living. Orpheus played a song so sad that Hades relented…on one condition: Orpheus had to lead Eurydice out of the underworld without turning around to look at her. Just when they were nearly free, Orpheus was unable to control himself any longer and stole a quick glance back at his love. Hades, true to his word, pulled Eurydice back to the underworld—this time forever. Orpheus roamed the Earth thereafter, playing heart-wrenching songs of mourning. Greek legend says that any time people write heart-breaking songs, they're hosting the spirit of Orpheus.

THE MAGICAL ZITHER

Country: Finland

Background: Väinämöinen was the Finnish god of songs, chants, and poetry. Called the "Eternal Sage," he was a wise old wizard who used music, cunning, and guile to thwart his foes. His tales were chronicled in an epic poem called the *Kalevala*.

Story: The *Kalevala* tells a famous tale of the evil mistress Louhi, who stole the Sampo, a magical talisman that ensured unlimited wealth for its owner. Louhi's greed brought misery and poverty to the people, so Väinämöinen and his followers sailed across the sea to stop her. Louhi threw a giant fish in front of their boat. But Väinämöinen killed it and used its bones to create the *kantele*, a kind of 5-stringed zither. Väinämöinen played the strange instrument and cast a spell over all the animals and people in the world. After Väinämöinen finished playing, the men guarding the Sampo were lost in blissful sleep, allowing him to to walk in and retrieve it. The Sampo was later destroyed in a fierce sea battle, as was the kantele, but Väinämöinen built a second kantele out of birchwood and the hair of a willing maiden. In the end, Louhi was defeated and the world was at peace. In the final verse of the *Kalevala*, Väinämöinen departed, leaving behind the kantele as his gift to the world, vowing to return one day…if he is needed. Today, the kantele is the national instrument of Finland.

AMAZING GRACE

*It's one of the most famous hymns in history—so famous that even
if you're not religious you probably know the first stanza by heart.
Here's the story that once was lost, but now is found.*

THE WRETCH

On May 10, 1748, John Newton, a sailor in the English
slave trade, was heading home to England when his ship
ran into a severe storm in the North Atlantic. So much seawater
poured into the cabin that it seemed the ship was about to sink;
Newton pumped water for nine hours straight and then, as his
energy finally gave out, he shouted, "Lord have mercy on us!"

Not long afterward, the weather began to clear and the bat-
tered ship was able to limp into port. Newton had never been a
religious man—in addition to working in the slave trade, he was a
gambler, a heavy drinker, and he cursed such a blue streak that
even other slave traders were shocked by the foulness of his language. "Not content with common oaths and imprecations, I daily
invented new ones," he recalled in his memoirs many years later.
But his deliverance from the storm changed him.

A NEW MAN

Convinced that his prayers had been answered in his moment of
need, Newton became an Evangelical Christian and gave up gambling, drinking, and swearing on the spot. Seven years later, when
an illness forced him to give up the seafaring life, he returned to
England and worked for several years as the surveyor of tides in Liverpool. There he met many of the most prominent Christians of the
day, including John Wesley, the founder of Methodism. Inspired by
their example, he became a minister in the Church of England and
was assigned to a church in the village of Olney, west of London.

It was in Olney that Newton met William Cowper (pronounced "Cooper"), one of the most popular poets of the 18th
century. Cowper, too, was a religious man, and he helped Newton
organize a weekly prayer meeting in the village. The two men set
a goal of writing a new hymn for every prayer meeting and took
turns doing it, each man writing one every other week.

In December 1772, Newton composed a hymn, which he titled "Faith's Review and Expectation," better known today by the first two words of the first stanza:

Amazing grace! How sweet the sound
That saved a wretch like me!
I once was lost, but now am found,
Was blind, but now I see.

AMAZING FACTS

• Newton wrote the words to the original seven stanzas; over the years, other contributors have added their own words to the hymn.

• No one knows who composed the melody; the hymn was sung to a number of other tunes before the current one became popular.

• In the more than 200 years since "Amazing Grace" was written, it has gone on to become arguably the most popular hymn of all time. It has become an anthem for all sorts of people struggling against injustice, even if they aren't Christians. Both sides sang it during the American Civil War; both sides sang it during the civil rights movement of the 1960s, too. Cherokee Indians sang it on the Trail of Tears in the late 1830s.

• To date, "Amazing Grace" has been recorded more than 1,000 times; it is so popular with contemporary black recording artists that it is commonly mistaken to be an old Negro spiritual.

MYTH-UNDERSTOOD

It's common for people to assume, when they learn that the author of this hymn of redemption was not a black man, but rather a former slave trader, that the song is addressing the issue of slavery. When Newton converted to Christianity, he must have left the slave trade and then written "Amazing Grace" to atone for his deeds, the logic goes. He's a "wretch" because he was a former slaver, and he "once was blind but now can see" because after he embraced religion he was finally able to see slavery for the evil that it was. There are even tales that when Newton experienced his religious conversion in 1748, he turned his ship around, sailed back to Africa, and set his slaves free.

STILL BLIND

That wasn't quite the case. Newton may have grown quickly as a composer of hymns—he composed 280, many of which are still sung today—but his spiritual growth took longer. After converting to Christianity, Newton returned to slave trading and spent the next five years buying slaves on the African coast and transporting them in bondage to British colonies in North America and the Caribbean. He worked his way up to captain of his own slave ship in the process, all the while devoting his free time to study and prayer.

According to historian Adam Hochschild, Newton and another Evangelical Christian slave ship captain once visited one another each evening for nearly a month. "A strange scene to imagine," he writes in his book *Bury the Chains*, "the two captains in their tricornered hats pacing the deck, earnestly talking of God and sin through the night, while slaves lie in shackles below them."

BETTER LATE THAN NEVER

Between 1764 and 1788 Newton wrote several books and delivered thousands of sermons, many of which were published and survive to this day. In them he frequently condemns adultery, usury, blasphemy, dishonesty, the size of the English national debt, and just about every kind of sin one can imagine. Except slavery—he doesn't condemn that even once.

It wasn't until 1788, when an antislavery movement was sweeping England, that Newton finally turned against slavery, condemning it in a pamphlet titled "Thoughts upon the African Slave Trade." In it, Newton makes a "confession, which comes too late," adding that "it will always be a subject of humiliating reflection to me, that I was once an active instrument in a business at which my heart now shudders."

Newton is often credited with devoting the remainder of his life to ending slavery, but that isn't true either. He published his pamphlet in 1788 and testified against slavery in Parliament the following year, but after that he dropped the subject. Though he lived until 1807 (the year that slavery was abolished throughout the British empire) and continued delivering sermons at a prodigious rate, he rarely mentioned slavery again. And he never wrote an antislavery hymn.

VENERATED VENUES

*You'll probably recognize most of the names on this list
—but do you know their histories?*

THE GRAND OLE OPRY

Where: 2802 Opryland Drive, Nashville, Tennessee
What: The Mecca of country music

Origin: In 1925 the National Life and Accident Insurance Company built radio station WSM ("We Shield Millions!") in its downtown Nashville office. (They wanted free publicity.) They hired radio pioneer George D. Hay away from WLS in Chicago, and on November 28, 1925, he started an hour-long show of old-timey music called the *WSM Barn Dance*. It was a huge success. So how did it get the "Opry" name? *The Barn Dance* followed a classical music and opera show, and one night in 1927 Hay said, "For the past hour, we have been listening to music taken largely from Grand Opera. From now on, we will present the Grand Ole Opry." The name stuck.

Making History: In 1932 the show went international when it boosted its output to 50,000 watts, making it receivable in most of the United States and into Mexico and Canada. In 1943 the show started broadcasting from the Ryman Auditorium, where it could handle the growing number of people who showed up, and in 1974 it moved to its present home, the 4,400-seat Grand Ole Opry House. It has been host to the royalty of country music for decades—from Hank Williams and Patsy Cline to Garth Brooks and Trisha Yearwood—and is still considered a must-stop on the country circuit. And it's the longest-running continuous radio show in the United States.

Sidenote: In 1954 a little-known, teenaged musician named Elvis Presley played at the Opry. The venue's manager, Jim Denny, told him afterward that he should keep his day job as a truck driver. Presley was so upset that he never played there again.

THE APOLLO THEATER

Where: 253 W 125th St., New York
What: The black Carnegie Hall

Tina Turner has sold more concert tickets than any other solo performer to date.

Origin: The Apollo's association with African-American musicians is undeniable, but it didn't start out that way. When the theater opened in 1914, it was a segregated burlesque hall; black patrons weren't allowed. The burlesque theater shut down in 1928, and the Apollo was purchased by theater promoter Sidney Cohen, who encouraged African-American artists to play there. In 1934 Cohen reopened the now-integrated theater and held its first amateur night—17-year-old Ella Fitzgerald was one of the finalists.

Making History: The theater's amateur night became its staple, and the Apollo was billed as "the place where stars are born and legends are made." They weren't kidding. Diana Ross, James Brown, Stevie Wonder, Billie Holiday, Jackie Wilson, the Jackson Five, Aretha Franklin, and dozens of other superstars got their starts on the show. Over the years, the Apollo fell into disrepair, but it was ultimately renovated and finally became a national landmark in 1983. Today, the theater still hosts concerts and shows...and amateur night: Every Wednesday night at 7:30, a new crop of performers steps onto the Apollo's stage and tries to fill the shoes of the stars and legends who came before.

In case you were wondering... You don't have to be black to perform at the Apollo; you just have to be a good musician. Buddy Holly played on the Apollo's stage in the 1950s, and the heavy-metal band Korn performed there in 1999.

CBGB

Where: 315 Bowery at Bleecker Street, Manhattan

What: The birthplace of punk

Origin: Founded in 1973 by Hilly Kristal, CBGB's music was originally supposed to be a little lighter; its name is an acronym for "country, blue grass, and blues." But Kristal couldn't find enough of those kinds of bands to book. Plus, the club's location in lower Manhattan, in a shabby neighborhood known as the Bowery, attracted a rowdier crowd. By 1974, when the Ramones played their first show there, CBGB had solidified its reputation as a haven for punks.

Making History: The experimental, minimalist, art-rock band Television started playing at the club regularly in 1974. Acts like Patti Smith, Blondie, the Ramones, and the Talking Heads followed, and when punk went big, CBGB went big with it—and was a must-play venue for hundreds of bands of all musical genres. A few of the acts that played there: AC/DC, the Black Crowes, the Cars, Elvis Costello, Guns N' Roses, Jeff Buckley, Nirvana, the Police, and Bruce Springsteen. CBGB closed its doors in 2006 when the owners couldn't reach an agreement with the building's landlords about the rent. But the club went out with a bang—Patti Smith played last show on October 15, with a marathon 3½-hour set—and the image of CBGB, with its low ceiling and stickered walls, remains a nostalgic fixture in music history. (Hilly Kristal passed away in 2007, and CBGB is slated to be converted into an upscale men's clothing boutique.)

CARNEGIE HALL

Where: 881 Seventh Avenue, New York

What: The most famous performance hall in the world

Origin: It was named for steel magnate and philanthropist Andrew Carnegie (he paid for it). Construction began in 1890 and opening day was May 5, 1891.

Making History: Although primarily a venue for showcasing classical music—Peter Ilyich Tchaikovsky played at the opening ceremony—Carnegie Hall has hosted some of the most important figures in popular music of all kinds. Just a few who made it a point to play Carnegie Hall over the decades: Leonard Bernstein, Enrico Caruso, Itzak Perlman, Luciano Pavarotti, Fats Waller, Louis Armstrong, Count Basie, Billie Holiday, Miles Davis, John Coltrane, Woody Guthrie, Harry Belafonte, Pete Seeger, Bob Dylan, Judy Garland, Nat King Cole, Frank Sinatra, the Beatles, the Rolling Stones, the Doors, Stevie Wonder, Wyclef Jean, Mary J. Blige.

THE FILLMORE AUDITORIUM

Where: The corner of Fillmore and Geary, San Francisco

What: The home of psychedelic rock

Origin: The Fillmore opened at the corner of Fillmore and Geary streets in 1912 as a dance hall, first called the Majestic Academy of Dancing. During World War II it was a roller rink. In the 1950s, the Fillmore became a live-music venue for the first time when local businessman Charles Sullivan started booking African-American acts—including Ike and Tina Turner and James

Brown—and the Fillmore (and San Francisco) got a reputation as a place that welcomed bohemians from all over the country. When Bill Graham took over as manager in 1965, he brought many of his counterculture artist friends with him and combined traditional greats like Miles Davis and B.B. King with up-and-comers like Jefferson Airplane and Janis Joplin. The mix proved both heady and successful, and the Fillmore helped solidify San Francisco's place in the American counterculture movement.

Onward: In 1968 Graham moved the venue to the corner of Market Street and South Van Ness Avenue, calling it Fillmore West (he opened Fillmore East in New York City that same year). It stayed there until after Graham died in 1991, and according to his wishes, the original Fillmore Auditorium was reopened in 1994. A list of the musicians who played the Fillmore in its heyday reads like a who's-who of 1960s and 1970s superstars: Jimi Hendrix, Pink Floyd, the Doors, Cream, Muddy Waters, the Who, Country Joe and the Fish, the Paul Butterfield Blues Band, Quicksilver Messenger Service, Led Zeppelin, the Grateful Dead, and hundreds of others. The Fillmore pioneered the use of psychedelic light shows to accompany the music. And its colorful event posters, commissioned by Graham, have become some of rock's most coveted collector's items.

*   *   *

RANDOM MOVIE QUOTE

Nigel Tufnel: It's part of a musical trilogy I'm working on in D minor, which is the saddest of all keys, I find. People weep instantly when they hear it, and I don't know why.

Marty DiBergi: It's very nice.

Nigel: You know, just simple lines intertwining—I'm really influenced by Mozart and Bach, and it's sort of in between those, really. It's like a "Mach" piece, really.

Marty: What do you call this?

Nigel: Well, this piece is called "Lick My Love Pump."

—Christopher Guest and Rob Reiner,
This Is Spinal Tap (1984)

Chevy Chase was an original member of Steely Dan.

METALLURGY

Who invented heavy metal? Most experts agree it was this group.

BACKGROUND

In the late 1960s, Birmingham was one of the bleakest areas in England, blackened with soot and grime from years of smog-spewing factories, which were beginning to close down, making the place even grayer. Out of this came local rock bands who parlayed that bleakness into music.

In 1967 Ozzy Osbourne (real name: John) and bassist Geezer Butler played together in a band called Rare Breed; guitarist Tony Iommi and drummer Bill Ward played in another band called Mythology. All four wanted to play harder, louder, blues-based rock (like Cream) instead of the progressive rock their bands were doing. So Iommi and Ward put an ad in the paper for a lead singer, Osbourne responded, and, together with Butler, they formed a new group called the Polka Tulk Blues Band (named after a store Osbourne liked). They changed their name to Earth in 1969 and played a variety of music, all of it loud and with heavy guitar distortion. Then it turned into a new kind of music: heavy metal. "We didn't really know what we were doing," said Iommi. "We had been through the pop, the blues, and everything else, but when we started putting our own music together, something else just happened."

THE ATTITUDE

As Earth, they played straight-ahead hard rock at first. One day while rehearsing in 1969, Iommi noticed a movie theater next door was playing a horror movie. The band started discussing how inexplicable and strangely funny it was that people would willingly pay money to see something that was supposed to scare them.

Sensing an untapped concept, this meshed perfectly with lead singer Osbourne's growing distaste for mainstream pop music, especially if it had a hippie flavor, which, being from a dreary part of England, he couldn't relate to. "If you ever go to San Francisco, be sure to wear a flower in your hair? Screw that. Let's go possess people!" Osbourne began to write lyrics about war, death, murder, the devil, and most often, mental illness.

Around the same time, Geezer Butler developed an interest in evil and magic. A friend gave him a book on the occult and while reading it one night, Butler claims a black-hooded ghost appeared at the foot of his bed. Rather than get freaked out, this made him start reading Dennis Wheatley novels about black magic, which influenced the band's songwriting. Butler wrote a song called "Black Sabbath," which Earth took on as its new name in late 1969.

THE SOUND

Another distinctive element of heavy metal: a strong "low end." Part of Black Sabbath's sound is a deep, buzzing, electrical drone. Geezer Butler says he was influenced by Cream bassist Jack Bruce, who improvised while he played and bent strings, things most bass players didn't do—most bassists just followed the drum parts, serving as part of the rhythm section. Butler's low, guttural, feedback-laden basslines were almost as menacing as lyrics about the devil.

Guitarist Iommi's sound came about by accident. While working as a welder, he'd accidentally cut off two fingertips. He used plastic sleeves made from a plastic detergent bottle over those fingers while playing guitar, but it still hurt to press down on thick, metal guitar strings. So Iommi strung his guitar with banjo strings. He didn't have to press down as hard, and it also allowed him to play faster. Then he lowered the tuning of his guitar—loosening the strings—which was easier on his fingers, but also made it sound "heavier."

THE RESULT

Black Sabbath released its first album, *Black Sabbath*, in early 1970. Songs included "The Wizard," "Behind the Wall of Sleep," and "N.I.B." (a love song written from the point of view of the devil). The cover reflected what the album sounded like: dark and scary. It showed Osbourne dressed in a black hooded cloak standing in a garden of red flowers in front of a decrepit house.

Surprisingly, audiences weren't freaked out. Black Sabbath's mixture of dark themes and heavy music struck a chord: *Black Sabbath* went to #8 on the British chart and #23 in America. Later in 1970, Black Sabbath released its second album, *Paranoid*, which contained some of its best-known songs, including "Iron Man," "Paranoid," and the antiwar "War Pigs." It went to #1 in the U.K. Heavy metal was born.

NEWSIC

News and music, all in one word (and in two pages).

SINGING IN THE...

In 2006 Energy Australia, one of that nation's biggest suppliers of electricity, issued a request to all its customers in the Sydney area: Please stop singing in the shower. The company had conducted a poll and found that customers were spending an average of seven minutes in the shower—because of frivolous activities like singing. That, they said, was wasting huge amounts of electricity. The UK's BBC news service then released a list of songs that might be shower-okay: the Pixies' "Crackity Jones" (1 minute, 22 seconds), Wire's "Three Girl Rhumba" (1 minute, 22 seconds), and the Dead Kennedys' "I Like Short Songs" (22 seconds).

(H)ARMLESS JOKES

In 1984 Rick Allen, drummer for the British metal band Def Leppard, lost his left arm in a drunk-driving accident. Amazingly, he continued to play with the band—with one arm—and still plays with them today. Over the years, a slew of jokes about the one-armed drummer have become popular. (Here's one. Q: What has nine arms and plays crappy music? A: Def Leppard.) In 2002 a reporter asked the band's guitarist, Phil Collen, how the band felt about the jokes. He said they had thick skin and knew it was all in fun...but added that if people overdo it in his presence, he'll just "beat the $@*#! out of them."

PLAY THAT (LUCKY) NUMBER

In July 2003, country singer Johnny Lee, best known for the #1 hit "Looking for Love," released a new CD. He released it, to be precise, on July 13th. And he titled it "The 13th of July." And he used 13 musicians to record it. And he had 13 investors behind him on the project. And he recorded it when his child was 13. And he had written the title track 13 years earlier. His lucky number, as you may have guessed, is 13. Luck prevailed; the album was his most successful in years.

Pet sounds? Igor Stravinsky said his music was "best understood by children and animals."

SHE TOOK THE TEE VEE

Country music superstar Kenny Chesney and actress Renee Zellweger were married in 2005. And then they were unmarried (the marriage was annulled) in 2005. In an interview with *Life* magazine later that year, Chesney explained—in country music terms—how much that hurt him. It was "like opening the door to your house," he said, "and having someone come in and take your bigscreen TV off the wall during the big game, and there's nothing you can do about it."

SINGS WITH THE FISHES

In October 2006, Georgian-Irish singer Katie Melua and her band were helicoptered to the Troll A oil-drilling platform 50 miles off the coast of Norway. They were then lowered down one of the rig's hollow concrete legs...to a depth of 994 feet, where the band played two hour-long concerts for oil workers. The deep-sea gig was part of an anniversary celebration for the platform, and was recognized by *Guinness World Records* as the deepest underwater concert ever performed in front of an audience. The 22-year-old Melua said it was "definitely the most surreal gig I've ever done."

COUNTRY FRAUD CHICKEN

In 2004 Troy Lee Gentry, half of the country music duo Montgomery Gentry, shot a black bear with a bow and arrow in Minnesota, then turned in papers to record the kill, and also had a video of the hunt made. But in 2005 some un-tough-guy news came out: Gentry had bought the bear. It was tame. Its name was "Cubby." And it was in a three-acre fenced enclosure (not shown in the video) when Gentry killed it. Gentry angrily denied the charge...at first. But days before facing trial on felony counts of possessing illegally obtained wildlife, he finally pleaded guilty to misdemeanor charges of falsely registering the bear as having been shot "in the wild." Gentry was sentenced to three months probation and a $15,000 fine, and had to give up the bear's hide (which was on display in his Tennessee home). The man from whom he bought the bear, Lee Marvin Greenly, faces up to five years in prison.

BATTLING THE BAND

They don't just make music. Some stars also make waves.

PEARL JAM VS. TICKETMASTER

The Feud: In the early 1990s, Pearl Jam was one of the most successful and popular rock bands in the world—led by singer Eddie Vedder, Pearl Jam has sold more than 30 million albums in the United States alone. In the summer of 1994, Pearl Jam decided to give something back to their fans—a low-cost tour. Concert ticket prices had gotten out of the reach of the average music fan, the band said, so most tickets for the tour would sell for just $20 (compared to the normal $40, $50, or even $100). But at the second show, the band discovered that Ticketmaster, the only agency licensed to sell tickets for most of the tour venues, was adding their standard $3 to $6 in processing fees to the price of each ticket. Pearl Jam asked Ticketmaster to lower its fees. The agency refused, so the band filed a complaint with the U.S. Justice Department, claiming that Ticketmaster was a monopoly. Congress investigated and even held hearings on the matter.

Who Came Out on Top? Ticketmaster. Pearl Jam ultimately canceled the 1994 tour and gave up its legal fight in June 1995. Ticketmaster continues to charge fees, and still controls ticket sales at more than 75 percent of all the major American concert venues. Nevertheless, the Justice Department dropped its monopoly investigation in 1995.

THE DIXIE CHICKS VS. COUNTRY RADIO

The Feud: In March 2003, the Dixie Chicks' album *Home* was on top of the music charts, they had a #1 single ("Travelin' Soldier"), and they'd sold out their upcoming U.S. tour. As a prelude to that tour, they played several clubs in Europe, including a show in London, where lead singer Natalie Maines, a Texan, told the audience, "Just so you know, we're ashamed the president of the United States is from Texas." The statement was met with cheers, so the band simply carried on, voicing support for the troops about to go to war in Iraq and launching into "Travelin' Soldier." But as the news media picked up the story, it became clear that many of the Dixie Chicks' American fans were not cheering.

At first, the Chicks (Maines, Martie Maguire, and Emily Robison) thought the whole thing would blow over. But they soon found themselves embroiled in a battle for their careers. They were called traitors for criticizing the president while they were in a foreign country, and many radio stations, primarily in the South, stopped playing their music. Angry fans sent death threats and heckled their shows. Local communities organized "stomp the Chicks" parties, inviting former fans to toss Dixie Chicks CDs into piles and watch as they were crushed by steamrollers.

Maines offered a public apology for "disrespecting the office of the president." But when that didn't stop the criticism, the band embraced the controversy, posing nude on the cover of *Entertainment Weekly*, their bodies covered only by stenciled phrases like "Saddam's Angels," "Dixie Sluts," "Big Mouth," and "Hero." The story eventually died down...until 2006, when the Chicks released the album *Taking the Long Way*, which included several songs about "the incident." The first single, "Not Ready to Make Nice," was an obvious snub at the people who had attacked them, and it further fueled the ire of many country radio stations. Said one station manager, "It's a four-minute @*&%-you to our format and our listeners. I like the Chicks, but I won't play it."

Who Came Out on Top? The Dixie Chicks. *Taking the Long Way* sold 400,000 copies its first week, went double platinum, and won five Grammys, including one for Record of the Year. *Time* magazine included the band on its 2006 list of the "Top 100 People Who Shape Our World." And the Dixie Chicks' 2006 tour—although its schedule had to be adjusted slightly and shows canceled in areas that remained hostile to the band—sold out most dates in the Northeast, the West, and Canada.

METALLICA VS. NAPSTER

The Feud: Before Napster, MP3 music files were hard to find. The music industry had been zealous about keeping its products off the Internet for fear that record sales would plummet if people could get their hands on digital music. In 1999 Shawn Fanning, a college kid from Boston, figured out how to put MP3s online and set up a system for sharing those files with others. He called his application Napster, and it quickly became popular with young music fans around the country. Music was expensive, after all, and older songs were sometimes hard to find. But thanks to Napster, everything from the entire Beatles collection to Limp Bizkit hits were just a mouse click away. And best of all, they were free.

Within a few months, the Recording Industry Association of America filed a lawsuit against Napster, claiming it was violating artists' copyrights. The next year, when Metallica discovered that one of its unreleased singles had been leaked to Napster and that its entire body of work was available for free download, the band joined the suit against Fanning and his company for copyright infringement.

Who Came Out on Top? Metallica...sort of. In 2001 the U.S. Court of Appeals ruled in favor of the record companies. Napster's free file sharing was considered a copyright violation, and legitimate music-sharing Web sites had to convert to pay systems. Many music lovers, though, were angry that free file sharing was being shut down, and they blamed Metallica. *Blender* magazine named the band in its Top 20 "biggest wusses" in rock. And fans ridiculed them as selfish and money-grubbing (especially ironic, since the group had found early success thanks to word-of-mouth and bootlegged concert recordings). To be fair, Metallica was just one of many artists who filed lawsuits against Napster: Madonna, Dr. Dre, and others were also involved. But Metallica was the most vocal and took the brunt of the criticism.

*   *   *

TV & FILM STARS WHO HAVE MADE ALBUMS

Marlon Brando	Farrah Fawcett	Sally Field
Walter Matthau	Cesar Romero	Ray Walston
Jack Lemmon	Joe Pesci	Butch Patrick
Gloria Swanson	Bubby Ebsen	Adam West
Rock Hudson	Dennis Weaver	Goldie Hawn
Sylvester Stallone	Joan Rivers	Fess Parker
Robert Mitchum	Phyllis Diller	Burt Reynolds
Orson Welles	Buddy Hackett	Jerry Mathers
Telly Savalas	Barbara Feldon	Patty Duke

As a session musician, Jimmy Page played with the Kinks, Joe Cocker, and Engelbert Humperdinck.

16 RANDOM LISTS ABOUT FRANK SINATRA

Frank Sinatra was an original—he contributed dozens of standards to the American songbook. But his music was often overshadowed by his turbulent personal life. And since we can't play his music here, we concentrated on that personal life.

9 VITAL STATISTICS

1. Born: December 12, 1915
2. Name at birth: Frank (not Francis) Albert Sinatra
3. Height: 5'7½"
4. Favorite color: orange
5. Drink of choice: Jack Daniels (straight)
6. Handgun of choice: .38 Smith & Wesson
7. Favorite meal: spaghetti pomodoro
8. Secret Service nickname (Nixon era): Napoleon
9. Epitaph: "The Best Is Yet to Come"

5 "OFFICERS" OF THE ORIGINAL RAT PACK

1. Frank Sinatra, Pack Master
2. Judy Garland, First Vice President
3. Lauren Bacall, Den Mother
4. Humphrey Bogart, Rat-in-Charge-of-Public Relations
5. Irving (Swifty) Lazar, Recording Secretary and Treasurer

5 MEMBERS OF THE LAS VEGAS RAT PACK

1. Frank Sinatra
2. Dean Martin
3. Sammy Davis Jr.
4. Peter Lawford
5. Joey Bishop

7 NICKNAMES

1. "The Frail Finch" (early in his career)
2. "The Voice"
3. "Chairman of the Board" (coined by deejay William B. Williams)
4. "The General"
5. "My Man Francis" (Sammy Davis Jr.'s pet name for him)
6. "Charlie Brown" (Mia Farrow's nickname for him)
7. "The Pope"

LOCATIONS OF HIS 3 STARS ON THE HOLLY-WOOD WALK OF FAME

1. Movies: 1600 Vine St.
2. Recordings: 1637 Vine St.
3. TV: 6538 Hollywood Blvd.

First African-American opera: *Treemonisha*, by ragtime composer Scott Joplin (1911).

3 IMPORTANT "ARMY" NUMBERS

1. Weight at his Army physical in 1943: 119 pounds
2. Draft designation: 4-F (because of a perforated eardrum, a condition later questioned by biographers)
3. Number of movies in which he played a serviceman: 11

2 QUOTES BY HIS FIRST WIFE, NANCY

1. "Frank, don't forget your galoshes." (That's what she called to him when he was leaving the house one rainy night. Sinatra claimed it was the reason he decided to leave her.)
2. "After *Sinatra?*" (Her response when asked why she never remarried.)

8 CATEGORIES OF PEOPLE WITH WHOM HE OFTEN HAD ALTERCATIONS

1. Columnists
2. Hecklers
3. Reporters
4. Musicians
5. Photographers
6. Publishers
7. Waiters
8. Anyone who he felt didn't show him respect

9 "ACQUAINTANCES" WITH INTERESTING NICKNAMES

1. Anthony "Tony Batters" Accardo
2. Willie "Potatoes" Daddano
3. Paul "Skinny" D'Amato
4. Charles "Trigger Happy" Fischetti
5. Joseph "Joe Fish" Fischetti
6. Sam "Momo" Giancana
7. Tommy "Three Fingers Brown" Lucchese
8. Carlos "Little Big Man" Marcello
9. Abner "Longie" Zwillman

4 THINGS HE COULDN'T STAND

1. Ashtrays filled with cigarette butts
2. Drawers left slightly open
3. Knives and forks not lined up perfectly in a place setting
4. Books in untidy heaps

6 WOMEN SINATRA ROMANCED...BUT DIDN'T MARRY

1. Marilyn Monroe
2. Marlene Dietrich
3. Gloria Vanderbilt
4. Lauren Bacall
5. Natalie Wood
6. Lana Turner

6 PEOPLE WHOSE HOSPITAL BILLS HE PAID

1. Buddy Rich
2. Joe Louis
3. Lee J. Cobb
4. Peggy Lee
5. Mabel Mercer
6. Billie Holiday

4 MEMBERS OF HIS ENTOURAGE

1. George Jacobs, valet/cook/chauffeur for 15 years. Fired without notice after Sinatra learned that he had danced with Mia Farrow at an L.A. disco. Jacobs went home that evening to find that the locks had been changed.
2. Brad Dexter, actor and close friend who once saved Sinatra from drowning. Sinatra never thanked him for saving his life and, after a falling-out, had him fired from a film he was producing.
3. Jilly Rizzo, best friend and bodyguard, in charge of confronting people who crossed Sinatra. He's buried near the Sinatra family plot.
4. A woman whose sole responsibility was to take care of his 60 toupees.

2 THINGS HE HAD TO HAVE

1. Clean hands and fingernails (another nickname: "Lady Macbeth," because he washed his hands so often)
2. Paper money that was new and crisp

3 LITTLE-KNOWN FACTS ABOUT SINATRA

1. While still a Democrat, he called Nancy Reagan "a dumb broad with fat ankles."
2. He carried cherry bombs to throw at paparazzi.
3. He had five model train sets at his Palm Springs home. He wore an engineer's hat (and blew a whistle) while playing with them.

4 BEQUESTS IN HIS LAST WILL AND TESTAMENT

1. $250,000 to his first wife, Nancy
2. $200,000 to each of his children (and his sheet music to Frank Jr.)
3. $1,000,000 in trust for his two grandchildren
4. Everything else (more than $3.5 million) to his fourth wife, Barbara

*   *   *

"Whatever else has been said about me personally is unimportant. When I sing, I believe. I'm honest."
—**Frank Sinatra**

LET'S PLAY THE NGARRRIRALKPWINA!

Or, as you Up Over *know it, the* didjeridu.

WHAT'S IN A NAME?

You may be familiar with the instrument known around the world as the didjeridu (often spelled *didgeridoo* or *didjeridoo*). It's an Australian instrument, a long, hollow wooden tube that's played by blowing into one end. The sound that it makes—an otherwordly, deep, rhythmic droning—may have been the reason why early 20th-century European settlers gave the instrument its unusual name. But the didjeridu is much older than that, and is known among the many different Australian Aboriginal tribes by many names: the Yolngu people in what is now Australia's Northern Territory call it the *yidaki*, or *yirdaki*. And on Groote Eylandt, an island off the country's northern coast, it's known as the *ngarrriralkpwina*.

THE TERMITE TREES

Traditional didjeridus are made the same way they've been made for thousands of years: from live trunks of young eucalyptus trees, or gum trees, as they're commonly called in Australia, that have been hollowed out by termites.

All termites eat cellulose, the main ingredient in trees and plants. Most of the termite species that eat live trees (as opposed to those that eat dead trees, like the lumber in your house) eat sapwood—the young, living, outer layer of the tree. They don't usually eat heartwood, the older, dead center of the tree, because it's too dense and contains fewer nutrients than sapwood. (And the heartwood of many trees contains compounds that are toxic or indigestible to termites.) But a few Australian termite species do eat heartwood, making them perfect didjeridu makers.

Termites are delicate creatures; they can't survive in the open air or when exposed to sunlight. While most termite species in Australia make their nests underground, in earthen termite mounds, or on the outside of trees, the didjeridu-making species build their nests inside the trees they're eating, making those gum trees their food *and* their shelter. It's a unique situation, without which the didjeridu might never have been invented.

THE MAKERS

Traditional didjeridu makers learn from a young age where to look for the right trees. An expert maker can tap on a tree and hear whether it's been hollowed out in such a way that would be good for a didjeridu. If the tree seems like a good candidate, it's chopped down and the *mudgut*, the substance the termites create to make their nests, is removed, and the hollow examined. The sound produced by any given didjeridu will be largely determined by the pattern carved out by the termites, which results in different tonal qualities and harmonics.

If the tube looks right, it's cut to the desired length—anywhere from three to eight feet—and taken back to the home or shop of the didjeridu maker. There the bark is removed, the ends are smoothed out, and the soon-to-be didjeridu is carved, etched, and painted—sometimes elaborately, according to the customs of the particular tribe or clan that the maker is associated with. Then a thick layer of beeswax is applied to the end to protect the player's mouth from the wood and to ensure a good seal when the instrument is played.

LET'S PLAY

Didjeridus are used for many purposes by Aboriginal peoples. They are the central instrument used for *corroborees*, ceremonies that range from secret and sacred to celebratory, usually with music and dancing. The music differs from tribe to tribe in its sound and purposes, but most often the didjeridu is played along with *clap sticks*—short pieces of wood that are struck together to make a sharp rapping sound. Didjeridus and clap sticks are both used to accompany singing and dancing.

But how does a didjeridu player get that trancelike, vibrating sound? It's produced by blowing through the lips, making something like a "raspberry," while the mouth is pressed tightly against the open end of the instrument. Using their lips, tongue, the shape of their mouths, and by humming or singing while blowing, expert players can make a surprisingly wide variety of sounds, from smooth, deep droning to sharp staccato notes, high yelps, and whirring, whistling sounds.

Europeans who first observed didjeridu players must have been astounded, because masters of the instrument can play for *nearly an hour* with no break in the sound. Nobody has that much breath in their lungs, nor can anyone survive that long without inhaling. The trick is the most difficult aspect of playing the didjeridu: *circular breathing.* An expert player can hold a bit of air in his cheeks and expel it manually while taking a breath through his nose—using his cheeks like the bag on a bagpipe—so the sound never stops.

RANDOM FACTS

• If you want to learn circular breathing, here's the technique: Puff up your cheeks and breathe through your nose; hold a mouthful of water (while leaning over the sink!) and, while breathing in through your nose, let a smooth stream of water out through your lips; or blow bubbles into a glass of water through a straw…while breathing in through your nose. Mastering those techniques, experts say, will make learning to play the didjeridu easier.

• Some of the preferred plant species used to make didjeridus: the woolybutt gum, the River Red gum, the stringybark, and bamboo.

• Nobody knows exactly how long the didjeridu has been around. Many stories put it as far back as the first human inhabitation of Australia—about 40,000 years ago—which would make it the oldest known instrument on Earth by far, but there is no solid evidence to support that. Petroglyphs in the Arnhem Land region show that they were being played there at least 2,000 years ago.

• A 2005 study by Swiss scientists concluded that taking didjeridu lessons several times per week can reduce sleeping disorders like snoring and daytime drowsiness.

• In 1991 the didjeridu-based rock band Yothu Yindi became a sensation in Australia with their album *Tribal Voice.* The song "Treaty," a plea to recognize the rights of Australia's Aboriginal peoples, was voted Australia's song of the year. Yothu Yindi would go on to international touring and acclaim, and along the way became one of the main reasons why the didjeridu is as popular as it is today.

QUOTIN' COUNTRY

*Here we examine the mythos and the hard
realities that make up country music.*

"You got to have smelt a lot of mule manure before you can sing like a hillbilly."

—**Hank Williams**

"Sometimes you don't realize how true country songs are until you find yourself in the middle of one."

—**Hank Williams Jr.**

"Country music to me is heartfelt music that speaks to the common man. It is about real life stories with rather simple melodies that the average person can follow."

—**George Jones**

"I've always felt that blues, rock 'n' roll, and country are just about a beat apart."

—**Waylon Jennings**

"While country and western music isn't classical, it is classically American."

—**Ronald Reagan**

"Country music has always been the best shrink that 15 bucks can buy."

—**Dierks Bentley**

"If you think that country is still about big hair and blue eye shadow, you haven't listened to it for 20 years—and you probably think that Elton John is still wearing platform shoes."

—**Trisha Yearwood**

"Back when I first started, in the late '50s, I rocked out a little. Somebody—I won't say who—came to me and told me, 'Hoss, you got to understand the difference between country music and that rock 'n' roll. In country music we want wet eyes...not wet crotches.'"

—**Bobby Bare**

"I think pure country music includes rock 'n' roll. I've never been able to get into the label of country-rock. How can you define something like that? I just say this: It's music. Either it's good or it's bad; either you like it or you don't."

—**Gram Parsons**

"Country music is three chords and the truth."

—**Harlan Howard**

First Grammy Award-winning country song: "El Paso," by Marty Robbins (1959).

JOHNNY CASH'S CAPTIVE AUDIENCE

*Johnny Cash was one of country music's first "outlaws," but the music
industry was still surprised in 1957 when he played a concert at Huntsville
State Prison in Texas. Over the next decade, Cash performed 30
prison shows and recorded albums during at least three of them.
(The shows at California's Folsom Prison and San Quentin
became the most famous.) Here are 10 little-known
facts about the Man in Black's prison concerts.*

**1. Columbia Records repeatedly rejected Cash's request to
record a prison concert.**
Cash started playing at prisons in response to fan mail from
inmates who identified with his songs (especially "Folsom Prison
Blues"). Soon he discovered that "prisoners are the greatest audience that an entertainer can perform for. We bring them a ray of
sunshine into their dungeon, and they're not ashamed to respond
and show their appreciation." He suspected that their excitement
and gratitude combined with the thrill of performing in a dangerous venue would create the perfect setting for an album. His record
company disagreed—they thought the concerts would kill Cash's
career and hurt the label's image. But when Columbia brought on
producer Bob Johnston—known for being a bit wild himself and
for bucking authority (as well as for producing Bob Dylan)—that
stance changed. Johnston readily approved the country star's idea.
Columbia remained tight-lipped about the performance and the
release of *Johnny Cash at Folsom Prison* in 1968, still believing the
album would never sell. But it did...an incredible 500,000 copies
in one year. Sales were boosted by Cash's tough-guy image (he
wore solid black clothing, used profane language, had a gravelly
voice, and fought an on-again, off-again addiction to drugs). To
help the cause along, Columbia released exaggerated ads claiming
Cash was no stranger to prison. Which brings us to...

2. Cash never served time at Folsom, or any other prison.
He did seven short stints in jail, though, for drug- and alcohol-
related charges. His song "Folsom Prison Blues" was instead

---

inspired by the 1951 movie *Inside the Walls of Folsom Prison*. According to biographer Michael Streissguth, another influence was Gordon Jenkins's song "Crescent City Blues," from which Cash "borrowed" so heavily that when his version was recorded on the *Folsom* album, the original artist demanded—and received—royalties.

3. Cash inspired future country star Merle Haggard.

Haggard was serving three years at San Quentin Prison for armed robbery and escaping from jail when Johnny Cash took the stage there in 1958. When Haggard later told Cash that he'd been at the concert, Cash said he didn't remember Haggard performing that day; Haggard replied, "I was in the audience, Johnny." In fact, he was sitting in the front row and was mesmerized by Cash. He and his fellow inmates identified with Cash's lyrics about loss and imprisonment. Haggard reminisced: "This was somebody singing a song about your personal life. Even the people who weren't fans of Johnny Cash—it was a mixture of people, all races were fans by the end of the show." Haggard also soon realized that he shared Cash's talent for making music and for speaking to the struggles of the working class. He joined the prison's country band shortly after Cash's concert and penned songs about being locked up. After his release in 1960, Haggard sang at clubs until he eventually became a country superstar himself.

4. The live "Folsom Prison Blues" was too grisly for radio play.

Cash's declaration "I shot a man in Reno/Just to watch him die," followed by an inmate's shriek of joy, was edited by radio stations. But the hollering wasn't real. It had been dubbed in by Columbia Records since the prisoners had been too enthralled by Cash's performance to whoop it up during songs.

5. Cash's band smuggled a gun into Folsom.

Johnny Cash and his bassist, Marshall Grant, often performed a comedy skit with an antique cap-and-ball gun that made smoke. It was a prop—but it was a real gun. Grant accidentally brought the weapon inside his bass guitar case to the 1968 show. A prison guard spotted it and politely took it to the warden for safekeeping until the concert ended.

6. Folsom Prison inmate Glen Sherley wrote the song "Greystone Chapel" and credited Cash with changing his life.

Glen Sherley was in Folsom for armed robbery, but he also loved music. Before Cash arrived for the 1968 show, Sherley recorded the song "Greystone Chapel" at the prison chapel. Appropriately, it was about a man whose body is imprisoned but his soul is freed by religion. Cash's pastor, who also counseled inmates, smuggled the tape out to Cash, who learned to play the song the night before the show. After seeing Cash perform his song, Sherley vowed to make a mark with the musician. Once he was released from Folsom, he went to work for Johnny Cash's publishing company, House of Cash. Sherley later remarked, "I was a three-time loser when John reached out his hand to me in 1968, and since then I sincerely believe that I have become a worthwhile person and can contribute to society."

7. Cash's concert at Folsom landed him his own musical variety show: *The Johnny Cash Show*.

Cash noted, "I've always thought it ironic that it was a prison concert, with me and the convicts getting along just as fellow rebels, outsiders, and miscreants should, that pumped up my marketability to the point where ABC thought I was respectable enough to have a weekly network TV show."

8. When Johnny Cash recorded *At San Quentin* in 1969, he didn't know the lyrics to one of his most famous songs.

It was the first time Cash had performed "A Boy Named Sue," written by poet Shel Silverstein, so he had to read the lyrics from a sheet he'd stained with coffee. And before playing "Starkville City Jail," Cash explained that he was thrown in the slammer for picking daisies and dandelions at two in the morning. (By other accounts, he was breaking curfew, drunk in public, and trespassing.)

9. Cash brushed up on his Swedish for a show overseas.

In 1972 Cash went to Stockholm, Sweden, where he recorded the album *Pa Osteraker* at a Swedish prison. Between songs, he impressed and thrilled the inmates by introducing some of his songs in their language.

10. At the 1969 show, Cash's song "San Quentin" nearly incited a riot there.

He'd just written the song the night before, and its inflammatory lyrics like, "San Quentin, may you rot and burn in hell," clearly struck a chord with the audience. The prisoners clamored and stomped until he repeated the song. Shrieking and jumping up on tabletops, they were so close to rioting that the guards drew and cocked their guns and the camera crew backed up toward the exit doors. According to producer Bob Johnston, Cash later said of that hair-raising moment, "I knew that if I wanted to let those people go all I had to do was say, 'The time is now.' And all of those prisoners would've broken...I was tempted." (But of course, he didn't.)

* * *

O, CANADA!

A few people who've been inducted into the Canadian Music Hall of Fame since its inception in 1978:

Guy Lombardo (1978)

Oscar Peterson (1978)

Hank Snow (1979)

Paul Anka (1980)

Joni Mitchell (1981)

Neil Young (1982)

Glenn Gould (1983)

The Crewcuts (1984)

Gordon Lightfoot (1986)

The Guess Who (1987)

The Band (1989)

Leonard Cohen (1991)

Ian and Sylvia (1992)

Anne Murray (1993)

Rush (1994)

Buffy Sainte-Marie (1995)

David Clayton-Thomas, Denny Doherty, John Kay, Zal Yanovsky (1996)

Gil Evans (1997)

Bruce Cockburn (2001)

Daniel Lanois (2002)

Ronnie Hawkins (2003)

The Tragically Hip (2005)

Bryan Adams (2006)

THE PLOT THICKENS

Opera combines beautiful music, virtuoso singing, gorgeous costumes, lush sets...and the most outlandish melodramatic plots imaginable. If you're not an opera fan, you may wonder what the heck they're singing about. Here's Uncle John's cheat sheet to the plots of five popular operas.

OPERA: *La Traviata* (1853)
COMPOSER: Giuseppe Verdi
PLOT: A beautiful prostitute named Violetta (who suffers from tuberculosis) falls in love with a respectable man named Alfredo, and moves in with him. Alfredo's father disapproves of the relationship (because Violetta is a former "courtesan") and demands that she leave Alfredo at once. Ashamed of her sinful past, Violetta agrees to leave, writing her boyfriend a tearful farewell letter and vanishing from their home. Alfredo returns to find the letter, but also finds a party invitation, and mistakenly assumes that Violetta has returned to her old life. So he tracks her down at the party and throws a wad of money at her as payment for her "services" during their time together. Eventually, Alfredo learns the truth and begs Violetta's forgiveness. But it's too late. Tuberculosis has consumed her, and after encouraging Alfredo to marry a "good" girl, she dies in his arms.

OPERA: *Madame Butterfly* (1904)
COMPOSER: Giacomo Puccini
STORY: A 15-year-old Japanese girl named Butterfly falls in love with Pinkerton, a U.S. Navy Lieutenant stationed in Japan. They get married, but Pinkerton is just toying with Butterfly's affection: He doesn't really want a Japanese wife and he secretly plans to marry an American when he goes home. Pinkerton is then sent off on a military assignment, leaving Butterfly alone (and pregnant) in Japan, where she waits...and waits...and waits for his return. When his ship finally comes into port, Pinkerton has a new wife in tow. He has come to Japan, he tells Butterfly, only to retrieve his child and then head for home. So the dumped and devastated Butterfly grabs a dagger and slashes her own throat, while Pinkerton (who suddenly regrets his two-timing ways) looks on in horror.

OPERA: *Carmen* (1875)
COMPOSER: Georges Bizet
STORY: The beautiful gypsy (and sometimes cigarette girl) Carmen is torn between two powerful men: police officer Jose and dashing bullfighter Escamillio. Eventually she chooses Escamillio, but Jose will not accept defeat: he confronts Carmen at one of Escamillio's bullfighting matches. The two argue, and an enraged Jose ultimately stabs her with his dagger. Escamillio wins the bullfighting match, and Jose feels really, really bad about killing his girlfriend.

OPERA: *Don Giovanni* (1787)
COMPOSER: Wolfgang Amadeus Mozart
STORY: Don Giovanni has slept with more than 2,000 women, but his exploits eventually catch up with him when he kills the father of one of them. His predicament worsens when he discovers that a multitude of vengeful women are after him. To protect himself from the mob, Giovanni swaps clothes with his servant and escapes. When he reunites with the servant—in a cemetery—a statue of the man Giovanni killed comes to life and threatens revenge. The statue follows Giovanni home and gives the lothario a final chance to repent. But when Giovanni laughs off his sins, the statue grabs him and drags him down to hell.

OPERA: *La Bohème* (1896)
COMPOSER: Giacomo Puccini
STORY: On a cold Christmas Eve, four roommates—Rodolfo, Marcello, Colline, and Schaunard—shiver together in their apartment. The friends are out of money for food and coal, so they decide to head to a local pub for drinks. Rodolfo stays behind just long enough to meet Mimi, a beautiful neighbor. While the two search for her lost key, they fall madly in love. Months later, with each of the roommates bemoaning his own love life (Mimi and Rodolfo have called it quits), Marcello's ex-girlfriend Musetta brings in Mimi, who collapses from tuberculosis. The boys rush off to buy Mimi warm clothes, food, and medicine, but they're too late. Mimi manges to tell Rodolfo she loves him one last time, swoons, and then dies.

WHO'S THAT BAND?

*Many bands changed their names before—or even after—they became
famous. See if you can match the bands on the left with their
original names on the right. (Answers on page 513.)*

1. ABBA

2. Badfinger

3. The Commodores

4. Green Day

5. Pink Floyd

6. Black Sabbath

7. Pearl Jam

8. Guns N' Roses

9. Goo Goo Dolls

10. Led Zeppelin

11. Nirvana

12. Radiohead

13. The Rolling Stones

14. Poco

15. Limp Bizkit

16. Stone Temple Pilots

17. Simon and Garfunkel

18. Creedence Clearwater
Revival

a) Mookie Blaylock

b) The Iveys

c) Tom and Jerry

d) On a Friday

e) Sex Maggots

f) The Mystics

g) Blues, Inc.

h) Pogo

i) Sweet Children

j) Sigma 6

k) Axl

l) The Blue Velvets

m) Björn and Benny

n) Lethal Injection

o) Pen Cap Chew

p) The New Yardbirds

q) Mighty Joe Young

r) Polka Tulk Blues Band

Do they sing "Fame"? Keanu Reeves, Johnny Depp, and Russell Crowe all play in bands.

THE STORY OF MUSIC, PART II

Over the last 3,000 years, Western music became steadily more complex and diverse. In Part II of our timeline, we provide some highlights of its development. (Part I starts on page 150.)

1000 B.C.: Psalm singing is a regular part of Jewish worship, and something akin to the hammered dulcimer is being played all over the Middle East ("dulcimer" comes from the Latin and Greek words *dulce* and *melos*—"sweet tune.")

600 B.C.: The Greek mathematician and philosopher Pythagoras discovers the concept of the "octave" and develops the first known scale based on mathematical ratios.

200 B.C.: The precursor to the pipe organ is invented in Greece.

100 A.D. : Psalms and hymns become part of early Christian masses, and music plays an integral role of the rituals associated with worship. The songs—and the rules for singing—are believed to have been only taught orally.

200: Greek astronomer Ptolemy writes *Harmonics*, the most substantial treatise on music to date. It outlines a system for determining the proper intervals to create scales (largely based on Pythagoras's work) and the construction of chords, among many other things.

325: Roman emperor Constantine declares Christianity the official religion of the empire. The development of Western music over the next 1,000 years will flow almost exclusively through the Church. Other types of music are still being played, but it is church music that later develops into classical music, and the rules devised in the church that become the basis for music theory.

MEDIEVAL PERIOD (476–1400)

521: Roman scholar Boethius writes his *Principles of Music*, considered one of the most influential and important books on Western music theory. Primarily a reintroduction of ancient

Blues singer? Every song title on Bobby Vinton's 1963 album Blue Velvet...

Greek musical thought, the book becomes a touchstone for European musical development over the next millennium. One of its innovations is to reintroduce Greek letters to notation, with some Roman letters...which will eventually lead to the modern A–G note-lettering system.

790: The Schola Cantorum—the Church's official school of music—is now well established, and branches soon open all over Europe, spreading the teaching of music theory. The organ, which had been virtually forgotten, is beginning to make a comeback.

800: The use of *neumes*, from the Greek *neuma*, for "sign" or "nod," the precursor of modern music notation, is spreading. In this system, accent marks are made over syllables of words in the texts of chants, possibly to remind the singer of the melody. By the 10th century, many such systems are in use all over Europe.

810: Charlemagne, Holy Roman Emperor, codifies how chanting, or *plainsong*, is to be performed in the Catholic mass. "Gregorian chanting," often attributed to the 7th-century Pope Gregory, is now the church norm.

850: The treatise *Musica enchiriadis* (music handbook), written by an unknown monk, introduces the first evidence of harmony used in Gregorian chants with a new style known as *organum*.

1000: The neume system evolves: Rather than marks made in a row above the text, they are now at varying distances above it— indicating higher and lower pitch for a melody line. (Picture the notes on a staff, but without the lines.)

1025: Benedictine monk Guido of Arezzo (in present-day Italy) is credited with the invention of the musical staff. His four-line system allows, for the first time, the notation of exact pitches. He also develops a system called *solfege*, the practice of singing sylla-bles to remember scale relationships. It will evolve some 900 years later into our "Do Re Mi" song.

1050: The *Chansons de Geste*, the French "songs of heroic deeds," become popular. (Think of the minstrel in *Monty Python and the Holy Grail*.) The most famous of these will be the "Song of Roland," believed to have been written in the mid-1100s, which tells the tragic (but heroic) story of 8th-century Frankish leader

Roland and his slaughter by the Muslims…over about 4,000 lines, which singers had to memorize. The hugely popular Chansons de Geste influenced the future of Western literature and music, and are called, perhaps not very accurately, the "first popular music."

1200s: The marks of the neumes system are replaced by square dots. These will evolve into our modern round notes (with their "tails"). The fame of Celtic musicians, especially harpists, is already widespread. Troubadours and minstrels from countries all over Europe are making secular music more and more popular.

1322: Pope John XXII bans polyphonal music (music with harmony) from services. A later pope will soon rescind the order.

1325: French composer and scholar Philippe de Vitry writes *Ars Nova*, which includes a system for the notation of exact, complex rhythms as well as melodies. It would remain the standard until the 1600s. The recorder is invented around this time.

RENAISSANCE PERIOD (1400–1600)

1400s: The printing press is invented, allowing for the much faster spread of musical styles. Composers from what is now northern France, the Netherlands, and Belgium—the "Franco-Flemish" school—become the most influential of the era with relatively complex, polyphonal compositions, mostly written for voice only, though some include music for instruments like the lute and the recorder. The most influential composer of the period: Guillaume Dufay.

1500s: The five-line staff is introduced in France. Sharps and flats are developed, adding new notes to the scale, moving toward the 12 we have today. The organ becomes extremely popular, and the guitar is invented. A four-string violin, meant to be held on the shoulder and bowed, is developed. (The oldest surviving example was built by Andrea Amati in Cremona, Italy.)

1570: The Florentine Camerata, a group of intellectuals and musicians in northern Italy, begins to meet. Believing that music has become too complex and unintelligible, they set about to correct it and end up inventing opera. Within a few decades, opera becomes one of the most popular styles of music in Europe.

For Part III, turn to page 443.

MORE SWAN SONGS

When someone dies, the last thing he or she did often seems poignantly appropriate. Here are more "last songs."

LOUIS PRIMA
Date of Death: August 24, 1978 (age 67)
Last Song: "Leaving You"
Story: Prima, one of the biggest stars of the swing era of the 1930s and '40s, was a star of the Las Vegas lounges in the 1950s and continued to perform and write until his death in 1978. These days he's probably best known for his iconic medley arrangement of "Just a Gigolo/I Ain't Got Nobody," and as the voice of King Louie, the orangutan in Disney's 1967 *The Jungle Book*. In 1975 Prima was diagnosed with a small brain tumor. Surgery for it left him in a coma until his death—three years later. The last song he recorded before the operation was the uncharacteristically slow and bluesy "I'm Leaving You." Radio stations in his hometown of New Orleans played it regularly during those three years. "And though my eyes are filled with tears," Prima sings, "I'm leaving you."

JOHNNY CASH
Date of Death: September 12, 2003 (age 71)
Last Song: "Like the 309"
Story: Recorded shortly before his death, the song was released in 2006 on the CD *American V: A Hundred Highways*. The "309" refers to a train, and in the song Cash sings, "Take me to the depot, put me to bed / Blow an electric fan on my gnarly ol' head / Everybody take a look, see, I'm doin' fine / Then load my box on the three-oh-nine."

WARREN ZEVON
Date of Death: September 7, 2003 (age 56)
Last Song: "Keep Me in Your Heart"
Story: The writer of such cult classics as "Werewolves of London" and "Roland the Headless Thompson Gunner" was diagnosed with

---

A 3,300-year-old stone carving shows a Hittite bard playing an instrument that looks like a guitar.

inoperable lung cancer in late 2002. The first song he wrote after learning this was "Keep Me in Your Heart" for his final album, *The Wind*, but recorded that song last. "Shadows are falling and I'm running out of breath," he sings, "Keep me in your heart for a while / If I leave you it doesn't mean I love you any less / Keep me in your heart for a while."

JEFF BUCKLEY
Date of Death: May 29, 1997 (age 30)
Last Song: "I Want Somebody Badly," recorded with the punk-rock band Shudder to Think
Story: On the day of his death, Buckley and his friend and roadie Keith Foti went to the Wolf River, a tributary of the Mississippi, near Buckley's home in Memphis, Tennessee. His band was arriving in town that day so they could start recording their new album. Buckley went swimming with his boots and clothes on…and disappeared. His body was found three days later, and his death was ruled accidental, not related to drugs or alcohol, as many in the press had stated. "I Want Somebody Badly" is the last known song he recorded, and, ironically, it was for a 1997 film called *First Love, Last Rites*.

JANIS JOPLIN
Date of Death: October 4, 1970 (age 27)
Last Song: "Mercedes Benz"
Story: Joplin wrote the song with Beat poet Michael McClure and recorded it on October 1, 1970. The a cappella number, captured on tape in one less-than-serious take, became one of her biggest hits. Also recorded that day: a one-minute version of "Happy Trails." It starts with Joplin saying, "Hello, John, this is Janis. We'd just like to wish you a very happy birthday." It arrived in a package at John Lennon's house on October 5, the day after Joplin died of a drug overdose. (Lennon's birthday was October 9.)

*　　*　　*

"Music—the one incorporeal entrance into the higher world of knowledge which comprehends mankind but which mankind cannot comprehend."
—Ludwig van Beethoven

Ray Charles was born sighted but went completely blind by the age of 7. (Cause unknown.)

THE KINGS OF THE SINGING COWBOYS

*If long-haired hippie freaks and skateboarders who won't
pull their pants up can have their own music eras,
then gosh dern it—we reckon cowboys can, too!*

BEFORE GENE AND ROY
Western movies of the 1940s and '50s may have popularized the image of the singing cowboy, but the tradition predates those films by about a half-century. Here are a few important dates:

• The first cowboy songbook, *Songs of the Cowboys*, was published in 1908, containing lyrics (no music) to songs by the anonymous pioneers who settled the western United States during the last decades of the 19th century. Sample songs: "What's Become of the Punchers?" "The Gol-Darned Wheel," and "Old Chisolm Trail."

• In 1910 celebrated American folklorist John Lomax published his first book, *Cowboy Songs and Other Frontier Ballads*, which included words and music. Fans like President Teddy Roosevelt helped make it popular, and it started a minor cowboy music craze.

• On May 7, 1925, Billy McGinty's Cowboy Band became the first cowboy group to appear live on the radio (KFRU in Bristow, Oklahoma). The band, later known as Otto Gray and his Oklahoma Cowboys, found success in vaudeville during the late 1920s and early 1930s.

• Texan Carl Sprague—a real cowboy—recorded "When the Work's All Done This Fall" in August 1925. It sold 800,000 copies, making it the first cowboy hit record.

• In 1933 a young unknown named John Wayne brought cowboy music to the big screen for the first time in the film *Riders of Destiny*—and for the next two decades the "Singing Cowboy" movie would be one of the most popular film styles in existence. Wayne made a few more of the films, but he couldn't sing—his voice had to be dubbed. The real stars of the genre were people who could sing—and write—cowboy songs. The first: Gene Autry.

Gene Autry recorded three of the most popular Christmas songs of the 20th century:...

IT'S IN HIS GENES

Between 1934 and 1955 actor, musician, and singer Gene Autry appeared in 93 feature films (that's about five per year), made 91 episodes of his own TV show, and recorded 640 songs. His recordings sold more than 100 million copies. He was the first king of music's—and film's—Singing Cowboy era.

Born in Texas in 1907, Autry saved up to buy his first guitar (from the Sears Roebuck catalog) when he was 12, and joined the Fields Brothers Marvelous Traveling Medicine Show while he was still in high school. But it was a chance meeting in 1927 that convinced him to pursue a career in music: One night, while working at an Oklahoma telegraph office, he picked up his guitar and started singing. A customer came in and heard Autry playing. After listening to a couple of songs, he handed Autry the message he wanted to send...and then encouraged him to quit his job and become a singer. The customer? Cowboy/ humorist Will Rogers.

Within three years, Autry had a new job singing on an Oklahoma radio station (under the name "Oklahoma's Yodeling Cowboy") and a contract with Columbia Records, and in 1932 he recorded the song that would make him a star. "Silver Haired Daddy of Mine," a twangy duet he cowrote and recorded with Jimmy Long, eventually sold more than 5 million copies.

By the time he filmed his first movie, Autry was already a huge star, so it was no surprise that his two scenes—as a singing cowboy—in the 1934 film *In Old Santa Fe* were tremendously popular with audiences. Over the next five years, he made more than 40 films, all musical Westerns, all with his trusty horse, Champion, and he was one of the country's top movie stars. A stint in the Army in World War II followed, then he was back to cowboy singing stardom, as well as radio (*Gene Autry's Melody Ranch*, where he introduced his theme song, "Back in the Saddle Again") and TV. In the 1950s, Hollywood's Singing Cowboy era pretty much dried up and he made his last film in 1953 (well, actually—he made six films that year).

THE OTHER COWBOY KING

Gene Autry was the original singing cowboy, but of course he wasn't the only one. In 1929 a skinny 18-year-old named Leonard

Slye showed up in Hollywood to become a singing star. It took a while, but in 1934 he and his band, the Sons of the Pioneers, had some hits with cowboy songs like "Tumbling Tumbleweeds" and "Cool Water." In 1935 he started getting work in films as a movie extra and stuntman for Republic Pictures, which was where Autry worked. (He even appeared, under the name Leonard Slye, in an Autry film.) In 1938 his big break finally came when Autry got into a contract dispute and Republic put Slye in a starring role in the film *Under Western Stars*. But he now had a new name—Roy Rogers. ("Rogers" as an homage to cowboy great Will Rogers and "Roy" just because it sounded good.)

By 1944 Rogers had starred in 55 films. In his 56th, *The Cowboy and the Senorita*, he met Dale Evans, an actress, singer, and songwriter nicknamed the "Queen of the West." The pair married in 1947 and would go on to star together in dozens of films, on radio, and, from 1950 to 1957, in the hugely successful television series *The Roy Rogers Show*. (It was Evans who wrote the couple's most famous song, "Happy Trails," which closed their television show every Sunday night.)

HONORABLE MENTIONS

• Rex Allen (called the "Arizona Cowboy" for his home state) was a singer and guitarist who found fame as a rodeo rider. Beginning in 1950, Allen starred as himself in 19 Westerns, and he wrote and recorded many songs, including "A Human Coyote Stole My Girl," and "Dude Ranch Polka."

• Herb Jeffries, the only African-American singing cowboy, was known as the "Bronze Buckaroo." He starred in four musical Westerns in the late 1930s and later went on to perform as a jazz singer with Duke Ellington's Orchestra.

• Tex Ritter began his career as a musician in the Men's Glee Club while he was a student at the University of Texas. He went on to tour the United States with his band and then became a featured singer in the Madison Square Garden Rodeo. Between 1936 and 1959, he made 85 movies, 78 of which were Westerns. He distinguished himself from other popular cowboy stars by singing traditional Western folk songs instead of contemporary tunes. His original hit songs include "Rye Whiskey," "I'm Wasting My Tears on You," and "High Noon."

BEHIND THE HITS

Here are a few "inside" stories about popular songs.

The Artist: Little Richard
The Song: "Tutti Frutti" (1955)
The Story: After a long, unproductive recording session in 1955, Little Richard couldn't get the sound his producer, "Bumps" Blackwell, wanted. Exasperated, they took a lunch break and went to the local dive, the Dew Drop Inn. The place had a piano, so Richard started banging on it and wailing out some nonsense words: "Awop-Bop-a-Loo-Mop a-Good @#!damn... Tutti Frutti, Good Booty!" It was the sound Blackwell was looking for.

Richard had actually written the song while he was washing dishes at a bus station in Macon, Georgia. "I couldn't talk back to the boss," he said. "So instead of saying bad words, I'd say, 'Wop-Bop-a-Loo-Bop-a-Lop-Bam-Boom,' so he wouldn't know what I was thinking." Blackwell cleaned up the lyrics ("good booty" became "aw rootie"), and they recorded it that day. The single reached #17 on the pop chart. (Believe it or not, Pat Boone covered the song and it outdid Richard's version on the hit parade.)

The Artist: Buddy Holly and the Crickets
The Song: "Peggy Sue" (1957)
The Story: The song was originally called "Cindy Lou"...until Crickets drummer Jerry Allison asked Holly to rename it so that he could impress his girlfriend Peggy Sue Rackham. It worked— Peggy Sue and Jerry eloped a year later, prompting Holly to follow up with "Peggy Sue Got Married."

The Artist: Aerosmith
The Song: "Walk This Way" (1975)
The Story: Guitarist Joe Perry and bassist Tom Hamilton were exhausted from rehearsing the new riff they had written, so they took a break to see a movie—*Young Frankenstein*. Says Hamilton, "There's that part in the movie where Igor says, 'Walk this way,'

and the other guy walks the same way with the hump and everything. We thought it was the funniest thing we'd ever seen." After the movie, they told singer Steven Tyler that the name of the song had to be "Walk This Way." Tyler rushed out and scribbled the lyrics to the song on the walls of the studio's stairway, and the band recorded the song right then.

The Artist: Los Del Rio
The Song: "Macarena (Bayside Boys Mix)" (1996)
The Story: Spanish duo Los Del Rio wrote this song about a girl named Macarena, a common name in their native Seville. Their original version was already a big hit in Spanish-speaking countries when Miami radio stations started getting requests for it. A local DJ and two friends made this American version because it was the only way the program director would play the song on the air. Working under the name "the Bayside Boys," they wrote English lyrics, restructured the melody (they used the Los Del Rio chorus and music tracks) and rerecorded it with a new singer—all in two days. It became a huge local hit, then a huge national hit, and was on the charts for an amazing 60 weeks.

The Artist: Led Zeppelin
The Song: "Whole Lotta Love" (1969)
The Story: While recording their second album, guitarist Jimmy Page came up with a bluesy riff and the rest of the band started jamming around it. Singer Robert Plant "improvised" some words, but they weren't really his. He borrowed them from a song called "You Need Love," written by blues legend Willie Dixon. And although Led Zeppelin had credited Dixon for two songs on their first album, they kept the writing credit on "Whole Lotta Love" for themselves. Why? "We decided that it was so far away in time," explained Plant. (Actually, it had only been seven years since Dixon wrote it.) "Whole Lotta Love" became the only Zeppelin song ever to reach the Top 10 in the United States. Fifteen years later, Dixon heard the song for the first time and noticed the resemblance. Dixon sued the band and settled out of court in 1987. He used the proceeds to set up the Blues Heaven Foundation to promote awareness of the blues.

MORE LAUGH TRACKS

Witty, clever, and not-so-clever quotes about this thing we call music.

"I want to do a musical movie. Like *Evita*, but with good music."

—Elton John

"I love to sing, and I love to drink scotch. Most people would rather hear me drink scotch."

—George Burns

"Last night at Carnegie Hall, Jack Benny played Mendelssohn. Mendelssohn lost."

—Harold C. Schonberg

"When I was in school in the first grade, the teacher told me, she said one and one was two. I said, now wait a minute, how do you know? And right then we had a big problem."

—Jerry Lee Lewis

"I still have people come up to me like, 'I really, really liked your last record.' 'Oh, thanks!' 'Are you going to do "Loser" tonight?' I'm like, 'Look, I'm six-foot-six. Beck is five-foot-six, all right?'"

—Thurston Moore, lead singer of Sonic Youth

"When she started to play, Steinway himself came down personally and rubbed his name off the piano."

—Bob Hope, on Phyllis Diller

"I'm glad there are a lot of guitar players pursuing technique as diligently as they possibly can, because it leaves this whole other area open to people like me."

—Richard Thompson

"Personally, being somewhat envious of Richard's songwriting and guitar playing, it's somewhat satisfying he's not yet achieved household-name status. It serves him right for being so good."

—David Byrne, on Richard Thompson

"There's people making babies to my music. That's nice."

—Barry White

"If you wanted to torture me, you'd tie me down and force me to watch our first five videos."

—Jon Bon Jovi

The Eagles sued the American Eagle Foundation for name infringement, but later dropped the suit.

THE PRODUCERS

*Songwriters and musicians create songs, but a producer brings
a song to life and to completion. Here's how a producer
makes a recording, and how some of the best do it.*

WHAT DOES A PRODUCER DO?

Behind most great recordings is a record producer who's responsible for getting the album made. Producers are, to varying degrees, involved with every aspect of a recording's construction, including artistically, technically, and mechanically. Overall the job is very simple: do whatever has to be done to get a great sounding album.

The mechanical duties include acquiring funding and sticking to the budget, selecting and renting a studio, scheduling rehearsals and recording sessions, hiring musicians, getting copyright clearance when necessary, and being a coach of sorts—even down to keeping the players' morale up and breaking up any disagreements (or fights) that might occur during recording, mixing, and mastering sessions.

What are the artistic and technical duties? Every producer is different. Many start out as recording engineers, so their abilities might center around the techinical aspects of recording—capturing good audio sound. But some of the most famous producers are intimately involved with the music, too, even if it's for established megastars like the Rolling Stones or U2. That means assisting with song selection, changing arrangements and lyrics, sometimes even telling the musicians what to play, and then overseeing mixing and mastering to give the entire project whatever overall feel it's supposed to have. Some people have a knack for it—and consistently get the best out of the musicians they work with. We chose some of the very best to highlight how it's done.

PHIL SPECTOR

Phil Spector formed a singing group in high school called the Teddy Bears. He wrote all the songs. The group recorded at Gold Star Studios—a Hollywood studio that included two chambers that created a unique echoing sound on recordings. The Teddy

First black record producer to produce a white artist: Tom Wilson, with Bob Dylan.

Bears' "To Know Him Is To Love Him" hit #1 in 1958, but Spector found that he was more interested in producing than performing. So, in 1961, after working as a recording supervisor on hit songs by the Drifters and Ben E. King under writer/producers Jerry Lieber and Mike Stoller, Spector started Philles Records. In six years, Spector produced (and largely wrote) 12 albums and 39 singles, including "He's a Rebel" and "Da Doo Ron Ron" by the Crystals, "River Deep Mountain High" by Ike and Tina Turner, "Christmas (Baby Please Come Home)" by Darlene Love, and "Be My Baby" and "Walkin' in the Rain" by the Ronettes. But his biggest hit was the Righteous Brothers' "You've Lost That Loving Feeling," the most-played song on American radio in the 20th century.

How he did it

Spector utilized L.A.'s top session musicians, lush arrangements that duplicated many parts on acoustic and electric instruments (to make them seem even more lush), and then added his signature production element: echo, inspired by Gold Star's unique echo chambers. Spector first recorded the musicians, then replayed the tape in the echo chamber, and then recorded that. On top of the basic track were layers of horns, strings, and choral backgrounds. The end result, known as the "Wall of Sound," influenced dozens of other artists, from Brian Wilson to Bruce Springsteen.

Spector went on to produce the Beatles' final album, *Let It Be*, George Harrison's *All Things Must Pass* (1970) and John Lennon's *Imagine* (1971). Lennon and Spector had numerous creative disagreements, and during one argument, Spector pulled out a pistol and shot a hole in the ceiling.

He continued to live up to his reputation as a difficult producer, but he still attracted big name musicians, including Harry Nillson, Cher, and others. In 1977, while working on Leonard Cohen's *Death of a Ladies' Man*, Spector reportedly aimed a loaded pistol at Cohen's head. In 1980, while working on the Ramones' *End of the Century*, Spector pulled a gun on frontman Joey Ramone and later made guitarist Johnny Ramone play the opening chord of a song for 10 straight hours. That was the last album Spector produced. He was inducted into the Rock and Roll Hall of Fame in 1989, and was tried for murder in 2007 after actress Lana Clarkson died of a gunshot wound at his home. (It ended in a mistrial.)

Feminists denounced the 1976 Rolling Stones album *Black and Blue* for "promoting violence."

QUINCY JONES

Jones was a trumpet virtuoso by the time he graduated high school and in the 1950s toured Europe in the bands of jazz greats Lionel Hampton and Dizzy Gillespie. In the late '50s, while working with his own band, Jones found himself broke. That's when he decided to work less as a musician and more on the other side of the music business. He took a job with Barclay, the French wing of Mercury Records, and by 1964 was vice president of the company. But he wanted to focus more on making music, so he moved to Los Angeles to score films, including *In Cold Blood*, *In the Heat of the Night*, and *The Italian Job* and TV shows like *Ironside* and *Sanford & Son*. While in Los Angeles, Jones also worked as an arranger and producer for vocalists such as Frank Sinatra and Ella Fitzgerald.

As a producer, Jones doesn't add a lot of effects or layers. He has a jazz background and tends to let the music "breathe"—he just lets the musicians play and encourages them to improvise and experiment, suggesting different techniques or offering new arrangements of songs. Jones is also known for mixing genres, such as his 1962 instrumental hit "Soul Bossa Nova" (best known as the theme song to the Austin Powers movies), which is a combination of American soul music and Brazilian bossa nova.

Jones greatest commercial success came in the 1980s. He produced Michael Jackson's first three solo albums *Off the Wall*, *Thriller*, and *Bad*, which sold a combined 158 million copies. He also produced and organized the "We Are the World" charity single. Today, he continues to produce albums in a range of genres, but in the last two decades, he's focused more on producing movies (*The Color Purple*) and TV shows (*The Fresh Prince of Bel-Air*) along with scoring films. Jones is one of the most honored individuals in American music, with 27 Grammys from 79 nominations.

BRIAN ENO

While in a "sound sculpture class" in art school in the late 1960s, Eno discovered the music of "minimalist" composers such as LaMonte Young and John Cage. Unlike pop music, which has melodies and logical chord progressions, minimalist has few or no chord changes and often employ repeated sequences of a few notes. Eno started experimenting with tape recorders, taking random noises and then manipulating, repeating, and layering them to create sound collages.

He also learned to play the keyboards, and joined the glam rock band Roxy Music in 1970. He left the band by 1973 because lead singer Bryan Ferry wanted to take the band in a more conventional rock direction. Eno wanted to work more with sound manipulation and minimalism, so he teamed up with Robert Fripp of the progressive rock band King Crimson. They developed a "tape-loop" system of recording guitar notes to electronically alter them, which they called "Frippertronics."

In 1975 Eno developed another innovation. While laying in bed recovering from a car accident, he couldn't turn up his stereo (he was listening to 18th century harp music) to drown out the rain. He realized the rain was just as interesting as the music. This inspired Eno to create "ambient music," music meant to blend into the background, reflect the environment, and soothe. He produced a series of 10 ambient recordings, most notably *Music for Airports*, a sound collage designed to soothe worried air travelers.

In the late 1970s, Eno applied his avant-garde approach to pop music.

• He produced the albums *Low*, *"Heroes,"* and *Lodger* for David Bowie. They were some of Bowie's most experimental projects, incorporating droning feedback and electronic instruments. The trilogy's sole hit was "Heroes," co-written by Eno.

• David Byrne invited Eno to collaborate with his group Talking Heads in 1981. Eno produced their albums *More Songs About Buildings and Food*, *Fear of Music*, and *Remain in Light*, cowriting the majority of the songs.

• In 1984 U2 wanted a moodier sound than their previous guitar-based albums and so they hired Eno to produce *The Unforgettable Fire*. By the time Eno produced the ten-million selling *The Joshua Tree* three years later, the band was using minimalist backgrounds on many of its songs. Eno's influence is most evident on U2's *Achtung Baby* (1991), which introduced electronic fuzz and drone to the mix. Eno continues to produce music, but today he considers himself a performance artist.

A FEW OTHERS

• **Phil Ramone.** A child prodigy on the violin, he opened up his own recording studio in 1959, where he did producing and engineering work. His work includes Paul Simon's "Still Crazy After All These Years" and seven albums for Billy Joel during Joel's commercial peak in the early 1980s. Other artists he's worked with: Tony Bennett, Ray Charles, Aretha Franklin, Natalie Cole, Kris Kristofferson, Elton John, Pavarotti, George Benson, Kenny Loggins, Lou Reed, Phoebe Snow, and Bob Dylan.

• **Peter Asher.** Asher got his start in music in the 1960s pop duo Peter & Gordon, who had a hit with "World Without Love." In the late 1960s, he moved into producing. He discovered James Taylor, produced Linda Rondstadt's first four albums, and helped craft the 1970s soft rock sound, producing albums for J.D. Souther, Bonnie Raitt, Andrew Gold, Cher, and Neil Diamond.

• **Butch Vig.** Vig produced three albums in the early 1990s that took "alternative rock" to mainstream popularity: *Dirty* by Sonic Youth, *Gish* by Smashing Pumpkins, and *Nevermind* by Nirvana. Vig added radio-ready sheen and smoothness with multitrack recording and overdubs to those bands, who were all previously lo-fi punk groups. Vig is also the drummer for the band Garbage.

• **Rick Rubin.** Rubin formed Def Jam Recordings in his NYU Dorm Room with Russell Simmons. Early rock 'n' roll was a mixture of white country music with black R&B music and Rubin did the same thing in the 1980s, mixing elements of white hard rock with black rap music. The result: Rubin molded early albums by Run DMC, the Beastie Boys, and the Red Hot Chili Peppers, and later worked with artists ranging from Johnny Cash and Tom Petty to Nine Inch Nails and Shakira.

* * *

DRAWN TO MUSIC

What do the Jackson 5, the Monkees, New Kids on the Block, MC Hammer, the Beatles, and the Bay City Rollers have in common? They all had their own Saturday morning cartoon shows.

MTV FACTS

What's your all-time favorite music video? "Sledgehammer"? "Money for Nothing"? "Thriller"? Since its debut in 1981, MTV has been a cultural phenomenon and a crucial part of popular music (and TV).

• MTV has banned 19 videos from the channel. Four of them were by Madonna: ("American Life," "Erotica," "Justify My Love," and "What It Feels Like for a Girl").

• MTV reaches nearly 500 million households worldwide.

• In 1988 MTV initially banned Neil Young's "This Note's for You," a satire that parodies the ads of many companies who bought commercial time on MTV. It was brought back to the network after it won the MTV award for Video of the Year.

• In 1984 MTV doubled the price it charged cable systems for carrying it. Result: Several cable companies asked TV mogul Ted Turner to start a music channel, which he called Cable Musical Channel. After a month of low ratings, CMC was bought out...by MTV, who turned it into VH1.

• Another competitor, The Box, was bought out in 2000 and turned into MTV2.

• First video on MTV2: Beck's "Where It's At" (1996). First video on VH1: "The Star-Spangled Banner," performed by Marvin Gaye (1985).

• First rap video played on MTV: "Rock Box" by Run DMC (1984).

• 75% of American teenagers regularly watch MTV.

• Three MTV Video of the Year winners: "Money for Nothing" by Dire Straits (1986), "Waterfalls" by TLC (1995), and "Hey Ya!" by Outkast (2004).

• In 1992 MTV pioneered the idea of reality television with its young-people-living-in-a-house documentary show *The Real World*. As of 2007, it's had 19 editions and more than 450 episodes.

• Highest-rated show in MTV history: the January 2002 premiere of *The Osbournes*.

• Most-requested video ever: Nirvana's "Smells Like Teen Spirit."

First video banned by MTV: "Girls on Film" by Duran Duran (it featured topless mud wrestlers).

IT'S A WEIRD, WEIRD WORLD (OF MUSIC)

The world is strange, and the world of music is stranger.

THOU SHALT NOT BEAR FALSETTO WITNESS
In 2007 radio stations in predominantly Orthodox Jewish sections of Israel banned the songs of Eliyahu Faizkov, a popular male singer. Faizkov sings in a high-pitched, falsetto voice which, according to the rabbinical scholars who pushed for the ban, is against the Jewish law that forbids men from listening to female voices.

NO STRINGS ATTACHED
What are the rarest, most coveted, and most valuable musical instruments in the world? Stradivarius violins. In fact, only a few hundred of the 17th-century marvels remain in existence, so it's big news when one turns up. Imre Horvath, a Hungarian chicken farmer, found one hidden in the rafters of his chicken coop in 2007. Horvath figures his father, a musician, hid it there for safe-keeping before he went off to fight in World War II. The elder Horvath died in the war and the violin was never discovered. Horvath, 68, found the violin by accident when cleaning. While he'd spent the last 50 years making a meager living selling eggs and poultry, Horvath now stands to earn $1 million from the sale of the violin.

THE KING OF KINGS VS. THE KING
In 1988 Mort Farndu and Karl Edwards of Portland, Oregon, opened the First Presleyterian Church of Elvis the Divine. The church became a tourist attraction in Portland, featuring amateur artwork of Presley, daily performances by an Elvis impersonator (and ordained minister), and actual religious "tenets." According to Farndu and Edwards, the King's 31 Commandments include things a person needs to do to be more Elvis-like, such as eating six meals a day, bowing to Las Vegas once a day, making a pilgrimage to Graceland, and fighting Michael Jackson, the "anti-Elvis."

IT'S EVEN LONGER THAN "IN-A-GADDA-DA-VIDA"

Avant-garde French composer Eric Satie wrote a piece called "Vexations" in 1803. The work is a list of piano chords to be played "very slow." The chord progression is supposed to last 90 seconds and then be repeated...840 times. "Vexations" should take exactly 21 hours to perform. It's been performed uninterrupted only once. In Iowa City, Iowa, in July 1994, 26 pianists convened to play "Vexations" (taking turns, of course).

GOD ONLY KNOWS

In 2006 St. Stephen's Church in Tonbridge, England, used its annual Christmas nativity play to pay tribute to *another* icon: the Beach Boys. In the play, Mary dresses as a surfer girl and sings "God Only Knows." The Three Wise Men (portrayed as Beach Boys Brian, Carl, and Dennis Wilson) perform "Fun Fun Fun" and "Good Vibrations" in honor of the baby Christ. The church's pastor approved the play, saying that this presentation "makes it more realistic."

STAYING CONNECTED

Reba Schappell is a country music singer based in Reading, Pennsylvania. She's also a conjoined twin: she and her sister Lori are attached at the head. "When I am singing, Lori is like any other fan," said Reba, "except she's up onstage with me." Lori doesn't play an instrument or sing back-up, and to reduce distraction and gawking, she's covered up with a blanket. "I do not ask for anything from Reba," said Lori. "I have to pay for a ticket just like every other fan."

UNCLE JOHN'S BAND

In 1992 the Grateful Dead planned to play a concert at the Deer Creek Music Center in Noblesville, Indiana. For the night of the show, local Judge William Hughes agreed to move his courtroom to a van outside the arena so the people inevitably arrested at the concert for drug possession could be booked and processed quickly, rather than waiting overnight in jail. "It's a courtesy to them," Judge Hughes said.

Bo Diddley was the first major act to have a female guitarist: Peggy Jones.

THE FOLK REVIVAL

Look out! It could happen again any year now...

TRADITIONAL TRANSITIONAL

Between the years 1958 and 1965, an unlikely music phenomenon known as the Folk Revival took hold of the country. At a time when rock 'n' roll acts like Elvis Presley, Bobby Darin, and Frankie Avalon were moving up the charts, traditional folk songs like "Tom Dooley" and "When the Saints Go Marching In" were right there with them—and sometimes even passing them.

Example: *Billboard*'s list of 1959's top 10 bestselling albums included four by a single group, the Kingston Trio. Not only that—two of their albums were in the top five, a feat that's been matched only three other times to this day. Rock 'n' roll was definitely in the fore, but the Kingston Trio's success made record company executives sit up and take notice—and the Folk Revival was officially on. But how did it all start?

THE COLLECTORS

The Folk Revival's main fuel, at least initially, was a desire to preserve the "old fashioned" aspects of American culture that seemed to be getting lost in the rapid modernization of the postwar boom. That same impetus had fueled a similar folk craze more than a century earlier.

In the 1800s, nationalism was gaining in popularity all across Europe. Everywhere people seemed to want to find the myths, legends, dances, dress, music, and whatever else made their nation unique. The old German folk tales collected and published by the Brothers Grimm in 1810 are an early and influential product of the era. Others delved into ancient Celtic legends of the Welsh, Scottish, Irish, and Bretons, still others into French hurdy-gurdy and fiddle songs. The term "folklore" itself comes from this folk revival era, coined by British writer William Thoms in 1846.

One of the most notable early collectors of traditional English-language music was Harvard's Francis James Child. "Child's Ballads," as they're known, are a collection of 305 English and

---

Walter Matthau, Goldie Hawn, and Sylvester Stallone all released albums. They all bombed.

Scottish songs dating from the 15th to the 18th century—one of the most celebrated of such collections in the world today.

THE NEXT GENERATION

The early folklorists were limited to preserving written versions of the songs that they collected, but with the introduction of phonograph recording technology in the early 1900s, they became able to make what they called "field recordings" of original folk sources.

One of the first American collectors to take advantage of this technology was another Harvard folklorist, John Lomax. In 1910 Lomax published the book *Cowboy Songs and Other Frontier Ballads*. The collection was an academic—and to some degree, popular—success, and it included actual recordings of some of the songs. Among the collection's fans was President Theodore Roosevelt who, in his enthusiasm for vigorous frontier life, celebrated American folklore. More importantly, it represented the first recordings of ballads like "Home on the Range," many of which would eventually become sing-along standards. (That particular recording was played by "negro saloon keeper" Bill Jack Curry in San Antonio, Texas, on an Edison cylinder.)

When commercial records and radio came along in the 1920s, niche markets for "hillbilly" songs, blues music—called "race music" —and cowboy records saw the material from academic field recordings enter the popular entertainment market. At the same time, people like John Lomax and his son Alan were touring the rural South, collecting tunes that would become part of the *Smithsonian Archive of American Folk Song*. One of their finds: an inmate in a Louisiana prison named Huddie Ledbetter—better known as "Lead Belly." Securing his release in 1934, they took him to New York and made him famous. From Lead Belly's 1930s recordings came such folk classics as "Goodnight Irene," and "The Midnight Special."

RISE UP SINGING

It was in the early 1900s that folk music also began to be linked to political activism. The most famous name from that time is Joe Hill, a union organizer, radical activist, and songwriter who would become one of the labor movement's martyrs. An excerpt from "In the Sweet Bye and Bye," which Hill published in 1911:

In 1987 Will Smith declared bankruptcy. In 1998 he was on *Forbes's* highest-paid entertainers list.

Long-haired preachers come out every night,
Try to tell you what's wrong and what's right;
But when asked how 'bout something to eat
They will answer in voices so sweet

You will eat, bye and bye,
In that glorious land above the sky;
Work and pray, live on hay,
You'll get pie in the sky when you die

Hill was charged with murder and executed in 1915. Supporters claimed he was innocent, convicted because of his activism, and he remains a symbol of the struggle of the "have-nots" against the "haves." The song "I Dreamed I Saw Joe Hill Last Night," made famous by Joan Baez, comes from a poem written in 1930 by American poet Alfred Hayes.

THIS LAND...

During the Depression and the WWII years, folk music took on an even finer political edge—and still managed to keep its popularity ...for a while. Protest-singers like Woody Guthrie and Pete Seeger got their starts during this era. Guthrie made a name for himself singing about Dust Bowl refugees, union organizers, and migrant farm workers in the 1930s. In the 1940s, he added songs like "Union Maid" and "This Land Is Your Land."

Pete Seeger, a Harvard dropout and privileged son of one of the early academic folklore collectors, had been involved with political activism since the late 1930s (he was born in 1919, Guthrie in 1912). In 1941 he and Guthrie became nationally known as members of the Almanac Singers, a group whose songs were tied to the politics of the day. In 1948 Seeger formed the Weavers and had huge hits with songs like "Goodnight Irene" and Guthrie's "So Long, It's Been Good to Know You."

Guthrie and Seeger, along with others like Lee Hays and Josh White, had set the stage for the Folk Revival. But their leftist politics brought the attention of Senator Joseph McCarthy and the House Un-American Activities Committee, and they found themselves blacklisted from performance venues, radio stations, and the growing medium of television. Some would see their careers irreparably damaged. But not all of them.

For Part II of the story, turn to page 468.

CLASSICAL OPINIONS

Quotes from critics, fans, and composers...sometimes about each other.

"Don't bother to look—I've composed all this already."
—**Gustav Mahler, to Bruno Walter, who was admiring the Austrian Alps**

"An intellectual is someone who can listen to the William Tell Overture and not think of *The Lone Ranger.*"
—**Dan Rather**

"I love Wagner, but the music I prefer is that of a cat hung up by its tail outside a window and trying to stick to the panes of glass with its claws."
—**Charles-Pierre Baudelaire**

"I have never acknowledged the difference between serious music and light music. There is only good music and bad music."
—**Kurt Weill**

"Wagner has beautiful moments but bad quarters of an hour."
—**Gioachino Rossini**

"Rossini might have been a great composer if his teacher had spanked him enough on his backside."
—**Ludwig van Beethoven**

"Berlioz says nothing in his music, but he says it magnificently."
—**James Gibbons Hunekar**

"To compose, all you need to do is remember a tune that nobody else has thought of."
—**Robert Schumann**

"There is no doubt that the first requirement for a great composer is to be dead."
—**Arthur Honegger**

"A good composer does not imitate; he steals."
—**Igor Stravinsky**

"I may not be a first-rate composer, but I am a first-class second-rate composer."
—**Richard Strauss**

"The aim and final end of all music should be none other than the glory of God and the refreshment of the soul."
—**Johann Sebastian Bach**

"I would rather play 'Chiquita Banana' and have my swimming pool than play Bach and starve."
—**Xavier Cugat**

France banned all rock concerts in the early '60s because the music was "socially subversive."

TWELVE RECORDINGS THAT CHANGED MUSIC

Sometimes an album, or even just a single song, can change a music genre forever—or create one that hadn't existed in the first place.

Album: *Elvis Presley* (1956)
Artist: Elvis Presley
Impact: In 1956 the worldwide phenomenon that was to be rock 'n' roll still wasn't fully formed—nobody even knew if it was going to last. Then this album came along, and it was such a huge success that record companies followed its lead…and its template. The sound—a pulsating blend of country and rhythm & blues, along with boogie woogie, gospel, and rockabilly—and the image of Elvis as the rebellious young heartthrob pretty much paved rock 'n' roll's road for decades. The *Rolling Stone Record Guide* says it contains "the seeds of everything rock 'n' roll was, has been, and most likely what it may foreseeably become." *Elvis Presley* was the first rock album to hit #1 on the Billboard chart, it stayed there for 10 weeks, and it was RCA's first million-selling pop album.

Albums: *King of the Delta Blues Singers* (1961)
Artist: Robert Johnson
Impact: Robert Johnson died in 1938 at the age of 27, and during his short life he recorded only 29 songs. Yet he remains one of the most influential bluesmen in history. The 17 songs on *King of the Delta Blues Singers* were recorded between 1936 and 1937, but the compilation album's release in 1961 sparked a renewed interest in the blues. The subject matter, guitar playing, and singing style on the album in classics like "Crossroad Blues," "Come On in My Kitchen," and "Kind Hearted Woman Blues," influenced nearly every great bluesman afterwards—including Muddy Waters, B. B. King, Mike Bloomfield, Albert King, and John Lee Hooker, just to name a few. But Johnson had an even bigger influence on the genre that was birthed by the blues—rock 'n'

Phoning it in: Robert Cassotto picked his stage name, Bobby Darin, out of a Bronx phone book.

roll—directly influencing acts that themselves became some of the most influential in the genre's history, the most obvious examples being the Rolling Stones, Cream, Led Zeppelin, and Eric Clapton, who has recorded versions of almost all of Robert Johnson's songs.

Album: *J. D. Crowe & The New South* (1975)
Artist: J. D. Crowe & The New South
Impact: Bluegrass music was born in the 1940s with Bill Monroe and the Blue Grass Boys, but experts on the genre say this album brought it to a new height and dramatically changed it. Banjo player J. D. Crowe, guitarist Tony Rice, dobro player Jerry Douglas, fiddler-mandolinist Ricky Skaggs, and bassist Bobby Slone loosened up the rigid rhythm of bluegrass, brought in some jazz influences for more sophisticated soloing, and Rice's soulful vocals were a big departure from the "high lonesome" style that had previously defined the genre. They also brought in a new audience by recording not only time-honored bluegrass traditionals, but also pop songs, including two by Gordon Lightfoot and "I'm Walkin'" by Fats Domino.

Album: *Bringing It All Back Home* (1965)
Artist: Bob Dylan
Impact: Dylan was already famous when he released his fifth album, *Bringing It All Back Home*, but he was known as a topical, political—and acoustic-guitar-playing—folk singer. *Bringing It All Back Home* let the world know that things had changed, with many of the songs, like the raucous "Subterranean Homesick Blues" and "Maggie's Farm," recorded with a full rock 'n' roll band. The lyrics were a major departure, too. Dylan's penchant for dark humor and abstract, near-hallucinatory imagery come into full force on songs like "Gates of Eden," "It's Alright, Ma (I'm Only Bleeding)," and "Mr. Tambourine Man." The album made Dylan an even bigger folk star (though many purists in the genre resented him for it), and for the first time a *rock* star. And, say experts, that record led to the more sophisticated lyrics that would appear on albums by other artists in the latter half of the 1960s (like those on the the Beatles' *Rubber Soul*, which came later that year.)

Album: *The Velvet Underground and Nico* (1967)
Artist: The Velvet Underground
Impact: Commercially speaking, *The Velvet Underground and Nico* was a flop: only a few thousand people purchased it in its first year. But as musician and producer Brian Eno later observed, almost all of those people must have gone out and started bands. This album, with its Andy Warhol–created cover (a peel-off banana sticker that revealed a phallic banana underneath) and explicit lyrics about the New York sex, drugs, and rock 'n' roll scene, is considered the progenitor of punk, glam, new wave, and the avant-garde New York music scene that thrived during the 1970s. The *New York Times* said the Velvet Underground "make 80 percent of today's popular rock groups seem pointless and amateurish."

Song: "P.S.K. What Does It Mean?" (1985)
Artist: Schoolly D
Impact: Philadelphia rapper Schoolly D, a.k.a Jesse B. Weaver Jr., wrote this song for his friends, a small Philly gang known as the Park Side Killers (hence the P.S.K.). "It was one of the easiest songs I'd ever written," he later said. "I wrote it sitting at my mom's dining room table, smoking some weed at 3 o'clock in the morning." The song featured heavily reverbed, booming bass and drum machine tracks, and lyrics celebrating the sex, drugs, and violence of the gang lifestyle. When Schoolly D listened to the song after an all-night recording session, he hated it. But everyone he played it for loved it. They included future megastars like Ice T and Dr. Dre, who took the style and turned it into the hugely successful music genre, gangsta rap.

Song: "I Wish I Was Single Again" (1954)
Artist: Walter "Li'l Wally" Jagiello
Impact: Jagiello was a concertina player and drummer in Chicago when he landed a deal with Columbia Records to make a recording of polka songs—in Polish—in 1947. He didn't like the big-label experience, so in 1951 he started his own company, Jay Jay Records, and started pumping out albums at a phenomenal rate. (He made 150 before he died.) In 1954 Jagiello recorded his first English-language song, "I Wish I Was Single Again." The style

was all Jagiello: He was a mainstay on Chicago's "Polish Broadway," a section of the city that was home to more than 50 polka clubs. In order to play the small taverns there, he reduced the size of his band and slowed down the normally frantic polka beat. When the song hit the pop chart, other polka artists imitated it, and soon the "Chicago style" polka Jagiello had created was a genre all its own. He later became a mainstay on the Lawrence Welk show and recorded some of the most famous American polka songs, including "No Beer in Heaven."

Album: *What's Going On* (1971)
Artist: Marvin Gaye
Impact: By the late 1960s, Motown Records was the most successful recording label in the business. That success was due in part to the label's formula for creating uncontroversial songs that sold to both black and white audiences—and a lot of them became hits. In 1971 Marvin Gaye, already an established Motown artist and soul singer, decided to do something a little different. He cowrote the album *What's Going On* with six other musicians, and used the nine songs on it to address the major political issues of the day: poverty, drugs, and the Vietnam War. The title track talks about the Vietnam War, protests, and police brutality. The album became a touchstone for the civil rights movement and introduced a new direction for soul music, which could now address difficult social issues rather than focus on fluffy dance tunes.

Album: *Sgt. Pepper's Lonely Hearts Club Band* (1967)
Artist: The Beatles
Impact: *London Times* critic Kenneth Tynan called *Sgt. Pepper's* a "decisive moment in the history of Western civilization." The album demonstrated that the recording studio was its own instrument. The Beatles spent more than 700 hours in the studio putting the record together, and when producer George Martin mixed it, he combined the band's playing and singing with electronic and nontraditional sounds—tapes of calliopes, clucking chickens, crowd noises, a steam organ, and a pack of foxhounds—to create a virtual "live" atmosphere. The album was also the first time that popular music was considered art. Whereas most rock music was

A photo of Queen Elizabeth taken by singer Bryan Adams was made into a Canadian postage stamp.

dismissed as just pop culture, *Sgt. Pepper's* proved itself to be cohesive (none of the songs were released as singles) and as fully imagined as a classical symphony. Artists from Frank Zappa and Jefferson Airplane to the Rolling Stones count *Sgt. Pepper's* among their primary influences.

Album: *Bitches Brew* (1970)
Artist: Miles Davis
Impact: *Bitches Brew* was recorded over three days in 1969, with Davis leading a group of jazz heavyweights including Wayne Shorter on soprano saxophone, Chick Corea on electric piano, John McLaughlin on electric guitar, and Billy Cobham and Jack DeJohnette on drums. Davis had just entered his "electric era," one that was marked by heavy use of electronics, studio effects, and the influence of rock 'n' roll and funk. The resulting recording was unlike anything the jazz world had ever heard before: mostly improvised, mostly long (up to 20-minute) free-form compositions featuring tape loops, reverb, heavy post-production editing—and whatever else was going on in Davis's head. Many called it a violent cacophony of senseless noise; others called it a masterpiece. In any case, it took the new genre of jazz fusion and brought it screaming into the limelight: Although sales figures are disputed, it is believed to be the best-selling jazz album of all time.

Album: *Trans-Europe Express* (1977)
Artist: Kraftwerk
Impact: *Trans-Europe Express* was Kraftwerk's sixth album. With this record, the band's sound, typified by 20-minute-long instrumentals on previous albums, started to distill down to pop-length songs. By moving from the esoterically avant-garde to the mainstream, their music was more widely heard—both in Europe and the United States. Through the use of a Moog synthesizer and vocoder-altered vocals, Kraftwerk created an entirely artificial sound and a new direction for pop music. The band's combination of driving beats and synthesized melodies became the template for techno and electronica, paving the way for everything from C+C Music Factory's upbeat techno to Nine Inch Nails' gritty industrial sound.

First live performers to appear on *American Bandstand:* The all-female group the Chordettes.

Album: *The Rise and Fall of Ziggy Stardust and the Spiders from Mars* (1972)

Artist: David Bowie

Impact: Says rock historian Chris Smith: "David Bowie never really considered himself a musician—or at least he considered his music secondary to his 'performance.'" And when it came to performance, Bowie was king. Using his background in theater and mime, he created Ziggy Stardust—an orange-haired, glitter-painted Martian who came to save Earth (based on an apocalyptic vision that Earth would be destroyed) through sex, drugs, and rock 'n' roll. But Bowie didn't limit his performance to the stage: He later said, "I thought I might as well take Ziggy to interviews as well. Why leave him onstage?" This integration of music and performance was what made the album's music so influential. David Bowie himself was so consumed by his stage persona that it spilled over into his real life; he said that the character "would not leave me alone for years...I really did have doubts about my sanity." It's a move that's been copied by many artists since: Ziggy Stardust paved the way for Prince, the Sex Pistols, Madonna, Boy George, Queen, Marilyn Manson, KISS, and every rock band that has been as much about stage presence as sound.

*　　*　　*

TOP 10 HITS OF 1973

1. "Tie a Yellow Ribbon" —*Tony Orlando & Dawn*
2. "Bad, Bad Leroy Brown" —*Jim Croce*
3. "Let's Get It On" —*Marvin Gaye*
4. "Killing Me Softly With His Song" —*Roberta Flack*
5. "My Love" —*Paul McCartney & Wings*
6. "Why Me" —*Kris Kristofferson*
7. "Will It Go Round in Circles" —*Billy Preston*
8. "Crocodile Rock" —*Elton John*
9. "You're So Vain" —*Carly Simon*
10. "Touch Me in the Morning" —*Diana Ross*

The professional career of Ritchie Valens of "La Bamba" fame lasted only eight months.

CONCERTS GONE BAD

Live entertainment can be very unpredictable.

HEADLINE: *Stapp Slobbers, Staggers, Sees Self Sued*
STORY: In December 2002, Scott Stapp, the singer for the rock band Creed, was on potent medication for a throat infection before a Chicago concert, but he still drank a bottle of whiskey before taking the stage. He mumbled through five songs, then went backstage to nap in his dressing room, thinking he'd performed a full concert. The band convinced him to come back out and continue singing...unfortunately, lyrics to songs they weren't playing. The show ended early—and four fans later sued Creed to get their money back. (The lawsuit was dismissed.)

HEADLINE: *Flaky Folkie Attacks Adoring Audience*
STORY: Folk singer Jewel performed at a casino in Hampton, New York, in May 2004. She played only five songs and spent the rest of the time making fun of people in the audience. Attendees say she insulted fans who were overweight or had bad teeth and said that drinkers and smokers were "sinners." For an encore, Jewel yodeled. One group of fans walked out of the show, demanded their money back, and drove by Jewel's tour bus, screaming obscenities at the singer.

HEADLINE: *U2's Lemon Is a Lemon*
STORY: U2's 1997 tour featured a number of absurdly huge stage props. One of them was a 40-foot-tall lemon with a giant hatch door that members would emerge from to play encores. At a stop in Oslo, Norway, one night, the lemon wouldn't open. Engineers tried to get it open, stagehands tried to get it open, and U2 tried to get it open from the inside. Unable to loosen the door, the band instead went out through the lemon's back opening (where they came in), climbed down some stairs, and walked around the lemon to the stage, at which point the song ("Discotheque") was over. Amazingly, the same problem happened during the same song a few months later at a concert in Osaka, Japan.

HEADLINE: *Starship's Slick Makes Sick Salute*

STORY: Jefferson Starship toured Europe in 1978, but on the first night in Hamburg, Germany, lead singer Grace Slick refused to perform due to an upset stomach. The concert was rescheduled for the next night, and Slick prepared by reportedly drinking all of the alcohol in her hotel room's minibar before taking the stage. She spent the evening fondling the band's guitarist, Craig Chaquico, and then, in an insult to the German crowd, marched in a Nazi goose-step and gave the "Heil Hitler" salute. She then jumped into the crowd and stuck her finger up a man's nose. Slick said her behavior was "retaliation for World War II concentration camps."

HEADLINE: *When Durst Went on First, Audience Cursed*

STORY: Rap-metal band Limp Bizkit landed a spot opening for Metallica during a tour in 2003. But unfortunately, most of the 40,000 fans who came to a concert in Chicago were *not* there to see Limp Bizkit. Allegedly egged on by a local radio DJ, hundreds of fans pelted Limp Bizkit's lead singer Fred Durst with garbage, fruit, and coins. Some were even waving "Fred Sucks" signs. Durst retaliated by saying that the fans had the same "lousy aim as the baseball teams" in Chicago. At that moment, a fan threw a lemon, which struck Durst squarely in the crotch. Durst stopped the show and retreated to the wings, where he continued to yell at the crowd, saying repeatedly that "Limp Bizkit is the greatest band in the world" before a stagehand forcibly took his microphone away.

HEADLINE: *Fiona Flails, Flips Off Fans*

STORY: Singer Fiona Apple was performing at New York's Roseland Ballroom in February 2000. Technical problems plagued the show, shutting off the singer's microphone several times. Apple flew into a rage: "You know, I just wanted to do real well in New York," she screamed, "but @#%*! I can't hear myself!" She played a few more notes of a song before stopping. "This song is dead! Just stop it! This is a nightmare!" she yelled. She then lashed out at music critics in attendance, warning that if any gave her a bad review, she'd "@#%*ing kill" them. Apple then began to cry, mumbled about how she needed to take a break, then left the stage. Concert over. (No critics were killed.)

IT BEGAN AS A JOKE

When Uncle John first wrote a book for the bathroom in 1987, he was just having fun, never dreaming of creating a "publishing phenomenon." The same thing happened with these three songs: a bit of messing around yielded a major hit.

PAINT IT, BLACK

Artist: The Rolling Stones

Just Playing Around: Sometimes, when a songwriting session isn't going anywhere, the best thing for the band to do is just jam. That's what the Stones did in a Los Angeles recording studio in 1966. They were trying to come up with "something funky," but nothing much was happening. As Mick Jagger tells it, "'Paint It, Black' was just going to be like a beat group number. If you'd been at the session, it was like one big joke. We put [bassist] Bill Wyman on piano and Bill plays in this funny style…And we just stuck the sitar on…'Oh, that'll sound good because it's got this thing that goes 'g-doing, doing, doing.'" At one point, Wyman got down on his hands and knees and started banging on the pedals of the Hammond B-3 organ with his fists to add more bottom to the bass line.

What they ended up with was a funky, uptempo melody featuring a weird array of instrumentation. Making it even weirder, Jagger added some of the saddest lyrics he'd ever written, penned from the point of view of a *very* depressed man: "I see the girls dressed in their summer clothes. / I have to look away until my darkness goes." He'd originally planned to turn those lines into a slow, mournful tune, but decided that the funky groove the band had just come up with would provide a great counterpoint to the sad lyrics.

It's a Hit! "Paint It, Black" has since become one of the most celebrated Rolling Stones songs in their four-decade career. It topped the charts for two weeks in the United States and one week in the U.K. Not bad for, as Keith Richards once called it, a "comedy track."

Is it "Paint It Black" or "Paint It, Black"? The Stones submitted the song to the record company without a comma. For some reason, when the single was released, it had a comma.

Country singers Loretta Lynn and Crystal Gayle are sisters.

CHECK ON IT

Artist: Beyoncé Knowles

Just Playing Around: "We were being silly in the studio," explained Knowles. "I'd gotten a really bad instrumental track from a producer and I couldn't write anything to it. So we started playing around, saying, 'Check on it, check on it!'" Knowles then moved on to other things, hardly giving another thought to the session.

A few months later, Knowles was asked to provide a single for the upcoming 2006 remake of *The Pink Panther*, in which she was starring with Steve Martin. After trying to come up with a few things, nothing really stuck, but that chant of "check on it, check on it" kept popping up in her head. "I thought, even though it's silly, it's fun. And this movie is a comedy and it's all about fun. So I finished writing it and put the Pink Panther theme music in the beginning."

It's a Hit! Just as it took Knowles some time to realize how infectious the phrase "check on it" was, it took 12 weeks before the tune hit #1 on the Billboard Hot 100 chart, but it stayed there for five weeks. In the mean time, the single went platinum and even became a crossover hit, reaching #1 on four separate Billboard charts, as well as breaking into the Top 5 on several European charts. For the record, Knowles says she's "never liked the song," but she's "thrilled" at how successful it's become.

OKIE FROM MUSKOGEE

Artist: Merle Haggard

Just Playing Around: While riding on their tour bus through Muskogee, Oklahoma, in 1969, Haggard and his band, the Strangers, were amazed at how much different life was in a small Southwestern town compared to the places they'd seen in the Northeast and on the West Coast, where legions of hippies were protesting the Vietnam War. Haggard's drummer, Roy Burris, casually commented, "I bet they don't smoke marijuana in Muskogee." Haggard agreed, and started writing some lines down. Muskogeeans don't "burn our draft cards down on Main Street." Instead, they prefer "livin' right and bein' free."

According to *L.A. Times* music writer, Robert Hilburn, Haggard has changed his tune a few times when talking about the song's origin. "In some interviews, he has said he wrote it for his father, saying, 'Dad was proud of being an Okie. That's where 'Okie From Muskogee' came from. He was the guy in the song.' In others, however, Haggard has maintained that it was just a joke that he came up with one night while riding the bus through Oklahoma."

Whichever story is true, Haggard has always maintained that he wrote the song tongue-in-cheek, as evidenced by the line, "A place where even squares can have a ball." But Haggard had no idea at the time just how much those "squares" would rally around "Okie from Muskogee."

It's a Hit! When Haggard debuted the song for soldiers at Fort Bragg, North Carolina, in the summer of '69, the crowd went completely wild, cheering after every line. That's how it went with conservatives all over America: "Okie from Muskogee" became a staple of country radio and spent four weeks at #1 on the country chart in late 1969. It went on to win country music's "Single of the Year" in 1970, and Haggard was named "Vocalist of the Year." President Nixon invited Haggard to sing "Okie from Muskogee" at the White House (he obliged). George Wallace even requested that the singer endorse his campaign (he respectfully declined, as he did when white supremacist David Duke requested the song be played at one of his rallies).

So how does Haggard, whose politics lean left, feel about writing a right-wing anthem? "If I was to do it over again, it would take a lot more thought...I thought [the song] was funny...It was like the epitome of the ignorance on certain subjects. But I'll be damned if people like Wallace and Nixon didn't take it for the truth."

*　　*　　*

GUITAR MAN

Lowell George, leader of the band Little Feat, was known as one of rock 'n' roll's most influential slide guitar players. He used a Sears Roebuck 11/16 socket wrench for a slide.

CHECK THE LABEL, PART II

On page 203, we told you the histories of some of music's most influential record companies. Here are a few more.

DEF JAM RECORDINGS

The Story: In 1984 Rick Rubin was a student at New York University. He played guitar in a punk band called Hose but also loved the hip-hop music that surrounded him on the streets of New York. One evening at a nightclub called Danceteria (which catered to both hard-core rockers and hip-hoppers), Rubin met Russell Simmons, who also loved rap and hip-hop and had already begun producing then-unknown local acts with names like Run DMC and Kurtis Blow in his basement. The two became fast friends, and after pooling their financial resources (about $4,000 each), they started their own record label in Rubin's dorm room. Def Jam was born.

Rubin wanted to merge genres, mixing rock and rap to create a new style of hip-hop. The first artist he produced was a young rapper named James Todd Smith III, also known as LL Cool J, whose first single, "I Need a Beat," included heavy-metal samples playing behind LL's rapping; it sold an impressive 100,000 copies. Seeing the success Rubin had with that single, Simmons decided to follow his friend's lead. Rubin also insisted that Def Jam's hip-hop records be concise and include hooks. Says Rubin, "Before Def Jam, hip-hop records were typically really long, and they rarely had a hook. Those songs didn't deliver in the way the Beatles did. By making our rap records sound more like pop songs, we changed the form. And we sold a lot of records." (For more on Rubin, see page 361.)

Over the next few years, Def Jam added acts like the Beastie Boys, Run DMC, and Public Enemy to its list of artists and churned out hit after hit. And it was Rubin's idea to produce the highly successful collaboration "Walk This Way," featuring Run DMC and the rock band Aerosmith in 1986. It was the first crossover rap single.

Angus Young of AC/DC tried out a gorilla suit before settling on his schoolboy look.

In 1988 Rubin left Def Jam (disagreements with other business partners caused a rift), but Simmons stayed on and saw Def Jam through some financial struggles in the 1990s. After changing hands a couple of times, Def Jam is owned today by Universal Music. Simmons left in 1999 to pursue other projects, and today, rapper Jay-Z serves as the label's president.

Major Recording Stars: Patti LaBelle, Public Enemy, Rihanna, Foxy Brown, Jay-Z, Kanye West, Redman, Ludacris, Ghostface Killah, Method Man, Ashanti

BLUE NOTE RECORDS

The Story: Jazz may be the only musical genre that is wholly American; it developed in New Orleans during the early 20th century. But the country's premier jazz record label was founded in 1939 by Alfred Lion, an immigrant from Germany. Lion first heard jazz music as a teenager in Berlin, and when he moved to the United States in the 1930s to escape the Nazis, he brought his love of the genre with him. In 1939, he established Blue Note Records in New York. The label's first artists were two Chicago-born pianists: Albert Ammons and Meade Lux Lewis.

It wasn't long before Lion partnered with photographer and fellow jazz lover Francis Wolff, also a German immigrant. When Lion was drafted into the army in 1941, Wolff ran the label until Lion could return. Throughout the World War II years, Blue Note picked up new talent but also supplemented its income by providing records to the military.

From the late 1940s until the 1960s, Blue Note was responsible for producing some of the biggest names in jazz. Everyone from Thelonious Monk to Charlie Parker to Miles Davis made records for the label, and these artists pioneered new types of jazz: bebop (a fast-tempo improvisational style) and hard bop (a style that mixed bebop with other musical styles like gospel, blues, and R&B). The label also employed one of the most innovative and meticulous sound engineers in music history, Rudy Van Gelder, whose recordings for Blue Note are renowned for their clarity.

In the 1960s and '70s, Blue Note changed hands several times, but the large corporations that bought the label (everyone from United Artists to BMI) had trouble maintaining Lion's original level of quality. Blue Note shut down in 1982 but reemerged in 1985 as part of Capitol Records. Today, Blue Note is still going strong, recording popular artists like Wynton Marsalis and Norah Jones.

Major Recording Stars: Duke Ellington, Billie Holiday, Benny Goodman, Count Basie, Etta James, Sarah Vaughan, Clifford Brown, Dizzy Gillespie, Herbie Hancock, John Coltrane, Ella Fitzgerald, Lou Rawls

DECCA RECORDS

The Story: Decca Records opened in 1929 in the United Kingdom when one-time stockbroker Edward Lewis bought a failing gramophone company and turned it into a record label. Over the next decade, Lewis continued to buy up other small British record companies, and by 1939, Decca was one of just two record companies left in Great Britain. (EMI was the other.) The label's American office opened in 1934 and had a huge hit eight years later with Bing Crosby's "White Christmas."

Throughout the 1940s, '50s, and '60s, Decca remained the premier record company in Great Britain. Its execs continued to find new artists and promote them to superstardom. Pat Boone, the Everly Brothers, David Bowie, the Rolling Stones, and many others recorded for the label. (There was one misstep, however. The execs at Decca turned down the Beatles in 1962.) Decca was also the first company to record albums of hit Broadway musicals. Its first: 1943's *Oklahoma!*

Decca's decline began in the 1970s when the Rolling Stones and most of the label's other stars left for other companies. By 1980 Polygram had bought the British arm of Decca. The American company continued and is now best known for its classical and Broadway albums (its most recent success was 2003's *Wicked*).

Major Recording Artists: Billie Holiday, Al Jolson, Andrea Bocelli, Luciano Pavarotti, Placido Domingo, Loretta Lynn, Sammy Davis Jr., the Animals, the Moody Blues

*   *   *

Random music trivia: Before they formed Nirvana, Kurt Cobain and Krist Novoselic played in a Credence Clearwater Revival tribute band called Sellout.

"COP KILLER"

Ice-T pioneered the genre of gangsta rap—graphically violent and politically charged songs about life in the ghetto. But one of his songs in particular has become synonymous with controversy.

ORIGINAL GANGSTER

Ice-T (real name: Tracy Marrow) grew up in the tough South Central neighborhood of Los Angeles, was a member of the notorious Crips gang as a teenager, and even worked as a pimp. In 1984 he decided to channel his stories of street life into music. Albums like *6 in the Morning* (1987) and *O.G.: Original Gangster* (1991) made him one of the bestselling and best known West Coast rappers.

In 1990 Ice-T wrote a song called "Cop Killer." Inspired by the 1977 Talking Heads hit "Psycho Killer" (a first-person narrative from the perspective of a murderer), the song is a young black man's account of being so fed up with racially motivated police brutality that he murders a police officer. Sample lyrics: "I'm 'bout to bust some shots off / I'm bout to dust some cops off / cop killer, better you than me."

A METALLIC TASTE

The song was so aggressive that Ice-T decided it wouldn't make a good rap song, but was perfect for his heavy-metal band side project, Body Count. Based on Ice-T's star power, the group signed with Sire Records (a division of Warner Bros.) and released their self-titled debut album in March 1992. The first single: "Cop Killer."

While the song didn't get much radio or MTV play (neither thrash metal nor hardcore rap generally do), it was a single by a major artist at the peak of his career, so Warner Bros. did a fair amount of promotion for *Body Count*, including selling the CD in tiny body bags instead of the usual long cardboard boxes CDs came in at the time.

But what really got "Cop Killer" noticed was its timing. In 1991 African-American motorist Rodney King had been severely beaten by several white L.A. police officers (and the incident was caught on videotape) and at the time of "Cop Killer's" release, those officers were on trial for the incident. In late April 1992, the four policemen were acquitted, enraging the African-American community. Los Angeles endured three days of riots, fires, and looting.

PROTEST

As pundits weighed in on the riots' causes, some blamed the song. The Dallas Police Association actually lobbied to get "Cop Killer" banned—it organized a boycott of all Time Warner products in an effort to force Warner Bros. to withdraw the album from stores because it "promoted violence" toward police. Decency crusader Tipper Gore publicly denounced the song, as did President George Bush and Vice President Dan Quayle (who also spoke out against the immorality of *Murphy Brown*, a TV sitcom about a single mother). Warner executives even reported receiving death threats.

On the other side, one major police organization, the National Black Police Association, supported "Cop Killer," arguing that the song accurately identified police brutality as the cause of the rise in anti-police sentiment. Other people said the song was blamed unjustly in the emotional aftermath of the riots. Criminologist Mark S. Hamm of Indiana State University pointed out that there was no controversy surrounding the Talking Heads' "Psycho Killer" or Eric Clapton's "I Shot the Sheriff," which was a #1 hit in 1974.

COUNTERPROTEST

Body Count was never actually banned or pulled from store shelves, but there were a few isolated incidents:
• A small record store in Greensboro, North Carolina, stopped selling it after local police told them they would no longer respond to emergency calls at the store if it continued to stock the album.
• When Body Count was scheduled to open for Metallica at a concert in San Diego, California Governor Pete Wilson demanded the band be dropped from the bill. As a compromise, the group was allowed to play under the promise that they wouldn't perform "Cop Killer." They took the stage...and played the song anyway.

Ice-T thought the controversy was absurd, because "Cop

Killer" was entirely a work of fiction. "I ain't never killed no cop," he said. "I felt like it a lot of times. But I never did it. If you believe that I'm a cop killer, you believe David Bowie is an astronaut" (in reference to Bowie's "Space Oddity").

A FORCED HAND

In late 1992, Ice-T asked Warner Bros. to pull *Body Count* from stores and re-release it—without "Cop Killer." Warner agreed, but not before it flooded stores with over half a million copies of the intact version of *Body Count*, ensuring there were plenty to meet demand for the "banned" album. Ultimately, it was one of the bestselling albums of Ice-T's career.

So why did Ice-T voluntarily recall "Cop Killer"? Strangely, it was out of respect for his record label. As he explained in his autobiography *The Ice Opinion*, "Warner never censored us. But when the cops moved on Body Count, they issued pressure on the corporate division. So even when you're in a business with somebody who might not want to censor you, economically people can put restraints on them."

Nevertheless, in 1993 Warner's corporate division tried to make the music division censor songs and artwork on Ice-T's next album, *Home Invasion*. In response to the pressure, Ice-T left Warner Bros. and signed with Priority Records, a small hardcore rap label. Body Count moved to Virgin Records.

AFTERMATH

The original 1992 recording of "Cop Killer" is no longer commercially available, although there is a version on a 2005 Body Count live album. And Ice-T has only recorded two albums in the last 10 years (along with two Body Count albums). Following an appearance in the hit movie *New Jack City* in 1991, he took on more and more acting roles. In 2000 he joined the cast of *Law and Order: Special Victims Unit*. The characters in both projects are, ironically, cops.

*   *   *

Music induces more madness in many than wine.

—Latin proverb

10 RANDOM LISTS ABOUT THE BEATLES

If you're a Beatles fan, you probably know everything about them. But maybe we can find a few things you don't know.

4 FACTS ABOUT THEIR NAMES

1. John's middle name: Winston.
2. Paul's real first name: James.
3. As a boy, Ringo was called "Ritchie."
4. George told reporters his haircut's name was "Arthur."

4 NAMES BETWEEN "THE QUARRYMEN" AND "THE BEATLES"

1. The Beatals
2. The Silver Beetles
3. The Silver Beats
4. The Silver Beatles

2 OPINIONS OF JOHN LENNON

1. **Little Richard:** "I developed an especially close relationship with Paul McCartney, but John and I couldn't make it. John had a nasty personality."
2. **Elton John:** "He's the only person in this business I've ever looked up to. The only person."

THE 5 SONGS THAT OCCUPIED THE TOP 5 SLOTS IN THE BILLBOARD HOT 100 DURING THE WEEK OF APRIL 4, 1964

1. "Can't Buy Me Love"
2. "Twist and Shout"
3. "She Loves You"
4. "I Want to Hold Your Hand"
5. "Please Please Me"

3 PEOPLE WHO DIDN'T GET ONTO THE COVER OF *SGT. PEPPER'S* BECAUSE THEY WERE TOO CONTROVERSIAL

1. Jesus
2. Gandhi
3. Hitler

7 FACTORS THAT LED TO THE BEATLES' BREAKUP (1970)

1. The death of manager Brian Epstein (1967).
2. The film *Magical Mystery Tour* was a flop (1967).
3. John was becoming more

The Beatles recorded their first album, *Please Please Me*, in 12 hrs. It cost about $1,000 to make.

interested in the avant-garde art scene.

4. George felt that his songwriting talents were underappreciated.

5. Their corporation, Apple Corps, was losing money.

6. Paul wanted his father-in-law, Lee Eastman, to be their new manager; the other three didn't (1969).

7. They argued over the songs and arrangements on *Let It Be.* (It didn't help that John insisted on letting Yoko participate in meetings about the album.)

6 BEATLES CHILDREN WHO ARE MUSICIANS

1. Dhani Harrison
2. Julian Lennon
3. Sean Lennon
4. James McCartney
5. Zak Starkey
6. Jason Starkey

4 LESSER-KNOWN PEOPLE WHO HELPED MAKE IT POSSIBLE

1. Bruno Koschmider, owner of several Hamburg clubs, who told them to *mach Schau,* or "make show," that is, let go and be outrageous.

2. Astrid Kirschherr, Stu Sutcliffe's girlfriend, who gave them their "mop-top" haircuts

and designed their signature collarless jackets.

3. Raymond Jones, who walked into Brian Epstein's music store and asked for a Beatles record. Legend says that this was the first time that Epstein had ever heard of them.

4. Alan Livingstone, president of Capitol Records, who decided to sign the Beatles after listening to a record sent by Brian Epstein.

7 MUSICIANS' OPINIONS

1. Roy Orbison: "I think that when their real success came, the Beatles were a bit disappointed...because they became big so fast. They wanted to conquer America, but we gave it to them on a silver platter."

2. Billy Joel: "Basically I'm a melody freak, and they were the masters."

3. Sting: "I think the Beatles are the reason I'm a musician."

4. Brian Wilson: "The Beatles looked sharp, especially compared to the silly, juvenile striped shirts and white pants the Beach Boys were wearing onstage. I suddenly felt unhip, as if we looked more like golf caddies than rock 'n' roll stars."

5. Bob Dylan: "Their chords were outrageous…and their harmonies made it all valid… I knew they were pointing to the direction where music had to go."

6. Kris Kristofferson: "What we admired about the Beatles was that they kept their personal and artistic integrity, and all their success didn't blow them away, like it killed Elvis."

7. Leonard Bernstein: "Three bars of 'A Day in the Life' still sustain me, rejuvenate me, inflame my senses and sensibilities. They are the best songwriters since Gershwin."

4 FAB QUOTES BY THE FAB FOUR ABOUT THEMSELVES

1. John: "None of us would've made it alone. Paul wasn't quite strong enough, I didn't have enough girl appeal, George was too quiet, and Ringo was the drummer. But we thought that everyone would be able to dig at least one of us, and that's how it turned out."

2. Paul: "Somebody said to me, 'But the Beatles were anti-materialistic.' That's a huge myth. John and I literally used to sit down and say, 'Now, let's write a swimming pool.'"

3. George: "The Beatles exist apart from my self. I am not really Beatle George. Beatle George is like a suit or shirt that I once wore on occasion and until the end of my life people may see that shirt and mistake it for me."

4. Ringo: "I became a drummer because it's the only thing I could do. But whenever I hear another drummer, I know I'm no good. I'm not good on the technical things, but I'm good with all the motions, swinging my head, like."

* * *

ISN'T IT IRONIC?

In 1987 the rock band Genesis (led by singer Phil Collins) was at the peak of its commercial success. Their video for "Land of Confusion" was nominated for Best Music Video of the Year at the MTV Video Music Awards. It ultimately lost to "Sledgehammer," by Peter Gabriel…who'd quit Genesis in 1975.

ODD HOMEMADE INSTRUMENTS

They're homemade, and they're cool. What else could you want?

T HE PENCILINA
Inventor: Brooklyn musician Bradford Reed
Description: The Pencilina features two wooden boards
that serve as guitar necks, mounted atop legs like a steel guitar.
One board is strung with six guitar strings; the other has four bass
strings. An array of six electric pickups gather the sound. Wedged
under the guitar strings are two drumsticks that can be moved to
change string length (and pitch) on either side of each stick.

Music: Reed—who used to play the electric zither with the Blue
Man Group—strikes, plucks, slides, or bows the strings on both
sides of the drumsticks, creating an amazingly wide variety of
sound textures and tones that the *Village Voice* said "sounds like
Jimi Hendrix and Buddy Rich playing 'Dueling Banjos.'"

THE CAR MUSIC PROJECT

Inventor: Emmy-winning sound designer Bill Milbrodt
Description: In 1994 Milbrodt decided that his '82 Honda
Accord's time was up. "It dripped oil, blew smoke, and made more
noise than a cement mixer," he said. So, with the help of metal
sculptor Ray Faunce III, he dismantled the entire car and proceeded to turn every piece of it into musical instruments.

Music: In 2005 he started a band called the Car Music Project.
Milbrodt plays the "Air Guitar"—a banjolike stringed instrument
made from the air filter, brake calipers, and part of the windshield
frame. Another member, William Trigg, plays "Percarsion" on
more than 50 percussion instruments made from springs, gears,
wheels, windows, pistons, and the crankshaft. Horn player James
Spotto plays the "Exhaust-aphone," made from the exhaust pipe,
and Wilbo Wright plays "Tank Bass," a stand-up bass made from
the gas tank. The New Jersey band has released a few recordings.
Their slogan: "You've never had a tune-up like this before!"

Gene Simmons of KISS financed Van Halen's first demo tape. He suggested...

THE GLOCKENMUNDHARMONIKA

Inventor: New Jersey resident Ernst Koch

Description: Patented in 1908, the name means "bell mouth harmonica" in German. Unlike a normal harmonica, this instrument didn't have any reeds—it had 22 little bells mounted inside.

Music: When you blew into the Glockenmundharmonika, tiny spring-loaded hammers would strike the bells. It's unknown if any were ever made, because none are known to exist today. There no recordings either, so nobody's exactly sure what it sounded like, although you can imagine it sounding "tinkly" if it worked.

THE MANDOCLETA

Inventor: Les Luthiers, an Argentine musical comedy group that specialized in making their own instruments from odd materials

Description: It's a stationary bicycle with a *bouzouki*, a Greek guitarlike instrument, mounted alongside the rear wheel of the bike. Attached to the wheel are picks that strike the bouzouki's strings as the wheel turns. A small keyboard is mounted on the handlebars. The keys control where the strings are fretted via cables attached to the neck of the bouzouki.

Music: The player simply sits on the bike, pedals, and plays the keyboards. And it sounds like a bouzouki.

NOMEOLBIDET

Inventor: Also from Les Luthiers

Description: It looks sort of like a bass fiddle. The body is a bidet, which sits on a short stand (a plunger, actually), with the opening facing the audience. A three-inch PVC pipe "neck" extends up from one end of the bidet. Two strings stretch from the other end of the bidet—attached to an actual cello tailpiece—across the open bowl top, and up the PVC pipe to two tuning pegs at the top.

Music: The player turns a crank that operates two wheels in front of the strings; a rubber band between the wheels "bows" the strings to make them produce sound, similar to the way a hurdy-gurdy works. The strings are "fretted" on the PVC pipe. The nomeolbidet's music sounds high and eerie like a hurdy-gurdy, but it has a lot more *bottom* end. (Just kidding—the sound is all very high. We just couldn't resist the bathroom joke.)

JAZZ IS...

Thoughts about jazz from those who know it best.

"Jazz came to America three hundred years ago in chains."
—Paul Whiteman

"Jazz is the big brother of Revolution."
—Miles Davis

"It's like a language. You learn the alphabet, which are the scales. You learn sentences, which are the chords. And then you talk extemporaneously with the horn."
—Stan Getz

"Jazz has always been like the kind of a man you wouldn't want your daughter to associate with."
—Duke Ellington

"I figured out the peculiar form of mathematics and harmonies that was strange to all the world but me."
—Jelly Roll Morton

"I don't know where jazz is going. You can't make anything go anywhere. It just happens."
—Thelonius Monk

"Life is a lot like jazz—it's best when you improvise."
—George Gershwin

"It's a shame that jazz is now being turned into dried fruit. It's becoming quantized, diced, and defined. To me, jazz is more like a process than it is a thing."
—Pat Metheny

"It bugs me when people try to analyze jazz as an intellectual theorem. It's not. It's feeling."
—Bill Evans

"Nothing else will ever so perfectly capture the democratic process in sound. Jazz means working things out musically with other people. You have to listen to other musicians and play with them even if you don't agree with what they're playing. It teaches you the very opposite of racism and anti-Semitism. It teaches you that the world is big enough to accommodate us all."
—Wynton Marsalis

Saxophones, invented in 1840, did not become popular until the rise of jazz in the 1920s.

THE WHO?

Ever wonder how rock bands get their names? So did we.
After some digging around, we found these "origin" stories.

PROCUL HARUM. Named after a friend's cat. It's Latin for "beyond all things."

10,000 MANIACS. Came from the cult horror film *2,000 Maniacs*. One of the band members misheard the film's name.

FOO FIGHTERS. Founder Dave Grohl has always been fascinated with UFOs. He named his band after the mysterious fireballs seen by American pilots in World War II.

DIRE STRAITS. Suggested by a friend who was concerned about the state of the band's finances.

MOTHERS OF INVENTION. Frank Zappa's group was originally just the Mothers. But their record company was concerned it would be interpreted as an Oedipal reference and insisted they change it. The band chose the name from the old saying, "Necessity is the mother of invention."

ALICE IN CHAINS. One day, band members were watching an episode of *The Honeymooners*. Ralph Kramden said he'd like to see his wife, Alice, in chains.

BEASTIE BOYS. "Beastie" supposedly stands for Boys Entering Anarchistic States Towards Inner Excellence.

BLUE ÖYSTER CULT. An anagram of "Cully Stout Beer." It was chosen by a band member one night as he was mindlessly doodling while at a bar with the band's manager. (They added the umlaut just because it looked cool.)

ZZ TOP. Said to be have been inspired by a poster of Texas bluesman Z.Z. Hill, and the rolling-paper brands Zig-Zag and Top.

DEVO. An abbreviation of "de-evolution," something that the members of the group believe is happening to the human race.

MATCHBOX 20. Took its name from the combination of a softball jersey bearing the number 20 and a patch that read "matchbox." The name is meaningless. "The two parts aren't even related," singer Rob Thomas has said.

COUNTING CROWS. A reference to an old British poem that said life is as meaningless as counting crows.

MARILYN MANSON. A combination of movie icon Marilyn Monroe and crime icon Charles Manson.

PEARL JAM. Singer Eddie Vedder claims he suggested the name in honor of his Aunt Pearl's homemade jam, supposedly a natural aphrodisiac containing peyote.

SOUNDGARDEN. In the band's hometown of Seattle, there's a modern art structure called *A Sound Garden* that creates a low hum when the wind blows through its many pipes and hollows.

RIGHTEOUS BROTHERS. The duo got their name when an audience member shouted, "Hey, that's really righteous, brothers!"

DEEP PURPLE. Named for the favorite song of guitarist Ritchie Blackmore's grandmother, the 1963 hit "Deep Purple" by April Stevens and Nino Tempo.

HOOTIE AND THE BLOWFISH. Singer Darius Rucker had two friends in his college choir with odd nicknames. Hootie (he had wide eyes like an owl) and Blowfish (he had puffy cheeks). Neither of them is in the band.

FLEETWOOD MAC. A combination of the last names of the band's founding members, Mick Fleetwood and John McVie.

MOBY. The singer sometimes claims to be a descendant of Herman Melville, author of *Moby Dick*, but other times insists Moby is an acronym for "master of beats, y'all."

THE WHO. According to legend, the group, first called the High Numbers, was looking for a new name. Every time someone came up with an idea, they jokingly asked, "The *who*?" Finally, a friend said "Why not just call yourselves 'The Who'?"

MAY THE FORCE
BE WITH YOU

After Uncle John saw Star Wars (12 times), he thought he knew all the characters. But BRI stalwart Jay Newman pointed out that there was one important character the wasn't listed in the cast—the music.

PRODIGY

He's won five Oscars and 18 Grammys, and he may be the most widely heard composer of all time. Who is he? John Williams, composer of the film soundtracks for blockbusters like *Star Wars, Jaws, Jurassic Park*, and the *Harry Potter* movies—and the televison themes for *The Today Show, NBC Nightly News*, and many of the "fanfares" heard during broadcasts of the Olympics since 1984.

By the time Williams achieved music superstardom in the mid-1970s, he was already a 20-year veteran of the TV and film scoring business. In fact, Williams had been immersed in music almost from the day he was born, on February 8, 1932, in New York City. His father, an accomplished jazz drummer and percussionist for the CBS Radio Orchestra, got his son started on piano lessons at six years old. The youngster soon added trombone, trumpet, and clarinet to his repertoire. Then, when he was 16, his father landed a job with the CBS Television Orchestra, and the Williams family moved to Hollywood.

HE SCORES!

Music was the only career that Williams ever pursued. He studied at UCLA in 1950, and progressed so quickly that when he was drafted into the military in 1952, the 21-year-old found himself conducting the Air Force Band. In another two years, he landed at the Juilliard School, where he studied under the world's greatest composers by day while playing piano in New York jazz clubs at night.

After Juilliard, Williams's show-biz roots brought him back to Hollywood, where he first worked as an orchestra pianist, but it was his skill as an orchestrator that garnered the attention of such

Joseph Williams, son of film composer John Williams, was a member of Toto in the 1980s.

film music legends as Bernard Herrmann (who composed the scores for *Citizen Kane*, *The Day the Earth Stood Still*, and many Hitchcock movies), Alfred Newman (*All About Eve*, *How Green Was My Valley*), and Franz Waxman (*Sunset Boulevard*, *The Philadelphia Story*). They utilized the young composer's skills to orchestrate musical cues for their film scores. After that, Johnny Williams (as he was credited) didn't have to look for work—it came looking for him.

Williams played on dozens of TV scores per year in the 1950s and started writing them in the 1960s, including *Checkmate* (1960), *Gilligan's Island* (1964), *Lost in Space* (1965), and *Land of the Giants* (1968). Writing music for movies came next. Starting in 1959, Williams turned out at least one score per year, at first for forgettable, lighthearted comedies such as *Gidget Goes to Rome* (1963) and *Not with My Wife You Don't!* (1966).

In 1967 Williams earned his first Academy Award nomination for the score of *Valley of the Dolls*...and never slowed down. So far, Williams has composed the music to more than 75 films. He's amassed 45 Oscar nominations (second behind Walt Disney for the most ever) and has won five of them. Director Alan Parker (*Angela's Ashes*) said in 2000 that, for a filmmaker, getting John Williams to score your movie is akin to "winning the lottery."

BLOCKBUSTER

So what is it about Williams's scores that have connected with so many filmmakers and moviegoers over the years? Of course, being in the right place at the right time has a lot to do with it—he scored the music to seven of the ten top-grossing films from 1976 to 1983. But it's fair to say that these films became so successful at least in part *because of* Williams's themes. Steven Spielberg calls him "the greatest musical storyteller of our time."

The Williams/Spielberg collaboration started in 1973 when the composer was 40 and the director was only 23. Williams was at the height of his disaster-score days (*The Poseidon Adventure*, *Earthquake*, and *The Towering Inferno*) and Spielberg wanted that bombastic feel for his first feature film, *The Sugarland Express*. The movie wasn't very successful, but the two men got along so well that Spielberg tapped Williams to come up with a really scary theme for his upcoming shark thriller, *Jaws*.

PRESENT TENSE

Jaws (1975) is a prime example of just how effective Williams can be at translating human emotions into musical notes: Instead of a sweeping melody (which Spielberg expected), Williams played two very low half-notes on the piano, back and forth, "Da...Duh," slow at first but then a little faster, "Da...Duh," the tension keeps building, "Da...Duh" and then when the tension is highest the crescendo hits, "DaDuhDaDuhDaDuh," and the viewer knows something really bad is about to happen to that poor woman swimming in the water.

Spielberg was amazed, and to this day credits Williams's primal score as a big reason that *Jaws* turned out to be such a phenomenal hit, and the first of the summer blockbusters that have come to define Hollywood (at the time, it was the highest-grossing movie ever). The two men have worked on more than 20 films together. Yet no score that Williams has done —before or since— has had as much impact on people all over the world as the music he composed for George Lucas's "space movie."

A NEW HOPE

It was Spielberg who told Lucas to seek out Williams for the *Star Wars* score. Lucas wanted the movie to buck the trend of 1970s science fiction films, which had been using "modern" sounds such as synthesizers and early drum machines, and return to Hollywood's golden age sound of a full orchestra. Lucas asked Williams to make the music the "emotional grounding point" of the film to offset the otherworldly characters and settings.

Williams understood Lucas's vision—and everything just seemed to click while he was writing the music. The composer recently tried to explain the experience of composing *Star Wars*:

> There's something sort of eerie about the way our hands are occasionally guided in some of the things that we do. It can happen in any aspect, any phase of human endeavor where we come to the right solutions almost in spite of ourselves. And you look back and you say that that almost seems to have a kind of—you want to use the word divine guidance—behind it. The Force was definitely with me.

UNCHAINED MELODIES

The movie, of course, was a runaway success, and so, too, was the

---

When he died in 1750, Bach was mourned mainly as an organist, not as a composer.

soundtrack—it was (and still is) the top-selling score-only movie soundtrack ever released. Even a disco version of the main theme (by Meco) made it to #1 on the pop chart. To understand just how integral Williams's music is to the movie, check out the original theatrical trailer—the one released in December 1976 before the score was completed (you can find it online). The visual images are there, but without Williams's melodies, the magic is definitely missing.

NEVER FORCE A THEME

While Williams may have benefited from a "guiding hand" in composing the music, he also utilized a time-tested technique: the *leitmotif*. Popularized in Richard Wagner's "Ring Cycle" in the 19th century, a leitmotif is a recurring theme assigned to a specific character, used intermittently throughout a work. Interestingly, very few Hollywood films used the leitmotif to its full potential up until that point (with a few notable exceptions, such as Max Steiner's *Gone with the Wind*). In *Star Wars*, however, Williams took the leitmotif to the next level, assigning themes not only to individual characters, such as Luke Skywalker (that one is also the main theme), but for abstract concepts such as the Force.

At its core, the "Force Theme" is a basic melody in a minor key, utilizing very few notes. The theme is heard not only whenever the Force is mentioned, but during the most intense emotional scenes: As Luke stares at the "Binary Sunset" early in the movie, the theme is introduced with a single French horn, invoking longing, and then crescendoes with a full string treatment, invoking hope. The theme returns when the Rebel ships attack the Death Star and Luke uses the Force, and finally, when the heroes receive their medals, the same set of notes is heard in the "Throne Room" march that concludes the movie.

The Force Theme would go on to become an important part of the two following sequels and then the three prequels, helping to tie the saga together. Just think of Luke at the beginning of *The Empire Strikes Back*, hanging by his feet in the ice cave and trying to reach his lightsaber. He shuts his eyes, extends his hand—and there's that theme, so familiar that the audience may wonder if Luke could use the Force without it. That's the power of Williams's "musical storytelling."

LEADER OF THE PACK

Even if he had retired after *Star Wars*, John Williams would still
be considered one of Hollywood's all-time greatest composers. But
he kept going, scoring phenomenal success with films such as
Superman (1978), *The Empire Strikes Back* (1980), *Raiders of the
Lost Ark* (1981), *E.T. the Extra-terrestrial* (1982, for which
Williams won an Oscar), *Home Alone* (1990), *Jurassic Park* (1993),
Schindler's List (1993—another Oscar), and the first three *Harry
Potter* movies. All those films carry on the leitmotif tradition that
Williams perfected in *Star Wars*. (Just think of the *Raiders* theme
when Indiana Jones is riding his horse and chasing the Nazis, or
the famous music that accompanies Elliot and E.T. when they fly
in front of the full moon.)

Williams has also remained active composing for television
(the Olympic fanfare and "The Mission," the NBC News theme)
and heading up the Boston Pops from 1980 to 1993. Along the
way, he's picked up 18 Grammys, 17 honorary degrees, 4 Golden
Globes, and 5 Oscars.

ONE LITTLE COMPLAINT

There are a few knocks against Williams, at least among film
music aficionados, the biggest being that he taps into that "universal melody" a bit too often. This is evidenced by very similar
melodies and phrasings that show up in completely different
movies that Williams has scored, especially when they're released
within a year of each other. (Detractors point to similar moments
in the scores to 1978's *Superman* and 1980's *The Empire Strikes
Back*, as well as 2004's *Harry Potter and the Prisoner of Azkaban* and
2005's *Star Wars Episode III: Revenge of the Sith*.)

Still, it's impossible to deny Williams' impact. His ability to
translate emotion into melody has made his work accessible to
people who aren't necessarily interested in "classical" music. Just
like Elvis and the Beatles, John Williams's influence has reached
far beyond his genre and touched millions. "So much of what we
do is ephemeral and quickly forgotten, even by ourselves," he said.
"So it's gratifying to have something you have done linger in people's memories."

Of the 88 keys on a piano, 52 are white, 36 are black. The lowest is an A, the highest is a C.

LEGENDARY SONGS

Odd lyrics or creepy sound effects in songs have given rise to some great urban legends. Here are a few of our favorite song-related myths.

SONG: "In the Air Tonight," by Phil Collins (1981)
LEGEND: The song is a public accusation of a man who didn't save a drowning victim.

THE STORY GOES: In the early 1980s, Collins was visiting a beach in England. While standing on a pier, he saw a man off-shore, drowning. Collins was too far away to help, but he ran out to the beach, only to discover that another man had been there all along and had done nothing to help the drowning man, who died. Collins wrote the song "In the Air Tonight" to directly accuse the man of the shameful act. Lyrics include "If you told me you were drowning / I would not lend a hand. I've seen your face before, my friend. But I don't know if you know who I am / I was there and I saw what you did…" Collins then invited the man to the concert where he premiered the song, sat him in the front row with a spotlight shining on him, and sang him the song. Police arrested the man after the show.

TRUTH: Collins has frequently denied that the song is about a real drowning. The drowning imagery is a metaphor, he says, for bitterness and hopelessness…and it's actually about his divorce from his first wife, Andy.

SONG: "Love Rollercoaster," by the Ohio Players (1975)
LEGEND: The scream heard during the song's instrumental break is the real scream of a murder victim accidentally recorded and left on the tape.

THE STORY GOES: While the band was recording the song, a woman burst into the studio and attacked them. The deranged woman was the model pictured on the cover of the album they were recording, *Honey*. In the photo, she's drenched in what appears to be honey, but the "honey" was actually liquid plastic, which severely damaged her skin when it was removed, ending her modeling career. Enraged, she attacked the band. The scream was hers—when the band killed her in self-defense.

TRUTH: The scream is from one of the Ohio Players—keyboard player Billy Beck—and it's *supposed* to be there.

SONG: "Mellow Yellow," by Donovan (1966)

LEGEND: The song is full of coded messages telling people to smoke dried banana peels, a powerful hallucinogenic.

THE STORY GOES: A few weeks after the song came out, musician Country Joe McDonald, a friend of Donovan's, told an interviewer, jokingly, that he smoked banana skins to get high. Some fans made the connection between that offhand comment and the song's lyrics, and a myth was born. Here's the song's last verse: "Electrical banana / is gonna be a sudden craze / electrical banana / is bound to be the very next phase. / They call it mellow yellow."

TRUTH: Despite being known for his trippy, psychedelic lyrics, Donovan says the song has nothing to do with drugs…or fruit. In 1966 he got sick with liver disease and developed jaundice, a yellowing of the skin and eyes. The song, Donovan says, is simply about that. And smoking banana peels won't get anyone high—that's another urban legend.

SONG: "Fire and Rain," by James Taylor (1969)

MYTH: It's about Taylor's girlfriend, who died in a plane crash while on her way to visit him.

THE STORY GOES: While Taylor was touring one year, some friends of his made plans to fly in his girlfriend, Suzanne, for a surprise visit at a concert stop. Her plane crashed en route (inspiring the lyric "sweet dreams and flying machines in pieces on the ground") and she died ("Suzanne, the plans they made put an end to you").

TRUTH: Despite the song's mournful lyrics, there was never a dead girlfriend. The song *is* autobiographical, but not quite so literally. Taylor says it's about several things: his reaction to the death of an old friend (named Suzanne) who committed suicide around the time when Taylor was becoming a successful pop star, his battles with depression and drug abuse, and his stay in a mental institution. "Flying machines in pieces on the ground" actually refers to Taylor's drug addiction, which led to the breakup of his first band…the Flying Machine.

THE AEOLIAN HARP

*Ancient Greeks wrote about a harp that was played by Aeolus,
the god of the wind. That's where we get the name for this
strange instrument that almost seems to play itself.*

A MIGHTY WIND

Legends about a magical harp played by the wind have been around for thousands of years. An ancient Hebrew text says that King David kept a kind of harp known as a *kinnor* mounted above his bed that would play music when the North Wind came through in the middle of the night.

No specimens from ancient times exist, and the first person known to make a serious study of such an instrument was German scholar and inventor Athanasius Kircher, and in 1650 he built his *machina harmonica automata*. It played "enchanting notes which defy description," Kircher wrote. "They are like the song of distant choirs. Gently rising and dying away again, more like a melodious vision of heavenly nature than the result of human artifice."

MUSIC BOX

Kircher's simple design is still used today. It's a rectangular box— about 42 inches long, 17 inches wide, and 8 inches deep. Along the face, 15 strings of the same length (about 40 inches), but of different thicknesses, were strung—all of them tuned to the same pitch. Under the right conditions, wind passing across the strings causes what has come to be known as the "aeolian vibration" of one or several of the strings. The harp then emits a high, eerie tone, described by many as "fairy music."

How does it work? Basically, the wind makes the strings vibrate in such a way that the *harmonics*, or *overtones*, are louder than the fundamental note. Example: If you have a string tuned to A and you pluck it—you hear the *fundamental* note—the A. But you will also hear other notes, including an A one octave higher, an E even higher, a C sharp still higher, that are softer than the A you hear. But they are there and our ears blend them all into a single note. That's what all musical instruments—even nonstringed instruments—do. The unique thing about the no-hands harp is

---

The band Queen spent more collective weeks on the U.K. album chart than the Beatles did.

that the aeolian vibrations cause the overtones to be louder than the fundamental, hence those eerie tones.

YOU ARE THE WIND BETWEEN MY STRINGS

The fact that the aeolian harp has strings of different thicknesses means that different wind speeds affect different strings differently. It also means that an aeolian harp might sit in your window or hang from a tree for long periods and not make a peep. That's just the way it is—and part of the charm of the instrument is that nature decides when to play it. When one does play, and when several strings sound with successive levels of harmonics, it can be a truly magical sound. It can also be haphazard and dissonant…but that's nature.

RANDOM AEOLIAN FACTS

• Aeolian harps, which were very popular in the 18th and 19th centuries in Europe and the United States, are still available today. You can buy one that will fit in your window or on your porch or patio.

• Aeolian vibration is a much-studied phenomenon because it causes power lines and bridge support cables to vibrate and weaken. It's also what causes them to occasionally "hum."

• In 1940 the Tacoma Narrows Bridge suddenly began to wiggle, sway, and "gallop" violently before finally collapsing completely, all caused by the wind creating aeolian vibration in its structure.

• Aeolian harps come in a very wide variety of shapes and sizes today, from window-sized to extra large. One sitting outside the Cornwall Harp Centre near Bude, England, is 9 feet tall, with 16 strings. One in New Mexico has 45 strings and stands 24 feet high. Another, on a deserted dune in a barren area of New South Wales, Australia, is made up of four separate triangular harps and a total of 107 strings, emitting its shimmering, wailing music almost constantly, day and night, over the Outback.

• In 1861 American poet Ralph Waldo Emerson used the aeolian harp as an analogy for the "Over-Soul," his depiction of a universal soul that played through all people. "Lift the sash / lay me within / lend me your ears and I begin / for gentle harp to gentle hearts / the secret of the world imparts."

AUTOPSIES OF THE RICH AND MUSICAL

Sometimes how a music star died is just as interesting as how they lived...and often much more mysterious

STAR: Rock 'n' roll pioneer J. P. "Big Bopper" Richards
UNOFFICIAL STORY: Richards died in one of music's most infamous tragedies: the 1959 plane crash that claimed him, aged 28; Ritchie Valens, just 17; and 22-year-old Buddy Holly. What many don't know is that a gun belonging to Holly was found in the wreckage, and some people believed there was foul play aboard the plane before it crashed, though investigators at the time found no evidence to support the claim. Other rumors said that the Big Bopper survived the crash and died trying to get help. So many stories floated around for so many years that in 2007, Jay Richardson, the Big Bopper's son, hired a forensic anthropologist to exhume his father's body from its grave in Beaumont, Texas, and perform an autopsy.
CORONER'S REPORT: "There was no indication of foul play," Dr. Bill Bass told the Associated Press. "There are fractures from head to toe. Massive fractures...(He) died immediately. He didn't crawl away. He didn't walk away from the plane." Richardson, who performs as the "Big Bopper Jr.," said that was just what he wanted to hear. "I was hoping to put the rumors to rest," he said.

STAR: Elliott Smith, American singer/songwriter
UNOFFICIAL STORY: Smith died on October 21, 2003, in his Los Angeles home at the age of 34. His girlfriend, Jennifer Chiba, later told police that she and Smith had been arguing and that she had locked herself in the bathroom. She heard Smith scream, so she ran out to find him with his back to her. When he turned around, she saw a knife sticking out of his chest. She called 911 and performed CPR on him, but he died at the hospital a short time later. He had, Chiba said, stabbed himself. Smith had reportedly had a long battle with depression.
CORONER'S REPORT: The autopsy report read, "The location

The first record to feature a Moog synthesizer was *Cosmic Sounds* by the Zodiac (1967).

and direction of the stab wound is consistent with self-infliction, but several aspects of the circumstances are atypical of suicide and raise the possibility of homicide. These include the absence of hesitation wounds, stabbing through clothing, and the presence of small incised wounds on the right arm and left hand (possible defensive wounds)." It was also discovered that Smith had been stabbed twice, once through a lung and the second through the heart. As of 2007, the police case is still not closed. Chiba insists that she was not involved in Smith's death.

STAR: The "First Lady of Country Music," Tammy Wynette, who was also the first female country artist to sell more than a million records with her 1968 hit "Stand by Your Man."

UNOFFICIAL STORY: Wynette died at age 55 while napping on a couch in her Nashville home in 1998. She'd had numerous medical problems over the years, as well as a prescription painkiller addiction, and had undergone several major surgeries.

CORONER'S REPORT #1: Wynette's doctor, Wallis Marsh, listed the cause of death as a blood clot in her lungs—but never performed an autopsy. The following year, Wynette's three daughters wrote to Nashville's medical examiner, Dr. Bruce Levy, and requested that their mother's body be exhumed and an autopsy performed. Levy refused. A few months later, the daughters filed a $50 million wrongful death lawsuit against Dr. Marsh for improperly prescribing narcotics to Wynette and against her husband/manager, George Richey, who, the suit said, had "maintained her narcotic addiction, administered narcotics to her, and failed to see that she would receive necessary medical treatment." Richey then requested an autopsy to defend against the allegations, and this time Levy complied.

CORONER'S REPORT #2: Levy's autopsy found that Wynette did die of heart failure due to blood clots in her lungs. But he couldn't determine whether the clots were caused by the prescriptions. "My belief is that the heart failure happened probably through a combination of natural disease and maybe or maybe not contributed to by the drugs," he said. Richey's name was dropped from the lawsuit, but in 2002, Marsh and the daughters settled the case for an undisclosed amount. "Both parties are quite happy that it's over and done with," Dr. Marsh's lawyer said.

Carl Perkins wrote the song "Blue Suede Shoes" on an old potato sack.

MUSIC MAKERS

From the harpsichord to the hurdy-gurdy, we've tracked down some of the most unique instruments that ever played a tune.

THE HARPSICHORD

The harpsichord has its roots in a dainty, harplike instrument from ancient Greece called the *psaltery*. In the 1300s, European instrument makers attached a keyboard-activated mechanism to the psaltery that used crow quills to pluck the strings. In the late 1500s, Hans Ruckers, patriarch of a Flemish keyboard-making family dynasty, made improvements to the harpsichord. He made the instrument larger, built a sturdier cabinet to house the strings, and increased the string tension, which gave it a richer sound. Other instrument makers copied his design, and by the late 1600s, the harpsichord had become the most popular instrument of its day.

The harpsichord's ethereal sound was employed widely in Baroque music. In fact, nearly all Baroque compositions include it, and composers like Bach wrote for it specifically. But the harpsichord was limited: Its strings were plucked internally (not hammered like later keyboard instruments), and that meant the musician couldn't control how loudly or how long the notes rang out. Harpsichords also were difficult to keep in tune. So in the 1700s they fell out of favor, replaced by the piano, which was louder, had a greater range, and allowed the musician more control.

Recently, though, the harpsichord has made a minor comeback—it shows up in songs from the Beatles' "She's Leaving Home" and the Doors' "Love Me Two Times" to the theme from *The Addams Family* and the Beastie Boys' "Remote Control."

Harpsichord Trivia: Henry Lim, a musician and artist in California, built a playable harpsichord out of Legos. It took him two years and 100,000 Lego pieces (in four colors: red, white, black, and tan). The only parts of the instrument not made from Legos are its wire strings.

THE HURDY-GURDY

As funny as its name sounds, the hurdy-gurdy started out in western Europe about 850 years ago with an even odder name: the *organistrum*. This three-foot-long guitar-shaped instrument had a stringed base attached to a long neck with keys. A hand crank turned a wheel inside the base, and the wheel ran along the strings the way a bow runs across a violin's strings. It took two people to play it—one turned the crank and one pressed the keys. But this made the instrument cumbersome, and it was relegated mostly to church music. Eventually, manufacturers made the organistrum smaller so that one player could both crank and press. It looked a little like a bulky violin and had a droning sound like an organ or a cello.

The instrument became popular with peasants, who played it at rural dances and festivals. In the 1600s, when royals started staging pastoral plays—plays that romanticized peasant life—the organistrum made its way to the courts of Europe. During the Renaissance, the instrument became a favorite of Louis XIV and Louis XV of France. Composers like Antonio Vivaldi even wrote music for it. By the late 17th century, however, royal tastes had changed; Louis XVI didn't appreciate music as much as his predecessors had, and the organistrum fell from favor.

About a hundred years later, it reappeared in Europe. The instrument's look and sound were the same, but it had a new name: the hurdy-gurdy. No one is sure how it got that name, but there are some theories:

• 1) It's related to the English term *hurly-burly*, which means "great noise."

• 2) It comes from two English words: *hurdy* (meaning "a person's backside") and *gurdy* (a type of crank used to reel in fish on a boat).

• 3) It's an onomatopoeia (a word whose name is the sound of what it describes) for wooden wheels rolling over a bridge. (The hurdy-gurdy is sometimes also called a "wheel fiddle.")

Obscure as it is, the hurdy-gurdy is still around today. It's mostly played in folk music or among hurdy-gurdy aficionados. But Donovan, a Scottish singer/songwriter ("Sunshine Superman," "Mellow Yellow"), wrote a song called "Hurdy-Gurdy Man," released in 1968, though no one actually plays the instrument on the recording. (The droning sound in Donovan's song comes from an Indian instrument called the *tambura*.)

THE BARREL ORGAN

Small mechanical organs in a box first appeared in France about 300 years ago, and their purpose was to teach songs to the canaries and other songbirds that belonged to society ladies. Street musicians, however, saw the tiny boxes as forms of portable entertainment and a good way to make a living. The organs were operated by wooden cylinders (or "barrels") with small pins or nails attached instead of a keyboard. As the player (or organ grinder) cranked the barrel, forcing it to turn, the pins opened valves that pushed air into the instrument's pipes.

Organ grinders often used animals to attract attention. Monkeys were favorites because they were cute and could hold small cups for coins. In the early 1900s, organ grinders and their animal companions were a common sight on New York's streets and in the city's parks, most of them immigrants trying to support their families. Many people regarded them as public nuisances, however, and in 1936, the city's mayor, Fiorello LaGuardia, banned them from the city limits. Forty years later, the law was repealed, but by then, the organ grinder, his music, and his monkey were passé.

THE PLAYER PIANO

Before the player piano, there was the piano player—not the human kind, but a portable mechanism known as the Pianola. The contraption looked like a large wooden box with two foot pedals at the bottom and a roller (for piano rolls) on top. A player would sit in front of the Pianola and push the pedals with his feet. This created suction, which caused small, felt-covered wooden "fingers" to hit the piano keys in time with the tiny holes punched in a revolving paper roll. Around 1900, Melville Clark, who owned a piano company in Illinois, figured out how to make the mechanism smaller and put it inside the piano. Thus, the player piano was born.

Early player pianos played only the 65 notes in the middle of the piano. (Most pianos play 88 notes.) But in 1908, piano rolls were upgraded to an 88-note standard. Two years later, lyrics were added to the piano rolls (called word rolls) so that people could sing along. One of composer George Gershwin's early jobs was as a piano roll writer, meaning he played a song and a machine recorded where the notes should be cut into the paper roll. (Then someone used a knife and ruler to actually cut the "notes" into the paper.) Between 1916 and 1927, Gershwin recorded more than 100 rolls, some of his own compositions and some of others.

Player piano sales peaked in 1923 at 194,855, but with the popularity of radio and records—and the onset of the Great Depression—demand dropped to only 2,744 in 1931. Over the next several decades, only antique buffs took an interest in player piano restoration. Today, a new generation of computerized player pianos use high-tech software to make music (instead of paper rolls).

CAN YOU KAZOO?

The kazoo has a reputation for being a child's toy, but rock bands from the Beatles to the Cure have incorporated the little buzzing instrument into their music. Based on an African instrument called a *mirliton*, the kazoo was developed in the early 19th century by Alabama Vest, an African-American entertainer from Georgia. (Slaves had brought the mirliton over from Africa, and Vest redesigned it.) In 1852 he teamed up with German clockmaker Thaddeus Von Clegg, who manufactured the kazoo based on Vest's specifications. The duo first demonstrated it at the Georgia State Fair, and it soon became popular in the region.

Around 1900, Emil Sorg, a traveling salesman, came across a kazoo while passing through Georgia. He, too, was intrigued by the little instrument, so when he returned home to New York, he called on his friend Michael McIntyre, a tool and die maker, to figure out how to mass-produce metal kazoos. In 1923 McIntyre patented his design, abandoned his partnership with Sorg, and teamed up with Harry Richardson, who owned a sheet-metal plant in upstate New York. McIntyre and Richardson established the Original American Kazoo Company to make and sell kazoos. The business still operates today in Eden, New York.

Did You Know? Classically trained musician Barbara Stewart (who studied at the Eastman School) is a professional kazooist who has played at Carnegie Hall and Lincoln Center. She's also the kazoo's (self-proclaimed) greatest supporter and has lobbied every president since Richard Nixon to make the kazoo America's national instrument. (They've all turned her down.)

STAGE FRIGHTS

Hold up your lighter and shout "Free Bird!" for some of the biggest—and strangest—concert spectacles of all time.

• In 1992 U2 staged "Zoo TV," a multimedia extravaganza designed to satirize multimedia extravaganzas. The stage featured 1,200 tons of equipment, including 40-foot video walls playing random images along with fake commercial slogans like "Taste is the Enemy of Art" and "Everything You Know Is Wrong." Lead singer Bono portrayed several characters, including the Fly, an egotistical rock star dressed in leather and sunglasses (a look Bono has since adopted permanently).

• In 1975 Rick Wakeman, keyboardist for the band Yes, recorded *The Myths and Legends of King Arthur and the Knights of the Round Table*, a concept album that told the story of King Arthur in music. Then he decided to stage it…on ice. He couldn't find any backers, so at his own expense, Wakeman rented out London's Wembley Stadium and produced the show in which all of the characters (King Arthur, Merlin, etc.) were portrayed by figure skaters.

• The centerpiece of funk band Parliament's 1976 "P-Funk Earth Tour" was a 50-foot-long spaceship called the Holy Mothership. At the beginning of the concert, the Mothership, complete with lights, sound effects, and pyrotechnics, descended from the arena's rafters (it looked a lot like the spaceship in *E.T.*). The band was already playing as frontman George Clinton would emerge from the ship as the character "Dr. Funkenstein."

• Pink Floyd's 1980 live version of its double album *The Wall* was so elaborate that it could only be staged in five cities worldwide. In addition to video screens, fireworks, and giant inflatable puppets, roadies used cardboard bricks to build a wall onstage between the band and the audience (to express the album's theme of the mental "wall of separation" caused by the anxiety of being a rock star). During the first half of the show, the wall was built. In the second half, the band played while almost completely obscured by cardboard bricks.

Actual dimensions of a record: a 12" disc (LP) is 11.89", and a 7" disc (45 rpm) is 6.89".

THE ORIGIN OF RAP

The definition of rap music is quite simple: it's essentially words spoken over a beat. As straightforward as that is, its origins are murky.

BACKGROUND
Rap hit the mainstream in 1980 with its first hit, "Rapper's Delight" by the Sugarhill Gang. Then Blondie included a rap in their 1981 song "Rapture," and the style quickly became a cultural phenomenon. But because rap seemed to explode into public consciousness fully formed, its origins were unclear. Music critics and historians have several theories about where it came from. Which one is right?

THEORY #1: Rap originated in Jamaica.
STORY: In the 1960s, the mobile discotheque was a popular form of entertainment in Jamaican ghettos. Two guys with a turntable, microphone, and generator would travel around and throw parties, playing all kinds of dance records. One guy, the DJ, would play the records while the other, a "chanter," would chant in rhyme to keep audiences entertained and engaged while the DJ switched records. Audiences ultimately liked the chanters better than the records, so the chanters started making their own recordings, speaking in rhyme to drumbeats. The first Jamaican rap records include "Ska-Ing West" by Sir Lord Comic and His Cowboys (1963), as well as songs by groups like Big Youth, U-Roy, and King Stitt the Ugly One.

THEORY #2: Rap came from "breakbeats."
STORY: DJ Kool Herc (or Kool DJ Herc, as he was sometimes billed) was a party DJ from the West Bronx who came up with what he called "breakbeating" in 1972. Herc would locate the instrumental "dance breaks" (or "breakdowns") in funk songs, then isolate and repeat them over and over by scratching, pausing, and repeating that section of the record (his favorites were Michael Viner's "Bongo Rock" and James Brown's *Sex Machine* LP). That meant that Herc could play the instrumental, percussion-heavy

funk bits through all-night parties. He got so good at it that his parties became hot Bronx attractions in the mid-1970s. To add to his show, he recruited a group of performers he called the Herculoids, who would psych the crowd up with rhyming chants delivered over the "breakbeats."

Where'd Herc get the idea? He was from Jamaica, and was familiar with mobile discotheque chanters. The breakbeat—and speaking in rhythm and rhyme—became the basis of rap music. Rap artists expanded their choice of breakbeats beyond funk records. For example, the beat in "Rapper's Delight" is from the disco song "Good Times" by Chic and the music in Afrika Baambaata's "Planet Rock" is from "Trans-Europe Express," by the 1970s German electronic music group Kraftwerk.

THEORY #3: It came from free-verse poetry.
STORY: In the late 1950s and early 1960s, African-American playwright and poet LeRoi Jones (who later changed his name to Amiri Baraka) performed political poetry in free verse (poetry without rhyme or specific structure) with accompaniment by the New York Art Ensemble's jazz improvisation. Then in 1969, a group of Black Nationalist poets from New York formed a group called the Last Poets. They recited politically-charged and provocative poetry (like "Black Wish," "Wake Up, N******," and "N****** Are Scared of Revolution") to conga drumbeats, and later to jazz and funk music. Their self-titled first album actually made it to the Billboard R&B Top 10 in 1970. Many music critics believe that rap came from these poetry movements because, like rap, they combined traditional black musical forms with spoken word that described the African-American experience.

THEORY #4: It came from hype men.
STORY: In the late 1970s, DJs usually played disco records at New York City house parties. To get people excited, the DJ would use a microphone to yell out and repeat phrases like "Clap your hands" and "Y'all ready to party?" and other chants about partying or having a good time. It evolved to where DJs would bring friends along with them to call these phrases into the microphone all night. At first the friends were called "hype men," but

later were called MCs (master of ceremonies). This arrangement—a DJ concentrating on spinning, mixing, and scratching records with an MC talking all night—made its way to dance clubs. With the music playing, the hype men naturally started to turn their observations about partying into rhythmic chants to match the music.

*   *   *

24 YEARS OF RAP HITS

1979: "Rapper's Delight" Sugar Hill Gang

1980: "The Breaks" (Kurtis Blow)

1981: "Drop the Bomb" (Trouble Funk)

1982: "The Message" (Grandmaster Flash)

1983: "Cookie Puss" (Beastie Boys)

1984: "Roxanne, Roxanne" (UTFO)

1985: "La-Di-Da-Di" (Slick Rick)

1986: "Walk This Way" (Run DMC)

1987: "Push It" (Salt N' Pepa)

1988: "Straight Outta Compton" (NWA)

1989: "Fight the Power" (Public Enemy)

1990: "Damn It Feels Good to Be a Gangsta" (Geto Boys)

1991: "Summertime" (DJ Jazzy Jeff & The Fresh Prince)

1992: "They Want EFX" (Das EFX)

1993: "Gin and Juice" (Snoop Dogg)

1994: "I Used to Love H.E.R."(Common)

1995: "Gangsta's Paradise" (Coolio)

1996: "Tha Crossroads" (Bone Thugs-N-Harmony)

1997: "Hypnotize" (Notorious BIG)

1998: "Hard Knock Life" (Jay-Z)

1999: "Guilty Conscience" (Eminem & Dr. Dre)

2000: "Ms. Jackson" (Outkast)

2001: "5 Million Ways to Kill a CEO" (The Coup)

2002: "One Mic" (Nas)

Crooner Michael Feinstein named his production company, Bing Clawsby Music, after his cat.

JOBRIATH

It's a story as old as the music business: the rising star who gets destroyed by the greedy people around him. Here's what happened to the singer who was supposed to be the next '70s superstar.

GLAMARAMA

After a year of acting in a Los Angeles production of the musical *Hair*, 24-year-old actor/singer Bruce Wayne Campbell decided to chase his dream of becoming a rock musician. So he moved to New York in 1970 and joined a progressive rock band called Pidgeon. They recorded one album that didn't sell well, so Campbell tried his hand at a solo career.

The hottest thing in rock music at the time was *glam*, a combination of guitar-driven pop and psychedelic rock performed by male singers in heavy makeup that made them look androgynous or even alienlike. Some of the most theatrical glam-rock acts were Marc Bolan and T. Rex, Gary Glitter, and David Bowie.

Campbell came up with a stage name, Jobriath (pronounced joe-bray-ith), and wrote and recorded a glam-rock demo tape. Every record label he sent it to thought it was terrible. Particularly critical was Columbia Records president Clive Davis, who called the music "mad and unstructured and destructive to melody."

Not helping Jobriath's marketability was the fact that he was openly gay. Despite the popularity of glam, the biggest rock stars of the day were macho men like Robert Plant of Led Zeppelin and Roger Daltrey of the Who. For the most part, in 1971, being gay meant being *secretly* gay.

LABEL MAKER

Music agent Jerry Brandt heard through the grapevine about an awful young glam singer trying to get a deal. He was particularly intrigued with Jobriath when he heard what Clive Davis had said about him. Brandt wondered what the music truly sounded like; if it was as raw and rebellious as Davis claimed, it might be marketable for just those reasons. In 1972 Brandt met with Jobriath,

---

London's Westminster clock tower (Big Ben) chimes part of Handel's *Messiah* on the ¼-hour.

and became convinced that the singer's strange music and shock-
ingly open homosexuality were going to make them both rich.
Jobriath was as flamboyant and effeminate as David Bowie, he
reasoned, but instead of hinting at sexuality, Jobriath would be
blunt about it. Brandt signed him to an exclusive 10-year management deal.

Brandt was an expert at making others believe his hype, and
Elektra Records president Jac Holzman bought the pitch. Elektra
signed Jobriath to a $500,000 contract—at the time, the largest
recording deal in history for a first-time artist.

MEDIA PUSH

In the 1950s and '60s, most rock and pop stars rose to fame slowly
and organically. Elvis Presley started by recording singles in a tiny
Tennessee studio and toured relentlessly to build up his name. The
Beatles made it big in England after years of playing clubs around
Europe, and then found success in the United States.

But in 1972, Brandt set out to make Jobriath the first mass-
marketed overnight success. He convinced Elektra to spend hundreds of thousands of dollars to promote Jobriath with full-page
ads in *Vogue*, the *New York Times*, and *Penthouse*, along with a 50-
by-50-foot billboard in Times Square depicting him shirtless.
Jobriath was booked to perform on the popular TV show *Midnight
Special*, and was set to embark on a nationwide concert tour upon
the release of his first album, scheduled for 1973. Meanwhile, custom drag-queen-meets-alien costumes were ordered from fashion
designer Stephen Sprouse for the upcoming concerts.

DON'T BELIEVE THE HYPE

Elektra Records, Brandt, and Jobriath himself were so confident
that Jobriath was the next big star that they openly dismissed the
inevitable comparisons to David Bowie. "Jobriath is as different
from Bowie as a Lamborghini is from a Model A Ford," Brandt
boasted. "They're both cars; it's just a question of taste, style, ele-
gance, and beauty."

The debut album, titled *Jobriath*, was released in 1973. Despite
nearly a year's worth of hype, the album—to the surprise of critics—wasn't bad. *Cashbox* gave it a rave review, while *Rolling Stone*
reported, "Jobriath has talent to burn."

But the record-buying public wasn't convinced. *Jobriath* ultimately sold fewer than 50,000 copies—a crushing disappointment compared to the millions it was expected to sell. The concert tour was canceled, along with a scheduled performance at the Paris Opera House. The world's first mass-marketed pop star was a complete and utter flop.

What went wrong? As Jac Holzman later reflected, "The music seemed secondary to everything else. It was lacking in any sense of reality. It's an embarrassment."

NO SECOND ACT

Not quite ready to give up on its huge investment, Elektra rushed a second Jobriath album, *Creatures of the Street*, to stores in 1974. Culled from unused, unfinished songs from the first album's recording sessions, it didn't get much marketing support from Elektra, and critics hated it. It sold only a few hundred copies.

Though Brandt had orchestrated every aspect of Jobriath's career, in 1975 he refused to work with the singer ever again. But the experience was such an embarrassment to Brandt that he held Jobriath to his 10-year contract, forbidding him to record again until 1983 (not that the music industry was interested anyway).

Jobriath went into semiretirement. He'd wisely held onto his windfall from the Elektra contract, and used the money to build a giant glass pyramid house on the roof of the Chelsea Hotel in New York. He went back to using his real name, Bruce Wayne Campbell, and auditioned for a role in the movie *Dog Day Afternoon* (the part of Al Pacino's transsexual wife, a role that went to Chris Sarandon instead).

THE END

Campbell built a modest recording studio in his home and actually recorded a third Jobriath album. But with his sales history, no record company wanted it (and the tapes were later lost). Campbell wrote a series of unproduced rock musicals, including an autobiographical one about his Jobriath years called *Pop Star*. Over the next few years, he occasionally performed in New York nightclubs and at parties in the guise of a cabaret singer named Cole Berlin.

Campbell died at home of AIDS in August 1983. He had become such a recluse that his body wasn't discovered for several days. Ironically, his 10-year contract had expired just a few weeks earlier.

Although he never found mainstream success, Jobriath earned the admiration of many hardcore fans. One of them was rock singer Morrissey, formerly of the Smiths. When Morrissey was preparing for a concert tour in 2004, he was hoping his old hero, Jobriath, would agree to be his opening act. But when he tried to track Jobriath down, he was shocked to find that the reclusive star had been dead for more than 20 years. As a tribute, Morrissey reissued Jobriath's two albums on a compilation CD called *Lonely Planet Boy*. And in 2007, Elektra included a Jobriath song on their five-CD collection, *Forever Changing: The Golden Age of Elektra 1963–1973*. His song, "World Without End," is song #117 in the set (the last song on disc 5).

* * *

TEST YOUR GRAMMY I.Q.

1. In 1965, the bestselling record of the year was "Satisfaction"; the Beatles recorded *Help!*; Motown was tearing up the charts. The Grammy winner that year for Best Vocal Group was:

  a) The Beatles **b)** The Supremes **c)** The Anita Kerr Quartet
  d) Steve Brummet & His Polka Pals **e)** The Mamas & the Papas

2. What performer won a Best Vocalist Grammy for a song she'd written about *not* receiving the award a few years earlier?

  a) Roseanne Cash **b)** Dolly Parton **c)** Carole King

3. In 1996 John Popper, harmonica player for Blues Traveler, pulled off a Grammy first when he jumped out of his seat to get an award, and…

  a) He tore a ligament in his leg **b)** His pants fell down
  c) He tripped and fell

ANSWERS

1. c. 2. a. 3. a.

Before it opened on Broadway, the original title of the musical *Oklahoma!* was *Away We Go!*

CRÉME de la CRUD

Here's a list of some of the worst records of all time. It's hard to believe, but all of these recordings are real. Why would anyone make them? We'll never know. Some mysteries are beyond human understanding.

MUSIC TO MAKE AUTOMOBILES BY. Volkswagen made this recording "to inspire their workers." It features the exciting sounds of an auto assembly line, backed by an orchestra.

"GRANNY'S MINI-SKIRT"
A bluegrass "rap" song from Irene Ryan, who played Granny on *The Beverly Hillbillies.* According to the lyrics, she decided to learn to Twist and Jerk, and started wearing a miniskirt. Only trouble is, the sight of her knobby knees is makin' ol' Grandpa sick.

SOUND EFFECT OF GODZILLA ONE. This Japanese import consists entirely of Godzilla sound effects. One critic said, "You can drop the needle anywhere and basically you'll hear Godzilla going 'Rarr...Rarr.' That's it."

SOUND EFFECTS: U.S. AIR FORCE FIREPOWER. Tracks include recordings of real Air Force attacks and exercises, including "Mass Napalm Attack by F-100s" and "Psychological Warfare, Public Address from C-47," where they announce (with helicopter sounds in the background) "Clear the village! We are about to strafe and bomb it!"

THE SOUND OF COMBAT TRAINING. Recorded live at the United States Army Training Center, Fort Knox, Kentucky. Tracks include: "Inoculation," "Mess Hall," and "Gas Chamber Exercise."

BOBBY BREAUX AND THE POT-BELLIED PIG. Drummer Bobby Breaux collaborated with a 450-pound boar named Rebel after noticing that his grunts sounded like he was humming a tune. Features "Amazing Grease" and "Hava Nasquela." Breaux backed the pig up on drums and synthesizer.

Most Tony Awards for a musical: 12, for *The Producers. Hello Dolly* is #2, with 10.

THE CREPITATION CONTEST (THE POWER OF POSITIVE STINKING). A whole album of nothing but farting. From the liner notes: "If you put your fingers in your ears, you can't hold your nose. If you hold your nose, you'll have to listen..."

NORAD TRACKS SANTA. A Cold War classic recorded in 1962. NORAD's (North American Air Defense) job was to protect the United States from enemy air attacks. Interspersed with standard Christmas music are NORAD reports on Santa Claus—basically, whether or not he's going to be shot down.

THE CANARIES: THE SONGS OF CANARIES WITH MUSIC. This album by the Artal Orchestra "mixes canary songs with waltzes such as 'Jeannie with the Light Brown Hair' and 'Wine, Women and Song.'"

MERRY CHRISTMAS FROM THE BRADY BUNCH. The six Brady kids were herded into a studio, where a producer barked out a list of songs that each would perform. He didn't bother to ask if they could sing. Barry Williams, who played Greg Brady, tells the story of being forced to sing the difficult "O Holy Night" despite the fact that his pubescent voice kept cracking: "I think I made the recording guy's ears bleed." He adds: "Should you ever come across this particular album in a record store, I suggest you run screaming in the opposite direction."

ADRIAN MUNSEY AND THE LOST SHEEP. The album features Munsey and a bunch of baaa-ing sheep recorded live in a small English studio. "There are thirty million sheep and nineteen million lambs in the U.K.," he intones, "This record is about three of them." Munsey's follow-up: a disco tune called "C'est Sheep."

PLANT TALK. The jacket says it all: "Treat yourself by listening to Molly Roth (a plant shop owner) talk to your Philodendron, Schefflera, Palm Tree, and many others." Sample: "Do you speak English, Ivy? What's the matter, why are you so droopy? Oh I see, your person really poured water to you. You don't like wet feet, do you?"

MUSICAL PRESIDENTS, PART III

The last installment of our musical tour of the White House takes us from the '60s to the present day. (Part II begins on page 289.)

RICHARD NIXON (1969–74)

"I have always had two great—and still unfulfilled—ambitions: to direct a symphony orchestra and to play an organ in a cathedral." In fact, during his tumultuous White House years, music was one of the few solaces for Nixon—who was skilled at both the piano and the accordion. Nixon loved all kinds of music, especially classical and jazz.

JIMMY CARTER (1977–81)

Colonel John Bourgeois, director of the United States Marine Band, said that "of all the presidents with whom I have worked, President Carter had the most extensive knowledge of classical music." Carter often used musical analogies to describe his job. "I think when you hear the *1812 Overture*," he said at a press conference, "it will remind you of the kind of breakfast that I have with the congressional leaders every two weeks." But his musical appreciation was more polished than his musical ability. "I'm not a good singer," he said. "On a few occasions I've been on the platform with Willie Nelson and he invites me to sing 'Amazing Grace' with him as a finale, he turns the microphone away so people can't hear me."

RONALD REAGAN (1981–89)

A novice piano player ("For a while there I almost convinced myself I could play"), Reagan took the road less traveled when it came to music...literally. "Once when I was a drum major leading my high school band in a parade, I was aware that the music was growing fainter and fainter behind me. Soon I knew they had gone one way and I another—and I had just marched out of my musical career."

GEORGE H. W. BUSH (1989–93)

"When I want to feel a surge of patriotism, I turn to country music."

BILL CLINTON (1993–2001)

Many credit Clinton's saxophone playing on *The Arsenio Hall Show* as one of the pivotal moments during his 1992 presidential campaign. His performances at rallies made him more appealing to younger voters. But Clinton's love of music wasn't just for show—he actually loves playing, and has for most of his life (during his two terms in office, Clinton often jammed with the Marine Band). When talking about music, he waxes philosophical:

> Music, to me, is kind of representative of everything I like most in life. It's beautiful and fun but very rigorous. If you want to be good, you have to work like crazy. My musical life experiences were just as important to me, in terms of forming my development, as my political experiences or my academic life.

GEORGE W. BUSH (2001–)

It's no secret that Bush, like his father, is a country music fan. But the public got a much more detailed look at the president's musical tastes when the contents of "iPod One" were leaked to the press in 2005. As expected, the country standards were there, including tunes by George Jones, Alan Jackson, and Kenny Chesney—but a few surprise artists showed up as well: Van Morrison, Bryan Adams, Robert Palmer, Joni Mitchell, John Fogerty (who campaigned for Bush's opponent in 2004), and the 1979 pop hit "My Sharona" by the Knack. These selections prompted the media to play "analyze the president" based on his song list. Here are some of the results:

• "This is basically boomer rock 'n' roll—safe, reliable feel-good music. The Sex Pistols it's not." —*Rolling Stone*

• "No black or gay artists, no world music, only one woman, no genre less than 25 years old, and no Beatles." —*London Times*

• "One of the lines in 'My Sharona'—'such a dirty mind / always get it up for the touch of the younger kind'—is inconsistent with Bush's image as protector of conservative values." —*Spin*

• "If any president limited his music selection to pro-establishment musicians, it would be a pretty slim collection. No one should psychoanalyze the song selection. It's simply music to get over the next hill." —Mark McKinnon, Bush's cycling partner

CHANNELING NATA2

*Have you been turned into a Satan-worshipping zombie by listening
to rock music? Neither have we. But you may have heard
that it can happen…according to some people.*

BACK(WARD)GROUND

The story of "backmasking," the studio technique of
recording music or other sounds, then playing them backward and rerecording them, began in the 1930s. But the concept
is much older.

> "This evening I found out something good. When the machine
> runs by regulated power the singing is sweet, but turning the cylin-
> der backward the song is still melodious in many cases and some of
> the strains are sweet and novel, but altogether different from the
> song reproduced in the right way."

That's Thomas Edison talking about his phonograph in 1878. But
he never recorded backward sounds. That would come a few years
later.

HARD CONCRETE

In the 1940s, French composer Pierre Schaeffer founded an
avant-garde music movement that he named *musique concrète*—
"concrete music." The idea behind it was that he and his fellow
composers took "concrete" or "unmusical" sounds like trains,
automobiles, animals, footsteps, etc., and manipulated them into
a new kind of music. Schaeffer had developed the technique in
the 1930s while working as a radio broadcaster and experimenting with the technology of magnetic tape recording, which had
just been invented in 1928. Schaeffer manipulated sounds by
manipulating tapes: he slowed them down, sped them up, cut up
sections of tape, and reassembled them haphazardly. In the midst
of such experimentation, he became the first known person to
record a sound, then turn the tape around and rerecord it, resulting in the sound being reversed. The musique concrète movement later influenced several pop artists, Frank Zappa and Pink
Floyd among them. But the first band known to use the reversed
technique in pop music (and it's not known whether they were

aware of Schaeffer's work) was the band that specialized in musical firsts—the Beatles.

RAIN MAN

In 1966 the Beatles released the song "Rain" as the B-side of the single "Paperback Writer." Said John Lennon: "After we'd done the session on that particular song—it ended at about four or five in the morning—I went home with a tape to see what else we could do with it. I was very tired, you know, not knowing what I was doing, and I just happened to put it on my own tape recorder and it came out backward. And I liked it better."

On the final mix of the song, they included a bit of John's vocals backward, making "Rain" not only the first pop song to be released with reversed sounds in it, but also the first with reversed *words*. During the last verse, the lyrics "Sunshine / Rain / When the rain comes, they run and hide their heads" (the words to the song's first verse) can be heard when the song is played backward. Anyone could do this on a phonograph by manually spinning a record backward with the needle on it. The band didn't do it to influence people (satanically or otherwise), but because they enjoyed experimenting with sounds in the studio.

The last song on the Beatles' 1966 album *Revolver*, "Tomorrow Never Knows," also contains backmasking—a lot of it—and is considered the first "psychedelic" song in music history. (Lennon later admitted that it was heavily influenced by his experiences with LSD.) The song features recordings of drums, guitar, orchestra, sitar, Mellotron, and vocals, most notably Paul McCartney screaming, all played backward.

DAED SI LUAP

Most of the reverse taping techniques employed by the Beatles were ignored by the larger public...until the "Paul is dead" phenomenon hit. On October 12, 1969, DJ Russell Gibb of WKNR-FM in Dearborn, Michigan, got a call from "Tom," a student at Eastern Michigan University, who claimed that Paul McCartney had been dead since 1966 and a substitute had taken his place. For proof, he told Gibb to play the 1968 song "Revolution 9" in reverse and listen for a phrase. Gibb did. And he heard, "Turn me on, dead man...turn me on, dead man...turn me on, dead man" Another clue: the words "Paul is a dead man, miss him, miss him, miss him" were heard when the song "I'm So Tired" was played backward.

Paul wasn't dead, but the "Paul is dead" story became *huge* news, and it made the subject of backmasking huge along with it. The technique began to be used more and more by popular musicians over the next decade, until it was noticed by people who not only didn't like it...they thought it was sinister.

HEAR NO EVIL

In the late 1970s, fundamentalist Christian churches in the United States, many of which had been against rock 'n' roll since its inception, began claiming that backward messages in songs were subconsciously influencing children in harmful ways. Many even said that satanists were involved and were using the technique to "recruit" children. The story became so big that it even made it onto the evening news on CBS, with Dan Rather playing Electric Light Orchestra and Led Zeppelin songs backward to listen for hidden messages. Sometimes there *were* messages hidden in the songs—because the bands put them there for kicks—but usually it only *seemed* as if they were...by people looking for them.

The antibackmasking debate became so charged that two states enacted legislation against it. A bill introduced in California in 1983 sought to prevent any reverse messages that "can manipulate our behavior without our knowledge or consent and turn us into disciples of the Antichrist." The bill passed. (It was later revoked.) Another was introduced in Arkansas, calling for albums with backmasking to include warning labels. It passed too, but was vetoed by Governor Bill Clinton.

EXTREME CASE

The furor over backward messages hit its peak when one band, England's Judas Priest, was actually sued over it. In 1985 two young men from Reno, Nevada, 20-year-old James Vance and 19-year-old Ray Belknap, shot themselves. Belknap died instantly; Vance survived, but was horribly disfigured. He overdosed on painkillers three years later. During those three years, a painfully depressed Vance said that he and his friend had been driven to make a suicide pact, in part, by heavy metal music. "I believe that alcohol and heavy metal music, such as Judas Priest, led us or even 'mesmerized' us into believing that the answer to 'life was death,'" he wrote in a letter in 1986. Vance's and Belknap's parents sued Judas Priest and at the trial claimed they'd found a subliminal message in the song "Better By You, Better Than Me" from the 1978 album *Stained Class*, one of Belknap's and Vance's favorites. The "message," which they said could be heard only when listening very carefully to the song backward, was "Do it. Do it."

The band seemed perplexed. In a documentary made about the case, lead singer Rob Halford said that if he was going to try to subliminally influence his audience, it would be with the message "Buy more records." The suit was dismissed by the judge.

BACKWARD TO THE FUTURE

In the 1980s, the dominance of CDs, which cannot easily be played backward, made the subject of backmasking virtually disappear. But when digital sound recording improved—and listening to music backward became easier than ever (you can do it with a click of a mouse today)—it regained some of its popularity. It has not revived a "Satan is coming for your children!" movement (yet), but it is finding its way back into popular music. Some modern examples:

• Beck's 1994 hit "Loser" has the words "I'm a loser baby / So why don't you kill me?" backward and forward in the song.

• Cake's 1994 song "Jesus Wrote a Blank Check" contains the backward words "Don't forget to breathe in."

• Tenacious D, the duo of Jack Black and Kyle Gass, put a hidden message at the end of their 2001 song "Karate." It says, "Eat donkey crap."

• The 2002 song "Stimulate" by Eminem has the message "I'm not here to save you / I'm only here for the ride / So let me entertain you / And everything will be fine."

*   *   *

"I have no pleasure in any man who despises music. It is no invention of ours: it is a gift of God. I place it next to theology. Satan hates music: he knows how it drives the evil spirit out of us."

—Martin Luther, 1483-1546

MOZART'S CONCERTO IN G MAJOR FOR PIANO AND STARLING

*Polly doesn't want a cracker—she wants a piano,
a pen, and some blank sheet music.*

SONGSTERS

European starlings have long been known as extraordinarily musical, and teachable, songbirds. Tales of their abilities go back to the ancient Greeks, and are even mentioned by Shakespeare (*Henry IV*). In 1990 Meredith J. West, Professor of Wildlife and Biology, and Andrew P. King, Professor of Psychology, both of Indiana University, published the results of a study in *American Scientist* magazine. Over the course of 10 years they studied 14 pet starlings in a variety of social settings—from a lot of interaction with humans, to nearly none. They compared recordings of the different birds to gauge whether they just mimicked—or if they created their own "music." Turns out they do both.

European starlings are amazingly good mimics. They regularly fool their owners with calls that can sound like such things as a door opening, a baby crying, silverware falling, and human voices so perfectly that you'd swear there was someone in the room with you. They even learn to use words at apt times: one regularly said "Goodbye" when someone put a coat on; one would fly around the kitchen sink crying "Water!"; another would shout "Defense!" when the TV came on (its owner was a basketball fan).

BASIC RESEARCH

As for music, the birds quickly learned melodies that were played or whistled to them. But the most curious thing West and King found was that regardless of what the starlings learned, once they learned it—they changed it and made it their own. They'd sing the beginning of a tune, then end it with part of another. Repeatedly.

They almost never played a tune as they had originally learned it from their owners. They were *improvising*. And they did it with human speech they'd learned, too. One bird had learned the phrase "basic research," and would mix it with other phrases he'd learned, coming up with things like "Basic research, it's true, I guess that's right."

So why were the birds rewriting songs and phrases? West cites another part of the finding: The birds in the study who had little contact with humans, but were played *recordings* of songs, did not improvise off of those songs. They did improvise with the calls of other birds they were kept with—but not recordings. That shows not only that starlings learn from those around them, but that they must "like" it, or get rewarded for it somehow. Some of that reward may be simply to stimulate social contact (and isn't that at least one reason humans make music?). Evidence strongly suggests that a give-and-take of that kind must have happened between Wolfgang Amadeus Mozart and his own pet starling.

THIS SONG'S FOR YOU

On May 27, 1784, Mozart waked into a Vienna, Austria, pet shop and bought himself a European starling. Later that day, the 28-year-old composer wrote a short note in his ledger next to a note about the purchase of the bird—a short, jotted musical score consisting of five measures and 17 notes, along with the words "*Das war schön!*" ("That was beautiful!").

Was it a tune the bird had sung? Music historians believe so… and it's also the melodic theme of the final movement of Mozart's Piano Concerto in G Major, which was catalogued as finished a month earlier, in April—but hadn't yet been performed in public. Did Mozart borrow the tune from the bird and add it to his concerto? Nobody knows for sure, but if he'd finished the piece with the melodic theme as it was, in April, why would he remark "Das war schön!" in May? We'll never know for sure what happened—but it does make you wonder. And it's not be the only time the bird is suspected of influencing the master's work.

FLY AWAY HOME

Mozart's pet starling died on June 4, 1787. He gave it a lavish funeral—several friends attended and hymns were sung as it was lowered into its grave. (Historians are quick to point out that the emotion may have been amplified by the fact that Mozart's own father had died just a week earlier.) He even wrote an elegy for the bird, a section of which reads:

A little fool lies here
Whom I held dear—
A starling in the prime
Of his brief time...

A month later Mozart finished a short composition for six instruments titled "A Musical Joke." It is, nearly all critics agree, incoherent, rambling, unstructured, off-key, and just plain bad. In other words, says Professor West of Indiana University, the piece contains "the compositional autograph...of a starling."

*　　*　　*

TWO CHARACTERS INSPIRED BY SONGS

• **Austin Powers.** Here's how comedian Mike Myers creates his characters: "Something hits my ear and it kind of happens. Usually it's music. I was driving home from hockey practice one day and I heard 'The Look of Love' [Burt Bacharach's sultry song, featured in the 1967 version of *Casino Royale*] and I wondered, 'What happened to swingers?'"

• **Scooby-Doo.** In 1969 Fred Silverman was in charge of children's programming at CBS. He pitched an idea to the network for a Saturday morning cartoon called *Who's Scared?* about five mystery-solving teenagers and their dog (who only had a small part). The network rejected it. Reason: too scary for kids. Silverman was stuck...until he heard the Frank Sinatra song, "Strangers in the Night," while listening to headphones on a plane ride. Silverman was struck by the nonsense line, "Scooby-dooby-doo." It suddenly struck him that it would be a great name for the dog—and they could switch the focus to Scooby (inspired by Bob Hope's cowardly movie persona). That would make the show funny instead of scary. The network agreed, and *Scooby-doo, Where Are You?* was born.

Julie Andrews had mastered a 4-octave singing range by age 8. Average person's range: 3 octaves.

TOILETTO!

Musical scores are loaded with Italian terms, directing the musicians how to play. Ever played in an orchestra? Then you probably won't recognize these, which are molto humoroso.

Adagio fromaggio: to play in a slow and cheesy manner.

Al Capóne: music played at machine-gun speed.

An Dante: a musical composition that is infernally slow.

Angus Dei: to play with a divine but beefy tone.

A patella: unaccompanied knee-slapping.

Approximento: a musical entrance that is somewhat close to the correct pitch.

Crashendo: the increasing sense of aggravation felt by band members as the percussionists keep dropping their cymbals on the floor.

Diminuendo: the process of hushing a rumor in the orchestra pit.

Kvetchendo: gradually—and annoyingly—getting louder.

Molto Bolto: head straight for the ending, but don't make it seemed rushed.

Mucho caffeinato: play loudly enough to wake up those sleeping in the audience.

OraToro: a lawn mower may be substituted for the original instrumentation at this point.

Pescado: fish around until you find the right note.

Poochini: when singing, to be accompanied by your dog.

Schmaltzando: a sudden burst of sickly-sweet music.

Spritzicato: plucking of a stringed instrument to produce a bright, bubbly sound, usually accompanied by sparkling water with lemon (wine optional).

Tempe Arizona: a particularly hot passage.

Tempo Tantrum: what a young orchestra is having when it's not keeping time with the conductor.

Toiletto: the reverberating effect heard when singing in small rooms with ceramic tiles.

Vesuvioso: a gradual buildup to a fiery conclusion.

Journalist Walter Winchell coined the term "disc jockey" for radio announcer Martin Block.

MAKE ROOM
FOR MOTOWN

*As one of the most influential record labels in the history of popular music,
Motown introduced the world to a talented group of artists who might
have gone unnoticed without the tenacity of Berry Gordy Jr.*

SHOP AROUND

The Gordys were one of Detroit's most prominent African-American families. Berry Gordy Sr. ran a construction business and all of his children, including Berry Gordy Jr., were musicians, earning the family the title of "America's Most Talented Family" in a 1949 issue of *Color* magazine.

Gordy Jr. wanted to be a both a songwriter and a boxer, but he pursued the latter when he dropped out of high school in 1946. He was drafted into the army in 1950, fought in the Korean War, and returned in Detroit in 1953, where he got married and realized that he couldn't support a family with boxing. So, while writing songs at night, he borrowed some money from his father and opened 3-D Record Mart, a jazz music store. The shop closed down in 1955 and Gordy got a job at the Lincoln-Mercury auto plant. But he kept writing songs.

THROUGH THE GRAPEVINE

Gordy's sisters introduced him to Al Green, the owner of the Flame Show Bar in Detroit. The city had produced a lot of R&B stars in the 1950s, and through Green, Gordy met R&B superstar Jackie Wilson, who in 1957 bought two songs Gordy had written. Both of them, "Reet Petite" and "Lonely Teardrops" became hits.

Gordy earned some songwriting royalties, but didn't think it was what he deserved (and he'd co-written "Lonely Teardrops," so he had to split the proceeds with his partner Billy Davis). He realized that the people truly making money in the industry were the people who owned the record labels.

Amazingly, Gordy turned down his first shot at running a record company. His sisters Anna and Gwen (along with Gordy's writing partner Billy Davis) started Anna Records in 1959 and asked him to be president. Not wanting to have to split the proceeds with three other people, Gordy turned down the offer and, with an $800 loan from his parents, started his own label, Tamla Records, which he later renamed after his hometown of Detroit, the "motor city": Motown.

AIN'T NO MOUNTAIN HIGH ENOUGH

Later that year, Gordy bought a house on West Grand Boulevard in Detroit. Gordy and his wife lived upstairs, and downstairs were the music studio and business offices of Motown. He nicknamed it "Hitsville U.S.A."

Because at the time there were no record labels that recorded predominantly African-American artists or music, and because there were a lot of African-American musicians in Detroit, Gordy made Motown a label for black R&B music. The first artists he signed were Mable John, Mary Wells ("My Guy"), and Barrett Strong, who sang Motown's first hit record (written by Gordy), "Money (That's What I Want)," which reached #2 in 1959.

The success of that song made Motown instantly successful. The label's first million-selling single was 1960's "Shop Around" by the Miracles and its first #1 national hit was "Please Mr. Postman" by the Marvelettes in 1961. Not only was Gordy the first African-American to own a record label, he was one of the most successful label owners...period.

UPTIGHT? EVERYTHING'S ALRIGHT

Motown defined R&B—and pop music—in the 1960s. From 1961 to 1971, Motown had 110 Top 10 hits by artists including Marvin Gaye, the Temptations, the Four Tops, the Supremes, and Stevie Wonder. How did Gordy ensure so many hits? A musical assembly line. Staff songwriters, including Smokey Robinson, Mickey Stevenson, Brian Holland, Eddie Holland, Norman Whitfield, and Lamont Dozier (as well as Gordy himself) wrote virtually every Motown single. Then the singer would record the track with Motown's band of session musicians, the Funk Brothers. Because of this, 1960s Motown hits have a distinctive, consistent sound, characterized by melodic bass lines and lots of snare drum, tambourine, and horns.

While the music was African-American oriented, Gordy want-

Sheryl Crow started her singing career as a backup singer on Michael Jackson's *Bad* tour.

ed it to appeal to as wide and diverse an audience as possible, so he hired model/beautician Maxine Powell to teach Motown acts to look impeccable and behave with poise, grace, and polish, to appeal to mainstream audiences. In this way, Motown developed a "look" as well as a sound. Two examples: the thick makeup and sequined, matching gowns worn by the Supremes, and the matching suits and synchronized dance moves of the Temptations.

WHERE DID OUR LOVE GO?

Motown was one of the most successful stories in music history, and songwriters Brian Holland, Eddie Holland, and Lamont Dozier were a major part of that. But in 1967 they accused Gordy of withholding owed royalties. Gordy wouldn't pay, so they left Motown and two new record labels, Hot Wax and Invictus. Without three of its most influential writers, the "Motown Sound" began to permanently change. Nevertheless, in 1969 Gordy signed one of its biggest acts ever, the Jackson 5.

Seeking more change and expansion, Gordy moved Motown out of Detroit in 1972, to Los Angeles. And he expanded from producing African-American-themed music into producing African-American-themed movies, including *The Wiz*, a soul-music version of *The Wizard of Oz* starring Michael Jackson of the Jackson 5, and *Lady Sings the Blues*, a movie about Billie Holiday starring Diana Ross of the Supremes.

But despite releases from superstars such as Rick James ("Super Freak") and Lionel Richie ("Hello"), by the mid-1980s, Motown's luster and prestige had faded and was losing millions of dollars annually. In 1988 Gordy sold Motown to MCA for $61 million. That might not seem much for such a record label that defined the music of an entire generation, but it wasn't a bad turnaround for Gordy, who'd started Motown on an $800 loan.

MOTOWN'S GREATEST?

The stories of some of Motown's most important artists.

Stevie Wonder

In 1962 child musical prodigy Stevie Wonder signed with Motown at age 12 and had a #1 hit a year later with "Fingertips, Part 2." The album, *The 12 Year Old Genius*, was Motown's first chart-topping album. He didn't have another hit until 1965, with "Uptight (Everything's Alright)," which may be one the definitive Motown song. In the 1970s, while still on Motown, Wonder grew both more experimental and more popular with some of the most influential R&B recordings of all time, including the albums *Talking Book*, *Innervisions*, and *Songs in the Key of Life*, and songs such as "You Are the Sunshine of My Life," "As," "Sir Duke," "Master Blaster," "Superstition," and "Higher Ground."

The Supremes
The Supremes—Diana Ross, Mary Wilson, and Florence Ballard—scored a then-record twelve #1 hits, including "Baby Love," "Come See About Me," "Stop! In the Name of Love," "You Can't Hurry Love," "I Hear a Symphony," "Someday We'll Be Together," and "Where Did Our Love Go?" The group signed with Motown in 1961 as the Primettes, a "female version" of another Motown act, the Primes (who later changed their name to the Temptations). Ross became the breakout star of the group and used her influence to get Ballard kicked out of the group in 1967, then changed the name of the group to Diana Ross and the Supremes in 1968, and ultimately left for a very successful solo career in 1970.

The Miracles
Smokey Robinson and the Miracles were the cornerstone of Motown; the band's 1960 hit "Shop Around" introduced the nation to the Motown sound. The label's most consistent hit makers, they had more than two dozen Top-40 hits in the 1960s, including "You've Really Got a Hold on Me," "Ooo Baby Baby," "The Tracks of My Tears," and "I Second That Emotion," and "The Tears of a Clown." At the center was Smokey Robinson's romantic tenor and his superb writing skills. (He also wrote #1 songs for Mary Wells and the Temptations.) Robinson left the group in the early 1970s and had several solo soft-rock hits, including "Cruisin'," "Being with You," and "Just to See Her."

The Temptations
The Temptations—Eldridge Bryant, Otis Williams, Paul Williams, Melvin Franklin, and Eddie Kendricks—came into being in 1961 as the Primes, and soon after David Ruffin replaced Bryant. The

group soon had its first Top-20 hit with "The Way You Do the Things You Do," the first of 37 hits, including "Ain't Too Proud to Beg," "My Girl," "Ball of Confusion," "Just My Imagination," and "Get Ready." Lead vocals rotated between Bryant, Ruffin, and Kendricks. The firing of Ruffin in 1968 for missing a performance began an era of personnel changes that left the group with only one original member—Otis Williams—in the 1990s. Individually, solo success was scattered: Kendricks had a #1 hit for Motown in 1973 with "Keep On Truckin'." Ruffin faded into obscurity and ultimately died of a drug overdose in 1991.

The Four Tops

Originally called the Four Aims, the group—Levi Stubbs, Abdul "Duke" Fakir, Renaldo "Obie" Benson, and Lawrence Payton— changed its name in 1956 to avoid confusion with the Ames Brothers. The lineup stayed constant from 1954 through 1997 (when Payton died of cancer). After a brief stint at Chess Records, the Four Tops joined Motown in 1963. When paired with Brian and Eddie Holland and Lamont Dozier, they started producing hits, including "Baby I Need Your Loving," "I Can't Help Myself," "It's the Same Old Song," "Standing in the Shadows of Love," and "Reach Out (I'll Be There)."

Jackson 5

A Motown executive discovered the group made up of brothers (Jackie, Tito, Jermaine, Marlon, and nine-year-old lead singer Michael) in 1968, but to drum up publicity, Gordy told reporters that Diana Ross had found them. The Jackson 5 signed to Motown in 1969. The group's first four singles ("I Want You Back," "ABC," "The Love You Save," and "I'll Be There") all went to #1, making them the first act ever to accomplish that. (Other notable hits: "Mama's Pearl," "Sugar Daddy," "Never Can Say Goodbye," and "Dancing Machine.") Their music bridged the tight, Motown R&B of the 1960s to bubblegum and into the dance and soul music of the 1970s. The Jackson 5 disbanded in 1975 when they left Motown (precipitated by Jermaine's marriage to Berry Gordy's daughter). Jermaine left the group and was replaced by brother Randy. The band was ultimately eclipsed in the 1970s and 1980s by Michael Jackson's solo career.

HAS ANYONE SEEN MY STRADIVARIUS?

Everybody knows a Stradivarius is the world's most valuable type of violin. (Read more on page 209.) So how could anyone lose one? Here are a few amazing stories of violins that got away.

VALUABLE VIOLINS

Master violin maker Antonio Stradivari created more than 1,100 instruments during his lifetime. The several hundred that survive are so valuable and so well documented, you'd think nobody would try to steal one because it would be immediately identified as stolen property. Considering their worth, you'd also think their owners would take good care of them. Guess again.

Missing! The Gruenberg Stradivarius, made in 1731; estimated value (1990): $500,000

Background: In July 1990, violinist Erich Gruenberg arrived at Los Angeles International Airport and was met by a friend. As he was loading his luggage into the friend's trunk, he let his violin case out of his sight for just a moment. When he looked back, it was gone.

Outcome: Police put out an international bulletin alerting the music world to the theft...and in April 1991, police in Honduras arrested 30-year-old Nazario Ramos when he tried to sell the violin to a member of a local orchestra. Police speculate that he was just a petty airport thief who didn't know what he was stealing until after he got it.

The violin was secretly flown back to Los Angeles. It was met at the airport by an armored car and taken immediately to a bank vault, where an insurance company executive verified that it was the genuine article. News of the violin's return was kept secret for several days. "We weren't going to give anyone a chance to steal it again," says police spokesman Bill Martin.

Missing! The Davidoff Stradivarius, made in 1727; estimated value: $3.5 million

There are 6 versions of Franz Schubert's "Die Forelle." (He made copies for friends from memory.)

Background: The Davidoff Stradivarius vanished from the Manhattan apartment of its owner, 91-year-old Erika Morini (considered one of the greatest violinists of all time) as she lay dying in a hospital a few blocks away. For years the former child prodigy had kept the violin locked away in a closet rather than in a safe, because she wanted it to be within close reach. While Morini was hospitalized, someone entered her apartment, unlocked the closet, and stole the violin, leaving an inferior violin in its place. It was insured for only $800,000.

The theft was discovered when Morini's goddaughter Erica Bradford and her daughter Valerie Bradford let themselves into the apartment to prepare it for Morini's return. Morini made it back home and lived out her last few days in the apartment, but the violin never did. Friends substituted a fake so that when she asked to see if the violin was safe, they could point to it and assure her that it was.

Outcome: The Davidoff Stradivarius is still missing. Reward: $100,000. According to news reports, Valerie Bradford "keeps failing lie detector tests and doesn't quite know why." The question she keeps failing: "Do you know who took the violin?"

"I guess I get nervous," she says.

Missing! The Duke of Alcantara Stradivarius, made in 1732; estimated value (1994): $800,000

Background: The Duke of Alcantara was owned by the University of California. On August 2, 1967, David Margetts, a second violinist with the UCLA string quartet, borrowed the violin from the university collection for a rehearsal in Hollywood. On his way home he bought some groceries and then stopped at a restaurant. When he got back to his car—which was *unlocked*—he realized the violin was gone. To this day, Margetts can't remember if he put the violin in the car after rehearsal—which would mean that somebody stole it—or if he simply left it on the roof of his car and drove off.

In January 1994, a violin dealer recognized the violin he was working on as an authentic Stradivarius. He looked it up in a reference book, found a photograph of the same violin, and discovered that it had been missing from UCLA for 27 years. It turned out the violin's "owner" was an amateur violinist named Teresa Salvato, who had gotten it from her ex-husband as part of their divorce settlement. He had gotten it from his aunt, who claimed to have found it beside a freeway in 1967. "That sort of matches the violin-left-on-the-top-of-the-car version," says Carla Shapreau, an attorney for UCLA.

Outcome: At first Salvato refused to give the violin back, but she eventually agreed to relinquish all claims of ownership in exchange for $11,500. She claims she only wanted to do the right thing for the instrument. "UCLA lost it once. They're really not very careful," she explains.

Missing! The Ex-Zimbalist Stradivarius, made in 1735; estimated value: $1 million

Background: In 1949 an NBC Symphony Orchestra violinist named David Sarser scraped together all the money he had and borrowed a little more so that he could buy the Stradivarius being sold by Efram Zimbalist Sr. (father of *The FBI* star Efram Zimbalist, Jr.). It cost him about $30,000.

"Buying that Strad got me a different life," Sarser remembers. "I was in the newspaper. I took it everywhere with me, and everyone was in awe." He planned on eventually selling the violin and living off the money in retirement, but his plans were dashed when the instrument was stolen from his studio in the mid-1960s.

Sarser says that at one point the FBI was close to solving the crime, but the instrument vanished a second time and was apparently sold to a buyer in Japan. The Ex-Zimbalist has since been photographed in Japan and even displayed in a department store, but Sarser hasn't been able to retrieve it or identify the new owner. "I have no desire to play any other instrument," he says. "It became part of me, and I became part of it."

Missing! The Gibson Stradivarius, made in 1713; estimated value: $1.2 million

Background: Polish virtuoso Bronislaw Huberman may be the only person ever to have the same Stradivarius stolen from him twice. In 1919 the Gibson was stolen in Vienna, then recovered a few days later when the thief tried to sell it to a dealer. In 1936 it was stolen from Huberman's dressing room while he was onstage at Carnegie Hall. He never saw it again—the violin was still missing when he died in 1947. Lloyd's of London paid him $30,000 for his loss.

In 1985 an ex-con and former café violinist named Julian Alt-

---

man summoned his wife, Marcelle Hall, to his deathbed and told her to take good care of his violin after he was gone. "That violin is important," he told her. He also instructed her to carefully examine the violin case. She did…and found newspaper clippings from the 1936 theft stuffed inside. She confronted her dying husband. At first he told her he had bought it from the thief for $100. Later he confessed that he'd stolen it by distracting a guard with a fine cigar, sneaking into the dressing room, and walking out with the Stradivarius under his coat. Unlike other thieves, he didn't want to sell it, he just wanted to play it. "Julian didn't get rid of it," Hall told reporters, "he played it for fifty years."

Outcome: After Altman died, Hall turned the violin over to Lloyd's of London. They must have believed Hall's claim that she didn't know anything about the theft until Altman confessed, because when they sold the Gibson Strad to a British violinist for $1.2 million, they paid her a $263,475 finder's fee.

"You know, Julian would tell people that his violin was a Stradivarius," remembers Altman's friend David Gartner. "They would just laugh at him. They thought he was kidding."

*   *   *

MORE IMPORTANT DATES IN MUSIC HISTORY

1943: The first Rodgers and Hammerstein musical, *Oklahoma!*, opens on Broadway.

1959: February 3rd becomes "The Day the Music Died." After playing a concert in Clear Lake, Iowa, the night before, Buddy Holly, Ritchie Valens, and the Big Bopper all die in a plane crash.

1966: *The Monkees*, a zany sitcom about a rock band (meant to mimic the Beatles' *A Hard Day's Night*) premiers. The show goes on to win Best Comedy Series at the Emmy Awards.

1988: Russian cosmonauts bring a copy of Pink Floyd's live album *Delicate Sound of Thunder* into space on a mission, making it the first album played in space.

MORE LAUGH TRACKS

Our final batch of amusing quotes by...and about...musicians.

"A gentleman is one who can play the accordion—but doesn't."
—George Bernard Shaw

Interviewer: "John, do you think Ringo is the best drummer in the world?"
John Lennon: "The best drummer in the world? Ringo's not even the best drummer in the Beatles!"

"I can't actually play any instrument properly. I can't read music. And here's the *New York Times* calling me the new Gershwin."
—Elvis Costello

"The difference between a violin and a viola is that a viola burns longer."
—Victor Borge

"I couldn't care less what your sexuality is—but of course, if you were gay, it would be fantastic!"
—Boy George, to Ricky Martin

"Sometimes you let the hair do the talking."
—James Brown

"The clarinet is a musical instrument—the only thing worse than which is two."
—Ambrose Bierce

"I'd love to see Christ come back to crush the spirit of hate and make men put down their guns. I'd also like just one more hit single."
—Tiny Tim

"To get your playing more forceful, hit the drums harder."
—Keith Moon

"We go home safe in the knowledge that we've deafened a few."
—Phil Taylor, of Motörhead

Interviewer: "What's the smartest thing you've ever heard anybody in rock 'n' roll say?"
Paul Simon: "'Be-bop-a-lula, she's my baby.'"

"'It's very hard to live in a studio apartment in San Jose with a man who's learning to play the violin.' That's what she told the police when she handed them the empty revolver."
—Richard Brautigan

Klezmer, the name for traditional Jewish music, is from Hebrew words meaning "vessel of music."

THE NEXT BIG THING

Ever since the Fab Four broke up in 1970, many other bands have been hailed by critics and audiences as "the new Beatles" or "the next big thing." They came...and they went.

BADFINGER (1969)

If you're heralded as the next Beatles, it helps to have an actual Beatle helping you out. Paul McCartney signed this Welsh pop band (formerly known as the Iveys) to the Beatles' Apple Records in 1969. McCartney gave them their name (the original title for the song "With a Little Help from My Friends" was "Bad Finger Boogie"), produced their first album, and wrote "Come and Get It," their first single. The result: Badfinger's guitar-riff-heavy, catchy pop songs sounded a lot like the Beatles. Between 1969 and 1972, Badfinger had four hit songs in the United States: "Come and Get It," "No Matter What," "Day After Day," and "Baby Blue." But after their initial success they released three more albums, which all sold poorly. Legal problems, contract disputes, and the suicide of group member Pete Ham led to the group's split in 1975.

THE BEE GEES (1967)

The brother act of Barry, Robin, and Maurice Gibb began performing in Australia in the late 1960s, combining folk music, harmonizing vocals, and psychedelic rock. Because they were young, British (they lived in Australia, but were born in Great Britain), played their own instruments, and played pop rock, they were often compared to the Beatles. Their debut album, *1st*, sold well and produced big hits like "New York Mining Disaster," "To Love Somebody," and "Holiday," bringing them critical acclaim in the U.S. and England. Throughout the late 1960s and early 1970s, the Bee Gees were a hit machine ("I Started a Joke," "I've Gotta Get a Message to You," "Lonely Days," and "How Can You Mend a Broken Heart"). But by 1973, interest in the band had waned. In the mid-'70s, the Bee Gees made a wise career move when they switched to disco: They recorded most of the songs for 1978's *Saturday Night Fever* soundtrack, which went on to sell 18 million

---

Muhammad Ali had a hit single on his 1963 album *I Am the Greatest*—a cover of "Stand by Me."

copies. At one point, songs written or performed by the Bee Gees occupied half of the spots in the Billboard Top 10. But when disco died, so did the popularity of the Bee Gees.

JULIAN LENNON (1984)

The mid-1980s brought a mini-Beatles revival, with George Harrison releasing "All Those Years Ago," a nostalgic tribute to his former band, and an unreleased John Lennon song called "Nobody Told Me" reaching the Top 5. Then in 1984, 22-year-old Julian Lennon, John Lennon's son, released his first album, *Valotte*. It was a smash, selling two million copies and producing two hit singles, the title track and "Too Late for Goodbyes." Lennon's instant popularity may have had something to do with the fact that he looked—and sounded—almost exactly like his father. The music press even speculated that the Beatles might reunite with Julian stepping in for the deceased John. The comparisons and the pressure made Julian Lennon uncomfortable (and he admitted he was still angry at his father for leaving his mother for Yoko Ono). The reunion never happened, and Lennon's second album, 1986's *The Secret Value of Daydreaming*, tanked with critics and didn't sell well.

THE KNACK (1979)

The Knack became a sensation in Los Angeles nightclubs in 1978 with their simple, catchy, stripped-down rock music. Capitol Records, sensing that audiences had grown tired of the disco fad, signed the band in 1979 and immediately started hyping the group as the saviors of rock 'n' roll. *Rolling Stone* agreed, calling them "the new Fab Four." The band happily played up the Beatles comparisons. The cover of their debut album *Get the Knack* (which sold a million copies in just seven weeks in the summer of 1979) featured a stark, black-and-white photo of the group in matching 1960s-style clothes, an homage to the *Meet the Beatles* cover. The Knack's first single, "My Sharona," stayed at #1 for six weeks. But apart from *Rolling Stone*, most music critics resented the group for the Beatles tribute cover and for their refusal to give interviews, which some critics thought was arrogant and foolish for a new band. For a few months, "My Sharona" seemed to be everywhere on the airwaves, but just as quickly as the band had risen to success (unsigned to #1 in nine months), they faded into obscurity. They rushed another album out just seven months after Get the Knack, called ...But the Little Girls Understand, which sold about a quarter as many as Get the Knack. A third album, 1981's Round Trip, bombed. The band broke up in January 1982.

OASIS (1995)

Oasis was the most popular band in England in the 1990s and broke through in the United States in 1995 with the hit ballad "Wonderwall." Group leader Noel Gallagher made no secret of his love of the Beatles and his desire to match their success: "With every song that I write, I compare it to the Beatles," he once said. "The thing is, they only got there before me." In fact, nobody compared Oasis to the Beatles more often than Oasis did. The band frequently and unabashedly borrowed from the Fab Four:

• The title of "Wonderwall" is taken from the George Harrison album Wonderwall Music.

• The piano hook on the single "Don't Look Back in Anger" was lifted from John Lennon's "Imagine."

• Gallagher got the title of the group's 1997 album Be Here Now from an interview in which John Lennon was asked to summarize the 1960s in one phrase.

• Oasis's ultimate Beatles homage: In 2004 Zak Starkey became the band's drummer. Zak's dad: Ringo Starr.

After two Top-20 songs, Oasis never had another hit in America. And their music was soon overshadowed by their tabloid exploits such as drunken, public fistfights between brothers/bandmates Noel and Liam Gallagher. Oasis is still extremely popular in England, where they've had eight #1 hits.

BAY CITY ROLLERS (1976)

In terms of hysteria and hype, the Bay City Rollers came closer than anyone else to being the next Beatles. Alan and Derek Longmuir founded the group in Edinburgh, Scotland, in 1967, picking a name by throwing a dart at a U.S. map, which landed on Bay City, Michigan. They hired manager Tam Paton, who created an image for the band: boys-next-door types who wore lots of plaid. An executive for Bell records saw them perform in an Edinburgh club and signed the band in 1971, leading quickly to a hit in the U.K. called "Keep on Dancing." Then, for two years…nothing. The Bay City Rollers seemed to be a one-hit wonder. But in 1973, the band's popularity suddenly surged with teenage audiences, and their next nine songs were U.K. Top-10 hits. They even got their own TV variety show and toured Europe, where their audiences were mostly throngs of shrieking teenage girls. Following the lead of Beatlemania (success first in England, then in the larger market in the U.S.), Paton booked Rollers performances via satellite on American TV shows (including *Saturday Night Live with Howard Cosell* and *American Bandstand*) so American audiences would see the hysterical crowds and follow suit. They did: In February 1976, the Bay City Rollers' plane landed at Kennedy Airport in New York, greeted by the national media and hundreds of screaming fans. A week later, their song "Saturday Night" was the #1 song in the U.S. Other hits followed, including "Money Honey" and "I Only Wanna Be with You." Then, at the height of "Rollermania," the stresses of touring and instant fame seemed to catch up with the band, and bassist Alan Longmuir quit the group. That led to the end of the Bay City Rollers phenomenon by 1977.

*   *   *

TELLING OFF THE MAN

In 1984 Johnny Cash, whose nickname was "The Man in Black," was trying to provoke a response from Columbia Records. Why? After more than 20 years with the label, he was still scratching out records but had lost his motivation and felt his work was being ignored. To get their attention, he recorded "Chicken in Black," a parody of himself. In the tune, Cash sings about getting a brain transplant from a bank robber; his old brain is implanted into a chicken who becomes a star.

Somehow, the single ended up more successful than his others at the time, peaking at #45 on the Billboard chart. What wasn't surprising is that Columbia Records declined to renew Cash's contract, and he happily went his own way.

On Emerson, Lake and Palmer's 1977 tour, they had 63 roadies, including a karate instructor.

THE STORY OF MUSIC, PART III

Here's the final installment of our whirlwind tour through the history of music (Part II is on page 346).

THE ART SCENE

Most musicologists divide the rest of the timeline of European Art Music—what we commonly call "classical music"—into four periods: Baroque, Classical, Romantic, and Modern. Each has its own distinctive characteristics.

Baroque (c.1600–1760): The growth of opera notwithstanding, the Baroque period sees instrumental music become the dominant form with the development of the *sonata*, which is to be "sounded," as opposed to the previous century's *cantana*—"to be sung"—and *concertos*, compositions written for orchestras and solo instrumentalists. The Baroque style is characterized as highly ornamented and decorative (mimicking the overall tastes of art during this time), with few changes in tempo or volume in a given piece. Strings are the most important instruments, and are divided into sections (first strings, second strings, etc.). Johann Sebastian Bach and George Frideric Handel are the two most important composers of the Baroque period. Some other highlights:

- Horns are first used in orchestras.
- Timpanis (kettle drums) are first used.
- In the 1650s, the oboe is invented in Paris.
- In 1666 the first Stradivarius violin is made.
- The *Italian overture*, commonly an instrumental prelude to an opera with three parts—quick/slow/quick in tempo—becomes popular.
- In 1690 the clarinet is invented.
- In 1720 the piano is invented.
- Italian becomes the accepted language for tempo notation (allegro, largo, etc.).

Classical (c.1750–1820): The Classical period is characterized by a "cleaning up" of art of all kinds. The music becomes more reserved, detailed, and "rational." Orchestras grow, with most of them numbering 30 to 50 players, and their newest member— the conductor—is employed to keep time. Haydn, Mozart, Beethoven, and Mendelssohn are the most famous composers of the period.

• The *symphony* (from the Greek for "sounding together"), grand, four-movement compositions, evolves from the Italian overture.

• The harpsichord disappears from orchestras.

• Instruments most commonly used: flutes, oboes, clarinets, bassoons, trumpets, timpani, violins, violas, cellos, and double basses.

Romantic (1815–1910): Music now becomes much more dynamic and expressive, and orchestra sizes balloon to more than 100 players. Tempo and volume now vary dramatically in a single piece, giving conductors a crucial role. Some of the famous names from this period: Wagner, Liszt, Chopin, Brahms, Dvorak, Tchaikovsky, and Rachmaninoff.

• Valves for horns are invented, making brass instruments much more playable and versatile.

• The Golden Age of flamenco music begins in Spain.

• Thomas Edison patents the phonograph.

• In 1880 the first American symphony to be published in the United States, John Paine's *In Spring*, debuts in Cambridge, Mass.

Modern (c.1900–Present): Changes spurred by technology—the ability to record and play back music, the accessibility and popularity of radio and television, and the development of electronic instruments—change music forever.

In classical music, the modern era is marked chiefly by an increased use of *dissonance*—simultaneously playing notes that don't sound "good" together—rather than the easier-to-listen-to sound of *consonance*. Many modern composers make their own rules regarding melody, rhythm, harmony, and instrumentation (and many non-western instruments were incorporated into their music). Some of the more prominent styles of the era:

• **Impressionism:** Spanning from the very late 1800s to the late 1930s, Impressionism is known for its "dreamy" and "unfinished"—

American composer Morton Gould wrote a concerto "for tap dancer and orchestra."

and, to many, "unmusical"—feel, and marked the bridge from the Romantic to the more dissonant modern era. The best-known impressionist composers are Frenchmen Claude Debussy and Maurice Ravel.

- **Neoclassicism:** This style, developed between the World Wars, is described as a return to the less emotional "strictness" of the Baroque and Classical eras, mixed with modern ingredients like experimental rhythms and melodic structures. Notables: early Igor Stravinsky, Leonard Bernstein, and Benjamin Britten.

- **Atonalism:** Over its entire history, Western music had been written with a "tonal center"—a key (or more than one). Atonal music, which ranges from about 1908 to the present, abandons this idea and allows the composer to change keys at any given time (resulting in music that some listeners find unpleasant). Notables: Alban Berg, Arnold Shoenberg, Igor Stravinsky (again), Pierre Boulez, Steve Reich, and Anton Webern.

- **Serialism:** In this style, which began around the 1950s, composers don't "write" the music in the traditional sense; they develop mathematical formulas for rhythm, melody, note length, volume, and so on. Notables: Igor Stravinsky (once more), Milton Babbitt, Karlheinz Stockhausen, and Walter Piston.

- **Indeterminism:** This is music left purely to chance. Its most famous composer is John Cage. His most famous work: *4'33"*, four minutes and thirty-three seconds of silence.

THE MODERN TIMELINE

With such a long history, the rules of Western music are the most popularly used ones in the world. But of course there are many other kinds of music, each with its own histories and stories, from the didjeridu players of Australia to the gamelan orchestras of Indonesia to the throat singers of Tuva in southern Siberia. In fact, the music of the timbila orchestras of Mozambique's Chopi people is considered to be the most sophisticated nonwritten music on the planet.

There are many others—and many more to come. Who knows? Maybe someday we'll have 59 notes in our scale and 25-part harmonies. Or we might just go back to chanting. We'll have to wait and see.

Tina Turner won a Grammy in 1971, was on food stamps in '76, and won another Grammy in '85.

THEY WROTE THE SONGS

You know the words, you know the tunes, but do
you know who wrote these famous songs?

SONG: "Auld Lang Syne"
SONGWRITER: Robert Burns
STORY: No one knows for sure who wrote the tune for this song, but poet Robert Burns wrote the lyrics during the late 18th century. Burns set his words to an old Scottish folk song that had been around since the 1400s. It implores listeners to remember times past—translated, the title is "old long since" or "days gone by." The song became a favorite among the Scots and English and later traveled to the United States with immigrants from those countries. Its widespread association with New Year's Eve comes from bandleader Guy Lombardo, who played "Auld Lang Syne" for the first time at the end of his 1929 New Year's Eve concert, which was broadcast on the radio. The public loved it so much that he ended every New Year's Eve concert with the song until the last concert in 1976 (on television). As a result, "Auld Lang Syne" has become the song to sing at the stroke of midnight every December 31st.

SONG: "The Stars and Stripes Forever"
SONGWRITER: John Philip Sousa
STORY: In 1896 Sousa and his wife were on a passenger ship, returning to the United States from a vacation in Europe. During the trip, the composer and bandleader (known as the "March King" because he found fame leading the U.S. Marine Corps Band) learned that his band's manager had died suddenly. Said Sousa, "I was pacing on the deck, absorbed in thoughts of my manager's death and the many duties and decisions which awaited me in New York. Suddenly, I began to sense a rhythmic beat of a band playing within my brain. Throughout the whole tense voyage, that imaginary band continued to unfold the same themes, echoing and re-echoing the most distinct melody." He didn't actually write the music down until he got back to the United States, but when he did, what came out were the music and (little-

known) lyrics to a patriotic march he called "The Stars and Stripes Forever." Soon after, Sousa started playing the song with his band and it was a huge hit—he played it at almost every concert until he died in 1932. Fifty-five years later, President Ronald Reagan signed a bill naming "The Stars and Stripes Forever" the official U.S. national march. (The only other song so honored is "The Star-Spangled Banner," which Congress designated as the U.S. national anthem in 1931.)

SONG: "Happy Birthday"
SONGWRITERS: Patty Hill and Mildred J. Hill
STORY: The Hill sisters were teachers in Kentucky in the 1890s, and they wanted an easy, fun song for their students to sing each morning. So they came up with "Good Morning to All." In 1893 the song appeared in a book called *Song Stories for the Kindergarten*, and soon, children across the country were singing it to their teachers each morning. It's unclear when the words changed from "Good morning to all" to "Happy birthday to you," and there's debate about who actually changed them—the Hill sisters or someone else. But in 1924, "Happy Birthday" appeared as the song's second verse in another book of children's songs. By 1935 it was everywhere, and a third Hill sister, Jessica, filed suit to protect the copyright. She won, and the music publisher she was working with (Chicago's Clayton F. Summy Company) became the owner of the song's copyright. Today, "Happy Birthday" remains a copyrighted song, and anyone who sings it in movies, on television (which is why you seldom hear it in movies or on TV), or on an album has to pay royalties to the Summy Company. You can still sing it for free at your kid's backyard party, though; the copyright laws apply only to people who profit from it.

SONG: "Over the Rainbow"
SONGWRITERS: E. Y. Harburg and Harold Arlen
STORY: In 1938 Harburg and Arlen were working as composers for MGM when they were hired to write the music for one of the studio's upcoming films: *The Wizard of Oz*. Director Victor Fleming and MGM's head honcho, Louis B. Mayer, wanted a wistful and dreamy song to highlight the talents of the film's star, Judy Garland. Arlen crafted the melody and then presented it to lyricist

"Yip" Harburg. Harburg thought the song was too slow, but with a little retooling (and some help from Ira Gershwin), Arlen was able to put together a melody that worked. Harburg, inspired by Franklin Roosevelt's New Deal optimism, wrote the hopeful lyrics. The song almost didn't make the film's final cut, however. During editing, MGM executives worried that the movie was too long and felt that the scene in the barnyard where Garland sings "Over the Rainbow" slowed down the action. But in the end, Fleming pushed for its inclusion and won out. And it's a good thing: The next year, "Over the Rainbow" won an Academy Award for Best Song, and it became Judy Garland's signature tune.

SONG: "Strange Fruit"
SONGWRITER: Abel Meeropol
STORY: Billie Holiday first recorded this antilynching song in 1939, but it was actually written a few years earlier by a school-teacher from New York. Abel Meeropol (a member of the Communist Party and the man who adopted the sons of Ethel and Julius Rosenberg after they were executed for espionage in 1953) wrote the lyrics after he saw a picture of two young black men lynched in the South. The verse was published in poem form in a 1937 edition of the New York Teacher's Union newsletter and was originally called "Bitter Fruit." Meeropol later set the poem to music and when he saw Billie Holiday perform at a nightclub in New York City in 1939, knew he'd found just the right person to sing his song. She sang it during her act every night for months. When she went to record it, though, her label (Columbia) refused; with lines like "Blood on the leaves and blood at the roots / Black bodies swinging in the Southern breeze," the song was too political and too provocative. But a smaller label, Commodore Records, agreed to record it. "Strange Fruit" never got much radio play: Southern stations banned it and Northern stations were afraid to stir up racial unrest. Some nightclubs even told Holiday she couldn't perform it during her concerts. Yet, the lyrics struck a chord with the public, and at one point, the song climbed to #16 on the Billboard chart. In the years since, "Strange Fruit" has been covered by everyone from Tori Amos to Sting to Siouxie and the Banshees, and it was an anthem of the civil rights movement during the 1950s and '60s.

SIX MORE
MUSICIAN JOKES

A few more jokes that musicians love…and hate…from the BRI's vault.

A musician calls the symphony office to talk to the conductor.

"I'm sorry, he's dead," comes the reply.

The musician calls back 25 times, always getting the same reply from the receptionist. Finally, she asks him why he keeps calling.

"I just like to hear you say it," he says.

♪   ♪   ♪

An anthropologist travels to a tropical island to study its natives. He hires a guide to take him into the jungle to the remote site where the natives live. On the second day of the trip, they begin to hear drums. The anthropologist asks the guide, "What are those drums?"

The guide turns to him and says ominously, "Drums okay, but very bad when they stop."

The drums go on for a few hours. Then they suddenly stop. The anthropologist grabs the guide and yells, "The drums have stopped! What does it mean?!"

The guide shakes his head and says, "Bass solo next."

♪   ♪   ♪

Three men walk up to the Pearly Gates.

"What did you do on Earth?" Saint Peter asks the first one.

The man says, "I was a doctor."

St. Peter says, "Okay, go right through those Pearly Gates. Next!"

The next man approaches and Saint Peter asks, "What did *you* do on Earth?"

"I was a schoolteacher," the man says.

"Great! Go right through those Pearly Gates. Next! And what did you do on Earth?"

"I was a musician."

Saint Peter looks at the guy and says, "Go around to the door in the alley, up the freight elevator, through the kitchen..."

♪ ♪ ♪

A drummer, sick of all the drummer jokes, decides to change instruments. After some thought, he decides on the accordion. He goes into a music store and says to the owner, "I'd like to look at the accordions, please."

The owner gestures to a shelf in the corner and says, "All our accordions are over there."

After browsing, the drummer says, "I think I'd like the big red one in the corner."

The store owner looks at him and says, "You're a drummer, aren't you?"

The drummer smiles and says, "How did you know?"

The store owner says, "That 'big red accordion' is the radiator."

♪ ♪ ♪

The doorbell rings. The lady of the house answers the front door to find a man with a toolbox standing on her porch.

"May I help you?" she asks.

"I'm the piano tuner," he says.

"But I didn't send for a piano tuner," she exclaims.

"No," he replies. "Your neighbors did."

♪ ♪ ♪

Q: What's the least-used sentence in the English language?
A: "Isn't that the banjo player's Porsche?"

WHY DISCO DIED

One of the shortest-lived phases in American musical history, disco took the nation by storm in 1977 and was declared "dead" just three years later. (For part I of the story, go to page XXX.)

SATURDAY NIGHT POSERS

When most people think of "disco music," they think of John Travolta in *Saturday Night Fever*. But most die-hard disco fans scoff at this. True disco, they maintain, was the underground dance-club scene of the early to mid-1970s, frequented primarily by gays and minorities, and fueled by deejays and independent record labels. So what's the problem with the 1977 film about a troubled Brooklyn kid named Tony Manero (Travolta) who goes to the discotheque every Saturday night? A lot, it turns out. "That movie was about a group of straight, homophobic, racist, Italian-American twenty-somethings in New York who went dancing wearing odd-looking clothes and probably too much aftershave lotion. They looked nothing much like people I saw or knew in gay discos." That review comes from disco historian Dennis Brumm, who's been active in the dance scene since the early 1970s. And many in the disco community feel the same way.

FROM FRAUD TO FAD

The idea for *Saturday Night Fever* came from a 1976 *New York* magazine article about the New York disco scene, written by British journalist Nik Cohn. Cohn later admitted that he made the whole thing up: He'd just arrived in the United States, and had no clue what the real "scene" was like when he was assigned to write about it. So he completely fabricated the character that eventually became Tony Manero.

Nevertheless, the film came out the next year, and the public ate it up: It earned $74 million, the third-highest gross of the year (after *Star Wars* and *Close Encounters of the Third Kind*). The soundtrack, featuring disco songs by the Bee Gees, was even more successful. It quickly became the highest-selling movie soundtrack ever, and was the highest-selling pop album until Michael Jack-

---

Rev. Jesse Jackson's PUSH organization launched a campaign against disco music in the 1970s.

son's *Thriller* eclipsed it six years later. Almost overnight, disco went from a fringe movement to a mainstream fad. And just as suddenly, the major funk and R&B record labels took an interest in the craze and began cranking out disco hits for all ages.

But in their book *Saturday Night Forever: The History of Disco*, Alan Jones and Jussi Kantonen try to set the record straight—that real disco was *not* the Village People, K.C. and the Sunshine Band, and Gloria Gaynor: "For every chart hit pounded into the public's consciousness, 50 far superior tracks from all over the world were being played at some hard-to-find basement club."

DISCO SUCKS

Disco started showing up everywhere:

• In 1978 the State of New York declared one week in June "National Disco Week."

• On television, *Dance Fever* and *Soul Train* were ratings hits.

• Film scores to popular movies like *Star Wars* and *Superman* were re-released in "disco mixes."

• Even Disney got into the act with the 1980 album *Mickey Mouse Disco*.

• Established rock artists added some disco elements to many of their songs in the late '70s, further angering die-hard disco fans— and alienating their own longtime listeners. Examples: the Rolling Stones ("Miss You"), Wings ("Silly Love Songs") and even the Grateful Dead ("Shakedown Street").

Slowly, a counter-movement began to spread throughout the United States. In the popular movie spoof *Airplane*, audiences cheered when the doomed plane knocked down a disco station's antenna. And on the sitcom *WKRP in Cincinnati*, rock deejay Dr. Johnny Fever regularly wore his "Disco Sucks" T-shirt. It was becoming cool to hate disco.

THE DAY THE DISCO DIED

On July 12, 1979, the anti-disco sentiment reached a fever pitch when the Chicago White Sox held "Disco Demolition Night" during a double-header at Comiskey Park. The event was the brainchild of Chicago radio deejay Steve Dahl, who had lost his previous job when his station went to an all-disco format. Now working for a rival station, Dahl wanted revenge. The rules for Disco Demolition Night: Fans who brought their unwanted disco records to the game only had to pay 98 cents to get in. Bonus: After the first game of the doubleheader, Dahl promised to blow up the records on the field. White Sox officials hoped for an additional 5,000 fans—but nearly 60,000 showed up, most of them with little interest in baseball. During the first game, drunk fans started flinging their disco records at each other and at the players on the field. After the game ended, Dahl put on an Army helmet and drove a Jeep around the field while the crowd chanted "Disco sucks! Disco sucks!" Then crates filled with more than 1,000 disco records were detonated in the outfield, ripping a hole in the grass. While players ran for cover, fans jumped the fences, stole the bases, toppled the batting cages, and tore up the infield. The White Sox were forced to forfeit the second game. And another nail was hammered into disco's coffin.

CONSPIRACY?

But was the "Disco Sucks" campaign just a natural backlash to a popular fad, or was there something more sinister behind it? Some claim the whole protest was manufactured by the executives of rock record companies, who secretly paid deejays to bad-mouth disco. Gloria Gaynor, known as the "Queen of Disco," sees no other way to explain the sudden outburst of hatred: "It was started by someone who felt that the popularity of disco was dipping into their pockets," she said. "Because, let's face it, young people...were buying my music instead of somebody else's. Certainly some record companies or producers may have been getting miffed, and I always believed that that whole thing was started by them."

So far, the theory's never been proven. But whether disco was murdered or died a natural death, it was still a target years later. Even in 1989, 10 years after the height of the backlash, the *Penguin Encyclopedia of Popular Music* defined disco as "a dance fad of the 1970s with a profound and unfortunate influence on popular music."

JUST KEEP ON DANCING

Yet to say disco "died" isn't completely accurate. Disco evolved into the mainstream dance music of the next two decades, such as house, drum and bass, and techno. All were more or less stripped-down versions of disco. Full orchestras were replaced by synthesizers, drum sets were replaced by programmed drum machines, and musical breaks were added by sampling pieces from funk, soul, and—appropriately enough—disco songs. All of these recording methods began in disco studios in the early 1970s and would flourish in years to come in dance, electronica, and even rap music.

GLAMOROUS GRAVEYARD

Meanwhile, true disco music never really died, either. It quietly went back to its underground roots, where it lives on at dance clubs today—even more so after the popularity of disco-fueled acts of the mid-1990s like Cher, Erasure, and the Pet Shop Boys. And like most fads, a couple of decades later, disco started to become cool again. Says Gloria Gaynor: "I always say that disco music is alive and well and living in the hearts of people all over the world. It simply changed its name to protect the innocent."

*   *   *

COSTA RICA'S PRISON ANTHEM

In 1852 the U.S. and Great Britain recognized the independence of the Central American nation of Costa Rica and notified them that diplomats would be arriving for a formal recognition ceremony. But there was a problem: Costa Rica didn't have a national anthem. What would they play at the ceremony? President Juan Rafael Mora summoned Don Manuel Maria Gutierrez, director of the Costa Rica national band, to quickly write an anthem. Gutierrez refused. He was a band master, he said, not a composer. Mora threw him in prison...but had the cell stocked with a desk and writing material and told Gutierrez he would be released as soon as he composed a worthy song.

After a few days of incarceration, Gutierrez suddenly discovered that he could write music after all, and, after a few more days, completed his task. On June 12, 1852, at the welcoming ceremonies for the arriving diplomats, "The Star Spangled Banner," "God Save the King," and, for the first time in its history, "Hino National de Costa Rica" was performed in public. (Don Gutierrez, who had been released from prison, was thanked for his work and returned to his position as director of the national band.)

The melody to "Twinkle, Twinkle, Little Star" is from a 1761 French song. The lyrics date to 1806.

LOST INSTRUMENTS

*They were loved in their heyday, but now they're found
mostly in museums. Here are some of the most
fascinating instruments that came...and went.*

THE THEORBO

This lutelike stringed instrument evolved from a need for deeper bass sounds to accompany a new style of music being developed in 16th-century Florence: opera. The *theorbo* had an egg-shaped, flat-faced body, a wide, fretted neck, and 14 strings. On top of that was a neck extension to accommodate several longer bass strings, making the entire neck a whopping four feet long. The resulting music: low, droning bass notes accompanying the delicate melodies that were plucked on the higher strings. The theorbo was a staple of classical music until the middle of the 18th century. It was (along with all lutes) then rendered obsolete by the louder, more versatile piano, which first gained widespread popularity in the late 1700s.

THE BUCCIN

In the 18th and 19th centuries, outdoor music parades were very popular in France. That led to loud, showy instruments like the *buccin* (pronounced "boo-san"). Similar to a trombone, this brass instrument had a slide. But the unusual part was its bell, which was located above the player's shoulder and was shaped like a snake's head, complete with teeth. The "head" was often painted bright red, green, or gold, with a metal tongue sticking out of the mouth...that flapped when the instrument was played. The only known score written for the buccin was by the French composer Hector Berlioz in 1824. By 1850, it had gone out of style.

THE SERPENT

This low-pitched horn is believed to have been invented in 1590 in Auxerre, France, by church official Edmé Guillaume, who wanted a mournful-sounding instrument to accompany choral singing during religious services. What he came up with was the "serpent," a tubular horn made of wood and brass played through a cupped mouth-

---

From 1950 to 1970, U.S. guitar sales grew from 228,000 to 2.3 million, a 1,000% increase.

piece (like a trumpet's). The wooden body of the instrument, which was usually covered in leather, snaked down in a serpentine shape (hence the name) before curving up at hip level in an unflared five-inch bell. Six finger holes were drilled into the curved body where it was held by the two hands. It was reportedly very difficult to master. In the 19th century, the serpent was replaced by a keyed brass instrument, the ophicleide (see below).

THE OPHICLEIDE

In 1817 Parisian bugle maker Jean Hilaire Asté set out to make a modern, brass version of the serpent to fit in better with the orchestras of the day. He called his new instrument the *ophicleide*, Greek for "keyed serpent." It was easier to play than the serpent, with keys and pads like its descendant, the saxophone, which it vaguely resembles. Composers like Mendelssohn, Verdi, and Wagner wrote specifically for the ophicleide, but it was gone by the 1920s, replaced by instruments like the trombone and French horn.

THE STROH VIOLIN

In 1899 German inventor Johannes Matthias Stroh patented a unique violin. It looked like a normal violin, but where the body would normally be it had a small metal resonator box and a large metal horn, similar to those found on old Victrola record players. The horn was crucial: The early 1900s were the first days of sound recording, and the primitive recording devices of the era had a hard time picking up the sound of string instruments. The Stroh violin made up for that by being *really* loud. Eventually, recording technology improved and conventional violins could be easily recorded, so Strohs were no longer needed. The last one was manufactured in 1943. Originals are very hard to come by today, but some companies are making new ones (Tom Waits used a one-string Stroh violin on his 2002 album, *Alice*).

THE CHAMBERLIN

This small, boxy organ was invented in 1946 by Harry Chamberlin of Los Angeles. But this organ was unusual: Under each key was a small tape playback unit with about eight seconds of pre-recorded sound on it, usually of an instrument like a violin or a clarinet.

When a key was pressed, that sound was played; when the key was released, the tape quickly rewound. In the first few years, about 100 Chamberlins were made in a workshop behind Chamberlin's garage, and after he built a factory in Ontario, California, he turned out another 600 or so. Chamberlins were used by many rock acts, including David Bowie and Brian Eno. The company folded in 1981, but there's more to the story...

THE MELLOTRON

In the early 1960s, a company in Birmingham, England, began selling Chamberlins under the name "Mellotron." How this came about isn't exactly clear, but it seems that an associate of Chamberlin's sold the idea to the British company without his knowledge (Chamberlin later sold the technology to the Mellotron company). The Mellotron featured some design improvements over the Chamberlin and actually became more popular with rock bands than the original instrument had been. The tapes could be changed fairly easily, so musicians could record their own sounds, making the instrument much more like a modern synthesizer. Mike Pinder of the Moody Blues—and also an ex-employee of the Mellotron company—made the Mellotron's sound world-famous in 1967 when he used one on the band's songs "Nights in White Satin" and "Tuesday Afternoon." (Pinder had earlier introduced the Mellotron to the Beatles, who first used it in 1966 on "Tomorrow Never Knows" and "Strawberry Fields Forever.") In 1977 a paperwork error gave a distributor rights to the name "Mellotron," forcing the company to change the brand name to "Novatron." Novatron went bust in 1986, when new sampling and synthesizer technology made the instrument obsolete. About 2,500 Mellotrons were built in the company's history, along with a few hundred Novatrons. Today the instruments are considered valuable collector's items.

*   *   *

STATES RIGHTS

Lynryd Skynyrd's biggest hit was "Sweet Home Alabama." The band is actually from Florida. And the song was later used in ad campaign for Kentucky Fried Chicken.

Inventor of multitrack recording: Les Paul. First song to use it: his "How High the Moon" (1951).

DEAD-HEADS

*Thoughts on the Grateful Dead...by
the Grateful Dead. Wow, man.*

"We were becoming aware that there was a group of people that was following the band around, and they weren't interested in coming in to the shows, they were just interested in hanging out outside and trying to break in."

—Phil Lesh

"Music is a hallucinogenic realm. When I'm singing and playing, I'm visiting another world. And when it gets really good, it's like there is a bright electric-blue white light that just radiates from everything and everybody. That's a place I go all the time. I like it there."

—Bob Weir

"The Grateful Dead should be sponsored by the government —a public service. And they should set us up to play at places that need to get high."

—Jerry Garcia

"Even though my hearing seems to have declined, I can still perceive things, although they tend to be loud, the things that I can perceive."

—Phil Lesh

"Being the focus of what amounts to a quasi-religious cult is just weird."

—Bob Weir

"It's pretty clear now that what looked like it might have been some kind of counterculture is, in reality, just the plain old chaos of undifferentiated weirdness."

—Jerry Garcia

"Being the new keyboardist in this band is like being the new guy in 'Nam."

—Vince Welnick,
the Grateful Dead's
third keyboardist

"Joseph Campbell was watching us play one night and he said, 'What you are is a conjurer.' I thought about it for a couple of months and decided, 'Yeah, you're right.'"

—Bob Weir

"Tipper and Al Gore came to a show the last time we were in Washington. They're nice people, a nice family. We made every effort not to frighten them."

—Jerry Garcia

He who cannot dance will say the drum is bad. —African proverb

HOW ALAN FREED THE MUSIC

The rise and fall of the man who brought rock 'n' roll to the masses mirrors the story of rock's formative years: youthful, rebellious, confident, scorned, controversial, and misunderstood.

RIGHT TIME, RIGHT PLACE

On July 11, 1951, a new voice came on the air on WJW Radio in Cleveland, Ohio: it belonged to an easygoing 29-year-old named Alan Freed. Up until that time, Freed had been a sportscaster, journalist, and disc jockey playing classical and jazz on east coast radio stations. A failed musician himself (his jazz trombone career was cut short when he suffered an ear infection years earlier), Freed loved new music, and was clamoring to play it.

Shortly after Freed arrived in Cleveland, a local record store owner named Leo Muntz told him that the new rage for white teenagers was black Rhythm and Blues music. At first Freed, who was white, balked at the idea of playing R&B, or "race music" as it was referred to—not because he didn't like it, but because the common practice at the time was to play covers of black R&B tunes by white artists. Radio, like the rest of the United States, was still segregated. But Freed felt that these white covers lacked the raw power and musical prowess of the original versions. So he followed Muntz's advice and started mixing in a few R&B tunes. And he got away with it, mostly because of where he was—a small, independent radio station. Freed had free reign because most of radio's biggest stars had moved over to television, taking their shows with them. In doing so they left a giant gap on the airwaves that needed to be filled. And WJW didn't have enough money to hire a live band, which was the common practice. Solution: Play records. So Freed took the night shift and was let loose to spin whatever he wanted.

MOONDOG

Freed's new format slowly started catching on in Cleveland. He tapped into a market that until that time had mostly been

---

Hold, please: Music was transmitted through a telephone line for the first time in 1876.

ignored: white teenagers. In addition to that, WJW had a very strong signal for an independent station, meaning kids in cities all across the Midwest could pick up the show.

And he didn't just play the music—he *lived* the music. Calling himself "Moondog," Freed began every show with his trademark intro: "Hello everybody, how y'all doin' tonight? This is Alan Freed, king of the Moondoggers!" As John Morthland describes Freed's manic style in *The Rolling Stone Illustrated History of Rock & Roll*:

> Freed yips, moans, and brays, gearing up for another evening host-
> ing the hottest rhythm and blues show in the land. Slipping on a
> golf glove, he bangs on a phone book in time to the music—maybe
> "Money Honey" by the Drifters, or "Shake a Hand" by Faye
> Adams. Swigging constantly from his trusty bottle of booze, he
> spins the hits and continues his manic patter throughout the night,
> spewing forth rhymed jive with the speed and inflections of a Holy
> Roller at the Pearly Gates. There had been celebrated disc jockeys
> before Alan Freed, but never anyone quite so crazed and obsessive.

WHEN ROCK MET ROLL

Knowing that he was treading on thin ice, because of the racial prejudices of the time, Freed never uttered the words "Rhythm and Blues" on his show. It was a major coup to play black artists for a white audience—even on an independent station. But Freed had to be careful. So instead of saying "R&B," he called the music he played "rock 'n' roll," a term he took credit for coining Some music historians argue that it was Leo Muntz, not Freed, who came up with the label as a way to describe the beat of the "race music." But one thing is certain, it was Freed who popularized the term, now calling his show "Moondog's Rock 'n' Roll Party."

Ironically, the term "rock 'n' roll" was far racier than "R&B." First appearing in the 1922 song "My Baby Rocks Me With One Steady Roll" by Trixie Smith—and in many other songs in subse- quent years—the term was black slang for sex. But it had never been used to describe a musical genre until Freed's show. He claimed he chose it because "it seemed to suggest rolling, surging beat of the music." He was also careful to wait for the wee hours of the morning to play the sexier songs, such as the Dominoes' "Sixty-Minute Man."

Freed became a celebrity in Cleveland, and sales of the black artists' records skyrocketed there. It was an early indication that radio play could bring enormous commercial success. This combination would lead Freed—and the music industry—down a slippery path in a few years. But for now, Freed lived the rock star lifestyle, drinking heavily and cavorting with musicians and women.

In March 1952, Freed organized what many consider the world's first rock concert, the Moondog Coronation Ball, which took place at the Cleveland Arena. Freed promoted the show for weeks, calling out all of his "Moondoggers" for a night of swinging and dancing to the music of the Dominoes, Tiny Grimes, the Rockin' Highlanders, Danny Cobb, and Varietta Dillard. The arena had a capacity of 10,000, yet more than twice that showed up—many of them young black kids. They rushed the gates, prompting the show to be cancelled by fire marshalls after just one song by Paul "Hucklebuck" Williams. The story received national attention, and rock 'n' roll music, though still in its infancy, was quickly becoming Public Enemy Number One.

SEGREGATION, RIOTS, AND THE BIG BEAT

Word of Freed's success on the radio spread nationwide, leading other stations to drop their formats and start playing rock 'n' roll records. Meanwhile, Freed's white audience grew and grew, and in 1954 he moved to a larger audience and a better job at WINS in New York City. Dropping the Moondog name (a blues artist called Moon Dog sued him), Freed maintained his manic style and kept pushing the "race music" to white teenagers, some of whom had picked up guitars and started wailing out their own tunes (including John Lennon and Paul McCartney, who heard Freed's later broadcasts on Radio Luxembourg). Freed promoted legendary concerts at New York's Brooklyn Paramount Theater, further fueling what most critics still considered just a passing fad. But not Freed, who said, "Anyone who thinks that rock 'n' roll is a flash-in-the-pan trend along the music road has rocks in their head, dad!"

Suddenly, Freed was rock 'n' roll's unofficial spokesman, appearing in a string of 1950s teen movies, including *Mr. Rock and Roll*, *Rock Around the Clock*, *Don't Knock the Rock*, and *Rock Rock Rock*, in which he famously proclaimed, "Rock 'n' roll is a river of music that has absorbed many streams: rhythm and blues, jazz, ragtime, cowboy songs, country songs, and folk songs. All have contributed to the Big Beat!"

TROUBLE BREWING

Unfortunately for Freed, that "river of music" would soon turn muddy, overrun by violence, racial politics, and money. The first sign of trouble came in 1957. ABC hired Freed to host a nationally televised rock 'n' roll show called *The Big Beat*, but it only ran for one episode. Why? Frankie Lymon, a black performer, danced with a white girl in front of a national TV audience. ABC's Southern affiliates were livid and dropped the show, leading many of the sponsors to pull their ads. When the network quickly gave it the axe, the message was clear: the Establishment did not like rock 'n' roll music.

Freed was increasingly finding himself the focus of the backlash against rock 'n' roll. In 1958 a concert he organized in Boston broke out in a riot, and Freed was criminally charged for inciting the violence (even though the fighting mostly took place outside of the arena by non-ticket holders). Ultimately, the charges were dropped. But both Freed and rock 'n' roll suffered serious blows from the event—Boston banned rock 'n' roll concerts and WINS fired their most famous deejay. Freed now had to scour local markets to find work.

Beleaguered, but still enthusiastic about rock 'n' roll, Freed landed a new job hosting a show on WABC radio in New York. That one didn't last long, either. Rock's biggest scandal to date was just around the corner, and once again Freed found himself at the center of it.

PAYOLA

After the potential of radio's power to sell records became apparent in the mid-1950s, record companies began paying radio stations and deejays to push their artists. Although the practice, dubbed "payola," had been around since the 1920s, the new demographic of post-war Baby Boomer teenagers promised dividends the likes of which had never been seen before. The kids—millions of them— liked rock 'n' roll, had access to money, and were willing to spend it on records. The laws surrounding payola were murky at the time. Many people was doing it, and they defended themselves by saying, "Everybody's doing it." Alan Freed had done it. He was mostly paid as a "consultant," listening to new records and telling executives which ones might fly with the kids. In some

---

The study of animal music, like cricket chirps and whale songs, is called *zoomusicology*.

cases he even accepted a co-writing credit on songs he played (which entitled him to profit from record sales), such as on Chuck Berry's "Maybelline." Yet since most of the dealings happened behind closed doors, no one is exactly sure to what extent Freed accepted cash and gifts. Through it all, though, Freed claimed, "I never played a record I didn't like."

Nevertheless, in November 1959 WABC ordered Freed to sign a statement that he never took money to play a song. Freed refused and was immediately fired. Soon after, Congress held hearings on the payola scandal. Although most of the nation's deejays were left alone, the high profile Freed was charged with 26 counts of commercial bribery. He was found guilty, fined heavily, and received a suspended sentence. Already nearly bankrupt from the massive legal fees surrounding the incident in Boston, the payola scandal effectively ended Freed's career.

Broke and despondent, Freed worked at a few California radio stations over the next few years, but was just a shadow of his former self. His liver was failing; his third wife left him; and those who had championed him in the past now abandoned him. After being charged in 1964 for tax evasion, Freed withdrew completely. Taken to a hospital in Palm Springs, California, Alan Freed died from uremia in January 1965. He was 43 years old.

THE BEAT LIVES ON

Freed's impact on rock 'n' roll is still felt today. Just listen to any rock deejay and you'll hear shades of the man who pioneered the form. But what Freed did in the 1950s had far more reaching ramifications than popularizing a new type of music. The Civil Rights Movement of the 1960s can be traced in part back to the dance halls that Freed integrated a decade earlier. Through music, he preached racial harmony. And music has, at times, been known to have a very loud voice.

In 1986 Freed was among the first group of inductees in the Rock and Roll Hall of Fame (which is located in Cleveland, considered the birthplace of rock—thanks to Freed's "Moondog Rock 'n' Roll Show"). And in 1988 Freed was inducted in the Radio Hall of Fame. "More than any other man," wrote Billboard's Paul Ackerman, "he brought us rock 'n' roll."

9 RANDOM MUSIC LISTS

Another page of carefully collected and numbered
musical information from the BRI trivia vault.

4 ACTS THAT LOST THE "BEST NEW ARTIST" GRAMMY TO MILLI VANILLI
1. Indigo Girls
2. Tone Loc
3. Neneh Cherry
4. Soul II Soul

9 ROCK STARS WHO MARRIED FASHION MODELS
1. John Mellencamp
2. Axl Rose
3. David Bowie
4. Billy Joel
5. Mick Jagger
6. Eric Clapton
7. Bruce Springsteen
8. Rod Stewart
9. Keith Richards

5 TYPES OF MARGARITAVILLE MERCHANDISE
1. Frozen seafood
2. Chicken wings
3. Tequila
4. Sandals
5. Margarita mix

4 DEFUNCT MUSIC MAGAZINES
1. *Melody Maker*
2. *Creem*
3. *Cash Box*
4. *Crawdaddy!*

7 SINGING DRUMMERS
1. Levon Helm
2. Phil Collins
3. Don Henley
4. Ringo Starr
5. Karen Carpenter
6. Mickey Dolenz
7. Sheila E.

4 SONGS ABOUT DOGS BY ARTISTS WITH ANIMAL NAMES
1. "Martha, My Dear" (The Beatles)
2. "Gonna Buy Me a Dog" (The Monkees)
3. "Old Blue" (The Byrds)
4. "Dog Eat Dog" (Adam Ant)

9 POP STARS WHO WON MUSIC OSCARS
1. Phil Collins
2. Elton John
3. Bruce Springsteen
4. Carly Simon
5. Lionel Richie
6. Stevie Wonder
7. Melissa Etheridge
8. Barbra Streisand
9. David Byrne

2 MUSICIANS WHO BECAME CONGRESSMEN
1. Sonny Bono
2. John Hall (Orleans)

5 CLASSIC SONGS THAT PEAKED AT #2
1. "Purple Rain" (Prince)
2. "Start Me Up" (The Rolling Stones)
3. "Daniel" (Elton John)
4. "What's Going On" (Marvin Gaye)
5. "Louie Louie" (The Kingsmen)

Before his career took off, Jackson Browne played with Blue Öyster Cult for two weeks.

WILLIE NELSON'S
"NIGHT LIFE"

It's a song that transformed Willie Nelson into a legendary country performer and made millions in royalties...for somebody else.

ODD JOBS

Back in the 1950s, long before Willie Nelson made his mark as a successful Nashville songwriter and country music performer, he was broke and living in Fort Worth, Texas. After a stint in the Air Force, he'd worked as a tree trimmer, dishwasher, and disc jockey. All the while, he wrote songs and tried to sell them to anyone who would buy them—often for as little as $10 per song.

In May of 1958, Nelson's first wife, Martha, gave birth to their third child. Nelson knew he needed to make more money to support his young family, and he knew that most country-music songwriters lived in Nashville. But the thought of moving to Music City intimidated him: "I got the feeling that if I went to Nashville right then, I would have been like a chigger on the butt of the abominable snowman," Nelson recalls. "I couldn't see any future in that direction."

So Nelson stayed in Fort Worth, and sold encyclopedias and vacuum cleaners and taught Sunday school at a Baptist church (he lost that job when the preacher found out he was moonlighting as a bar singer). But he didn't prove to be much of a salesman, and soon found himself in debt. So Nelson decided to try his luck in Houston, and packed up his family to move there. "We didn't have any money," he said, "but I did have some new songs I thought I could sell."

SONGS FOR SALE

On his way into Houston, Nelson stopped at a bar called the Esquire Club and talked to a musician named Larry Butler, who was rehearsing with his band. "When they took a break, I got Larry off to the side and told him I wanted to sell him some songs.

The first #1 album on the Billboard 200 was *Belafonte* by Harry Belafonte.

I told him I'd take $10 apiece for them. I sang him 'Mr. Record Man' and some other good songs...and when I finished I said, 'How many do you want to buy?' Larry said, 'You mean you want to sell "Mr. Record Man" to me for ten dollars for me to put my name on it and claim I wrote it?'" That was *exactly* what Nelson wanted. At the time, he looked at songs like paintings: "You finish one and you sell it for whatever you can get, and then you do another," he later said. But Butler refused to buy any. "You don't like 'em?" Nelson asked. "Hell, I love 'em," Larry responded. "But these songs are too good for you to sell like this. Hang onto them, and one day they'll be hits."

GET A JOB

Larry Butler saw enough promise in Nelson to give him a $50 loan and a job playing in his band. Nelson also looked up an old friend, guitarist Paul Buskirk, who found him a few jobs teaching guitar lessons. "Paul Buskirk was my mentor," Nelson remembers. "He taught me a lot about life and about music. He knows his instruments and knows what he's doing...my playing is a lot of leaping off into space and seeing if I can hit the ground running."

Buskirk was also in the market for new songs for his country band, so he bought two of Nelson's—"Family Bible" for $50, and "Night Life" for $150. "Family Bible" was later recorded by singer Claude Gray, and reached #1 on the country chart. Willie never received any royalties on the song, which was published with Gray, Buskirk, and Walter Breeland as the songwriters.

Similarly, though Nelson performed on Paul Buskirk's original recording of "Night Life," Buskirk got the songwriting credit. At the time, Nelson had a recording contract with a small Houston studio called D Records. The studio didn't want him to record "Night Life" because they didn't think it was a country song. But when Buskirk and Nelson went to another studio to record it, D Records threatened to sue Nelson. So he changed his name in the credits of the song to "Hugh Nelson" to head off the lawsuit.

RIGHTS ARE WRONGS

"Night Life" turned out to be one of the most-recorded songs in history. More than 70 artists from genres as varied as blues, pop, jazz, and even opera have performed it, and it's sold more than 30

The metronome, invented by Dietrich Winkel in 1812, was first used by Beethoven.

million records worldwide. But all Willie Nelson ever received for it was $150, since he'd sold all the rights to Paul Buskirk. "At the time, I needed the money," Nelson said years later. "Suppose I'd been stubborn and waited and maybe never sold it at all?" Philosophically, he says of both "Night Life" and "Family Bible," "The fact that both songs became hits encouraged me to think I could write a lot more songs that were just as good."

NEW LIFE

Nelson's success in Houston gave him the confidence to finally make his move to Nashville. In a beaten-down 1950 Buick that he owed five payments on—and with a siphon for stealing gas—he hit the road for Tennessee. He made it as far as downtown Nashville...where the car belched smoke and died. But he'd arrived, and over the next few years he sold those songs Larry Butler had refused to buy—and many others—and was on his way to one of the most legendary careers in music history.

*   *   *

THREE OF THE WEIRDEST ALBUMS OF ALL TIME

Sammy Petrillo: *My Son, the Phone Caller.* Petrillo was a Jerry Lewis impersonator who starred in a few B-movies, including *Bela Lugosi Meets a Brooklyn Gorilla.* This album features him doing moronic phone pranks like calling hospitals and saying that he's got a pregnant pet gorilla in labor, then asking how to deliver the baby.

The National Gallery: *Performing Musical Interpretations of the Paintings of Paul Klee.* Four beatniks from Cleveland introduce listeners the German Expressionist painter Paul Klee by performing "rock-art" song versions of his paintings. Lyrics include: "Boy with toys, alone in the attic / Choking his hobby horse, thinking of his mother."

Mr. Methane: *Mr. Methane.com.* The anonymous Mr. Methane is a "fartiste"—he breaks melodic wind. Here he poots his way through classics like "The Blue Danube," Beethoven's Ninth Symphony, and "Greensleeves," proving conclusively that he doesn't have to be silent to be deadly.

THE FOLK REVIVAL, PART II

*In Part I of the story (see page 365), we told you about
the early pioneers of folk music. But how did folk
fuel the politically charged 1960s? Read on.*

TRAIN KEPT A-ROLLIN'

While some political folk musicians were forced to take an involuntary hiatus in the late 1940s and '50s by the House Un-American Activities Committee, a nonpolitical interest in preserving the folk tradition continued to build the groundwork of the Folk Revival. One of the most important builders was a Polish immigrant and radio deejay named Moses Asch. He started recording folk singers in the early 1940s, and in 1948 founded Folkways Records. His records, like the *Anthology of American Folk Music*, a 1952 compilation of hillbilly and "race" recordings from the 1920s and '30s, kept folk music's popularity up until in the late '50s, when it finally exploded—not as a protest movement but as a celebration of Americana. The Folk Revival began as a clean-cut, collegiate sing-along, with the Kingston Trio leading the way.

HOOTENANNY

In 1957 three young college grads from Palo Alto, California—Dave Guard (guitar), Bob Shane (banjo), and Nick Reynolds (guitar)—landed a deal with Capitol Records and released their self-titled album *The Kingston Trio*. One song from the album, "Tom Dooley" (written around 1868 and based on the true story of a convicted murderer named Tom Dula), started getting regular radio play around the country, and the song was rereleased in July 1958 as a single. By October it was in the Billboard Top 10, and in November it hit #1. The song won a Grammy for Best Country & Western Performance (no folk category existed yet—and it was the first award for "country" music of any kind). And it sold more than three million copies.

In 1959 the band made not one, but *four* more albums—*Stereo Concert*, *...from the Hungry*, *At Large*, and *Here We Go Again*.

They won two more Grammys, were named Best Group of the Year by both *Billboard* and *Cashbox* magazines—and they even made the cover of *Life* magazine. Big record companies started pumping out albums by folk (and mostly nonpolitical) acts like the Limeliters, the Highwaymen, the Chad Mitchell Trio, the Journeymen, the Tarriers, and the New Christy Minstrels. Folk acts were all over the radio, and were appearing regularly on TV shows like *The Ed Sullivan Show*, and specialty shows dedicated solely to folk music, like ABC's *Hootenanny*.

THE TIMES THEY ARE, UH, CHANGIN'

Until about 1963, popular folk music retained its apolitical image. But that didn't last. McCarthy was gone, the Red Scare era was over, and the left-leaning singers were no longer blacklisted. The older protest singers like Seeger, Hays, and Odetta burst back onto the scene, singing at gatherings for the burgeoning civil cights movement and, with the Vietnam War escalating, the peace movement. (In 1963 Pete Seeger even got his own TV show on PBS, *Rainbow Quest*, on which he hosted musical guests like Richard and Mimi Farina, Tom Paxton, and Johnny Cash.)

About this time a new category of folksinger began to emerge within the larger Folk Revival. Performers like Dave van Ronk, Malvina Reynolds, Fred Neil, Eric von Schmidt, and Tom Paxton became the new folk stars, and with a new twist: their own newly written songs (not old folk standards), often with biting political commentary. Many of them did quite well, and some are still cult heroes, but none of them ever became the major superstars that the Kingston Trio were. Except one.

In 1962 Columbia Records found their next star in a young Greenwich Village-based (and Woody Guthrie-influenced) balladeer by the name of Bob Dylan. The first album had 11 covers of traditional songs and two nonpolitical originals. It didn't do very well. His next album, *The Freewheelin' Bob Dylan*, had two covers and 11 originals, including some of the most enduring antiwar songs ever penned, "Blowin' in the Wind," "A Hard Rain's Gonna Fall," and "Masters of War." The album made the *Billboard* chart and began the meteoric rise of the Folk Revival's longest-lasting and biggest star. Ironically, Dylan also helped bring the era to an end.

FOR WHAT IT'S WORTH

Other things were happening in the early 1960s: The Beatles and
the Rolling Stones were taking rock 'n' roll to artistic and commercial heights nobody could have foreseen. Even some folkies
were picking up electric guitars. This drove folk purists nuts...and
splits in the folk movement quickly appeared.

The symbolic end of the Folk Revival came at the 1965 New-
port Folk Festival, when Dylan went onstage with an electric guitar
and a full rock 'n' roll band. He may as well have smashed all the
folkies' acoustic guitars with a hammer (if he'd had a hammer).
Result: folk music was never the same. Seeing that the times were
passing them by, purists started fragmenting into specialty groups
(bluegrass, old timey, etc.), and forming preservation societies dedicated to their own favorite folk styles. They dwindled into obscurity, and rock and pop took over. The Folk Revival was done.

LEGACY

Folk music record labels continued on as they always had; big labels
pretty much gave up on folk—but not altogether. For years they
continued to sign artists like John Prine, Loudon Wainwright III,
and Bruce Springsteen, hoping to find the "next Bob Dylan" (see
page 153). And although the Folk Revival was finished, its effects
would be long felt. Songwriters, especially Dylan, influenced rock
'n' roll songwriting for decades, with acts as diverse as the Beatles,
Neil Young, Lou Reed, Joni Mitchell, Dire Straits, R.E.M., Oasis,
and Nirvana (just to name a very few) claiming inspiration from the
Folk Revival era. And new folkies—all influenced by the Folk
Revival—have come on the scene and made their mark. A few of
the bigger names over the years: Gordon Lightfoot, Stan Rogers,
Michelle Shocked, Ani DiFranco, Greg Brown, Jeff Buckley, Billy
Bragg, and Suzanne Vega.

FOLK HEROES

Some more notable figures of the Folk Revival era:

• **Josh White (1914–1969).** The first big-time black folk singer.
In the 1930s, he became nationally known and even became
friends with President Franklin Roosevelt, performing at his
inauguration in 1941 and again in 1945. And this was while
White was singing songs that were openly hostile to government

---

In 1941 the town of Berwyn, Oklahoma (population 99) changed its name to Gene Autry.

policies, especially segregation. White continued to perform until his death in 1969. Biggest hits: "St. James Infirmary" and "House of the Rising Sun."

• **Elizabeth Cotten (1895–1987).** She wrote her most famous song, "Freight Train," at the age of 12. But she got a boost in the Folk Revival, too. Mike Seeger, Pete's brother, produced her first album in 1957, when she was in her 60s, and by the mid-1960s she was an American folk legend. She won the 1984 Grammy for Best Ethnic or Traditional Recording for her album *Elizabeth Cotten Live.*

• **Malvina Reynolds.** Most famous for the suburbia-lampooning "Little Boxes" and the antinuclear weapons song, "What Have They Done to the Rain?"—both written in 1962.

• **Eric Anderson.** He hit the Greenwich Village folk scene in 1964 and is best known for his folk classic "Thirsty Boots."

• **Tom Paxton** has written hundreds of songs, many of which have become standards, including "Bottle of Wine," "Last Thing on My Mind," and "Rambling Boy." He's still regularly performing.

• **A few others:** Dave van Ronk (folk music's "Mayor of MacDougal Street" in Greenwich Village), Phil Ochs ("Draft Dodger Rag" and "I Ain't Marching Anymore"), Ian and Sylvia ("Four Strong Winds"), Tom Rush ("No Regrets"), Fred Neil ("Everybody's Talkin'"), and Tim Buckley, David Blue, John Sebastian, Tim Hardin, John Hartford, Buffy Sainte-Marie, and Leonard Cohen.

• **Legendary folk music moment:** In 1967 Pete Seeger wrote and recorded an anti-Vietnam War song called "Waist Deep in the Big Muddy." Columbia Records—which controlled the fate of the album for which Seeger recorded it—refused to send it to stores. Later that year Seeger was invited by Tom and Dick Smothers to sing the song on the *Smothers Brothers Comedy Hour.* He did… and CBS refused to air it. The Smothers brothers responded by sending letters to newspapers, saying "CBS censors our best jokes. They censored Seeger's best song. It ain't fair!" It worked: In January 1968, the Smothers called Seeger again. "On 48 hours' notice I flew to California and taped the song," Seeger recalled years later. "And this time seven million people saw it." It was Seeger's first time on network television since being blacklisted 17 years earlier.

THE BATHROOM ALBUM

Uncle John's fantabulous list of classic songs written about his favorite room. You might be surprised at how many you know.

"**Splish Splash (I Was Takin' a Bath),**" Bobby Darin, 1958. That year, Darin was living at the home of now-legendary New York disc jockey Murray "the K" Kaufman. Kaufman's mother, Jean Kaufman, suggested a song called "Splish Splash"— and Darin wrote it on the spot. Murray and his mother both got writing credit on the song; they're listed as cowriter "Jean Murray," a combination of their names.

"**Smokin' in the Boys' Room,**" Brownsville Station, 1973. This teenage anthem would probably be controversial today because of its "pro-smoking" message, but back then it went to #3 in the chart. Guitarist Michael "Cub" Koda wrote it in half an hour.

"**She Came in Through the Bathroom Window,**" the Beatles, 1968. According to Beatles lore, Paul McCartney was inspired to write the song after a female fan climbed up to his bathroom window.

"**The Plexiglas Toilet,**" Styx, 1974. This song isn't listed in the liner notes of the album *The Serpent Is Rising*, but it runs right after the end of the fourth song, "As Bad as This." Chorus: "Don't sit on the Plexiglas toilet / Said the momma to her son / Wipe the butt clean with the paper / Make it nice for everyone / But don't sit down on the Plexiglas toilet—yeah."

"**Fat Man in the Bathtub,**" Little Feat, 1973. "Throw me a line, throw me a line," growls legendary singer and slide-guitar player Lowell George, "'cuz there's a fat man in the bathtub with the blues. I hear you moan, I hear you moan…"

"**Flushed from the Bathroom of Your Heart,**" Johnny Cash, 1968. Besides the title, Cash croons these classic country lines: "In the garbage disposal of your dreams I've been ground up, dear / On the river of your plans I'm up the creek / Up the elevator of your future I've been shafted / On the calendar of your events I'm last week."

YOU CAN COUNT ON BASIE

Despite a deceptively simple piano style (one band member commented, "Count don't do nothin'. But it sure sounds good."), there was no hotter jazz musician than Count Basie in the 1930s. Here are four facts to help you get to know the Count.

1. HE WANTED TO PLAY DRUMS

Bill Basie's first instrument wasn't the piano—he played drums with his school band, but when it turned out that another kid in school played the drums better, Basie got discouraged and quit. Fortunately for him, his mother was an enthusiastic amateur pianist and encouraged him to take up the keys. The piano suited Basie well, and by 1924, when he was 20, he had gone to Harlem to study with legendary jazz pianist Fats Waller. Waller recommended Basie to a traveling vaudeville show, and for the next couple of years, the young pianist traveled the country playing jazz. In 1927 the vaudeville tour folded, leaving Basie stuck in Kansas City, Missouri. He stayed there until 1936. Then he and his orchestra headed for New York and national fame. (Incidentally, the kid who played drums better than Basie was Sonny Greer, who went on to play drums for Duke Ellington.)

2. HE WASN'T REALLY A COUNT

He was the son of a coachman and a laundress. But the reason he's known as "Count" Basie dates back to the 1930s, when he formed a band from the remnants of two earlier bands (Walter Page's Blue Devils and Bennie Moten's Kansas City Orchestra) and performed with the group on a local Kansas City shortwave radio station. The announcer, riffing off the royalty names of jazz greats Duke Ellington and Earl Hines, dubbed Basie a count...and the nickname stuck. (Other nicknames: "The Jump King" because of his band's driving rhythm, and "The Kid from Red Bank" because he grew up in Red Bank, New Jersey.)

3. HE WAS SWINDLED BY HIS RECORD COMPANY

Modern musicians like to complain about the dog-eat-dog nature of the music industry. But today's music companies have nothing on the greedy tactics of the music industry in the 1930s. Basie's first recording contract is a good example of how musicians got manhandled: In exchange for 24 "sides" (this was in the days of 78-rpm records, which played one song on each side) over three years, Basie earned a mere $750. Royalties? He got none. Basie never made additional money from early hits like "One O'Clock Jump," and "Jumpin' at the Woodside."

4. HIS CAREER IS DIVIDED INTO TWO "TESTAMENTS"

Basie's career has an "old testament" (prior to 1950) and a "new testament" (everything after 1952). The dividing line falls during the two-year gap when the bottom seemed to drop out of the market for swing and jazz orchestras. For economic reasons, Basie had to disband his full orchestra in 1950 and continue with just an eight-piece group. In 1952 things picked up again, and Basie was able to rehire a full orchestra.

On either side of this gap, Basie's orchestras were substantially different. The old testament musicians relied on memorizing arrangements (known as "head arrangements") rather than reading music. They also focused mostly on a swing sound. The new testament orchestras, on the other hand, played primarily blues and were filled with sight readers (players who not only read music but read it well enough to play it right away), which gave Basie more flexibility with his arrangements.

Which testament is better? That's a personal choice, of course. But both testaments were known for their excellent musicians. Old testament musicians included Lester Young (often regarded as the best tenor saxophonist in jazz history), trombonist Dicky Wells, and even singer Billie Holiday, who joined Basie for a stint in 1937. New testament standouts included saxophonist Frank Wess, trumpeter Thad Jones, and vocalist Joe Williams.

*　　　*　　　*

"We all do *do-re-mi*, but you have to find the other notes yourself."

—Louis Armstrong

In 2004 the first "robot conductor" led the Tokyo Philharmonic. They played Beethoven's 5th.

THE KILLER VS. THE KING

When you've been around as long as Uncle John has, you'll probably start to assume you've heard every story there is about pop music. Wrong! Here's one that was new to all of us.

OLD FRIENDS

Elvis Presley was the "King of Rock 'n' Roll"; Jerry Lee Lewis was the first person to be inducted into the Rock and Roll Hall of Fame. They were both hugely influential in formulating the sound of rock 'n' roll music—both were raised singing gospel music in the Pentecostal church, and they both got their start at Sam Phillips's famous Sun Studios in Memphis, Tennessee. Presley and Lewis were good friends early in their careers, and were even known to go on motorcycle rides and double dates together.

During one of Lewis's recording sessions in late 1956, Presley, who had moved on to record for RCA, stopped by to see his old friends at Sun. Rockabilly pioneer Carl Perkins was also hanging around, and a jam session broke out with the three. Sam Phillips quickly called his other big star, Johnny Cash, to join in, and the star-packed session became known as the "Million Dollar Quartet." As Presley's and Lewis's careers took different paths, double dates and motorcycle rides gave way to gold records and international tours. They never again had the same day-to-day friendship they had during the Sun Studio years, but their relationship was still amicable.

"THE KILLER" IS COINED

In 1957, while Presley was selling millions of records and starring in movies, Lewis made the headlines by marrying his 13-year-old third cousin (and the daughter of his bass player), a move that virtually ended his rock 'n' roll career. In 1973 he rose from the ashes to become a successful country music performer, but bad publicity from his erratic behavior continued to dog him.

"The Killer" was a nickname that Lewis lived up to—thanks to both his aggressive piano style and a number of highly publicized violent incidents. In 1958 on Alan Freed's *Big Beat Show*, a dispute broke out between Lewis and Chuck Berry over who would close the show. When promoters decided that Berry would be the closer, Lewis protested by pouring a Coke bottle full of gasoline on the piano and lighting it ablaze after his finale—"Great Balls of Fire." In 1976 at his 41st birthday party, he accidentally shot his bass player in the chest, later claiming that he didn't know the gun was loaded. More tragedy: Lewis's fourth wife drowned in a swimming pool in 1982, and the following year his fifth wife died shortly after their wedding from a drug overdose. But Lewis's strangest incident of violence was aimed at his old friend, Elvis Presley.

GUNPLAY AT GRACELAND

At 2:50 a.m. on November 22, 1976, Jerry Lee Lewis unexpectedly pulled up to the front gate of Graceland in a brand-new Silver Shadow Rolls-Royce and asked to see Presley. The King's cousin, Harold Loyd, was working the guard's booth and told Lewis that Presley was sleeping. Lewis thanked Loyd and drove away, leaving Loyd puzzled by the event. Later that morning, Lewis was arrested for driving without a license, driving while intoxicated, and reckless driving after rolling his Rolls-Royce while rounding a corner in the Memphis suburb of Collierville. (Drunk and reckless driving must have been popular in the Lewis family—when Lewis was arrested and taken to Hernando Jail, his father Elmo was there on similar charges.)

RETURN ENGAGEMENT

Ten hours later, Lewis was out on bail and at it again. He was drinking at a popular Memphis nightspot called the Vapors when, for reasons that are still disputed between the King's and the Killer's camps, he left the bar and decided to make his way back to Graceland. He got there at 2:50 a.m., almost the exact time he'd arrived the night before, but this time he was driving a brand-new Lincoln Continental...and he was in a different mood.

"He was outta his mind, man. He was screamin', hollerin', and cussin'," Loyd recalled. Lewis was angry, drunk, and armed with a Derringer pistol. "Get on the @#$%&* phone!" Lewis yelled at Loyd, waving the pistol. "I know you got an intercom system. Call up there and tell Elvis I wanna visit with him! Who in the hell does he think he is? Tell him the Killer's here to see him!"

LITTLE SISTER

Lewis's sister, Linda Gail, recalled that "Jerry was really havin' one big party at the time," that he admitted he'd been "partyin' and drinkin'," and that he was out of it. But Gail swears that Lewis just wanted to visit with Presley. Cousin Harold read the situation differently.

He went into the guard booth and called up to the main house. He was told to call the cops, which he did immediately. Then the King himself called down to the guard booth. Loyd remembered the conversation exactly, including how badly Presley would stutter when he was nervous. "Wh-wh-what the hell's goin' on down there, Harold? Wh-wh-what's that @#$%&* guy want? I-I-I don't wanna talk to that crazy sonofab#$@%. Hell no, I don't wanna talk to him. I'll come down there and kill him! You call the cops, Harold. When they get there, tell 'em to lock his butt up and throw the key away. Okay? Thank you, Harold."

JAILHOUSE ROCK

When Officer Billy J. Kirkpatrick arrived, he ordered Lewis out of the car, but the Killer wouldn't comply. "[Kirkpatrick] had to pull him out of the car," Loyd recalled. "He told him to keep his hands on the steering wheel where he could see 'em. Jerry said he just wanted to see Elvis, but Kirkpatrick told him to shut up. Now Jerry, he had tried to hide his pistol by puttin' it in between his knee and the door. When Kirkpatrick opened the door, the damn gun fell out onto the floorboard. Kirkpatrick picked up the gun, and it was cocked and loaded!"

Kirkpatrick also found that the front passenger window of Lewis's car was smashed out and that Lewis had a deep gash on his nose, which he concluded was due to "broken glass resulting from [Lewis] attempting to jettison an empty champagne bottle thru the closed window of his '76 Lincoln." Kirkpatrick and four other policemen arrested Lewis and took him to jail, ironically, just as Lewis's father, Elmo Lewis, was being bailed out. The elder Lewis arrived at Graceland just as the wrecker arrived to tow away Lewis's Lincoln. "Ha! Ain't this some crap, man?"

Loyd remembered Elmo saying when he arrived on the scene. "I just got word that they've taken my son to jail. I just got me outta the Hernando Jail, and Jerry done gone ahead."

SUSPICIOUS MINDS

Word soon got out that "the Killer" was trying to kill "the King," but Lewis's sister Linda Gail believes that Presley called Lewis at the Vapors and invited him to come to Graceland, that Harold Loyd never told Presley that Lewis was there, and that Lewis became belligerent because he thought Presley would get mad at him if he didn't take the invitation seriously. "I believe, really and truly, that the people who were associated with Elvis at that time were trying to manipulate him," Gail says. "He was supporting all of them financially, and it was in their best interest to keep him isolated. If him and Elvis had started runnin' the roads together, can you imagine what that would have been like? It probably would have been more than Memphis could handle."

LAST MAN STANDING

After the incident, the Killer and the King's friendship was never the same. When Elvis Presley died in 1977, Lewis said, "I'm glad. Just another one outta the way. What the @#%* did Presley ever do except take dope I couldn't get ahold of?" Then after Johnny Cash died in 2003, the 71-year-old Lewis televised an all-star tribute concert called *Last Man Standing*, a reference to his being the last surviving member of the "Million Dollar Quartet."

*　　*　　*

TWO-HIT WONDERS

While they've sold millions of albums, these music giants each have had only two Top-40 songs, making them "two-hit wonders."
- Spencer Davis Group ("Gimme Some Lovin'," "I'm a Man")
- Pink Floyd ("Money," "Another Brick in the Wall")
- Nirvana ("Smells Like Teen Spirit," "Come as You Are")
- Elvis Costello ("Everyday I Write the Book," "Veronica")
- The Clash ("Train in Vain," "Rock the Casbah")

The world's largest playable electric guitar is 43' 7 ½" long and weighs 2,244 pounds.

LA TRIVIATA

Fascinating facts behind some of history's greatest operas.

BOO-CCINI. *Madame Butterfly* wasn't well received when it premiered at La Scala in Milan, Italy, in 1904. The audience apparently thought the second act was too long. Composer Giacomo Puccini stood in the wings of the opera house, listening to the patrons' boos and hisses, and muttered, "Louder, louder, you beasts! You'll see who's right. This is the best opera I've ever written!" He was right. By making a few alterations (he actually split the second act into two parts), Puccini had the last word. Audiences raved when *Madame Butterfly* was rereleased a few months later.

HE WAS CARMEN AND GOING. In April 1906, the famous tenor Enrico Caruso performed in *Carmen* at San Francisco's Tivoli Opera House. Just hours after the performance, at 5:12 a.m., he was roused from bed when an earthquake shook the city. The fires caused by the 1906 San Francisco earthquake destroyed the famous Palace Hotel where Caruso and his touring company were staying. The opera house was destroyed as well, and the company lost all of its costumes and stage sets. Caruso fled the burning city and vowed never to return. (He kept his word.)

CLOSING TIME. The audience at the 1786 Viennese premiere of *The Marriage of Figaro* received the opera so enthusiastically that the encores lasted almost two hours (the opera was four hours long). The cast may have thought that was a good thing, but Austrian emperor Joseph II didn't. He was exhausted, and wanted to go home. After one duet was performed three times in the encore, the exasperated emperor enacted a law forbidding all encores at performances of *Figaro*.

WHERE AM I? Many onstage misadventures have added unexpected excitement to the opera *Tosca*. One performance was interrupted when the diva's wig caught fire after she leaned too close to a lit candle. Another time, a knife failed to retract during a dra-

---

Patsy Cline didn't like "Walkin' After Midnight," saying it was "just a lil' old pop song."

matic murder scene and actually stabbed one of the actors. One classic 20th-century performance made the newspapers when baritone Tito Gobbi suddenly broke out in uncontrollable laughter on the floor following his character's murder. What was so funny? Soprano Maria Callas, nearly blind without her glasses (she couldn't wear contacts), was wandering around, unable to find her way off the stage.

NO NO, RIGOLETTO. Composer Giuseppe Verdi and his librettist Francesco Maria Piave had to censor themselves while writing this opera based on Victor Hugo's 1832 play *Le Roi S'amuse*. Austro-Hungarian authorities found the work insulting to the crown and required extensive revisions to make it acceptable, so much that *Rigoletto* was almost unrecognizable from its original form. Required alterations: The setting was changed from a royal court to a small territory in Italy, the characters were renamed, scenes were cut, and even the title was changed. (It was unofficially known as *The Curse*.) Regardless, when it premiered in Venice in 1851, the audience loved it. Today, *Rigoletto* is the sixth most frequently performed opera at the Metropolitan Opera House in New York.

CONSPIRACY THEORY. When Mozart died at the age of 35 in 1791, *The Magic Flute*—his final opera—was already a success. Audiences flocked to it, filling the opera houses. In fact, just 13 months after it premiered, the opera celebrated its 100th performance. Sadly, Mozart didn't live to see this milestone; he died from an unexplained illness just two months after *Magic Flute* premiered. Some historians believe that Mozart may have been murdered by the Freemasons, a secret society to which he belonged and by which he had been heavily influenced. According to this theory, Mozart had revealed too many of the group's secrets, and they had him executed. Whether that's true or not, Freemasons today do acknowledge that many symbols and allusions in *The Magic Flute* are related to Freemasonry ideas, rituals, and initiation processes—specifically, the many references to the number three, a symbol of the Freemasons. (The meaning behind the symbol is still a mystery because the Freemasons remain a secret society.)

LIBERACE

*Just when rock 'n' roll was on the rise, something a lot more
square was insanely popular with a lot of people: Liberace.*

LITTLE TINKLER

Wladziu Valentino Liberace was born in West Allis, a suburb of Milwaukee, Wisconsin, in 1919. His mother was a
Polish immigrant who played piano and his father worked as a
French horn player for Milwaukee dance bands and orchestras.
They demanded their children take music lessons, so Wladziu's
brother, 12-year-old George, took up the piano. Wladziu, then just
four years old, quickly learned to play by ear; he'd listen to George
play and pick out the notes on the piano.

Wladziu was a natural: By age seven, he'd memorized the hard-
est compositions by Mendelssohn and his skill level had exceeded
that of his teacher (a next-door neighbor). That same year, the
Liberace family received a visit from the Polish concert pianist
Ignacy Paderewski.

Liberace's mother had worked in Paderewski's lesson studio in
Poland. She wrote to the master pianist when he toured the United
States in 1926, asking that if he remembered her, perhaps he could
come to her home and encourage her son. Sure enough, Paderewski
showed up at the house wearing a red velvet cape and accompanied by a large entourage. Wladziu played selections by Liszt and
Chopin for Paderewski, who was so impressed he remarked, "Perhaps someday when I am gone, you will take my place."

As a teen, Walter (nobody could pronounce Wladziu) Liberace's skills quickly progressed. He played piano at high school
dances, dance recitals, and fashion shows around Milwaukee, as
well as his own classical recitals around Wisconsin. By 20, he'd
landed a spot as a soloist with the Chicago Symphony Orchestra
and was studying on a scholarship at the Wisconsin College of
Music. His future as a successful classical pianist seemed assured.

BORING PARTS LEFT OUT

But at a 1939 recital in La Crosse, Wisconsin, something changed.
After playing a classical program, the young pianist took requests

from the audience for an encore. He expected that they'd want to hear more classical music, but someone asked for "Three Little Fishes," a novelty song about a fish-eating whale by bandleader Kay Kyser that was the #1 song in the country at the time. Liberace played the song, grinning and winking to the audience to let them know how audacious it was for a classically trained pianist to play something so "beneath" him (and especially in the presence of a snooty local music critic who was reportedly in the audience).

The audience loved the song and the over-the-top way he played it. "I realized after that incident that my heart was not in concertizing, but in entertaining," Liberace later said. He immediately changed his act to incorporate popular songs and humorous takes on classical pieces. He called it "pop with a bit of the classics" or "classical music with the boring parts left out."

To hone the routine, Liberace took a job as house entertainer at Wunderbar, a nightclub in Warsaw, Wisconsin, performing under the name "Walter Busterkeys." After a few months, he decided to go to New York and try to make it on the nightclub scene there. He got a job at the Persian Room in the Plaza Hotel, where *Variety* favorably reviewed his show, saying, "He should snowball into box office."

Liberace's rise to fame was interrupted in 1946 when the Musicians Union found out he was playing humorous musical counterpoints to records being played over the sound system at the Persian Room. The union banned him from playing there, so he decided to move to Los Angeles, where he dropped the stage name and began to perform under only his last name—Liberace.

SIGN ALONG WITH MITCH

Liberace's move to California paid off when Decca Records executives saw him perform at a Hollywood bar. Intrigued by his unique act and engaging, self-deprecating stage persona, they signed him to a record deal with the intention of making him into the next big bandleader, like Glenn Miller or Guy Lombardo. That idea never took off, but in 1950 Columbia Records bought out his contract. Columbia executive and record producer Mitch Miller (who later starred on the TV show *Sing Along with Mitch*) didn't think it was a good idea to mold Liberace into something he wasn't. Miller reasoned that nightclub audiences enjoyed Liberace's act for exactly what it was: pop music played in a classical style, with stories and jokes thrown in. In 1950 Miller produced a Liberace live album and a single called "September Song." Both became national hits and led to a film appearance as the master of ceremonies in *Footlight Varieties*, a filmed variety show made up of old vaudeville acts. Liberace was a rising star.

In 1952, with network television in its early stages, TV executives wanted to create shows based on performers who had already established themselves in music, theater, or even vaudeville. So in the summer of 1952, NBC quietly debuted *The Liberace Show*, a 15-minute program of Liberace doing his act. Airing on Tuesday and Thursday nights, it was a summer replacement for the very popular *Dinah Shore Show*, and was meant to last only eight weeks. But it turned out to be the most-watched TV show of the summer. *The Liberace Show* returned as a regular half-hour program in 1953 and stayed on NBC for five years. In addition, another version of *The Liberace Show* was syndicated to local TV stations two years later, giving the pianist two simultaneous TV shows. Combined, Liberace was seen on more TV stations than *I Love Lucy* in the early 1950s.

Liberace later said the secret to his success was the way he flirted with the camera. "I looked it right in its one big eye just the way I'd look you in the eye. When I winked, everyone in the whole television audience could see for themselves that I was winking right at them."

Thanks mostly to the TV show, Liberace was the biggest musical act in the United States in the early 1950s. In 1953 alone he sold two million albums, received 5,000 fan letters per week, and regularly made hundreds of women faint at his public appearances. But unlike earlier idols such as Frank Sinatra, Liberace wasn't making the teenage girls swoon—middle-aged and elderly women were usually the ones screaming and passing out.

A FABULOUS BREAKTHROUGH
In 1953 Liberace was scheduled to play for an audience of 20,000 at the Hollywood Bowl, the premier outdoor concert venue in the United States. He worried that in such a large stadium, the crowd at the back wouldn't be able to see him because his concert attire—traditional pianist clothes of black tie and tails—wouldn't stand out

against the black tuxedos of the orchestra behind him. Solution: he wore all white. And at his next concert, he wore gold lamé.

From that point on, Liberace's costumes became shinier, sparklier, more expensive, and more garish, and became a signature part of his act—along with a golden candelabra atop the piano. Eventually he incorporated lace, huge rings, silks, medallions, sequins, diamonds, furs, and capes. Some of his more notable costumes included a 40-pound rhinestone jacket, a jewel-encrusted fox fur cape, and black velvet dress tails with "Liberace" spelled out in diamonds. By his own estimates, he spent more than $100,000 per year on costumes.

Liberace's popularity kept increasing throughout the 1950s. In 1955 he starred in the musical melodrama *Sincerely Yours* as a deaf concert pianist. He was mentioned by name in the Chordettes song "Mr. Sandman" ("and lots of wavy hair like Liberace"), published his own cookbook, and in addition to his TV show, started playing a regularly scheduled show in Las Vegas at the Riviera casino. For that, he earned $50,000 per week (the equivalent of $360,000 today). He also played another sold-out Hollywood Bowl concert and performed for Queen Elizabeth three times. By 1957 there were 160 official Liberace fan clubs—with 250,000 members.

OFF TO CAMP

By the mid-'50s, rumors began to circulate that Liberace was gay, but he usually dodged the question. When asked by a British reporter if he had a "normal" sex life, he replied, "Yes. Do you?" But in 1956, William Connor, who wrote a gossip column for the London tabloid *The Daily Mirror* under the pen name Cassandra, wrote: "Liberace is a deadly, winking, sniggering, snuggling, chromium-plated, scent-impregnated, luminous, quivering, giggling, fruit-flavored, mincing, ice-covered heap of mother love." Connor did everything he could to suggest Liberace was gay, without actually saying it (he didn't want to get sued). Liberace successfully sued the paper for libel anyway, testifying in court that he wasn't gay. Privately, all his friends and family knew that he was, but he asked them to keep it a secret until his death.

By the late 1950s, after rock 'n' roll began to dominate popular music, Liberace's career faded. His TV show ended in 1959 and he tried to play off his campy image to some success: In the mid-'60s he appeared on *Batman* (as a mincing villain and as himself on *The Monkees*). He also tried to branch out into nonmusical acting, getting good reviews for his role as a crooked funeral home director in the 1965 dark comedy *The Loved One*. He was back in the public eye and seemed set to enjoy a TV comeback. A new version of *The Liberace Show*, made to look exactly like his 1950s show, aired in 1969, but it was canceled after only seven episodes.

VIVA LAS VEGAS

In the 1970s, Liberace started performing on the road—especially in Las Vegas—full time. His wallet didn't suffer: He made $300,000 per week at the Las Vegas Hilton, published several cookbooks, and opened an antique store in Beverly Hills and a three-story Liberace Museum in Las Vegas to display his costumes and memorabilia. He also appeared on television frequently, performing on talk and variety shows.

His sexual orientation remained an open secret until 1982, when his live-in boyfriend, Scott Thorson, sued him for $113 million in palimony after they broke up. Liberace still denied being homosexual, but he settled the suit for $95,000.

Liberace played his last concerts—a sold-out, weeklong stand at New York's Radio City Music Hall, in November 1986. He was noticeably thinner, which he attributed to "going overboard on a watermelon diet." Three months later, Liberace died at age 67 from complications due to AIDS, one of the first major public figures to die from the disease. He was buried in Hollywood's Forest Lawn cemetery in a massive marble tomb surrounded by trees… bent to look like candelabras.

*   *   *

GETTING BUGGED

Ever see one of those old Warner Bros. cartoons where Bugs Bunny sits down at the piano, plays a few notes, then looks up and says, "I wish my brother George was here"? That's a Liberace reference. George Liberace played violin occasionally on *The Liberace Show*. When he didn't, Liberace would utter that line, and it briefly became a catchphrase.

In 2 episodes of TV's *Batman*, Liberace played the villain Chandell (*and* his twin brother Harry).

WHY DO INSTRUMENTS SOUND DIFFERENT?

It's not as silly a question as it might at first sound.

BACKGROUND NOISE

Strike a single note on a guitar, say the A string. Now blow the same note on a clarinet. They're both the same note... but they don't sound the same. Why? Because, although it may sound like it, that's not the only note you're hearing. Each instrument produces, simultaneously with its A note, other (and quieter) notes known as *overtones*. Our brains don't interpret these as separate notes—we blend them all into that single A note, giving it a tone or personality that a listener might interpret as "dark," "bright," "mellow," "harsh," or "warm." This tonal quality is known as the *timbre* (TAM-ber) of a sound. The trick is that each instrument is creating those overtones in a way that's unique to its physical structure—and that's what makes each instrument sound different.

GOOD VIBRATIONS

The source of all sound is *vibration*. A vibrating object pushes air molecules around it, which push against air molecules around them, and so on, causing *sound waves* to radiate through the air away from the object. This is true for anything that makes a sound, whether it's a musical instrument or a book that you drop on the floor. But how they vibrate—or how waves move through them—is very different.

When you drop a book on the floor, it creates vibrations in the book (and the floor) that cause sound waves to move through the air—but only for a very short time. That's because a book isn't very *resonant*, meaning that it doesn't build up waves inside it, and it stops vibrating very quickly. A guitar string, on the other hand, is very resonant. When a string is plucked, waves travel up and down the length of the string, creating a sustained tone. That's what musical instruments do. They trap waves, creating what is the necessary ingredient in what we think of as musical tone—*standing waves*.

Here's the important part: Different instruments create different kinds of standing waves (and in different combinations), and those multiple standing waves are what produce the overtones that define an instrument's sound.

THE OVERTONE SERIES

Here's a basic description of how it works.

• When you pluck an A string on a guitar, standing waves exactly as long as the string are created, which is just another way of saying it vibrates back and forth along its entire length. The physical characteristics of a guitar's A string determines that it vibrates back and forth 440 times a second, or at 440 *hertz*, emitting the sound we hear as an A note. This is referred to as the *fundamental*.

• At the same time, standing waves exactly *half* the string's length are created. (Only waves that "fit" in this simple, fractional way—being half, a third, a fourth, a fifth, and so on, of the string's length—can become standing waves. Waves that don't fit like that are simply cancelled out.) This half-sized wave vibrates at twice the speed of the fundamental: 880 hertz. That creates a note twice as high. It's an A note again, but an octave higher than the fundamental. That's the *first overtone*.

• Another standing wave exactly one third the string's length is also being created. It vibrates three times faster than the fundamental—at 1320 hertz. That's an E note, much higher than the fundamental A, and it's the *second overtone*.

• This goes on and on—1/4 the length (the fourth overtone), 1/5 the length (the fifth overtone), 1/6 the length (the sixth overtone), ad infinitum—with each successively shorter wave vibrating faster, creating higher and higher pitches. (But they quickly leave human hearing capability, which ends at about 20,000 hertz.)

This is known as the *overtone series*. All musical instruments operate on these rules. Wind instruments obviously don't have strings—they have columns of air that vibrate, but they produce standing waves and overtones based on the length of the column instead of the length of the string.

TIMBRE!

Now back to our original question—why do a clarinet and a guitar playing the same note sound different? The answer is that while all instruments produce standing waves and their corresponding overtones, they all do it differently. In nearly all of them, the fundamental tone—for example, the A note produced by an A string on a guitar—is much louder than the overtones. Beyond that, overtones sound different on different instruments. Some instruments produce many overtones loudly, some produce only a few, some produce only the lower ones, some only the higher, and so on. But our brains merge them with the fundamental note, and they all add up to each instrument's unique timbre. Some examples:

• Steel-string acoustic guitars generally sound all the overtones strongly, and many, especially the higher ones, diminish quickly, which is why the tone of acoustic guitars "mellows out" after a short time.

• Clarinets sound the fundamental, but only the even-numbered overtones—the second, fourth, sixth, and so on. Because of its physical makeup, the clarinet simply doesn't create the standing waves that would produce the odd-numbered overtones. That's what gives the clarinet its unique sound.

• A flute produces almost *no* overtones. The fundamental is virtually the only note heard, resulting in that very "pure" tone we associate with the flute.

• An oboe produces all the overtones—but produces all of them with amplitudes in inverse proportion to the fundamental: the second overtone is half as loud as the fundamental; the third is one-third as loud, etc. Interestingly, that's what violins and violas do, too. That's one reason why they produce similar sounds, even though oboes are, obviously, very different from violins and violas.

OTHER FACTORS

The overtone profile is primarily used to describe an instrument's timbre, but there are other factors that influence it.

• *Vibrato* refers to periodic changes in tone; *tremolo* to periodic changes in amplitude or volume. These are generally considered pleasing sounds, especially in singing, though they can be overdone (think of someone with an especially warbly singing voice).

Jimmy Page wasn't the first: Bows were commonly used to play guitars until the 1500s.

An indication of how natural these effects are: good synthesizers have the ability to add vibrato and tremolo to more realistically duplicate natural sounds.

• *Attack* and *decay* describe how the sound begins and ends. A sharp, hard strike on a piano that is quickly muted creates a very different sound qualitatively than that of a key being gently struck and allowed to ring. Thus attack and delay are important parts of sound quality too. (The attack can also affect the overtones. A sharp picking of a guitar string, for example, produces louder high overtones.)

RANDOM NOTES

• Overtones are also known as *harmonics*.

• Harmonics and overtones are also known as *partials*, since their corresponding standing waves are *parts*, or fractions, of the fundamental standing wave's length.

• You may have noticed that while we've been discussing "musical instruments," we certainly haven't included all instruments—only those with vibrating strings and vibrating columns of air (more precisely known as *chordophones* and *aerophones*). That leaves two more types of (non-electronic) musical instruments: *membranophones* and *idiophones*.

• *Membranophones* are instruments with vibrating membranes (like drums); *idiophones* are instruments in which the body of the instrument itself vibrates to produce sound (like bells, xylophones, and gongs). So what do they do with overtones?

• Many percussion instruments, like snare drums, do not create standing waves at all, and therefore don't produce "tones," but simply emit erratically-patterned sound waves. It is the rhythm that makes them "musical."

• Some types of drums do create standing waves along their membranes in very complex patterns, and have a discernable pitch. You can hear this in hand drums like congas, for example.

• *Idiophones*, such as gongs, steel drums, and many types of bells, produce standing waves and are very resonant, creating tones that last for a long time. But they produce *inharmonic* standing waves, meaning they don't have the simple fractional relationships in the overtone series we described. That being said, they still produce what most people hear as a nice sound.

In 2007 Garth Brooks passed Elvis Presley to become the best-selling solo artist in U.S. history.

BANJO RISING

When you hear banjo picking, images of mountains and barn dances come to mind. It may surprise you, then, to learn that this seemingly most "American" of instruments began as an African folk instrument ...and came to the New World aboard slave ships.

FIRST CONTACT

While traveling through the Gambra River area of West Africa in 1620, British explorer Richard Jobson noticed some local people playing musical instruments he'd never seen before. He wrote about one of them in his journal:

> That which is most common in use is made of a great gourd, and a necke thereunto fastned, but they have no manner of fret, and the strings they are either such as the place yeeldes, or their invention can attaine to make, being very unapt to yeeld a sweete and musicall sound, notwithstanding with pinnes they winde and bring to agree in tunable notes, having not above six strings upon their greatest instrument.

Although that "great gourd" was the first written mention of the banjo in the Western world, nearly every ancient culture had a musical instrument made of a hollow drum (a gourd or turtle shell) attached to a neck (a stick), with strings across it. In Africa, these instruments were known by many similar names: *banjar, banjil, banza, bangoe,* and *banshaw.*

Of all the early drum-and-string instruments that the Africans played, the most likely direct ancestor of the American banjo was the *akonting,* which originated near Gambia. Many early North American slaves came from Gambia and, according to music historians, the bamboo used to make the akonting's neck was called *bangoc,* pronounced "ban-joo."

SPREADING THE SOUND

While the akonting may have been the banjo's predecessor, it's doubtful that any of them made their way to North America. Most African slaves arrived in the New World with few or no possessions, so they constructed new instruments the same way they had for centuries—with whatever materials they could find. In

America, they often used a bowl-shaped calabash gourd with the top half sawed off and the skin of a groundhog, goat, or cat stretched tightly around it to make a drum. The final touch was a fretless wooden neck that held three or four strings, usually made from gut, twine, or hemp.

To the white colonists, the banjo was an exotic oddity, but many were drawn to its music in spite of its reputation as a "slave instrument." In time, slaves taught many white people to play it. By the mid-1700s, white banjo players had become popular entertainers in traveling music shows.

THE SWEENEY MINSTRELS

The first acclaimed American banjoist was Joel Walker Sweeney. When he was 13 years old, he learned how to play the banjo from slaves on his father's farm in the Virginia town of Appomattox Court House. A gifted musician and natural showman, Sweeney traveled around Virginia and North Carolina in the 1830s, putting on shows and charging a few pennies for admission. He could sing, dance, imitate animal sounds, and, legend has it, play the fiddle and banjo at the same time. Eventually, Sweeney began wearing blackface (made from the ash of burned cork) and performing in minstrel shows—troupes of white performers who sang and played songs, performed skits, and did magic tricks. And always at the heart of his minstrel show was the banjo. In the 1840s, the Sweeney Minstrels spread the banjo sound even farther when they toured New York City, England, Scotland, and Ireland. Sweeney also popularized the rhythmic "clawhammer" playing style that the slaves had taught him—hitting the strings hard with the fingernails on the downstroke, then strumming with the thumbnail on the upward motion. Clawhammer would be the standard playing style for the next 50 years.

FOUR STRINGS OR FIVE?

Sweeney is often credited with another innovation that's still in use: the five-string banjo. Most early banjos had only four strings, but Sweeney added a fifth string to his instrument to get a fuller sound. The result was something like the modern banjo: four strings that went all the way from the bridge to the end of the neck, and a shorter, high-pitched "drone" string that ran to a tuning peg only halfway down the neck. In the 1840s, Sweeney contracted with a Baltimore drum maker named William Boucher to build the first five-string banjos available for sale. The modern banjo was beginning to take shape: The gourd was replaced with an open-backed drum, and steel strings took the place of gut, producing a louder, brighter sound. But two more ingredients for the modern banjo—the resonator and the fretted neck—were still many years away.

A BANJO CULTURE

Another of Sweeney's lasting legacies was his enthusiastic work as an instructor: He taught the banjo to scores of people, some of whom became famous players themselves. Billy Whitlock, a Sweeney student, led the Virginia Minstrels (along with Dan Emmet, who wrote "Dixie") to great success in New York City, where Sweeney soon followed and found a built-in audience. Whitlock, in turn, taught Tom Briggs, who soon became a famous picker, but more importantly published the *Briggs Banjo Instructor*, the instrument's first instruction book (still in print today).

By the time the Civil War broke out, banjo playing was so popular that many army regiments had their own minstrel groups to keep up morale. Sweeney's own son, Sam, made a name for himself as Confederate General Jeb Stuart's personal banjo player, and performed shows for the Army of Northern Virginia. And Sweeney's students—now much in demand as entertainers—all added their own style to the banjo, creating a staggering array of strumming patterns and tunings. Banjo music was growing more diverse every year.

"THE DEPTH OF POPULAR DEGRADATION"

After the Civil War ended, the instrument's popularity continued to spread, but mainly in rural areas. Most of high society shunned the twangy banjo, preferring the guitar, which had a fuller sound and was easier to play because it had only one standard tuning, while the banjo could have dozens. Once associated with slaves, the banjo had become a symbol of the poor and uneducated. Soon, even the press was scorning it. The *Boston Daily Evening Voice* linked the banjo to "the depth of popular degradation fit only for the jig-dancing lower classes of the community."

Trying to bring the instrument more respectability, many players cut back on the rhythmic clawhammer styles and developed more refined fingerpicking techniques similar to those of the guitar. Instead of playing in restaurants, saloons, and train stations, the banjo players of the late 1800s played in people's homes, leading to the fad of "parlor music" and to what some have called the banjo's "classical period." (Before the phonograph and the radio, parlor music was the only way for nonmusicians to hear music at home.)

One parlor musician, Henry C. Dobson, made his mark on the music world by asking a banjo builder to add the last pieces to the modern banjo: frets for more precise intonation, a resonator for amplification, and a tone ring—a metal shell in the banjo's body that helped balance the sound. Now the banjo could do anything a guitar could do...almost.

STEWART'S BANJEAU

As the banjo's popularity began rising again, some players thought that the instrument belonged in one place it hadn't yet been: the classical orchestra. Leading the charge was Samuel Swain Stewart, a Philadelphia instrument maker who had built thousands of banjos. Stewart believed that the banjo should be taught to educated musicians via sheet music, unlike the learn-by-ear method of the early minstrels and slaves. So he distributed banjo sheet music and instruction manuals to music and book stores all over the country. He also published a magazine, *Stewart's Banjo and Guitar Journal*, which included articles like "The Banjo Philosophically: Its Construction, Its Capabilities, Its Evolution, Its Place as a Musical Instrument, Its Possibilities, and Its Future." Stewart even tried to change the spelling to "banjeau" in an attempt to make the instrument sound more refined.

Stewart also used his considerable wealth to sponsor many of the 19th century's greatest banjo players, including Horace Weston, a freeborn black man from Connecticut. A virtuoso player, Weston started in minstrel groups, but later found great success as a parlor musician—so much, in fact, that he became the first African American musician to headline a show in Europe when he toured with a production of *Uncle Tom's Cabin* in 1873.

AIN'T GOT THAT SWING

By 1900 the banjo was nearly as popular in America as the guitar, and its repertoire of music was diverse enough to please almost any audience. But the clawhammer strumming style that had started it all was now nearly extinct. A 1915 article in the *New York Clipper* pulled no punches: "The banjo playing of the old-timer was something that would not be tolerated at present. It was banging and twanging and plunketty plunk, used probably for plantation songs of a hilarious or noisy order." Clawhammer style was *supposed* to be noisy, to help the banjo project over a band. But the style had outgrown its usefulness: The new plectrum banjo (designed to be played with a guitar pick), along with resonators and steel strings, had made the instrument loud enough to be heard in dance bands. And the widespread use of fingerpicks, which made the clawhammer style obsolete, was pushing the instrument to the peak of its popularity.

If the banjo was so popular 100 years ago, why is it a niche instrument today, associated primarily with country and bluegrass music? Mostly because of jazz. When jazz bands became popular in the 1920s and '30s, the guitar, with its lighter-gauged strings, proved better than the banjo for creating the complex rhythms needed. And the guitar blended better with the jazz sound compared to the twang of the banjo, which tended to overwhelm other instruments. That isn't to say there weren't banjo players in early jazz bands—there were. But they were steadily being replaced by guitarists. In order to survive, the banjo had to travel a different road.

BLUEGRASS

By the time of the Great Depression in the 1930s, the banjo craze had all but ended. And when factory closures halted the production of steel strings, it nearly disappeared altogether. It wasn't until the postwar boom of the 1940s that the banjo would make yet another resurgence.

That resurgence came mainly from the work of one man: Earl Scruggs. Born in North Carolina in 1924, Scruggs grew up playing hillbilly songs in a musical family, and was taught a three-finger banjo technique by a North Carolina picker named Snuffy Jenkins. Scruggs took this style and sped it up, creating his own specialty, now called "Scruggs style." In the 1940s, Scruggs and his new style led to a new genre of music. In traditional old-timey music, every instrument takes the melody and supports it. If there is a solo, it's usually performed by one player, only once in a song. In jazz, however, the players trade off—one instrument takes the lead while the rest take the melody, and every player gets at least one solo in any given song. Scruggs fused the sound of old-timey music with the style of jazz by making the banjo a lead instrument. And voilà—modern bluegrass was born.

Although the bluegrass genre can be traced back to 1939 with the formation of Bill Monroe and his Blue Grass Boys, the style took off when Scruggs joined the band in 1945. He proved that when let loose, the banjo is a formidable instrument for soloing. Scruggs became the 20th century's most famous banjo player and has influenced scores of pickers after him.

KEEP ON PICKIN'

Shortly after it found a new home in bluegrass, the banjo became the center of another popular subgenre in the late 1950s: folk music. Pete Seeger, a Harvard dropout, helped start the folk movement in the 1940s, and he did it on the banjo. Seeger favored "roots" music, pre-bluegrass slave and minstrel styles such as clawhammer. Combining these old-style sounds with pop-song structures and socially conscious lyrics, Seeger wrote or cowrote such folk classics as "Where Have All the Flowers Gone?" and "If I Had a Hammer," and adapted the spiritual hymn "We Shall Overcome"—which later became the unofficial anthem for the civil rights movement.

In the 1960s, the banjo branched into another genre when a New York teenager named Béla Fleck first heard Earl Scruggs's banjo playing on the theme song to *The Beverly Hillbillies*. By the 1970s, Fleck was hooked, and became a banjo virtuoso by his midtwenties. He would go on to combine bluegrass with jazz fusion, and is one of today's best-known banjo players, introducing the instrument to a whole new generation.

BACK HOME AND BEYOND

All through its fragmented and tumultuous history, one place where the banjo never went out of style was the South. "The banjo fit in perfectly with the Southerners' love of homemade music," writes Mike Seeger, one of the 20th century's most prolific banjo pickers (and half-brother of Pete Seeger). "Banjo playing became a fad in the North, but in the South this robust expression of African American tradition became a vital part of Anglo American music."

Today, the banjo is as versatile as ever, picking its way into many musical genres, from rock (Beck) to blues (Taj Mahal), and even to eclectic "world" music (Kaleidoscope). In recent years, there's been a resurgence of African American banjo pickers: Players such as Otis Taylor, Alvin Youngblood Hart, Don Vappie, the Ebony Hillbillies, and Guy Davis are bringing the instrument full circle, proving that the "great gourd" with the humble origins is alive and well.

*　　*　　*

RANDOM ORIGINS OF ROCK BAND NAMES

THE B-52'S. They weren't named after an Air Force jet. "B-52" is a Southern term for a tall bouffant hairdo, which the women of the band wore early in the group's career.

GENESIS. Named by record producer Jonathan King, who signed the band in 1967. He chose the name because they were the first "serious" band he'd produced, and his signing them marked the official beginning of his production career.

CREAM. Eric Clapton, Jack Bruce, and Ginger Baker considered themselves the cream of the crop of British blues musicians.

THEY MIGHT BE GIANTS. Named after an obscure 1971 B-movie starring George C. Scott and Joanne Woodward.

RADIOHEAD. They were originally called On a Friday (because they practiced on Fridays). But the EMI execs who signed them in 1992 feared that On a Friday might be confusing to some, so the band quickly chose a new name. Their inspiration: an obscure Talking Heads song called "Radio Head."

DAVID BOWIE. David Robert Jones changed his last name to Bowie to avoid being mistaken for Davy Jones of the Monkees. He chose Bowie after the hunting knife he'd seen in American films.

BY THE TIME WE GOT TO WOODSTOCK

The Woodstock Music and Arts festival was an event like no other in the 20th century. Nearly half a million young people gathered in upstate New York on a hot, rainy weekend in 1969 to watch one of the most impressive musical lineups in history. But what they got was much more than a concert—Woodstock was both a cultural milestone and the end of an era.

TENSE TIMES

In the late 1960s, the United States was a divided nation. The war in Vietnam had put people on one of two sides: pro-war or anti-war. And both sides were vehement in their beliefs. By 1969 the anti-war movement felt completely marginalized by the media—it seemed like the only way left to spread the message of peace was through music. San Francisco was the West Coast headquarters of the hippie movement; on the East Coast, it was New York City. But after a while, the hustle and bustle of the cities became too much for musicians to deal with—especially for recording music—so a lot of them started moving to the country.

About 100 miles north of Manhattan, the rural town of Woodstock, New York, had been a pastoral retreat for artists and musicians for nearly a century. Bob Dylan, Janis Joplin, and Van Morrison, to name a few, decided to build homes and record there. Young people liked Woodstock for its back-to-nature appeal, but the local farmers weren't too thrilled to see long-haired hippies rolling into town. Because there were only a few at first, the locals just shrugged it off. They had no idea what was about to hit them.

THE FANTASTIC FOUR

There was one thing Woodstock lacked: a state-of-the-art recording studio. In the spring of 1969, four entrepreneurs—all young men in their 20s—decided to build one.

• Michael Lang, the oldest of the four at 26, was a stereotypical longhair, described by his friends as a "cosmic pixie." A year earlier, he had produced Florida's largest-ever rock concert—the two-day Miami Pop Festival, which drew 40,000 people.

• Artie Kornfeld was a vice president of Capitol Records and an accomplished songwriter with 30 hit singles to his credit, including Jan and Dean's "Dead Man's Curve."

• John Roberts, heir to a toothpaste fortune, was the one with money. The only concert he'd ever seen was a Beach Boys show.

• Joel Rosenman was a Yale Law School graduate, but he cared more about playing guitar in a lounge band than practicing law.

LET'S PUT ON A SHOW

Kornfeld and Lang were friends who shared a New York City apartment and a love for progressive music. One of their dreams was to put on a huge music festival. When they heard of the exodus up to Woodstock, they wanted to be a part of it, and building a studio would be their in. They thought a rock concert might be a good way to raise money and generate publicity for the studio—but first they needed money to put on the concert.

Meanwhile, in another New York City apartment, Roberts and Rosenman were busy thinking up new business ideas. They had some money, but true to the times they wanted to use it for some unconventional, cutting-edge venture. But what? They decided to produce a television sitcom about two oddball businessmen who got into a different wacky business venture every week. For plot ideas, they put an ad in the *New York Times* in March 1968:

Young Men with Unlimited Capital looking for interesting, legitimate investment opportunities and business propositions.

MEETING OF THE MINDS

The show never made it off the drawing board. The ad, however, caught the eye of Lang and Kornfeld's lawyer, who knew his clients were looking for business partners to put on their concert. A meeting was arranged in February 1969. Although they came from different backgrounds—Roberts and Rosenman were buttondown college graduates; Kornfeld and Lang were tie-dyed flower children—they all agreed that the summer of 1969 in Woodstock, New York, would be the time and place for an unprecedented festival, what they called "three days of peace and music." They expected between 40,000 and 50,000 people to show up.

"Battle Cry of Freedom" (1862) was so popular that 14 printing presses couldn't meet the demand.

FINDING A FIELD, PART I

The four men formed Woodstock Ventures, and in the spring of 1969, started scouting around for a concert site in or near Woodstock. In Wallkill they found an abandoned industrial park that was the right size (300 acres), was in a good location (right off the highway), and had all the utilities in place. Roberts shelled out $10,000 to rent it.

But although the industrial park had all the amenities the four were looking for, the "vibe" didn't feel right. Lang, for one, hated it: the industrial feeling was a far cry from the back-to-nature theme he'd envisioned for the concert. The people of Wallkill were wary of the prospect of a few thousand hippies converging on them, but Rosenman assured town supervisor Jack Schlosser that it would be a low-key folk festival. Schlosser reluctantly agreed, and so did Lang. Even though the site wasn't perfect, it was the only one they had.

FINDING THE ACTS

As spring turned to summer, the four men went to work trying to book the biggest folk and rock acts of the day. Performers were understandably hesitant—Woodstock Ventures had never put on a concert before, and now they were trying to put on the largest one of the year. "To get the contracts," remembered Rosenman, "we had to have the credibility, and to get the credibility, we had to have the contracts." They got the contracts the only way they could think of: they promised incredible sums of money to performers. First, Jefferson Airplane agreed to play for $12,000, twice their usual fee. Then Creedence Clearwater Revival and The Who signed for similar fees. That gave the show the credibility it needed. Other acts soon began to follow: the Grateful Dead and the headliner, Jimi Hendrix. (The musician they wanted most, Bob Dylan, couldn't make the show—he had already signed on to play the Isle of Wight Festival in England on the same weekend.)

With all the wheels in motion, an army of longhaired hippies descended upon Wallkill to begin setting up the site and start construction on the largest sound system ever created. The influx proved to be too much for the already suspicious locals—they reneged on the agreement and ran Woodstock Ventures out of town—one month before the concert was scheduled to begin.

Most expensive concert ticket ever: $1,530. (Front row, Barbra Streisand's 2000 Australia tour.)

FINDING A FIELD, PART II

Losing the site was a huge blow. The people at Woodstock Ventures were disconsolate; some were even packing up their stuff to go home. But then the press found out about what happened in Wallkill, and that changed everything. The story of the town that reneged on its concert deal made headlines everywhere. Suddenly, Woodstock was a part of a national conversation. And that may have been the best thing to happen to the festival. Many think that if the concert had gone on in Wallkill, it would have turned out badly—tensions there were high, and some Wallkill citizens had threatened to "shoot the first hippie that walks into town."

But the fact remained that Woodstock still had no venue. Then, sometime during the week of July 20, when most of the people of the world were focused on the first moon landing, Lang heard about Max Yasgur, an eccentric old pipe-smoking dairy farmer in the town of White Lake, who owned a 600-acre farm and might be willing to rent it. Lang went to the field and fell in love with it. "It was magic," he said. "The sloping bowl, a little rise for the stage. A lake in the background. The deal was sealed right there in the field."

HERE IT COMES

Rosenman maintained that at most 50,000 people would show up. That's what he told Wallkill and that's what he told the people of White Lake, even though he expected five times that many. At that point he would've said anything to make the show happen. But Max Yasgur was shrewd—he tallied up his expenses for lost crops and destruction of his land and charged $75,000 in advance …and got it. The bands were misled, too. There was supposed to be a $15,000 cap on artists' fees, but word leaked out that Jimi Hendrix had been promised $32,000. Rosenman explained that it was because Hendrix, the headliner, was slated to do two sets. In the end it didn't matter: few of the acts were ever paid in full, anyway.

A week before the start of the festival, the citizens of White Lake and Bethel realized the full magnitude of what was about to happen. There were at least 1,000 people on the site building the stage, sound towers, clinics, tent cities, and two huge ticket booths. Outside, tens of thousands of people were driving up Route 17B, inundating the small town of Bethel. White Lake town officials "freaked out" and pulled the permits just a few days before the

---

First Fender electric guitar: the 1950 Esquire. Only about 60 were released under that name.

event. But by this point, it was too late. The "Stop Work" signs were ripped down almost as soon as they were put up. Like it or not, Woodstock was going to happen.

FRIDAY, AUGUST 15

By evening, close to half a million hippies had converged on the site. Estimates say that half a million more tried to get to Woodstock, but never made it past the 20-mile traffic jam leading into Bethel. In the end, thousands of people just abandoned their cars and walked to the farm. And when they got there, instead of going in through one of the two gates, the kids trampled the fence and walked right in. While Woodstock Ventures were overjoyed by the turnout, they were equally dismayed when they found that very few of the concertgoers had paid. The largest concert of the century had suddenly become a free concert. And Rosenman, Lang, Kornfeld, and Roberts had no clue how they were going to pay for it.

When they got the word on Friday afternoon that the bands couldn't make it through the gridlock, Woodstock Ventures rented a fleet of Army helicopters to ferry them in. But that would take time, and hundreds of thousands of kids were screaming for music. The only artist who had shown up—folkie Richie Havens—was ushered onto the stage at 5:00 p.m. His band hadn't arrived yet, so he played solo…for three hours. Every time he tried to stop, the promoters threw him back onstage. Next up was John Sebastian, who wasn't even scheduled to perform, but happened to be there. Lang was afraid that if the music stopped, the kids might riot. For that reason, the plan to stop playing every night at midnight was abandoned. If all went well, the music would go nonstop until Sunday evening.

SATURDAY, AUGUST 16

When the sun rose on Max Yasgur's field on Saturday morning, Woodstock was the third largest city in New York State. It was also one of the muddiest: five inches of rain had fallen during the night. On the surface, the entire event looked like a mess. Greil Marcus, a reporter who covered the event for *Rolling Stone*, described the troubles: "The sanitation facilities were breaking down and overflowing; the water from six wells and parked water tanks were proving to be an inadequate supply.…the food concessions were sold out and it was impossible to ferry in any more through the traffic."

But despite the adversity, the music kept going through the afternoon and people banded together for survival. The Hog Farm, a group of communal hippies, had been hired to manage the crowds, run interference, help people make it through bad drug trips, and keep the message of love flowing. Their leader, known as Wavy Gravy, when asked how he intended to maintain law and order, replied, "With seltzer bottles and cream pies." Instead of the police force, they called themselves the "Please force." Woodstock Ventures would later maintain that the $16,000 they spent to get the Hog Farm to Woodstock was the best money they ever spent. Even the locals, many of whom had tried to stop the event, pitched in when they heard how little food there was for so many people. Through it all, the music kept playing. And then at five in the afternoon on Saturday, it started raining again. Heavily.

But the rain was the least of their problems. The three main acts for Saturday night—the Grateful Dead, Janis Joplin, and The Who—threatened to not play unless they were paid in advance, in cash. That added up to more than $30,000. Roberts didn't have that kind of money on him, so he pleaded with Charlie Prince, the owner of a local bank, to give him a cash advance. Roberts promised that he was good for it (he had a $1 million trust fund), but Prince was still skeptical. Then Roberts informed him that if the music stopped, they could be faced with the largest riot in American history. Prince conceded, and the music went on.

SUNDAY, AUGUST 17

As the sun came up, the Who were just concluding the perform-ance of their rock opera *Tommy*. Arriving by car (barely) the night before, they didn't realize how big the crowd was until dawn. As they were singing "Listening to you, I feel the music," the band saw almost half a million people looking back at them. Pete Townshend says it's one of the most amazing things he's ever expe-rienced. (Less than an hour before, Townshend had another strange experience: yippie activist Abbie Hoffman ran onstage and started preaching politics. Townshend, not recognizing Hoffman, bonked him on the head with his guitar.)

By noon, torrential rain had given way to baking sun. All of the extra space at the festival, even the dressing rooms, had been converted to hospitals. Someone had spiked the water supply with LSD, so the Hog Farm was helping thousands of kids (and many band members) through bad trips. Local medics were treating people for heatstroke, cut feet (from all of the broken glass), pneumonia (from being drenched), and even blindness (several tripped-out kids had been lying on their backs and staring at the sun).

The food situation was dire; supplies were woefully short. And by this time, the portable toilets were unusable. Max Yasgur's field looked like a disaster area. The situation was so bad, in fact, that New York governor Nelson Rockefeller threatened to send in National Guard troops to break up the festival. But luckily for everyone involved, calmer heads prevailed.

And still, the music went on. Audiences were treated that day and throughout the night to sets by Crosby, Stills & Nash, Ten Years After, Johnny Winter, and Joe Cocker. Woodstock's final act, headliner Jimi Hendrix, didn't even get to start his set until 9 a.m. on Monday morning. His instrumental version of "The Star-Spangled Banner" woke up the dozing crowd and gave them one last electrifying—but underappreciated—performance as they packed up their muddy belongings and left Yasgur's farm. The Woodstock Music and Arts Fair was over, but for the four men who formed Woodstock Ventures, that weekend would consume them for years to come.

AFTERMATH

The largest concert in history also left one of the biggest messes in history. It took several months and $100,000 to clean up all the garbage left behind—and it was years before Max Yasgur's land recuperated. The festival also left at least three people dead: one a 17-year-old boy who was asleep under a tractor trailer when it started up and pulled away, and two more people who died of drug overdoses. The final tally for those treated for medical problems was around 5,000. There were eight reported miscarriages, along with rumors of several babies being born. And with all of the free love, who knows how many babies were conceived at Woodstock.

By the festival's end, Woodstock Ventures was $1.3 million in debt. Promotional and production expenses had gone way over budget. Throughout the 1970s, Woodstock Ventures was mired in lawsuits and faced criminal charges for illegal drug use, breach of contract, and even "illegal burning" for the plumes of smoke that rose over the field for weeks as all the trash was burned. Another lawsuit came from the town of White Lake for disturbing the peace (an ironic charge for an event whose goal was to promote peace), but that suit was dropped in 1978. So was it worth it? Yes, says Lang—the whole ordeal of organizing Woodstock was like "living a dream. My idea was just to get it done, whatever it took. We had a vision, and it all came true."

The saving grace for the concert promoters' monetary woes came from the movie *Woodstock*. Warner Bros. made a film of the event (edited by Martin Scorsese) and Woodstock Ventures was entitled to residual royalties. Because of this, Woodstock Ventures broke even—in 1980. (Want to see Mrs. Uncle John? She's in the movie. She the cute brunette behind the guy freaking out.)

Twenty-five years later, on August 12, 1994, around 300,000 people showed up in Saugerties, New York, to attend Woodstock '94, which was produced by Woodstock Ventures, still headed by Michael Lang, Joel Rosenman, and John Roberts.

A CULTURAL LEGACY

Woodstock came at a time when the United States was at a crossroads, but did it really change anything? On the day after the event, the *New York Times* ran an editorial that called Woodstock a "colossal mess." But just a day later, the paper changed its tune, calling it a "phenomenon of innocence. They came, it seems, to enjoy their lifestyle that is its own declaration of independence."

One thing is for sure: as the summer of 1969 came to an end, the optimism that stemmed from seeing men land on the moon and 450,000 people gather peacefully in the rain was running out. On December 6 of that year, the Rolling Stones headlined the Altamont Festival in Livermore, California. The event was scarred by a near-riot and the stabbing death of an 18-year-old man at the hands of the Hells Angels. Altamont has since been called "the day the '60s died" and "the anti-Woodstock." And as the '70s rolled in, the nation would soon be rocked by the Watergate scandal and then an energy crisis, making that weekend in White Lake seem like a distant memory.

The tune of Little Peggy Marsh's "I Will Follow Him" is from the French song "Chariot."

WHAT A LONG STRANGE TRIP

But Woodstock is by no means forgotten. It's one of the most enduring images of the 1960s. And it's likely there won't be a concert again of its magnitude. The original site now holds a monument to the event and an amphitheater that seats 16,000… comfortably. And as for the recording studio that sparked the whole idea in the first place, it was never built.

"I think you have proven something to the world—that half a million kids can get together and have three days of fun and music and have nothing BUT fun and music. God bless you all!"

—Max Yasgur to the crowd at Woodstock

* * *

THE LINEUP AT WOODSTOCK

Friday
Richie Havens
John Sebastian
Country Joe McDonald
(with "Fixin-to-Die-Rag")
Swami Satchadinanda
(the guru)
Bert Sommer
Sweetwater
Tim Hardin
Ravi Shankar
(quit due to rain)
Melanie
Arlo Guthrie
Joan Baez

Saturday
Quill (threw stuff
at the audience)
Keef Hartly
Santana
Mountain
Canned Heat

The Incredible String Band
Grateful Dead
Creedence Clearwater Revival
Janis Joplin
Sly and the Family Stone
The Who
Jefferson Airplane

Sunday/Monday
Joe Cocker (followed by
a huge rainstorm)
Max Yasgur (with a speech)
Country Joe & the Fish
Ten Years After
The Band
Blood, Sweat & Tears
Johnny Winter
Crosby, Stills & Nash
(joined for a few songs
by Neil Young)
Paul Butterfield Blues Band
Sha-Na-Na
Jimi Hendrix

The hillbilly singing group in the 1969 film *Paint Your Wagon* was the Nitty Gritty Dirt Band.

FINAL THOUGHTS

Some great words on music.

"Ninety-nine percent of the world's lovers are not with their first choice. That's what makes the jukebox play."

—Willie Nelson

"It's easy to play any musical instrument: all you have to do is touch the right key at the right time and the instrument will play itself."

—J. S. Bach

"There is one god—Bach—and Mendelssohn is his prophet."

—Hector Berlioz

"I refuse to slap some stupid words on the stupid paper just so we have a stupid song finished."

—Suzanne Vega

"What makes rock 'n' roll so great is that someone like me can be a star."

—Elton John

"A composer is a guy who goes around forcing his will on unsuspecting air molecules, often with the assistance of unsuspecting musicians."

—Frank Zappa

"The sonatas of Mozart are unique; they are too easy for children, and too difficult for artists."

—Artur Schnabel

"You gotta dare to suck in order to be great."

—Ricky Martin

"There'll always be some arrogant little brat who wants to make music with a guitar. Rock 'n' roll will never die."

—Dave Edmunds

"There are still so many beautiful things to be said in C major."

—Sergei Prokofiev

"Some songs are just like tattoos for your brain—you hear them and they're affixed to you."

—Carlos Santana

"Too many pieces of music finish too long after the end."

—Igor Stravinsky

"Without music life would be a mistake."

—Friedrich Nietzsche

ANSWER PAGES

NAME THAT FICTIONAL MUSICIAN
(Answers for page 53)

THE SAX MAN

Answer: "Bleeding Gums" Murphy

Story: He's the jazz saxophone player from *The Simpsons*. You can see him in every show—Bart passes him on the street while riding his skateboard in the opening credits. He was a main character in a handful of episodes, mostly involving his protégé, Lisa. In the last episode he appeared in, 1995's "Round Springfield," Lisa finds the aged musician is in the hospital. They play Carole King's "Jazzman" together, and he tells her his life story.

THE OLD-TIMEY BAND

Answer: The Soggy Bottom Boys

Story: They're the band from the 2000 film *O Brother, Where Art Thou?*, played by George Clooney, John Turturro, and Tim Blake Nelson, joined by guitarist Chris Thomas King. The song they recorded with the blind DJ (Stephen Root) was "Man of Constant Sorrow," written in 1913 by American songwriter Dick Burnett. The name of the band pokes fun at bluegrass legend Flatt and Scruggs' backup band, the Foggy Mountain Boys. The fictional Soggy Bottom Boys, and the other great music in the film, were such a hit that Dan Tyminski and the other musicians who played on the soundtrack toured to support the album. The film's version of "Man of Constant Sorrow," sung by Tyminski, won the 2001 Grammy for Best Country Collaboration with Vocals.

THE UNIVERSAL BLASTER BAND

Answer: Disaster Area

Story: They're the band from *The Restaurant at the End of the Universe*, the second book in Douglas Adams's classic series, *The Hitchhiker's Guide to the Galaxy*. Adams said he got the inspiration for the band's elaborate stage effects—which include crashing a spaceship into the Sun to create a solar flare for the audience's amusement—from Pink Floyd. As for the name of Disaster Area's

---

"March King" John Philip Sousa composed 136 patriotic marches....

lead singer, Hotblack Desiato, Adams told the BBC in 2000: "One day I was driving down the street and there was this new estate agency opened up called Hotblack Desiato. And I just thought it was such a wonderful name I nearly crashed the car."

THE SWEETHEARTS OF FOLK

Answer: Mitch and Mickey

Story: The fictional folk duo of Mitch Cohen and Mickey Crabbe was played by Eugene Levy and Catherine O'Hara in Christopher Guest's 2003 "mockumentary" *A Mighty Wind*, a spoof on the '60s folk music scene. Their song "A Kiss at the End of the Rainbow" was nominated for an Academy Award—and won a Grammy. It was written by Michael McKean, who played David St. Hubbins in Guest's 1984 film *This Is Spinal Tap*. McKean wrote it with his wife, actress Annette O'Toole, while they were driving from Los Angeles to Vancouver (where O'Toole was filming for her role in the hit TV show *Smallville*) shortly after the attacks on September 11, 2001, when there were no airline flights.

THE FOLK TOON SINGER

Answer: Jimmy (Ray) Thudpucker

Story: He's been a character in Garry Trudeau's comic strip *Doonesbury* since 1970. But his music is in the real world, too: In 1977 Trudeau produced an album of Jimmy Thudpucker songs, mostly written and played by L.A. studio musician Jimmy Brewer. And in 1999 Trudeau made an animated music video of Thudpucker singing a song called "Too Poor," voiced by Fred Newman, the sound-effects man on the radio show *A Prairie Home Companion*.) You can download the songs at Trudeau's Web site...for free.

THE VANISHING STAR

Answer: Eddie Wilson

Story: He's "Eddie" in the 1983 film *Eddie and the Cruisers*, played by Michael Paré. Was Eddie murdered in the film? Did he commit suicide? Does he come back in the sequel? You'll have to rent them and see. The film music was performed by the Beaver Brown Band, with singer John Cafferty. The band had a #7 hit with a song from the soundtrack, "On the Dark Side." (Many thought it was a Bruce Springsteen song. It wasn't.)

...One march, "The Liberty Bell," was used as the theme song for *Monty Python's Flying Circus*.

THE "DISCOVERED" MASTER

Answer: P.D.Q. Bach

Story: In the 1960s, composer and satirist "Professor" Peter Schickele came up with this character for a laugh. Schickele has written several dozen classical works for symphonies and choral ensembles, but he's best known for "discovering" the music of P.D.Q. Bach, whom he describes as the "youngest and oddest of the twenty-odd children" of Johann Sebastian Bach. P.D.Q., (it stands for "pretty damned quick") is a joke on the fact that many of Bach's actual children had three-part names that were shortened to initials, such as C.P.E. or J.C.F Bach.

HITS OF THE 1970s: A QUIZ
(Answers for page 163)

1. a) In 1978 Gary Guthrie, a disc jockey for WAKY-AM in Louisville, Kentucky, was in the process of breaking up with his wife. One night, a friend played them the new Neil Diamond album. Guthrie recalls: "When it got to 'You Don't Bring Me Flowers,' my wife started crying. I knew it was special, but I couldn't help feeling there was something missing. A few days later, the new Barbra Streisand LP came into the radio station, and she was doing the song too. It set off this image in my mind, in *The Sound of Music*, when Christopher Plummer and Julie Andrews were onstage singing 'Edelweiss'…and a lightbulb! It needed two people singing it to each other."

The Diamond and Streisand versions happened to be in the same key. Guthrie spent sixteen hours splicing the songs together to create a duet. "After five days, I came out with my finished product of 'You Don't Bring Me Flowers.' I put it on the radio as a going away present for my wife," he continues. "I called her up and played it for her, and the phones started going crazy: 'What is that song?'" So many people asked for it at local record stores that the stores finally demanded the station stop playing it.

When Columbia Records got wind of the uproar in Louisville, they got the two stars together to duplicate Guthrie's recording. The "official" duet version reached #1 in five weeks. Guthrie ended up without a wife…or a song. Claiming he'd been wronged by the company after selling them the idea for the duet, he filed a $5 million breach of contract lawsuit against CBS.

Lynyrd Skynyrd was named for their high-school gym teacher, Leonard Skinner—whom they hated.

2. a) The session in which Led Zeppelin recorded "Stairway to Heaven" was pretty spontaneous. Drummer John Bonham worked out his part on the spot...and singer Robert Plant made up the lyrics as he was getting set to record them. Although he later cited a book called *Magic Arts in Celtic Britain* by Lewis Spence as his inspiration, Plant also admitted that he didn't really know what they meant. They were just words he put together in a hurry. "Really," he said, "I have no idea why 'Stairway to Heaven' is so popular. No idea at all. Maybe it's because of its abstraction. Depending on what day it is, I still interpret [the song] a different way—and I wrote those lyrics." How do people turn that into devil worship? Simple—"automatic writing." The reason, some people say, that Plant doesn't know the meaning of his own song is that Satan guided his hand when he was writing it, and if you play it backward, you can hear evil messages.

For the Record: It wasn't released as a single—a decision that boosted the sales of the album by an estimated 500,000 copies.

3. c) The group, from Rockford, Illinois, had been trying to get recognition in the United States for several years. They'd released three albums, all of which bombed. They couldn't make it in Europe, either. In fact, the only place they were popular was Japan.

There, they were heroes with hit singles and tremendously successful tours. When the group's third album flopped in the States, they headed for Japan to tour again. Their record company, Epic, decided to tape their performances in Osaka and Tokyo and come out with a quickie "live" album exclusively for the Japanese market. But for some reason, *Live at Budokan*—which wasn't released anywhere except Japan—caught on in America, and the live version of "I Want You to Want Me," complete with screaming, became Cheap Trick's first hit. It was a twist on a classic rock 'n' roll story. Jimi Hendrix and the Stray Cats had to go to England to become popular in America; Cheap Trick went to Japan.

4. a) It seemed so tailored to Captain & Tennille that no one thought to ask what it was really about. For over 20 years, Neil Sedaka had cowritten songs with his high-school buddy, Howard Greenfield. Their hits included "Calendar Girl" and "Breaking Up Is Hard to Do." But by 1973, their Midas touch had worn off and they decided to break up the team. "Our last song together was

Shinji Kanki composed the album *Music for Dolphins* based on music dolphins seemed to like.

called 'Love Will Keep Us Together.'" says Sedaka. "It was actually written about us and our collaborating."

5. b) "Brand New Key" was banned from some radio stations for being "too suggestive." It was interpreted as promoting drug use (a "key" being a kilo of marijuana) or sexual freedom (a wife-swapping club in L.A. used it as a theme song). Actually, the inspiration was an impulsive visit to McDonald's.

Melanie's search for enlightenment and purification had inspired her to go on a 27-day fast in which she drank nothing but distilled water. Coming off the fast, she was eating transitional food—grated raw carrots, a sip of orange juice—when suddenly she felt an incredible urge, like an "inner voice," telling her to go get a McDonald's hamburger and french fries. After three years of following a strict vegetarian diet, she gave in to what she assumed to be "the voice of spiritual awareness." "I ran down," she says, "and got the whole meal. And then on the way home, in the car, I started to write 'Brand New Key.' So if you are what you eat... (laughs)... I totally connect the McDonald's meal and the song."

6. b) The Bee Gees had a #1 record in 1972. But by 1974, they had released two stiff albums in a row and two years passed without a single in the Top 40. They had fallen so low that they were relegated to the oldies circuit when they toured.

Arif Mardin, Atlantic's superstar producer, had produced their *Mr. Natural* album. It flopped (peak: #178 on the chart), but the band developed a good rapport with him and requested that he produce their next album as well. Mardin accepted, and advised them to open up their ears and get back in touch with what was happening in pop music. Then he said, "I'm going away for a week. I want you to write while I'm away." It was a do-or-die situation.

Luckily, Barry Gibb's wife, Linda, took Mardin's advice seriously. "We used to go over this bridge every night on the way to the studio," she told a critic later. "I used to hear this 'chunka-chunka-chunka' just as we went over the railroad tracks. So I said to Barry, 'Do you ever listen to that rhythm when we go across the bridge at night?' He just looked at me." That night, as they crossed the Sunny Isles Bridge headed for Miami's Criterion Studio, Linda brought it up again. "I said, 'Listen,' and he said, 'Oh, yeah.' It was the chunka-chunka. Barry started singing something and the brothers joined in." It became "Drive Talking," which became "Jive Talkin'," which became a #1 record and the first step in the Bee Gees' astounding comeback.

7. a) The song was originally written as "Le Moribund" (literal translation: "The Dying Man") by Jacques Brel in 1961, and adapted to English by Rod McKuen in 1964. Jacks heard it on a Kingston Trio record, and in 1972, he took it to a Beach Boys' session he was involved with. The Beach Boys recorded it but didn't release it, so Jacks, who was distraught over a friend's death, decided to do his own version of it. He rewrote the last verse.

One day a year later, he was playing his recording of it when the boy who delivered his newspapers overheard it; the boy liked it so much that he brought some friends over to Jacks's house to listen to it, and their enthusiastic response inspired him to release it on his own Goldfish label.

WOMEN WHO ROCK
(Answers for page 220)

1. Pat Benatar. Benatar's Billboard hit "Hit Me with Your Best Shot" was written by a man (Eddie Schwartz, who had written for Carly Simon, Joe Cocker, and others) and originally included the line "put another notch in your lipstick case." The only word Benatar changed when she recorded the song was to turn "your" into "my."

2. Debbie Harry. So many people thought that the name "Blondie" referred to Debbie Harry as a solo act that, in 1979, she started handing out buttons at her shows that said "Blondie is a group." (The band's name came from the fact that truck drivers used to lean out their windows and call out "Hey, Blondie!" as Harry walked by. Before that, she'd planned to call the band Angel and the Snakes.)

3. Chrissie Hynde. Despite his having drastically different political views, Hynde allowed conservative talk show host Rush Limbaugh to use part of her song "My City Was Gone" as the theme song to his radio show…provided that he donated all the royalties to her favorite charity: PETA.

4. Joan Jett. Joan Jett was the

first female musician to establish her own record label.

5. Courtney Love. Mythconception: In 2003, rumors swirled that Marlon Brando was the grandfather of Courtney Love, whose mother had been adopted at birth. Fact: They're not related.

6. Shirley Manson. Manson's father is a geneticist, and he was one of the scientists who cloned Dolly the sheep in 1996.

7. Janis Joplin. "Me and Bobby McGee," one of Joplin's best-known songs, only became a hit after she died in 1970. It was posthumously released as part of the 1971 album *Pearl*, and she sang the song only four times live before she died.

8. Patti Smith. If imitation is the sincerest form of flattery, Gilda Radner loved Patti Smith. In a 1978 *Saturday Night Live* episode, Radner played a character called Candy Slice, who was based on Smith.

9. Siouxsie Sioux. Her real name is Susan Janet Ballion.

10. Grace Slick. Slick and former president Richard Nixon's daughter, Tricia, were both alumni of New York's Finch College. When Slick was invited to an alumni event at the White House in 1970, she brought activist Abbie Hoffman as her date. The Secret Service wouldn't clear the two because of Hoffman's radical ideology, so the pair had to leave

THEY'RE UNREAL, MAN!
(Answers for page 310)

1. c   2. m   3. i   4. j   5. k   6. b   7. d   8. f   9. g
10. h   11. n   12. o   13. l   14. a   15. p   16. e

WHO'S THAT BAND?
(Answers for page 345)

1. m   2. b   3. f   4. i   5. j   6. r   7. a   8. k   9. e   10. p
11. o   12. d   13. g   14. h   15. n   16. q   17. c   18. l

...A. Jimi Hendrix.

UNCLE JOHN'S BATHROOM READER CLASSIC SERIES

Find these and other great titles from the *Uncle John's Bathroom Reader* Classic Series online at **www.bathroomreader.com**. Or contact us at:

Bathroom Readers' Institute
P.O. Box 1117
Ashland, OR 97520
(888) 488-4642

Also available
from *Uncle John's
Bathroom Reader!*

THE LAST PAGE

FELLOW BATHROOM READERS:
The fight for good bathroom reading should never be taken loosely—we must do our duty and sit firmly for what we believe in, even while the rest of the world is taking potshots at us.

We'll be brief. Now that we've proven we're not simply a flush-in-the-pan, we invite you to take the plunge: Sit Down and Be Counted! Become a member of the Bathroom Readers' Institute. Log on to *www.bathroomreader.com*, or send a self-addressed, stamped, business-sized envelope to: BRI, PO Box 1117, Ashland, Oregon 97520. You'll receive your free membership card, get discounts when ordering directly through the BRI, and earn a permanent spot on the BRI honor roll!

If you like reading our books...
VISIT THE BRI'S WEB SITE!
www.bathroomreader.com

- Visit "The Throne Room"—a great place to read!
- Receive our irregular newsletters via e-mail
- Order additional *Bathroom Readers*
- Become a BRI member

Go with the Flow...

Well, we're out of space, and when you've gotta go, you've gotta go. Tanks for all your support. Hope to hear from you soon. Meanwhile, remember...

Keep on flushin'!